Visual Basic 6 Bootcamp

All-in-One Certification

Exam Guide

McGraw-Hill Books on Certification

BOONE, Barry: *Java 1.1 Certification for Programmers and Developers.* 0-07-913657-5

CADY, Dorothy: *Accelerated NetWare 5 CNA Study Guide.* 0-07-134532-9

CADY, Dorothy: *Accelerated NetWare 5 CNE Study Guide.* 0-07-134531-0

GATLIN, Anthony : *The Complete Microsoft Certification Success Guide, 2nd Edition.* 0-07-913201-4

GILES, Roosevelt: *Cisco CCIE Exam Guide.* 0-07-913728-8

KINNAMAN, Dave: *Accelerated MCSE Networking Essentials.* 0-07-067685-2

KINNAMAN, Dave: *Accelerated MCSE TCP/IP.* 0-07-067686-0

KINNAMAN, Dave: *Accelerated MCSE Windows NT 4.0 Server.* 0-07-067697-6

KINNAMAN, Dave: *Accelerated MCSE Windows NT 4.0 Workstation.* 0-07-067683-6

KINNAMAN, Dave: *Accelerated MCSE Windows NT 4.0/Server in the Enterprise.* 0-07-067684-4

MARTINEZ, Anne: *Get Certified and Get Ahead.* 0-07-041127-1

MEYERS, Michael: *A+ All-in-One Certification Exam Guide.* 0-07-913765-2

MILLER, Stewart: *SAP R/3 All-in-One Certification Exam Guide.* 0-07-134161-7

MUELLER, John Paul; WILLIAMS, Robert A.: *CNA/CNE Study Guide: IntranetWare Edition.* 0-07-913619-2

NEAL, Patrick Terrance: *Accelerated MCSE Study Guide: Windows 98 (Exam 70-98).* 0-07-134555-8

NET GURU TECHNOLOGIES, Inc.: *WebMaster Administrator Certification Exam Guide.* 0-07-913287-1

NEW TECHNOLOGY SOLUTIONS: *Visual Basic 5 Bootcamp: Everything You Need to Pass Microsoft's Visual Basic 5 Certification.* 0-07-913671-0

NEW TECHNOLOGY SOLUTIONS: *Visual Basic 6 Bootcamp All-in-One Certification Exam Guide.* 0-07-134534-5

OLIVER, Steve: *Accelerated Domino Web Development and Administration Study Guide.* 0-07-134533-7

PARKS, Sarah T.; KALMAN, Bob: *The A+ Certification Success Guide for Computer Technicians.* 0-07-048596-8

PARKS, Sarah T.; KALMAN, Bob: *A+ Certification Success Guide for Computer Technicians, Revised and Expanded.* 0-07-048618-2

THOMAS, Scott L.; PEASLEY, Amy E.: *Lotus Notes Certification Exam Guide: Application Development and System Administration.* 0-07-913674-5

TOTAL SEMINARS LLC: *Accelerated A+ Certification: Core Exam.* 0-07-044466-8

TOTAL SEMINARS LLC: *Accelerated A+ Certification: Operating System.* 0-07-134216-8

TOTAL SEMINARS LLC: *MCSE NT4 All-in-One Certification Exam Guide.* 0-07-913739-3

VISUAL BASIC 6 *BOOTCAMP*
ALL-IN-ONE CERTIFICATION
EXAM GUIDE

NEW TECHNOLOGY SOLUTIONS

McGraw-Hill

New York   San Francisco   Washington, D.C.
Auckland   Bogotá   Caracas   Lisbon   London
Madrid   Mexico City   Milan   Montreal   New Delhi
San Juan   Singapore   Sydney   Tokyo   Toronto

McGraw-Hill

A Division of The McGraw·Hill Companies

1 2 3 4 5 6 7 8 9 0   AGM/AGM   9 0 4 3 2 1 0 9

P/N 134535-3

PART OF ISBN 0-07-134534-5

The sponsoring editor for this book was Judy Brief and the production supervisor
was Clare Stanley. It was set in Times New Roman by Patricia Wallenburg.

Printed and bound by Quebecor/Martinsburg.

DEDICATION

To Nancy, Ashley, and Matthew
for helping me be a better person.

—Scot

To Roberta, without whom I am incomplete.

—Dan

ACKNOWLEDGMENTS

In many ways, this book was the most challenging title we have created. As we mature as authors, we find that our expectations increase proportionally. All the challenges seem to arise when these higher expectations meet the realistic demands of timetables and marketing. However, we remain committed to creating works that add value to the Visual Basic community. This book represents that effort.

Before you begin any instructional book, you should understand the philosophy of the instructors. Our belief is that certification comes from mastering the Visual Basic product. This book is created to that end. This book is not an effort to give all of the questions you must memorize to pass the tests. Instead, you will find comprehensive instruction that will lead you to an understanding of Visual Basic that is more than sufficient to pass the exams. We have taken the liberty to cover areas of Visual Basic that are not likely to be on the exam, but represent knowledge that an expert will need. We have also made considerable effort to go into more detail than the VB5 version of this book. Indeed, this book is several hundred pages longer than its predecessor and includes an excellent exam matrix in Appendix A.

Although we cannot possibly guarantee that this book has no errors, we are committed to providing corrections as required. To that end, please visit our Web site to find appropriate errata including a downloadable certification exam that will be updated for VB6. You'll find us at www.vb-bootcamp.com.

This list of acknowledgments is long and begins with those that have read our previous books and provided constructive feedback that has helped us grow. After suggestions, however, real work must begin. In this arena, many people stand out. We would like first to thank Gary Shomsky and Patrick Babcock for their technical reviews of this work. These two read every line in the book—more than once—and actually worked each and every exercise multiple times to ensure their accuracy. Additionally, Gary Shomsky is responsible for the companion CD-ROM in its entirely. This CD contains solutions to all of the exercises in the book cataloged for easy reference. Thanks to both of you.

Many other people read chapters and provided feedback where they could. This list includes other employees at New Technology Solutions as well as our students who were routinely used as "crash dummies" for the exercises. All of you have helped insure the quality of this book.

On the publishing side, we have had many people help with this book. We have had no less than two editors for the work—Judy Brief and Michael Sprague. Both of them worked hard to get this book out the door. Additionally, we would like to thank the copyeditors and technical editors at McGraw-Hill for their efforts.

Finally, no list would be complete without mentioning our families. They are always supportive. Without them, we could accomplish nothing.

Scot Hillier
Dan Mezick

New Technology Solutions Incorporated
info@vb-bootcamp.com
www.vb-bootcamp.com

CONTENTS

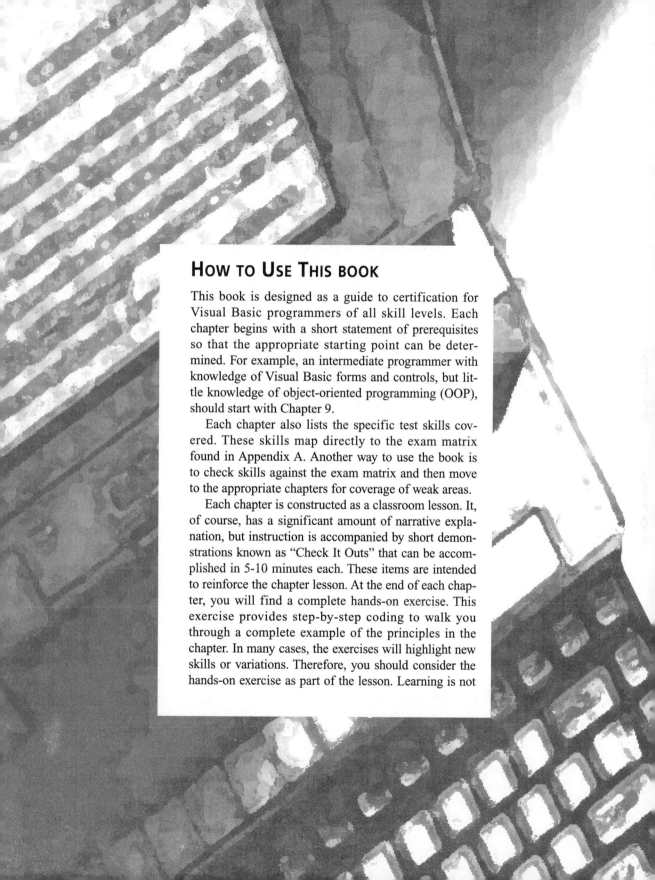

How to Use This book

This book is designed as a guide to certification for Visual Basic programmers of all skill levels. Each chapter begins with a short statement of prerequisites so that the appropriate starting point can be determined. For example, an intermediate programmer with knowledge of Visual Basic forms and controls, but little knowledge of object-oriented programming (OOP), should start with Chapter 9.

Each chapter also lists the specific test skills covered. These skills map directly to the exam matrix found in Appendix A. Another way to use the book is to check skills against the exam matrix and then move to the appropriate chapters for coverage of weak areas.

Each chapter is constructed as a classroom lesson. It, of course, has a significant amount of narrative explanation, but instruction is accompanied by short demonstrations known as "Check It Outs" that can be accomplished in 5-10 minutes each. These items are intended to reinforce the chapter lesson. At the end of each chapter, you will find a complete hands-on exercise. This exercise provides step-by-step coding to walk you through a complete example of the principles in the chapter. In many cases, the exercises will highlight new skills or variations. Therefore, you should consider the hands-on exercise as part of the lesson. Learning is not finished until the exercise is complete. After the exercise, there are advanced exercise topics that can be performed on your own. These are listed under the "For the Certified Pro" section.

Each chapter ends with suggested reading topics and a quiz. The quiz is designed to give you some idea of what the certification exam is like. Typically, the certification exam consists of two types of questions: check box and option button. Check box questions have more than one answer while option button questions have only one answer. In the case of the book, you should pick all correct answers for a given question. The answers to the questions are found after the test.

The book contains a CD-ROM with complete answers for every "Check It Out", hands-on exercise, and "Certified Pro" exercise. The CD-ROM also contains an installable exam program that provides a timed test similar to the true certification exam. You should use this program as your "final exam" before attempting certification.

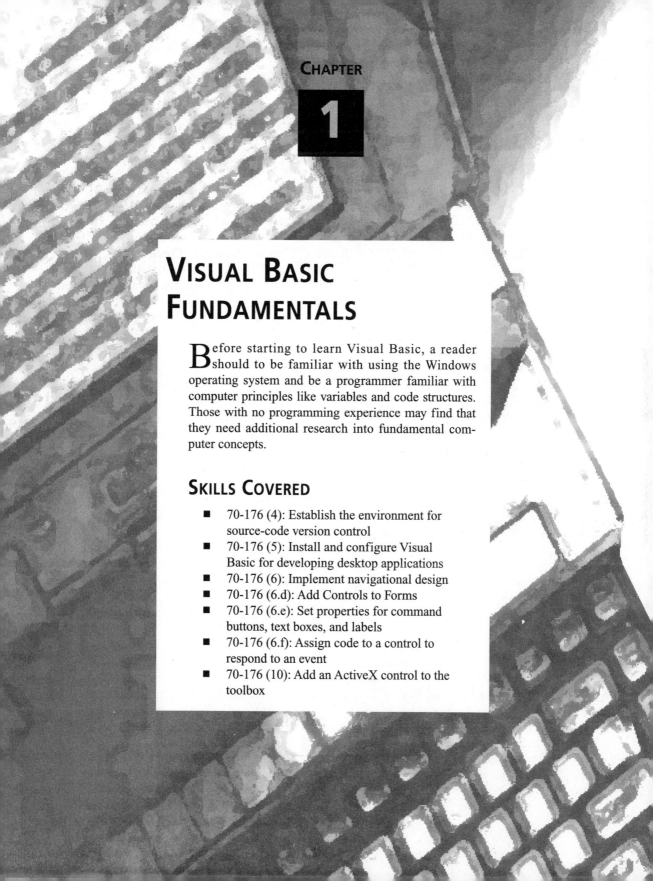

VISUAL BASIC FUNDAMENTALS

Before starting to learn Visual Basic, a reader should to be familiar with using the Windows operating system and be a programmer familiar with computer principles like variables and code structures. Those with no programming experience may find that they need additional research into fundamental computer concepts.

SKILLS COVERED

- 70-176 (4): Establish the environment for source-code version control
- 70-176 (5): Install and configure Visual Basic for developing desktop applications
- 70-176 (6): Implement navigational design
- 70-176 (6.d): Add Controls to Forms
- 70-176 (6.e): Set properties for command buttons, text boxes, and labels
- 70-176 (6.f): Assign code to a control to respond to an event
- 70-176 (10): Add an ActiveX control to the toolbox

- 70-176 (24): Given a scenario, select the appropriate compiler options
- 70-176 (25): Control an application by using conditional compilation
- 70-176 (5): Establish the environment for source-code version control
- 70-175 (6): Install and configure Visual Basic for developing distributed applications
- 70-175 (9): Implement navigational design
- 70-175 (9.d): Add controls to forms
- 70-175 (9.e): Set properties for command buttons, text boxes, and labels
- 70-175 (9.f): Assign code to a control to respond to an event
- 70-175 (13): Add an ActiveX control to the toolbox
- 70-175 (44): Given a scenario, select the appropriate compiler options
- 70-175 (45): Control an application by using conditional compilation

Visual Basic 6.0 continues Microsoft's pursuit of object programming in a *Rapid Application Development* (RAD) environment. A programmer new to objects may be surprised to discover that Visual Basic relies heavily on object programming. Everything in Visual Basic, however, assumes a complete understanding of object principles. This may seem scary at first since the words "object oriented" bring to mind terms like *polymorphism*, *abstraction*, *encapsulation*, and *inheritance*. While these terms are important to understand—and we will provide definitions later—using VB means primarily understanding mechanisms that are used to manipulate objects. In this book, we define an object as a unit of functionality that can be manipulated in fundamentally the same way as objects in the real world. To that end, readers will learn to describe and manipulate objects just as they would a pencil, a computer, or an automobile.

A Quick Tour of Visual Basic

VB has several modes of operation that allow creation of applications. *Design time* is the mode used to create graphic user interfaces (GUI) and code. *Run time* is the mode that actually executes the application while break mode is used to debug applications. When Visual Basic first starts, it is always in design time, ready for the creation of a new application.

Manipulating VB's various design time windows is how to get things done when using VB. The more important windows include the Project window, also known as the Project Explorer, the Properties window, the Toolbox, and the work area. (See Figure 1-1).

The Project Explorer is the heart of project management in Visual Basic. This window shows which project is active as well as the elements that make up that project. These elements include graphical components called *forms*, and code components called *classes* and *modules*. The Visual Basic interface is a multiple document interface (MDI). This means that VB has the capability to work on more than one project at a time. This is clear in the Project Explorer where multiple projects can be opened. At first, the idea of working on more than one project sounds strange; however, VB can use multiple projects in the same application, known as a Project Group. This makes it possible to build powerful component-based applications that we will examine as the book continues.

The Project Explorer is where all the elements of a project are contained and displayed. For example, in the Project Explorer all the items added to the project can be viewed. Double clicking on any program object will bring up a window for that object. Double clicking on a module will bring up its code window. Double clicking on a form will bring up its Form Designer window. To insert new items in the project, select the Project menu command, where there are further choices for inserting various program objects such as forms, modules, MDI forms, and class modules.

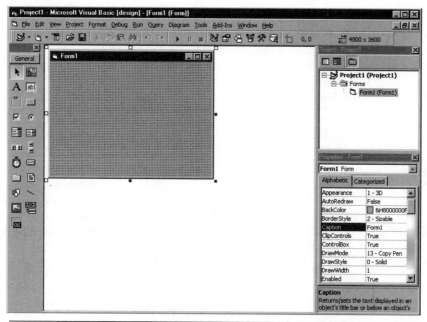

Figure 1-1 Important elements of the Visual Basic (VB) design environment include the Toolbox, the Properties window, and the Project Explorer.

Forms are windows that will appear in the application's user interface, or UI. Modules are special files that hold data and procedures typically accessible from the entire application. These data items and procedures are said to be globally accessible from the entire application. A class module is a special kind of module that serves as a plan or blueprint for a homegrown, custom object. This will be discussed in detail in Chapter 13, and is the basis for object-based programming in VB. Finally, an MDI form is a special kind of form that can contain subordinate "child" forms. In this book we will use all of these project components.

Check It Out 1-1: Inserting Several Key Program Items into Your Project

Many project components can be inserted in the Project Explorer. Here we will look at three key ones: a form, a module, and a class module.

1. Start a new Standard EXE project in Visual Basic. Select the **PROJECT/ADD FORM...** menu command. (Note: If the **Add Form** dialog box is visible, simply push the **OK** button.) The form will appear inside VB's Form Designer, in the main area of the VB display, a child window in the VB MDI design environment.

2. Close the form now. If it is maximized, close it by clicking on the icon that appears next to the File menu, and selecting **Close** from the system menu that drops down. If the form is normalized, close it by clicking the icon that appears in the upper left corner of the Form Designer, and selecting **Close** from the system menu that drops down.

3. Select the **VIEW/PROJECT EXPLORER** menu command. Form2, the form just created, will be visible, inside the Project window. It is under the folder called *Forms*. Try opening and closing this folder with the mouse now.

4. Select the **PROJECT/ADD MODULE** menu command. (Note: If the **Add Module** dialog box is visible, simply push the **OK** button.) A code window will appear. (We describe code windows later.) Close it just as the previously created form was closed, by clicking on the icon that appears next to the File menu and selecting **Close** from the system menu that drops down. Look in the Project window, where Module1 appears under a folder named *Modules*. More modules can be added and the Modules folder can be opened and closed by double clicking on it.

5. Select the **PROJECT/ADD CLASS MODULE** menu command. (Note: If the **Add Class Module** dialog box is visible, simple push the **OK** button.) A code window will appear. Close it just as the form and module previously created were closed. Look in the Project window, where the class module named Class1 appears under a folder named *Class Modules*. Class modules are covered in depth in Chapter 13. More class modules can be added in the same way as Class1. VB will name the next class modules Class2, Class3, and so on. Later we will discuss how to override the default name. The Class Modules folder inside the Project window can be opened and closed by double clicking on it as usual.

Visual Basic saves a project as a series of text files. Each item added to the project whether a form, module, or class, is saved as a separate file and one file is saved to track the project. Each item has its own special file extension to indicate what is saved. Table 1-1 shows the different types of files available and the associated extension for each type.

Table 1-1 File Extensions for VB projects

Project Component	File Extension
Project Group	VBG
Project	VBP
Form	FRM
Module	BAS
Class	CLS

When a new project is created in Visual Basic, no work is initially saved. To first save work, select **FILE/SAVE PROJECT** from the menu; VB will prompt for a name for each of the components in the project along with a name for the project itself. Once a project is saved, subsequent saves do not engender prompts unless a new form, module, or class is added.

Projects are normally saved into a separate directory for each new project. Going to this directory using the File Explorer will reveal the text files for the project. These files may be opened in any text editor, including Notepad, where the files can be examined. You can also see how VB stores information. Listing 1-1 shows a typical project file saved with a VBP extension. Notice how this file refers to the forms, modules, and classes that constitute the project. The component files can also be opened to view their internal storage format.

Listing 1-1 A Typical VBP file

```
Type=Exe
Form=Form1.frm
Reference=*\G{00020430-0000-0000-C000-000000000046}#2.0#0#..\WINNT\
          System32\StdOle2.tlb#OLE Automation
Form=Form2.frm
Form=Form3.frm
Startup="Form1"
Command32=""
Name="Project1"
HelpContextID="0"
CompatibleMode="0"
MajorVer=1
MinorVer=0
RevisionVer=0
AutoIncrementVer=0
ServerSupportFiles=0
VersionCompanyName="New Technology Solutions Incorporated"
CompilationType=0
OptimizationType=0
FavorPentiumPro(tm)=0
CodeViewDebugInfo=0
NoAliasing=0
BoundsCheck=0
OverflowCheck=0
FlPointCheck=0
FDIVCheck=0
UnroundedFP=0
StartMode=0
Unattended=0
```

```
Retained=0
ThreadPerObject=0
MaxNumberOfThreads=1
```

The Properties window is where to alter the settings for the appearance or behavior of an object. Properties are like adjectives used to describe an object. Just as real-world objects are described using adjectives, software objects can be described using properties. Understanding properties is a key objective of this chapter.

Check It Out 1-2: Changing the Properties of a Form

A form's appearance can be changed at design time. Try this:

1. Start up VB. If prompted to select a project template, select a Standard EXE.
2. Select the **VIEW/PROPERTIES WINDOW** menu command. The Properties window will appear if it is not visible now.
3. Select the **BackColor** property of the form by clicking on the name of the property. Click on the drop-down button that appears to be pointing down to see a tabbed dialog with two tabs: System and Palette. Note the background color of the form. Also note the hexadecimal value for BackColor. (The hexadecimal value represents the Red-Green-Blue mix of colors that make up the shade selected.)
4. Now change BackColor by clicking a color on the palette. Note how both the background color of the form and the hexadecimal value of the property change.

The code window is where Visual Basic is programmed. For the form object, display its code window by double clicking on the form in Form Designer. Or click on the item in Project Explorer and press the **View Code** button that appears at the upper left of the Project window. The code window will be explored in detail throughout this book.

Check It Out 1-3: Viewing the Code Window for a Form and Module

Forms and modules can contain Visual Basic code. This code is edited from the code window, where VB code can be edited. Try these steps:

1. Double click on the name **Form1** in the Project window. It will appear in Form Designer. Double clicking on the form will bring up a code window for the form. Two drop-down combo boxes appear at the top of the window. The left one contains the objects in this form, including the form itself (more on this later). The Form object appears by default. The right combo box contains built-in event procedures for the Form object. The `Form_Load` event procedure appears by default. This is known as the *default event*. Click on the drop-down combo boxes now.
2. Close the code window. Close the Form window.
3. A code window for a Form can also be displayed by clicking the leftmost button at the upper left of the Project window. Point the mouse there now to display a ToolTip labeled View Code. Click on the name **Form1** in the Project window, and

then click on the **View Code** button. This series of actions will also display a code window for a selected Module.

4. Select the **PROJECT/ADD MODULE** menu command. A code window will appear for the new module. The [General][Declarations] section is displayed. A *module* is a library that contains VB code and data variables. There will be more about modules in the topics that follow.

The Toolbox is where the reusable, visual components called *ActiveX controls* are displayed for use. The Toolbox is displayed by selecting the **VIEW/TOOLBOX** menu command of VB. This window is used to select (ActiveX) controls for use on a VB form object. When the Toolbox is visible and a form is displayed, CommandButtons, ListBoxes, and other visual objects can be dropped onto the form directly from the Toolbox.

Check It Out 1-4: Dropping Controls

Controls are added to forms like this:

1. Display Form1. (Click on **Form1**, then click on the **View Object** button at the top of the Project window, or just double click on **Form1** from the Project window.)
2. Select the **VIEW/TOOLBOX** menu command, making the Toolbox appear.
3. Double click on the **Label** control (the one with the capital letter A on it). This will place a Label control of a default size, centered on Form1.
4. Click on the **Label Control** icon in the Toolbox, then left-click on the form, dragging the mouse from upper left to lower right, holding the mouse button down. This will "draw" a Label control on Form1, of whatever size and location is chosen.

New custom controls can be added to the Toolbox by selecting the **PROJECT/COMPO-NENTS** menu command. This will display a list of installed controls from which new controls can be selected.

To add a new control, click the checkbox next to the control name and click on the **OK** button. The new control will be added to the project. Remove controls from the Toolbox in the same way. If a control is currently in the toolbox, just click on it to clear the checkbox and press **OK**. The control will disappear from the Toolbox.

Check It Out 1-5: Adding and Removing Controls from the Toolbox

The Toolbox may be customized to include favorite controls (see Figure 1-2). Try this:

1. Select **FILE/NEW** from the VB menu. Do not save the previous project. Click on **No** when prompted about saving work.
2. A set of standard project templates will appear. Select **Standard EXE** and press **OK**. This is now a new project, consisting of a single form named Form1. If the Toolbox is not visible, select the **VIEW/TOOLBOX** menu command to display it.
3. Select the **PROJECT/COMPONENTS** menu command. When the dialog appears, scroll to the Microsoft DataGrid Control 6.0 (OLEDB), and click on the checkbox that appears next to it.

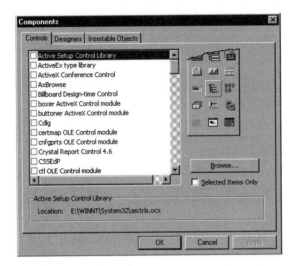

Figure 1-2 The Toolbox may be customized by selecting from the list of installed controls, making them available for use in your project.

4. Move the dialog so that both the Toolbox and the Components dialog are visible. Clicking on the **OK** button on the Components dialog will append Microsoft DataGrid Control 6.0 (OLEDB) to the Toolbox. It can be removed the same way it was added.

Controls can be added and removed from the Toolbox using the PROJECT/COMPONENTS dialog. Chapter 16 will discuss creating controls using VB. These controls, when properly constructed, will appear in the Components dialog, right alongside all the Microsoft controls that ship with VB.

Try deselecting all of the controls in the Components dialog and see what happens. The Toolbox does not become empty—some controls remain in the Toolbox. These remaining controls (such as CommandButton, ListBox, and Label) are known as *intrinsic controls*. They are always there because they reside in the VB runtime Dynamic Link Library named MSVBVM650.DLL. These controls have been optimized for speed and are always part of any VB application created. For these reasons, it is smart to use them whenever possible.

The Toolbar is a panel of buttons displayed beneath VB's menu. These buttons form a subset of VB's menu functions and can be used in place of the corresponding menu command. For example, there is a button for saving the project. Clicking on this button is the equivalent of selecting the **FILE/SAVE PROJECT** menu command. The Toolbar can be toggled off and on by selecting the **VIEW/TOOLBARS/STANDARD** menu command. Turning it off will provide more screen real estate. This is recommended, since the menu provides all of the Toolbar's functions.

VB also provides a Preferences dialog for handling developer settings. This dialog is located under VB's menu as the TOOLS/OPTIONS... dialog. It provides many settings that can be customized to set up VB to look and work as required. For example, the font name and size can be set for the code window, and colors for code and comments can be specified.

Check It Out 1-6: Setting VB Design Environment Options

VB provides a way to set the environment to preferences. Try this:

1. Select the **TOOLS/OPTIONS...** menu command.
2. The Options dialog will appear. It has several tabs. Select the **Editor Format** tab.
3. From the Editor Format tab, change the font name and font size for the code that will appear in the code windows during editing. Alter the font name and size to suit.
4. Click on the **OK** button. Now display Form1, and double click on it to display its code window. The editor settings should be in effect.
5. Again select the **TOOLS/OPTIONS...** menu command.
6. Explore the other tabs on the Options dialog, but do not change anything. When done, press **Cancel**, in case some setting was changed during exploration. At the end of this chapter, you will find a section covering all of the VBIDE options.

When a new VB project begins, there is a list of templates. These provide a convenient way to get started with the many types of specialized projects possible in VB. For now, select the **Standard EXE** template for all examples and exercises. From VB it is possible to create stand-alone EXEs, components called ActiveX servers, ActiveX controls, and other types of output, such as ActiveX documents.

Quite often developers will use Visual Basic, as members of a team. This means that several programmers are creating various parts of the total application. Learning to share and control code is an essential part of team development. Visual Basic is designed to support team development through the Visual SourceSafe product. Visual SourceSafe provides a tool to manage code and version control while sharing files among many developers. VB interfaces to Visual SourceSafe through an add-in. When properly installed, SourceSafe automatically prompts to store code in SourceSafe when saving a project. When files are saved in SourceSafe, they must be "checked-in" and "checked-out". Checking a file out locks the file so that other developers cannot change the code. For more information, refer to the Visual SourceSafe documentation.

No discussion of using VB would be complete without some mention of the Help file. Clicking on the **HELP/CONTENTS** menu command will reveal an HTML help viewer. Select the **Index** tab and type in the topic desired. The Help file will perform an incremental search (Figure 1-3), showing all of the topics available based on the text, as you enter it.

Those who understand the Project, Properties, and Toolbox windows, and have a clue about code windows and the VB editor, are ready to begin learning the whole product. Understanding how to add forms and modules to the Project window is vital.

We have covered certain important design time basics. We have seen the Project, Properties, and Toolbox windows. We have worked with code windows and the VB editor. We have learned how to add forms and modules to the Project window. We have also found some important menu commands under the menu bar headings of View, Project, Tools, and of course, Help.

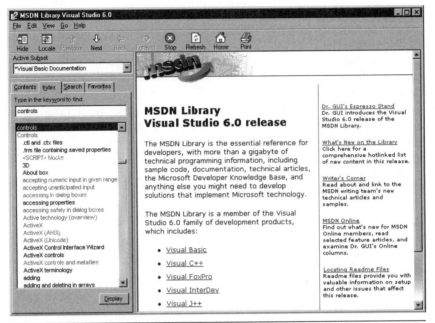

Figure 1-3 The Index tab of VB's Help dialog does an incremental search for a topic
as you type.

PROPERTIES, EVENTS, AND METHODS

Properties, Events, and Methods are the foundation of Visual Basic. In fact, every VB application from the simplest demo to the most complicated multi-user application is, at the heart, just properties, events, and methods. These are the interfaces to objects in Visual Basic. Understand these interfaces, and nothing is impossible. Those who choose to dive in and not learn these fundamental topics may never really understand VB completely. Those who are new to VB development will want to study this section carefully.

PROPERTIES

A *property* is a characteristic or attribute of an object that typically describes the object's appearance or behavior. Think of a property as an adjective that describes an object.

BACKGROUND

Almost everything manipulated in VB possesses properties. The ListBox control, for example, has a property named BackColor, which describes the appearance of the ListBox. It also has a property named MultiSelect, which determines whether multiple items can be selected in the list. Besides controls, there are other *system objects*, such as the App object, which also have many properties. Understanding the various properties of each object manipulated in VB code is absolutely essential to competency in Visual Basic.

In our quick tour of VB, we learned that VB has three modes of operation: Design mode, Run mode, and Break mode. Design time is for establishing forms, adding controls to forms, and getting the visual appearance right for the application. This is also when code is defined for execution at Run time. Run time, or Run mode, is the mode in which to test the application before compilation. A third mode, Break mode, is used for debugging the VB application. This mode and the debugging process will be addressed in Chapter 6.

Why discuss this now? Because some properties of some objects, such as the ListBox object, are "Run-time only." This means it is not possible to manipulate or *see* the property at design time. Other properties may be "read-only at run time." The upcoming sections will demonstrate that all properties are not created equal. Some are not available at design time, and others cannot be set at run time. Without a mental model of how properties work, there will be frustrating error-messages VB issues when the program runs. Understanding how properties work is central to understanding almost everything in Visual Basic.

Changing Properties at Design Time

Most properties can be changed via the Properties window (Figure 1-4), which lists the properties of an object in alphabetical order, or arranges them by category, depending on the tab selected. At the top of the Properties window is the Object box. This drop-down combo box displays the name and class name of the currently selected object. The class name is the control or object type. Select the properties of an object from the object box, or click on an object on the form to view its properties.

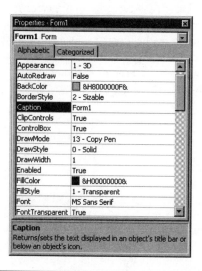

Figure 1-4 The Properties Window is used to change the characteristics of the selected object.

Check It Out 1-7: Working with Design Time Properties

The Properties window displays the design time properties of an object. Start getting familiar with the properties of some commonly used objects.

1. Start a new project and drop a Command Button, a ListBox, and a Label control on Form1.
2. Bring the Properties window into view by selecting the **VIEW/PROPERTIES** Window menu command.
3. Click **CommandButton**. Note the display in the Properties window. It shows the properties of the CommandButton named Command1.
4. Click **ListBox**. Note the display in the Properties window. It shows the properties of ListBox named List1.
5. Click **Label**. Note the display in the Properties window. It shows the properties of the label named Label1.
6. Click the form. Yes, once again, note the display in the Properties window. It shows the properties of the form named Form1.
7. Now check out the object box of the Properties window. Drop the list down by clicking on the down-arrow button. Four objects will appear: Command1, Form1, Label1, and List1. Select **List1**. Note how the focus on the form shifts to ListBox and its properties are displayed when List1 is selected. Selecting **List1** from the object box of the Properties window produces the same results as clicking on **ListBox**.
8. Select **Command1**. Click on the **Categorized** tab of the Properties window. The same properties are listed under both the Alphabetic and the Categorized tabs, but in a different order.
9. Notice the bold headings of the categories (Appearance, Behavior, Font, etc.). These headings are not properties. Click on the **minus sign** in the box to the left of each heading, collapsing the list down to view only the headings.
10. Select **Label1**. Which categories are still expanded? Click on the **minus sign** next to each heading to collapse the Properties window down to headings only.
11. Select **List1**. Which category is still expanded? Collapse the Properties window down to headings only.
12. Select **Form1**. Which category is still expanded?
13. Change the BackColor property of Form1 to white.

CHANGING PROPERTIES AT RUN TIME

Most properties of controls and forms can be changed at design time. Most properties of controls can also be changed at run time. Changing a property at run time requires code, and code is typically placed under event procedures. For example, the form object has an event procedure named `Form_Load`. This event procedure executes when the form is loaded into memory. Code can be placed under this event procedure. Experiment with changing a property of the Label object at run time. This is done with code placed under event procedures. For example, the Label object has a property named Caption that contains the text on the Label. The displayed text in the Label can be altered with the following line of VB code:

```
Form1.Label1.Caption = "VB BOOTCAMP"
```

This code specifies that the Caption property of the control named Label1 located on Form1 will be changed from its current value to VB BOOTCAMP. Specifying a property in this way (i.e., `FormName.ObjectName.PropertyName`) is known as *full qualification*. When this code executes, the Caption property of Label1 changes.

Check It Out 1-8: Changing Properties at Run Time

Properties that may be changed at run time can be manipulated in VB code, typically inside an event procedure. Try this:

1. Bring Form1 into view (if it is not already) by selecting **Form1** from the Project window and clicking on the **View Object** button of the Project window. (Or double click on **Form1** to make it visible.)
2. Now double click on **Form1**. A code window will appear displaying the `Form_Load` event procedure of Form1.
3. Now enter the following line of VB code inside the `Form_Load` event procedure:

   ```
   Form1.Label1.Caption = "VB BOOTCAMP"
   ```

4. Now select the **RUN/START** menu command. Tell VB not to save the changes. Now move from design time into run time, and VB displays Form1.
5. Label1 should be displaying the text VB BOOTCAMP because the value of Label1's Caption property was changed at run time. Click the **RUN/END** menu command to return to design time. Note that the caption of Label1 will revert back to the original design time value.

The event procedure named `Form_Load` executed when the application was started. This is because Form1 is the default Startup Object. Event procedures execute when certain events take place, such as a form loading into memory. Other examples of events include mouse clicks and mouse moves by the user. Event procedures are covered in more detail later in this chapter. For now, understand that event procedures are part of most controls and objects such as forms, and code can be placed under the procedure to respond to events and user actions. The code inserted under the `Form_Load` event of Form1 can change a property at run time. The Caption property of the Label object is an example of a property that can be changed both at design time and, with code, at run time.

Learn about all of the properties related to the Label object by referring to the VB Help file. To do this, click on the **Label** object on Form1 and press the **F1** key. The Help topic for the Label object will appear, and at the top of the listing there will be a hyperlink labeled Properties. Click on that hyperlink to get more information on all of the properties related to the Label object. Examine the Help file *often* when learning VB, so as not to miss important information.

READ-ONLY AT RUN TIME PROPERTIES

Some properties are read-only at run time. The value can be sampled, but not altered in any way. Attempting to change a property that is read-only at run time will provoke an error message. For example, the ControlBox property of the Form object can be set to either True or False at design time, specifying whether or not a system menu appears in the form to the upper left corner of the form.

If the ControlBox property is set to False, the system menu will not appear. The ControlBox property of the Form object can be changed at design time. An attempt to change the Control-Box property of a form at run time will produce a compile error as depicted in Figure 1-5. This is because the ControlBox property of the form object is *read-only* at run time. Search the Help file by selecting the **HELP/CONTENTS** menu command and search on "ControlBox" to access the Help file for this property. Note the help file indicates the property is read-only at run time.

Unlike the Caption property of the Label object, the ControlBox property of the Form object cannot be changed both at design time and at run time. The ControlBox property can only be sampled at run time, it cannot be altered. It is read-only at run time. There are many properties of numerous controls that fit into this category. When exploring the properties of a control, start thinking about how the properties behave at design time and run time. Unfortunately, the important fact that a property is read-only at run time is usually just a small detail in the Help topic. It is vital to understand the significance of any limitations imposed on the run-time behavior of a property being explored in Visual Basic.

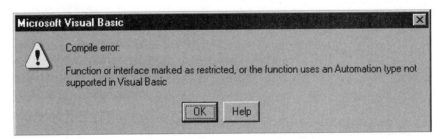

Figure 1-5 This is the error message associated with attempting to change a read-only property. It appears when there is an attempt to run the code, and halts the application.

The Default Property of a Control

The following line of code will change the caption of a label at run time:

```
Form1.Label1.Caption = "VB BOOTCAMP"
```

This line of code will do the same thing, and without an error, even if the Caption property is not specified. The following two lines of code are equivalent:

```
Form1.Label1.Caption = "VB BOOTCAMP"
Form1.Label1 = "VB BOOTCAMP"
```

Notice that in the second line of code no property is specified. Coding in this way will cause the default property of the Label object to get the assignment. This means that the Caption property of Label1 will get assigned VB BOOTCAMP, even though no property has been specified.

Coding in this manner, using implied functionality such as the default property, should be avoided because anyone who maintains this code will have to (a) know the name of the default property of the Label object or (b) stop and slog through the documentation or Help file looking for this detail. Avoid implicit coding and keep things obvious to all, unless it is necessary to write *career-secure* code, which is typically written by consultants; the excuse commonly used being "performance." Career-secure code is code that no one can comprehend—except the coder. Maintainability and good coding practice will be discussed as this book unfolds. For now, avoid the default property.

As a matter of historical note, the default property of most controls has been either poorly documented or is totally undocumented. This is because custom control writers could not define a default property when custom controls first came into vogue. Microsoft subsequently introduced the ability to define a default property as an optional feature that custom control writers could choose to implement at their discretion. Some writers did, some did not. Most did not update their Help files to call out the property with this special status. As it stands now, some controls have a default property, and some do not. Those that do rarely document the default property as they should. This has only made matters worse for new VB programmers. Do not use the default property of any control, even if you actually know what it is.

DEPENDENT PROPERTIES

Some controls have dependencies established across two or more properties. The Timer object, for example, has a property named *Interval* and a property named *Enabled*. The Interval property is used to specify how many milliseconds should elapse before the Timer's only event procedure, called the *Timer event procedure*, executes. The timer control is good for things done periodically. One use for it is to check the file system for the existence of a particular filename. Say, for example, that the VB application needs to know when some other application concludes processing. One solution is to have the other application write a certain file to a certain directory to indicate it is finished. VB can then check at intervals to see if the file is there. If it is there, it can be deleted and other processing performed. All of this can happen under the Timer event procedure using standard VB code. Shut the Timer off by setting the Enabled property to False at run time so that the Timer will not tick. Even if the Interval property is set to a valid value, it does not matter, because the Interval property of the Timer object is dependent upon the value of the Enabled property.

Many third-party custom controls possess property dependencies. Again, like the default property, this material is typically poorly documented. Be on the alert for dependencies across the properties of third-party custom controls.

DESIGN-TIME ONLY PROPERTIES

Design-time only properties are another property type. Some controls have properties such as "(About)" or "(Custom)" displayed in the Properties window. These typically lead to a dialog box, and are design-time only properties. Attempting to access these properties at run time produces an error. Try this:

Check It Out 1-9: Design-Time Only Properties

A design-time only property like "(Custom)" has obvious value at design time. Try this:

1. Add the **Microsoft DataGrid Control 6.0 (OLEDB)** to the Toolbox using VB's **PROJECT/COMPONENTS** menu command. Click on this menu command and examine the dialog.
2. The list of components that appears is actually the list of all custom controls installed on the machine. Note how many are free with Visual Basic. (It was not always this way.) Scroll down the list to the listing titled Microsoft DataGrid Control 6.0 (OLEDB). Click on the checkbox to its left, and click on the **OK** button on the dialog. The SSTab control will add itself to VB's Toolbox.
3. Select the **SSTab** from VB's Toolbox and drop one of these controls on the form. Bring up the Properties window. Click on the **Alphabetic** tab, and find the **"(About)"** property. Double click on it, and watch what happens.
4. Dismiss the About dialog and double click on the **"(Custom)"** property in the Properties window. The window that comes up is called a *property sheet*. This dialog provides a point-and-click interface for the setting of properties on the control.
5. Change the Caption property to "VB Bootcamp" and press the **Apply** button. What happens?
6. Experiment with other settings on the property page that appears when the "(Custom)" property is selected.

Understanding how to use custom controls means understanding the interfaces that the control exposes. Properties are a big part of the total interface exposed by a control. Learning how to use objects will lead to learning to build objects for use by others. Examples include ActiveX EXEs, ActiveX DLLs, and ActiveX controls, all of which can be constructed in VB. Building reusable components and controls will define properties as part of the interface. Understanding design-time and run-time properties, the default property, dependent properties, and property pages becomes critical, because these features will be incorporated into the properties of homegrown components.

GETTING HELP

Properties can be confusing. Fortunately, the Visual Basic help system is one of the best resources. Visual Basic documentation is part of the Microsoft Developer Network (MSDN) and is included as a separate application which contains help on all Microsoft's development tools, plus white papers and samples. The Help file can be accessed in several different ways including using the **F1** key, browsing the contents, or performing a search.

Check It Out 1-10: Leveraging the Help File During Development

There are several ways to get to the information in VB help. Try these:

1. Start with a new Standard EXE project by selecting **FILE/NEW PROJECT** from VB's menu. Drop a ListBox on Form1.
2. Click on the **ListBox** and expose the Properties window. Click on the **List** property and then press **F1**. What happens? It is possible to click on any property in the Properties window and then press **F1** to get Help on that property. Close VB Help.
3. Next, click on the **CommandButton** on the Toolbox. Now press **F1**. What happens? It is possible to click on any control in the Toolbox and press **F1** to get help on that control. Close VB Help again.
4. Now, go back to the ListBox. Double click on it and a code window will appear, displaying the Click event procedure. Inside this Click event, type in the word **MsgBox**. Next, click on that keyword, and then press **F1**. What happens? It is possible to click on any code in VB with a valid keyword in the code, and VB will provide the Help topic for that keyword.

Developers probably do not read documentation on the principle that we can figure it out ourselves. VB's design-time environment makes it easy to skip reading the documentation and Help file. Those who succumb to this obvious temptation will be in complete ignorance of things that are useful but invisible at design time. For example, in upcoming sections we will explain system objects like the App, Screen, and Printer objects.

Get in the habit of examining the Help file and reading the documentation. VB ships with full documentation in the MSDN application, and we strongly recommend they be installed in total. VB's Help menu command provides access to MSDN as a menu option, and a search engine is provided. This is a great resource, a required resource in the bag of tools for learning VB. Those in a rush may go off and start looking for jobs in VB, and may even immediately get them after they digest this book. There will be a strong temptation to "go build something" and skip the ongoing study we recommend here. They will eventually have to go back and do it anyway. Trust us. Develop a balanced VB brain.

EVENTS AND EVENT-HANDLING ROUTINES

It is important to note that the whole purpose of VB is to create Windows programs fast and without a fuss. A Windows program is created by programming in VB. Also remember that Windows is an event-driven, message-based programming environment of great complexity. Writing Windows programs in VB is simple, largely because VB reduces the complexity of Windows programming significantly by providing event procedures where custom code can be placed to make the program come to life.

BACKGROUND

> **Event Procedure:** A predefined, empty procedure in which to put custom code.

During the lifetime of the program, there are many events. The first form loads. Then the first control on that form gets the focus. Then the user moves the mouse and clicks it on a button. In VB, there are empty event procedures that will execute when specific events take place, like the ones we just described. Those who care about the occurrence of the event write code in the corresponding event procedure, which is initially empty. Event procedures are provided by VB so that programmers can react to specific events during the execution of the application.

For each item programmed, there may be a predefined set of event procedures, or there may be none at all. The form object, for example, has many event procedures, while the timer control (discussed earlier when we talked about property dependency) has only one: the Timer event procedure. As we will see, some controls have very few event procedures, while others have many. Event procedures are optional—do not expect every object programmed to have them. Other books on VB will have the terms *event* and *event procedure* used interchangeably. Instead, we define an event as something that occurs, and we define an event procedure as a predefined procedure that executes *in response* to a specific event, such as the user clicking the mouse. Events happen; event procedures execute in response.

THE DEFAULT EVENT PROCEDURE

Start a new project and drop a ListBox, a Timer, and a Label on Form1. Next, double click on the **Form**. This will bring up a code window. The code window will display the `Form_Load` event procedure. This is because the `Form_Load` event procedure is defined as the default event procedure. Double click on the **ListBox** control and see the `List1_Click` event procedure displayed. For any control, there is a default event procedure defined. This is the procedure that appears first when a code window for the control is displayed.

Double click on **Form1**: `Form_Load` is displayed—the default event procedure. Click on the dropdown combo to the upper right of the code window. All the event procedures that are defined for the Form object will display in the dropdown. (See Figure 1-6.) All these procedures are empty, waiting for custom code. Think of event procedures as notifications. When an event happens, the corresponding event procedure executes, providing the opportunity to react to the event.

Check It Out 1-11: Event Procedures of the Form Object

We will look at some of the most fundamental event procedures found in Visual Basic: the event procedures of the Form object. The Form object has many event procedures of interest. Two are the *Load* and *Unload* event procedures.

1. Start a new project and double click on **Form1** to display a code window. The `Form_Load` event procedure will appear. It is the default procedure for the Form object.

2. Add the following code to the `Form_Load` event procedure:

```
MsgBox "FORM LOAD"
```

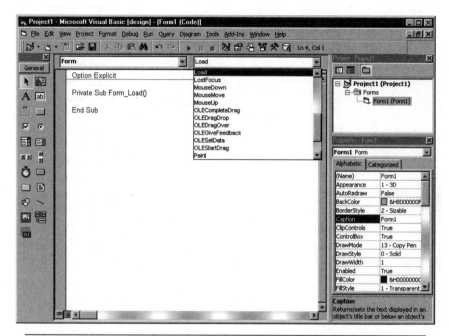

Figure 1-6 The right side dropdown box of the form's code window displays the event procedures of the Form object.

3. Now select the **Unload** event procedure by clicking on the **Procedure** dropdown that appears to the upper right of the code window, and click on **Unload** from the list. Add the following code in the Unload event procedure:

```
MsgBox "FORM UNLOAD"
```

4. Now click on the **RUN/START** menu command. The output from the `Form_Load` event procedure's MsgBox statement is: a modal dialog box displaying the text FORM LOAD. What is visible is the Load event procedure executing. This happens when the form comes into memory, but before it goes on screen.

5. Click the **OK** button of the MsgBox dialog. Now the form is visible. Click the **ControlBox** on Form1, and from the system menu, select the **Close** command. Now the `Form_Unload` event procedure executes and displays a dialog with the text FORM UNLOAD. The Unload event procedure of the Form object executes before the form leaves memory, and before it goes off screen.

6. The Form object has many other interesting and important event procedures that are well documented in the Help file. (How can this important online documentation for the Form object be found?)

EVENT PROCEDURE FIRING ORDER

The event procedures of the Form object are well documented. What is *not* well documented is the relationship between all the individual event procedures that are part of the Form object.

Check It Out 1-12: Analyzing Event Firing Order

To understand the order in which various event procedures execute, do some experimentation.

1. Double click on **Form1** to bring up its code window.
2. Add the following MsgBox statement under the Activate event procedure:

```
MsgBox "FORM ACTIVATE"
```

3. Add similar MsgBox statements with appropriate descriptive text under the Initialize, Paint, and Resize event procedures.
4. Now run the project. What happens? What is the event firing order?
5. Now experiment. Resize the form to be smaller. Resize the form to be larger. Minimize and then restore the form. What happens?

The Initialize, Load, Resize, Paint, and Activate event procedures are interrelated. When the form loads, they all execute in a certain order. Knowing the order is important for a competent VB developer, though this important knowledge concerning the event firing order of event procedures is very poorly documented in VB manuals and the Help file. We hope that is not the case now that this book is published.

USING DEBUG.PRINT

For many event procedures, it is possible to experiment with placing MsgBox statements inside, and then fiddling with the control or form to see what happens. However, the Form_MouseMove event procedure will cause trouble if MsgBox statements are put under it to see what it does because the MouseMove event procedure executes every time the mouse is moved one pixel. Putting a MsgBox statement under the MouseMove will cause it to execute and appear on screen. Click on the **OK** button to dismiss it—but that will move the mouse a pixel, which will execute the MouseMove event procedure again. This type of behavior can occur with several other events as well.

Clearly, the MsgBox statement is not an all-purpose solution when experimenting with event procedures. Use Debug.Print instead. A Debug.Print statement will write text to the *Immediate window* (also known as the *Debug window* by crusty, veteran VB 1.0 developers).

Check It Out 1-13: Printing to the Immediate (Debug) Window

Using the same project with the MsgBox statements, see what happens when sending output to the Immediate window.

1. Double click on **Form1** to bring up its code window.

2. Click on the procedure dropdown to the upper right. The event procedures will appear in the dropdown. Note that, for each event procedure under which code has been placed, that event procedure name is represented as bolded text. This indicates that it contains something—probably some code, but at least a comment.

3. For each event procedure with a MsgBox statement under it, replace it with a `Debug.Print` statement instead, such as:

```
Debug.Print "FORM LOAD"
```

4. Run the application, and then select the **VIEW/IMMEDIATE WINDOW** menu command. This will bring up the Immediate (or Debug) window. What is visible?

5. Form1 is still running, as a separate application. Switch the window to Form1 and close it. Which event procedure executes now? It may be necessary to use the **VIEW/IMMEDIATE WINDOW** menu command again, since you are back to design time. (Note: Clicking inside the Immediate window may have repositioned the cursor within that window. This would affect the position of the output of any `Debug.Print` statements that followed.)

6. Now put similar `Debug.Print` statements under these events: Deactivate, QueryUnload, and Terminate.

7. Observe what happens, and in what order the application is started and stopped. To clear the contents of the Immediate window and start over, select its contents (in design time) and delete it.

Read the Help file for each of the event procedures of the form object tested. This technique of exploring the event firing order of event procedures is valuable to those beginning to write production VB applications. For example, if you assume that the Resize event procedure executed only when the form was resized would be wrong, even though that assumption would be a reasonable one to make. This experiment has shown that the Resize event executes right *after* the form loads. Short-circuiting the default behavior and making VB obey will come later. Understand the relationships between event procedures of the form object. They execute in a predefined order, which must be known *before* starting to do serious work in Visual Basic.

Event procedures impose a rigid set of rules on a developer. An event procedure cannot be deleted or added. The name of an existing event procedure cannot be changed; nor can the return value (if any) of an event procedure. Most event procedures do not include passed parameters, but some do. (Investigate the Unload and QueryUnload event procedures for examples of this.) All event procedures consist of a name and a set of parentheses, which are typically empty, having no parameters passed in by VB or Windows. New passed parameters cannot be inserted between the parentheses, nor can any passed-in parameters that may appear between the parentheses be removed. The name or data type of any passed-in parameters cannot be changed.

In short, there are two choices: Place code under event procedures of interest, or ignore the event procedure and do nothing with it whatsoever. Events execute whether or not code is placed under them. Event procedures make it easy to write event-driven Windows applications, but the rigid rules must be obeyed. That is the price for the convenience of programming in Visual Basic.

An event procedure executes when a specific event occurs. Visual Basic objects provide empty event procedures. To respond to that particular event, put code inside that event procedure. Events have a specific firing order. Understanding the firing order is key to successful VB development. VB has reduced the complexity of Windows programming, and with that come certain restrictions concerning the use of event procedures.

METHODS

A *method* is a routine that has a name and is part of the object being programmed. It is a procedure that performs an action upon the object to which it belongs. For example, the AddItem method of the ListBox control appends a new item to the visible display of the ListBox object. By way of comparison, the RemoveItem method of the ListBox object deletes text items from the ListBox.

BACKGROUND

A method is a callable procedure that is part of an object such as a form, ListBox, or scroll bar. The method can be thought of as a kind of verb, or action, that can be performed upon the object.

METHOD EXAMPLES

Methods often come in pairs. For example, the ListBox object contains AddItem and RemoveItem methods. These are complementary opposites. The Form object supports a Show method, which displays the form, and a Hide method, which hides it from view. For a complete list of the methods of the form or ListBox, examine the Help file for each object.

The syntax of a method call is very similar to the syntax of a property of an object. Compare the following two lines:

```
ObjectName.PropertyName = value
ObjectName.MethodName argument
```

How is it possible to tell the difference between a property and a method? The first thing to notice is that the property name will be a description of an attribute of the object. The method name will identify an action to be performed on the object. It will usually make obvious sense for the property to have a value that represents a quantity (a number) or a state (True or False, for example). In grammatical terms, a property is like an adjective that describes; a method is like a verb that does an action.

Check It Out 1-14: Methods of the ListBox control

It is time to experiment with the ListBox control and some typical examples of methods.

1. Start with a new project. Drop a ListBox on Form1.
2. Double click on **Form1**. Add the following code to the Form_Load event:

```
Form1.List1.AddItem "Thing1"
Form1.List1.AddItem "Thing2"
Form1.List1.AddItem "Thing3"
```

3. Run the application. List1 will display the text added to List1 with the AddItem method calls, which are coded under the `Form_Load` event procedure.
4. End the application by clicking on the **RUN/END** menu command.
5. Drop a CommandButton on Form1. Attach the following code to the Click event of this button:

```
Form1.List1.RemoveItem 0
```

6. When clicked, this button will remove the first item from List1. The `RemoveItem` method requires an integer value specifying the ordinal number of the item to remove. Since the first item in a ListBox starts with the number zero, this is what we have specified to delete the first item. Run the applilcation. Click on **Command1**. What happens?
7. Click on **Command1** to delete all of the items, then click once more. There is an error because of the attempt to delete the first item, and there is no first item to delete. We are now in VB's Break mode, which will be covered later. For now, click on **End** in the modal error message dialog box to return to design time.
8. Drop another button on Form1, and attach this code under the Click event procedure:

```
Form1.List1.Clear
```

9. Run the application. Click on **Command2**. What happens?
10. End the application. Click on **List1**, and press **F1** to bring up the Help. For further study, check out all the methods of the ListBox object.

The `AddItem` and `RemoveItem` methods of the ListBox object are typical of the way methods operate on an object. Knowledge of the methods of one control may be applicable to many controls. The ComboBox control, for example, also has AddItem, RemoveItem, and Clear methods, just like the ListBox control. Common methods will become clear, and it will be easy to identify the unique features with each new control learned.

A method is a *callable procedure*. Methods do the work on an object and often come in pairs, like the `AddItem` and `RemoveItem` methods of the ListBox control. A typical use of method calls is in event procedures, to make the object do its actions. In the exercise to follow, we will consider more of how properties, events, and methods interact.

A large part of the interface of a control is its properties, or attributes of the object. Events fire event procedures in a specific order. It is possible to call methods from within event procedures to get work done.

Properties, events, and methods are the interfaces to each control. The interface exposed is the control. Mastering the fundamentals of the properties, events, and methods of each control is essential to use a control properly.

ADVANCED IDE FEATURES

NOTE

Many of the features covered in this section are related to advanced programming concepts. Bookmark this section and return to it regularly as more skills are learned.

The Visual Basic *Integrated Debugging Environment* (IDE) provides a main work area and tool windows that are dockable alongside the border of a *multiple document interface* (MDI) design. The MDI design, as its name implies, means that more than one Visual Basic project may be open at a time. At first, the advantages of multiple projects may be unclear. We need to change our definition of an application. Normally, most developers think of an application as a monolithic pile of code compiled as a single entity and then distributed. This is no longer true. An application is now defined as a set of distributed software components that work together to perform a function. Many of these components may participate in more than one "application" at a time by performing a common function like database services.

Visual Basic 6.0 reflects the reality of distributed object applications through a concept known as the *program group*. Program groups are made up of many VB projects. Each project is a separate software component that performs a function in a distributed application. The complete application is the collection of all these projects or the program group. In Visual Basic 6.0, individual components are created as VB projects, and run together as a group when they are complete.

Check It Out 1-15: Using Program Groups

1. Start a new Visual Basic Standard EXE by selecting **FILE/NEW PROJECT...** from the menu and choosing **Standard EXE** from the project dialog.
2. This project, with its form support, might be used as a front end for an application.
3. Now add a new project by selecting **FILE/ADD PROJECT...** from the menu. This time add an ActiveX DLL from the project dialog.
4. Notice that both projects are visible in the Project window. Use the mouse to toggle between the projects.
5. Right-click on one of the projects and note the menu that appears. Visual Basic permits setting a project as the startup project. This means that the selected project is the one to run first when selecting **RUN/START** from the menu. All of the other projects can be accessed by the startup project.
6. Save the group by selecting **FILE/SAVE PROJECT GROUP...** from the menu. The project group allows keeping the projects together that work together.

THE COMPONENTS DIALOG AND TOOLBOX

Managing ActiveX controls in Visual Basic is accomplished through the toolbox and components dialog. Viewing the toolbox is done by selecting **VIEW/TOOLBOX** from the menu, whereas selecting **PROJECT/COMPONENTS** reveals the Components dialog. VB provides several new features and ActiveX controls for projects.

The toolbox is used to manage the components that are currently part of a program group. Components appear in the toolbox because one of the projects in the group uses the control. The contents of the toolbox remain unchanged from project to project as long as they remain within the same program group. Controls may also be grouped in Visual Basic using the new tabbed toolbox feature.

The toolbox supports grouping by adding up to four additional tabs along with the General tab that exists by default. The new tabs can be used to sort existing or new controls within the program group. They remain as part of the toolbox permanently, but the controls placed in the tabs are present only as long as their respective projects are open.

The Components dialog permits adding new controls to a Visual Basic project. VB supports more than just ActiveX controls, however. The Components dialog also lists the Insertable objects and Designers available at design time. Insertable objects are not new. They existed in VB 4.0, but many developers are still not familiar with them. Insertable objects are ActiveX components that represent objects available from other applications on the operating system. This includes Excel spreadsheets, Word documents, Paintbrush images, and so on. All of these components can be embedded into a Visual Basic form.

Check It Out 1-16: Insertable Objects

1. Start a new Standard EXE project in Visual Basic by selecting **FILE/NEW PROJECT...** from the menu.
2. Open the Components dialog by selecting **PROJECT/COMPONENTS...** from the menu.
3. In the Components dialog, select the **Insertable Objects** tab.
4. Locate the Insertable object titled **Bitmap Image**, which is part of the Paint program. Select the checkbox and push the **OK** button. An icon should appear in the toolbox for the Insertable object.
5. Select the new icon from the toolbox and draw it onto Form1 so that it covers the entire form.
6. Run the project by selecting **RUN/START** from the menu.
7. Double-click on the **Insertable** object to start the Paint program. Now draw inside the work area.

Designers are additional components that make it possible to create software graphically. Visual Basic ships with several designers that may be added to the VBIDE by simply selecting them in the Components dialog. When added to the VBIDE, the designers do not appear in the toolbox, but on the menu under PROJECT. Once added, the designers are a permanent part of the environment.

PROJECT TEMPLATES AND THE NEW PROJECT DIALOG

With every new project in Visual Basic, notice that VB prompts a selection from a collection of predefined projects. The project templates are presented in the New Project dialog, which contains templates for all the different projects that VB can create, but can also contain templates for created projects. All of the templates are kept in the templates directory, which is C:\PROGRAM FILES\MICROSOFT VISUAL STUDIO\VB98\TEMPLATE by default. It is possible to change the templates directory in the Options dialog found under the TOOLS/OPTIONS menu selection.

Check It Out 1-17: Creating a Template

---

1. Start a new Standard EXE Project in Visual Basic.
2. Place a command button on Form1.
3. In the Click event of Command1, add the following code:

```
MsgBox "This is My First Template!"
```

4. Change the name of Form1 to frmFirst.
5. Save the project by selecting **FILE/SAVE PROJECT** into the TEMPLATE\ PROJECTS directory as specified in the options dialog. Use the following file names:

```
First.frm
My First Template.VBP
```

6. After saving, select **FILE/NEW PROJECT** from the menu. Examine the New Project dialog. The new template should be visible. Select this project.
7. Run the new project and verify that the template works correctly.

THE CODE WINDOW

The Code window has many features designed to speed coding. These begin with the most noticeable of all: Auto List Members and Auto Quick Tips. Auto List Members and Auto Quick Tips provide hints to programmers as they write code. If an object or function is selected, then these features give the programmer a list of choices to complete the line of code.

The VB Code window also supports drag-and-drop coding. With this feature, it is possible to highlight a line of code in the Code window and drag it to another location in the window or to make a copy of the code by holding the **Ctrl** key while dragging the code. The code can even be dragged to the Debug window during break mode for evaluation.

The Code window also has a gray margin area where breakpoints and bookmarks are set. Setting a breakpoint is now a simple matter of clicking in the margin next to the line of code where the breakpoint is required. Bookmarks are set using the Edit menu. They can be turned on and off from the Edit menu and make it possible to navigate between the bookmarks that have been set. Neither bookmarks nor breakpoints are saved when a project is saved.

During Break mode, it is possible to gain access to the values of variables by simply putting the mouse over the variable in the Code window. Highlight expressions and see their value in the same way. Locals and Watch windows are also available for viewing variable values.

FORM DESIGN FEATURES

Visual Basic provides a number of formatting features for use with forms. Most are available directly off of the Format menu. VB provides alignment tools that make it possible to align groups of controls on left, top, right, center, middle, or bottom edges. These options will help line up buttons and text boxes on forms, and to make groups of controls the same size either horizontally, vertically, or both.

PROJECT PROPERTIES

Many key aspects of a Visual Basic project can be controlled through the Project Properties dialog, which is accessed through the Project menu. Select **PROJECT/PROJECT1 PROPERTIES...** to display the tabbed dialog. Each tab of the dialog controls a specific set of project features.

THE GENERAL TAB

The General tab configures many fundamental aspects of a project. The Project Type dropdown box is used to set the type of project-Standard EXE, ActiveX EXE, ActiveX DLL, or ActiveX control. This value is set when a project template is chosen from the New Project dialog and can be changed at any time.

The Startup Object box permits selecting the component within a project that will be the first to execute. In a Standard EXE this can be any form in the project or Sub Main. With ActiveX components, there can be no startup object; simply activate the component when it is called by a client.

The Project Name, Description, and Help file can also be set in this tab. This information is important, particularly in ActiveX components, since the name and description will appear in tools such as the object browser.

Selecting Upgrade ActiveX Controls will convert any controls in the project that conform to the VBX standard with the equivalent OCX. This will only affect a project if it was previously created in VB 4.0, 16-bit version, or VB 3.0. In these cases, upgrade the controls or they will not be recognized in VB 6.0. Selecting **Require License Key** permits requiring a license for the ActiveX controls created. Selecting **Unattended Execution** means that components will not have a user interface. Selecting **Retain in Memory** allows created components to stay in memory even after they finish running so they will start faster.

THE MAKE TAB

The Make tab contains information about the current build of the project. In this tab, set the version number and ask Visual Basic to automatically increment the build version each time the project is compiled. Automatic incrementing is limited to the smallest revision number only. Changing the major and minor values must be done by hand.

Version number and version information can be embedded into the compiled project. All the embedded information is available at run time through properties of the App object. This eases building of splash screens and About boxes that can be used in every project.

Any VB application that you create can be executed not only from an icon, but also from the command line. When an application is executed from a command line, Visual Basic accepts command line arguments that are passed in to a special variable in VB called `Command$`. `Command$` contains all the arguments that can be read and then parsed to modify the application's behavior. The Make tab provides a way to pass these arguments at design time by simply typing them into the Command Line Arguments textbox.

Check It Out 1-18: Using Command Line Arguments

1. Start a new Visual Basic Standard EXE.
2. Open the **Project Properties** dialog and click on the **Make** tab.
3. In the Command Line Arguments dialog, enter the following test arguments:

```
/s /u
```

4. Close the **Project Properties** dialog.
5. In the Load event of Form1, add the following code to read the arguments:

```
MsgBox Command$
```

6. Run the project and verify that Command$ receives the command line arguments specified.

In addition to command line arguments, Visual Basic also supports Conditional Compilation, which makes it possible to designate certain parts of code to compile based on a specified argument. A number of different editions can be created for a component from just a single code base. Imagine, for example, wanting to create a Standard, Pro, and Enterprise edition of some software. To accomplish this, specify Conditional Compilation constants and set their values in the Make tab as follows:

```
Standard = -1:Pro = 0:Enterprise = 0
```

The values for the constants are set as either True or False. Visual Basic recognizes –1 as True and 0 as False. In this case, only the Standard constant is True. You can then use the constants in code to block out functions reserved only for the Pro or Enterprise editions.

```
#If Standard Then
  'Code for Standard Edition
#Else
  'Code for Pro and Enterprise
#End If
```

The number/pound sign (#) indicates to the VB compiler that the If...Then statement is a preprocessor command. In other words, VB looks at the Conditional Compilation blocks before the compiler runs. Any code that does not meet the test is not compiled. The code left out is simply treated as a comment.

THE COMPILE TAB

The Compile tab makes it possible to control all the native compile features of Visual Basic. Projects can be compiled into p-code or native code using the appropriate options. Several options and optimizations are available to enhance project speed or size.

Optimize for Fast Code is perhaps the most frequently used option. This will produce the fastest possible executable, but the size of the program in memory will be larger than with other optimizations. The memory footprint may not be a concern in most applications, but may be an issue for clients constrained by available resources.

Optimize for Small Code causes the memory footprint of the application to be as small as possible. The small-memory footprint will cause the program to run slower than code optimized for speed, but will use fewer resources. This may help components load and initialize faster.

No Optimization removes all optimizing features, while Favor Pentium Pro produces software specifically targeted at the Pentium Pro processor. Creating Symbolic debug information will allow the application to be debugged in Visual C++ and create a special file containing debug information to go along with the component.

THE COMPONENT TAB

The Component tab is used to specify features of the software component that affect its use and compatibility. The Start Mode option is used by VB to identify projects in the design environment that are dependent on other projects, such as DLLs. Selecting the ActiveX component allows the projects to stay running in the design environment so they can be debugged. This option has no effect after the project is compiled.

The Remote Server files option creates a special file for use with servers that will be distributed on a network. The created file, with extension .VBR, contains information required by clients connecting to distributed ActiveX components.

Version compatibility determines how ActiveX components behave as they are modified, compiled, and distributed. Components that set the Project Compatibility option allow clients to maintain a reference to them in the References dialog even after the component code is modified. This is primarily for debugging purposes. The Binary Compatibility option ensures that when the component is modified and compiled, it is completely backwards compatible with clients that have used a previous version of the component. Binary compatibility can only be maintained if the function signatures of all properties and methods are left unchanged across versions.

THE DEBUGGING TAB

The Debugging tab is used to determine how to start various components in a project while they are being debugged. Some components may start in a web browser. Others may not start until they are needed. We will explore these options.

VBIDE OPTIONS

Project properties are responsible for managing features of the project. VBIDE options are used to manage options associated with the Visual Basic environment itself. The options are accessed by selecting **TOOLS/OPTIONS...** from the menu.

THE EDITOR TAB

The Editor tab sets options that affect the code window behavior. The Auto Syntax Check option causes Visual Basic to check the syntax on a line of code when exiting the line. If the line is incorrect, VB pops an error dialog. At first, the Auto Syntax Check seems like a good idea, but actually it is not. If the Auto Syntax Check is off, then VB still checks the line of code, but when it is wrong, no message box is displayed—the line of code simply turns red. This is a much more useful way to identify problematic code. Our recommendation is to turn off Auto Syntax Check.

The Require Variable Declaration option causes Visual Basic to place the keywords *Option Explicit* at the top of every form and module in a project when they are first added. Option Explicit tells the Visual Basic compiler that every variable in the application must be explicitly declared before it can be used. This is an excellent feature that eliminates typographical errors. Our recommendation is to have the Require Variable declaration on.

Auto List Members, Auto Quick Tips, and Auto Data Tips enable the popup lists for the code window discussed earlier. Our recommendation is for all of the features to be on.

Auto Indent tells the VB text editor to automatically indent the next line of code to the level of the previous line. This feature makes it possible to create *block indented* code that enhances readability and nesting. Our recommendation is to have Auto Indent on.

The Window settings features enable display features of the code window discussed previously. These useful features should all be on.

THE EDITOR FORMAT TAB

The Editor Format tab is where the text editor display features are configured. In this dialog, the font style, size, and color for the Text Editor are set. The code window margin can be enabled. The margin area supports placing breakpoints and bookmarks in the code.

THE GENERAL TAB

The General tab contains a number of options not easily grouped under another tab. The Form Grid Settings permit configuring the grid pattern that appears on a form. This pattern is used to help align controls when building a GUI. The pattern density can be altered with the Height and Width numbers. If the grid is disabled, then controls can be moved one pixel at a time.

The Form Grid also supports two useful keyboard shortcuts for resizing and repositioning controls. After a control is selected, it can be moved by holding down the **Ctrl** key and pressing the arrow keys. Resizing occurs when the **Shift** key is held and the arrows are pressed.

The error trapping options are also available from this tab. Break on All Errors disables all of the On Error GoTo statements in the code. This can be very useful in debugging since it forces VB to enter Break mode rather than handle the error in a trap. Break in Class Module causes errors raised by ActiveX components to force VB into Break mode inside the component instead of in the calling client. Break on Unhandled Errors is the normal error handling mechanism that will only break if no error handler is coded into the routine.

The Compile On Demand option is used only while running code in the VB environment and tells Visual Basic to compile just the next few lines of code necessary to continue running an application. With this option unchecked, VB will fully compile the entire project before running it. If Background Compile is selected as well, VB will not only compile on demand, but will also do it in the background while the user is not interacting with the application. Our experience is that Compile On Demand can be confusing, since it often raises compile-time errors, such as undeclared variables while the program is executing. Our recommendation is to turn this option off.

Show Tool Tips simply turns on the tool tips for the toolbox. Collapse Proj. Hides Windows causes the code modules and forms to disappear when the project tree in the project window is collapsed.

THE DOCKING TAB

The Docking tab is fairly simple. Here it is possible to specify which windows are dockable in the VB environment. All dockable windows can also be easily undocked by grabbing them and pulling with the mouse.

THE ENVIRONMENT TAB

The Environment tab specifies options that affect the entire VB environment. When starting VB, it is possible to choose to have it create a default project (Standard EXE) or prompt with the New Project dialog. When a project is subsequently run, VB can be instructed how to handle unsaved changes. They can be ignored and VB can prompt to save the project, or the changes can be automatically saved without prompting. We recommend at least setting this option to receive a prompt from VB when the project is dirty.

The templates discussed previously can be managed from this tab. Select the available templates and template directory in this tab.

THE ADVANCED TAB

The Advanced tab contains only three options. Background Project Load instructs VB to load project files in the background. This feature makes it easy to get to work faster. "Notify when changing shared project items" makes it possible to receive notification when a shared item such as a form or class is changed in one project. The same form or module can be used in many projects, but if one project changes the component, all other projects must be synchronized with the change. Finally, an HTML editor can be specified for use with Web projects in VB.

Exercise 1-1: ListBox Manipulation

The following exercise allows practice using properties, events, and methods for ListBox manipulation. Notice how a method is called from within an event procedure, but is conditional upon the value of a property.

Step 1

Start a new Standard EXE project. Immediately save the project to a directory named **VB BOOTCAMP\EXERCISE1-1**. The VB BOOTCAMP directory will hold all of the projects created in the exercises in this book. Properties, Events, and Methods is the first project. All the elements of this first project will be saved to the **EXERCISE1-1** directory.

Step 2

Make Form1 visible if it is not already. Add two ListBoxes and one Button to the form. Figure 1-7 shows the completed interface. Double click on it to reveal a code window and add the following code under the `Form_Load` event:

```
Form1.List1.Additem "Thing3"
Form1.List1.Additem "Thing2"
Form1.List1.Additem "Thing1"
```

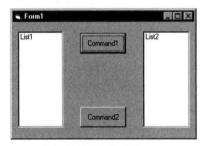

Figure 1-7 This is the form with two ListBoxes and two CommandButtons.

Step 3

Run the application by selecting the **RUN/START** menu command. List1 should display the three items added in the previous step. End the application by clicking on the **RUN/END** menu command to return to design time.

Step 4

Double click on the **Command1** button to reveal the Click event of Command1. Code will be placed under the Click event of Command1.

Step 5

The purpose of Command1 is to move the selected item from List1 to List2. Add the following code to the Click event procedure of Command1:

```
'CHECK TO SEE IF AN ITEM IS SELECTED:
If Form1.List1.ListIndex = -1 Then Exit Sub
'COPY THE SELECTED ITEM FROM LIST1 TO LIST2:
Form1.List2.AddItem Form1.List1.List(Form1.List1.ListIndex)
```

Step 6

Run the application. Click on the first item in List1, and then click on **Command1**. What happens? The selected List1 text should appear in List2. End the application and return to design time.

Step 7

Search the Help file for the following properties of the ListBox control:
- a. ListCount Property
- b. List Property
- c. ListIndex Property

Step 8

Also, search the help for the following methods of the ListBox:
- a. AddItem Method
- b. RemoveItem Method
- c. Clear Method

Step 9

Now search the help for this VB command:
- a. Exit Sub Satement

Step 10

The code attached to the `Command1_Click` event procedure performed the task of copying the selected text from one list box to another. One additional step remains. Remove the text from List1, the source list box. Double click on **Command1** and append the following code lines to the very end of the event procedure:

```
'DELETE THE SELECTED ITEM FROM LIST1
Form1.List1.RemoveItem Form1.List1.ListIndex
```

Step 11

Run the application and click the first item on List1. What happens?

Step 12

With nothing selected in List1, click on **Command1**. What happens? Why?

Step 13

The application being coded is common to setup and initialization programs—there is a list of possible choices to select from in order to arrive at the final list of selections. Those who have seen this type of user interface in the past know that there is usually not just one button between the list boxes, but four. One button moves selected items from left to right, and another moves selected items from right to left. Two more buttons are used to move everything in one direction or the other. In this exercise, we will create buttons to move only a single selected item at a time. We just created the first button that moves a selected item from left to right. Now we will move it back.

Step 14

Add a second CommandButton. Now we will work with the second button. We will copy code from Command1 and change it slightly.

Step 15

Command2 will do everything Command1 does, but it will move selected text form List2 into List1. The code in Command1 will be useful to do this. All we have to do is make a few changes. Double click on **Command1**, then select all the code entered in the previous steps. Click on the **EDIT/COPY** menu command. This will copy the selected code to the Windows clipboard.

Step 16

Now close the Code window and double click on **Command2**. The Command2_Click event will display in the code window that appears. Click anywhere *inside* this event procedure and select the **EDIT/PASTE** menu command. This (in effect) copies the code from Command1 to Command2, by way of the clipboard. Save the work by clicking on the **FILE/SAVE PROJECT** menu command. *Remember to save often!*

Step 17

Now, edit the code that was pasted. Carefully change it so that this code moves the selected text in List2 to List1. *Be careful* and deliberate. Change the comments to reflect what the code should do. Change every reference to List1 to List2, and vice versa. The effect of these edits will be to enable Command2 with the functionality to move the selected item in List2 directly into List1. Save work by clicking on the **FILE/SAVE PROJECT** menu command.

Step 18

Run the application. Click on the first item in List1 and click on **Command1** to move it to List2. Now select the first item in List2, and click on **Command2**. Is everything working? If Command2 does not work, return to design time. Go back to the code under Command2_Click and check it over. Is it a good idea to copy code this way?

Step 19

Notice that items in both ListBoxes do not appear in sorted order, something that most users have come to expect. Click on **List1** and change the Sorted property to True. Do the same for List2.

Step 20

Save the work and run the application. All items should appear sorted in both ListBoxes, regardless of the order in which they were added to the ListBox.

Exercise 1-2: Creating a Spin Control

A spin control is a combination of a TextBox and a Slider. The Slider causes a numeric range of values to be set into the TextBox. The value can also be changed by typing directly into the TextBox.

Step 1

Begin by creating a directory underneath the VB BOOTCAMP directory for the new project using the File Explorer. The directory should be **VB BOOTCAMP\EXERCISE1-2**.

Step 2

Start a new Visual Basic Standard EXE project. Immediately save the project under the directory created.

Step 3

On Form1, place a TextBox and Horizontal Scroll Bar as shown in Figure 1-8. Use the information below to set the properties for each control at design time.

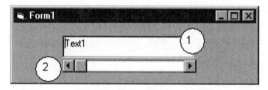

Figure 1-8 This is the form used to create the spin control.

Item1—TextBox

Name	Text1
Text	<blank>

Item2—Horizontal Scroll Bar

Name	HScroll1
LargeChange	10
Max	100

Step 4

Once the form is built, add code to the project to make the spinner work. Double click on the **scroll bar** to enter the code window. The event handler for the Change event will appear. This event is Hscroll1_Change. Add the following code to display the current value of the scroll bar in the TextBox.

```
Text1.Text = HScroll1.Value
```

Step 5

Run the application by selecting **RUN/START** from the Visual Basic menu. The form will appear. Try clicking on the left and right arrows of the scroll bar. The value in the TextBox should change. Now try moving the center part of the scroll bar called the *thumb*. Note the value of the TextBox as the thumb moves. The value will not change until moving finishes.

Step 6

Try changing the behavior by using a different event. Enter the same line of code from step 4 in the Scroll event of the scroll bar. Run the application and move the thumb again. This time the TextBox values change as the thumb moves.

Step 7

Now add code to change the value by typing directly into the TextBox. When the value in the TextBox changes, the Change event fires. Add the follwing code to the `Text1_Change` event to set a new value for the scroll bar.

```
HScroll1.Value = Text1.Text
```

Step 8

Run the project and type the value **50** into the TextBox. The scrollbar thumb should move halfway across. Now move the thumb. The TextBox value should change.

Step 9

With the project still running, type the letter **A** into the TextBox. What happens? This is a problem because our scroll bar does not expect to deal with letters.

Step 10

In order to mask out unwanted input to a TextBox, use the **KeyPress** event. This fires when a key on the keyboard is pressed, but before the value actually appears in the TextBox. The event also receives an integer representation of the key pressed, called an *ASCII*. ASCII represents every key on the keyboard with a unique number. We can then detect what key was pressed and ignore it if we do not want it.

Step 11

Add the following code to the `Text1_KeyPress` event to reject non-numeric values. Whenever you mask, remember to allow users to use the BackSpace key. Search the help file for keycode constants to see all of the available ASCII key constants.

```
'This code is used to mask
'out unwanted values
If KeyAscii = vbKeyBack Then Exit Sub

If KeyAscii < vbKey0 Or KeyAscii > vbKey9 Then
 KeyAscii = 0
End If
```

FOR THE CERTIFIED PRO

Pro 1-1: Searching a List

1. Create a Standard EXE with a TextBox and a ListBox.
2. When a user types into the TextBox, search the ListBox for an item starting with the entered text and highlight the item.

Pro 1-2: Masking a TextBox

1. Create a TextBox that can accept just numbers or just letters. Use option buttons to set the preference.

PREPARING FOR CERTIFICATION

Topics for further reading include:
> Welcome to Visual Basic
> Designing a Form
> Understanding Properties, Events, and Methods
> Your First Visual Basic Application.

CERTIFICATION QUIZ

1. The Properties window is used to:
   a. alter the appearance of an object such as a form.
   b. change settings related to an object's behavior.
   c. view the current settings of the properties of an object.
   d. All of the above

2. Which main menu command leads to submenu commands that add new program objects such as forms, modules, and class modules?
   a. File
   b. Edit
   c. View
   d. Project

3. Which property sets a value that determines whether a form can be moved?
   a. MDIChild property
   b. FixedMode property
   c. Movable property
   d. ScaleMode property

4. The StartUpPosition Property identifies where
   a. a form will be displayed when first shown.
   b. a control will be displayed when first shown.
   c. the data control will set its first record at start up.
   d. the current cell of the MSFlexGrid will start off.

5. The DisabledPicture Property sets a reference to a picture to display in which of the following controls when the control is disabled?
   a. CheckBox control
   b. OptionButton control
   c. CommandButton control
   d. PictureBox control

6. The Style property of a ListBox control determines
   a. whether it will be a pull-down list box or a standard list box.
   b. whether graphical images can be displayed instead of a list of text.
   c. whether graphical images (icons) can be displayed next to each text item.
   d. whether a checkbox will appear to the left of each item to show if it is selected.

7. Which properties may be changed for a form from the Form layout Window?
   a. Top and left
   b. Width and height
   c. StartUpPosition
   d. WindowState

8. Which of the following statement(s) is/are true about the ToolTipText property?
   a. It may be set to True in order to enable, or False in order to disable the ToolTip feature.
   b. The ShowTips property must be set to True to display ToolTips.
   c. Any value of text in the ToolTipText property will enable the ToolTip feature in most controls.
   d. The maximum length of a ToolTip text is 255 characters.

9. The ItemCheck Event of the ListBox control
   a. occurs when a list item is highlighted.
   b. occurs when a list item is selected.
   c. occurs when the checkbox of the list item is selected.
   d. occurs when the checkbox of the list item is cleared.

10. The MultiLine property applies to which of the following controls?
   a. Line control
   b. ListBox control
   c. Label control
   d. TextBox control

11. The MultiLine property is
   a. not available at run time.
   b. read-only at run time.
   c. read/write at run time.
   d. None of the above

12. The Change event applies to
   a. the ComboBox control.
   b. the DirListBox and DriveListBox controls.
   c. the Hscrollbar and Vscrollbar controls.
   d. the Label control.

13. The Activate and Deactivate events occur
   a. only when moving the focus from another application.
   b. only when moving the mouse from another application.
   c. only when moving the focus within an application.
   d. every time the mouse moves to another form in the application.

14. The left, right, and middle mouse buttons may be distinguished in which events?
   a. Click event
   b. MouseDown event
   c. MouseUp event
   d. MouseMove event

15. KeyDown and KeyUp events never occur for which of the following keys?
   a. Enter
   b. Delete
   c. Tab
   d. Escape

16. Which of the following event procedures have parameters that indicate the physical state of the keyboard?
   a. KeyDown
   b. KeyUp
   c. KeyPress
   d. KeyPreview

17. Which of the following methods may invoke a Paint event?
   a. Paint method
   b. Repaint method
   c. Show method
   d. Refresh method

18. Which event(s) occurs as a user repositions the scroll box on a scroll bar?
   a.   Scroll event
   b.   Change event
   c.   Reposition event
   d.   All of the above

19. The Clear method
   a.   clears all property settings of the Err object.
   b.   clears the contents of a ListBox, ComboBox, or the system Clipboard.
   c.   clears all objects in a collection.
   d.   clears graphics and text generated at run time from a Form or PictureBox.

20. The Circle Method applies to which of the following objects?
   a.   Form object
   b.   PictureBox control
   c.   Image control
   d.   Shape control

ANSWERS TO CERTIFICATION QUIZ

1. d
2. d
3. c
4. a
5. a, b, c
6. d
7. a, c
8. c
9. c, d
10. d
11. b
12. a, b, c, d
13. c
14. b, c, d
15. c
16. a, b
17. c, d
18. a
19. a, b
20. a, b

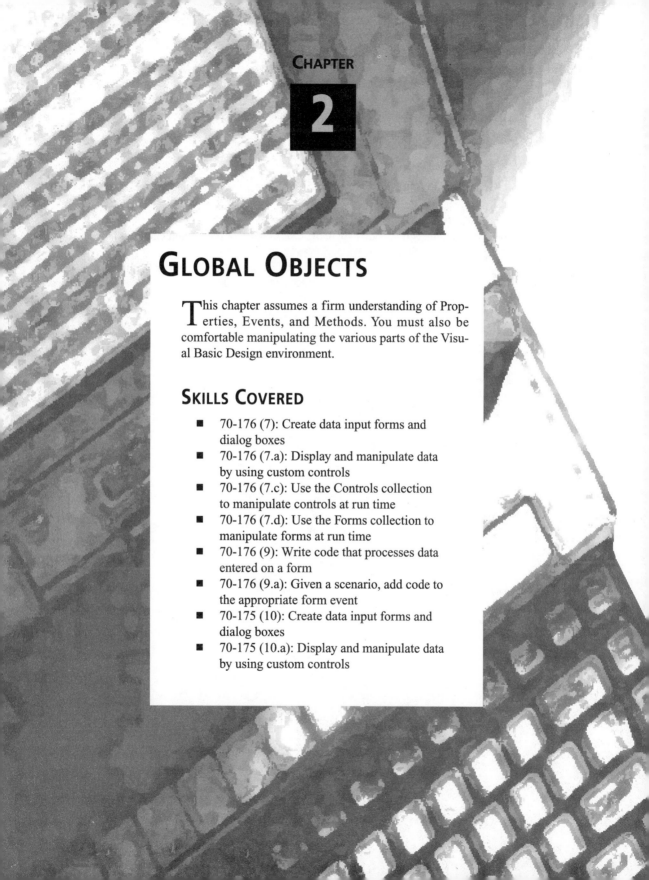

GLOBAL OBJECTS

This chapter assumes a firm understanding of Properties, Events, and Methods. You must also be comfortable manipulating the various parts of the Visual Basic Design environment.

SKILLS COVERED

- 70-176 (7): Create data input forms and dialog boxes
- 70-176 (7.a): Display and manipulate data by using custom controls
- 70-176 (7.c): Use the Controls collection to manipulate controls at run time
- 70-176 (7.d): Use the Forms collection to manipulate forms at run time
- 70-176 (9): Write code that processes data entered on a form
- 70-176 (9.a): Given a scenario, add code to the appropriate form event
- 70-175 (10): Create data input forms and dialog boxes
- 70-175 (10.a): Display and manipulate data by using custom controls

- 70-175 (10.c): Use the Controls collection to manipulate controls at run time
- 70-175 (10.d): Use the Forms collection to manipulate forms at run time
- 70-175 (12): Write code that processes data entered on a form
- 70-175 (12.a): Given a scenario, add code to the appropriate form event

Even beginners in the programming world have heard people extolling the virtues of object programming. We are told that objects are easier to build, maintain, and reuse. The problem with most object-oriented languages, however, is that they generally require a significant amount of experience before users can take advantage of their object concepts.

Visual Basic eases the burden on new developers by providing many prebuilt objects. We have seen how one group of these objects, known as *controls*, simplifies constructing user interfaces. VB also provides many built-in objects; some have graphical interfaces and some do not. In this chapter, we discuss pre-built objects which can be used by the entire application. Because they can be used by the entire program and require no special work to make them available, we call them *Global objects*.

Form Objects

Forms are the first software objects encountered by new Visual Basic developers. Like all software objects, forms have properties, events, and methods which are used to manipulate them. The Form object has *properties* that change its appearance, like BackColor and BorderStyle, as well as *methods* that cause forms to be displayed or removed, called Show and Hide. A complete understanding of these properties, events, and methods will facilitate making the most of forms in applications.

A project may consist of one or many forms. Adding a new form to a project is done by selecting **PROJECT/ADD FORM**. When a new form is added to a project, Visual Basic presents the **Add Form** dialog (Figure 2-1), which makes it possible to select from the standard form, or one of many predefined forms.

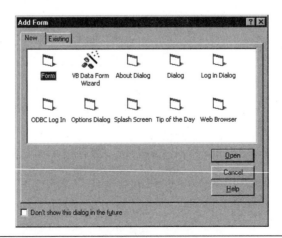

Figure 2-1 The Add Form dialog allows you to pick from several pre-defined forms.

When a form is added to a project, it is part of a child window and is generally fixed in the window at design time. The run-time position of a form is therefore not readily apparent. To set the form's run-time position, use the **StartUpPosition** property, which may be set to 0-Manual, 1-CenterOwner, 2-CenterScreen, or 3-WindowsDefault. Manual positioning permits setting the startup position through the use of the Form Layout window (Figure 2-2), which displays the exact startup location of a form relative to the screen. Access this window by selecting **VIEW/FORM LAYOUT WINDOW...** from the menu.

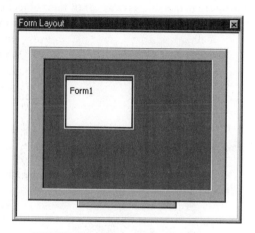

Figure 2-2 The Form Layout window.

Centering a form in its owner will cause the form to appear in the center of the form that called it. Centering in the screen causes the form to appear in the middle of the screen regardless of screen resolution. Windows default allows the operating system to place the form. This setting is typically used for child windows in an MDI application like Word or Excel.

Causing a form to display is normally done from code and is accomplished through the Show method, which results in immediate display of a form. A form may be displayed as *modeless*, which means it is an independent form with independent behavior, or it may be displayed as *modal*, which means that a user cannot interact with any other form until the modal form is dismissed.

Check It Out 2-1: Using Multiple Forms

1. Start a new VB project. Add a new form, resulting in two forms for the project: Form1 and Form2.
2. Both forms will display in the same location at run time, so Form1 must be moved. Click on the **VIEW/FORM LAYOUT WINDOW** menu command to reveal the Form Layout window. Click on the form that appears (this will be Form2) and drag it to the lower right. Form1 should remain to the upper left. For more information on Form Layout, search Help for "Form Layout."

3. Drop a button on Form1. Add this line under the click of Command1:

```
Form2.Show
```

This code will bring up Form2 after a click on **Form1.Command1**.

4. Run the application and click on **Command1**. See Form2? Size Form2 smaller and position it on Form1. Now click anywhere on Form1. Form2 disappears. To where? Move Form1, and Form2 will appear behind Form1, which obscured it. Form2 allowed this because it was not shown "modally."

5. End the application and search Help on Show.

A *modal form* is one that halts execution of the application when it is displayed. Some file operations have similar behavior. An attempt to copy files from the hard drive onto a floppy disk that is write protected engenders a Windows error message similar to that shown in Figure 2-3. This dialog exhibits modal behavior because it requires users to push the **OK** button before continuing work.

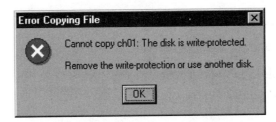

Figure 2-3 A modal dialog from File Explorer.

The Visual Basic command MsgBox (Message Box) is similar to the Windows modal dialog. The MsgBox statement displays a modal dialog box with the message constrained inside. When the Msgbox displays, execution of the application halts. Forms display modal behavior in the same manner as the Msgbox statement.

Check It Out 2-2: Showing Modal Forms

1. Double click on **Form1.Command1** to reveal a code window with the `Command1_Click` event displayed for editing. Change this line:

```
Form2.Show
```

to this:

```
Form2.Show vbModal
```

2. Run the application. Size and position Form2 to sit on top of Form1. Now click on **Form1**, attempting to obscure Form2. What happens? Form2 is now being displayed modally. Close the window for execution to resume. Click on the **Control-**

Box (located in the upper left corner of Form2) and click on the **Close** system menu command to dismiss Form2.

Before a form can be displayed, it must first be loaded. Loading a form consists of reading the form from disk and creating it in memory at run time. The Show method will load the form if it is not already loaded, meaning that a single line of code can be used both to load and to display a form. The Load event of a form is an initializing event, and is frequently used by Visual Basic programmers to prepare a form for use. Since the Load event fires before the form is visible, programmers may use the event for such actions as connecting to a database or filling a list.

Dismissing a form from the screen is accomplished by unloading the form. Unloading a form causes it to be removed from the active project so that it has to be loaded to be displayed again. A click on the system menu and selection of the Close command fires the Unload event procedure. Unloading is a terminating event often used by programmers to clean up after a form. In this event, it is possible to capture and save information or disconnect from a database.

Check It Out 2-3: Implicitly Loading a Form

1. Add this code to the Load event procedure of Form2:

```
MsgBox "FORM2 LOADING"
```

2. Add this code to the Unload event of Form2:

```
MsgBox "FORM2 UNLOADING"
```

3. Run the application. Click on **Form1.Command1**. What happens? The Show method is automatically loading Form2, firing the Load event procedure, and executing the code.

4. Click on the **system menu** of Form2 when it appears. Click on the **Close** menu command. What happens? Clicking on the **Close** menu command automatically fires the Unload event procedure and executes the code. Now the form is no longer in memory.

5. End the application and return to design time.

Adding significant code to the Load and Unload events is fine for simple applications, but code added to event procedures of the form increases the size of the form. Also note that any code attached to event procedures of controls located on the form bloats the size of the form. A form can grow quickly in size, which will slow the load time. It is better to preload key forms into memory when the entire application loads, and keep them in memory for the lifetime of the application. This way, the form will appear faster when the Show method is executed.

Visual Basic permits specifying how an application should start by selecting the *StartUp Object*, a VB option that allows users to pick a form that will be the first form loaded. You can also elect to start the application from a special routine known as "Sub Main," a user-created routine that must be built inside a module. A module can be added to the project by selecting **PROJECT/ADD MODULE** from the menu.

A module is essentially a code window with no graphic user interface. Routines that can be called from anywhere in the application can be placed in this code window. Adding routines to the window can be done by typing in a new procedure, or by using the procedure dialog box; the latter helps create new procedures for a code. Access the procedure dialog by selecting **TOOLS/ADD PROCEDURE...** from the menu (Figure 2-4).

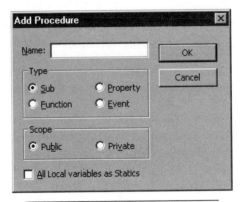

Figure 2-4 The Add Procedure Dialog.

Sub Main must be located in a module and must be declared public. When an application has a Sub Main, and a user indicates to VB that Sub Main shouldbe the Startup object (see Figure 2-5), VB will run the procedure `Sub Main()` and execute all VB program statements found there. It is therefore possible to preload the most important forms when the entire application loads for the first time, by the Load function in the `Sub Main()` procedure. Load causes a form to be placed in memory, but not be displayed. This way, all the important forms can be loaded into memory when the application starts; this will speed later access to the forms.

Check It Out 2-4: Using Sub Main

1. Click on the **PROJECT/ADD MODULE** menu command. Visual Basic will add a module named Module1 to the project.

2. Now click on the **TOOLS/ADD PROCEDURE** menu command. The Add Procedure dialog will appear. Specify **Main** as the name of the procedure, and make sure it is specified as **Public** (not Private) and as a **Sub** (not a Function). Click on **OK** when done.

3. Add these lines to Sub Main:

```
Load Form1 'Preload Form1
Load Form2 'Preload Form2
Form1.Show 'Show startup form
```

4. Sub Main has been defined and statements for application startup have been included, but there is one more thing to do: specify to VB that Sub Main should be used as the Startup object.

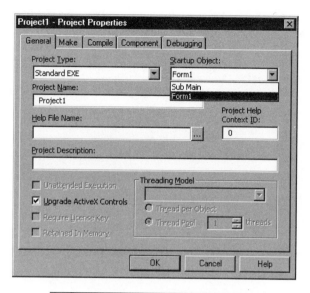

Figure 2-5 Specifying the Startup Object.

5. Click on the **PROJECT/PROJECT1 PROPERTIES** menu command; a modal dialog will appear.

6. Click on the **Startup Object** dropdown combo. Select **Sub Main** as the Startup object.

7. One last thing: Add this line of code under the Load event procedure of Form1:

```
Msgbox "FORM1 LOADING"
```

8. Run the application. Form1 and Form2 are loading from Sub Main. Form1 is showing from Sub Main. The Msgbox statements under the Load event procedures of Form1 and Form2 execute as a result of `Sub Main()` executing as the Startup object.

9. If **Command1** is clicked on Form1, Form2 will not load, because it is already in memory.

10. Dismiss Form2 by closing it. What happens? Form2 unloads and leaves memory.

11. Click **Command1** on Form1 again. Why does Form2 load? Because it is no longer loaded, and the Show method therefore loads it automatically.

12. End the application. Return to design time.

Loading and unloading a form can be a very expensive operation. If the form has many controls and significant code, it can take several seconds to load and initialize a form. This delay can result in unacceptable performance that destroys a user's perception of the application. Often we want to make a form leave the screen while keeping it in memory. This eliminates the need to load the form the next time we want to display it. The Hide method is used to accomplish this task. Hiding a form is a simple method call.

```
Form2.Hide
```

The right way to manage forms is to understand that a few forms need to be preloaded in memory all the time. The startup form, the forms that implement major function points, and so on, need to be preloaded from `Sub Main()` to ensure fast and responsive performance. Forms such as Preference dialogs and About boxes need not be in memory all the time. In other words, 20% of the forms are typically used often, while the remaining 80% are barely used at all. The 20% need to be preloaded from `Sub Main()` and then hidden and shown using the Hide and Show methods.

Unlike forms, most objects do not have a graphical component. Instead, they are more likely simply to be functional objects that perform a useful service. Visual Basic supports a host of global objects that perform services for applications. Like all global objects, they require no special action, and are available by default to every application created. We refer to these special global objects as the *system objects*. They provide information and affect behavior for a wide variety of features. The Screen object, for example, returns key information about the current display. The following code returns the height and width of the display.

```
Msgbox "The screen is " & Screen.Width & " by "& Screen.Height
```

Every application written in VB has access to the system objects through similar code. Learn more by searching on "Screen object" in the Help file. In this section of the book we cover all the system resource objects free with every VB application.

- **App Object:** Provides access to system and project information
- **Screen Object:** Provides information on the display
- **Clipboard Object:** Reads from and writes to the Windows clipboard
- **Error Object:** Provides info on run time errors
- **Debug Object:** Assists in finding code bugs
- **Printer Object:** Writes output to a printer
- **Forms() Collection:** Provides access to every loaded form in the project
- **Controls() Collection:** Provides access to every control on a form
- **Printers() Collection:** Provides access to installed printers on the system

All these objects are available to all VB applications all the time. Note the last three items are actually collections of other objects. These will be covered last as an introduction to the concept of a Visual Basic collection, a kind of list of objects in VB programming.

Keep in mind that this discussion of the system objects is designed to introduce these VB application resources. Examine the Help file concerning each object, study the example code in the Help file, search the MSDN, and do the exercises that follow to get a good grip on how to use these objects. The Printer object, for example, is very large, and a thorough treatment would take a great many pages. An exhaustive treatment of each object is beyond the scope of this book. Explore, experiment with, and understand these objects through hands-on exercise and a complete reading of the applicable VB documentation.

THE APP OBJECT

The App object is designed to represent the application. It provides properties and methods that give information or affect behavior. Table 2-1 shows a partial list of the properties and methods associated with the App object, features that will be most useful immediately.

Table 2-1 Key Members of the App Object

Member	Purpose	Usage
EXEName	Returns the name of the running application without the file extension	`App.EXEName`
TaskVisible	Returns or sets a value indicating if the application appears in the Windows task list	`App.TaskVisible`
Comments, CompanyName, LegalCopyright, LegalTrademarks, Major ,Minor, ProductName, Revision, Title	Gives access to properties set in the project properties dialog	`App.Property`
LogMode, LogPath, StartLogging, LogEvent	Properties and methods that allow an application to write to a text log file or the Windows/NT event log	`App.Method Argument` `App.Property`
HelpFile	Specifies the name of the help file for this application	`App.HelpFile = filename`
PrevInstance	Indicates if this application is already running	`App.PrevInstance`

One of the more useful properties of this object is the Path property. It reveals where the application is located in the file system on the computer. This is essential for a programmer who needs to find secondary resources related to an application.

Imagine that an application is shipped with a windows bitmap to be shown. Further imagine trying to load this bitmap into a picture control by using a complete path to the picture location (a bad coding practice known as *hard coding*). The hard-coded process might look like this:

```
Picture1.Picture = LoadPicture("C:\MyFiles\balloon.bmp")
```

The problem is that users who install this application on their machines do not have to put it in the same directory. When they subsequently run the program, it crashes. How are they to figure out where the bitmap is located? The answer is the Path property of the App object. `App.Path` will always return a complete path to the associated executable. For example, if the application is located in the directory named **C:\VBBOOTCAMP\MYAPP**, then the following line of code will produce the output shown in Figure 2-6.

```
MsgBox "This app was launched from: " & App.Path
```

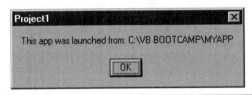

Figure 2-6 Msgbox showing the use of App.Path.

With the knowledge of the location of the executable, we can easily find the bitmap by ensuring it is in the same directory as the executable. The correct code to load the picture control is shown below. Note the use of the backslash because App.Path does not generate it as a natural part of its output.

```
Picture1.Picture = LoadPicture(App.Path & "\balloon.bmp")
```

In addition to identifying the location of the application, the App object can also retrieve other key information entered into the project properties dialog. This series of properties—Comments, CompanyName, LegalCopyright, LegalTrademarks, Major Minor, ProductName, Revision, and Title—make it easy to create splash screens and "about" boxes for applications.

Check It Out 2-6: Building an About box for An Application

1. Start a new Visual Basic Standard EXE project.
2. Open the project properties dialog by selecting **PROJECT/PROJECT1 PROPERTIES...** from the menu.
3. Click on the **Make** tab in the dialog.
4. Change the Title Box to read **My First VB App**.
5. Locate the **Version Information** frame. Find the **Product Name** entry in the list and change it to **My Product**.
6. Note the other entries in the dialog and see how they correspond to properties of the App object. Close the properties dialog.
7. Add three label controls to Form1.
8. Add the following code to the Form_Load event to display information about the project:

```
Label1.Caption = App.Major & "." & App.Minor & "." & App.Revision
Label2.Caption = App.Title
Label3.Caption = App.ProductName
```

9. Run the application.

Another extremely useful set of App object members makes it possible to create log files from the application. A *log file* is a file into which the application can write information. For example, if a serious error occurs, it may be desirable to record key information about the error in a log for later review. This is especially useful when supporting an application used by non-technical people. Many of VB's error messages are cryptic at best and users will not remember the error an application presented just before they called on the phone.

To set up logging within an application, use the `StartLogging` method. `App.Start-Logging` determines where events will be written. Visual Basic can write to a text file or to the Windows/NT event log. Once the location for writing the information is established, use the LogEvent method to write the data.

Check It Out 2-7: Writing to a Log File

1. Start a new Visual Basic Standard EXE project.
2. Using Form1, create an interface with one TextBox, 3 Options Buttons, and 1 CommandButton, as shown in Figure 2-7. Use the list below to set specific properties in the Properties window.

   Item 1—TextBox
   Name Text1
   Item 2—Option Button
   Name Option1
   Caption   Error
   Item 3—Option Button
   Name Option2
   Caption   Warning
   Item 4—Option Button
   Name Option3
   Caption   Information
   Item 5—CommandButton
   Name Command1
   Caption   Log It

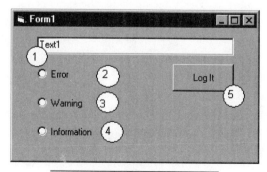

Figure 2-7 The Form for logging.

3. In the `Form_Load` event of Form1, add the following code to setup logging to a text file.

```
App.StartLogging App.Path & "\events.log", vbLogToFile
```

4. Now add the following code to the click event of Command1 to actually log the data typed into Text1.

```
If Option1.Value = True Then
  App.LogEvent Text1.Text, vbLogEventTypeError
ElseIf Option2.Value = True Then
  App.LogEvent Text1.Text, vbLogEventTypeWarning
ElseIf Option3.Value = True Then
  App.LogEvent Text1.Text, vbLogEventTypeInformation
End If
```

5. The logging features of the App object work only if the application is compiled. This is designed to prevent excess entries in the log. Therefore, compile the application by selecting **FILE/MAKE PROJECT1.EXE...** from the menu. We will cover creating and distributing EXE files in detail later.

6. Start the Windows File Explorer and locate the file **PROJECT1.EXE** just created. Run the application and test out the logging capabilities. When an entry is made, a new file called **EVENTS.LOG** will appear in the File Explorer. Open this file in Notepad to examine the entries.

THE SCREEN OBJECT

The Screen object provides useful information about the screen's resolution and state, access to the form and control with the focus, and other information such as the fonts supported. The properties are useful for providing a consistent behavior to the application, regardless of the monitor type of the end-user.

The Height and Width properties of the Screen object return the height and width of the display area. This can vary depending upon the resolution of the target monitor. Knowing the Height and Width can allow a programmer to adjust the size of a form for best display. The following example reports the resolution of the screen in pixels:

```
MsgBox "Screen is " & Screen.Width / Screen.TwipsPerPixelX _
& " wide in pixels."
```

This example introduces new information. First, the *continuation character* in VB is a single blank followed by an underscore. The "space underscore" tells VB that this line of code continues on the following line in the code module. This example also introduces a new measure of screen resolution called the *twip*. The terminology is from the world of typography, where a point is defined as $1/72$ of an inch. The twip is $1/72$ of a point, or $1/1440$ of an inch. The default unit of measure for VB is the twip. For example, the screen and the form object use the twip as the default unit of measure.

The screen provides the TwipsPerPixelX and TwipsPerPixelY properties. These allow programmers to derive the number of pixels on the screen by dividing the twip-measured width by TwipsPerPixelX. A similar calculation can be done to determine the vertical pixels of the screen. Visual Basic supports several different measuring systems, including such familiar units as inches, centimeters, and pixels. Find out about the different measuring systems by examining the ScaleMode property in the Help file.

Along with information about the display, the Screen object also provides information about the objects being displayed. Most important, the active form and the active control properties of the Screen object return the current form and control that the user is manipulating. In the Windows operating system, an active form or control is said to have the *focus*. The following code will report the window title of the form in the project that currently has the focus:

```
Msgbox _
"The Caption of the form with the focus now is " & _
Screen.ActiveForm.Caption
```

Note how `Screen.ActiveForm` is equivalent to specifying the name of the form. When `Screen.ActiveForm` is specified, all the properties and methods of that form are available to a program. It is possible to determine the name of the active form by sampling the name property, like this:

```
MsgBox _
"The Name of the form with the focus now is " & _
Screen.ActiveForm.Name
```

Find which control has the focus by sampling the value of the ActiveControl property. This property provides access to the properties and methods of the control that has the focus on the active form. For example, this code will report on the name of the control with the focus on the active form:

```
MsgBox "The active control right now is: " & _
Screen.ActiveControl.Name
```

Identifying the active form and control is useful in applications that have many forms similar in appearance. A word processor is a good example of such an application. In a word processor, the menu choices like "Save" or "Spell Check" function exactly the same on each document. The only question is which document to work on. The ActiveForm property answers this need.

In performing functions in an application, a programmer will want to change the mouse to reflect a busy state. This is most commonly done by changing the mouse to an hourglass. The Screen object makes it possible to change the mouse through the MousePointer property. This property permits selecting from several built-in mouse pointers. For example, the following code changes the mouse pointer to an hourglass and back to the default when the function is complete.

```
Screen.MousePointer = vbHourGlass
'Perform Work
Screen.MousePointer = vbDefault
```

Along with using built-in mouse pointers, Visual Basic will also let users create their own. The MouseIcon property of the Screen object permits specifying a custom icon to be used as a pointer. Create a personalized icon with any tool that creates ICO files, or choose from the many graphics that ship with VB. Once this property is set, set the MousePointer property to use the new pointer.

```
Screen.MouseIcon = LoadPicture(App.Path & "\myicon.ico")
Screen.MousePointer = vbCustom
```

THE CLIPBOARD OBJECT

The Windows clipboard is a shared area of memory that all applications on the Windows desktop can read from and write to. It has probably been used many times from Word, Excel, or other applications. The basic idea with the Clipboard object is to copy text and even images to this area of memory; other applications can paste this information into their own documents or forms. Here is a simple example to try:

Check It Out 2-8: Writing to the Clipboard

---

1. Start a new Standard EXE project. Drop two TextBoxes and two CommandButtons on Form1. The control names should be Text1, Text2, Command1, and Command2 by default. Do not rename the controls, just stick with the VB-assigned names.
2. Under the **Click event procedure of Command1**, add this code, which will copy the TextBox text from Text1 to the Clipboard:

```
Private Command1_Click()
 Clipboard.Clear  'Clear the Clipboard contents
 If Text1.Text <> "" Then 'if Text1 contains something...
   Clipboard.SetText Text1.Text 'Copy Text1.Text to the Clipboard
   MsgBox "Text1.Text contents is now in the Clipboard."
   MsgBox "You can start NotePad or Word and select Edit/Paste!!"
 Else
   Msgbox "NOTHING in Text1 to copy to clipboard."
 End If
End Sub
```

3. Run the application. Enter some text into **Text1** and click on **Command1**. The contents of Text1 will be copied to the Windows clipboard. Next, run a word processor such as Write, NotePad, WordPad, or Word and select the **EDIT/PASTE** menu command. The contents of the clipboard will be copied into the document. The data from the VB application should be visible in the word processing document. Data from the VB application have been copied into another Windows application with just a few lines of code.
4. Pasting from the clipboard does not clear it out. It is possible to paste from the clipboard into any application that supports such data transfers. The same text can

be pasted eight times to the same document. The clipboard data can even be pasted into a VB application. This is the next step. Add this code under the Click event procedure of the second button named Command2:

```
Private Sub Command2_Click()
   Text2.Text = Clipboard.GetText(vbCFText)
                   'get text from clipboard
   'vbCFText indicates the format of the text to copy
End Sub
```

5. Run the application. Add some text to Text1, then click on **Command1** to copy it to the Clipboard. Next, click on **Command2**, which will copy whatever is in the Clipboard to Text2.Text.

We have seen that it is simple to write to, and read from the Windows clipboard. Keep in mind that the Clipboard object is simply the VB programmer's interface to what is in essence a Windows desktop facility, shared by all applications.

THE ERROR OBJECT

The Error object is interesting and is covered completely in Chapter 6. For now, understand that the Error object is used to manage errors raised by VB. An error can also be *raised* in VB code, but when doing this be sure to use an error code that is not reserved by VB itself. There is a way to print out all the error codes reserved in VB; we will learn to do this shortly.

The most important properties of the Error object are the Number and Description properties. Err.Number gives the code for the error, and Err.Description provides the associated descriptive text that matches the code. Table 2-2 lists the members of the Error object.

Error information is typically sampled when a trappable error occurs. You do this by reading the Err.Number and Err.Description properties of the Error object. You can create and then raise your own custom error code by using the Err.Raise method. You do not need to be too concerned about this right now, because this book contains a section that deals with these issues completely. Later, you will learn the ins and outs of trapping errors. For now, be aware that the Error object exists and that you can exploit it to good effect in your VB applications later in the learning program, when you learn how to trap errors.

The Raise method sets the Err.Number to the number you specify. This has the effect of allowing you to add new errors to the syntax and processing errors that VB already supports. For example, you could use one of the unreserved error codes to force an error that will be trapped by your program. The idea here is that your application-defined error can be responded to by your error trapping procedure, just like the standard trappable VB runtime errors. Don't be too concerned about trapping errors at this point, as the subject is covered in a complete manner in a subsequent chapter. For now, understand that the Error object exists, it comes for free with each VB application, and it is very useful when the time comes to handle trappable runtime errors in your VB programs.

Table 2-2 Members of the Err Object

Member	Purpose	Usage
Description	Returns a text description of the last error that occurred.	`Err.Description`
HelpContext, HelpFile	Set a help file and topic that can be accessed by the user when an error occurs	`Err.HelpFile` `Err.HelpContext`
LastDLLError	Returns an error code from a called dynamic link library	`Err.LastDLLError`
Number	Returns the numeric code for the last error that occurred	`Err.Number`
Source	Specifies the class name object that generated the last error	`Err.Source`
Clear	Clears the properties of the Err object	`Err.Clear`
Raise	Causes an error condition to be raised in the code	`Err.Raisenumber`

THE DEBUG OBJECT

The Debug object provides two useful methods for discovering bugs in VB code: *Print* and *Assert*. The Print method writes text output to the Immediate window, which is like a log file except that it is never written to disk. We cover all of VB's debugging facilities in Chapter 6, but for now the following code shows how to print to the Immediate Window.

```
Debug.Print "This is a sample of writing to the Immediate window."
```

The Print method makes it possible to see how code is functioning as it runs. What is printed may be a status message or the value of a variable at a key point in the code. Just use the `Debug.Print` statement. The Immediate window may be used as a quick and easy way to view program output that might otherwise go to the printer. The following exercise lists error numbers and descriptions to the Immediate window.

Check It Out 2-9: Debugging Basics

1. Start a new Standard EXE project. Drop a button on Form1; it will be named Command1 by default.
2. Place the following code under the click of Command1. This code will list out the first 100 reserved VB error codes to the Debug window:

```
Private Sub Command1_Click()
  Dim i As Integer
```

```
      For i = 1 To 100
         Debug.Print i, Error(i)
      Next i
   End Sub
```

3. Now run the application. Select the **VIEW/IMMEDIATE WINDOW** menu command. This will display the Debug (or Immediate) window. Size and position the Debug window and Form1 to be side by side.

4. Click on **Command1** and 100 lines of output will come out of the Debug window. When the 100th item prints, check out the contents of the Debug window. These are error codes reserved by VB. Note that some of these may say `Application-defined or object-defined error`. These are codes that are unreserved and not currently used by VB.

The Assert method of the Debug object is used to cause an application to enter break mode whenever a key condition is reached. The syntax is simple and straightforward. Any condition that evaluates to False will cause the application to enter break mode. In the following code, a `For...Next` loop is used to increment a variable I from 0 to 100. Break mode is entered as soon as the value of I reaches 50.

```
Dim I As Integer
For I = 0 To 100
    Debug.Assert I < 50
Next
```

At first, the Assert method may seem of only moderate value; however, asserting conditions is a powerful mechanism for ensuring that an application runs within its designed parameters. Use asserts to test the values passed into functions and ensure they are within required limits. Asserts should be added regularly anywhere in the code where variables are expected always to be within a certain range.

THE PRINTER OBJECT

The Printer object is the largest system object available to the programmer. It has more properties and more methods than any of the other system objects. The Printer object is an output-only object; all we can do is write to it. Many of the Printer object's properties and methods are similar to the properties and methods of the Form object. For example, the Printer object has Circle and Line methods just as the Form object does. To send output to the printer using the Printer object, use the Print method. Windows will make an attempt to send output to the printer designated as the default printer. If that printer is properly connected, the printer will receive the output.

```
Printer.Print "YOUR MESSAGE HERE"
Printer.EndDoc
```

The Print method queues up printed output for a page. The EndDoc method causes the queued print commands to be flushed to the printer. At this point the printer creates the output. The Printer object allows specification of many attributes of the printed page; including orientation (landscape and portrait), font style, and size.

NOTE   A valid question here is: "Speaking of the printer, exactly how do I get a printed program listing?" Although it is directly related to programming the Printer object, there is a facility for printing out source code. The File/Print menu command provides a small dialog that makes it possible to specify the current module or form. There is also an option for printing the entire project.

THE FORMS() COLLECTION

In addition to the system objects that come with every VB project, there is also a group of resources known as *collections*. These are lists of items useful in VB programs. There is a list of every loaded form in the project, maintained automatically by the system in the Forms() collection.

To examine the contents of the Forms collection, use the For Each...Next looping construct that is part of the VB language. For any array or collection, the For Each...Next construct makes it possible to iterate over the entire list without knowing the number of items it contains. Here is an example:

```
Dim FormItem as Form
For Each FormItem in Forms()
   MsgBox "Form " & FormItem.Caption & " is in the Forms() collection."

Next
```

Since the entire VB language is covered in a subsequent chapter, a brief discussion of this bit of code is in order. This line:

```
Dim FormItem as Form
```

reserves storage for a variable named FormItem. This variable can contain a reference to a form object because it is declared as type Form. (The variable can be named anything, not necessarily this name.) The variable is used for referring to a particular Form object. The Forms() collection contains all of the forms in the project that are currently loaded. This line:

```
For Each FormItem in Forms()
```

sets up the loop so that each item in the list will be processed. With each iteration through the collection, FormItem is assigned a reference to a form in the collection. The first, then the second, then the next form is referred to by the variable FormItem. This permits addressing each item in turn until all the items are processed.

For example, this line:

```
MsgBox "Form " & FormItem.Caption & " is in the Forms() collection."
```

uses `FormItem.Caption` to refer to the Caption property of each item in the collection, one per iteration, and report the value of the Caption property via a simple MsgBox statement.

Check It Out 2-10: The Forms Collection

1. Start a new VB project. Add three more forms. They will be named Form2, Form3, and Form4.
2. Add this code to the `Form_Load` event procedure for Form1:

```
Load Form2
Load Form3
Load Form4
```

3. Close the code window and display Form1. Drop a button named Command1 on Form1. Add this code to the Click event procedure of Command1:

```
Dim FormItem as Form
For Each FormItem in Forms
  MsgBox FormItem.Caption & " is in the Forms() collection."
Next
```

4. Start the application, and click on the **Command1** button. What happens? There should be a MsgBox with the form caption for each form loaded in the project. (Note: The order that VB reports these forms is not predictable. Which item is first, for example, can vary. Usually VB reports the forms in the order in which the project loaded them.)
5. End the application with the **RUN/END** menu command.
6. Now go back to the `Form_Load` of Form1 and erase or remark out this line:

```
Load Form4
```

7. Run the project again. What happens? Form4 is in the project, but not loaded, so it is not part of the `Forms()` collection.
8. End the application and return to VB design time.

Collections like the Forms(), Printers, and Controls collections are free with each VB project. Each works in the same way as the `Forms()` collection we just discussed. Iterate over all the items with the `For Each...Next` loop construct.

THE CONTROLS() COLLECTION

The Controls collection is a part of each form. Iterate over the `Controls()` collection as with the `Forms()` collection, but note that the Controls collection is part of a form, not part of the entire project. Each form has a `Controls()` collection. For example, to report all the controls on a form, place this code under a button on the form, and click on the button:

```
Dim ControlItem As Control
For Each ControlItem In Form1.Controls()
  MsgBox "Form1 contains this control: " & ControlItem.Name
Next
```

In this example, we report the Name property rather than the Caption property. The Name property is used in code to refer to the object, while the Caption is simply descriptive text displayed on the object as a kind of label.

There is a way to dynamically add new controls to a VB form at run time. Be sure to examine the `Controls()` collection to refer to each control dynamically added. (There is also a way to add new forms to the application dynamically at run time. More on this later.)

The Printers() Collection

The Printers collection provides a simple way to access all the printers installed in Windows, not just the one currently set as the default. Iterate over the Printers collection as over the `Forms()` and `Controls()` collections, by using the `For Each...Next` looping construct.

Searching the Help file on Printers will reveal more information. Here is a simple code sample that reports the names of all the installed printers and specifies which one is the default:

```
Dim PrinterItem As Printer 'This is a VB reserved word
For Each PrinterItem In Printers
  MsgBox PrinterItem.DeviceName & " is installed."
    'The Printer object points to the default printer...
    'PrinterItem is the current printer.
    'Question: Are they one and the same?
  If PrinterItem.DeviceName = Printer.DeviceName Then
  MsgBox PrinterItem.DeviceName & " is also the DEFAULT."
  End If
Next
```

Attach this code to the click of a button on a form and see the results in a couple of minutes. This will list every installed printer and tell which one is the default.

The Help file has more to say about the Printer object and the Printers collection, but we will not address these other details now. Those who are comfortable with what has been presented so far concerning the Printer object and the Printers collection are in great shape.

All these system-supplied programmable objects are extremely useful. The new VB user typically discovers these assets after six months or more of VB use. The main reason for this is that no self-respecting developer examines the printed documentation. This is unfortunate, because the documentation has much useful information for exploiting the full power of the product.

Exercise 2-1: A Simple Word Processor

This exercise will explore the Printer object to create a small but functional word processor. We will show how to read and write text files from the disk as an additional lesson in this exercise.

CREATING THE USER INTERFACE

Step 1

Create a directory named **VB BOOTCAMP\EXERCISE2-1**. Start a new Standard EXE project and immediately save everything to this directory. Build a GUI on the form as shown in Figure 2-8. Refer to the list below for properties that should be set at design time.

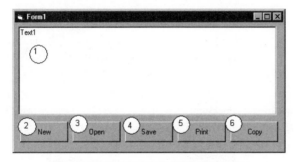

Figure 2-8 The Simple Word Processor.

Item 1—TextBox

Name	Text1
Height	2220
Width	6630
MultiLine	True
ScrollBars	Both

Item 2—CommandButton

Name	Command1
Caption	New

Item 3—CommandButton

Name	Command2
Caption	Open

Item 4—CommandButton

Name	Command3
Caption	Save

Item 5—CommandButton

Name	Command4
Caption	Print

Item 6—CommandButton

```
Name           Command5
Caption        Copy
```

Step 2

The New button clears out the text so that we can start a new document. Under the Command1_Click event procedure, add this code:

```
Text1.Text=""
```

WRITING TEXT OUTPUT TO A FILE

Step 3

In this step we will enter some text and then to write that text to a file. For simplicity, we will always write to and read from the same text file. The name of the file will be **SAMPLE.TXT**, and it will be written to your project directory. To write out the text to a file, we'll use the buttons added to the form. To write out the text entered as a file, perform text file operations. Under the Command3_Click event procedure, add this code:

```
'Write the text to a file
'Open the file for output, overwriting any existing text
'Note the use of App.Path
Open App.Path & "\SAMPLE.TXT" For Output As #1
'Write the data
Print #1, Text1.Text
'Close the file
Close #1
'Notify user
MsgBox "Text saved."
```

Step 4

Simple file I/O is based on a file *channel* or *handle*. This is nothing more than a number that specifies to VB an open connection to a specific file for input or output. We are using **#1**. The Print statement uses this file handle to do the job of writing out the text to the file. Once this is done, the file handle is closed using the **Close** keyword. Now look over the Help for these search items: "Open Statement," "Close Statement," "Write Statement," and "Print Statement."

Step 5

Run the application. Type some text. Click on **Command3**. If everything went well, it should be possible to open this file using NotePad. Be sure to search for the file in the project's directory, since App.Path was used to specify the location. (Note: If the project was not saved, then App.Path will refer to the directory in which the VB EXE is installed.) Start NotePad (Windows 95 and NT clients both contain this application in the Programs/Accessories menu command) and be sure the file SAMPLE.TXT exists and can be opened. If the file contents are visible using NotePad, this was done the right way.

READING TEXT INPUT FROM A FILE

Step 6

Reading the file from the disk is very similar to writing. In fact, it is the exact opposite, since we want to get the text and insert it into Text1 for editing. Place this code under the Command2_Click event procedure of Form1:

```
Text1.Text = "" 'Clear Text Box text
Close #1 'no error if already closed, so always do this.
Open App.Path & "\SAMPLE.TXT" For Input As #1
Dim FileText As String 'Temp variable for each line
Do While Not EOF(1) 'Until no more lines in file
  Input #1, FileText 'Get the next line
   'Rebuild the text, tack on a carriage return/linefeed
  Text1.Text = Text1.Text & FileText & vbCrLf
Loop 'While there is still data in the file to read
Close #1 'Close the file
```

Step 7

Run the application. Click on **Command2** to copy the contents of **SAMPLE.TXT** into the text box. We dimension a variable with this statement:

```
Dim FileText as String
```

This creates a variable we need to hold each line in the file as we process it. For each line in the file, we move it to the variable, and then assign it to Text1.Text. This is because the Input statement will not simply accept Text1.Text as the place to store the file text. We need to use a variable temporarily, and then copy the variable contents to Text1.Text.

This code also demonstrates the use of the Do...Loop construct. We are using Do While, which specifies a condition. While EOF(1) is not True, we continue to process the file. This line accomplishes that:

```
Do While Not EOF(1)
```

The EOF(1) is a function built into VB. The (1) indicates testing for End of File on the file indicated as open on file handle #1. As long as this file still has contents to process, the iterative loop continues, processing each item in the file until EOF(1) evaluates to True.

This statement:

```
Input #1
```

reads the text until a carriage return/line feed is encountered. This end-of-line marker is dropped by the Input statement during processing. Our program therefore needs to append it to each line as we process it and assign it into the variable FileText. The VB constant vbCrLf contains the ASCII character sequence for a carriage return/line feed combination. We tack this value onto the end of each line processed so that the restoration of the text into Text1.Text is complete.

PRINTING TEXT TO THE PRINTER

Step 8

If a printer is attached, the default printer should be active and working. Test this by firing up NotePad and then trying to print a sample page. If that test works, proceed to try to print some text under VB program control.

Step 9

The Printer object will point to the default printer. Under the Command4_Click event procedure insert the following code:

```
Printer.Print Text1.Text
```

This one simple statement will spew the contents of Text1.Text to the default printer. This statement is quite simple. Powerful printing techniques may be built around this simple statement.

The default behavior is for VB to send it to the printer when the application ends. Since this is rarely the desirable behavior, add the following line of code after the Print statement to make it print immediately:

```
Printer.EndDoc
```

COPYING APPLICATION DATA TO THE CLIPBOARD

Step 10

In many applications, it may be desirable to implement simple cross-task data transfer abilities. For example, users may request that portions of a form's displayed data be accessible to any word processor they are using. This is best accomplished with the Clipboard object, which makes it possible to read from and write to the Windows clipboard. This last part of the exercise shows how to write to the Windows clipboard from the application, making the application's data available to all applications.

Switch to **Form1** and add the following code to the Command5_Click event procedure:

```
Clipboard.Clear
Clipboard.SetText Text1.Text
```

Close the code window and run the application. Enter text into Text1 and then click on **Command5**. Then minimize the application and fire up NotePad or Word. From the word processor, use the **EDIT/PASTE** menu command to get a copy of the current Clipboard contents into the word processor being used.

FOR THE CERTIFIED PRO

Pro 2-1: Showing Forms

1. Create an application with two forms. After clicking a button on the first form, display the second form.
2. Make the second form an About box that shows key project information.

Pro 2-2: Sizing Forms

1. Create a form that will size itself to cover exactly ¼ of the display area regardless of the screen resolution.

PREPARING FOR CERTIFICATION

Topics for further reading

    Screen
    Printer
    App
    Debug
    Err
    Clipboard
    Forms Collection
    Controls Collection

CERTIFICATION QUIZ

1. To write text data to the Clipboard:
   a. use the GetFormat method followed by the SetData method.
   b. use the SetData method followed by the SetText method.
   c. use the SetText method.
   d. None of the above

2. To determine the resolution of the screen, the VB program must:
   a. sample the Width and Height properties of the Screen object.
   b. sample the Width and Height properties of the Screen.ActiveForm.
   c. sample the Width and Height properties of the Screen.ActiveControl.
   d. sample pertinent properties of the App object.

3. To force the printer to eject a page:
   a. execute the Printer.Eject method.
   b. execute the Printer.KillPage method.
   c. execute the Printer.NewPage method.
   d. set the Printer.NewPage property to True.

4. The App object:
   a. has a property that indicates how long the application has been running.
   b. has a property that indicates if the application was started as a component instead of a standalone executable.
   c. has a property that contains information about the application's version information.
   d. a and c only

5. The Clipboard may contain many data formats. How does the application determine the format of the data currently in the Clipboard?
   a. The GetText method of the Clipboard object must be executed.
   b. The GetData method of the Clipboard object must be executed.
   c. The GetFormat method of the Clipboard object must be executed.
   d. The GetInfo method of the Clipboard object must be executed.

6. The primary purpose of the Debug object is to:
   a. provide a way for the application to trap errors that may occur.
   b. provide a way to set and clear breakpoints in the VB code.
   c. provide an interface between the program and the Immediate window.
   d. None of the above

7. Before retrieving graphical data from the Clipboard object, it is wise to:
   a. execute the GetFormat method of the Clipboard to be sure the data in the Clipboard are the expected format.
   b. execute the GetData method to be sure the data in the Clipboard are the expected format.
   c. execute the Clear method of the Clipboard object.
   d. sample the FormatName property of the Clipboard object to be sure the data in the Clipboard are the expected format.

8. The Screen object's ActiveForm property indicates:
   a. which form has the Windows focus at run time.
   b. which form was last loaded.
   c. which form received the last mouse click.
   d. a and c only

9. If the Screen.MousePointer is set to the value of 99, this indicates:
   a. the Screen has a MousePointer that looks like an hourglass.
   b. the screen has a MousePointer that looks like a pointer.
   c. the screen has a MousePointer that is defined by the user.
   d. none of the above

10. The Raise method of the Err object:
   a. sets the error number and produces a trappable error.
   b. sets the error text and produces a trappable error.
   c. Both a and b
   d. Neither a nor b

ANSWERS TO CERTIFICATION QUIZ

1. c
2. a
3. c
4. b, c
5. c
6. c
7. a
8. a
9. c
10. c

MENUS

This section assumes knowledge of the VB form object and how to use the Show method to navigate from form to form. A solid understanding of how to use methods and event procedures will be necessary to understand how to implement right mouse button menu support.

SKILLS COVERED

- 70-176 (6): Implement navigational design
- 70-176 (6.a): Dynamically modify the appearance of a menu
- 70-176 (6.b): Add a pop-up menu to an application
- 70-175 (9): Implement navigational design
- 70-175 (9.a): Dynamically modify the appearance of a menu
- 70-175 (9.b): Add a pop-up menu to an application

USING THE MENU EDITOR DIALOG

A *menu* is a set of dropdown commands that can be installed into a form. In VB, one form may possess only a single menu structure. There is no simple way to install a new menu structure within a form. Each form in a VB project can be thought of as a kind of container for a menu. A menu in VB can have many submenus, up to four levels deep. Menus allow users to interact with the VB application in all of the same ways they interact with any other Windows application.

MENU FUNDAMENTALS

Constructing menus in Visual Basic is done with the Menu Editor (Figure 3-1). There are two ways to bring up the Menu Editor. One is to select the **TOOLS/MENU EDITOR** menu command. The other is to right-click on a form in your project, which brings up a context menu.

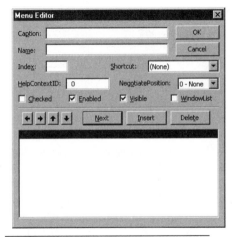

Figure 3-1 The Visual Basic menu editor.

Context Menu: a menu that appears as a result of clicking the right mouse button.

BACKGROUND

Check It Out 3-1: Getting to the Menu Editor

1. Start a new VB project.
2. Right-click on **Form1**. A context menu appears for the Form object. Select the **Menu Editor** command from this context menu to bring up the Menu Editor.
3. Click on the **Cancel** button of the Menu Editor to dismiss it.
4. Click on **Form1** to give it the focus. Now display the Menu Editor by selecting the **TOOLS/MENU EDITOR** menu command. After it appears, click on the **Cancel** button to dismiss it.

5. If the Toolbox is not visible, make it appear by clicking the **VIEW/TOOLBOX** menu command. Now click on the **Toolbox**, which will give it the focus. Next, try to select the **TOOLS/MENU EDITOR** menu command again. It will be disabled or grayed-out because a form does not have the focus—the Toolbox does.

6. Now click on **Form1**. Try to select the **TOOLS/MENU EDITOR** command one more time. Since Form1 now has the focus, the Menu Editor command will be enabled. Dismiss the menu dialog after it appears by clicking on the **Cancel** button.

The Menu Editor creates menu objects. Menu objects have several properties, but only a single event, the *Click* event. After menu objects have been created with the Menu Editor, it is possible to view and change the properties of each menu object from the Properties window of VB itself. The menu objects will appear in the Object box of the Properties window, where they can be selected easily.

Once the Menu Editor is visible, we can start to create a menu for the form. Look at the menu editor dialog and notice it has entries such as Name and Caption. These items represent the properties of the menu items. The Menu Editor provides a convenient way to edit these properties for many menu items, making it easy to build an entire menu at once.

In order to define a new menu item, at least fill out the Name and Caption properties, to cause Visual Basic to build a representation of the menu structure in the lower half of the Menu Editor. For each item in the menu, add a Name and Caption property, then click the **Next** button to create a new item. Figure 3-2 shows the Menu Editor with File, Edit, and View menus defined.

Figure 3-2 File, Edit, and View menus in the Menu Editor.

Once the main item in the menu is defined, subitems underneath each menu can be defined by using the **Insert** button to make room for a new entry and creating an item. Typical items can include New, Open, Save, or Save As. The menu editor identifies a subitem as a child of another menu when the arrow buttons are used to indent the item. The indented hierarchy of the editor makes it possible to see the relationships between all the menu items on the form.

A complete menu structure supports several features that enhance navigation. These features include accelerators and shortcuts. For an example of a full-featured menu, we will again look to Visual Basic, which has a file menu that supports typical menu features. The File menu has the following structure

New Project Ctl-N
Open Project... Ctl-O
Add Project...
Remove Project
Save Project
Save Project As...

Note several things about these menu items. First, some menu items have three dots (ellipsis) following the menu command text. This UI device is used to signal the user that a dialog box will follow, allowing a way to back out if necessary. This device is common to many applications and users are familiar with it. Indicating the ellipsis is always done in the Caption property and requires nothing more than typing in the three dots.

Second, each menu command has an underlined character, the *accelerator key*. This key, when pressed concurrently with the **Alt** key, selects the menu item with the keyboard instead of the mouse. For example, holding down the **Alt** key and pressing **f** (for File) and **o** (for Open) selects VB's **FILE/OPEN PROJECT** menu command. This is a keyboard alternative to using the mouse to select menu commands. All Windows applications are required to support keyboard navigation.

Third, some items in the menu structure support *shortcuts*—key combinations that, when pressed, take you directly to the menu item, without the need to navigate the menu at all. It makes execution "go to" that menu command. For example, the Open Project menu command can be accessed directly by holding down the **Ctl** key and pressing **o**. The effect of a shortcut on a menu command is to make it simple to select that menu command with one keystroke.

The menu editor permits specifying accelerators and shortcuts for menus. Accelerator keys are designated by placing an ampersand in front of the accelerator character in the Caption property. Thus, creating a file menu is normally done by using a Caption property of &File. Accelerators should be unique across all menus or groups of submenus. An *accelerator* can also be any letter in the Caption. For example, you can make the letter **x** the accelerator for an Exit menu by using the Caption E&xit.

Shortcuts are normally associated with the most-used menu items. Specifying a shortcut key is done by selecting the menu item of interest in the editor and choosing a shortcut combination from the dropdown list in the Menu Editor (See Figure 3-3). Each shortcut combination can only be used one time.

Each menu item created with the Menu Editor possesses three properties based on the True-False Boolean data type: Visible, Checked, and Enabled. The Visible property of the menu object, if set False, makes the menu item invisible. Setting any menu item's Enabled property to False makes it appear gray and makes using the menu item impossible. Do this according to the state of the application. For example, when a VB project is run, many of VB's menu items will be disabled and appear gray because VB recognizes that certain menu items do not apply in Run mode, so it grays them out. Do the same for created applications. The Checked property is used to place a check mark next to a menu item. The Visible, Checked, and Enabled properties are available both in the Menu Editor and at run time through code.

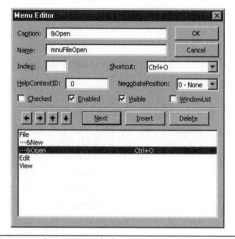

Figure 3-3 Accelerators and Shortcuts in the Menu Editor.

The Boolean menu properties are often used to show the state of various devices in an application. For example, the Checked property can be used to show when a toolbar is available. Visual Basic does this with its toolbar under the VIEW menu. Selecting to view a toolbar places a check next to the item when the toolbar becomes visible (see Figure 3-4). The check goes away if the toolbar is hidden.

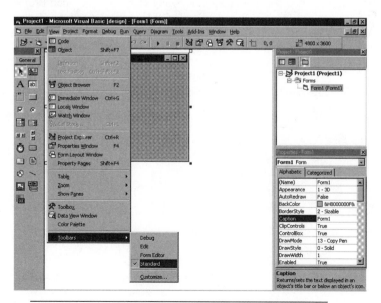

Figure 3-4 Showing a check mark when a toolbar is visible.

Check It Out 3-2: Toggling Boolean properties

1. Start a new Standard EXE project in Visual Basic.
2. Bring up the menu editor by selecting **TOOLS/MENU EDITOR...** from the menu.
3. In the menu editor, add a **View** menu and name it **mnuView**.
4. Under the View menu, add a sub item **Toolbar** and name it **mnuViewToolbar**. Click on the checked property to start off with the item checked in the menu. Figure 3-5 shows the Menu Editor entries.

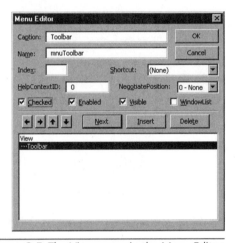

Figure 3-5 The View menu in the Menu Editor.

5. Close the Menu Editor.
6. Locate the toolbar control by selecting **PROJECT/COMPONENTS...** from the Visual Basic menu. In the components dialog (Figure 3-6), select the **Microsoft Windows Common Controls 6.0** and close the dialog. The common controls contain many of the useful common Windows controls.
7. In the toolbox, locate the toolbar control and drop it onto Form1.
8. With the toolbar selected, locate the **Custom** property in the properties window. Push the ellipsis for the Custom property, which will show a tabbed dialog that permits construction of a toolbar (Figure 3-7). Select the **Buttons** tab.
9. In the Buttons tab press the **Insert button** button several times to add new buttons for the toolbar. When several buttons are visible, close the custom dialog. (See Figure 3-8).
10. Open the code window for Form1. Now enter the simple code for displaying the toolbar and checking the menu item. Add the following code to the mnuViewToolbar_Click event.

```
'Toggle Check Mark
mnuViewToolbar.Checked = Not (mnuViewToolbar.Checked)
```

```
'Toggle Toolbar Visibility
Toolbar1.Visible = mnuViewToolbar.Checked
```

11. Run the project and try selecting the **VIEW/TOOLBAR** menu from Form1.

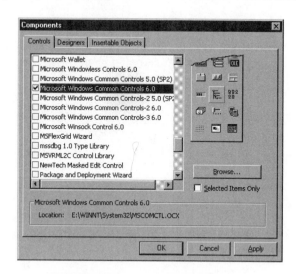

Figure 3-6 The Components Dialog.

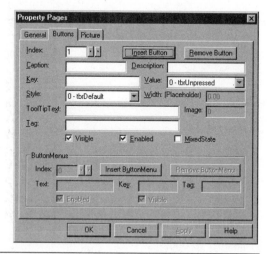

Figure 3-7 The Custom dialog for the toolbar control.

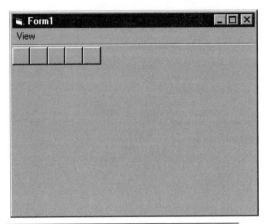

Figure 3-8 Form1 with a Toolbar and Buttons.

Menus are part of the overall user interface of an application. As such, they should adhere to a standard look and feel. For example, in most Microsoft Office applications, there will always be these standard menu options:

```
File    Edit    View    Help
```

Users grow accustomed to this standard ordering of menu choices and programmers should adhere to this familiar look. Along with standard naming, there are standard accelerators, shortcuts, and grouping. Grouping is accomplished in part through the use of menu *separators*, lines within a menu that separate groups of functionality. The menus of various commercial products, including VB, will show extensive use of menu separators. Visual Basic's File menu command, for example, makes use of no fewer than six menu separators. Menu separators are supported in the Menu Editor through the use of a dash character in the Caption property (see Figure 3-9). This dash is interpreted by VB as a menu separator at run time. Along with the special dash Caption, the menu separator must have a unique Name just like any other menu item.

Check It Out 3-3: Using Menu Features

1. Start a new Standard EXE VB project.
2. Right-click on **Form1**. Select Menu Editor from the context menu. The Menu Editor appears.
3. In the textbox labeled Caption, enter this text: **&File**
4. In the textbox labeled Name, enter this text: **mnuFile**
5. Now add two items under the File menu command. Press the **Next** button that appears in the Menu Editor. This creates a space for a new menu item. Now click on the **right-arrow** button. This indents the currently selected menu item by one level. Clicking on this button defines the next menu item as an indented item of the File menu command.

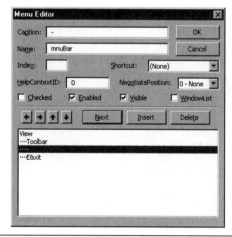

Figure 3-9 Building menu separators is done with a dash in the Caption property.

6. Now define the Caption and Name for this menu item. In the textbox labeled Caption, enter this text: **&New**. In the textbox labeled Name, enter this text: **mnuFileNew**.

7. Now define one more indented menu item under File. Click on the menu item labeled **New** and then click on the **Next** button. This creates a new indented item that will appear under the File menu item. Set the new menu item's Caption to **&Open** and the Name to **mnuFileOpen**.

8. Click on the **OK** button of the Menu Editor and fiddle with the menu. Clicking on the File menu command causes the menu items New and Open to drop down.

9. Now click on the **FILE/NEW** menu command—while in VB's design time. A code window will appear, displaying the menu command's only event procedure: the Click event procedure. Add the following code to this event procedure:

```
MsgBox "File/New menu command clicked"
```

10. Now run the project and click on the **FILE/NEW** menu command. Does the MsgBox output appear when this menu command is clicked?

11. Return to design time. Now define an Exit item separated by a bar.

12. Click on the menu command labeled **Open**, and then click on the **Next** button. This creates a new menu item. Next, define the Caption and Name for the menu item. Set the Caption to a **dash** (–) and the Name to **mnuFileBar1**.

13. Create one more submenu item by clicking on the **Next** button. This creates a new menu item at the same level as the previous one. Set the Caption of this menu item to **E&xit** and the Name to **mnuFileExit**.

14. Click on the **OK** button of the Menu Editor to dismiss it.

15. Now examine the menu. There should be several items and an exit menu separated with a bar.

Once a menu structure is defined in a form, the menu items can be accessed in many ways during VB's design time. We know that the Properties window contains the object box; a dropdown combination box. Clicking on it reveals the name of the form and every item contained on the form—including the menu items (see Figure 3-10). Try it. Clicking on any menu item from the Properties window Object box will display all the properties of that menu item. From the Properties window make changes to the properties of any menu item on a form. Thus, the Menu Editor is where menu items are created and the Properties window is where the properties of menu items are edited and/or maintained.

Figure 3-10 Menu items in the Properties window.

It is possible to add code to the Click event procedures of menu items by clicking the menu item at design time; this will display the Click event procedure in a Code window for the menu item clicked. Once a Code window is displayed, a dropdown combo box will appear in the upper left of the Code window. This is the object box of the Code window. Clicking on it will reveal all the menu items defined on the form, and selecting one will arrive at the Click event procedure for that menu item.

Although the menu item is a control and has properties and events, it is not in the toolbox. It is not available to click and drop onto the form. There is no simple way to install a new menu structure into a VB form without modifying the .FRM file that contains the form definition. Any menu defined for the form is saved as text in the form's .FRM file in the project directory. After a menu is defined for a form, it is instructive to examine the .FRM file after the form has been safely saved to disk. Examine the form file (using a text editor like NotePad) and notice the menu structure saved in the form file as text. The Menu Editor is the only facility in VB that reads and writes this information to the form file.

Be careful when editing a menu structure that already has code in the Click event procedures. If there is a top-level menu item with no subordinate menu items, there is probably code in the Click event procedure. If a user asks to subdivide the top-level menu command called *Tools* into three or four subordinate menu items, it may be better to add the subitems under the Tools menu using the Menu Editor. Then, of course, test the menu at run time. The original code under the Tools menu *short-circuits* the new submenu items. That is, a click on **Tools** causes the original code under the Click event procedure to execute; the new options defined for users may never be visible. The only way to fix this situation is to bring up a Code window for the form, click on the **Object** box dropdown, select the Click event procedure for the Edit menu object, and remove the original code.

Each menu item is a control with both Caption and Name properties. It is best to avoid duplication of names on more than one menu control. Duplication of the Caption property may cause confusion to users. Duplication of the Name property may confuse the programmer because of the way VB wants to handle that situation. When two objects have the same name, VB assumes creation of a control array. Control arrays are arrays of similar controls (or menu objects) that share the same name and a common event procedure and are covered in Chapter 7. There are beneficial uses of menu control arrays, but for now, be careful to name each menu item with a unique name. Notice we named menu items starting with the prefix mnu. For example, mnuOpen refers to the menu object used as the Open menu command. Always use prefixes for the Menu object, variable, and control naming. Naming standards will be fully covered in Chapter 7.

POPUP MENUS

With the advent of 32-bit operating systems like Windows 95 and Windows NT workstation, right mouse button support has become mandatory for all applications. Users have grown accustomed to context menus appearing when the right mouse button is clicked. VB has right mouse button support. Try clicking on any VB window to get an idea of how this works. Right mouse clicking on the Toolbox reveals a context menu for the Toolbox, while right mouse clicking on any form gives a context menu for the form. Try it and see. The context menus that appear list commonly needed menu options in a convenient and natural format.

Context menu support is easy to implement in VB. First define a menu on any form. Next, add code to the MouseDown event procedure to enable right mouse button support. Under the MouseDown event, call the PopupMenu (see Figure 3-11) method of the form object, specifying the menu name to be displayed.

Check It Out 3-4: Creating Popup menus

1. Start a new Standard EXE project in Visual Basic.
2. Open the Menu Editor by selecting **TOOLS/MENU EDITOR...** from the menu.
3. In the menu editor, construct a menu called Pop named mnuPop. This menu will have the following structure with sub menus Item1 and Item2.

Name	Caption
Pop	mnuPop
Item1	mnuPopItem1
Item2	mnuPopItem2

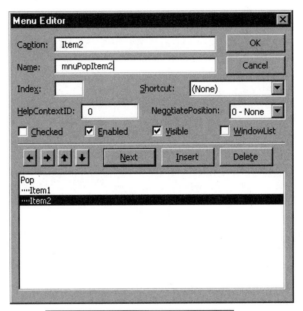

Figure 3-11 The Pop menu structure.

4. Set the Visible property of `mnuPop` to **False** by removing the check mark from its visible property in the menu editor.

5. Close the Menu Editor.

6. We want the Pop menu to show only when someone right clicks on our VB form. Therefore we will code this functionality in the MouseDown event of Form1. Locate the `Form1_MouseDown` event and add the following code.

```
'Button tells which mouse button
'was pressed, and PopupMenu
'displays the menu.
If Button = vbRightButton Then
    PopupMenu mnuPop
End If
```

7. Run the application and click on **Form1** with the right mouse button.

Some commonly used menu items can easily be supplied with powerful functions. FILE/OPEN, for example, is a menu command supported by many applications. It typically displays an Open dialog and is available with the CommonDialog control. It provides a VB application with a simple way to display familiar dialogs, such as for selection of File, Font, or Color. With the CommonDialog control, it is simple to display the same dialogs that appear in applications like Excel, Word, and Visual Basic.

Check It Out 3-5: Showing a Common Dialog Box

1. Start a new Standard EXE VB project.
2. Click on the **PROJECT/COMPONENTS...** dialog to find a list of all the custom controls that can be added to a project. Select the **Microsoft Common Dialog Control 6.0** by clicking on the checkbox and then clicking on **OK**. VB will add the new control to the Toolbox and dismiss the **PROJECT/COMPONENTS...** dialog.
3. The Common Dialog control will appear at the bottom of a Toolbox. Double click on it now to place one of these controls on Form1.
4. Place a button on Form1. Double click on it and place this code under the Click event procedure of the button:

```
Form1.Commondialog1.ShowOpen
```

5. Now run the project (with the **RUN/START** menu command) and click on the button. What happens? There is a fully functional File Open dialog—all accomplished with one line of code under the click of a button.
6. Return to design time. Try using the ShowColor and ShowFont methods of the CommonDialog control. Search VB Help for more information on how to do this.

Menus are strongly supported in VB by accelerator keys, shortcuts, submenus, and various adornments such as menu separators and checkmarks. VB also has the ability to support context menus via the PopUpMenu method and MouseDown event procedure of the form object. Menus are an important part of the overall application UI, and should be defined for every application developed.

Exercise 3-1: Menu Construction and the CommonDialog Control

In the following exercise, the features of the menu editor and common dialog control will be used to create a standard menu facility. Start by building a menu structure that simulates the VB menu structure. When it is finished, it will look like Figure 3-12 on the form. This same menu structure, when completely defined using the Menu Editor, will be represented as Figure 3-13 in the Menu Editor:

Step 1

Create a new directory named **VB BOOTCAMP/EXERCISE3-1**. Start a new Standard EXE project in VB with the **FILE/NEW PROJECT...** menu command. Save it immediately to the new directory using the **FILE/SAVE PROJECT** menu command. Be sure periodically to save work during the exercise.

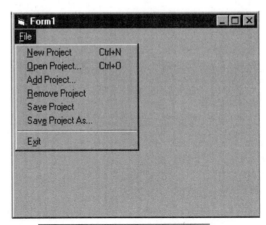

Figure 3-12 The Menu on Form1.

Figure 3-13 The Menu in the Menu Editor.

Step 2

Now begin work with the Menu Editor. Right-click on **Form1**. Select the **Menu Editor** menu command that appears in the context menu. This displays the Menu Editor.

Step 3

Now define the File menu command, and then all the subordinate items beneath it. Define the File menu command by specifying the following attributes:

Caption: &File
Name: mnuFile

Step 4

Now define the subordinate items that will appear with a click on the **File** menu command. Click on the **Next** button. The selection will move down one line, from File to a blank line.

Step 5

All the subordinate menu items need to be indented one level. The indent buttons of the Menu Editor appear together and display arrow-shaped icons pointing left, right, up, and down. For the first item defined in the next step, click the right-arrow indent button. This will indent the menu item under the File menu command.

Step 6

Now, define the Caption and the Name of this menu item as follows:

Caption: &New Project

Name: mnuFileNew

Step 7

Click on the **OK** Button of the Menu Editor, then run the project. A click on the **File** menu will show the **FILE/NEW PROJECT** menu command. Return to VB design time.

Step 8

Go back into the Menu Editor and add the following items. Be sure each one gets one level of indentation, so they appear under the File menu command. Also, be sure to press the **Next** button after the Caption and Name are defined for each menu item. This sets up the Menu Editor to define the next menu item. Notice how the same level of indentation is assumed for the next item.

Step 9

Define the following items:

Caption: &Open Project...   Name: mnuFileOpen

Caption: A&dd Project...   Name: mnuFileAdd

Caption: Sa&ve Project   Name: mnuFileSave

Caption: Sav&e Project As...   Name: mnuFileSaveAs

Step 10

The next item to add is a menu separator, which is a horizontal line that logically groups menu items. It is not possible to click on a menu separator; its function is cosmetic only. The separator must have a name, even though it has no function. By convention in VB, any menu item whose caption is the hyphen, minus sign, or dash (–) is automatically assumed to be a menu separator. Add a separator to the menu now and add an Exit menu item right under it.

Step 11

While still in the Menu Editor, begin the definition of a new menu item by pressing the **Next** button. Now, define a menu separator by specifying the following:

Caption: – (this is a single dash or hyphen character)

Name: `mnuSeparator1`

Step 12

Now press the **Next** button again, to define one more item. Specify the Caption and the Name as follows:

Caption: `E&xit`

Name: `mnuFileExit`

Step 13

The menu structure should appear as follows in the Menu Editor:

```
&File
____&New Project
____&Open Project...
____A&dd Project...
____Sa&ve Project
____Sav&e Project As...
____   -
____E&xit
```

From here, insert one final item in the menu. In the previous steps, new items were added one after the other. With production VB applications, it will often be necessary to insert new menu items after the initial structure is defined, for example, to add new items or regroup existing items, or add one or more menu separators. The menu structure will be edited often. VB provides a way to insert new menu items, with the Menu Editor's Insert button, located adjacent to the Next button.

Step 14

To insert a new menu item, click on the menu item *under* the location where the new one will be inserted. We want to insert a menu item *before* the Save Project menu item, so click on this and then press the **Insert** button. This opens up the menu so that a new item can be inserted.

Step 15

Define the new menu item as follows:

Caption: `&Remove Project`

Name: `mnuFileRemove`

Notice what happens if the name is left blank. Blank out the Name text just entered and press the Menu Editor's **OK** button. VB complains, with the error message `Menu control must` have a name. Clicking on **OK** will make VB place the cursor on the Name textbox. Reenter the text **mnuFileRemove** in the Name textbox of the Menu Editor and then click on **OK**. Everything should be fine. Remember, every menu object must have a Name. This allows VB to display the menu object's Click event procedure in the Code window. It also allows VB to display the menu object's properties in the Properties window.

Step 16

A shortcut key allows the user to get to a menu item with a single key combo such as **Ctl-O** or **Ctl-N**. VB provides a simple way for this to function. In the Menu Editor, click on the **Open Project** menu command, and then click on the dropdown combo box labeled **Shortcut** within the Menu Editor. (It appears to the upper right of the Menu Editor dialog.) Scroll all the choices. Then, select **Ctl-O** as the shortcut for this menu item by clicking on it. Next, look at the menu hierarchy. See how the menu shortcut is attached to the menu command?

Step 17

Click on **OK**, then click on the new menu structure on Form1. Now run the project and click on the menu again. Although the menu structure is defined and will display, it has no functionality. Now we will add some functionality to the menu.

Step 18

At design time with the Menu Editor closed, click on the **FILE/EXIT** menu command. A Code window will appear. Add the following lines to the Click event of the mnuFileExit menu command:

```
Msgbox "App closing down..." End (this is a special VB reserved word
that kills the application)
```

Step 19

Now run the project and click on the **FILE/EXIT** menu command. See how the application just stops executing?

Step 20

Now click on the **FILE/OPEN** menu command; this brings up a Code window displaying the mnuFileOpen_Click event procedure. Add the following line of code under that event procedure:

```
MsgBox "You have clicked the File/Open menu command."
```

Step 21

Now run the application. Click on **File**, then click on **Open**. This should display the message box just defined. Dismiss the message box.

Step 22

Now hold down the **Alt** key and press **f** followed by **o**, all the while holding down the **Alt** key, using the keyboard accelerators defined for this menu item. Again, dismiss the message box.

Step 23

Another way to execute the Click event procedure of the FILE/OPEN menu command is to hold down the **Ctl** key and press **o**. (This is the shortcut for FILE/OPEN, defined earlier.) Clicking with the mouse, using the Alt accelerator keys, or using the shortcuts—these are the three ways to select menu commands from applications.

Step 24

In most commercial applications with menus, ellipsis characters follow some of the commands, and signify that a dialog box will appear with at least a set of OK and Cancel buttons, and maybe more functions and choices that are optional. When a menu command is followed by three dots, start thinking, "Here comes a dialog box. If I click on this option, I can back out without any problem." Some of the menu commands in this exercise are followed by the ellipsis. Under one of these, we will display a Common Dialog box.

Step 25

Click on the **PROJECT/COMPONENTS...** dialog. A list of all the custom controls that can be added to the project appears. Select the **Microsoft Common Dialog Control 6.0** by clicking on the checkbox and then clicking on **OK**. VB will add the new control to the Toolbox and dismiss the PROJECT/COMPONENTS... dialog.

Step 26

The Common Dialog control will appear at the bottom of the Toolbox. Double click on it now to place one of these controls on Form1.

Step 27

Now click on the **FILE/OPEN PROJECT** menu command of Form1 (not VB's menu, but Form1's menu-in the project!) while still in VB design time. A code window will appear for adding the following lines line of code to the `mnuFileOpen_Click` event procedure:

```
Form1.CommonDialog1.ShowOpen
MsgBox "File selected was : " & Form1.CommonDialog1.FileName
```

Step 28

The Msgbox line of code just listed takes a string (`"File selected was : "`) and a string-valued property (`Form1.CommonDialog1.FileName`) and mashes them together to form one string. Computer scientists call this *concatenation*. In VB, the concatenation operator is the ampersand. This is why the "&" character appears between the two items following the Msg-Box command. Be sure to type the line exactly as shown.

Step 29

The CommonDialog control will not appear on the form at run time because this control simply provides services to an application and does not need to be displayed. The CommonDialog does, however, display various familiar dialog boxes (known as *common dialogs*) when one of its methods, such as ShowOpen, is called.

Step 30

Run the project and click on the **FILE/OPEN** menu command. See the File Open dialog? Use this dialog to specify a file in the list. When a valid file is selected, a message box will appear, displaying the value of the Filename property of the CommonDialog control. What actually happens is that the ShowOpen method will fill in the FileName property if the user selects a file via the dialog display.

Step 31

Return to design time by clicking on the functional **FILE/EXIT** menu command.

Step 32

Now search the Help file for ShowOpen, ShowSave, ShowPrinter, and ShowColor. Experiment with these methods of the Common Dialog control by calling them under some of the other menu items defined. For example, add this line under the Add Project... menu command:

```
Form1.Commondialog1.ShowColor 'Showcolor example
```

FOR THE CERTIFIED PRO

Pro 3-1: Toggle Operations

1. Create an application with a View menu. Have a sub item that permits toggling on and off a status bar at the bottom of the form.

Pro 3-2: Popup menus

1. Create a form with a command button. Create a popup menu for the form and a separate one for the button.

Pro 3-3: Common Dialog

1. Create a form with some controls.
2. Use a CommandButton to show a Font dialog. When the dialog closes, apply the font to all controls on the form.

PREPARING FOR CERTIFICATION

Topics for further reading
   Menu Basics
   Creating menus with the Menu Editor
   Using menus in your application

CERTIFICATION QUIZ

1. The PopupMenu method of the Form object:
    a.   provides a way to specify where a popup menu will appear on the form.
    b.   provides a way to specify that only a click of the middle mouse button will result in a menu click.
    c.   provides a way to specify that only a click of the right mouse.
         button will result in a menu click
    d.   a and c only

2. Which property of the Commondialog control will be populated with the name of a file selected by the user after the ShowOpen method is executed?
    a.   File
    b.   Path
    c.   Filename
    d.   Pathname

3. The Enabled property of a menu item may be accessed via:
    a.   the Tools/Options/Settings dialog box.
    b.   the Menu Editor dialog.
    c.   the Properties window.
    d.   b and c only

4. Is it possible to bold a menu item in a Popup menu made visible with the Popup-Menu method?
    a.   Yes
    b.   No

ANSWERS TO CERTIFICATION QUIZ

1. a
2. c
3. d
4. a

VARIABLES AND STRUCTURES

This chapter assumes fundamental knowledge of programming concepts and an understanding of how variables and programming code work from some other programming language. Readers should also be familiar with the Visual Basic design environment.

SKILLS COVERED

- Cert (1): Write code using the Visual Basic Language
- Cert (1.a): Use code structures to control program flow
- Cert (1.b): Use built-in functions to manipulate programmatic data
- Cert (1.c): Create custom functions to process data
- Cert (1.d): Use variables of differing data types to store and manipulate values
- Cert (1.e): Use constants to simplify code maintenance

As with any programming language, the heart of Visual Basic lies in declaring variables and writing code structures. Visual Basic provides a large set of data types and code structures to use when creating applications. Generally, before a variable can be used in VB, it must be declared. The generic syntax for variable declaration in a VB project looks like this:

```
{Public|Private|Dim|Static] variablename [As datatype]
```

where `Public`, `Private`, `Dim`, and `Static` define the variable "scope" and `datatype` can be any of the intrinsic types, custom data types, or objects. An actual declaration would appear as follows:

```
Private strAppName As String
```

This code defines a `Private` variable named `strAppName` whose data type is `String`. The `Private` keyword specifies that this variable is only available to code written in the same code module where the variable is declared. The prefix `str` on the variable name is a coding convention used by many programmers to denote the data type of the variable within the variable name. This is known as Hungarian notation, in part because a prolific Microsoft programmer named Charles Simonyi, of Hungarian descent, came up with the prefixing scheme as a way to make code more readable. Finally, the `As String` clause specifies that the variable is capable of holding text.

Visual Basic supports three different categories of data types. The first encompasses the *primitive* data types, those that can hold simple data like numbers or text. Primitive data types include Byte, Boolean, Integer, Long, Single, Double, and String.

The Byte data type is exactly as named—it holds one byte of data and can represent values between 0 and 255. Naturally, the Byte data type requires one byte of memory.

A Boolean type is used to hold True/False values. Visual Basic recognizes the keywords `True` and `False`. The Boolean data type requires two bytes of memory for storage. The two bytes may seem unusual at first since a true/false value can be represented by a single bit; however, VB actually uses the numeric values of −1 and 0 to represent true and false respectively. In hexadecimal notation, 0 is represented as 00000000 and −1 is FFFFFFFF. Boolean data types can be set to any of these values: True, False, 0, −1, 00000000 Hex, and FFFFFFFF Hex.

The Integer data type represents integers between −32K and +32K. It takes two bytes to hold an integer. It is obvious that a Boolean data type is just a special representation of an integer. The Integer data type is a general-purpose type used commonly for program data and loop indexes.

The Integer's big brother, the Long, occupies 4 bytes and can hold −2M to +2M. The Long, like the Integer, only holds integer values. The Long is commonly used to represent primary keys in database tables.

A special form of the Long data type is the Enumeration. Enumerated data types permit specifying a set of values for a data type instead of a range. A property like `MousePointer` is a good example of an enumeration. This property provides several discrete possible values that translate to different mouse pointers. Enumerations are created with the `Enum` keyword.

```
Enum GolfClub
  Iron
  Wood
  Putter
  Chipper =100
End Enum
```

In this enumeration, the entries `Iron`, `Wood`, and `Putter` correspond to values 0, 1, and 2, respectively. `Chipper` is given a specific value of 100. Variables may now be declared as type `GolfClub` and will support values of 0, 1, 2, and 100. Furthermore, these values can be specified in code by name.

```
Dim MyClub As GolfClub
MyClub = Wood
```

Enumerations considerably improve readability, though they have a significant limitation. At first, it may seem that an enumeration will only accept the values specified, but remember the enumeration is really a Long. Therefore, even though we have specified an enumeration to have values of 0, 1, 2, and 100, the truth is that it can hold any Long value. So the following code is also valid.

```
Dim MyClub As GolfClub
MyClub = 5000
```

This behavior of enumerations is not immediately obvious and calls into question the utility of the structure. Enumerations are primarily good for improving maintainability and readability of code. They are virtually useless for validating data.

Floating point arithmetic begins with the Single data type. The Single is a four-byte data type that can represent values between approximately ±3.4E38. The Double data type is an eight-byte data type used to hold values between approximately ±1.8E308.

The String data type is used to represent text. Visual Basic string data types use the UNICODE format. UNICODE is a two-byte-per-character standard that replaces the old ASCII standard of one byte per character. The purpose of UNICODE is to make it possible to localize a Visual Basic program to any country in the world. Localization becomes a major issue when writing applications for Asian countries that use non-Latin character sets called ideographic characters. In these countries, Microsoft operating systems use a special system to represent these character sets called the double-byte character set (DBCS). U.S. operating systems recognize UNICODE or ASCII depending upon which system is used. For example, Windows 95 is not UNICODE compliant while Window/NT 4.0 supports UNICODE. Because of varying support for ASCII, UNICODE, and DBCS, Visual Basic must internally convert from UNICODE to the standard supported by the operating system. The good news, however, is that none of these issues affects the way VB handles string manipulations if internationalization is not required. For the most part, these peculiarities can be ignored.

Visual Basic supports a number of string manipulation functions that help parse and manage strings. The Left, Right and Mid functions return portions of a string. The `InStr` function determines if one string is contained as part of another. Text comparison can be performed in

Visual Basic by testing to see if one string is equal to another. By default, text comparisons are case sensitive, meaning *A* is not equal to *a*; however, the Option Compare Text statement can be used in a code module to force case-insensitive comparisons.

The primitive data types represent the fundamental types needed to construct a program. However, VB supports other special data types that represent data of particular interest to programmers, including the Date and Currency.

The Date data type holds a date and time. The format of the date may be any legitimate date format. All of the following lines are legal VB statements:

```
Dim MyDate As Date

MyDate = "1/1/99"
MyDate = "1/1/1999"
MyDate = "January 1,1999"
MyDate = "1 January 1999"
```

Regardless of the format used to set a Date variable, the default presentation format is dd/mm/yy. This means that all of the above code results in 1/1/99 when displayed in a TextBox or message box. To change the format of the date, use the Format function. This can change the format of any data type for presentation, but is especially useful for formatting dates. The syntax for the Format function is:

```
Format(expression[, format[, firstdayofweek[, firstweekofyear]]])
```

The function accepts an expression to format a date variable. The format argument is a string that represents the format to apply. In this argument, specify one of many built-in formats such as Long Date, Short Date, or Scientific or also use custom formats.

Visual Basic Date types are year-2000 compliant. It is wise to understand exactly how VB dates are maintained before they are used. Essentially, Visual Basic dates are managed as Double data types. That is, they are represented internally as a floating point number. Zero is midnight, December 31 1899. Numbers to the left of the decimal represent whole days while numbers on the right of the decimal represent fractions of days. Since a Double has a range in excess of ±1.8E308, do not fear running out of dates any time soon. There is one caveat when using dates with two-digit year formats like 1/1/99: VB assumes the date must be between 1930 and 2029; therefore two-digit years are only compliant until 2029. This may seem a long time, but that was the thinking that brought about the Y2K issue in the first place. Always use four-digit years!

Visual Basic also supports math for dates. The `DateDiff()` and `DateAdd()` functions permit adding and subtracting time from a date. The difference between two dates can be found and a number of days added to a date with these functions.

Currency is the data type used for money; it always maintains four digits of decimal precision. This data type is also known as a scaled integer. As with the Date data type, it will be desirable to use the Format function when displaying these data. Visual Basic also provides the `FormatDateTime` and `FormatCurrency` functions, which may be easier for using the default formats for a particular region.

Check It Out 4-1: Working with dates

1. Start a new Standard EXE project.
2. Place a TextBox and a CommandButton on Form1 as shown in Figure 4-1. Properties for the controls are listed below.

Figure 4-1 Simple Form with TextBox and CommandButton.

Item 1—TextBox
Name   Text1
Item 2—CommandButton
Name   Command1
Caption   Validate

3. When the button is clicked, verify that the entry in the TextBox is actually a date using the IsDate function. If the entry is a legitimate date, then it is reformatted to a standard display. Add the following code to `Command1_Click` to validate the data.

```
'Check to see if the entry is a date
If Not IsDate(Text1.Text) Then
  MsgBox "The entry is not a date", vbOKOnly + vbExclamation
  Exit Sub
Else
  Text1.Text = Format$(Text1.Text, "Long Date")
End If
```

4. Run the project and try entering both valid and invalid date formats.

The user-defined type (UDT) is a data type made up of other data types. It is created with the Type keyword in the [General][Declarations] section of a form or module. For example, to define a UDT that represented an employee, start with this Type statement:

```
Type Employee
  LastName As String
  FirstName As String
  EmployeeID As Integer
  BirthDate As Date
```

```
End Type
```

Once a UDT is defined, it can be used like a new data type for variable declarations. Thus, a new employee could be declared using the following code.

```
Private e As Employee
```

Doing this automatically gets all the items associated with the type. To assign the employee an employee number, use the following code.

```
e.EmployeeID = 23456
```

Reading the values is a simple matter of setting a variable equal to the UDT value. The following code reads the birth date and stores it in a variable.

```
Dim DOB As Date
DOB = e.Birthdate
```

The beauty of the UDT is that it facilitates keeping related data together in one compact package. The problem with the UDT is that while it contains related data, it offers no mechanism for packaging the functions that work on the data. For this reason, we will need a new and more sophisticated structure, known as a Class, that contains both variables and functions so it is much more efficient that a UDT.

Classes in Visual Basic can be represented with the Object data type, which is capable of representing any object in VB. This includes forms, controls, and custom classes. All of the following statements are legal in VB.

```
Set MyObject = Form1
Set MyObject = List1
Set MyObject = Text1
Set MyObject = Screen
Set MyObject = App
```

The Object data type is useful as a generic representative of an object, but whenever possible, we prefer to use a more specific data type. Visual Basic supports declaring a variable as a more specific object such as a form or control. This is done using the Form and Control keywords. When a variable is declared as Form or Control, it is specified that the variable can represent any form or control in the system. The following declarations are legal in VB.

```
Private MyVar As Form
Private MyVar As Control
```

Although Form and Control narrow the possible values for the variable, we can easily be more specific in our declarations. Visual Basic will allow us to declare variables as exact forms and controls. In this case, we can declare variables that are capable of representing only one object. The following lines of code are legal declarations of specific object types.

```
Private MyVar As Form1
Private MyVar As ListBox
```

```
Private MyVar As TextBox
Private MyVar As List1
Private MyVar As Text1
```

The Variant data type is the most generic data type in Visual Basic and is capable of representing any data whether primitive or objects. The Variant is also the default data type in VB, and is the slowest of all the data types. If the data type is not specified for a variable when it is declared, the result is a Variant. For example, both of these lines declare a variable of type Variant

```
Dim v As Variant 'Explicit declaration is best, but....
Dim MyVariant 'Here, you get a variant by default!
```

The Variant data type can have data of any type assigned into it. When string data are assigned into a Variant, for example, string operations can be performed on the Variant, just as if it were actually a string variable. Because of the extremely flexible nature of Variants, they occupy much memory and can be very slow.

Because a Variant can represent any type of data, the Variant tracks the true underlying data type as the *subtype* of the Variant. Thus, if a String is assigned to a Variant, it is said to have a string subtype. The subtype of any Variant can be determined using the VarType function, which returns a numeric value indicating the subtype of a Variant.

When a Variant is first created, it has no data and therefore no subtype. The value of a newly created Variant is the keyword `Empty`. As soon as any value is assigned to the Variant, it takes on the appropriate subtype of the data assigned. To clear the data in the Variant, set it to the keyword `Null`.

Because Variants can represent any kind of data, they actually have the ability to morph the underlying data into a different data type if the situation warrants. This phenomenon is known as Evil Type Coercion (ETC). Consider the following code which declares Variants, attempts to add two of them, and place the result in a third.

```
Dim x,y,z As Variant
x=10
y="15"
z=x+y
```

If the code above is run and then the VarType function is used to determine the subtype of the variables, VB sees x as an Integer and y as a String. This is not surprising, since we explicitly set them to a numeric and text value respectively. However, when we attempt to add the values together, VB actually creates a Double subtype for z and adds the values so that the resulting value of z is 25. This implicit conversion among a String, Integer, and Double is unusual in a programming language and can lead to subtle bugs in code.

ETC is not limited to Variants—it can affect many operations in VB. To rewrite the above code to be very explicit we will declare the variables as specific primitive data types in an attempt to generate a run time error when we try to add the String and Integer.

```
Dim x As Integer
Dim y As String
```

```
Dim z As Integer
x=10
y="15"
z=x+y
```

It may be surprising that the code above works well in VB. Visual Basic assumes that a numeric value based on the data type assigned to the variable z is desired and simply adds 10 and 15 to get 25. In this case, however, we have controlled the data type of z and forced it to be an Integer whereas the Variant case made z a Double subtype. Throughout Visual Basic code, be careful of ETC because of the bugs it can engender.

If a variable is referred to for the first time in code without a specific declaration, by default Visual Basic will create a Variant. This is known as implicit variable declaration. Implicit declaration is fraught with peril and should be avoided at all costs. Consider a trivial line of code where a variable A is set to a value of one.

```
A=1
```

In the absence of any other code, VB immediately creates a Variant for A and sets its value. To a beginner, skipping the variable declaration step may seem convenient, but actually can cause serious problems. What if later, in an attempt to change the value of the variable, instead of typing A, S is hit? Visual Basic responds by immediately creating a new Variant named S. VB is happy—but the programmer is not. The most difficult bugs to find are created by implicit declaration because VB never generates an error message in this situation.

Because implicit declaration is so dangerous, it is a good idea to stop Visual Basic from ever creating variables in this way. This is accomplished by placing the code `Option Explicit` in the [General][Declarations] section of every form and module in a project (see Figure 4-2). This code tells Visual Basic that every variable must have an explicit declaration line or else an error must be generated.

Because Option Explicit can prevent so many difficult bugs, never develop an application without using it. This means the statement must be placed in every form and module. Fortunately, VB provides an option that will ensure automatic placement. This option is found in the Options dialog by selecting **TOOLS/OPTIONS...** from the menu. In the Options dialog, simply check the option **Require Variable Declaration** (Figure 4-3) and VB does the rest. Each time a new form or module is added to a project the `Option Explicit` statement is automatically coded. Visual Basic does not, however, add the statement to any existing modules in a project. If modules are already open in the project, the statement must be added manually.

Check It Out 4-2: Investigating implicit declaration

1. Start a new VB project. Show a code window for Form1, and navigate to the [General][Declarations] of the Form. Make sure no `Option Explicit` line is coded there. Then, add this code to the `Form_Load` of Form1:

```
V = 10
MsgBox V
```

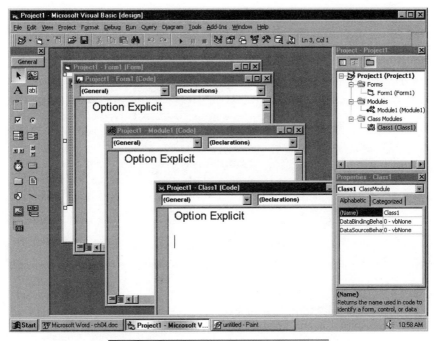

Figure 4-2 Option Explicit in code modules.

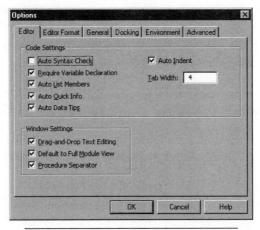

Figure 4-3 Requiring Variable Declaration.

2. Run the application. What is happening is referring to a variable that has not been declared *at all*. In this case Visual Basic creates a new Variant and hands it over for use in the program. Thus, the code works.

3. Now go back to the [General][Declarations] of Form1 and add this line:

```
Option Explicit
```

4. Now run the application again. This time, there is a compiler error (see Figure 4-4) in the Form_Load of Form1, because Option Explicit tells VB that undeclared variables are invalid.

Figure 4-4 Undeclared Variable compilation error.

5. Select the **TOOLS/OPTIONS...** menu command and click the **Editor** tab.
6. Check the box labeled **Require Variable Declaration**. Click on the **OK** button. Now, every time a module or a form is added to the project, VB will automatically add the Option Explicit statement, which will force variable declaration in the module or form.
7. Remember, changing the TOOLS/OPTIONS Editor tab setting *does not* have any effect on existing forms or modules. The Option Explicit statement must be typed into each existing module or form where variable declaration is required. If Require Variable Declaration was not checked before, now that it has been checked, the existing Form1 will still need Option Explicit added manually.

Even with Option Explicit present in the code module, there can still be problems through incomplete or incorrect variable declarations. This is because Visual Basic allows several short-hand declaration mechanisms that are often confusing to new programmers. These techniques include declaration without explicit typing, multiple declarations, and symbolic declarations.

Variants can be declared explicitly by using the *As Variant* clause or by declaring without a specific type. To declare without a specific type, omit the *As* clause. These declarations always result in a Variant.

```
Private MyVar
```

Failing to declare the *As* clause is often a result of hurried coding. However, the *As* clause can be unknowingly omitted when multiple variables are declared on the same line. VB allows multiple declarations, but the data type must be explicitly specified.

```
Dim x As Integer, y As String, z As Double
```

Failing specifically to call out data types in a multiple declaration results in the creation of Variants. This is a true trap because many languages allow multiple declarations without typing each member. In Visual Basic, however, the following code results in five Variants and one Integer—not six Integers as might be expected.

```
Dim a, b, c, d, e, f As Integer
```

All the variable types supported by Visual Basic can be declared as arrays. The arrays can support multiple dimensions and be declared as fixed or dynamic sizes. The syntax for declaring an array is similar to that for declaring a single variable except that information about the size is specified. The following code declares an array of Integers.

```
Public KeyCodes(10) As Integer
```

Examining the above code may lead to the belief that the array will have ten elements. By default, there will be not 10 but rather 11 items in the array because all arrays in VB start with an index of zero. In order specifically to declare a range of allowable indexes, they must be used in the declaration. The following lines of code are all legal declarations and specify both the lower and upper bounds of the array.

```
Public KeyCodes(1 to 10) As Integer
Private MyData(5 To 35) As String
Dim Numbers(0 To 14) As Long
```

It is possible to force all the arrays declared to begin with an index of one instead of zero. This is done with the "Option Base 1" statement placed in the [General][Declarations] section of a form or module. Like all Option statements, this one works only for the form or module in which it is written. Therefore, the code will need to be added to each form and module.

Visual Basic will also allow declaration of arrays with multiple indexes, by separating each index with a comma. Just as with single indexes, a range of allowable values can be specified. The following lines are all valid declarations of multiple index arrays.

```
Public KeyCodes(1 to 10,50) As Integer
Public MyVar(10,100,100) As Single
Private MyData(5 To 35, 16 To 25) As String
Dim Numbers(0 To 14, 0 To 14) As Long
```

In addition to static ranges, a dynamic array can be created whose size can change at run time. These types of arrays are particularly useful if a programmer is not sure of the size, or if the array may need to grow as an application runs. This often happens during data entry. The syntax for a dynamic array leaves out the index declaration. The following code declares a dynamic array of Strings.

```
Private MyNames() As String
```

Resizing dynamic arrays is accomplished through the use of the ReDim keyword. ReDim permits specifying a new size for an array. When specifying the size, remember that by default VB supports zero-base arrays. This means the actual size is always one greater than the value specified by the ReDim statement. The following code resizes the array to have an upper bound of 100.

```
ReDim MyNames(100)
```

One surprising result of resizing an array is that the data in the array are not saved. Resizing an array always causes the data in the array to be lost. This is true if the array is made larger or smaller. To preserve the original contents of the array while making it bigger or smaller, use the Preserve clause of the ReDim statement. This statement resizes the array and maintains all the existing data. When using the Preserve keyword, however, understand that maintaining the data in an array is an extremely expensive operation because when VB resizes an array, it actually recreates the entire array rather than simply adding or subtracting space to the original. Preserving data requires a complete copy of each item from the old array to the new one. Therefore, use the Preserve keyword sparingly.

```
ReDim Preserve MyNames(150)
```

When working with arrays, it will often be necessary to know the upper and lower bounds of the array. Visual Basic provides the functions Ubound and Lbound for determining array size. These are especially useful in loops for processing all members of an array, or when it is desirable to resize the array. The following code will add one new member to an array regardless of its size.

```
ReDim Preserve MyNames(Ubound(MyNames) + 1)
```

SCOPING

Scoping is a concept that affects two characteristics of a variable. It determines how long a variable exists in an application and what parts of the code are able to access the variables. Visual Basic uses the keywords Public, Private, and Dim to set variable scope.

Variables declared as Public are available to the entire application. They may be read and written by any function or event procedure. These types of variables may only be declared in the [General][Declarations] section of a form or module. If declared in a module, the variables are available from application startup until application shutdown. If declared in a form, they are available as long as their parent form is available.

Check It Out 4-3: Module Declarations

1. Start a new VB project. Click on the **PROJECT/ADD MODULE** menu command to add a module. **Module1** will be the default name. A Code window will appear displaying the [General][Declarations] section of the Module. Add this line to that section now:

    ```
    Public strAppName As String
    ```

2. Drop two CommandButtons on the Form1. Under the click of Command1, add this code to write a value into the variable:

    ```
    strAppname = "VB BOOTCAMP"
    ```

3. Under the click of Command2, add this code to read the value of the variable:

```
MsgBox "Value of strAppName = " & strAppName
```

4. Run the application. Click on **Command1**, then click on **Command2**. This is writing and reading a global variable (declared Public in Module1) from a form in the application.

Variables can also be declared as Private. Variables declared Private are not available to the entire application, but only to the procedures that reside in the code module where they are declared. Private variables are often referred to as member variables. The typical use of these variables is as support for the processing contained in related procedures, such as event handlers. The advantage of Private variables is that they can hide data from other parts of the application. This can prevent erroneous changes to critical variables. We discuss data hiding in more detail when we build class modules in Chapter 13.

Check It Out 4-4: General Declarations on a Form

1. Start a new Standard EXE project. Double click on **Form1** to reveal a code window for Form1. Notice that `Form_Load` is what appears in the code window. This is because the Form object has event procedures and `Form_Load` is the default event procedure. The author of the Form object designated the Load event procedure as the default event procedure—one that would appear in the code window first.
2. Often new VB developers who do not read the documentation miss the fact that the form object has a place to declare variables. To see the [General][Declarations] of Form1, click on the **Object:** dropdown that appears to the upper left of the code window. The items in the list will be Form and [general]. Click on the **[general]** item in the dropdown list.
3. The next thing visible is the [General][Declarations] area of the Form object. Here it is possible to define variables for use in the form. Variables declared here as Private can be accessed only by procedures (such as `Form_Load`) located within the form itself.

The `Dim` statement in VB is used to declare variables used at the procedure level. This means that if a variable must be used inside the `Form_Load` event procedure, the `Dim` keyword will be used. Dim is short for *dimension*. Variables declared in a procedure with `Dim` come into existence when the procedure starts executing and are destroyed when the procedure is terminated with `End Sub` or `Exit Sub`. This type of variable is known only to the procedure that declares it, and is often called a *local* variable.

The `Static` keyword is closely related to `Dim`. With the `Dim` statement, variables are initialized each time the procedure is called. However, variables declared with the `Static` keyword retain their value from the procedure's previous execution. This makes it possible to declare variables that have local scope but persistent values.

Check It Out 4-5: Dim Versus Static

1. Start a new Standard EXE project. On Form1, drop a command button. Under the Command1_click event procedure, add this code:

```
Dim countA As integer 'Dim an integer
Static countB As integer 'Statically declare an integer
countA = countA + 1 'Increment countA by 1
countB = countB + 1 'Increment countB by 1
'Report the results of incrementing both variables:
MsgBox "countA = " & countA & " ...countB = " & countB
```

2. Run the application and click on **Command1** several times.
3. Notice that the variable declared `Dim` is reset to zero each time the `Click` procedure executes. The variable declared `Static` retains its last value, and each execution of the `Click` procedure increments it by one. `Static` variables are useful for counting the number of executions of a procedure and a variety of other tasks.

Using Public, Private and Dim is not restricted by the type of component being coded. Variables of any scope can be declared in either form or module. When a Public variable is declared in a module, that variable is available by name to the entire application. However, when a Public variable is declared in a form, it is available to the entire application only through a special syntax which uses the name of the form to qualify the variable.

```
[Formname].[variablename]
```

This coding syntax is known as *full qualification* and is required when accessing any Public variable in a form from another component. Full qualification is optional for modules, but will work fine if used. Consider a module named *Module1* with a variable *I* and a form named *Form1* with a variable *S*. The following code could be used to access the variables.

```
Module1.I
Form1.S
```

A first exposure to full qualification may not reveal all the advantages. It would be possible to place all variables in modules and never use full qualification. This type of programming results in a traditional procedural application as might be written in COBOL. Visual Basic, however, is all about objects. Therefore, we want to write code that can be used efficiently in an object-based environment. A look at the syntax for full qualification might reveal the similarity to object-dot-property syntax we used to access properties like the Caption of a form. This syntax is not an accident and reaches its fruition in the use of classes.

Since full qualification makes it possible to access any component variable, it stands to reason that variable names could be duplicated between modules. Visual Basic permits declaring two Public variables by the same name in any number of components. There could easily be ten modules and ten forms in an application all with a Public variable declared as *I*. In this case, VB absolutely relies on full qualification to reconcile which variable should be addressed.

To those not familiar with object-oriented programming principles, the notion of declaring variables with the same name seems outrageous. The truth is that objects often have data members by the same name. Just as both the Label control and the form have a Caption property, so may other objects—including self-built ones. There will be more about this as we progress. For now, understand that variables can be declared with the same name and Visual Basic deals with this through full qualification. If multiple Public variables are declared with the same name, and are not fully qualified, VB generates an error (see Figure 4-5).

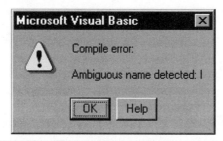

Figure 4-5 Error Generated with duplicate named variables
"I" and no full qualification.

Another scenario involving variables of the same name is referred to as *shadowing*. It is possible to declare two variables with the same name at two differing levels of scope. For example, one variable named intCount could be declared as Public in a module and another with the same name as a local variable in the same module. In this case, Visual Basic always references the variable with the least scope.

Consider an application with one form and one module. Imagine that a variable *I* is declared as Public in Module1 and Public in Form1. Additionally, a local variable *I* is declared in the form load event of Form1. Figure 4-6 shows this situation.

Now imagine writing the code I = 10. If the code is written in the Form_Load event, the local variable in the event will be changed. If it is written in Form1, but in some other event, then the Public variable in Form1 would be changed. Finally, if this same code is written in another form or module, then the Public variable in Module1 would be changed. VB always searches for unqualified variable names in the order local, private in the same code window, public in the same code window, then public in modules.

Check It Out 4-6: Variable Shadowing

1. Start a new Standard EXE VB project. Click on the **PROJECT/ADD MODULE** menu command to add a new module. Declare this variable in the [General] [Declarations] of Module1:

   ```
   Public iMyInt As Integer
   ```

2. Now navigate to the [general][declaration] of Form1. Add this declaration there:

   ```
   Public iMyInt As Integer
   ```

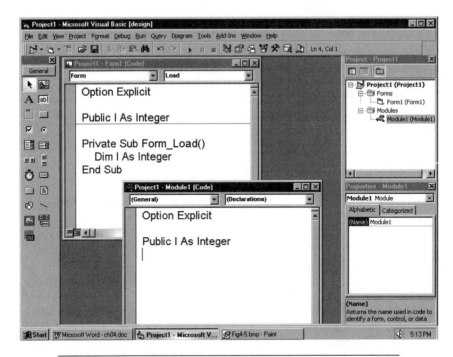

Figure 4-6 Variables named "I" declared at different levels of scope.

3. There are now two variables with the same exact name. One is global because it is Public in a module. The other is declared Public in the form named Form1.

4. Now drop a button on Form1 and double click on the button. This creates a code window displaying the `Command1_Click` event procedure. Add this code to the event procedure:

```
Dim iMyInt As Integer
```

5. The question now is: When referencing `iMyInt`, which variable gets the assignment? The global one, the form-local one, or the one just defined at the procedure level? The lowest level of scope gets the assignment.

6. Add this line to the `Command1_Click` procedure to alter the variable defined in the procedure:

```
'The local one gets the assignment
iMyInt = 10
```

7. To access the form-level variable, use a qualified reference. Append this line to the Click event procedure of Command1:

```
'This one is declared in the Form1 [General][Declarations]
Form1.iMyInt = 20
```

8. Why the qualification? Since the variable is declared Public to the form, what is the need for the qualified reference `Form1.iMyInt`? The Click procedure also has a variable with this same name, so qualification is necessary to make sure the intended variable gets the assignment.

9. In this scenario, it is even possible to reference the global variable. Simply qualify the reference with the module name. Append this line of code to the list of lines that now reside in the `Command1_Click` event procedure:

```
'This one is declared in the Module1 [General][Declarations]
Module1.iMyInt = 30
```

10. Add message boxes to display the values. The entire `Command1_Click` should now look like this:

```
Private Sub Command1_Click()
Dim iMyInt As Integer
'The local one gets the assignment
iMyInt = 10
'This is the one declared in the Form1 [General][Declarations]
Form1.iMyInt = 20
'This is the one declared in the Module1 [General][Declarations]
Module1.iMyInt = 30

MsgBox "iMyInt = " & iMyInt
MsgBox "Form1.iMyInt = " & Form1.iMyInt
MsgBox "Module1.iMyInt = " & Module1.iMyInt

End Sub
```

11. Run the application and click on **Command1** to see all of the values. End the application.

12. Now change the scope of the variable declaration in Form1 from Public to Private. Run the application and the compile error `Method or Data Member not found` will appear. When full qualification is used, VB looks for the variable from the outside even though the code is in the same component. The only way to resolve this is to change the declaration back to Public or change the name of the local variable.

Prefixing a variable name with *i* as in `iMyInt` helps to make it clear that the variable holds an integer. The prefix, however, does not indicate the level of scope. Many teams will add this information into the standard prefix for naming variables. For example, all globals may start with a *g*, followed by characters indicating the data type. This additional scope information in the prefix can make the variable scope and data type immediately obvious to maintenance programmers who examine the code later. Another immediate benefit is that the duplication of variable names at multiple levels of scope is impossible by virtue of the naming standard. However, another school of thought says that long prefixes are bad because they render variable names unreadable. We disagree. We are in favor of prefixes up to four characters long. Maintainability is always a central concern. Adopt a naming standard for variables and stick to it.

FUNCTIONS AND SUBS

Functions and subroutines are procedure types that can be created and used in VB. Both types of procedures can receive zero or more arguments, which are data variables passed to the procedure. Both procedures return to the calling program when the processing in the procedure completes. In the case of a procedure coded as a function, a value will be returned. Both subs and functions can receive arguments, but only functions return a value.

Creating functions and subs in VB is fairly simple. To create a function that is accessible from the entire application, define it as a Public function in a module. The same scope rules apply to procedures that apply to variables; the rules are consistent across data variables and procedures created. With respect to creating a procedure, there are two options. Type the function declaration directly into the [General][Declarations] of a module or use the Add Procedure dialog.

The first and most pressing concern is how to write a function the application can access on a global basis. We will now create a globally accessible function that accepts a single argument consisting of text in a string variable. The function will convert the text to uppercase and return the converted text via the function's return value. Here is how the function will look when completed:

```
Public Function fCapitalize(strTEXT As String) As String
    'UPPERCASE WHATEVER IS PASSED
    'FUNCTION NAME = RETURN VALUE
    fCapitalize = Ucase$(strTEXT)
End Function
```

There are a couple of things to note here. First, the function name is `fCapitalize`. The prefix *f* is our standard for denoting that this was a function created in-house. A subroutine or function can originate from a variety of places. It could be created in-house or be a built-in VB function or an API call, or it could come from a third-party Dynamic Link Library, or even from a reusable component. Using the prefix *f* for custom functions we write makes it simple to see in code where the function comes from. (We use *s* for subroutines.) Decide how far to go with prefixing and naming schemes. We know it aids maintenance programmers who must examine our code.

Second, functions take arguments which are listed between the parentheses. Our `fCapitalize` function takes one argument of type `String`. Also, the `As String` portion of the declaration indicates that this function shall return a string to the calling program. Once properly defined, this function may be called by setting a variable of type String returned by the function to the name of the function.

```
Dim r As String
r = fCapitalize("vb is fun indeed!")
```

```
MsgBox "The return value is " & r
```

Functions can be called by either returning the value to a variable or simply evaluating the function as an argument to another statement. This processing is known as *in-line* function calling. It is useful when the return value of the function is to be processed immediately by another function. This works because the entire function call resolves to a string, and a string is expected after the ampersand.

```
MsgBox "The return value is " & fCapitalize("VB is fun indeed!")
```

Check It Out 4-7: Functions and Subs

1. Start a new Standard EXE project, and click on the **PROJECT/ADD MODULE** menu command to add a module named Module1. When the code window is displayed, click the **TOOLS/ADD PROCEDURE** menu command. (Note that this menu item will be disabled unless a code window is active.) The Add Procedure dialog is depicted in Figure 4-7.
2. Click on the option button labeled **Function** in the Add Procedure dialog and type **fCapitalize** for the procedure name. Click on **OK** and VB will automatically insert the function declaration into the code window.

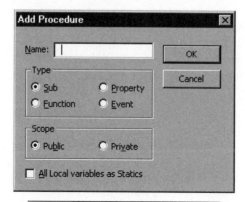

Figure 4-7 The Add Procedure dialog.

3. When VB creates a function with the Add Procedure dialog, the code it creates must be edited. VB does not define the arguments (if any) passed in, and does not specify the data type of the returned value. Edit the function to (a) accept a string and (b) return a string. It should look like this:

```
Public Function fCapitalize(strTEXT As String) As String
'UPPERCASE WHATEVER IS PASSED
'FUNCTION NAME = RETURN VALUE
fCapitalize = UCase$(strTEXT)
End Function
```

4. Now go to the form and drop a Command button; it will be named **Command1**. Add this code to the click of the button. The code will alter the Caption of Form1.

```
Form1.Caption = fCapitalize("VB Bootcamp!!")
```

5. Run the application and click the button. The window title should change from Form1 to **VB BOOTCAMP!!** when the button is clicked.

6. End the application. Display the code window for Module1. Now bring up the Add Procedure dialog again by clicking on the **TOOLS/ADD PROCEDURE** menu command.

7. Define a subroutine named **MakeRecord** by (a) clicking on the option button labeled **Sub**, (b) specifying **MakeRecord** for the subroutine name, and (c) clicking on the **OK** button.

8. So far, a function and a subroutine have been defined using the Add Procedure dialog. The function or subroutine declarations can also be typed directly into the [General][Declarations] section of a module or form. With the code window up for Module1, navigate to the [General][Declarations] section and enter this line:

```
Public Sub MySub
```

9. Press **Enter** and watch VB complete the subroutine declaration by adding End Sub automatically. Functions can also be entered in this manner.

10. Now click on the Procedure dropdown located at the upper right of the code window. The dropdown will list all of the procedures (both functions and subroutines) defined inside Module1. As procedures are added, this dropdown permits navigation from procedure to procedure.

The rules regarding the scope of a procedure are exactly the same as the rules for variables. We have not mentioned this yet, but procedures can be defined within forms as well as within modules. These procedures in forms can be declared as Public or Private. If they are Private, they are callable only from another procedure (such as an event procedure) inside that same form. If a procedure defined in a form is declared Public, it can be called from anywhere in the application, with full qualification, like this:

```
[formname].[procedurename(argument list)]
```

If the procedure is being called from inside the form where it is defined, the qualification is not needed when specifying the procedure name. Note that these rules for referencing procedures are completely consistent with what we have discussed regarding the scoping rules for data variables declared Public and Private in forms and modules.

Interestingly, Visual Basic does not require accepting the return value of a function when it is called. It is possible just to call a function and ignore the return value. This effectively turns a function into a subroutine since the only real difference between a function and a sub is that a function returns a value.

Just as functions can be called in different ways, VB offers several ways to call subroutines. Use the VB keyword Call before the name of a sub, in which case the arguments must be enclosed in parentheses, or omit the `Call` keyword and do not enclose the arguments in parentheses. Neither syntax is technically superior and both have staunch advocates. Some programmers like the `Call` syntax because they believe it is more readable. Others like to omit the parentheses because it looks more like a true method call. The following sub calls are equivalent.

```
Public Sub sEchoParms(Name As String, Age As Integer, IDNUM As_
String)
  MsgBox "Name is " & Name
  MsgBox "Age is " & Age
  MsgBox "IDNUM " & IDNUM
End Sub

sEchoParms "Dan", 29, "333448888"
Call sEchoParms("Dan", 29, "333448888")
```

When arguments are passed to a function or a sub, just list them between the parentheses in the procedure definition. These arguments are then required from the code that calls the procedure. Visual Basic has the capability to pass arguments to a function in one of two ways: by value or by reference. When an argument is passed by reference, a memory location corresponding to the data is sent to the routine. This means that in order to get the real data, the procedure uses the memory address to find the value needed. This is an excellent method when data are voluminous. Imagine a 32K array. Would it be preferable to pass all 32K into a function or just a 4-byte memory address?

Although passing by reference is fast, it has a significant disadvantage. Because the memory location is passed to the function, if the value of the data is changed by the function, the original value of the variable changes as well. This is like defaulting on a loan from a loan shark. If the loan shark has the defaulters address, he can be changed in interesting ways because the shark knows where he lives.

Contrast this with by-value argument passing. In passing by value, a copy of the data is passed to the function. This means that if the function does any damage to the input argument, it happens to a copy of the variable and not to the real data. This is like having a clone deal with the loan shark. If anyone is going to get hurt, it may as well be a clone.

VB passes arguments by reference unless a programmer specifies otherwise with the `ByVal` keyword. In passing by reference, the procedure that receives the passed argument can alter the contents of the variable in a permanent manner, producing very bad effects if the programmer is not careful. To ensure that the variables used to pass data to a procedure are protected from alteration by the procedure, use the `ByVal` keyword when defining the procedure. For example, this definition of the `sEchoParms()` procedure specifies *by value* argument passing, by using the `ByVal` keyword in front of each argument:

```
Public Sub sEchoParms( _
  ByVal Name As String, _
  ByVal Age As Integer, _
  ByVal IDNUM As String)
End Sub
```

By specifying `ByVal`, this procedure makes private copies of the contents of the arguments passed and uses the copy of each passed argument to perform any processing. If the value of an argument is changed, only the local copy gets affected. When the procedure is complete, these private variables are destroyed. Any variables used to call the procedure are preserved when `ByVal` is used.

Check It Out 4-8: Passing Arguments

1. Start a new Visual Basic Standard EXE project.
2. Open the code window for Form1. Select **TOOLS/ADD PROCEDURE...** from the menu to open the procedure dialog box. Create a Public Function named **IsEven** and press the **OK** button. (See Figure 4-8).

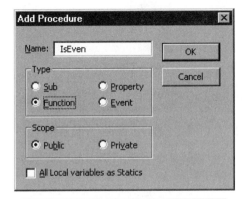

Figure 4-8 Defining the IsEven function.

3. After Visual Basic adds the function, finish it by specifying the input argument and output type. This will be sending in a Double and receiving a Boolean function indicating whether the input argument is even. The complete function should appear as follows:

```
Public Function IsEven(dblInput As Double) As Boolean
End Function
```

4. In order to determine if the input value is odd or even, we divide the number by 2 and see if we have a whole number remaining. This is done by comparing the result to the same result using the Int function. The Int function truncates a number and returns an Integer value. Add the following code to the IsEven function to test the input argument and return a value:

```
dblInput = dblInput / 2
If dblInput = Int(dblInput) Then
  IsEven = True
Else
```

```
   IsEven = False
End If
```

5. After the function is defined, add the following code in the `Form_Load` event to call the function and display results.

```
Dim d As Double
d = 10
MsgBox "The Function Returned " & IsEven(d)
MsgBox "The value of d is " & d
```

6. Now run the code. As expected, the first message will indicate that the function returned true. However, the second message will indicate the value of d is 5, not an even number, and not even the number passed in.

7. Now try changing the function definition to pass the argument by value. This is done by adding the `ByVal` keyword in front of the argument in the function definition.

```
Public Function IsEven(ByVal dblInput As Double) As Boolean
End Function
```

8. Now run the code again. This time the results are correct.

Regardless of whether arguments are passed by value or by reference, they can always be passed by name. When they are passed by name, they can be in any order, and Visual Basic sorts them by the name used. Returning to our `sEchoParms()` example, here is the declaration:

```
Public Sub sEchoParms( _
  ByVal Name As String, _
  ByVal Age As Integer, _
  ByVal IDNUM As String)
```

This procedure can be called by naming the arguments. The arguments must be specified using this syntax: `[keyword]:=[value]`

The interesting thing about named arguments is that the argument list can be specified in any order. This example specifies the arguments defined for `sEchoParms()` in reverse order of their definition in the sub declaration:

```
Call sEchoParms(IDNUM:="232324", Age:=34, Name:="Scot")
```

As an alternative, this can be written:

```
sEchoParms IDNUM:="232324", Age:=34, Name:="Scot"
```

Nothing special need be done to begin using named arguments except to comply with the syntax. Be sure to note the colon and equals sign (:=) which must be used; a simple = will only produce an error.

Named arguments make code more readable and easier to maintain because the actual argument names are used in `keyword:=value` format to evoke the procedure. This notation automatically makes the intent more evident. If the function writer knows that the procedure will be called by name, the author is more likely to use meaningful names for the arguments defined in the procedure declaration. Named arguments, combined with the Call statement and procedure name prefixing, make code easier to debug and maintain.

Along with named arguments, VB supports the definition of optional arguments. Optional arguments are, as the name implies, not required, but may be optionally passed into the procedure. For example, the sub sEchoParms coded with the IDNUM argument optional would look like this:

```
Public Sub sEchoParms( _
  ByVal Name As String, _
  ByVal Age As Integer, _
  Optional ByVal IDNUM As String)
  MsgBox "Name is " & Name
  MsgBox "Age is " & Age
  MsgBox "IDNUM " & IDNUM
End Sub
```

Now the IDNUM is optional and not required. Note that if ByVal is used, Optional comes before the ByVal keyword (VB will enforce this). If an Optional argument is used, the default value for the argument can be set to be used when the argument is not passed. This prevents errors in the body of the procedure. For example, the following routine has an Optional argument with a default value:

```
Public Sub sMyProc(Optional ByVal intTest As Integer = 1)
```

What if the argument is not passed in and not set by default? Any reference to the Optional argument will produce an error. For example, this line in sEchoParms() will produce an error if the optional IDNUM is not passed in:

```
MsgBox "IDNUM " & IDNUM
```

The way around this problem is to test for the argument and see if it is missing. VB provides a function to do this. The IsMissing() function returns True when the argument is missing and False otherwise. Here is how it is used in a procedure to test for the existence of an argument that is declared Optional:

```
If IsMissing(IDNUM) Then
  MsgBox "IDNUM is MISSING!!!"
Else
  MsgBox "IDNUM " & IDNUM
End If
```

In some cases, optional arguments do not provide enough flexibility. Instead, it may be desirable to specify an indeterminate number of input arguments. This is accomplished through the use of a `ParamArray`. An argument array is a single argument with a name that can hold several individual data items. An argument declared as a `ParamArray` is actually an optional array of Variants. Because a `ParamArray` is an array of Variants, it will accept any input values. When using `ParamArray`, specify the argument with a set of empty parentheses to signify that it is an array. The `ParamArray` must also be the last argument in any procedure definition.

```
Public Sub PA_Sample(ParamArray Items() As Variant)
```

Check It Out 4-9: ParamArrays

1. Start a new Standard EXE VB project. Double click on **Form1**, to get a code window. Click on the **TOOLS/ADD PROCEDURE** dialog, and add a procedure named sPA_Sample. Make it a subroutine.

2. Edit sPA_Sample to look like this:

```
Public Sub sPA_Sample(ParamArray Items() As Variant)
'NOTE THE PARENTHESES AFTER "ITEMS"
   Dim v As Variant
   For Each v In Items
      MsgBox "This item has a variant subtype of " & VarType(v)
   Next
End Sub
```

3. Now make Form1 visible and drop a button on Form1. We will test out the procedure with a call to sPA_Sample under this button. Add this code under the Click of Command1:

```
Call sPA_Sample("Bill",10)
```

4. Run the application; click on **Command1**. What should appear are the subtypes for the two arguments passed in as Variants to sPA_Sample via the `ParamArray`. The procedure should report an 8 for the first argument (indicating the String subtype) and a 2 for the second argument (indicating the Integer subtype.)

5. Search Help now on VarType and become familiar with what this function does.

6. Modify the code found in the Click of Command1 so that it has another argument, this time a number with a fractional, decimal portion:

```
Call sPA_Sample("Bill",10, 99.99)
```

7. Run the application again. Can you see how the procedure accepts the new item without any additional supporting code required? This is the major advantage to the `ParamArray`.

`ParamArray` will seem even more significant when we discuss building ActiveX servers.

THE VISUAL BASIC LANGUAGE

The Visual Basic language looks a lot like previous versions of Basic. It contains dozens of intrinsic functions and subroutines. There is also a rich set of flow-of-control statements, the focus of this section. We finish with a brief description of the built-in intrinsic functions and the always-available predefined constants supported by VB. This part of the book assumes readers are programmers, and for that reason it is relatively short. The looping constructs are well documented in the VB Help file. The Help file is a primary resource for understanding this part of the language.

For...Next

The primary purpose of the For...Next construct is to iterate over a list of known size. For example, this For...Next loop displays the contents of an entire array filled with information. Note the use of the UBound() function, from which the array size can be derived:

```
Dim intLastOne As Integer
Dim c As Integer
intLastOne = UBound(strADDRESSES())
For c = 1 to intLastOne
  Debug.Print "Item " & c & " contains this: " & strADDRESSES(c)
Next c
```

For...Next loops can go backward through a list. The Step clause specifies how many to advance with each iteration, and also the direction. For example, to report the contents of strADDRESSES() in reverse order, write:

```
Dim intLastOne As Integer
Dim c As Integer
intLastOne = UBound(strADDRESSES())
For c = intLastOne To 0 Step -1
    Debug.Print "Item " & c & " contains this: " & strADDRESSES(c)
Next c
```

Do...Loop

The Do...Loop construct is the most flexible of all the available loops in VB.
This code provides an endless loop:

```
Do
Debug.Print "Looping..."
Loop
```

The following code iterates 100 times, using an If statement to test a variable incremented by one each time through the loop. It uses the Exit Do statement to terminate the loop based on the condition:

```
Dim c As Integer
Do
```

```
   c = c + 1
   If c = 101 Then Exit Do
Loop
```

It is possible to Do While a condition is True or Do Until a condition is True. The While or Until test can also be performed at the bottom of the loop by specifying the While or Until clause with the Loop keyword (at the bottom of loop) instead of with the Do keyword (at the top of the loop). VB provides the option for testing at the bottom of the loop should it be desirable to guarantee at least one iteration. Testing at the bottom makes this guarantee possible.

The following code guarantees one iteration and ends when the variable *c* exceeds the value 10:

```
Dim c As Integer
Do
  c = c + 1
Loop Until c > 10
```

Select Case

The Select Case statement is used to implement a multiway branch. For example, to test a variable for one or more possible values and perform processing based on the value, use this statement:

```
Select Case intMyVar
Case Is = 10
  MsgBox "That's a 10"
Case Is = 20
  MsgBox "That's a 20"
Case Is = 30
  MsgBox "That's a 30"
Case Else
  MsgBox "What is it?"
End Select
```

Once one of the cases evaluates to True, processing under that Case statement executes. When the processing is done for that case, the rest of the construct is skipped and execution goes to the first line under the End Select. Note the Case Else, which is the default case. If none of the cases evaluate to True, the default case is executed.

One interesting use of the Select Case construct involves the use of the MsgBox function. The MsgBox statement takes two optional arguments. One specifies the overall style of the MsgBox window, including the buttons and icon that will appear. The other specifies the window title that will appear in the MsgBox window. For example, this statement specifies a MsgBox that will have Yes, No, and Cancel buttons and a window title that says **VB BOOTCAMP**:

```
MsgBox "Your message here", vbYesNoCancel, "VB BOOTCAMP"
```

The second argument specifies `vbYesNoCancel`. This is a predefined constant that VB provides. A constant is a symbol that evaluates to a value; the symbol is easier to remember and recognize, and is therefore superior to a hard-coded value. VB supplies a good many constants that are used for a variety of purposes. You will learn more about constants later in this chapter. The second argument also specifies the style of the window that will appear. A search of Help on "MsgBox function" will find documentation on most of the values that are valid as part of the second argument to the MsgBox function. For example, this code provides an "exclamation" icon and also makes the second button the default button, in addition to defining Yes, No, and Cancel buttons and specifying the window caption:

```
MsgBox _
"Your message here", _
vbYesNoCancel + vbExclamation + vbDefaultButton2, _
"VB BOOTCAMP"
```

The constants `vbYesNoCancel`, `vbExclamation`, and `vbDefaultButton2` all evaluate to numbers. These numbers are added together to form the second argument to the MsgBox function, which determines the style and look of the MsgBox that appears. One interesting thing to note is that `vbDefaultButton2` makes the No button the one that VB thinks was clicked on if the user simply presses the **Enter** key.

The MsgBox function returns an integer indicating the button pressed. How will the program test the return value and take appropriate action? The `Select Case` construct is best for this task.

Check It Out 4-10: Select...Case

1. Start a new VB project, and drop a button on Form1. Add this code to the Click event of Command1:

    ```
    Dim intRetValue As Integer
    intRetValue = MsgBox( _
       "Your message here", _
       vbYesNoCancel + vbExclamation + vbDefaultButton2, _
       "VB BOOTCAMP")
    MsgBox "That was a " & intRetValue
    ```

2. Run the application. Click on **Form1 Command1**, and the MsgBox will appear with Yes, No, and Cancel buttons. Click on **Yes, No,** and **Cancel** in turn. This will reveal the values returned by the MsgBox function for Yes (6), No (7), and Cancel (2).

3. Now append this additional code to the code that already appears under Form1's `Command1_Click`:

    ```
    Select Case intRetValue
    Case Is = 6 'or you can say vbYes rather than 6
        MsgBox "That's a YES"
    ```

```
Case Is = 7 'or you can say vbNo rather than 7
    MsgBox "That's a NO"
Case Is = 2 'or you can say vbCancel rather than 2
    MsgBox "That's a CANCEL"
End Select
```

4. Run the application and observe the behavior. Notice what happens when the **Enter** key is hit when the MsgBox comes up. Try the **Escape** key.
5. Try this last technique: Since `Select Case` needs an expression or a variable, evoke the MsgBox function in-line with `Select Case`:

```
Select Case MsgBox("Your message here", _
vbYesNoCancel + vbExclamation + vbDefaultButton2, _
"VB BOOTCAMP")
Case Is = 6 'or you can say vbYes rather than 6
    MsgBox "That's a YES"
Case Is = 7 'or you can say vbNo rather than 7
    MsgBox "That's a NO"
Case Is = 2 'or you can say vbCancel rather than 2
    MsgBox "That's a CANCEL"
End Select
```

Observe how this works. Why does it work?

With Statement

This construct is used to provide a concise notation for the setting of object properties. The `With` statement makes it simple to refer to an object once, and then refer to properties of the object.

For example, here is a way to change several properties of a ListBox object on Form1:

```
With Form1.List1
  .Height = 500
  .Width = 400
  .ListIndex = 1
  .Visible = True
End With
```

In previous versions of VB, the `With` statement did not exist, and consecutive properties of an object would be set thus:

```
Form1.List1.Height = 500
Form1.List1.Width = 400
Form1.List1.ListIndex = 1
Form1.List1.Visible = True
```

The `With` statement makes this kind of thing easier to do by referring to the object once.

For Each...Next

The `For Each...Next` statement is used to iterate over arrays and collections. The key to using this construct is to remember to define a variable that will be used to refer to the current item in the list or collection when the loop iterates. The variable must be a Variant if there is iteration over an array, even if the array is declared to hold just integers or strings. To iterate over a collection, use a Variant, or the Object data type, or a more specific object type such as Control or Form.

This example displays all the controls located on Form1:

```
Dim ctl as Control
For Each ctl in Form1.Controls()
  Debug.Print "The Control named : " & ctl.Name & " exists in Form1"
Next
```

This next example lists all of the strings in the array `strMyNames()`:

```
Dim strMyNames(3) as String
strMyNames (0) = "Attila the Hun"
strMyNames (1) = "Hannibal"
strMyNames (2) = "Napolean"
strMyNames (3) = "McArthur"
Dim v as Variant
For Each v in strMyNames
  Debug.Print "strMyNames() contains " & v
Next
```

If...Then... Else Statement

The basic form of the statement for taking a single action based on a condition is

```
If [condition] Then [Action]
```

If multiple actions are contemplated, multiple program lines will probably be used. In that case, use the `If` with the `End If`, like this:

```
If [condition] Then
  [Action Line 1]
  [Action Line 2]
  [Action Line 3]
End If
```

The condition can be any expression, variable, or literal that evaluates to True or False. What if the expression evaluates to False? In such cases, the `Else` is provided so that processing can be forced for when the condition is False. This example uses the `If...Then...Else` statement to test the return value from a `MsgBox()`:

```
Dim r As Integer
r = MsgBox("Do you want to continue?", vbYesNo, "Confirm")
If r = 6 Then
  MsgBox "You pressed YES"
Else 'Not a Yes, must be a NO
  MsgBox "You pressed NO"
End If
```

Leftovers from the Cretaceous Period of the BASIC Language

There are several leftover portions of BASIC that were useful in years gone by. Now we have little use for them. One such example is the use of the word "Let." These two statements are equivalent:

```
MyVar = 10
```

Or you can say it this way:

```
Let MyVar = 10
```

You will have little use for the `Let` keyword.

Visual Basic also uses symbols to define the return value of functions and the data types of variables. These two statements are equivalent:

```
Dim Zipcode$
```

This is the preferred way to do it:

```
Dim Zipcode As String
```

In past years, there was no `As` [datatype] syntax, and symbolic declaration was the only option. There are symbols for string, integer, long, and so on, but do not bother using them. Some code reviewed from others may date back to VB3, and the symbols used for procedure declarations may appear. This function will accept a string and return a string:

```
Public Function fCapitalize$(UserText$)
```

This more modern function declaration is equivalent:

```
Public Function fCapitalize(ByVal UserText As String) As String
```

Other Old Language Not to Use

While...Wend

`While...Wend` is a looping construct. It works like this:

```
'While Form1.Visible = True
'Call sBigProcedure
```

The big procedure may set Form1.Visible to False:

```
'Wend 'While End
```

GoTo

It is possible to GoTo anywhere in a procedure; but this should be avoided. The only legitimate use of GoTo is to branch to a single exit point in a procedure or to branch to an error trapping portion of the code. GoTo remains a valid and dangerous reserved word. Avoid it.

GoSub...Return

GoSub also remains a valid reserved word. GoSub branches execution to a code block within the same procedure and returns to the calling statement when the Return statement is encountered. The Help file provides more detail. GoSub has been largely superseded by the Call statement.

Built-in (Intrinsic) Functions

VB provides an impressive set of built-in functions which can be thought of as part of the language. For example, UCase$() is a function that will uppercase whatever text is passed in as an argument:

```
Dim strMyText As String
strMyText = "daniel joseph mezick"
strMyText = Ucase$(strMyText)
```

There are many other built-in functions. See the Help search strings later in this chapter for more detail.

String Functions

The String functions manipulate strings. To find a string within a string, use the InStr$() function. To get the leftmost or rightmost text in a string, use Left$() and Right$(). To extract some text from the middle of a string, use Mid$().

Conversion Functions

Visual Basic provides many useful functions to convert one data type to another. Most of these start with *C*. For example, to convert a string to an integer, use the CInt() function. To convert a Variant to a Double, use CDbl(), and so on.

The IIf() Function

Visual Basic provides some interesting functions that appear in other languages. IIf() evaluates any expression that can be evaluated to True or False, and then it permits specifying what will be returned from IIf() in each case. For example, to return "Dan" if the Integer variable MyVar is greater than 10 expression is True, and "Scot" otherwise.

Code IIf() like this:

```
Dim r As String
r = IIf(MyVar > 10, "Dan", "Scot")
```

IIf() is known as the Immediate If. It is useful as a compact and lightweight way to evaluate an expression and return a value.

Financial Functions

Visual Basic provides a set of financial functions, which make it possible to obtain the present value of an annuity, calculate interest, and so on. Functions such as `IPmt()`, `IRR()`, and `Rate()` are part of the financial library. Search the Help file as described later in this chapter to learn more about these functions.

CONSTANTS

Constants and the Object Browser

Does VB support values with symbolic names, *constants*, which make code easier to read? Yes. Learn about VB's support for constants by examining VB's Object Browser, accessible from the VIEW/OBJECT BROWSER menu command.

Check It Out 4-11: Constants

1. Start a new standard VB project and click on the **VIEW/OBJECT BROWSER...** menu command. The Object Browser will appear.
2. There will be a list of items in the list box to the left of the Object Browser; it will be labeled **Classes**. In this box will be many items, among them Constants. (The list is generally in a group order and then in alphabetical suborder.) Click on **Constants**, a part of the VBA type library.
3. The Object Browser will now list all the members of the class named Constants. One of these will be `vbCrLf`. Most of the built-in VB constants start with the prefix *vb*. Click on the constant **vbCrLf** and look to the bottom of the Object Browser, scrolling if necessary. There will be useful information that `vbCrLf` is the equivalent of `Chr$(13)+Chr$(10)`.
4. There is a button with a yellow question mark on the Object Browser. Click on this button now to reveal more detailed help on the `vbCrLf` constant.

The Object Browser is actually providing a lens into the many objects available to VB programs. At the top of the object browser is a dropdown combination. Hover the mouse over this dropdown and see a yellow ToolTip with the text Project/Library; dropping down this list provides access to objects such as VB, VBA, and VBRUN. The working project is listed in this dropdown box. Each item in this dropdown has members accessible to this program.

Click on `<All Libraries>` in the Project/Library dropdown and see various classes; some will contain the string "constant" in the name. Click on any of these classes to explore the many constants available.

Searching Help for a given function or keyword will often provide you with some useful information on constants that apply to that particular function or procedure.

Check It Out 4-12: Constants Help

1. Start a new Standard EXE project; double click on Form1 to reveal a code window.

2. Type MsgBox in the `Form_Load` to index into the Help. Click on the keyword MsgBox with the mouse and press the **F1** key to index into the Help for the Msg-Box keyword.
3. Examine the Help, which describes the constants that can be used in conjunction with the MsgBox function. Be sure to scroll all the way to the bottom.

Defining Custom Constants

Custom constants can be defined in VB. To make an application-wide global constant, define the constant in the [General][Declarations] section of a module, like this:

```
Public Const gcAppName As String = "My Little Application"
```

`Const` is the keyword used to define a constant. Constants differ from variables in that they cannot be changed. The scoping rules concerning the use of `Public`, `Private`, and `Dim` are the same as for variables. Think of constants as read-only variables.

In this chapter we covered all the data types, wrote procedures, and learned about the VB language. Those who have a good grip on this material, are now in good shape to dive into the more advanced topics. We discussed all the VB data types and all of the places where VB code can reside within a project.

Exercise 4-1: Variables and Functions

This exercise will make it possible to work with variables and functions. We will investigate scoping rules, argument passing, calling conventions and work with a ListBox to employ some of the key elements in the Visual Basic language.

EXPLORING THE SCOPING OF VARIABLES

Step 1

Start a new VB Standard EXE project and add a module. In the module add custom constants accessible from the entire application. Add the following code to Module1:

```
Public Const gcAppName As String = "My Little Application"
Public Const gcVersion As String = "1.0"
```

Now add this code to the Form_Load of Form1:

```
Form1.Caption = gcAppName & " Version " & gcVersion
```

Run the application. Because there is access to the constants, the values appear in Form1's window title.

Now return to Module1 and make the constants Private instead of Public. Run the application. What happens? Why?

Step 2

Change the constant declarations in Module1 back to Public declarations. Next, try this line as the first line under the `Form_Load` of Form1:

```
gcAppName = "Your error will occur here." _
    & "Constants cannot be changed."
```

Run the application and see what happens. Can the constant be changed? Comment out this line of code now.

Step 3

The next step is to work with a variable that is local to a form. One common use of a variable that is Private to a form is for communicating between procedures. Explore this use of a Private, form-level variable now.

Add this line to the `Form_Resize` of Form1:

```
MsgBox "FORM RESIZE"
```

Step 4

Now run the application. When the form loads, the Resize event procedure executes. This can be suppressed, but only if the Resize event procedure can be sure that the `Form_Load` just executed. This is fairly simple to program. Set up a variable on the form and make sure that the `Form_Load` sets it to a value. Later, the `Form_Resize` can examine the variable and take action based on the value.

Step 5

Declare a Boolean variable Private to Form1. Name it `FromFormLoad`, like this:

```
Private FromFormLoad As Boolean
```

Next, set this variable to True in the `Form_Load` of Form1, like this:

```
FromFormLoad = True
```

So far, this Boolean local has been set to Form1, and `Form_Load` sets it to True. Now test the value in `Form_Resize` and exit the resize procedure if the `Form_Load` just executed. Place this code under the `Form_Resize` of Form1:

```
If FromFormLoad = True Then
  FromFormLoad = False
  Exit Sub
End If
MsgBox "FORM RESIZE"
```

Now run the application. Execution of the Resize event procedure will not be visible when the form loads, but if Form1 is resized, the Resize event procedure will execute, as evidenced by the MsgBox that appears. The effect is accomplished by using a variable so that the Load event procedure can communicate to the Resize event procedure. Since both of these procedures reside in Form1, it makes perfect sense to use a variable private to Form1. There is no need for the entire application to know about this variable.

EXPLORING PROCEDURES AND PROCEDURE WRITING

Step 6

Now we will write a procedure that uses the intrinsic string functions of VB. This procedure will accept a string of text and return that same text with each word capitalized. This part of the exercise shows how to use some of the intrinsic functions, and also how to write a custom procedure that can be called from the entire application.

Bring up Module1 in a code window, and then click on the **TOOLS/ADD PROCEDURE** menu. Define a Public Function named UpperAllWords(). Set it up so it will accept a string and return a string. The function declaration should look like this:

```
Public Function UpperAllWords(TEXTIN As String) As String
```

Here is the complete function. Note that it does not handle a single word in a string (it only handles multiple words in a string), and does not capitalize the first letter of the last word. Add this functionality if you have time.

```
Public Function UpperAllWords(ByVal TEXTIN As String) As String
Dim strWORD As String
Dim strFINAL As String
Do While InStr(TEXTIN, " ") <> 0
  'Isolate the first word in TEXTIN
  strWORD = Left(TEXTIN, InStr(TEXTIN, " "))
  'Chop the first word off the TEXTIN
  TEXTIN = Right(TEXTIN, Len(TEXTIN) - InStr(TEXTIN, " "))
  'Uppercase the 1st letter
  strWORD = UCase(Left(strWORD, 1)) & Right(strWORD, _
            Len(strWORD) - 1)
  'Append results to final string
  strFINAL = strFINAL & strWORD
Loop
'Return Results Capitalized
UpperAllWords = strFINAL & " " & TEXTIN
'WARNING: This function can't handle a single word, and
'does not uppercase the last word. You need to
'consider fixing this.
End Function
```

Step 7

The procedure UpperAllWords() accepts a stringful of words and returns those words capitalized. The next step is to test the procedure. Drop a TextBox on Form1, and then drop a CommandButton. Under the CommandButton, add this code:

```
Form1.Caption = UpperAllWords(Text1.Text)
```

Run the application, and enter a sentence using all lowercase letters in Text1, and click on Command1. The uppercase text should appear in the window title of Form1.

Step 8

Alter the code in the procedure to handle (a) an input string with only one word inside, and (b) setting the first letter of the last word to an uppercase.

A SIMPLE SELECTION LIST BOX

Step 9

One of the more common things in installation and setup applications is the selection list box arrangement. Here, two list boxes are provided. The one to the left is the source box, and is filled with items. The one on the right is populated dynamically, click on items for inclusion, from the source list box. Typically, these boxes have a set of buttons between them as depicted in Figure 4-9.

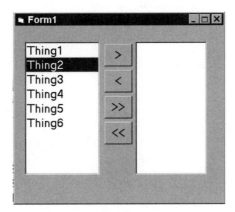

Figure 4-9 Form and Controls.

The > button moves a single item from left to right.
The < button moves a single selected item from right to left.
The >> button moves everything from left to right.
The << button moves everything from right to left.

Start a new VB Standard EXE project. Drop two list boxes on Form1; these will be named List1 and List2 by default. Also, drop two buttons and label with > and < respectively. In this exercise, only implement these two buttons. Next, add this code to the Form_Load of Form1:

```
List1.AddItem "Thing1"
List1.AddItem "Thing2"
List1.AddItem "Thing3"
```

```
List1.AddItem "Thing4"
List1.AddItem "Thing5"
List1.AddItem "Thing6"
```

Run the application to be sure that List1 fills with information.

Step 10

Now add functionality to the buttons. Add this code to the Click event procedure of Command1:

```
'BE SURE SOMETHING IS SELECTED, Exit Sub if not
If Form1.List1.ListIndex = -1 Then Exit Sub
'COPY SELECTED TEXT FROM SOURCE TO DESTINATION
Form1.List2.AddItem Form1.List1.List(Form1.List1.ListIndex)
'DELETE TEXT FROM SOURCE
Form1.List1.RemoveItem Form1.List1.ListIndex
```

Be sure to examine the Help file for the ListBox properties and methods used here. They include List(), ListIndex, AddItem, and RemoveItem.

Step 11

Test the application. Click on an item in List1 and then click on the Command1 button labeled > and see if the selected data *moves* from List1 to List2. It should. Moving data in the opposite direction is just a matter of moving this code under another button (Command2) and renaming some items so that the selected item in List2 gets moved to List1. Select the code with the mouse, and click on **EDIT/COPY**. Then, open a code window to the Command2_Click, and click on **EDIT/PASTE**. Now alter the code so that the data movement is from List2 to List1. The completed code under Command2 should look like this:

```
'BE SURE SOMETHING IS SELECTED, Exit Sub if not
If Form1.List2.ListIndex = -1 Then Exit Sub
'COPY SELECTED TEXT FROM SOURCE TO DESTINATION
Form1.List1.AddItem Form1.List2.List(Form1.List2.ListIndex)
'DELETE TEXT FROM SOURCE
Form1.List2.RemoveItem Form1.List2.ListIndex
```

Step 12

Test the application. The data should move in both directions. Some functionality works, and has been completed, but essentially with duplicate code. This was done needlessly. The processing under Command1 and Command2 is similar. In fact, it would be nice if we could call a procedure to move the data. This can be done by passing in the ListBoxes as arguments. In this last part, we will write a procedure as a subroutine that moves the data from a source list box to a destination list box. The key to this is that controls can be passed around just like variables. Create a new procedure by clicking on the **TOOLS/ADD PROCEDURE** menu. (It can be set up as Public in Module1 or as Public or Private in Form1.) Create a subroutine and name the procedure MoveData. The completed procedure should look like this:

```
Public Sub MoveData(SOURCE As ListBox, DEST As ListBox)
'BE SURE SOMETHING IS SELECTED, Exit Sub if not
If SOURCE.ListIndex = -1 Then Exit Sub
'COPY SELECTED TEXT FROM SOURCE TO DESTINATION
DEST.AddItem SOURCE.List(SOURCE.ListIndex)
'DELETE TEXT FROM SOURCE
SOURCE.RemoveItem SOURCE.ListIndex
End Sub
```

This procedure moves data between any two arbitrary ListBoxes. Now call the procedure by replacing all that code under Command1 with this single line of code:

```
Call MoveData(Form1.List1,Form1.List2)
```

Test it out. Now replace all the lines of code under Command2 with this single line, reversing the order, making List2 the source ListBox:

```
Call MoveData(Form1.List2, Form1.List1)
```

Exercise 4-2: Passing Arguments

In this exercise, we will investigate the fundamentals of argument passing in Visual Basic and work with the `ByVal` keyword, optional arguments, and the `ParamArray`.

BY VALUE VS. BY REFERENCE

Step 1

Arguments may be passed to Functions and Subroutines in one of two ways: by value or by reference. When an argument is passed by reference, a pointer to the location in memory of the argument is passed to the procedure. In contrast, when an argument is passed by value, a copy of the argument is passed to the procedure. This difference is important, because when arguments are passed by reference, the values may be accidentally changed by the procedure.

Step 2

Create a new directory in the File Explorer called **VB BOOTCAMP/EXERCISE 4-2/BYVAL**. Start a New Standard EXE project in Visual Basic.

Step 3

On Form1, place a Text Box, Labels, and two Command Buttons so that Form1 looks like Figure 4-10. Refer to the item list for details on properties that should be set at design time.

Item 1—CommandButton

Name	cmdByVal
Caption	By Value

Item 2—CommandButton

Name   cmdByRef

Caption   By Reference

Item 3—TextBox

Name   Text1

Item 4—Label

Name   lblBefore

Item 5—Label

Name   lblInSub

Item 6—Label

Name   lblAfter

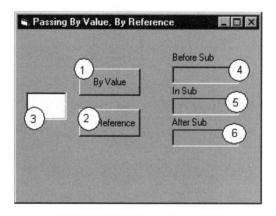

Figure 4-10 Form1 and controls.

Step 4

Add a new Subroutine to the Form by selecting **TOOLS/ADD PROCEDURE** from the menu. This procedure will be used to demonstrate passing arguments by reference.

Procedure Name: ByRefTest
Procedure Type: Sub
Procedure Scope: Public

Step 5

Add the following code to the ByRefTest subroutine to pass an argument by reference. The routine will add 2 to the passed value and update the display in Form1.

```
Public Sub ByRefTest(iNumber As Integer)
   iNumber=iNumber+2
   lblInSub.Caption = Str$(iNumber)
End Sub
```

Step 6

Add a new Subroutine to the Form by selecting **TOOLS/ADD PROCEDURE** from the menu. This procedure will do the same thing as the last procedure added except the argument will be passed by value.

Procedure Name: `ByValTest`
Procedure Type: `Sub`
Procedure Scope: `Public`

Step 7

Add the following code to the `ByValTest` subroutine to add 2 to the passed value and update the display in Form1.

```
Public Sub ByValTest(ByVal iNumber As Integer)
 iNumber=iNumber+2
 lblInSub.Caption = Str$(iNumber)
End Sub
```

Step 8

Notice the only difference between these two subroutines is that the `ByVal` keyword appears in the argument list of the `ByValTest` subroutine which causes the argument to be passed by value. Add the following code to the Click event of `cmdByRef` to call the procedure:

```
Public Sub cmdByRef_Click()
 Dim iNum As Integer
 iNum = Val(Text1.Text)
 lblBefore.Caption = Str$(iNum)
 Call ByRefTest(iNum)
 lblAfter.Caption = Str$(iNum)
End Sub
```

Step 9

Add the following code to the Click event of `cmdByVal` to call the procedure:

```
Public Sub cmdByVal_Click()
Dim iNum As Integer
iNum = Val(Text1.Text)
lblBefore.Caption = Str$(iNum)
Call ByValTest(iNum)
lblAfter.Caption = Str$(iNum)
End Sub
```

Step 10

Run the Project. Enter a Value of 10 into the Text Box and Press the `ByRef` button. The Values that result are:

Before Sub: 10
In Sub: 12
After Sub: 12

Step 11

When the value is passed by reference, the subroutine can easily change the value of the actual argument since the subroutine has a pointer to the location in memory where the argument resides.

Step 12

Now press the ByVal button. The results are:

Before Sub: 10
In Sub: 12
After Sub: 10

Step 13

The difference in the after-sub value is due to the fact that by-value passing sends a copy of the argument to a procedure. This copy can be manipulated by the procedure, but the copy is destroyed after the procedure is complete. This does not mean that by-value passing is better than by-reference passing—they are just different. For example, if there is a 30-member array to pass, would it be better to pass it by value (making a 30-member copy) or by reference (passing a simple 4-byte pointer)?

OPTIONAL ARGUMENTS

Step 14

Create a new directory called **VB BOOTCAMP/EXERCISE 4-2/OPTIONAL**. Start a New Standard EXE Project in Visual Basic.

Step 15

On Form1 place controls so that the form looks like Figure 4-11. Refer to the Item list for details on properties you should set at design time.

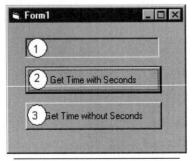

Figure 4-11 Form1 and controls.

Item 1—Label

Name   lblTime

Item 2—CommandButton

Name   cmdWith

Caption   Get Time With Seconds

Item 3—CommandButton

Name   cmdWithout

Caption   Get Time Without Seconds

Step 16

Add a new procedure to Form1 by selecting **TOOLS\ADD PROCEDURE** from the menu.

Procedure name: GetTime
Procedure Type: Sub
Procedure Scope: Public

Step 17

Add the following code to the GetTime procedure with one optional argument. Notice also that all of the arguments are passed by reference which is the default in VB.

```
Public Sub GetTime(Hour As String, Minute As String, Optional Second
As String)
'The Third Argument is optional--we can decide
'whether or not to pass in a third argument.
'Once the OPTIONAL keyword is used, all following
'arguments must be Optional.
'The IsMissing function determines whether or not an Optional
'argument was passed
If IsMissing(Second) Then Second = ""

Dim ThisMoment

ThisMoment = Now

Hour = Format$(ThisMoment, "hh")
Minute = Format$(ThisMoment, "nn")
Second = Format$(ThisMoment, "ss")

End Sub
```

Step 18

Under the cmdWith button, place the following code to call the procedure and pass the optional argument. Notice that we can display the variables after the call because the GetTime routine changes the arguments which are passed by reference.

```
Private Sub cmdWith_Click()

Dim ThisHour As String
Dim ThisMinute As String
Dim ThisSecond As String

Call GetTime(ThisHour, ThisMinute, ThisSecond)
lblTime.Caption = ThisHour & ":" & ThisMinute & ":" & ThisSecond
End Sub
```

Step 19

Under the `cmdWithout` button, place the following code to call the procedure without the optional argument. This displays the time with no seconds.

```
Private Sub cmdWithout_Click()

Dim ThisHour As String
Dim ThisMinute As String
'In this case we are not using the Third Argument
'which is designated in the procedure definition
'as "Optional"
Call GetTime(ThisHour, ThisMinute)
lblTime.Caption = ThisHour & ":" & ThisMinute
End Sub
```

Step 20

Run the Project. Notice that it is not necessary to provide the "Second" argument since it is specified as optional.

THE PARAM ARRAY

Step 21

Create a new directory called **VB BOOTCAMP/EXERCISE 4-2/PARAM**. Start a New Standard EXE project in Visual Basic.

Step 22

Place controls on Form1 so that it looks like Figure 4-12. Refer to the Item list for details regarding properties to set at design time.

Item 1—ListBox

Name   lstNames

Item 2—CommandButton

Name   cmdFillList
Caption   Fill List

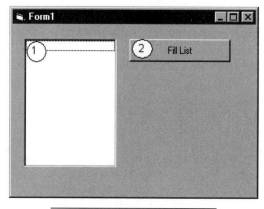

Figure 4-12 Form1 and controls.

Step 23

Add a New Procedure to Form1 by selecting **TOOLS/ADD PROCEDURE** from the menu.

Procedure Name: `FillList`
Procedure Type: `Sub`
Procedure Scope: `Public`

Step 24

Add the following code to the `FillList` procedure.

```
Public Sub FillList(ParamArray Names() As Variant)

'When using ParamArray, the array data type must
'always be a variant and the array must always be
'the last argument.

Dim MyName As Variant

For Each MyName In Names()
 lstNames.AddItem MyName
Next
End Sub
```

Step 25

The ParamArray permits passing an indeterminate number of arguments to a procedure. Add the following code to the Click event of `cmdFillList`.

```
Private Sub cmdFillList_Click()
'This Subroutine accepts any number of arguments
Call FillList("Dan", "Gary", "Scot")
Call FillList
Call FillList("Bill")
End Sub
```

Step 26

Run the program and fill the List box. Notice how the code under the button passes a varying numbers of arguments to the `FillList` procedure.

FOR THE CERTIFIED PRO

Pro 4-1: Passing Objects as arguments

1. Create a subroutine that takes a form as an argument and centers it on the screen.

Pro 4-2: Sorting arrays

1. Create a function that finds the largest value in an array of Integers and returns it from the function.

PREPARING FOR CERTIFICATION

Topics for further reading
Introduction to variables, constants, and data types
Introduction to procedures
Introduction to control structures

CERTIFICATION QUIZ

1. A function created in a Class module by declaring with the Friend keyword is visible
   a. inside the Class module, only
   b. to the entire project
   c. outside the project
   d. none of the above

2. A function created in a standard module by declaring with the Friend keyword is visible
   a. inside the Class module only
   b. to the entire project
   c. outside the project
   d. none of the above

3. Which of the following statements are true about the decimal data type?
   a. A variable can be declared to be of type Decimal.
   b. The Decimal data type is a subtype of the Variant data type.
   c. The Decimal data type is derived from the Currency data type.
   d. A Variant data type can be created whose subtype is Decimal using the CDec function.

4. Which statements are true for a subroutine?
   a. It remains idle until called upon to respond to events caused by the user or triggered by the system.
   b. It must be explicitly invoked by the application.
   c. It can be either Public or Private. It is Private by default.
   d. It may return a value to the calling procedure.

5. Which statements are true for a function?
   a. It must be explicitly invoked by the application.
   b. It may return a value to the calling procedure.
   c. It remains idle until called upon to respond to events caused by the user or triggered by the system.
   d. It can be either Public or Private. It is Public by default.

6. Which statements are true of the ByRef keyword?
   a. If neither ByVal nor ByRef is specified, this is the default.
   b. When used, it passes the address of the argument to the procedure.
   c. The Option Explicit statement forces this to be the default method of passing arguments.
   d. It can be used with Call whenever the procedure being called must be forced to accept arguments by this method.

7. The Static statement is used at which level?
   a. Procedure level
   b. Module level
   c. Form level
   d. Property procedures

8. In VB, once a user-defined type is declared using the Type statement, declaring a variable of that type can be declared using which of the following?
   a. `ReDim`
   b. `Public`
   c. `Friend`
   d. `Private`

9. Which is used at module level to declare the default lower bound for array subscripts?
   a. `Option Bounds`
   b. `Option Base`
   c. `Option Compare`
   d. `Option Explicit`

10. In VB, which of the following are valid variable declarations?
   a. `Dim a, b, c As Integers`
   b. `Dim Static a As Integer`
   c. `Static Dim a As Integer`
   d. `ReDim b As Interger`

11. A Variant data type may contain which of the following?
    a. String arrays
    b. Integer arrays
    c. Variant arrays
    d. User-defined data types

12. If an arithmetic operation is performed on a Variant data type and the result exceeds the normal range for the original data type:
    a. the result is truncated to the maximum value the data type may hold
    b. the result is promoted within the Variant to the next larger data type, if it exists
    c. it will result in an Arithmetic Overflow runtime error
    d. None of the above

13. What keyword indicates that the Variant variable intentionally contains no valid data?
    a. New
    b. Empty
    c. Nothing
    d. Null

14. What keyword denotes a Variant variable that has not been initialized?
    a. New
    b. Empty
    c. Nothing
    d. Null

15. According to the largest positive values allowed in the range of each data type, which groupings are arranged from smallest to largest?
    a. Boolean, Byte, Integer, Long
    b. Currency, Single, Double, Long
    c. Integer, Long, Single, Double
    d. Byte, Integer, Currency, Variant

16. A variable of Boolean data type is True when it contains which of the following values?
    a. −1
    b. 0
    c. 1
    d. 32767

17. Which set of statements repeats a block of statements while a condition is True or until a condition becomes True?
    a. `If...Then...Else`
    b. `Select Case`
    c. `Do...Loop`
    d. `While...Wend`

18. A variable of what data type may be used to iterate through the elements of an array using a `For Each...Next` statement?
    a. String
    b. Variant
    c. Decimal
    d. Long

19. Which of the following statements are proper uses of the Exit statement?
    a. `Exit Loop`
    b. `Exit For`
    c. `Exit Sub`
    d. `Exit Next`

20. An uninitialized Boolean variable contains what value?
    a. Null
    b. Empty
    c. Nothing
    d. 0

21. Which of the following may be valid assignment statements?
    a. Let X = Y + Z
    b. Let X = Y And Z
    c. Let X > Y If X = Z
    d. X = Z And Y = Z

ANSWERS TO CERTIFICATION QUIZ

1. b
2. d
3. b, d
4. b
5. a, b, d
6. a, b
7. a
8. a, b, d
9. b
10. a, b, c
11. a, b, c, d
12. b
13. d
14. b
15. c, d
16. a, c, d
17. c, d
18. b

19. b, c
20. d
21. a, b, d

INTRODUCING DATA ACCESS

BASIC KNOWLEDGE REQUIRED

Those beginning this chapter should have a fundamental knowledge of relational database concepts, and be completely familiar with the Visual Basic language, data types, and scoping rules. A working knowledge of Structured Query Language (SQL) is not required, but is useful.

SKILLS COVERED

- 70-176 (11): Use data binding to display and manipulate data from a data source
- 70-176 (23): Access and manipulate a data source by using ADO and the ADO Data Control
- 70-175 (15): Use data binding to display and manipulate data from a data source

- 70-175 (33): Access and manipulate a data source by using ADO and the ADO Data Control
- 70-175 (41): Write SQL statements that retrieve and modify data
- 70-175 (42): Write SQL statements that use joins to combine data from multiple tables

The history of data access in Visual Basic is a long one with many twists and variations. As VB has matured, so have the data access methodologies. In Visual Basic 6.0, data access represents a significant and capable body of knowledge. This chapter introduces data access in Visual Basic and prepares the way for the more complicated discussions which follow.

Unlike other RAD tools, Visual Basic never shipped with an intrinsic database technology. VB was always intended to be a jack of all trades when it came to data access, and Microsoft built the tool to ensure maximum flexibility. The closest thing VB ever had to a native database was Microsoft Access.

Visual Basic ships with the run-time engine for Microsoft Access known as the *Joint Engine Technology* (JET) database engine. JET was one of the first object-oriented database engines, and as such was a perfect partner for VB. The latest version of JET ships with Visual Basic 6.0 and is still run-time royalty free which means that VB can use Microsoft Access databases right out of the box. The object interface used by Visual Basic to access JET is known as the *Data Access Objects* (DAO).

JET is a good database engine for desktop solutions that have a single user, but its performance degrades as users and data are added. For this reason, JET does not represent a good solution for multi-user database applications. Opinions vary as to exactly how much data and how many users are appropriate for JET, but in the end, JET will always be more limited than other solutions. Nonetheless, JET is often a good starting point for new VB programmers because its simplified data access scheme relieves programmers of the burden of security and distribution issues.

As Visual Basic and data access matured, more programmers wanted the ability to build true client/server applications that provided a high degree of security and scalability. For this reason, Microsoft provided support in Visual Basic to access relational databases that complied with the *Open Database Connectivity* (ODBC) standard. ODBC is a specification intended to provide access to high-end relational databases like SQL Server and Oracle. In fact, ODBC can be used to access almost any database in use today, including Microsoft Access and even mainframe databases like IBM DB2. The object interface used by Visual Basic to access ODBC is known as the *Remote Data Objects* (RDO).

DAO and RDO are technologies that provide the ability to work with many relational databases. However, with the release of Visual Basic 6.0, Microsoft has provided a new and more powerful tool for accessing data, known as OLEDB (pronounced OLAY – D B). OLEDB is a specification that defines how data are to be accessed from both relational and nonrelational data stores. This includes databases like Access, Oracle, and SQL Server, but also includes nonrelational sources like Excel, Microsoft Index Server, Microsoft Exchange, and the Active Directory. In fact, OLEDB can access any facility that stores data. This concept of one specification defining access to all data stores is known as *Universal Data Access* (UDA). The object interface used by Visual Basic to access OLEDB sources is known as the *ActiveX Data Objects* (ADO).

Visual Basic provides many facilities for accessing data through DAO, RDO, and ADO. The natural question for any programmer is: Which to use, when, and why? From the Microsoft perspective, UDA is the goal of Visual Basic 6.0 and ADO is clearly the weapon of choice. Many people will say that DAO and RDO are obsolete technologies and no one should ever use anything except ADO. While it is true that DAO and RDO represent only a subset of ADO capabilities, many existing VB applications are written using DAO and RDO, and therefore, they are still critical technologies. Furthermore, at this writing, OLEDB does not yet enjoy widespread support among all the popular database vendors. In some cases, an RDO solution may be superior to an ADO solution. As the book progresses, we will examine each of the technologies in increasing detail.

The simplest way to access data from Visual Basic is through a data control. Visual Basic provides data controls for DAO, RDO, and ADO. These controls are specially designed to provide a simple set of properties, events, and methods through which to access the facilities of JET, ODBC, and OLEDB. Since JET was the first database engine used by Visual Basic, the data control associated with JET is simply referred to as the *Data Control*; however, to avoid confusion, we will refer to it as the *JET Data Control*. The control used with RDO is logically called the *Remote Data Control* (RDC), and the data control associated with ADO is called the *Active Data Control* (ADC). Each of these controls has a similar interface. They use a VCR-style metaphor with arrow buttons for first, next, last, and previous records (See Figure 5-1).

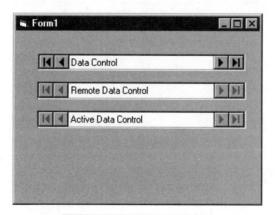

Figure 5-1 The data controls.

THE JET DATA CONTROL

The JET Data Control allows simple data access to JET with almost no coding. Using the JET Data Control can require as little work as setting three or four properties for controls. Once set up, the control gives access to a table or set of records based on settings. In order to connect to an Access database using the JET Data Control, first designate the database using the "DatabaseName" property (Figure 5-2). Clicking on the **DatabaseName** property at design time will bring up an ellipsis that makes it possible to search the hard drive for databases to view.

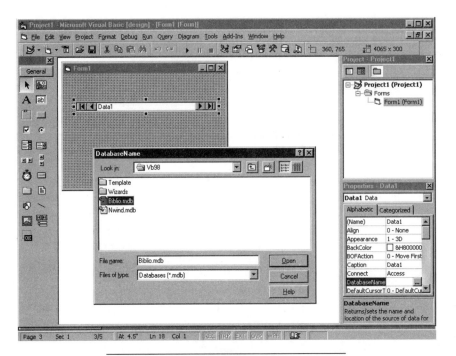

Figure 5-2 Setting the DatabaseName property.

When the DatabaseName property is set, Visual Basic initially wants to locate a file with an MDB extension, the extension for Microsoft Access databases. Although the JET Data Control suggests Microsoft Access, the truth is that the Data Control can talk to many other databases. The JET Data Control has a "Connect" property which initially defaults to the value "Access," but can be set to see many other databases (see Figure 5-3). It is possible to pick from databases in the list, but the JET Data Control will accept a value for the Connect property of "ODBC," which permits connecting to any ODBC database like Oracle or SQL Server.

This is where new VB programmers get confused. These are three different technologies for accessing data—JET, ODBC, and OLEDB—yet already the JET Data Control has the ability to access not only JET, but also ODBC. The reason for the overlap is that Microsoft added significant functionality to the JET engine as VB matured. By the time RDO emerged to allow ODBC access, JET already had an ODBC component. This is typical of Microsoft, where an emerging standard is incorporated into all technologies, old and new. Although the JET Data Control can access ODBC, the RDC is better suited for the task. We will focus on working with Microsoft Access databases with the JET Data Control.

Once the DatabaseName property is set, select a table from the database with which the JET Data Control should connect. Selecting the table is done with the RecordSource property (Figure 5-4). Once a database is selected, the RecordSource property provides an ellipsis and drop-down box to select the table of interest.

Figure 5-3 Setting the Connect property.

Figure 5-4 Setting the RecordSource property.

Once the DatabaseName and RecordSource property are set, the JET Data Control can be used to present the data on a form. Data presentation is accomplished with a Data Control through a process known as *data binding*, which associates a display control like a TextBox or grid with a data control. Data binding has been available in Visual Basic for a long while, but Visual Basic 6.0 increases its capabilities. The product will help users find new ways to connect data display mechanisms with data source mechanisms.

The simplest way to display data from the JET Data Control is through a TextBox control, which is capable of binding to any of the three data controls. This is accomplished through the DataSource property which is set to the name of the data control acting as the data source (Figure 5-5). Many controls support a DataSource property that allows a data control to pass information to them for display. This communication requires no new code and is the essence of data binding. Any control which has a DataSource property and supports binding is referred to generically as a "bound" control.

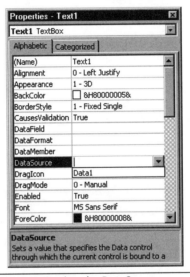

Figure 5-5 Setting the DataSource property.

Once the DataSource property is set, the field TextBox display must be designated through the DataField property (Figure 5-6). This is because the TextBox can only display one field. Other controls, like grids, can display multiple fields and records, and therefore may not have a DataField property. If the JET Data Control is properly bound to a TextBox, all the fields will appear in a dropdown list.

When the DatabaseName, RecordSource, DataSource, and DataField properties have been set, the project is ready to run. With no new code, the appropriate table will be bound to the selected display control. Figure 5-7 shows a JET Data Control bound to both a TextBox and a grid.

Check It Out 5-1: Using the JET Data Control

---

1. Start a new VB Standard EXE project. Drop a JET Data Control on Form1 named Data1.
2. Drop a TextBox control on Form1 named Text1. It is a data bound control and will have data displayed.

Figure 5-6 Setting the DataField property.

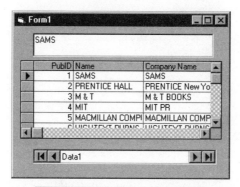

Figure 5-7 A data-bound project.

3. Click on **Data1**. Set the DatabaseName property so that it points to BIBLIO.MDB in the VB installation directory. To do this, click on the **DatabaseName** property in the Properties window and click on the button that appears with the ellipsis. A dialog box will appear. Navigate to the VB installation directory and click on the file **BIBLIO.MDB** to specify this Access database as the one that will appear in the DatabaseName property of Data1. Click on the **BIBLIO.MDB** and then on **OK**; the full pathname of the BIBLIO database will be written into the Databasename property of Data1 in the Properties window.

4. The next property to set on Data1 is the RecordSource. Click the **RecordSource** property of Data1 in the Properties window; then click on the dropdown button that appears. All of the tables in BIBLIO.MDB will appear in the dropdown list.

Select **Publishers** and this table will be indicated for the RecordSource in the Properties window.

5. Now Data1 is set up to point to a table in BIBLIO.MDB. The next step is to display some of the data. Click on **Text1** and set the DataSource property to Data1 and the DataField property to Company Name. (The Datafield will expose a list of available fields. Drop down the list and select one.) Setting up the data access with the Data Control is now complete.

6. Run the application and click some of the Data Control buttons. Navigate to the first, last, previous and next records using the buttons on the Data Control. When a button is clicked, the user interface updates automatically. If the data are edited before another record is accessed, that edit is saved to the database.

7. End the application and return to design time.

The major advantages of the JET Data Control are automatic updates of the user interface as the data are scrolled, and automatic updates of the database during editing. The Data Control contains a ReadOnly property and an Exclusive property. The former makes the data read-only; the user cannot make updates when this property is True. The Exclusive property gives an application exclusive use of the data and locks out other users until the application breaks the connection.

The JET Data Control also has events. The Validate event fires during navigation from record to record. It executes before a different record becomes the current record, making it possible to examine the record under program control before it is written back to the database with changes. The Reposition event fires after a record has become the current record, permitting examination before display.

The JET Data Control maintains a container called a *Recordset*; the Recordset object can contain a Table, a Snapshot, or a Dynaset. It is possible to specify which object. Table is the default. The table-type Recordset is read-write. The Snapshot-type Recordset gives a copy of the database records as of the time the query executed; Snapshots are fast, but read-only. The Dynaset type of Recordset is a collection of indexes that point to the data, not the data themselves. This means that if other users change the underlying data, the changes are visible in rescrolling those records. Dynasets can be slow and should be avoided for performance reasons.

The JET Data Control makes it simple to access data without programming, but this access is not without cost. The JET Data Control does not allow full access to the database; it is not possible to add a new table to the database or a new field to a table.

DATA ACCESS OBJECTS

The JET Data Control provides a graphical interface to the functionality of the JET engine. However, for many applications, more database control is required than the JET Data Control provides. In order to gain maximum flexibility, write code directly to the object interface of the Data Access Objects (DAO). DAO provides properties, events, and methods access to JET, so that VB programmers can leverage existing knowledge to exploit the power of the Access run-time database engine. Think of the DAO as a bag of objects, each object with its own set of properties and methods. DAO sits below the Data Control and above the Access runtime engine. The objects contained within the DAO make data access easy in Visual Basic. Keep in mind that with the DAO there is no automatic user interface update and no automatic database update provided by the Data Control.

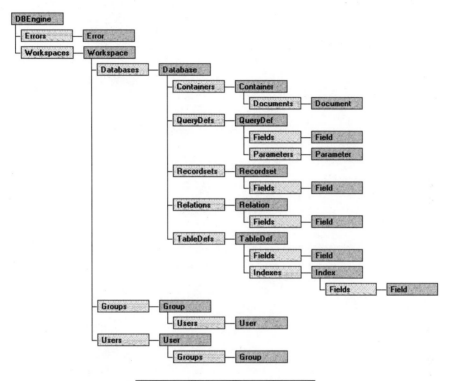

Figure 5-8 The DAO Object Model.

The objects that make up DAO are presented through an *object model* (Figure 5-8). Object models are hierarchical representations of a set of objects. The object model shows both the names of the objects and their relationships to each other. The vertical presentation is designed to show one-to-many and dependent relationships. Thus, the model shows that a single database can have many recordsets associated with it. It also suggests that in order to use a recordset object, there must first be a database object available. The relationships between objects in DAO are typically implemented via methods of the objects.

Before using DAO, establish a reference to the DAO model. This reference makes all the objects in the DAO available to a program. Do this by clicking on the **PROJECT/ REFERENCES** menu command to see the References dialog (Figure 5-9) that displays all the reusable components available on the computer. When VB installs, it also installs the DAO reusable component. For this reason, the references dialog displays the DAO as an available item for use by a project. Clicking the item titled **Microsoft DAO 3.5 Object Library** makes the objects in the DAO available to a program.

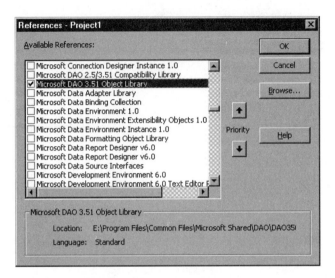

Figure 5-9 The References Dialog.

Check It Out 5-2: Using DAO

1. From the Windows Explorer, BIBLIO.MDB is found in the VB installation directory to the root directory of the computer. By placing the file in the root or topmost directory, we are simplifying the task of opening it under program control, because it will not be preceded by a long pathname.

2. Start a new VB Standard EXE project. Make sure the Microsoft DAO 3.51 Object Library entry in the VB References is checked before proceeding to the next step. Get to the references by clicking on the **PROJECT/REFERENCES** menu command.

3. Now drop a button on Form1. Clicking on this button will indicate how many rows of data are in the Publishers table of the BIBLIO.MDB copied to the root directory. Experiment with DAO programmability under the click of this button.

4. Add this code to the `Command1_Click` event procedure:

```
Dim db As Database
Dim rs As Recordset

Set db = OpenDatabase("C:\BIBLIO.MDB")
Set rs = db.OpenRecordset("Publishers")

MsgBox "Publishers table contains " & rs.RecordCount & _
       " rows of data."

rs.Close
db.Close

Set db = Nothing
Set rs = Nothing
```

5. Run the application and see what happens. Click on **Command1**. There should be a MsgBox telling how many rows of data are in the Publishers table.

Before using any object model, first declare variables to represent the objects from the model. These variables are referred to as *object variables*, and may be declared in code after a reference to the appropriate model is set. There are two new keywords required to use these object variables: *Set* and *Nothing*. The Set statement is used here because db is declared as an object variable. Object variables always require the use of the word `Set` when initializing them to a value or when using them in assignment. Thus the following code is used to establish a connection to a JET database and use an object variable to represent that connection.

```
Dim db As Database
Set db = OpenDatabase("C:\BIBLIO.MDB")
```

Once the database connection is established, the object variable makes all the properties and methods of its associated object available to a program. In the case of a database connection, we can use a method of the Database object to return a Recordset. The OpenRecordset method allows us to specify that the Recordset will contain the data from a given table. Thus the following code accesses a table.

```
Dim rs As Recordset
Set rs = db.OpenRecordset("Publishers")
```

After the table is accessed, the object variable may be used to read and write data to the table. We can also use it to gain information about the table such as the total number of records. After we have finished using the object variables, we must clear the resources used to create them. This is done with the Nothing keyword. The following code tells Visual Basic to release the resources used by the two object variables.

```
Set db = Nothing
Set rs = Nothing
```

The Database and Recordset objects are the workhorses of DAO. However, there are many other objects in the model that can be used to perform special functions. DAO supports JET security features through the Users and Groups objects. It is possible to access pre-compiled queries through the QueryDefs object and discover information about the database structure through the TableDefs object. Object models like DAO exist for all the data access technologies including ODBC and OLEDB. In Chapters 11 and 12, we will investigate these object models fully.

Check It Out 5-3: The TableDefs Collection

---

1. Start a new Standard EXE project. Go to the references and make sure that Microsoft DAO 3.5 Object Library is checked off.
2. Drop a ListBox and a CommandButton on Form1. Add this code under the `Command1_Click` event procedure:

```
Dim db As Database
Dim td As TableDef
Set db = DBEngine.Workspaces(0).OpenDatabase("C:\BIBLIO.MDB")
'ITERATE OVER THE TABLEDEFS COLLECTION
For Each td In db.TableDefs
    Me.List1.AddItem td.Name 'Add the .Name to List1
Next
```

3. Run the application and click **Command1**. List1 should populate with the name of every table definition in BIBLIO.MDB.

OPEN DATABASE CONNECTIVITY

Understanding the RDC begins with understanding the Open Database Connectivity (ODBC) specification. ODBC is a database communication standard that aims to provide database independence, a concept that allows access to any database, regardless of manufacturer, through a single common data manipulation language known as *Structured Query Language* (SQL). A single unified language for data access provides enormous benefits to developers who can easily migrate data from one source to another without recoding the applications that are accessing the data.

Achieving database independence is the job of the ODBC driver, a middleware component that translates the standard SQL statements of database front ends to the proprietary language of the particular back end. In this way, a single SQL statement can be run on any proprietary server that supports SQL.

The reality is, of course, slightly less perfect than the theory. Although SQL is widely supported, not all databases have the same level of support. The most fundamental SQL support is known as *Core SQL*. All data sources that claim to support ODBC must support Core SQL. However, SQL has several different additional levels that may or may not be supported. Discover to what degree a target data source supports SQL prior to beginning any project.

In order to write Visual Basic code against an ODBC-compliant database, first establish an ODBC data source, or DSN (Figure 5-10). A data source is simply the definition of a database and ODBC driver under a single alias that can be accessed through code. Establishing the ODBC data source is the job of the ODBC Administrator, an application found under the Control Panel as the ODBC icon.

Starting the ODBC Administrator will facilitate viewing all the ODBC data sources on the machine as well as establishing new ones. ODBC sources may be built against any database for which there is a driver such as SQL Server, Microsoft Access, or Oracle. When a data source is built, an alias name is provided; this can be used to access the source later from code. This name has no significance and can be nearly anything. Typically, the name is closely related to the actual database name.

ODBC data sources may be created with varying levels of scope. A DSN may be a User, System, or File DSN. User data sources are available only to the user who created the source. System data sources are available to all the users on a machine and the Windows NT services that run on the machine. File data sources are available to any machine that has security access to the DSN and the appropriate drivers available. In a nutshell, User, System, and File data sources provide individual, machine, and enterprise scope respectively. Visual Basic also supports the concept of DSN-less connections that make it possible to specify a data source without using the ODBC Administrator.

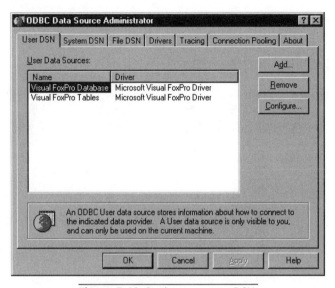

Figure 5-10 Setting up a new DSN.

Check It Out 5-4: Creating a DSN

1. Before using the ODBC API, set up an ODBC data source for use.
2. Establishing the data source is not a Visual Basic function, but one in Windows OS. Setup is done using the ODBC Administrator utility in Windows. Click on Start, Settings, then Control Panel. In the Control Panel, there will be an icon labeled ODBC. Double click this icon to start the ODBC Administrator.
3. The Data Sources dialog box will appear, listing all the ODBC data sources currently available on the machine. To create a new data source, select the **System** tab and push the **Add** button.
4. When you push the **Add** button, you will see the Create New Data Source dialog listing all the ODBC drivers available on the machine. For this exercise, select the **Microsoft Access ODBC driver** from the list and press **Finish**.
5. The ODBC Setup dialog box will appear. This dialog is for defining the new data source. First, provide a name for the data source. This can be any name, but for this exercise, name the data source **BIBLIO**.
6. Next, select the **BIBLIO.MDB** database by pushing the **Select** button and navigating the file system look for the BIBLIO.MDB file. Select this file and then push the **OK** button and back out of the ODBC Administrator. The data source has now been defined.

Once a DSN is established, use the RDC to access the data in much the same way the JET Data Control helped access the BIBLIO.MDB file. Connect to Microsoft Access databases through either JET or ODBC. When ODBC is used, the JET engine is not required. The database is being accessed through ODBC and the Microsoft Access ODBC driver. Anyone wanting to use the application must also have the appropriate drivers.

STRUCTURED QUERY LANGUAGE

Knowledge of how to create a DSN must be accompanied by knowledge of how to write queries using the Structured Query Language (SQL) supported by the ODBC specification. The scope of SQL makes complete coverage impossible, though we will try to give enough of the fundamentals to foster successful use of ODBC. Those who are already familiar with SQL and aggregate functions can skip this section. As with most of our data access topics, our coverage of SQL will increase in complexity as the book progresses.

SQL is a straightforward language made up of statements and clauses that form the basis of a standardized request to add, edit, or delete data inside a database. Any database accessible through ODBC recognizes some form of SQL. For our discussion of data controls, we will limit our coverage of SQL to statements that return records for display.

The backbone of SQL is the SELECT statement used to compose queries and obtain results. All the data controls are capable of executing SELECT statements to generate sets of records that can be bound to display controls. The syntax for the SELECT statement is shown below.

```
SELECT [DISTINCT] column1, column2, column3...
[FROM {table1, table2, table3...}
[JOIN table ON column1 = column2]
[WHERE clause]
[GROUP BY clause]
[HAVING clause]
[ORDER BY clause]
```

The SELECT statement tells the database that we intend to return a set of rows to our application and begins by specifying the columns from the database we want to return. The DISTINCT keyword tells the database to omit any repeated rows. If the same entry appears more than once, it will be sent to our application only one time. Column names can be used directly, or the asterisk can be a wildcard to indicate that all rows should be returned. Thus, if the database has a table named Customers with fields CustomerID, FirstName, and LastName, the following statements are equivalent.

```
SELECT CustomerID, FirstName, LastName FROM Customers
SELECT * FROM Customers
```

The FROM clause is used to specify the tables involved in the query. This may be as simple as a single table like our Customers example, or it may be a more complex relationship like a join. The JOIN and ON keywords indicate which tables are joined and the keys that make up the join. If a Customers table has entries in an Order table and a relationship on the field CustomerID, the following statement will join the tables and return the results.

```
SELECT * FROM Customers INNER JOIN Orders
ON Customers.CustomerID = Orders.CustomerID
```

One of the most useful clauses in the SELECT statement is the WHERE clause. WHERE permits filtering the records returned based on some parameter. This filter can be on any field in the table. For example, the following statement will return customer information for customers with an identification number greater than 100.

```
SELECT * FROM Customers WHERE CustomerID > 100
```

The WHERE clause can be used to specify a host of filters and perform Boolean algebra on them. Use AND, OR, NOT, and XOR to join separate comparative conditions in the clause. WHERE also supports string searches through the use of the LIKE keyword. LIKE is useful for returning data when only part of a text entry is known. LIKE operators permit substituting a wildcard character for text. In ODBC, the percent sign (%) is used to represent any number of characters. Therefore, the following statement returns customer information for all customers whose names begin with *B*.

```
SELECT * FROM Customers WHERE LastName LIKE 'B%'
```

TIP Although the % sign is the common wildcard for ODBC, be aware that JET uses the * character to accomplish the same function. Therefore, use the * character to specify a similar SQL statement to JET. The JET Data Control can accept SQL statements in the RecordSource property.

In addition to filtering data, the SELECT statement can also sort data through the ORDER BY clause. This specifies a field against which the records should be sorted. The following statement sorts the customer data alphabetically.

```
SELECT * FROM Customers ORDER BY LastName
```

Many programmers are aware of the fundamentals of SQL statements and are capable of creating the necessary queries for a business application. However, not all programmers are aware of some of the additional features of the SELECT statement that make it especially useful. These additional features make it possible to return data that do not actually reside in the database, but rather are calculated from the data. These are known as *aggregate functions*. Use aggregate functions to find averages, minimum values, maximum values, add numbers, and count entries.

As an example of aggregate functions, we will evaluate the *pubs* database that ships with SQL Server. This database is well known to developers because it is a demo database for testing queries. Pubs is to SQL Server as `Biblio.mdb` is to Microsoft Access. Like Biblio, pubs has publishers, titles, and author information. We can calculate some aggregate functions using pubs. For example, the following statement returns the average price of a book in the Titles table.

```
SELECT AVG(Price) FROM Titles
```

Note that this query does not return a set of records, but rather returns only one piece of data. This is how the aggregate functions work—they return information about data. Retrieving the average price is good, but what if more detail is required? SQL supports the GROUP BY clause which permits sorting the averages. The following statement can be used to find the average price of a book from every category in the Titles table.

```
SELECT Type, AVG(Price) FROM Titles GROUP BY Type
```

Data can be categorized and they can also be filtered based on aggregate functions. The HAVING clause is used to specify a condition upon which data should be returned. The following statement returns only the categories with an average price greater than $15.

```
SELECT Type, AVG(Price) FROM Titles GROUP BY Type HAVING AVG(Price)
> $15
```

 TIP   The examples used in this section are largely from Transact-SQL, the variety of SQL used by SQL Server. Although the fundamental statements shown here are widely supported, check database documentation for any special features.

THE REMOTE DATA CONTROL

The RDC is the data control used primarily with ODBC. This control was a follow-on to the JET Data Control and retains much of its look and feel. However, because the use of ODBC is different from that of JET, it does have some unique properties that must be carefully treated.

In order to use the RDC, add it to the toolbox if it is not already there. Unlike the JET Data Control, the RDC is not built in to the Visual Basic run time engine, but is a separate file. It must be added through the components dialog by selecting **PROJECT/COMPONENTS...** from the menu. In the components dialog, choose **Microsoft Remote Data Control 6.0** and press **OK**.

Once the control is in the toolbox, it can be added to a form. Since the RDC is designed to use ODBC, be sure that any required DSNs have been set up before the control is used. In fact, the first property set when using the RDC selects the DSN to connect with. This DSN is set in the "DataSourceName" property (Figure 5-11). Click on this property and see a dropdown list of available DSN entries.

Once the DataSourceName is set, create an SQL statement to indicate what records to return. A table cannot be accessed directly; instead, use an SQL statement. The RDC provides an "SQL" property for entering SQL statements. This property is available at run time, which means that it can be changed to retrieve different results as the application runs. When the SQL statement is changed at run time, call the Refresh method to cause the new statement to execute.

With the RDC, it is not enough to set the DataSourceName and SQL properties, because most high-end servers require a log-in to access the database. The RDC makes it possible to specify log-in information through the UserName and Password properties. As with the SQL property, these properties may be set at run time so they can be retrieved from a log in dialog. If the UserName and Password are forgotten, ODBC will help. The ODBC Administrator will pop a dialog requesting a log-in if the application has not provided enough infor-mation (Figure 5-12). This is the default behavior of ODBC. This dialog can be suppressed by changing the Prompt property of the RDC.

Figure 5-11 Setting the DataSourceName property.

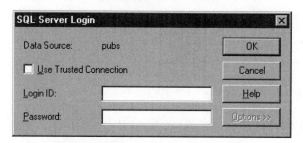

Figure 5-12 The ODBC Prompt dialog.

Once connection to the DSN is established, controls can be bound to the RDC in exactly the same way as they are bound to the JET Data Control. Like the JET Data Control, the RDC also supports a variety of properties, events, and methods that affect the cursor type and update fea-tures. These will be covered in more detail as the book progresses.

Check It Out 5-5: Using the Remote Data Control

1. Complete the previous Check It Out exercise that established a system DSN named Biblio.
2. Start a new Standard EXE project in Visual Basic.

3. The RDC may not be in the Visual Basic toolbox on startup, so add it through the Components dialog. Select **PROJECT/COMPONENTS...** from the menu to display the components dialog. In the dialog select add the **Microsoft Remote Data Control 6.0** and the **Microsoft FlexGrid Control 6.0**. Press **OK** to add them to the toolbox.

4. Place an RDC and FlexGrid control on Form1. Select the **RDC** and set the DataSourceName to Biblio.

5. Set the SQL property of the RDC to **SELECT * FROM Publishers**.

6. Select the **FlexGrid** control and set the DataSource property to point to the RDC which will have the name MSRDC1.

7. Run the project and the grid will display the information from the Publishers table in Biblio.

THE ACTIVE DATA CONTROL

Like the other data controls, the ADC is designed to return data and allow controls to display through binding. The big difference is that the ADC can be used to bind to any database supported by the JET Data Control and RDC plus a host of non-relational databases. As with the RDC, however, the ADC must be added manually to the toolbox by selecting **Microsoft ADO Data Control 6.0 (OLEDB)**.

OLEDB does not have an equivalent to the ODBC Administrator. Instead, all connection information is provided as straight text to the `ConnectionString` property or saved in a file known as a Data Link file. This information specifies the OLEDB provider and the database to connect with. When the `ConnectionString` property is set, there is a prompt to specify the text information for connection or the Data Link file containing the equivalent information.

Examine the `ConnectionString` dialog (Figure 5-13). You will notice that it also provides an option to select an ODBC driver. This is Microsoft's way of trying to ease the transition burden between ODBC and OLEDB. OLEDB has a built-in ODBC/OLEDB bridge which allows it to use any ODBC DSN as well as OLEDB provider. As we stated earlier, OLEDB is still not widely supported, so an ODBC capability means the ADC can be used with any database, even if that database does not have an OLEDB provider.

Check It Out 5-6: Creating a Data Link File

1. Data Link Files are created in the File Explorer. Start the file explorer and create a new directory named **VB BOOTCAMP/DATA LINK**.

2. Select this new directory and choose **NEW/MICROSOFT DATA LINK** from the File Explorer menu.

3. Rename the file **TEST.UDL** and press **Enter**.

4. Right click the new file and select **PROPERTIES...** from the popup menu. (See Figure 5-14.)

5. Click on the **Provider** tab and choose **Microsoft JET 3.51 OLE DB Provider**.

6. Click on the **Connection** tab. Use the ellipsis under **Select or Enter Database Name** to locate the BIBLIO.MDB database.

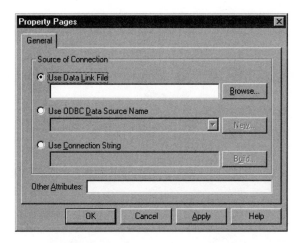

Figure 5-13 The ConnectionString dialog.

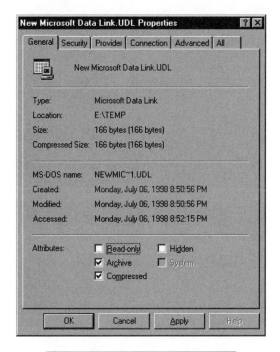

Figure 5-14 The Data Link Properties.

7. Press the **Test Connection** button to test the new Data Link.
8. Press **OK** to save the Data Link file for use with the ADC.

In order to retrieve records with the ADC, set the **RecordSource** property (Figure 5-15). This accepts an SQL string just as the SQL property of the RDC does. Keep in mind that OLEDB has the ability to access not only relational sources, but also non-relational data stores. When the RecordSource property is selected, Visual Basic presents a dialog to specify how to form the query. In the ADC, a query may be formed as text or a precompiled query may be used like a stored procedure. For simple SQL statements, pick the command type as text and enter the SQL.

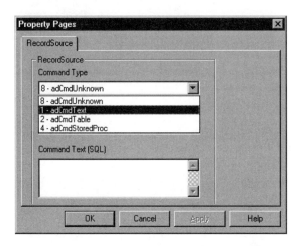

Figure 5-15 Setting The RecordSource property.

Once a connection is established, use bound controls with the ADC just as with the JET Data Control and RDC. However, not all of the controls that can be bound to the other data controls work with the ADC. Generally, the controls must be specifically designated for use with OLEDB. Look for the OLEDB designator in the components dialog to help identify these special controls.

Check It Out 5-7: Using the Active Data Control

1. Start a new Standard EXE project in Visual Basic
2. Open the components dialog by selecting **PROJECT/COMPONENTS...** from the menu. In the components dialog, select **Microsoft ADO Data Control 6.0** and **Microsoft Hierarchical Flex Grid Control 6.0 (OLEDB)**. Push the **OK** button.
3. With the ADC and Flex Grid controls in the toolbox, add one of each to Form1 so that the form looks like Figure 5-16.
4. Click on the **ADC** and view its properties; select the **ConnectionString** property. Use the ConnectionString property to reference the DataLink file created previously.
5. In the RecordSource property, select to add a text command and enter the SQL statement **SELECT * FROM Publishers**.

6. Click on the **Flex Grid** control and set the DataSource property to bind the grid to the ADC.
7. Run the project.

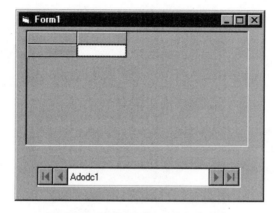

Figure 5-16 The ADC and Flex Grid.

Visual Basic ships with a family of bound controls to be used with the data controls. These include not only text boxes, but ListBoxes, ComboBoxes, and grids as well. Together with the data controls, the bound controls provide a methodology for rapidly creating data access solutions in Visual Basic. Most of the standard VB controls support data binding, for instance to the PictureBox, Label, TextBox, CheckBox, ComboBox, ListBox. Image, and OLE Container. In addition to these controls, Visual Basic supports special controls with enhanced binding features, including the Data Bound and Flex Grids, the Data Bound List, and the Data Bound Combo.

In addition to the bound controls, Visual Basic also provides a wizard designed for rapid creation of data control solutions, known as the *Data Form Wizard*. This is available as an add-in to the Visual Basic environment. Select **ADD-INS/ADD-IN MANAGER...** from the menu. In the Add-In Manager (Figure 5-17), double click the **Data Form Wizard**. Once the Add-In Manager is closed, the Data Form Wizard will be available as a menu item under the ADD-INS menu.

Check It Out 5-8: Using the Data Form Wizard

1. Start a new Standard EXE project in Visual Basic.
2. Right click the blank Form1 in the Project Explorer and select **Remove Form1** from the pop up menu. A form is unnecessary because the Data Form Wizard will add one.
3. Open the Add-In Manager by selecting **ADD-INS/ADD-IN MANAGER...** from the menu. In the Add-In Manager, double click the **Data Form Wizard** entry and close the Add-In Manager.
4. Start the Data Form Wizard by selecting **ADD-INS/DATA FORM WIZARD...** from the menu.

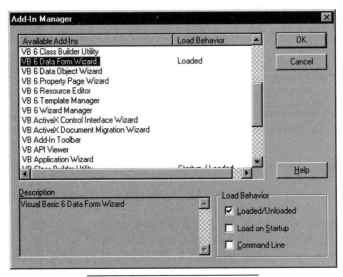

Figure 5-17 The Add-In Manager.

5. When the Data Form Wizard starts, it will prompt for a profile. Leave the profile set to **none**. Press the **Next** button.

6. Now the Wizard will prompt to select the database type for the project. Select to access a Remote database. Press **Next**.

7. Now the Wizard will prompt for ODBC connecting information. Using the DSN set up earlier in this chapter, select the **BIBLIO** database. Press **Next**.

8. Now the Wizard prompts for a form name, form layout, and data binding methodology. Set the Form name to **frmWizard**. Select the form layout as **MS HflexGrid**, and select the binding type as **ADO Data Control**. Press **Next**.

9. Now the Wizard will prompt for a RecordSource and Fields to display. Select **Titles** from the RecordSource list and include all the fields from the Titles table in the display. Press **Next**.

10. Now the Wizard asks what type of grid to use. Select an **outline grid**. Press **Next**.

11. Now the Wizard asks for a grid style. Choose **contemporary**. Press **Next**.

12. Now the Wizard allows changing the column order. Do not change the column order. Press **Next**.

13. Now the Wizard allows you to edit the column headers. Do not change the column headers. Press **Next**.

14. Now the Data Form Wizard has finished. The settings in this screen may be saved. When ready, press the **Finish** button to create the application.

15. Open the Project Properties dialog by selecting **PROJECT/PROJECT1 PROPERTIES...** from the menu. In the Properties dialog, set the Startup object to **frm Wizard**. Close the dialog.

16. Run the application.

Exercise 5-1: ADC Data Binding

In this exercise we will build an application that uses the Active Data Control and several data-bound controls to create a complete solution. This exercise assumes the SQL Server database *pubs* is available. If it is not available, Exercise 5-2 uses DAO and a Microsoft Access database which can be run from any machine.

CREATING THE DATA LINK FILE

Step 1

Create a new directory for this project using the File Explorer. Name the directory **VB BOOT-CAMP\EXERCISE5-1**.

Step 2

Before we can use the ADC, we have to create a Data Link file for the pubs database in SQL Server. Data Link files are normally stored under the \PROGRAM FILES\COMMON FILES\SYSTEM\OLE DB\DATA LINKS directory. Open this directory in the File Explorer.

Step 3

In the File Explorer, select **FILE/NEW/MICROSOFT DATA LINK** from the menu. Immediately rename the created file **PUBS.UDL**.

Step 4

Right click **PUBS.UDL** and select **PROPERTIES** from the popup menu.

Step 5

In the Provider tab, choose **Microsoft OLEDB Provider for SQL Server**. In the Connection tab, specify the name of the server running SQL Server. Enter a log-in name for the properties dialog and select the pubs database. When finished, check the connection by pressing the **Test Connection** button. Close the dialog

CREATING THE APPLICATION

Step 6

Start a new Standard EXE project in Visual Basic. Open the Components dialog by selecting **PROJECT/COMPONENTS...** from the menu. In the Components dialog, select to add the **Microsoft ADO Data Control 6.0**, **Microsoft DataGrid Control 6.0 (OLEDB)**, and **Microsoft DataList Controls 6.0 (OLEDB)**. Close the Components dialog.

Step 7

Create a graphic user interface on Form1 as shown in Figure 5-18. Use the following item list to set design time properties for the controls.

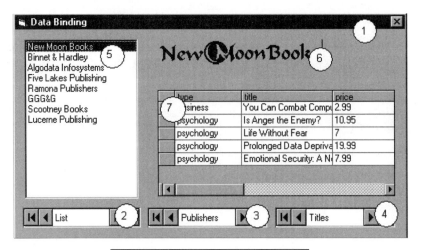

Figure 5-18 The graphic user interface.

Item 1—Form

Name   frmBind

Caption   Data Binding

BorderStyle   3-Fixed Dialog

Item 2—ADC DataControl

Name   datList

Caption   List

Visible   False

Item 3—ADC DataControl

Name   datPublishers

Caption   Publishers

Visible   False

Item 4—ADC DataControl

Name   datTitles

Caption   Titles

Visible   False

Item 5—DataList

Name   lstPublishers

Item 6—Image

Name   imgPublishers

Item 7—DataGrid

Name   grdTitles

Step 8

Each of the three data controls must be set to access the pubs database. Using the Connection-String property of each control, select to connect using a Data Link file. Select the **PUBS.UDL** file for each of the controls.

Step 9

Each of these controls will also use an SQL statement to define the recordset to return. Therefore, set the CommandType property to `adCmdText` for each data control.

Step 10

Each of the data controls will need an SQL statement entered in the RecordSource property to start. Add the SQL statements to the RecordSource property of each control as shown:

```
datList
SELECT pub_id, pub_name FROM Publishers
datPublishers
SELECT pub_id, logo FROM pub_info WHERE pub_id = '0000'
datTitles
SELECT type, title, price FROM Titles WHERE pub_id = '0000'
```

Step 11

When the application loads, we want to display a list of all publishers in the data-bound list control. This can be accomplished by setting the RowSource and ListField properties. RowSource points to a data control containing the records for the list. ListField is the field to display. For lstPublishers, set the RowSource to `datList` and the ListField to `pub_name`.

Step 12

Save the work and run the application. The list should be filled with publisher names.

Step 13

When a publisher is selected from the list, we want to use the `pub_id` value for that publisher to retrieve specific information for the other data controls. The data-bound list gives us a way to return the `pub_id` when someone clicks on the `pub_name`. This is done through the BoundColumn property, which returns the field value specified here through a property called BoundText. Set the BoundColumn property of lstPublishers to `pub_id`.

Step 14

In order to update the data controls, we must change their CommandText property and call the Refresh method. We want this update to occur when the list is clicked. In the `lst-Publishers_Click` event, add the following code to update the data controls.

```
'Populate the other data controls
datPublishers.RecordSource = _
"SELECT pub_id, logo FROM pub_info WHERE pub_id = " _
& Chr$(39) & lstPublishers.BoundText & Chr$(39)
```

```
datPublishers.Refresh
datTitles.RecordSource = _
"SELECT type, title, price FROM Titles WHERE pub_id = " _
& Chr$(39) & lstPublishers.BoundText & Chr$(39)
datTitles.Refresh
```

Step 15

Now that the data controls are updated, we can use them to bind with. First bind the image control to the `datPublishers` control. Set the DataSource property of `imgPublishers` to `datPublishers` and the DataField property to `logo`.

Step 16

Now bind the grid to the remaining data control. Set the DataSource property of `grdTitles` to `datTitles`.

Step 17

Save the project and run it. Select various publishers from the list and verify the data changes in the grid and image.

Exercise 5-2: DAO Query Builder

In this exercise we will build an application that uses DAO extensively to explore .MDB databases. The application will allow selection of an .MDB for examination, browsing of available tables and fields within any selected table, the execution of freeform SQL queries, and the saving of SQL queries by name into the database. This database browser will also be able to browse existing queries stored in the database, and even examine the SQL that makes the query work.

SELECTING A DATABASE TO VIEW

Step 1

Make a directory named **VB BOOTCAMP\EXERCISE5-2**. Fire up VB and immediately save the new project to this directory. Do not forget to save often during development. The first thing is to set up a menu that looks like this:

```
File
Open...
_____
Exit
```

Build this menu. Name the menu objects `mnuFILE`, `mnuOPEN`, and `mnuEXIT`.

Step 2

Drop a Common Dialog control on Form1. Name it `dlgDATABASE`. (It may be necessary to select it from the PROJECT/COMPONENTS dialog to make it available to the project.)

Examine the Help for the common Dialog control. Press **F1** with focus on it to get this Help page. Check out the methods available. Check out `.ShowOpen`. Also check the `.Filename` property.

We will display a common dialog to select an .MDB file for browsing. Add this code under the `mnuOPEN_Click()` event:

```
dlgDATABASE.filename = "*.mdb"
dlgDATABASE.Filter = "Access DBs (*.mdb)|*.mdb"
dlgDATABASE.ShowOpen
Data1.DatabaseName = dlgDATABASE.Filename
```

BUILDING THE GRAPHIC USER INTERFACE (GUI)

Step 3

Drop a DBGrid control on the form. This is the Microsoft Data Bound Grid found under the Components tab of the Components dialog. Be sure it is checked within the Components dialog. This will make the control available in the Toolbox. (This dialog can be reached via the PROJECT/COMPONENTS menu command.) Also drop a TextBox and a Data Control on the form. Use the default names `DBGrid1`, `Text1`, and `Data1`.

Set properties as follows:

```
Item1 - TextBox
Name     Text1
Multiline = True
Scrollbars = 3 (both vertical and horizontal)
Item2 - DBGrid
Name     DBGrid1
Datasource = Data1
Font.Name = SmallFonts
Font.Size = 6
```

Step 4

Now add a button next to the Text1 textbox. Keep the default name Command1. Set the .Caption to **Run Query**. Command1 will be used to execute the SQL statement typed into Text1. To make a query entered into Text1 actually work, assign it to the `.Recordsource` property of the Data Control Data1, like this:

```
Private Sub Command1_Click()
Data1.Recordsource = Text1.Text
Data1.Refresh
End Sub
```

Step 5

Search the Help on the Refresh method to learn how it works with bound controls. Next, under the Exit menu's `mnuExit_Click` event, enter the following line of code:

```
End
```

Start the application. Select the **FILE-OPEN** menu command and select **VB98\BIBLIO.MDB**. Then, type this SQL into the Text box:

```
SELECT * FROM PUBLISHERS
```

Click on **Command1** to make it start. The grid named DBGrid1 should fill up with the results from the query.

BUILDING THE DATABASE EXPLORER

So far this project allows the user to open an .MDB database and run some queries. Now we will do more interesting things. For example, for any database opened, what are the table names? That would be useful information in constructing a query. The next step finds the information.

Step 6

To iterate through all the tables using DAO syntax first, create a database object and a table object. Add this code to the [General][Declarations] of Form1:

```
Private db As DAO.Database
Private td As DAO.TableDef
Private qd As DAO.QueryDef
Private fld As DAO.Field
```

Step 7

These variables will be used extensively in this exercise. Now, display all the tables in a list box. To do this, a valid database object will be necessary. Add this code to the FILE/OPEN menu command:

```
If UCase(Right(dlgDATABASE.filename, 3)) <> "MDB" Then
  MsgBox "File name selected is not an Access database."
Else
  On Error Resume Next
  db.Close
  On Error GoTo 0
  Screen.MousePointer = vbHourglass
  'Open the Database using a method of the Workspace Object
  Set db = DBEngine.Workspaces(0).OpenDatabase(dlgDATABASE.filename)
  Form1.Caption = "DAOQUERY: Browsing " & dlgDATABASE.filename
  Screen.MousePointer = vbDefault
  Data1.DatabaseName = dlgDATABASE.filename
End If
```

Step 8

Search the Help for each item to understand what is going on in this code. We have a database object named db that can now be used to fill a list box with table names in the user-selected database.

Drop a list box on the form. It will be named List1. Under the File-Open Menu command, add the following code to fill the list box. *All of this code must be placed just before the* End If *statement:*

```
'Fill List Box with names
List1.Clear
For Each td In db.TableDefs
 List1.AddItem td.Name
Next
```

Run the application. The list box should fill with table names that are in the selected database.

Step 9

Drop another list box on the form. It will be named List2. Now go to the click event of List1 and add this code:

```
Private List1_Click()
'FIND THE RIGHT TABLEDEF IN THE COLLECTION IN THE DB
Set td = New TableDef
For Each td In db.TableDefs
  If td.Name = Me.List1.List(Me.List1.ListIndex) Then
    Exit For
  End If
Next
'NOW DISPLAY THE FIELDS IN THAT TABLE's DEFINITION
List2.Clear
'LOAD LIST2 WITH FIELDS
For Each fld In td.Fields
  List2.AddItem fld.Name
Next
End Sub
```

Step 10

If everything is working, it should be possible to open a database, which will fill List1 with table names. Clicking any one table name in the list should fill List2 with field names. This information is useful for constructing queries. In the next section, we will list any queries stored in the selected database. (Note: Tables that start with the letter MSys are system or *catalog* tables and are not part of this exercise. Clicking on these tables *will not* display any fields in List2.)

Drop another list box on the form. It will be named List3 by default. Then, add this code to the FILE/OPEN menu command just before the End If statement:

```
List2.Clear
List3.Clear
Text1.Text=""
```

```
For Each qd In db.QueryDefs
List3.AddItem qd.Name
Next
```

Step 11

This code iterates through the collection of QUERYDEFS that are part of each .MDB database. Now, run the application, select **BIBLIO.MDB,** and notice what shows up in List3. There should be query definition names defined inside BIBLIO.MDB.

Add this code under the click of List3:

```
'FILL TEXT1.TEXT WITH QUERY SQL
For Each qd In db.QueryDefs
  If qd.Name = List3.List(List3.ListIndex) Then
    Text1.Text = qd.SQL
  End If
Next
```

Run the application, open **BIBLIO.MDB,** and click on **List3.** What happens?

Step 12

For the last part of this exercise, we will save a query to the selected database. The basic idea is to test some SQL; when it is right, save it by name to the database as a `QueryDef`.

Drop a new button on the form, and name it Command2. Set the `Caption` to **SAVE QUERY**. Add this code under the Click event of this button:

```
Private Sub Command2_Click()
  'PLACE THE SQL INTO A QUERY OBJECT
  Set qd = New QueryDef
  qd.SQL = Trim$(Text1.Text)
  MsgBox "Query to Save is " & qd.SQL
  'SAVE THE QUERY WITH A NAME
  qd.Name = InputBox("Specify a QUERY NAME: ")
  db.QueryDefs.Append qd
End Sub
```

Step 13

Run the application. It should be possible to select **BIBLIO.MDB,** specify a query, run it, and then press this button to save the query to a specific name as a `Querydef` in the database. To be sure it worked, reopen the database. The saved query should be visable in List3.

FOR THE CERTIFIED PRO

Pro 5-1: Remote Data Control

1. Using the RDC, populate a list of authors from the BIBLIO.MDB database.
2. When a user clicks on an author, show the titles written by that author in a grid.

Pro 5-2: Active Data Control

1. Create a Form with three TextBoxes—one for author name, one for publisher, and one for book title.
2. Allow a use to enter one or more partial strings in the TextBoxes and use an ADC to populate a grid of the book titles that contain the partial search strings.

PREPARING FOR CERTIFICATION

Topics for further reading
    Using Data Access Objects
    Microsoft DAO 3.51
    Using Remote Data Objects and the Remote Data Control
    Using the Active Data Control

CERTIFICATION QUIZ

1. Which method must be executed when the JET Data Control has had any property changes at runtime?
    a.   The Update method
    b.   The AddNew method
    c.   The Refresh method
    d.   The FindLast method

2. Which DAO collection contains all of the SQL statements stored in the database?
    a.   The Recordset collection
    b.   The QueryDefs collection
    c.   The TableDefs collection
    d.   none of the above

3. To add a new record to a recordset maintained by a JET Data Control when the user scrolls to the end of the recordset, it is necessary to:
    a.   execute the AddNew method.
    b.   execute the NewRow method.
    c.   set the EOFAction property of the Data Control to 2-AddNew.
    d.   none of the above

4. An instance of the DAO recordset object can be obtained via the:
   a. OpenRecordSet method of the Database object.
   b. OpenResultSet method of the Database object.
   c. CreateRecordset method of the Database object.
   d. CreateResultSet method of the Database object.

5. A User DSN is available to:
   a. the user who created it.
   b. any user on the machine where it was created.
   c. any user on the network.
   d. any service on the machine where it was created.

6. A System DSN is available to:
   a. the user who created it.
   b. any user on the machine where it was created.
   c. any user on the network.
   d. any service on the machine where it was created.

7. A File DSN is available to:
   a. the user who created it.
   b. any user on the machine where it was created.
   c. any user on the network.
   d. any service on the machine where it was created.

8. The property of the RDC that establishes a connection is:
   a. DatabaseName
   b. DataSourceName
   c. ConnectionString
   d. CommandText

9. The property of the RDC where a query is defined is:
   a. RecordSource
   b. SQL
   c. DataSourceName
   d. CommandText

10. A Data Link file is created:
    a. in Visual Basic.
    b. in the ODBC Administrator.
    c. in the File Explorer.
    d. in the Control Panel.

11. The ADC may connect to a data source using
    a. a connect string.
    b. an MDB file.
    c. a Data Link File.
    d. an ODBC DSN.

ANSWERS TO CERTIFICATION QUIZ

1. c
2. b
3. c
4. a
5. a
6. a,b,d
7. a,b,c,d
8. b
9. b
10. c
11. a, c, d

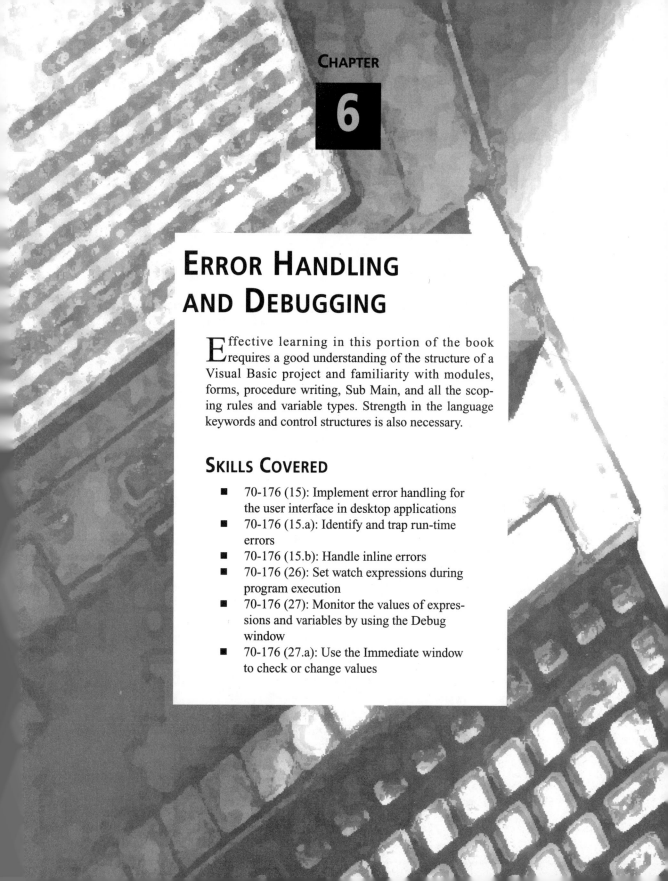

6

ERROR HANDLING AND DEBUGGING

Effective learning in this portion of the book requires a good understanding of the structure of a Visual Basic project and familiarity with modules, forms, procedure writing, Sub Main, and all the scoping rules and variable types. Strength in the language keywords and control structures is also necessary.

SKILLS COVERED

- 70-176 (15): Implement error handling for the user interface in desktop applications
- 70-176 (15.a): Identify and trap run-time errors
- 70-176 (15.b): Handle inline errors
- 70-176 (26): Set watch expressions during program execution
- 70-176 (27): Monitor the values of expressions and variables by using the Debug window
- 70-176 (27.a): Use the Immediate window to check or change values

- 70-176 (27.b): Use the Locals window to check or change values
- 70-176 (29): Given a scenario, define the scope of a watch variable
- 70-176 (34): Fix errors, and take measures to prevent future errors
- 70-175 (19): Implement error handling for the user interface in distributed applications
- 70-175 (19.a): Identify and trap run-time errors
- 70-175 (19.b): Handle inline errors
- 70-175 (19.c): Determine how to send error information from a COM component to a client computer
- 70-175 (46): Set watch expressions during program execution
- 70-175 (47): Monitor the values of expressions and variables by using the Debug window
- 70-175 (47.a): Use the Immediate window to check or change values
- 70-175 (47.b): Use the Locals window to check or change values
- 70-175 (49): Given a scenario, define the scope of a watch variable
- 70-175 (57): Fix errors, and take measures to prevent future errors

ERROR HANDLING FEATURES

Run-time error handling is required at some point in any programming language. A programmer cannot possibly control all situations that may lead to run-time errors. For example, one cannot programmatically prevent a user from trying to copy files to the floppy drive with no disk inserted. In these cases, run-time error handling becomes critical in creating a well-behaved program. Visual Basic error handling provides a competent facility for handling such errors. However, the structures used to handle errors have not changed much since the days of BASICA and GW BASIC. Visual Basic also has the tremendous disadvantage of causing an immediate program termination if an untrapped run-time error occurs.

Check It Out 6-1: Unhandled Errors

1. Start a new VB Standard EXE project. Add these lines to the `Form_Load` event procedure of Form1:

```
Dim names(3) As String
Names(99) = "This causes a VB error #9"
```

2. Create an executable application by selecting **FILE/MAKE PROJECT1.EXE** from the menu.
3. Close Visual Basic and run the **EXE** from the desktop. The attempt to address the 99th element in the `names()` array causes an error #9, "Subscript out of range." This produces an error message that comes from VB. VB then terminates the application.

Run-time errors are handled in Visual Basic by defining an error *trap*, a code container that protects routines from run-time errors. An error trap starts with the statement On Error

GoTo and ends with the `Resume` statement. The `On Error` statement tells VB to jump to a specified label when an error is encountered. The label identifies the error trapping code. The following code defines a typical error trap.

```
On Error GoTo MyTrap
    'Procedure Code to protect
Exit Sub
MyTrap:
    MsgBox _
      "Error # " & Err.Number & " Description: " & Err.Description
    Resume Next
```

The `On Error GoTo` statement begins the trap by defining a line label where Visual Basic should go if any run-time error should occur. The label jumped to must be within the same procedure as the code being protected. After the `On Error GoTo` statement above, any run-time error will cause Visual Basic immediately and unconditionally to jump to the line label specified. Line labels in Visual Basic are designated by placing a colon after the label. In the above code `MyTrap:` is a line label. Line labels do not execute, but simply represent bookmarks in the code.

The `Exit Sub` line prevents execution from falling into the error trapping routine. Generally, error-handling code is placed at the end of a routine after the `Exit` keyword. In this way it will never run unless explicitly entered due to the `On Error GoTo` statement.

Visual Basic provides information about run-time errors through the `Err` object, whose Number property contains the last error number; `Err.Description` contains the error text. The `Err` object also contains additional properties that report the source of external errors in DLL calls or provide a help file that can be accessed when an error occurs. The `Err` object also permits causing custom errors to occur through the use of the Raise method.

Once the trap is sprung, the error condition must be handled. Error conditions can be handled as simply as by displaying the error in a `MsgBox`; more complex handling might be writing to the event log, or sending e-mail. In all cases, there is the full power of Visual Basic to take whatever action is required to clear the error. After the error is handled, Visual Basic must re-enter the code processing through the `Resume` statement.

The `Resume` statement comes in three different flavors—Resume, `Resume Next`, and `Resume` label. Just plain `Resume` without the `Next` clause will cause execution to branch back to the line where the error occurred. This usage of `Resume` without the `Next` clause assumes processing was performed in the error trap which will allow the line to execute without error. The more typical setup is to `Resume Next`, effectively skipping over the problem line of code. Finally, it is possible to resume at some other line label once the error is cleared.

Check It Out 6-2: Trapping a Runtime Error

1. Start a new Standard EXE VB project and add this code to Form1's `Form_Load` event procedure:

    ```
    On Error GoTo Form1_ErrTrap
    Dim names(3) As String
    ```

```
'THE FOLLOWING LINE CAUSES AN ERROR
'AND JUMPS TO THE DEFINED ERROR TRAP:
names(72) = "Error #9 encountered here!"
'RESUME NEXT IN THE TRAP TAKES EXECUTION TO HERE:
names(3) = "No Error here!"
'THIS LINE STOPS EXECUTION FROM 'FALLING IN'
'FROM ABOVE:
Exit Sub
'THE ONLY WAY INTO THIS TRAP IS IF YOU
'JUMP BECAUSE OF AN ERROR:
Form1_ErrTrap:
MsgBox _
     "Error # " & Err.Number & " Description: " & Err.Description
Resume Next
```

2. Run the application and watch how it issues a message and recovers from the error to display Form1.

3. Now stop the application and comment out this line:

```
'COMMENT OUT THIS LINE:
On Error GoTo Form1_ErrTrap
```

4. Run the application now, without the benefit of error handling, to see what VB does when an error is encountered without the benefit of an error trap.

There will be times when it will be desirable to shut off the error trap for certain program lines. One example might be when opening a text file; if the file does not exist, the program can create it later using VB code. In such a case, it does not matter if the "File not found" error occurs when an attempt is made to open the file. To shut error handling off for a group of program lines, use the `On Error Resume Next` statement. The code snippet that follows shows how the program might shut off error handling momentarily, and then continue processing and trapping any errors encountered.

```
'SHUT ERROR HANDLING OFF TEMPORARILY,
On Error Resume Next
Close #1
Open App.Path & "\MYAPP.TXT" For Input As #1
Line Input #1, strCOMPANY 'get file data
Line Input #1, strADDRESS 'get file data
Line Input #1, strZIP 'get file data
Close #1
'RESTORE ERROR HANDLING FOR THIS PROCEDURE:
On Error GoTo MYAPP_ErrorTrap
```

To shut off all error trapping, use `On Error GoTo 0`. This VB line is so ugly because in the early days of the BASIC language, `On Error GoTo` could branch only to program line numbers, not labels. The convention was if the line were specified zero, that meant, "shut error handling off." The syntax survives to this day. Using this line will produce only the default VB error processing when the application encounters an error. There will be times during debugging error traps, for example, when this kind of setup will be desirable.

Experienced VB programmers know that if they provide an error trap for each procedure, their program cannot crash. This dangerous strategy can lead to sloppy coding. Include an error handler in each procedure where it is possible that an unhandled error can occur. But do not use run-time error handling as a substitute for debugging.

Error handlers can protect not only the procedure they are written in but also any procedure called from it. Visual Basic searches the current call stack for error handlers before it terminates the application. If the procedure with the error has no caller, VB ends the search and reports the error, producing *break* mode if testing is in progress, or terminating the program in the case of an executable. If there is a caller to the procedure with the error, VB looks to that caller to see if it contains an active error handler (See Figure 6-1). If the calling procedure has an error handler active, VB will use it. If the calling procedure has no error trap, VB will look to the caller of *that* procedure, if any, for an error handler. VB traverses the list of procedures in the Call list, checking each one for an error-handling procedure. If the procedure has no callers or none of the calling procedures has an error handler, then VB does the default handling with all of the dire consequences associated with an untrapped error.

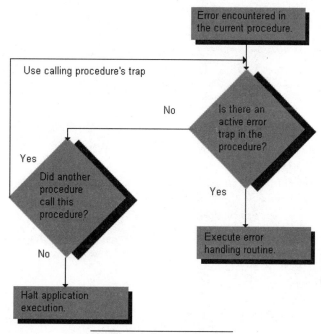

Figure 6-1 Error processing.

VB provides a set of preformatted error numbers with associated text descriptions. These error codes and descriptions can be found in the Help file. It is also possible to print them with the following simple loop.

```
Dim i as Integer
For i = 1 to 100
  Err = I
  Debug.Print Err, Error$
Next i
```

`Err` and `Error$` are the VB3 reserved words that correspond to `Err.Number` and `Err.Description`, respectively, in VB6. We are using these now to clarify the VB error codes. These are rarely used and are supported in VB6 only for backward compatibility. Running the above code reveals that some of the error numbers are not reserved by VB. This leaves values that can be assigned as custom error codes just for the application. Since VB does not specifically know about custom errors defined, these must be tripped using the Raise method of the Err object.

The Raise method requires at least the error number. This value is written into the `Err.Number` property before the error is raised. Use *any* number, but it is wise to stick with error numbers not currently in use by Visual Basic. It is also an option to specify the Source and Description properties. The Source property specifies the name of the application that caused the error. There can also be a Help file that the user may access as the error is reported.

Check It Out 6-3: Defining an Error-Handling Routine

1. Start a new Standard EXE VB application. Add a module to the project and add this routine, which will be called from all error traps:

```
Public Sub MyErrHandler(errno As Integer, errdesc As String)

'DONT TRAP ERRORS HERE
On Error GoTo 0
Select Case errno
  Case 1001
    MsgBox errno & " :" & errdesc & _
        ". This error can only come from Command1"
  Case 1002
    MsgBox errno & " :" & errdesc & _
        ". This error can only come
from Command2"
  Case Else
    MsgBox "Unrecognized error."
End Select
End Sub
```

2. The first thing to do in an error-handling subroutine is to shut off all error handling so as not to enter a recursive loop by mistake if there is an error while in the error-handling routine. This routine gets the error number passed in and then checks against all the codes it recognizes; 1001 and 1002 are unreserved by VB and used by this application.

3. Now drop two buttons on Form1. Place this code under Command1:

```
On Error GoTo Command1_Err
       'MAKE AN ERROR HAPPEN WHEN CLICKED:
       Err.Raise Number:=1001, Description:= _
          "Custom error from Command1"
       'ERROR TRAP:
       Exit Sub
Command1_Err:
       Call MyErrHandler(Err.Number, Err.Decription)
       Resume Next
```

4. Now, place this code under Command2:

```
On Error GoTo Command2_Err
       'MAKE AN ERROR HAPPEN WHEN CLICKED:
       Err.Raise Number:=1002, Description:= _
          "Custom error from Command1"
       'ERROR TRAP:
       Exit Sub
Command1_Err:
       Call MyErrHandler(Err.Number, Err.Decription)
       Resume Next
```

5. Now run the application and click each button. The click of **Command1** will produce a trappable error 1001, which will be handled by Command1's error trap. The click of **Command2** will produce a trappable error 1002, which will be handled by Command2's error trap. Both traps call `MyErrHandler`, which is set up to recognize both custom error codes 1001 and 1002.

Often when we introduce students to error handling, they are surprised that all error handling is local to a procedure. With the exception of searching the call stack, Visual Basic will not look anywhere except the current routine for an active handler. Searching the call stack has its limits as well. Visual Basic will not, for example, search outside of the current form or module for an error handler and an error handler cannot be used in Sub Main to trap all the errors in the application. In the end, if an error handler must protect a routine, write it into the routine.

When the routine is processed, it is acceptable to jump to a centralized location. For example, there may be a common error-logging system to be used whenever any application error occurs. In this case, it would be possible to jump to the logging routines for every error. In jumping from the error trap, be sure to pass the error data as arguments to the new routine since `Err.Number` and `Err.Description` are only valid for the routine in which the error occurred.

Check It Out 6-4: Common Error Logging

1. Start a new Visual Basic Standard EXE project.
2. Add a Module to the application. In Module1 add a new procedure by selecting **TOOLS/ADD PROCEDURE...** from the dialog. Add a sub named `LogError` that takes four arguments. Make the sub definition look like the following:

```
Public Sub LogError( _

    lngNumber As Long, _
    strDescription As String, _
    strModule As String, _
    strProcedure As String)

End Sub
```

3. In the `LogError` routine, add code to show the error in the immediate window while debugging is proceeding, or log it to a text file after it is compiled. Add the following code to finish the routine.

```
On Error GoTo 0

'This line only runs when you
'are debugging
Debug.Print _
    "Error: " & lngNumber & "; " & strDescription & vbCrLf & _
    "Module: " & strModule & vbCrLf & _
    "Procedure: " & strProcedure

'This code only runs after
'the project is compiled
App.StartLogging App.Path & "\errors.log", vbLogToFile
App.LogEvent _
        "Error: " & lngNumber & "; " & strDescription & "; " & _
    "Module: " & strModule & "; " & _
    "Procedure: " & strProcedure
```

4. Now test the application by placing an error in the `Form_Load` event of Form1. Add the following code to the Load event to generate an error.

```
On Error GoTo LoadErr

    'Show Form
    Show

    'Try to open a bad file
```

```
Open "ZZ:\BadFile" For Input As #1
Close #1

Exit Sub


LoadErr:
    Call LogError(Err.Number, Err.Description, "Form1", _
        "Form_Load")
    Resume Next
```

5. Run the application. Notice that the form loads fine, but there should be a message in the immediate window telling of the bad file-name error.

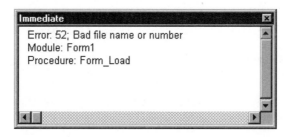

Figure 6-2 Error Logging to the Immediate Window.

6. Now compile the application into an executable by selecting **FILE/MAKE PROJECT1.EXE...** from the menu.
7. Locate and run the EXE from the desktop. After the EXE runs, examine the directory where it was created. Here there will be a file ERRORS.LOG. Open the file, and a logged entry for the error should be visible.

Error handlers should be added to the application as a routine part of the normal development cycle. This discipline is important to the overall success of any application. In our experience, developers typically do not add error handling to the application until after much of it is complete. This is a serious mistake because an application under development may have many opportunities for an untrapped run-time error. Quite often during development, installable previews of the work will be requested for customers and supervisors. Imagine the embarrassment of providing code that explodes when it is used. Proper error-handling development of the program can prevent this situation.

When adding error-handling routines, be careful about masking problems that should be fixed, as when a logic or code error is committed. In this case, an error handler can mask the problem by trapping an error that should never occur. Always separate the errors that cannot be controlled from those that can be. Sometimes it will be desirable to disable error handling in the application to force VB into break mode instead of trapping the error. This can easily be done through the Options dialog. The General tab of the Options dialog permits turning off error handling for the application by selecting **Break on all errors**. This option effectively disables all the error traps in the application. It works only during debugging and has no effect on the final compiled project.

DEBUGGING FACILITIES

In addition to errors needing handling when they occur at run time, there will be plenty of errors to clear up as the application is created. This is where the debugging capabilities of Visual Basic come into play. These include breakpoints, informational windows, and variable watches.

Check It Out 6-5: Debugging

1. Start a new VB Standard EXE project. Enter this code into the Form_Load event procedure of Form1:

```
Dim I As Integer, j As Integer
For i = 1 To 100
    j = j + 1
    Call MySub
Next
```

2. Now define the sub named MySub. Add a subroutine procedure to Form1 that looks like this:

```
Public Sub MySub()
   Dim names(2) As String
   names(0) = "Thing1"
   names(1) = "Thing2"
   names(2) = "Thing3"
   MsgBox "MySub Called"
End Sub
```

This sub does nothing except execute; we will use it to demonstrate basic debugging techniques.

3. Now set a breakpoint; the line with the breakpoint, when executed, will drop the application into VB's Break mode. From inside the Form_Load of Form1, click on the line **j = j + 1** and then click on the **Debug/Toggle Breakpoint** menu command. This will set a breakpoint on that line of code.

4. Run the application. It will now be in VB's Break mode. Watch the execution of the application, line by line. To go line by line, click on the **Debug/Step Into** menu command. Click this menu command once to advance the execution point one line. **F8** is the shortcut key for this menu command.

5. When **F8** is pressed, the execution point moves. When the call to MySub is hit, the execution point drops down into the subroutine. What if MySub() is already debugged? What if MySub calls SomeOtherSub()? For these situations, VB provides the Debug/Step Over menu command.

6. Keep pressing **F8** until the next line to execute is the call to MySub(), then select the **Debug/Step Over** menu command. This will execute MySub(), but will not

trace the code. The code display will stay at the caller. This is a good situation if it is not desirable to drop into debugged procedures when debugging at a higher level. **Shift-F8** is the shortcut key combination for the Debug/Step Over menu command.

7. Do not reinitialize the project as it will be used again shortly. Return to design time.

Breakpoints are not saved with code, so if much time has been spent determining where the breakpoints should be set, it is a good idea to comment the lines with a code such as MYBP or something similar so that it will be easy to find the breakpoint lines later to reestablish them. To churn out some output while debugging to the Immediate window use the `Debug.Print` statement. Although `Debug.Print` lines are advertised not to affect executables, they can and they should always be commented out prior to final compilation.

It is possible to force VB into Break mode with the Stop statement. Test a variable for a value and then conditionally go to Break mode with the Stop statement. Experimentation is strongly encouraged. Note that the Stop statement, if encountered by a user, will terminate the application. For this reason use the Stop statement with great care.

The execution of various routines can be checked by examining the call stack, a list of all of the procedures that VB is processing which shows what procedures have called other procedures.

Check It Out 6-6: Viewing the Call Stack

1. Using the last example worked with, get the `For...Next` loop going up to the sub-routine call to `MySub`. Press **F8** to step into the procedure `MySub()`.

2. Click on the **View/Call Stack** menu command. The dialog depicted in Figure 6-4 will be visible.

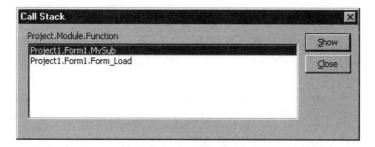

Figure 6-4 The Call stack.

3. Try setting a breakpoint by clicking inside the left margin of the code editor. Clicking sets a breakpoint; clicking again clears the breakpoint.

4. Try dragging and dropping the execution point from one place in the code to another using the mouse. Visual Basic supports this. The default color for the line execution indicator is yellow. Try clicking on the **yellow arrow** in the margin while the application is in Break mode, and moving it to another location in the loop.

5. Return to design time.

Visual Basic provides several ways to get information about the variables in the application. The Immediate window can be used to find the values of variables and also to alter variables. Executable lines such as this one are valid:

```
J = J + 99
```

However, lines such as the following are invalid in the Immediate window because the statement is declarative, not executable.

```
Dim foo As Integer
```

Check It Out 6-7: Exploring the Immediate Window

1. Return to the project you were checking out before. Set a breakpoint in the code found under the `Form_Load` event procedure. When the application pauses, click on the **View/Immediate Window** menu command.
2. The Immediate (or Debug) window appears. Find the values of variables in the program from this window. Try typing the following lines into the Immediate window:

```
Print "I = " & I
Print " J = " & j
? I
? j
I = I + 90
```

All these lines are valid in the Immediate window. So is this call to `MySub()`:

```
Call MySub()
```

3. When the following line is typed it into the Immediate window, it will cause an error since declarative statements are invalid in the Immediate window:

```
Dim myvar as String
```

Try typing this in. What message from VB appears? It should be `Compiler Error. Invalid in Immediate Pane`.
4. Click the **VIEW/LOCALS WINDOW** menu command. This shows the name and current value of all the variables local to the current procedure.
5. Return to design time.

Visual Basic permits flagging certain key places in code through the use of *bookmarks*, placeholders that can be set in the code window. It will often be desirable to skip around all the bookmarked portions of code, to pick up information, view the source, and so on. While not strictly a debugging feature, bookmarks are a natural way to keep tabs on code.

Check It Out 6-8: Bookmarks

1. Using the current project, display the code from Form1's `Form_Load` event procedure in a code window. Click any line inside the `For...Next` Loop.
2. Click the **View/Toolbars** menu command and select the **Edit** submenu. This will make a floating toolbar appear. Click the button with the blue flag to set a bookmark in the code.
3. Dock the Bookmarks toolbar under VB's menu.

Bookmarks provide an easy way to set placeholders in code, and the Bookmarks toolbar makes it easy to keep track of bookmarks, with the ability to scroll forward, scroll back, and clear all bookmarks.

Debugging and error handling are essential skills to acquire for basic knowledge for building larger and more robust applications. This chapter has introduced the most important features of error handling and debugging. Now apply this knowledge with a search of the Help and MSDN as well as some hands-on experimentation.

Exercise 6-1: Error Handling

In this example, we are going to demonstrate the types of runtime error situations that are possible in a project and how to effectively rig the project for error handling. This first part of the exercise starts with error-handling basics. The next part shows how to set up an error handler for each routine in a project and how to disable error handlers.

PART 1: SETTING UP AN ERROR HANDLER

Step 1

Start a new project in Visual Basic. Using VB's Tools menu, add a new Public Sub called `CalledSub` into Form1. In this new procedure, add code so that the procedure appears as here:

```
Public Sub CalledSub( )
  Dim MyVar As Integer
  MsgBox "Attempting to assign a value to MyVar."
  MyVar = "This Integer Var will not accept a string."
  MsgBox "MyVar = " & Format$(MyVar)
End Sub
```

Step 2

In Form1's `Form_Load` event procedure, add the following line of code:

```
'The error will occur inside CalledSub
MsgBox "Starting Sub CalledSub."
Call CalledSub
MsgBox "Sub CalledSub is finished."
```

This is a good place to save the project. Create a directory **VB BOOTCAMP\EXERCISE6-1** and save the following files into the new directory:

```
Save Form1 as FORM1.FRM
Save Project as DEBUG.VBP
```

Step 3

Now run the project. Visual Basic gives a message box affording the opportunity to debug the problem. *Do not* try to solve the problem at this time. Click **RUN/END** and return to design time.

Make an executable called **DEBUG.EXE** by selecting the **FILE/MAKE DEBUG.EXE** menu command. Making and distributing applications will be discussed later. For now think of the EXE as a final version of the application that can be given to others to run.

Run the EXE by locating it in the Windows File Explorer and double clicking on it. (The file DEBUG.EXE will be in the working directory if the project was saved.) Notice that an attempt to run the executable engenders a message box, and then the application simply goes away. This is exactly what should not happen when the application is distributed.

Before we go any further, we will review what happened when the application ran. First, the Form_Load event fired, which caused Sub CalledSub to be called. There was a message just before the variable was to be assigned a value. Then, you received the standard VB error message for an unhandled error when the variable was attempted to be assigned. Finally, VB's default action occured when it ran into an unhandled error—the application just terminated. Notice that the lines after the variable assignment did not even get a chance to execute. If they had, there would have been the message, MyVar = 0 and Sub CalledSub is finished.

Step 4

Now we are going to add error handling to the Form_Load event. Add code so that the Form_Load event appears as below:

```
Private Sub Form_Load ( )
On Error GoTo MyFirstHandler
  'The error will occur inside CalledSub
  MsgBox "Starting Sub CalledSub"
  Call CalledSub
  MsgBox "Sub CalledSub is finished."
ExitRoutine:
  Exit Sub
MyFirstHandler:
  MsgBox "Form_Load - This error occurred: " & Err.Description
  Resume ExitRoutine
End Sub
```

Step 5

Now save and run the project. Notice that instead of VB giving a message, a personal message appears. This is what happens when an error is *handled*. Also, notice that the error is handled in the `Form_Load` procedure. This is because `Sub CalledSub` inherits the error handler from the `Form_Load` event because `Sub Form_Load` is calling `Sub CalledSub`.

Step 6

Remake the `DEBUG.EXE` executable using `FILE-MAKE DEBUG.EXE`, and run it. This time, the application continues in spite of the error. Now the application is more robust.

PART 2: ERROR HANDLERS FOR EACH ROUTINE

Step 7

Currently, everything called by the `Form_Load` event has its errors handled by the `Sub Form_Load`'s error handler. But what if `Sub CalledSub` is to have its own error handler? Simply add an error handler to `Sub CalledSub`. `Sub CalledSub`'s error handler will override the error handler in `Sub Form_Load` until `CalledSub` is finished. When `Sub CalledSub` is finished, error handling control reverts to `Form_Load`. As long as `Sub CalledSub` does not call any other procedures or any procedures called by `Sub CalledSub` have their own error handler, it is possible to ensure that `Sub CalledSub`'s error handler will be active *only* when that procedure is actually running.

Change `Sub CalledSub` so that it appears as here:

```
Public Sub CalledSub( )
  Dim MyVar As Integer
On Error GoTo CalledSubHandler
  MsgBox "Attempting to assign a value to MyVar."
  MyVar = "This Integer Var will not accept a string."
  MsgBox "MyVar = " & Format$(MyVar)
CalledSubExit:
  Exit Sub
CalledSubHandler:
  MsgBox "CalledSub ( ) - This error occurred: " & Err.Description
  Resume CalledSubExit
End Sub
```

Step 8

Save and run the project. Replace `Resume CalledSubExit` with `Resume` and run the project. This will cause the execution to go back to the error line and retry. This will produce an endless loop of execution as the error line pings control back to the error-handling routine. When this happens, press the **Ctrl** and **Break** keys at the same time to get control back. That will exit the loop. Remember, the `Resume` statement returns control to the error line.

Now replace `Resume` with `Resume Next` and run again. No more endless loop. This is because `Resume Next` resumes execution at the next available line after the error line, not at the error line itself. Notice that for the first time in this entire exercise, there is the message, `MyVar=0`.

Step 9

Error handlers should be created while the application is developed. Do not wait until it is nearly complete. However, when error handlers are placed in the application before it is fully debugged, they can cause unnecessary headaches by trapping errors that should actually be debugged. Fortunately, Visual Basic allows us to turn off all error handlers in the application.

Click on the **Tools/Options** menu command and then click on the **General** tab. In the General tab, select the **Break on All Errors** option from the Error Trapping section of the tab. Run the project again. All the error handlers should be disabled, and the VB default error processing should happen.

FOR THE CERTIFIED PRO

Pro 6-1: Error Handling

1. Create a central error-handling routine that logs to the Windows/NT event log.
2. Pass an argument to the routine that permits specifying whether the error is critical or informational.

Pro 6-2: Debugging

1. Write a routine to calculate the area of a circle.
2. Use the Assert method of the Debug object to verify that the radius of the circle is never a negative number.

PREPARING FOR CERTIFICATION

Topics for further reading
  Error Handling
  Debugging
  Trappable Errors

CERTIFICATION QUIZ

1. How can all error handling be shut off when running the VB application?
   a. Use the On Error Off statement.
   b. Use the On Error Resume Next statement.
   c. Use the On Error GoTo 0 statement.
   d. Error handling cannot be disabled.

2. When trapping errors with the On Error GoTo statement, it is necessary to:
    a. be sure no other error handlers are active.
    b. specify a properly formatted label to jump to within the On Error GoTo statement.
    c. make sure that the error trap can only be entered via an On Error GoTo jump, and not executed as part of the normal program flow.
    d. Both b and c

3. Bookmarks in the code editor are used primarily for:
    a. locating placeholders to jump to or scroll in serial order.
    b. establishing breakpoints.
    c. applying annotations to the code that the bookmark denotes.
    d. None of the above

4. The main reason for trapping errors in code is to:
    a. write a log of program exceptions to a file using the App.WriteLog method.
    b. examine the state of the program's error status by checking the Err.LastErrNumber property, and take action.
    c. prevent users from experiencing a program termination.
    d. execute the global error handling subroutine.

5. When debugging, press the **Shift-F8** key sequence to:
    a. dump variables to the Immediate window.
    b. execute but not view code from called procedures.
    c. single step inline code in the same manner as pressing **F8**.
    d. both b and c

6. Use the Stop statement to:
    a. shut off error handling.
    b. skip over error lines and ignore any trappable errors.
    c. send the program into Break mode when the statement is encountered.
    d. None of the above

7. Use the On Error Resume Next statement to:
    a. shut off error handling.
    b. skip over error lines and ignore any trappable errors.
    c. send the program into break mode when the statement is encountered.
    d. None of the above

8. The Debug/Step Out menu command performs what action?
    a. It skips out of the current loop or the current procedure and continues.
    b. It concludes the debug session.
    c. It moves the execution point to the cursor location.
    d. None of the above

9. To set a breakpoint,
   a. select the Debug/Toggle Breakpoint menu command.
   b. select the Debug/Step Into menu command.
   c. click on the left margin of the code window at the program line where the breakpoint should be set.
   d. Both a and c

10. The Call Stack informational dialog shows which procedures are active during execution. View the Call Stack by:
   a. clicking on the **View/Call Stack** menu command at run time or clicking on the **Toolbars/Debug** menu command and clicking the **Call Stack** button from the Debug toolbar.
   b. pressing the **Ctrl-L** shortcut key.
   c. clicking on the **View/Call Stack** menu command at design time or run time.
   d. Both a and b

ANSWERS TO CERTIFICATION QUIZ

   1. c
   2. d
   3. a
   4. c
   5. d
   6. c
   7. b
   8. a
   9. d
   10. d

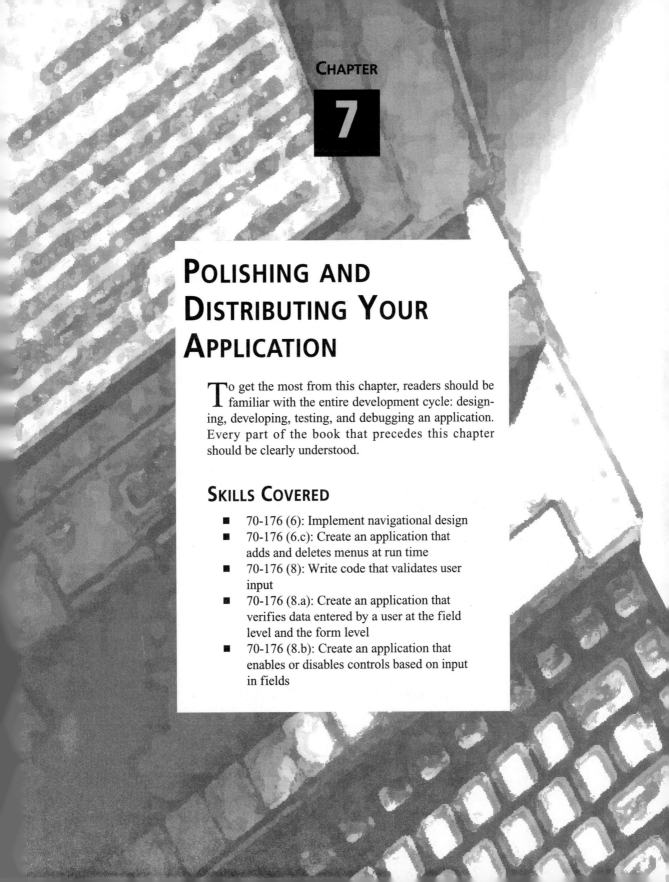

POLISHING AND DISTRIBUTING YOUR APPLICATION

To get the most from this chapter, readers should be familiar with the entire development cycle: designing, developing, testing, and debugging an application. Every part of the book that precedes this chapter should be clearly understood.

SKILLS COVERED

- 70-176 (6): Implement navigational design
- 70-176 (6.c): Create an application that adds and deletes menus at run time
- 70-176 (8): Write code that validates user input
- 70-176 (8.a): Create an application that verifies data entered by a user at the field level and the form level
- 70-176 (8.b): Create an application that enables or disables controls based on input in fields

- 70-176 (7): Create data input forms and dialog boxes
- 70-176 (7.b): Create an application that adds and deletes controls at run time
- 70-176 (14): Implement online user assistance in a desktop application
- 70-176 (14.a): Set appropriate properties to enable user assistance
- 70-176 (14.b): Create HTML Help for an application
- 70-176 (30): Use the Package and Deployment Wizard to create a setup program that installs a desktop application, registers COM components, and allows for uninstall
- 70-176 (31): Plan and implement floppy disk-based deployment or compact disk-based deployment for a desktop application
- 70-176 (33): Plan and implement network-based deployment for a desktop application
- 70-176 (35) Deploy application updates for desktop applications
- 70-175 (10): Create data input forms and dialog boxes
- 70-175 (10.b): Create an application that adds and deletes controls at run time
- 70-175 (9): Implement navigational design
- 70-175 (9c): Create an application that adds and deletes menus at run time
- 70-175 (11): Write code that validates user input
- 70-175 (11.a): Create an application that verifies data entered by a user at the field level and the form level
- 70-175 (11.b): Create an application that enables or disables controls based on input in fields
- 70-175 (18): Implement online user assistance in a distributed application
- 70-175 (18.a): Set appropriate properties to enable user assistance
- 70-175 (18.b): Create HTML Help for an application

After the application has been developed and debugged, it is time to compile, package, and distribute the completed work. This chapter explains several topics: the basics of understanding VB executables, how to package and distribute a VB application, and how to add online Help features to the application. We also examine several techniques used in developing programs; knowledge of these will be necessary for certification.

NAMING STANDARDS

Consistent naming clarifies code. The basic technique of prefixing variables with a short lower-case code that denotes the data type is a powerful, self-documenting way to clarify code. This technique can also be effective when applied to procedures and controls. Variables always have a data type. As such, this type can be denoted in the variable name. For example, a variable that will hold the sum of a person's annual salary with all bonuses could be declared like this:

```
Public sngTotalPay As Single
```

There are many religiously held arguments both for and against the use of prefixing (also known as *Hungarian notation*). Some like only three-letter prefixes; others argue for a postfix notation. Pick a standard for naming and stick to it, because it clarifies code. For example, here a prefixed variable is used in an expression, making it easy to see the data type.

```
dblResult = (sngTotalPay * .10)/12)
```

Prefixing makes it easy to see the data type of variables used in expressions and to see what the programmer intended regarding the data type of the return value. This speeds comprehension of the code and greatly aids maintainability, something we strongly favor. Gaining a nanosecond of processing speed may seem sexy, but often that blazing code is impenetrable in terms of comprehension. We favor maintainability over incremental performance enhancements that render the code unreadable.

On the same subject, note that VB variables are traditionally named using mixed case. This means that the first letter of a major word is capitalized while the prefix and all other letters remain in lower case. However, it is much more important actually to *have* a standard than to argue over the exact details of the standard.

Like variables, procedures should also conform to a naming convention. In this case an *f* might prefix a function while an *s* might prefix a subroutine. Some shops also show the return data type for a function. A function that returns an Integer might have a prefix *fint*. Table 7-1 lists a set of suggested prefixes for variables and procedures.

Table 7-1 Suggested Variable Prefixes

Data Type	Prefix
Byte	byt
Boolean	bln
Integer	int
Long	lng
Single	sng
Double	dbl
String	str
Date	dte
Currency	cur
Variant	var
Object	obj
User-Defined Type	udt
Enumeration	enm
Function	f
Sub	s

Scope can also play a roll in naming. Take the variable `sngTotalPay`. If this same variable had global scope, it might be declared with a *g* as part of the prefix. Here, the *g* denotes that the variable has global scope. The prefix can convey both datatype and scoping information to a maintenance programmer. All this is accomplished without the use of comments in the code.

```
Public gsngTOTALPAY As Single
```

Sometimes a naming standard can become so complicated that it is no longer useful. Therefore, be careful when creating a standard to present information without passing the point of diminishing return. Furthermore, a standard would do well to leverage the existing knowledge of VB developers. For example, most object methods do not have prefixes, so adding many prefixes to methods can make them hard to read. Consider the `ListCount` property of a ListBox. This method has no prefix, but imagine if we could force it to have one. Which line of code is preferable? The answer will go a long way to stating what kind of prefixing scheme you should use.

```
MyVar = List1.ListCount
MyVar = List1.gflngListCount
```

Some level of prefixing applies to nearly all aspects of VB code, even forms and controls. Typically, developers name forms and controls to indicate the type of control. For example, `txt` could be used for TextBox, `cmd` for CommandButtons, and so on. Forms and controls do not vary in scope, so scoping information is not typically presented in the prefix. Table 7-2 lists suggested prefixes for various objects in Visual Basic.

Table 7-2 Suggested Control and Form Prefixes

Control Type	Prefix
PictureBox	pic
Label	lbl
TextBox	txt
Frame	fra
CommandButton	cmd
CheckBox	chk
OptionButton	opt
ComboBox	cbo
ListBox	lst
Horizontal Scrollbar	hsb

continued on next page

Control Type	Prefix
Vertical Scrollbar	vsb
Timer	tmr
DriveList	drv
DirectoryList	dir
FileList	fil
Shape	shp
Line	lin
Image	img
Data	dat
OLE Container	ole
Forms	frm
MDI Forms	mdi
Standard Modules	bas
Class Modules	C
Interfaces	I

Naming controls is important for maintenance; it is also important for relating code to a control. A potentially troublesome situation arises when renaming a control that has associated code. Let us suppose a button named Command1 has code already attached to the Command1_Click event. If the control is renamed cmdCancel, the code becomes *orphaned*. That is, the event procedure Command1_Click remains in the form, but unattached to any control, since there is no longer a control with the name Command1. If the control is renamed, (a new CommandButton is dropped), it will get the name Command1. The previously orphaned code will attach itself to that new button.

Check It Out 7-1: Orphan Code

1. Start a new Standard VB project. On Form1 drop four CommandButtons. These will be named Command1, Command2, Command3, and Command4 by default.
2. Now delete **Command2** and drop another button. What does VB name it?
3. Now add this code to Command1_Click:

```
MsgBox "ISNT THIS SPECIAL?"
```

4. Run the application, click on **Command1**, and see the MsgBox output. Command1 works. End the application.

5. Now go to the Properties window and set the Name property of Command1 to **cmdSample**.

6. Now run your application again and click on that button you just renamed. Shouldn't you be seeing MsgBox output?

7. End the application and double click on **cmdSample**, which is still labeled Command1. There is no code under the Click event procedure. Where is it?

8. Navigate to the [General][Declarations] of Form1. Click on the **Procedure** dropdown. See the procedure `Command1_Click`? This is orphan code.

9. Now drop a button on Form1. The name will be Command1 by default. Double click on it to show a code window. See the orphan code? Command1 has just *adopted* it because it has the name Command1.

NOTE   The first thing to do in dropping a control is to name it properly. If code is attached to a control which is subsequently renamed (or deleted), the code becomes orphaned in [General][Declarations]. Orphan code can and will bloat the size of an EXE if it is not removed prior to compilation.

Throughout this manual, we have been suggesting that maintainability is a virtue, and specific techniques make code more readable. The summary statement of fact here is that code that is explicit is good, and code that uses implicit knowledge is bad. Consider this line of code:

```
AppName = Label1
```

This is career-secure code that no one else can understand, not even the original programmer after about 4 weeks. However, since no one else can read the code, people come to the programmer when a maintenance fix is needed. With career-secure code, everyone else has to do detective work to find out what is going on, because everything is implied. What is the data type of AppName? It is probably a string, but could be variant and still work. What about the scope of AppName? We have to find it, adding time to the maintenance task. Now, consider Label1. It sits on the form in which this code resides. Taken to extremes, career-secure code that uses implicit techniques at every turn can be impossible to maintain. The preceding is a very simple example of what can become complex very fast.

The Caption property of the Label object is the default property of that object. This is the property used if no property is specified. So actually, this is going on:

```
AppName = Label1.Caption
```

This code can be improved with prefixing and some simple explicit coding techniques. How about this?

```
gstrAppName = Me.Label1.Caption
```

Here it is possible to understand what is going on and what is intended by the original coder. The *gstr* in `gstrAppName` says that this is a string declared to be global in scope, and known to the entire application. We also know that the Caption property of Label1 is intended to be assigned into `gstrAppName`. It seems so simple, but is hard to do. Multiple programmers, contract programmers, multiple versions—all of these things work against the application and enforcement of a standard for the naming of variables, procedures and controls. The same is true for forms, which should be prefixed with *frm*.

Develop a standard set of naming prefixes and stick to it. Code will be more readable and require few, if any, comments. Comments are rarely revised, and become misleading when a maintenance change is made to the code. Keep comments in a single block at the start of a procedure, and use consistent naming to write self-documenting code instead. Consistent naming practices used from the start of a project through to completion of the code will result in code clarity.

One final note: This is a book that teaches VB in such a way that programmers get to know the entire product by going through the entire book. We use all the default names (Form1, Command1, etc.) to keep things simple. If we were writing an application instead of a book, we would definitely be sure to practice what we are preaching.

APPLICATION-BUILDING TECHNIQUES AND TRICKS

The mark of true professional is complete knowledge of the pros and cons of all the tools. Visual Basic is full of many shortcuts and tricks, and much strange behavior. In this section, we catalog a number of these tricks and tips. Some of these have actually been part of certification exams in the past.

TRICK: CALLING AN EVENT PROCEDURE

Event procedures are nothing more than procedures that are Private to the form in which they reside. They can be called any time, just like any other procedure. This raises many interesting possibilities. It would be possible to have some code under a button that performs a useful task. That code can then be executed by calling the Click event procedure, perhaps from a menu item. This has the effect of enabling the same functionality in two places on a form. A little imagination applied here will present all sorts of possibilities for creative ways to reduce the code size and increase the functionality of the applications.

Check It Out 7-2: Calling an Event Procedure

1. Start a new VB Standard EXE application. On Form1, drop two CommandButtons. Under Command1_Click, add this code:

```
MsgBox "Command1 CLICK event fired!!!!"
```

2. Now run the application and click on **Command1** with the mouse.

3. Return to design time, and add this code to Command2:

```
MsgBox "Here I am clicking Command2, which 'clicks' Command1!!!"
'Command1 will now think someone 'clicked' it!!!
Call Command1_Click
```

4. Run the application and click on **Command2**. (Make sure to click on **Command2**, not Command1.) What happens? Command1's Click event procedure gets called from VB code.

5. Return to design time.

It is even possible to click on a button on another form! To do this, change the Click event procedure from Private to Public so that it will be callable from outside the form. Then click the button, but remember, the rule for Public procedures in a form applies: qualify the procedure name with the name of the containing form.

From somewhere in Form1, click on the button named **Command1** on Form99. Be sure the Click was modified so that it was Public, and use the code to click on the button:

```
Form99.Command1_Click
```

This technique has many applications.

It is also possible to click a button on another form, even if that form is not loaded. The next section explains the important difference between initializing a form and loading a form.

TRICK: ACCESSING THE PROCEDURES AND DATA ON AN UNLOADED FORM

Suppose a form with required procedures is not yet loaded into memory. You can attempt to access an event procedure that is modified to be Public, or attempt to call a Public procedure in the form. This is because the procedures and variables that are Public in the form are available immediately after the `Form_Initialize` event of the form executes. When a Public procedure or a Public variable on a form is accessed from outside the form, the Initialize event procedure executes. This makes the Public procedures and data in the form available to a program. The form does not have to load.

Check It Out 7-3: Using Procedures and Data in an Unloaded Form

1. Start a new VB Standard EXE project. Add a new form. It will be named Form2. Now add this MsgBox to the `Form_Load`:

```
MsgBox "FORM2 LOADING"
```

2. Also add this code to the `Form_Initialize` of Form2:

```
MsgBox "FORM2 INITIALIZING"
```

3. Click on the **TOOLS/ADD PROCEDURE** and add this procedure to Form2:

```
Public Sub MyTest()
```

```
    MsgBox "MyTest Procedure executing"
End Sub
```

4. Now switch to Form1. Drop a button on Form1. It will be named Command1. Add this code to `Command1_Click`, which will execute the `Form2.MyTest` procedure:

    ```
    Call Form2.MyTest
    ```

5. Run the application and Form1 will appear with Command1 on it. Click on **Command1**. The Initialize event procedure of Form2 executes. The Load event procedure of Form2 does not. This is the default behavior when Public procedures or Public data are accessed from a form that has not yet been initialized.
6. Click on **Command1** again. This time, the Initialize event procedure does not execute, because this event only executes once.
7. Add another CommandButton to Form1. Under the Click event for this button, add the following code.

    ```
    MsgBox "Form2 Caption is " & Form2.Caption
    ```

8. Run the application and click on **Command2**. If any predefined property or method of the form is used, then the form will receive the Initialize *and* Load event.

This is what happens if Public procedures and data are accessed from a form that has not yet been loaded.

TRICKS: SORTING WITH A LISTBOX AND THE CLICK OF THE LISTBOX WITH LISTINDEX

It might occasionally be necessary to sort some strings. One way to accomplish this is to use the Sorted property of a list box. The basic idea is to set this read-only at run time property to True during design time. Then load it with the text to sort. Finally, pull the text out after the list box sorts it. Assume the strings are in an array named `MyText()`. Here is the code to load the list box:

```
'LOAD THE LISTBOX
Dim i As Integer
Dim max As Integer
max = UBound(MyText): MsgBox max
For i = 0 To max
  Me.List1.AddItem MyText(i)
Next
```

Remember, the list box has a Sorted property set to True. This means all the items in the list box will be in sorted order. Here is the code to reload the array with the sorted data:

```
'UNLOAD THE LISTBOX
Dim i As Integer
Dim max As Integer
max = Me.List1.ListCount
For i = 0 To max - 1
  MyText(i) = Me.List1.List(i)
  Debug.Print MyText(i)
Next
```

The key to the effective use of this technique is to set the Visible property of the list box to False, so users cannot see the list box. Just use it as a cheap but effective sorting machine for text.

TECHNIQUE: DATA VALIDATION

A key skill for any Visual Basic programmer is the ability to validate user input. Data entered into a form can be validated in one of two ways: field-level or form-level. Field-level data validation is accomplished by using the LostFocus event. This fires whenever a data input field, like a TextBox, has the focus and then the user tabs away from the field. In this event, it is possible to write code to check data. As an example, the following code is used to check and see if a valid date is entered into a TextBox named txtDate. If the data are valid, it is converted to short date format, otherwise a message is displayed.

```
Private Sub txtDate_LostFocus()
  If IsDate(txtDate.Text) Then
    txtDate.Text = Format$(txtDate.Text, "Short Date")
  Else
    MsgBox "Not a Date!"
  End If
End Sub
```

Form-level validation is done by waiting for the press of a button on a dialog box. In this strategy, the user is allowed to enter data in the form without validating until an **OK** button is pressed. When the button is pressed, the value of each field in the form can be checked. In this scenario, the properties of controls are changed if any of the data are invalid. For example, one might change the BackColor of a TextBox to red if it contains bad data.

MULTIPLE DOCUMENT INTERFACE

The notion of a Multiple Document Interface is easy to understand. The *Multiple Document Interface* (MDI) style of user interface is in popular applications like Word and Excel. In applications that use the MDI interface, there is one dominant window and one or more sibling (or *child*) windows. The child windows are always contained in the containing (or *parent*) window. The parent window is a special kind of VB form called an *MDIForm*.

To create an MDI application, first add a single MDIForm to the application. Selecting **PROJECT/ADD MDI FORM** from the VB menu does this. Only one MDIForm per application can be added, so the menu item will be disabled after an MDIForm is added to your application. The child windows that will inhabit the MDIForm are just regular VB forms with their MDIChild property set to True. Therefore, the forms will always display as subordinate, fully-contained windows of the MDIForm in the project.

Even after an MDIForm is added to the project and the MDIChild of other forms in the project is set to True, there are more steps to perform. First, go to PROJECT/PROJECT PROPER-TIES and set the Startup object to the name of the MDIForm. This makes the MDIForm the startup form for the project, so that it will load and show to start things off. Using the `Show` method to show a child window before the MDIForm will cause the child window to force the MDIForm to load also. However, any additional child windows will not automatically load. A control cannot be dropped on an MDIForm unless it has an `Align` property, which forces the control to align itself along the top, bottom, left, or right of the parent window. Search Help on Align Property and check the controls in the Applies To link.

When building MDI applications, ask for the Window List to appear in the menu in the MDIForm by specifying that the Window list should appear in the Menu Editor. Figure 7-1 shows the Menu Editor and the WindowList checkbox. Figure 7-2 displays a menu within an MDIForm with the Window list displayed. The Window list displays the window title of each child window as a menu item. With the Window list feature, the focus can be shifted from one child window to another by clicking an item in the Window list.

Figure 7-1 Setting the WindowList property.

If a child form is created with its own menu, the menu will appear on the parent MDI form when the child receives the focus. This process is know as *menu negotiation*. Menu negotiation permits using child forms that perform different functions, and thus change the mode of the application. Although this feature exists, be careful not to abuse it. Users find modal applications confusing and limited. Use this feature sparingly.

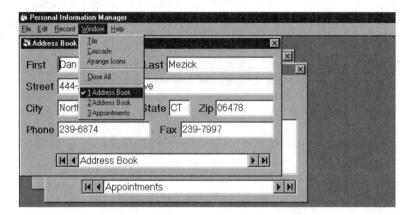

Figure 7-2 Using the Window List.

Check It Out 7-4: Child Form Menus

1. Start a new VB Standard EXE project. Add an MDIForm by clicking on **PROJECT/ADD MDI FORM**.

2. The MDIForm does not become the Startup object by default. Specify that from PROJECT/PROJECT1 PROPERTIES. Click on this menu item now and set Startup Object to MDIForm1.

3. Start the application. MDIForm1 will appear, but will not have any child windows. Add them now.

4. Return to design time. Add a form to the project named Form2.

5. Set the MDIChild property of Form2 to True. Also set the MDIChild property of Form1 to True. This makes both forms subordinate to MDIForm1. In the Project window, the icon of both Form1 and Form2 will change slightly to reflect the new status of these forms.

6. Do not run the application yet, because the children will not automatically appear in the parent. They must first be loaded. Add this code to the `MDIForm_Load` of MDIForm1:

```
Load Form1
Load Form2
```

7. Now run the application. Form1 and Form2 will appear as child windows within MDIForm1. Fiddle with each window. Try normalizing, maximizing, and minimizing Form1 and Form2.

8. Return to design time. Now set the AutoShowChildren property on MDIForm1 from True to False. Run the application. Where are the children?

9. Now back in design time, comment out the Load statements, and add the following statements that use the form's Show method.

```
Form1.Show
Form2.Show
```

10. Run the application and see the children again. Return to design time. Change the AutoShowChildren property back to its default value, and replace the Show methods with the Load statements again.

11. Now explore menu behavior under MDI. Add a single menu item captioned MDIForm1 MainMenu to MDIForm1 using the Menu Editor. Also, check the WindowList option for this menu item of MDIForm1. Finally, add a single menu item to Form1 with a caption as Form1 Child Menu.

12. Run the application. Click on the menu of MDIForm1. The Window list will appear, displaying Form1 and Form2. Notice the menu that currently appears; it belongs to MDIForm1. Now, click on **Form1** or select it from the Window list. What happens? Form1's menu appears until the focus shifts to Form2 by clicking on it.

13. Return to design time. Set Form1 as the StartUp object in the PROJECT/PROJECT1 PROPERTIES dialog. Run the application. MDIForm1 will appear with Form1 and Form2 contained as child windows because when a child window is loaded, it drags its parent along.

MDI applications are more structured than independent, form-based applications that do not impose the structure of MDI. Just remember the simple rules: (a) set the MDIForm as the Startup Object, (b) set the MDIChild property to True for each child window, and (c) set the MDIForm's AutoShowChildren property for the desired results.

CONTROL ARRAYS

A *control array* is a set of controls of the same class that shares a common set of event procedures and a common name. The Index property of each control array element differentiates it from all others and is passed in to the common event procedures they all share. The classic example of a control array is calculator buttons. Calculator buttons all share the same purpose—to input data. The only thing that differs among the buttons is the value. Therefore, it makes sense to share the click event for each button and use the control array index as the data input. This makes the code and application more compact.

Check It Out 7-5: Creating Control Arrays

1. Start a new VB Standard EXE project. Drop a CommandButton on Form1 named Command1.

2. Drop another button on Form1 named Command2. Go to the Properties window and change the name to Command1. The prompted message "You already have a

control named 'Command1.' Do you want to create a control array?" will appear. Click on **Yes** in response to this dialog. The dialog appears in Figure 7-3.

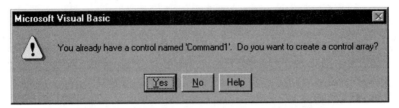

Figure 7-3 The prompt about creating a control array.

3. Now double click on the first button and look at the Click event. The parameter Index As Integer is passed in by the system. This parameter has the value of the Index property of the CommandButton that was clicked by the user. Enter this code in the `Command1_Click` event procedure:

```
MsgBox "Index of button clicked is " & Index
```

4. Run the application. Click on the first button, then click on the second button. What happens? The first button has an Index of 0, while the second button has an Index of 1.
5. Return to design time. Open up the Properties window to see both the Name property and the Index property. Drop yet another CommandButton on Form1. Name it Command1 from inside the Properties window. Notice there is no prompt about the control array, because this has already been created in the previous step. Also, notice that as soon as the name Command1 is given, VB automatically sets Index to the value 2.
6. Run the application. Click on the third button. What happens now?
7. Control arrays can be created in many ways. Drop a TextBox on Form1. Click on it so it gets the design time focus.
8. Now go to the VB menu and click on the **EDIT/COPY** menu command. The control has just been copied to the clipboard.
9. Now click on **EDIT/PASTE**. This will copy the contents of the clipboard to the form. Doing this is the equivalent of trying to paste another Text1 onto Form1. The result will be the prompt shown in Figure 7-3. Specify **Yes** to create a control array, and the new control will have the value 1 for its Index, while the original control it was based on will now have an Index of 0. This is another way to create a control array at design time.

Once a control array is defined, new controls can be added to the array dynamically at run time. Place a control with an Index of zero on the form, and make it invisible. This item is the base element of a control array that can grow dynamically at run time. In VB code, new controls are added to the control array and appear dynamically at run time. Use the Load command to do this. The Load command is not just for loading forms.

Check It Out 7-6: Adding Members to a Control Array

1. Start a new VB project. Drop a TextBox control on Form1. Set the Index property to zero. This makes it the base element in a control array.
2. Set the Visible property of Text1 to False and set both the Left and Top properties to zero.
3. Drop a button on Form1. When this button is pressed, code in the Click event will create new TextBoxes. Add this code under the `Command1_Click` event:

```
Static c As Integer
'THIS WILL BE USED AS THE INDEX OF THE NEW ELEMENT:
c = c + 1
'THIS LINE CREATES THE NEW CONTROL ARRAY ELEMENT:
Load Text1(c)
'THIS LINE MAKES THE TEXT BOX VISIBLE:
Text1(c).Visible = True
'THIS LINE POSITIONS THE TEXT BOX ON THE FORM:
Text1(c).Top = Text1(c - 1).Top + 600
```

4. Run the application and click the button to create new TextBoxes.

Since all control array elements share a common name, the notation used in code to refer to an individual element in the array must include the array index, such as `[ArrayName]` `(ArrayIndex). [property | method]`. The code just shown uses a `Static` variable incremented by one each time the button is clicked. This variable's value is used as the index for the new item created with the Load command.

New menu items can be added to a menu in the same way a new control can be added to a form.. Create a menu item with an Index of zero, making it a base element in an array of menu items. Then, in code, use the Load command to add a new menu item to the menu, change the Caption of the new item, and set the Visible property of the new menu item to True. All the menu items will share a common Click event. The system will pass in the Index value to the Click event procedure so that it is possible to tell which menu item was clicked.

Check It Out 7-7: Dynamic Menus

1. Start a new VB Standard EXE project. Add this menu to Form1 using the Menu Editor:

Caption:	Name:
File	mnuFILE
Open	mnuOPEN
Menu Array	mnuARRAY

2. For mnuARRAY, set the `Visible` property to False and set the `Index` property to zero, all from the Menu Editor.

3. Drop a Textbox and a CommandButton on the Form. Add this code to the
    `Command1_Click` event procedure:

```
Static c As Integer
c = c + 1
Load mnuARRAY(c)
mnuARRAY(c).Caption = Text1.Text
mnuARRAY(c).Visible = True
```

4. Run the application. Enter a name into Text1 and click on the **Command1** button,
    then click on the menu. That name should appear in the menu. Type in other names
    and check the menu after each click on Command1.
5. Each menu item shares a common event procedure for the Click event. Add this
    code under the `mnuARRAY_Click(Index as Integer)` event procedure:

```
MsgBox "That was menu array item number " & Index
```

6. Run the application to add dynamic menu items as done previously, and then click
    those dynamic menu items. See how the system passes in the Index of the menu item
    clicked? This makes it possible to perform conditional processing based on the Index.

In addition to adding controls through the Load function, you can also add controls to your form
through the Add method of the Controls collection. The add method takes as an argument the type
of control you want to add and a name for the new control. When added in this way, the control
does not explicitly become part of a control array, but stands alone. The following code shows how
TextBoxes might be added to a form at run time.

```
Dim MyTextBox As VB.TextBox
Static intNumber As Integer
intNumber = intNumber + 1

Set MyTextBox = Me.Controls.Add("VB.TextBox", "Text" & intNumber)
MyTextBox.Text = MyTextBox.Name
MyTextBox.Visible = True
MyTextBox.Left = 0
MytextBox.Height = 0
```

HELP FILES

Visual Basic does not supply a utility for creating Help files, though the Visual Studio '98 suite
ships with the HTML Help Workshop (Figure 7-4) which can be used to create Help files for
Visual Basic applications. The HTML Workshop is functional, but has very few features. In
fact, one part of the utility actually requires creation of a C++ header file. Fortunately, there
are several third-party tools on the market to help fill the void left by this tool.

In most organizations, programmers do not create the Help file but instead incorporate it in
the application. Incorporating help into an application requires the use of Help files made up

of help topics referenced by *context identifiers*. The Help context ID is an integer that can be used programmatically to retrieve and display specific Help topics in the Help file. The author of the Help file defines both the topical content for the file and the associated context IDs for each individual Help topic in the file.

Specify the Help file that an application will be using by clicking on the **PROJECT/PRO-JECT1 PROPERTIES** menu command and navigating to the General tab. There is a text box provided to specifying the full path to the Help file. This is not a recommended approach (even though the facility is provided) because the result is a hard-coded pathname to the Help file. This could be a problem if a user installs to a nonstandard directory when installing the application. A better approach is to assign a string specifying the location of the Help file to the Helpfile property of the App object. The code that follows uses `App.Path` as the pathname when specifying the Help file that will be used in the application. This code is typically executed in the Load event of the first form, or from within `Sub Main`.

```
App.Helpfile = App.Path & "\MYHELP.CHM"
```

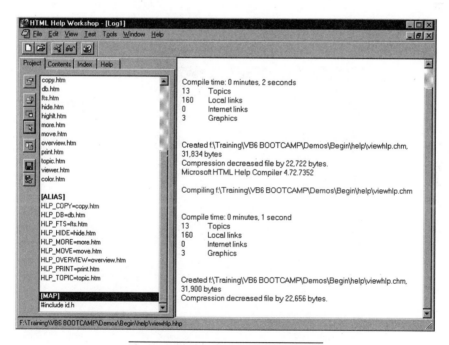

Figure 7-4 The HTML Help Workshop.

By specifying the Help file location at run time with an assist from the `Path` property of the App object (Figure 7-5), the application will always be able to find the Help file. The only caveat is that the Help file must reside in the same directory as the executable. The Help file specified in `App.Helpfile` is the default Help file for the entire application until this is changed. Once `App.Helpfile` points to a valid Help file name, the application can begin using it. A user who presses the **F1** key from anywhere in the application will receive the first page of the Help file, which usually has a Help context ID of zero.

In addition, many controls also have a `HelpContextId` property, which can contain the index of the Help topic in the Help file that is most pertinent to the control. For example, if `App.Helpfile` points to a valid Help file name and `Command1.HelpContextId` points to a valid `Help context ID` within that file, the topical text and graphics associated with the `HelpContextId` will appear when the user places the focus on Command1 and then presses the **F1** key to obtain Help on that control. A developer needs a mapping of topic names and Help context IDs to apply the context sensitivity to an application. This is typically provided by the author of the Help file.

Check It Out 7-8: Incorporating Help Files

1. Start a new Standard EXE project in Visual Basic.
2. Open the properties dialog by selecting **PROJECT/PROJECT1 PROPER-TIES...** from the menu. In the General tab, push the **ellipsis** next to the Help File entry. Locate the help file on the CD-ROM called **VIEWHLP.CHM**. This file is an HTML help file.

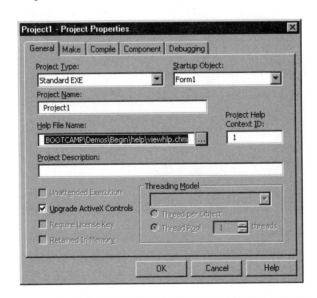

Figure 7-5 Specifying the help file in the project properties.

3. In this file, we have associated help context IDs with certain topics. The overview topic is associated with an ID of 1. Set this ID into the `HelpContextID` property of the project. Press the **OK** button.
4. Run the project. When the project starts, press **F1** and the overview topic should appear in a window.

5. Stop the project and return to design mode.
6. Now add three buttons to Form1. Under each button, set the `HelpContextID` property to 2, 3, and 4, respectively.
7. Run the project again. Click on a button and then press **F1**. The topic shown for each button should be different. In this way, it is possible to map a topic to a certain control in the application to give targeted assistance where needed.

Beginning with Windows 95, a new kind of Help access was made available: "What's this?" help (see Figure 7-6). This kind of Help floats above the item clicked, rather than appearing in the standard Help display window format. Visual Basic supports "What's this? help" by showing a special button on the title bar for forms that have this feature or through the `WhatsThisHelpMode` method.

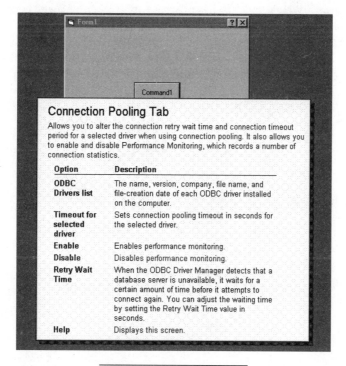

Figure 7-6 What's this? help.

Check It Out 7-9: What's this? help

1. Start a new Standard EXE project in Visual Basic.
2. Open the Properties dialog by selecting **PROJECT/PROJECT1 PROPERTIES...** from the menu. In the General tab, push the **ellipsis** next to the Help File entry. Locate the help file **ODBCINST.HLP** in the Windows or Winnt directory. A file search may be needed to locate this file.

3. Open the properties for Form1.

4. Set the `BorderStyle` property to **3-Fixed Dialog**. This is one of the allowable form states in which the What's this? button will appear in the form's title bar.

5. Set the `WhatsThisHelp` property to True to allow the form to use the special pop-up window available for "What's this?" help.

6. Set the `WhatsThisButton` property for Form1 to True. This property shows the special What's this? help button in the title bar of Form1 at run time.

7. Drop a button from the toolbox onto Form1. In the properties for the button, set the `WhatsThisHelpID` to a value of 100. This is the topic that will appear when "What's this?" help is activated.

8. Run the application. Push the **What's this? help** button and then try clicking on the button to get more information. A pop-up similar to Figure 7-6 should appear.

9. Sometimes "What's this?" help is activated off of a pop-up menu instead of the button in the title bar. We can easily add that functionality to a project.

10. Return to design mode and open the properties for Form1. Set the `WhatsThis-Button` property to False so that it will no longer appear in the title bar.

11. Now open the Menu Editor by selecting **TOOLS/MENU EDITOR...** from the menu. In the Menu Editor, create a pop-up menu as seen in Figure 7-7. Refer to the Item list for the specific properties of each menu.

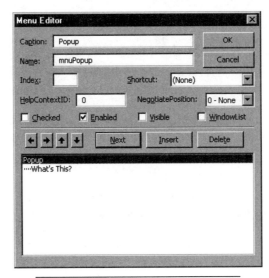

Figure 7-7 The Pop-up Menu for Form1.

Item 1—Menu

Name	`mnuPopup`
Caption	`Popup`

Visible	False

Item 2—Menu

Name	mnuWhatsThis
Caption	What's This?

12. We want to enter "What's this?" mode whenever a user right clicks on the form. At the same time, we will pop up a menu that allows the user to show the Help file associated with the item currently active on the form.

13. In the `Form_MouseDown` event, add the following code to enter "What's this?" mode and show the menu.

```
If Button = vbRightButton Then
   WhatsThisMode
   PopupMenu mnuPopup

End If
```

14. Now we need to show the appropriate help topic when the user clicks on the menu. In this case, we will show the help for the currently-active control. Add the following code to the click event of `mnuWhatsThis` to activate the help topic.

```
Screen.ActiveControl.ShowWhatsThis
```

15. Run the application. Right click on the form and pick **"What's this?"** from the menu.

When implementing a Help file into an application, remember to alert the setup wizard to this fact while building the installation. The setup wizard provides a step in the process for files to be added, and the Help file must be added to the list at that point. Also, be sure to install the Help file in the application's installation directory. When this is done, the application can use the `App.Path` property to find the Help file without any problems.

RESOURCE FILES

Visual Basic 6.0 supports the creation and use of resource files, special files that contain binary and text data for use in an application. This might include graphic images or text strings. Resource files are useful because they allow inclusion of application data as part of the final executable as opposed to having to obtain separate BMP, GIF, JPG, or WAV files. This eases distribution and protects the data from alteration. Text shipped in a resource file, called a *resource string*, is useful for localizing applications. Phrases in several languages can be stored; the correct language for a locale can then be selected.

Resource files are created in Visual Basic using the VB6 Resource Editor (Figure 7-9), an add-in that can be activated through the Add-In Manager (Figure 7-8). Once loaded, the Resource Editor is available from the TOOLS/RESOURCE EDITOR menu item.

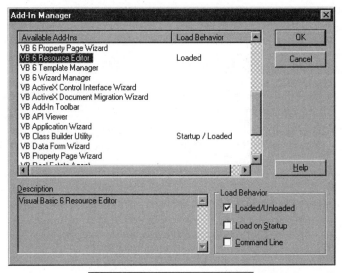

Figure 7-8 The Add-In Manager.

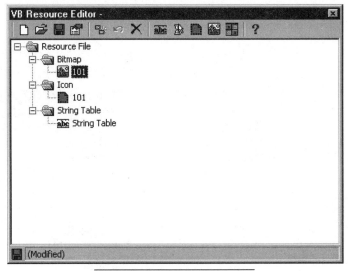

Figure 7-9 The Resource Editor.

Visual Basic limits resource files to a single file per application. Once the Resource Editor has been started, create a new file and save it. Saving a resource file automatically adds that file to the application. Creating a new one will delete any previous file and add the new one to the project. In the Resource Editor, text or binary resources may be added to the same file.

Adding resources to the file is a simple matter of clicking the appropriate button on the toolbar. Adding resource strings is done by creating a *string table* (Figure 7-10). String tables associate string entries with a unique integer value that can be used later to access the data entered in the table, for example, to display a greeting in one of several different languages. The greetings could be added as part of the resource file and a number could be assigned to each greeting. Later in the application, the number could be used to retrieve the appropriate greeting. Cursors, bitmaps, and icons are used in a similar way.

Once resources are saved in the file, retrieve them by using the `LoadResString`, `LoadResPicture`, and `LoadResData` functions. The `LoadResString` function takes an integer as an argument and returns the string from the resource file that corresponds to the number. The `LoadResPicture` takes an integer as the first argument and a format argument that indicates if a bitmap, icon, or cursor is being loaded. The `LoadResData` function also takes an integer and a format argument, though this function can load any kind of binary data to be saved.

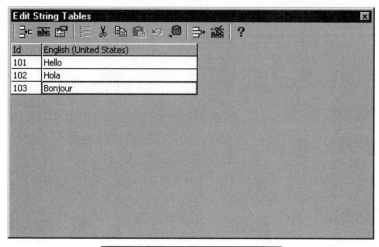

Figure 7-10 Creating a string table.

Check It Out 7-10: Using Resource Files

1. Create a new directory called VB BOOTCAMP/RESOURCE.
2. Start a new Visual Basic Standard EXE project.
3. Open the Add-In Manager by selecting **ADD-INS/ADD-IN MANAGER...** from the menu.
4. In the Add-In Manager, load the VB6 Resource Editor. Close the Add-In Manager.
5. Start the Resource Editor by selecting **TOOLS/RESOURCE EDITOR...** from the menu.
6. In the resource editor, start a new string table. In the table add the following resource strings.

```
101   Hello
102   Hola
103   Bonjour
```

7. Now select to add an icon to the resource file. To add icons, locate the files to add. All the files to be added are on the CD-ROM. Add the files shown in the list below.

```
101   CTRUSA.ICO
102   CTRMEX.ICO
103   CTRFRAN.ICO
```

8. Save the project into the directory created. The resource file needs to be saved before the application is run.

9. Select **Form1** from the project window and make it visible. Add a ListBox, CommandButton, and Image Control to Form1 so that it looks like Figure 7-11. Refer to the Item List for information on the properties to set at design time.

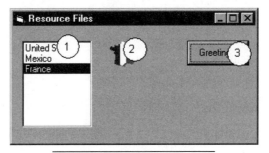

Figure 7-11 Form and Controls.

Item 1—ListBox

Name   lstCountries

Item 2—Image

Name   imgFlag

Item 3—CommandButton

Name   cmdHello

Caption   "Greetings!"

10. When the project first starts, we want to add the possible countries to a list. Under the Form_Load event, add the following code to fill the list.

```
lstCountries.AddItem "United States"
lstCountries.ItemData(lstCountries.NewIndex) = 101
lstCountries.AddItem "Mexico"
lstCountries.ItemData(lstCountries.NewIndex) = 102
lstCountries.AddItem "France"
lstCountries.ItemData(lstCountries.NewIndex) = 103
```

11. After a country is selected, we want to use the resources to show a greeting. Under the click event for `cmdHello`, add the following code to show the greeting.

```
If lstCountries.ListIndex = -1 Then Exit Sub
Set imgFlag.Picture = _
  LoadResPicture(lstCountries.ItemData(lstCountries.ListIndex),
  vbResIcon)
MsgBox LoadResString(lstCountries.ItemData(lstCountries.
    ListIndex))
```

12. Run the application. Select a country from the list and display the greeting.

COMPILATION, PACKAGING, AND DISTRIBUTION

The word *executable* in VB is something of a misnomer. What comes out of VB requires the VB runtime file MSVBVM60.DLL. When an EXE is created, all the forms, modules, and class modules in the project are used to create a single file with an EXE extension. The default name of the EXE is the name of the project. It is possible to override the default and provide a custom name. To build an executable, click on the **FILE/MAKE EXE** menu command. Visual Basic will insert the name of the project in the menu command. For example, if the project name is Project1, Make Project1 EXE... will appear as a menu command from the File menu. Clicking on this option will show the name of the EXE and where it will be written by VB when completed. To alter the properties of the EXE that will be created, click on the **Options...** button that appears on the dialog. Figure 7-12 shows the Make options accessible from the Options... button of the Make EXE Dialog.

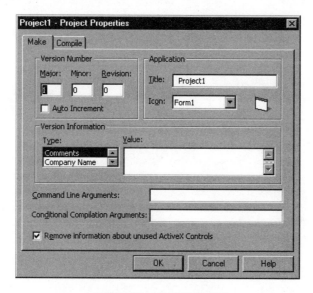

Figure 7-12 Make Options.

Note that the dialog that appears as a result of clicking the **Options...** button displays two tabs, Make and Compile. These are the same tabs visible when the **PROJECT/PROPERTIES...** menu command is selected. The Make and Compile tabs allow alteration of the various properties of the executable before it is generated. These properties can be altered from either location within VB's menu structure.

The Make tab is where version information is set for the EXE and where the project name and desktop icon for the application are specified. The Compile tab is where *p-code* or *native code* compilation of forms, modules, and class modules is specified. Select native code to drill deeper into the options for the executable by clicking on the **Advanced Optimizations...** button and further fine-tune the EXE output. P-code is actually a conversion from VB language to a set of tokens. Each token represents a particular keyword or coding construct of the language. This is *pseudo-code*, hence the slang term p-code. Native code is actual machine language statements understood by the target CPU, usually the Intel architecture in the case of Visual Basic; however, VB is supported on the Alpha platform as well. The default setting is to compile to native code, which is faster than p-code but is not platform-independent.

Regardless of the compile option, the VB EXE will require the distribution of MSVBVM60.DLL, the file containing the VB runtime module. Even the natively compiled EXE will require this file, since it will be making calls into the functions found in this DLL. This requirement means that the minimum VB application (as distributed to end users) must include both the EXE and the VB runtime module. VB does not create standalone EXEs.

Prior to building the EXE, there are several options. The first set of options pertains to versioning information about the executable. From the Project/Properties menu command access the Make tab of the Project Properties. Here, the major version, minor version, and revision version numbers can be set and the copyright information that will be compiled into the executable can be defined. Many of these values will become the default values for properties of the App object. For example, `LegalCopyright` is a property of the App object. The value of this property is set using the Make tab of the Project Properties dialog prior to compilation.

The Compile tab of the Project Properties dialog permits specifying p-code or native code compilation. If compilation to native code is specified, there are further options. You can optimize the compile for speed or size, for example. Or favor the Pentium Pro processor, though doing so will hurt performance on previous Intel processors. Likewise, favoring speed over size will result in a larger generated EXE, while favoring size will most likely result in a slower but smaller application executable.

When generating the executable is finished, it is time to consider the installation process. Simple applications require the executable plus the VB runtime module. Even so, creating a convenient and simple setup and installation disk is something users have come to expect. For this reason, programmers need to be familiar with the Packaging and Distribution Wizard, another add-in available through the Add-in manager. The Packaging and Distribution Wizard can build setup disks for products or send components to a Web server for distribution via the Internet. In this chapter, we will examine the standard packaging facilities.

For most applications, there will be a large number of additional files beyond the EXE and the VB runtime module. To call functions in a DLL that does not reside on the target user's machine, it will be necessary to distribute and install the DLL. There are INI files, data files, bitmaps, and any runtime DLLs such as the DLLs associated with Data Access Objects and the

Data Control. The Packaging and Distribution Wizard (Figure 7-13) helps manage the gathering, setup, and distribution of the many files that make up the VB application.

When beginning to create the installation disks, start the Packaging and Distribution Wizard from within the project. When the Wizard starts, it assumes distribution of the current project is desired. The Wizard also gives a choice between packaging for distribution via traditional medium, like floppy or CD-ROM, and deploying through a Web server. For standard packaging, select the **Package** button.

Figure 7-13 The Package and Deployment Wizard.

The first step in creating a package is to choose the *packaging script* for the Wizard to use (Figure 7-14). Packaging scripts are essentially macros that repeat a packaging process so it is not continually necessary to rerun the Wizard when changes are made to the application. The Wizard provides a standard script for plain vanilla packages to use for most setups.

After you select a script, the Wizard will prompt you to select a location to build the installation files. The Wizard packages files in cabinet (CAB) files, a standard Microsoft compressed file format, are closely related to ZIP files. All Microsoft software uses CAB files for distribution so applications behave much like any Microsoft application. CAB files are a departure from previous versions of Visual Basic which compressed each file separately.

Once a location for CAB files is selected, the Wizard will create a list of files that belong with the application. At this point, add files that need distribution. Files added will include any separate data files like Help files, initialization files, or small Microsoft Access databases. Files can be removed from the list by unchecking the file name in the wizard.

As the wizard progresses, it prompts to specify whether the application is to be distributed as a single CAB or in multiple CAB files. Multiple files are used through floppy disks whereas a single CAB could be used for a CD-ROM or network installation. Further options permit specifying the program groups and icons for the application, a nice improvement over previous distribution tools.

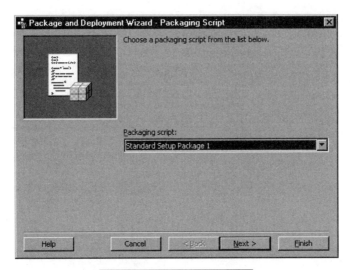

Figure 7-14 Selecting a script.

One of the most important steps in the Wizard involves specifying the locations for file installation (Figure 7-15). The Wizard identifies many different files for distribution and tries to make logical decisions about where they should go on a client machine. These choices can be edited for application files. The Wizard provides a list of files that make up the application and the ability to select from a dropdown list to indicate the installation location. Note that the list of files only includes the EXE and associated data files. The Wizard automatically sets the locations for key files like MSVBVM60.DLL.

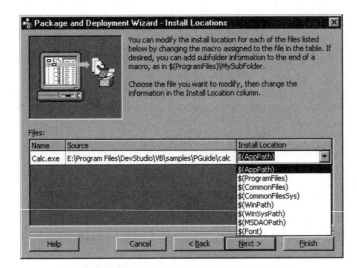

Figure 7-15 Selecting installation locations.

The Wizard builds the CAB files. Two other files will be created along with the CAB, the bootstrap program `SETUP.EXE`, which the user will run to start the installation process, and `SETUP.LST`, a list of files and locations used by the setup routines. Under the directory where CAB was created will be a subdirectory called *\Support*. This contains all the files in the CAB. There will also be a batch file with a BAT extension. This file can be run to recreate the CAB files without rerunning the Wizard. This is useful if changes are made to one of the files in the CAB. After the Wizard is complete, use the CAB files, `SETUP.EXE`, and `SETUP.LST` to install the project on any client machine.

Exercise 7-1: Help Desk Request

This application creates a Help Desk Request wizard which users can run to record a request to a company help desk. The application uses several of the advanced techniques taught in this chapter. This application will also be used in the next exercise to create distribution medium.

Step 1

In the File Explorer, create a new directory called VB BOOTCAMP/EXERCISE7-1. Then open Visual Basic 6.0 and start a new Standard EXE project.

Step 2

The interface for this application consists of three Label controls, three TextBoxes, and three CommandButtons. The controls are arranged in a control array. This requires creating an array of Labels, then one of TextBoxes, and finally, one of CommandButtons. The final interface should look like Figure 7-16. Refer to the item list for details on the properties to be set at design time for each control.

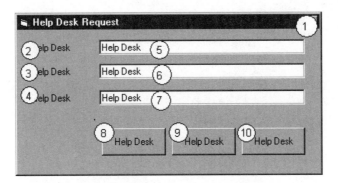

Figure 7-16 The help desk form.

Item1—Form

Name	`frmHelpDesk`
Caption	Help Desk Request
BorderStyle	3-Fixed Dialog

StartUpPosition   2-Center Screen

Item 2—Label

Name   `lblHelp`

Caption   Help Desk

Index   0

Item 3—Label

Name   `lblHelp`

Caption   Help Desk

Index   1

Item 4—Label

Name   `lblHelp`

Caption   Help Desk

Index   2

Item 5—TextBox

Name   `txtHelp`

Text   Help Desk

Index   0

Item 6—TextBox

Name   `txtHelp`

Text   Help Desk

Index   1

Item 7—TextBox

Name   `txtHelp`

Text   Help Desk

Index   2

Item 8—CommandButton

Name   `cmdHelp`

Text   Help Desk

Index   0

Item 9—CommandButton

Name   `cmdHelp`

Text   Help Desk

Index   1

Item 10—CommandButton

Name   `cmdHelp`

Text   Help Desk

Index   2

Step 3

Notice that the controls on the form all have the same text displayed in them. This is because we intend to use a resource file to change the displayed text on the form as the user works through the wizard. In order to create the resource file, load the Resource Editor by starting it in the Add-in manager. Start the Add-in manager by selecting **ADD-INS/ADD-IN MANAGER...** from the menu. In the Add-in manager, double click the entry for the resource editor and close the Add-in manager.

Step 4

Start the Resource Editor by selecting **TOOLS/RESOURCE EDITOR** from the menu. Open the String Table Editor by clicking on the **abc** icon in the Resource Editor. The Editor will display the string table. The first entry is set to an integer of 101, but we want to start at 1. Change the ID of the first string to 1 and add the text "First Name." Continue adding strings until the string table looks like the one below.

ID	Resource String
1	First Name
2	Last Name
3	Employee ID
4	Cancel
5	Disabled
6	Next
7	Phone
8	Serial #
9	Problem
10	Cancel
11	Back
12	Finish

Step 5

Save the resource file by clicking on the **disk** icon in the resource editor. Close the Resource Editor and save your project.

Step 6

Open the Code window for the form. In the [General][Declarations] section create a user-defined type to hold the data for the user's request. Add the following code to create the data type:

```
Private Type udtRequest
   FirstName As String
   LastName As String
   EmployeeID As String
   Phone As String
   Serial As String
   Problem As String
End Type
```

Step 7

In the [General][Declarations] section of the form, declare two variables. One will be for the user-defined type created above, while a second variable will keep track of which step the wizard is on. Add the following code to declare the variables:

```
Private m_StepIndex As Integer
Private m_Request As udtRequest
```

Step 8

In this application, the use of consecutive steps and control arrays could be confusing if we coded using actual integer values. Whenever there is a sequence of consecutive numbers or fixed values, it is a good idea to declare constants to represent the values. In the [General][Declarations] section of the form, add the following code to create constants for the steps and control arrays.

```
'Constants
Private Enum enmSteps
   ntsStep1 = 1
   ntsStep2 = 2
   ntsStep3 = 3
End Enum

Private Enum enmIndexes
   ntsLeftButton
   ntsMiddleButton
   ntsRightButton
End Enum
```

Step 9

This application uses just one form and set of controls to create a multi-step wizard. This is because the resource file keeps track of the text to display in each element. Therefore, we need to create a routine that will update the form display based on what step the wizard is executing. The strategy is to read elements out of the resource file based on a step number. Create a subroutine called `UpdateDisplay` by selecting **TOOLS/ADD PROCEDURE...** from the menu. In the routine, add code so that the completed routine appears as follows.

```
Public Sub UpdateDisplay()

  Dim i As Integer

  'Make sure the StepIndex is in bounds
  Debug.Assert m_StepIndex = 1 Or m_StepIndex = 2

  For i = 0 To 2

    'Labels
    lblHelp(i).Caption = LoadResString((m_StepIndex - 1) * 6 +
                         (i + 1))

    'Buttons
    cmdHelp(i).Caption = LoadResString((m_StepIndex - 1) * 6 +
                         (i + 4))
    If UCase$(cmdHelp(i).Caption) = "DISABLED" Then
      cmdHelp(i).Visible = False
    Else
      cmdHelp(i).Visible = True
    End If

    txtHelp(i).Text = ""
  Next

End Sub
```

Step 10

When the application first starts, we obviously want to be on Step 1. Add the following code to the Form_Load event to initialize the application.

```
'Initialize Form
m_StepIndex = 1
UpdateDisplay
```

Step 11

Whenever a button on the wizard is clicked, the wizard is moving from one step to another. As with all wizards, users can move forward or backward in the wizard. All the buttons are in a control array, so they share a click event called cmdHelp_Click. In the shared click event, add the following code to save data and switch between steps.

```
'Save Data
Select Case m_StepIndex
  Case ntsStep1
```

```
      m_Request.FirstName = txtHelp(0).Text
      m_Request.LastName = txtHelp(1).Text
      m_Request.EmployeeID = txtHelp(2).Text
   Case ntsStep2
      m_Request.Phone = txtHelp(0).Text
      m_Request.Serial = txtHelp(1).Text
      m_Request.Problem = txtHelp(2).Text
End Select

'Handle Buttons
Select Case Index
   Case ntsLeftButton
      'Cancel Request
      End
   Case ntsMiddleButton
      'Move backward
      m_StepIndex = ntsStep1
      UpdateDisplay
   Case ntsRightButton
      'Move forward
      m_StepIndex = m_StepIndex + 1
      If m_StepIndex = ntsStep2 Then
         UpdateDisplay
      Else
         SendRequest
      End If
End Select
```

Step 12

After the wizard is finished, it writes all its data out to a text file. In this case a routine named
SendRequest is called. Add this procedure through the **TOOLS/ADD PROCEDURE...**
menu selection. In this procedure, add code to write all of the collected data out to a text file.
The final procedure appears as follows:

```
Public Sub SendRequest()

On Error GoTo SendErr

   'Get a file handle
   Dim intFile As Integer
   intFile = FreeFile()
```

```
'Write Request
Open App.Path & "\request.txt" For Output As #intFile
  Print #1, "First Name: " & m_Request.FirstName
  Print #1, "Last Name: " & m_Request.LastName
  Print #1, "EmployeeID: " & m_Request.EmployeeID
  Print #1, "Phone: " & m_Request.Phone
  Print #1, "Serial #: " & m_Request.Serial
  Print #1, "Problem: " & m_Request.Problem
Close #intFile

MsgBox "Your Request has been sent!", vbOKOnly + vbInformation, _
  "Help Desk Request"
End

Exit Sub

SendErr:
  MsgBox Err.Description, vbOKOnly + vbExclamation, "Help Desk
Request"
  Exit Sub

End Sub
```

Step 13

Save and run the application. Fill in the TextBoxes and save a request. Open the request file in Notepad to see the results.

Exercise 7-2: Creating Installations

Creating installation disks is a critical part of distributing any Visual Basic application. Fortunately, VB provides an excellent utility for creating setup disks, the Packaging and Deployment Wizard. This utility will help create a professional setup quickly. However, there are a few things to keep in mind. In this exercise, we will use the setup utility to distribute a VB application and then customize the setup for a company.

USING THE PACKAGE AND DEPLOYMENT WIZARD

Step 1

Open the Help Desk application created in Exercise 7-1. If you did not do this exercise, locate the completed exercise on the CD-ROM. Once the project is open, load the Package and Deployment Wizard from the Add-in manager by selecting **ADD-INS/ADD-IN MANAGER** from the menu. Once the Wizard is loaded, start it from the menu by selecting **ADD-INS/PACKAGE AND DEPLOYMENT WIZARD**.

Step 2

A Visual Basic setup requires many files. In fact, these files will generally require two floppy disks before *any* of the code is distributed to the target machine. The good news, however, is that most of these files are *shared* files, which means that they only have to be on a computer one time and all Visual Basic applications can use them simultaneously. Shared files are generally stored in the \WINDOWS\SYSTEM directory.

Step 3

From the first step of the Wizard, we can perform a traditional packaging or a deployment to an Internet site. For our application, we will build a typical product installation for CD-ROM. Push the **Package** button.

Step 4

If the application has not already been compiled, the Wizard will prompt to compile it now. If necessary, compile the application and save the project when prompted.

Step 5

Now the Wizard asks whether to create a standard setup package or a dependency file. Dependency files are lists of files that components rely upon for distribution. For this exercise choose **Standard Setup Package**. Push the **Next** button.

Step 6

Now the Wizard will ask for a location to build the CAB file for the setup. Select to create a new directory underneath the HelpDesk application called \PACKAGE. Choose this directory. Push the **Next** button.

Step 7

The next step shows all the files that will become part of the installation. The Add... button here is used to bring up a dialog permitting inclusion of more files such as bitmaps, icons, or data files. Since the Wizard cannot know everything about the project, supply the names of additional files, if any. In this example, we have no additional files, so just investigate the Add... button by clicking it and then push the **Cancel** button. Push the **Next** button.

Step 8

In this step the Wizard asks if a single CAB or multiple CAB files are required. A single CAB is for CD-ROM distribution while multiple CABs are used for floppy disk distribution. For our exercise, select a single CAB file. Push the **Next** button.

Step 9

In this step, the Wizard asks for a title to appear when the setup runs. This entry is not critical, so call this Help Desk Request. Push the **Next** button.

Step 10

In this step, the Wizard asks for information about icons. It offers a standard group and icon which will work fine for the application. Those who are operating in Windows/NT should make sure that the program group created by the Wizard is a common group. This can be done by selecting the program group and pushing the **Properties** button. Push the **Next** button.

Step 11

In this step, the Wizard will allow us to change the installation target of the executable. We normally choose to install an application in AppPath$, which means the EXE file will be installed in a directory selected by the user during installation. Push the **Next** button.

Step 12

In this step, the Wizard asks about installing any files as *shared* files. Shared files can be used by more than one application. The operating system keeps track of the number of applications using the files. Shared files are only removed from the system if all applications using them are also removed. For our exercise, we do not need to check any boxes in this step. Push the **Next** button.

Step 13

Now the Wizard is finished. We can save a macro of our work by a key name. For our exercise, just accept the default name provided by the Wizard. Push the **Finish** button. The installation program is ready.

INSTALLING THE APPLICATION

Step 14

Before running the setup, go to the Windows Explorer and navigate to the \PACKAGE directory to view the files created by the Wizard. There are several key files here. All the files used by the application have been built into one single CAB file. The Wizard has created a bootstrap file called SETUP.EXE that users actually run to install the software.

Step 15

The Wizard has also created a third file called SETUP.LST. This file contains all the information necessary to properly install the files. Using the setup wizard is what generates this file. To change the application name that appears in the setup, realize that the setup gets the name from SETUP.LST. During the processing, the Wizard picks up the Application Title specified and writes it to SETUP.LST. Later, SETUP1.EXE reads this file, a simple text file that can be viewed in any text editor. To view this file, run NotePad from the Accessories group and open the file SETUP.LST. Be careful not to change the contents.

Step 16

After examining the contents of the \SETUP directory, run the file SETUP.EXE from the command line. The setup utility prompts for all the steps necessary to install the software. Follow the directions and when done, run the application to verify that it works.

UNINSTALLING SOFTWARE

Step 17

Windows 95 and Windows NT both support the concept of uninstalling software. Uninstall is supported by Visual Basic applications with no special work from the programmer. Go to the Settings\Control Panel and select **Add\Remove Software**. A dialog appears with several programs listed. To uninstall the application, double click on **Help Desk Request**. The uninstall runs and removes the program. Notice that all the files are removed.

CUSTOMIZING SETUP

Step 18

Although the Wizard provides a fairly good setup right out of the box, quite often we want to customize the look of an installation program. In this section, we will add a custom banner to the setup. When the Wizard builds a setup, it actually creates a Visual Basic application. In VB 6.0 the file is SETUP1.EXE. Start up Visual Basic. Locate the Visual Basic project built by the Wizard. The project is called SETUP1.VBP and is located in the \VB98\WIZARDS\PDWIZARD\SETUP1 directory. Open this project.

Step 19

The designers of this SETUP1 project have created it so that all customization can be accomplished using the form named frmSetup1. Select this form in the project window and push the **View Form** button. A form will be visible as a rectangle with a blue background and some label controls on it. Upsize this.

Step 20

With the form frmSetup1 visible, drop a new label control on the blue portion of the form. Select the label control and change its properties as follows:

Left	100
Top	100
Height	45
Width	600
BackStyle	0-Transparent
ForeColor	White
Font-Size	18
Caption	Your Company Name

Step 21

Now we have to build the distribution file by hand, since we are overriding the files created by the Wizard. Build an executable of the custom setup by selecting the **File/Make EXE** menu command. When prompted, select to replace the existing SETUP1.EXE file in the \SUPPORT directory with the new one.

Step 22

Close Visual Basic. What we just did was alter the file SETUP1.EXE, which is gathered during the processing of the setup wizard. The startup form of SETUP1.EXE now has the company name.

Step 23

Now we have customized the setup. Run the PROJECT1.BAT file in the \SUPPORT directory to build a new CAB file. Run the new installation to see the customized setup.

FOR THE CERTIFIED PRO

Pro 7-1: Resource Files

1. Create an animated stop light using three stop light icons found on the CD-ROM: TRFFC10A, TRFFC10B, TRFFC10C.
2. Put the icons in a resource file and read them out one at a time using a timer control.

Pro 7-2: Package and Deployment Wizard

1. Customize the Package and Deployment Wizard to use a company logo.
2. Create a setup with the customized installation.

PREPARING FOR CERTIFICATION

Topics for Further Reading
  Visual Basic Coding Conventions
  Working with Control Arrays
  Adding Help to an Application
  Distributing Visual Basic Applications

CERTIFICATION QUIZ

1. The primary purpose of compiling to native code as opposed to p-code is:
    a. security, since native code cannot be readily decompiled, making the code more secure.
    b. runtime speed of execution.
    c. the ability to optimize the code for speed or size.
    d. Both a and c

2. When calling a function in an API:
   a. use a Declare Function or Declare Sub statement in the [General] [Declarations] of the form that contains the call to the API procedure.
   b. always pass any arguments "by value."
   c. use a Declare Function or Declare Sub statement to establish the dynamic link between the application and the API procedure.
   d. None of the above

3. The setup wizard relies upon what EXE that ships with Visual Basic to perform installations that are customized by the user?
   a. SETUP.EXE
   b. COMPRESS.EXE
   c. SETUP1.EXE
   d. All of the above

4. When a VB executable is created, to which default directory does the EXE get written?
   a. The root directory
   b. The VB installation directory
   c. The project directory
   d. The /SWSETUP directory

5. The name of the runtime module for VB version 6 is:
   a. VMVBMS60.DLL
   b. VBVMMS60.DLL
   c. MSVMVB60.DLL
   d. MSVBVM60.DLL

6. When an application is looking for a DLL, the first place it looks is:
   a. the root directory
   b. the /WINDOWS/SYSTEM directory
   c. the working directory for the application
   d. memory

7. The VB project that can be customized by the user before beginning the setup creation process is located in:
   a. the VB installation directory.
   b. the /SWSETUP directory.
   c. the WIZARDS\PDWIZARDS\SETUP1 directory found under the VB installation directory.
   d. the /SETUPKIT/SETUP directory found under the VB installation directory.

8. Every VB application has an application title and is set from the Project/Properties menu command of VB. What is the title used for, within the context of creating the setup for the application?
   a. It is used as the name of the setup's EXE.
   b. It is used in the setup screen to label the setup with the name of the application that is being installed.
   c. Both a and b
   d. None of the above

9. Which files distributed with the VB application do not appear anywhere in the application's VBP file?
   a. Custom controls
   b. Reusable ActiveX components
   c. Dynamic Link Libraries
   d. None of the above

ANSWERS TO CERTIFICATION QUIZ

1. d
2. c
3. a, c
4. c
5. d
6. d
7. c
8. b
9. c

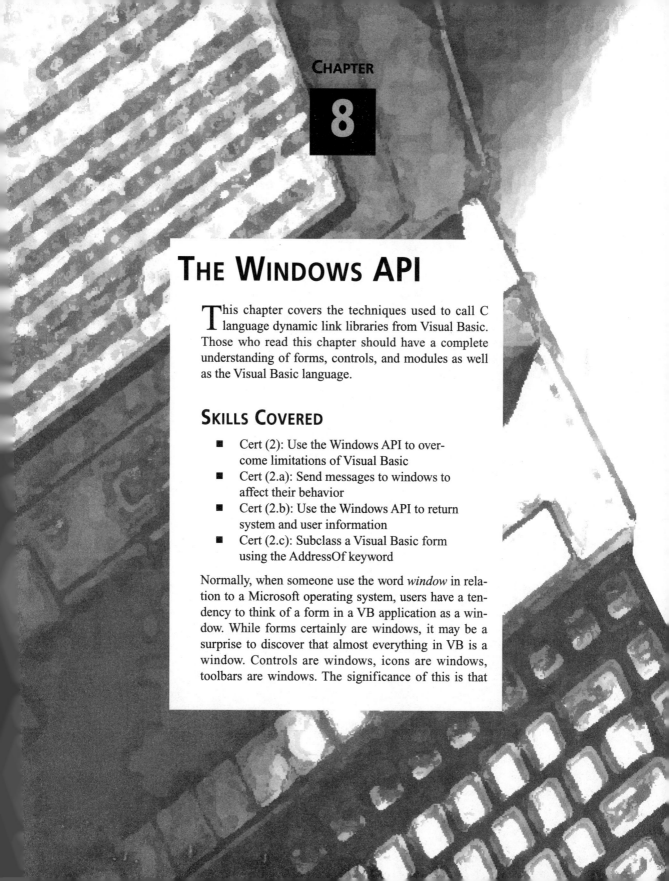

8

THE WINDOWS API

This chapter covers the techniques used to call C language dynamic link libraries from Visual Basic. Those who read this chapter should have a complete understanding of forms, controls, and modules as well as the Visual Basic language.

SKILLS COVERED

- Cert (2): Use the Windows API to overcome limitations of Visual Basic
- Cert (2.a): Send messages to windows to affect their behavior
- Cert (2.b): Use the Windows API to return system and user information
- Cert (2.c): Subclass a Visual Basic form using the AddressOf keyword

Normally, when someone use the word *window* in relation to a Microsoft operating system, users have a tendency to think of a form in a VB application as a window. While forms certainly are windows, it may be a surprise to discover that almost everything in VB is a window. Controls are windows, icons are windows, toolbars are windows. The significance of this is that the windows operating system functions by sending streams of communications called *messages* between windows in the system. Visual Basic 6.0 is tightly integrated with the Windows operating system. In fact, the events recognized by Visual Basic map directly to messages sent between windows. The functionality provided by Visual Basic is really just a subset of the overall features provided by the Windows operating system. Normally, the features of Visual Basic are sufficient for many types of applications; however, VB does not support all of the functionality provided by the Windows operating system. When Visual Basic's native functionality is not sufficient for our needs we can make calls directly to the operating system and overcome many limitations..

Every user of a VB application is by definition a Windows user. Users have on their desktops the functionality of the Windows Application Programmer's Interface (API). The Windows API function libraries are Dynamic Link Libraries (DLLs) containing over 800 individual function calls available to the VB application. Since VB is a Windows programming language, almost all the functions in the API are available to the program. Many of these functions have the potential to enhance the application and reduce the number of files that must be installed with the EXE.

The Windows API is a vast store of functions. Within the API is support for initialization files, Windows messaging, drawing, and memory management. The core functions of the API are contained in three libraries: KERNEL32, USER32, and GDI32. These files contain substantially all the functions in the Windows API. Unfortunately, the documentation on how to use these functions does not ship with VB. This means the theory of operation on the API functions must be learned from some other source. There is some help in the form of books and periodicals that focus on VB. Documentation is also available from the Microsoft Developer Network CD-ROM, which includes all the tools and documentation Microsoft publishes to create Windows applications. In this chapter, we will examine some of the best uses for the API by solving common programming problems.

Although the Windows API resides in a set of Dynamic Link Libraries—which normally have a DLL extension—the 16-bit libraries KERNEL, USER, and GDI all end with .EXE. This curiosity is explained with a brief history lesson. In the early days of Windows programming, the .EXE extension was used for all libraries. Later, Microsoft adopted the .DLL extension for function libraries that linked at run time—*dynamic linking*. However, independent software vendors had already created applications with calls to the KERNEL, USER, and GDI so to this day, the core DLLs that hold the Windows API end with .EXE, not .DLL. Increased programming experience will cause almost every DLL connected to VB programs to end with .DLL. These files are usually written in the C or C++ languages, but can be written in Pascal, Delphi, or any programming system that supports DLL output.

When Windows starts, it loads KERNEL32, USER32, and GDI32 into memory. These are DLLs. A DLL can be shared by many applications which make calls to the functions in these libraries that are loaded into memory. Since one copy of the DLL serves many applications, each application makes calls as needed to the functions in the library. This is accomplished through dynamic linking. Unlike static linking, in which the functions called are linked with the program to form an executable program, dynamic linking takes a different approach. With dynamic linking, each application that wants to call a function in a library can link to that library dynamically at run time. Each application contains a statement that is declarative in nature. This statement specifies the library name, function name, arguments passed in, and return value. Armed with this information, each application can link dynamically to the function library and call the functions that reside within the DLL. The first place an application looks for a DLL it wants to link to is memory. Thus, when a VB application attempts to link to USER32, it looks to memory, finds the library, links to it, and obtains services in the form of callable functions. (If the specified DLL is not in memory, the VB application will use the Windows search path to find the DLL and load it, looking first in the /SYSTEM directory of the Windows installation.)

Running the Windows operating system will show the Windows desktop, but that is not really the operating system. The desktop is just a Windows application. The desktop application could be terminated and other applications would still remain running. The desktop is just an instance of an application that calls into the functions found in the Windows API. Similarly, VB applications can use these functions.

Since VB is a complete language for Windows programming, it supports calls to functions in DLLs. This is accomplished via the Declare Function statement, which specifies all the pertinent details needed to link to the DLL and call a specific function. The Declare Function statement typically is coded in the [General][Declarations] of a standard module although it may exist as a private member of a class. As an example, the API makes it possible to determine the directory where Windows is installed on the current machine, with the GetWindowsDirectory function.

```
Public Declare Function GetWindowsDirectory _
    Lib "kernel32" Alias "GetWindowsDirectoryA" _
    (ByVal lpBuffer As String, ByVal nSize As Long) As Long
```

The Declare Function statement specifies the function name as it will be used by the application and also specifies the module name where the function is defined. In this case, the function is found in the KERNEL32 library. The Alias clause is optional and used only when the name used to refer to the function differs from the actual name. The actual name always follows the Alias clause, which may seem counterintuitive. The Alias clause is useful in many situations when it is impossible to use the actual name in a program because of conflicts with reserved words, other procedure names, and so on. In this case the alias has a secondary purpose. The 32-bit version of Windows supports two types of function calls—one for ASCII text and one for UNICODE. These functions are known as ASCII and *wide* functions respectively. In the API, are functions subscripted with *A* for ASCII and *W* for wide. VB always converts its string data types to ASCII when they are sent to an external function, therefore always use the *A* functions from Visual Basic.

After the function is declared, an argument list follows. The prefix *lp* means *long pointer*; this is Hungarian prefixing, used by C programmers. The Windows API is for the most part written by and for C and C++ developers. As a result, most of the documentation follows C coding conventions, down to the prefixing. All the arguments are passed by value, which is the C default for arguments passed in. The GetWindowsDirectory takes two arguments: the first is a String and the second is a Long.

GetWindowsDirectory works by returning a string which is placed inside the variable passed to the function. The function, like many API functions, needs to know the length of the String being passed. Typically, we pass a fixed-length string to a function like this which is subsequently filled by the API call. A fixed-length string used to return data from a function is referred to as a *buffer*. The Windows API defines many informational function calls that write data to a buffer. These include not only GetWindowsDirectory, but also GetTempPath, GetSystemDirectory, GetLogicalDriveStrings, GetCurrentDirectory, GetComputerName, and GetUserName.

The key to understanding the function declaration process is to recognize that any function from any DLL may be declared in a similar format. The problem for programmers trying to use this functionality, however, is that they are not sure exactly *what* functions to declare even if they understand *how* they are declared. Visual Basic can help through the use of an add-in called the *API Viewer* which contains all the function declarations likely to be needed in VB programs. To use the API Viewer, type the first few letters of the function required and the viewer yields the declaration.

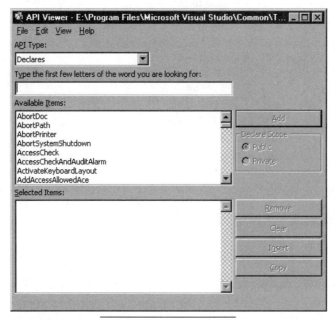

Figure 8-1 The API Viewer

Check It Out 8-1: Returning System Information

1. Start a new Visual Basic Standard EXE project. Add a module to the new project by selecting **PROJECT/ADD MODULE...** from the menu.
2. Load the API Viewer add-in through the Add-In Manager by selecting **ADD-INS/ADD-IN MANAGER...** from the menu.

3. Once the API Viewer is loaded, run the viewer by selecting **ADD-INS/API VIEWER**.
4. The API Viewer uses a text file to hold function declarations. Load the appropriate text file into the viewer by selecting **FILE/LOAD TEXT FILE** from the viewer menu. From this item, locate and load the file **WIN32API.TXT**.
5. Once the API declarations are loaded, use the Available Items list to locate the following functions:

```
GetWindowsDirectory
GetTempPath
GetSystemDirectory
GetCurrentDirectory
GetComputerName
GetUserName
```

6. Add the declarations into the Selected Items list. When all the declarations are added, press the **Insert** button to copy them to Module1.
7. Close the API Viewer and open the Code window for Module1. The following code should be visible:

```
Public Declare Function GetUserName Lib "advapi32.dll" _
   Alias "GetUserNameA" _
(ByVal lpBuffer As String, nSize As Long) As Long
Public Declare Function GetWindowsDirectory Lib "kernel32" _
   Alias "GetWindowsDirectoryA" _
(ByVal lpBuffer As String, ByVal nSize As Long) As Long
Public Declare Function GetTempPath Lib "kernel32" _
   Alias "GetTempPathA" _
(ByVal nBufferLength As Long, ByVal lpBuffer As String) As Long
Public Declare Function GetSystemDirectory Lib "kernel32" _
   Alias "GetSystemDirectoryA" _
(ByVal lpBuffer As String, ByVal nSize As Long) As Long
Public Declare Function GetCurrentDirectory Lib "kernel32" _
   Alias "GetCurrentDirectoryA" _
(ByVal nBufferLength As Long, ByVal lpBuffer As String) As Long
Public Declare Function GetComputerName Lib "kernel32" _
   Alias "GetComputerNameA" _
(ByVal lpBuffer As String, nSize As Long) As Long
```

8. Each of the informational functions above takes a string buffer and its length as arguments. However, the order of the arguments is reversed in several of the calls. When each call is made, we fill a buffer with blank spaces and the call writes the data into the buffer. Add the following code to the Form_Load event for Form1 to show the items in message boxes.

```
Dim strBuffer As String * 255
Dim lngReturn As Long

'Get UserID
strBuffer = Space$(255)
lngReturn = GetUserName(strBuffer, 255)
MsgBox "User Name: " & _
  Left$(strBuffer, InStr(strBuffer, Chr(0)) - 1)

'Get Windows Directory
strBuffer = Space$(255)
lngReturn = GetWindowsDirectory(strBuffer, 255)
MsgBox "Windows Directory: " & _
  Left$(strBuffer, InStr(strBuffer, Chr(0)) - 1)

'Get Temp Directory
strBuffer = Space$(255)
lngReturn = GetTempPath(255, strBuffer)
MsgBox "Temp Directory: " & _
  Left$(strBuffer, InStr(strBuffer, Chr(0)) - 1)

'Get System Directory
strBuffer = Space$(255)
lngReturn = GetSystemDirectory(strBuffer, 255)
MsgBox "System Directory: " & _
  Left$(strBuffer, InStr(strBuffer, Chr(0)) - 1)

'Get Current Directory
strBuffer = Space$(255)
lngReturn = GetCurrentDirectory(255, strBuffer)
MsgBox "Current Directory: " & _
  Left$(strBuffer, InStr(strBuffer, Chr(0)) - 1)

'Get Computer Name
strBuffer = Space$(255)
lngReturn = GetComputerName(strBuffer, 255)
MsgBox "Computer Name: " & _
  Left$(strBuffer, InStr(strBuffer, Chr(0)) - 1)
```

9. Run the application and view the information.

WINDOW HANDLES

An informational function such as `GetWindowsDirectory` is a simple example of functions that perform a useful task. However, much of the Windows API relies upon a programming device known as a window handle which is used to identify, manipulate, and communicate with a window. In Visual Basic, the window handle can be obtained from the `hWnd` property which returns a Long integer (the system handle for the window). Since most controls in VB are also windows, there will be `hWnd` properties for controls like ListBoxes, TextBoxes, and many others. After the handle is obtained, it can be used to manipulate the associated window.

Check It Out 8-2: Creating a top most window

1. Start a new Visual Basic Standard EXE project. Add a module to the new project by selecting **PROJECT/ADD MODULE...** from the menu.
2. Load the API Viewer add-in through the Add-In Manager by selecting **ADD-INS/ADD-IN MANAGER...** from the menu.
3. Once the API Viewer is loaded, run the viewer by selecting **DIAGRAM/API VIEWER**.
4. The API Viewer uses a text file to hold function declarations. Load the appropriate text file into the viewer by selecting **FILE/LOAD TEXT FILE** from the viewer menu. From this item, locate and load the file **WIN32API.TXT**.
5. Once the API declarations are loaded, use the Available Items list to locate the following function:

   `SetWindowPos`

6. Add the declaration into the Selected Items list. When all the declarations are added, press the **Insert** button to copy them to Module1.
7. Close the API Viewer and open the Code window for Module1. Paste the function declarations into the code window. The following code should be visible:

   ```
   Public Declare Function SetWindowPos Lib "user32" _
   (ByVal hwnd As Long, ByVal hWndInsertAfter As Long, _
   ByVal x As Long, ByVal y As Long, ByVal cx As Long, _
   ByVal cy As Long, ByVal wFlags As Long) As Long
   ```

8. The `SetWindowPos` function takes a window and moves it or resizes it. In and of itself, moving and resizing a window is not extremely useful, though this call can also set the Z-order of the window. This will allow us to create a window that floats on top of all other windows. This kind of floating window is referred to as a *top most* window.
9. The first argument for `SetWindowPos` is the handle of the window to act on. The second argument is the operation to perform. Remember, `SetWindowPos` will perform many functions, but we are only interested in making it float. The next four arguments are *x* and *y* coordinates for moving and resizing. We will set

these values to zero and ignore them. The last argument is for setting options. Here is where we will tell the function to ignore sizing and moving.

10. In general, it is always a good idea to declare constants for function calls. In the [General][Declarations] section of Module1, add the following constant declarations.

```
Public Const ntsTopMost = -1
Public Const ntsNoMove = 1
Public Const ntsNoSize = 2
```

11. Now add a new form to the application by selecting **PROJECT/ADD FORM...** from the menu. We will use this form to show how Form1 floats.

12. Now open the Code window for Form1. In the `Form_Load` event of Form1, add the following code to show both forms, but make Form1 *top most*.

```
Form1.Show
Form2.Show


Dim lngReturn As Long
lngReturn = SetWindowPos(Me.hwnd, ntsTopMost, _
              0, 0, 0, 0, ntsNoSize Or ntsNoMove)
```

13. Run the application. Note how Form1 is in front of Form2. Try clicking on **Form2** to make it the active form. Notice that the title of Form2 changes color indicating it is active, but it will not move in front of Form1. That is because Form1 occupies the *top most* position. Only one form can be topmost at any time. Do not confuse this behavior with modal behavior. Modal forms prevent other forms from becoming active. In this case, Form2 can be made active, it just will not move in front of Form1.

The hWnd property in VB makes it simple to perform operations on forms and controls in an application. To perform an API operation on a window that is part of another application such as Excel or Notepad it will be necessary to call an API function to obtain the window handle. One function that performs this operation is called `FindWindow()`. As an example, let us say NotePad is running and the window caption of NotePad should be changed to the name of the application. Here are the steps:

1. Obtain the handle of NotePad's main window by calling the API function `FindWindow()`. This function returns the handle to the window specified.

2. Use the NotePad window handle to call the `SetWindowText()` API function. This function places new text in the window caption of the specified window.

Check It Out 8-3: Changing the Text of an Application's Window Caption

1. Start a new VB Standard EXE project.
2. Add a standard module to the application. Start the API Text Viewer.

3. Use the Text Viewer to find the Declare statements for the functions `FindWindow` and `SetWindowText`. Insert the declarations into Module1.

4. Now drop a CommandButton on Form1 and add this code under the `Command1_Click` event. This will call the `FindWindow()` API function to retrieve the window handle. The code displays it with a MsgBox:

```
Dim hWndNOTEPAD As Long
hWndNOTEPAD = FindWindow(vbNullString, "Untitled - Notepad")
MsgBox hWndNOTEPAD
```

5. Start Notepad. Run the application and click on **Command1**. A nonzero number should be displayed by the MsgBox. This number is not used directly but is passed along to API functions that require the value. This step is just to verify the window handle. Also, note the use of the `vbNullString` constant as the first parameter passed to `FindWindow()`. This parameter specifies the window class, something we do not cover here. Specifying `vbNullString` tells `FindWindow()` that we are not specifying the window class name. The second parameter specifies the window title we are looking for. Before running this test code, make sure that NotePad is started and that the title **Untitled-Notepad** is the window caption for this application's main window. If it is not, be sure to use the precise text displayed by NotePad when running this sample code. If the text does not exactly match, `FindWindow()` will return zero. Make sure there is a nonzero value for the window handle before proceeding to the next step.

6. Now use the window handle to manipulate NotePad, changing the title of the NotePad window to VB BOOTCAMP.

7. `SetWindowText()` is the function used to alter the caption of a window. This is analogous to saying `Form1.Caption = "My title"` in VB code, but uses an API call to deal with a window not in the application. The first parameter to `SetWindowText()` is the handle of the window to edit. The second parameter is the new window text. Add this code to the code already found under Form1's `Command1_Click`:

```
Dim r As Integer
r = SetWindowText(hWndNOTEPAD, "VB BOOTCAMP")
```

8. Bring NotePad into view as the application is run. When Form1 appears, click **Command1** and watch what happens. The window title of the NotePad window should change to VB BOOTCAMP. Now reset the title bar by selecting **FILE/NEW** from the Notepad menu.

9. It is also possible to *nest* the function calls to make the code more compact. This completed code would work under Command1:

```
Dim r As Integer
r = _
SetWindowText(FindWindow(vbNullString, _
            "Untitled - Notepad"), "VB BOOTCAMP")
```

Using the API can be simple if the programmer knows what to accomplish, understands the mechanics, knows the API calls to execute, and also knows the details of the arguments passed to each function. Teaching every aspect of the Windows API is beyond the scope of this book. However, we did just learn the details of the FindWindow() and SetWindowText API calls while learning more about window handles. API programming is an advanced topic. An understanding of the concepts and facilities of calling API functions, and especially the Declare Function statement is required in order to create or modify production VB applications.

WINDOWS MESSAGES

Messages are the primary communication mechanism in the Windows environment. They are sent between windows to request activity, set attributes, and announce events. Messages are also integral to the functions of Visual Basic. VB has the ability to listen to the messages sent from various components, such as buttons and textboxes, and respond when a key message is heard. For example, double clicking on a list box in a Visual Basic application causes a Windows message to fire, which in turn causes the DblClick event code to execute. The event model in Visual Basic is one of listening to the message stream and responding by executing event code.

The Windows API allows us not only to listen to the various messages, but also to send our own messages. This latter can be useful in accessing functionality that has not been exposed in Visual Basic itself. Sending messages is accomplished through the SendMessage and PostMessage functions.

Before programmers can understand how the SendMessage and PostMessage functions work, they must understand how a window processes a message. All windows have a special function for processing messages known as the Window Function. The Window Function is responsible for receiving and processing messages sent to a window. The messages themselves are little more than long integer values processed by the Window Function. Think of it as a large Select Case statement that takes a different branch for each unique message received.

Because a window may receive more than one message at a time, every window supports a message queue for keeping messages that have not yet been processed by the Window Function. Messages sent to a window may be sent either directly to the Window Function or to the message queue. The SendMessage function sends a message by calling the Window function directly. The call to the window does not return to the client application until the message has been processed by the Window function. The PostMessage on the other hand, sends a message to the message queue for later processing by the window. The call to PostMessage returns to the calling client immediately after the message is placed in the queue but before the message is actually processed.

THE SENDMESSAGE FUNCTION

The SendMessage function is part of USER and can be declared using the following syntax:

```
Public Declare Function SendMessage Lib "user32" _
      Alias "SendMessageA" _
```

```
(ByVal hwnd As Long, ByVal wMsg As Long, ByVal wParam As Long, _
lParam As Any) As Long
```

The hWnd argument for the SendMessage function is the window handle for the window that will receive the message, an identifier used by Windows uniquely to represent every window in the operating system. This argument can be accessed for any form or control in Visual Basic by simply referencing the hWnd property.

The wMsg argument for the SendMessage function is the actual message to send. The available messages are many and varied. A complete description of every message that can be sent is beyond the scope of this book; this chapter will show examples for some of the more common messages.

The wParam and lParam arguments essentially provide a mechanism for passing additional information with the message. The type of information sent using these arguments varies based on the message being sent. Again, the possible values for these arguments are many, but once the function is declared, it is a simple matter of calling the function from Visual Basic to send the appropriate message. As an example, consider the message LB_SELECTSTRING, which can be sent to a Visual Basic ListBox. This message forces a ListBox to search for and highlight an entry matching a text string provided. The declaration for the message constant is this:

```
Public Const LB_SELECTSTRING = &H18C
```

Searching a ListBox named List1 requires making a call to SendMessage with the appropriate arguments. The following code shows how to search List1 for the text string "New Technology Solutions":

```
Dim lngReturn As Long
lngReturn = SendMessage(List1.hwnd, LB_SELECTSTRING, ByVal -1, _
ByVal "New Technology Solutions")
```

THE POSTMESSAGE FUNCTION

The PostMessage function is similar to the SendMessage function and has the following syntax:

```
Public Declare Function PostMessage Lib "user32" _
      Alias "PostMessageA" _
(ByVal hwnd As Long, ByVal wMsg As Long, ByVal wParam As Long, _
ByVal lParam As Any) As Long
```

Note that the arguments for the PostMessage function are identical to those for the SendMessage function. The only difference is when the message is processed. The PostMessage function should be used in cases where the return value of the function is not important. This is because PostMessage cannot return a meaningful value since the message was not processed by the Window Function before the call returned.

SUBCLASSING WINDOWS

Although every window provides a Window Function for processing messages, it may some-times be desirable to provide custom message processing. In this case, Visual Basic allows sub-stitution of a custom function for the default Window Function. The process of creating a sub-stitute Windows Function is known as *subclassing* a window. Subclassing relies on SetWindowLong function to specify the function that will act as the Window Function. The SetWindowLong function is declared as follows:

```
Public Declare Function SetWindowLong Lib "user32" Alias _
"SetWindowLongA" (ByVal hwnd As Long, _
ByVal nIndex As Long, ByVal dwNewLong As Long) As Long
```

The SetWindowLong function is used for changing the attributes of any particular window for which there is a handle. The hWnd argument is the window handle for the window to subclass. The nIndex argument specifies the type of window information to set. The constant GWL_WNDPROC tells the function to set the address for the Windows Function, and dwNewLong is the address of the new Window Function.

Notice that SetWindowLong relies on knowing the address in memory of the function to be the new Window Function. Until version 5.0, function addresses could not be retrieved for Visual Basic functions. However, in VB 5.0, the AddressOf keyword was added to return the address in memory of a custom function. The only restriction is that the new Window Function should be declared inside a Standard Module and not a form or Class Module.

As a simple example of subclassing, we have created a spy tool that displays all the mes-sages received by a Visual Basic form. This example simply shows messages sent to a form inside a TextBox. The new Windows function is declared inside a Standard Module using the following code:

```
Public Function WindowProc(ByVal hw As Long, ByVal uMsg As Long, _
ByVal wParam As Long, ByVal lParam As Long) As Long
  'This is the CallBack function that will intercept
  'all of the messages from the subclassed
  'window.
  frmSpy.txtMessages.Text = _
  "Message: hWnd(" & hw & "), Msg(" & uMsg & _
  "), wParam(" & wParam & "), lParam(" & lParam & ")" _
  & vbCrLf & frmSpy.txtMessages.Text
End Function
```

The arguments of the new procedure are strictly defined and match the arguments passed by the SendMessage function. This makes perfect sense since the new function will be called directly by any SendMessage call. Inside the function, the messages are simply printed in a textbox and the function exits. In most cases, however, it will not be desirable to exit after examining a message; the message will need to be passed along to the previous Window Func-tion. This allows the window to process the message after the code is complete. Passing the message to the original Window Function is done with the `CallWindowProc` function, which is declared as follows:

```
Public Declare Function CallWindowProc Lib "user32" Alias _
"CallWindowProcA" (ByVal lpPrevWndFunc As Long, _
ByVal hwnd As Long, ByVal Msg As Long, _
ByVal wParam As Long, ByVal lParam As Long) As Long
```

This function takes as arguments the same arguments that were passed by `SendMessage` with the addition of the `lpPrevWndFunc` argument. The `lpPrevWndFunc` argument is the address of the original Window Function, which is returned by the call to `SetWindowLong`. Therefore, in order to subclass a window, call `SetWindowLong` and save the return value that refers to the original function. This is called *hooking* the window. The following code hooks the window and sets the Window Function to `WindowProc` using the `AddressOf` keyword:

```
lpPrevWndProc = SetWindowLong(frmSpy.hWnd, GWL_WNDPROC, _
AddressOf WindowProc)
```

When the application is closed, we also want to unhook the window, that is, set the Window Function back to the original function because our application is no longer available. Unhooking the window is done with another call to `SetWindowLong`, but this time we pass the original function address.

```
Dim lngTemp As Long
lngTemp = SetWindowLong(frmSpy.hWnd, GWL_WNDPROC, lpPrevWndProc)
```

Subclassing windows makes it essentially possible to create events in Visual Basic that are not normally supported. Hook a window and then examine the message stream that enters the function. When a given message is detected, execute code much as Visual Basic fires an event. It might even be desirable to use the `RaiseEvent` keyword to fire a custom event in code. Custom events are discussed in detail in Chapter 13.

RECEIVING CALLBACKS

A callback is another technique that utilizes the `AddressOf` keyword. It makes it possible to send a pointer to a custom function and have Windows call that function periodically. Windows provides many functions that use callbacks and some of the most common are the *enumerated* functions.

Enumerated functions are designed to make callbacks and provide data. For example, the function `EnumChildWindows` makes a call to the callback function once for each child window of a parent window specified. In this way, callbacks are used to provide a list of data to the program. To use an enumerated function, declare it just as for any API call. The following is the declaration for `EnumChildWindows`:

```
Public Declare Function EnumChildWindows _
```

```
Lib "user32" (ByVal hWndParent As Long, _
ByVal lpEnumFunc As Long, ByVal lParam As Long) As Long
```

This function accepts as arguments the window handle of the parent window, a pointer to the callback function, and a user-defined parameter that holds data of interest. Once the function is declared, the callback function must be created.

Enumerated functions have specific requirements for the arguments provided in a callback. The argument list varies according to each enumerated function. For EnumChildWindows, the callback function must provide three long data types to return the window handle of each child window and associated data. The following is the declaration for a callback used with EnumChildWindows:

```
Public Sub Enumerate(ByVal lngHandle As Long, ByVal lngData As Long, _
lngReturn As Long)
```

Exercise 8-1: Using Messages

The Windows API is a collection of C-Language function calls housed in several DLLs. These libraries provide all the functions associated with the Windows OS. The primary libraries inside Windows are KERNEL32, USER32, and GDI32, which may be accessed directly from Visual Basic projects. In this exercise, we will use the functions of the Windows API to add functions to a standard VB list box. In particular, we will add an incremental search feature and a horizontal scroll bar.

When calls are made using the Windows API, there is no error handling. This means that incorrect code will cause the system to crash. Save this project before running any part of it so as not to lose all the work!

THE API TEXT VIEWER

Step 1

Create a new directory in the File Explorer called **VB BOOTCAMP\EXERCISE8-1**. Start a new Visual Basic Standard EXE project. Add a Standard Module to the project by selecting **PROJECT/ADD MODULE** from the menu. The Standard Module is used to keep the declaration statements for API calls.

Step 2

Add a Sub Main to the project by selecting **TOOLS/ADD PROCEDURE** from the menu. Set the project up to start from Sub Main by changing the Start Form option under the PROJECT/PROPERTIES... menu.

Step 3

In the Add-in manager, load the API Text Viewer, which can subsequently be accessed by selecting **ADD-INS/API VIEWER**. When the API Text Viewer is visible, load the declarations by selecting **FILE/LOAD TEXT FILE...** and selecting **WIN32API.TXT** as the file to load. When the file is loaded, all the API declarations are available.

Begin typing **Send Message** until the item is selected in the **Available Items** list. Then click **Add** to put the declaration in the Selected Items list. Now press the **Insert** button to add the declaration to the project. This function permits sending a message to any component in the Windows OS.

The types of messages that can be sent to the list box are defined as constants in the API Text Viewer. Copy these message constants to the clipboard as well. In the API Type box, select **Constants**. The message constants will load and can be selected from the list. Select the following constants:

```
LB_SELECTSTRING
LB_SETHORIZONTALEXTENT
```

Step 4

Now click the **Insert** button to paste the declaration in the [General][Declarations] section of the Standard Module. The declarations tell VB about the function to call, which is part of the Windows API. The following code is pasted in:

```
Declare Function SendMessage Lib "user32" Alias "SendMessageA" _
(ByVal hwnd As Long, ByVal wMsg As Long, ByVal wParam As Long, _
lParam As Long) As Long
Public Const LB_SETHORIZONTALEXTENT = &H194
Public Const LB_SELECTSTRING = &H18C
```

The constants defined represent the actual messages being sent using this API. These messages will actually cause the incremental searching behavior and allow a horizontal scroll bar to appear.

INCREMENTAL SEARCH

Step 5

On Form 1 place a TextBox and a ListBox. Call the textbox **txtAPI** and the list box **lstAPI**. In the Sub Main routine, display this form and add text entries by coding. Remember to set Sub Main as the Startup Object in the Project Properties dialog.

```
Form1.Show
Form1.lstApi.AddItem "Dan"
Form1.lstApi.AddItem "Dave"
Form1.lstApi.AddItem "David"
Form1.lstApi.AddItem "Davidson"
```

Step 6

Implementing the incremental search is now as simple as calling the SendMessage function. Add the following code to the txtAPI_Change event so that the incremental search occurs while we type:

```
'Make sure something is in the box
If Len(txtAPI.Text) = 0 Then Exit Sub
Dim lngResult As Long
'Make the call to search the List Box
lngResult = SendMessage(1stAPI.hwnd, LB_SELECTSTRING, _
ByVal -1, ByVal txtAPI.Text)
```

This code uses the window handle for the list box (given by the hWnd Property) to send a message to search for the given text in the list box. Accessing the handle is a matter of using the hWnd property of the list box. Many components in VB have hWnd properties that allow messages to be sent to them. Investigate the hWnd property in the VB Help file.

HORIZONTAL SCROLL BAR

Step 7

The standard Visual Basic list box provides a vertical scroll bar whenever the list of items is too long to be seen in the box. However, the list box does *not* provide a horizontal scroll bar if the entries are too wide to be read in the box. Adding a horizontal scroll bar is possible, however, if we send the list box a message telling it to produce one. In this section, we will add a horizontal scroll bar to the list box.

Step 8

First, add items that are particularly wide in order to test the horizontal scroll bar. In the Sub Main procedure, add the following code to place wide entries in the list box:

```
Form1.1stApi.AddItem "Microsoft Access"
Form1.1stApi.AddItem "MicroSoft Exchange Server"
Form1.1stApi.AddItem "Microsoft FoxPro"
Form1.1stApi.AddItem "Microsoft SQL Server"
Form1.1stApi.AddItem "Microsoft Systems Management Server"
Form1.1stApi.AddItem "Microsoft Visual Basic"
Form1.1stApi.AddItem "Microsoft Visual Basic Script"
Form1.1stApi.AddItem "Microsoft Visual C++"
```

Step 9

Now save and run the application. Look at the list box and make sure the entries just placed in the box are wider than the list box. If not, shut down the application and make the list box smaller until the new entries are clipped.

Step 10

Add a button to the form and call it **cmdAPI**. Change the caption of the button to **Scrollbar**. In the Click event of the button, add the following code to send a message to the list box:

```
'This routine makes a call to set the virtual width of
```

```
'the list box. This is known as the "Horizontal Extent".
'In this case, we set it to 3 times the physical width.
Dim lngReturnValue As Long
Dim lngExtent As Long
lngExtent = 3 * (lstAPI.Width / Screen.TwipsPerPixelX) _
lngReturnValue = SendMessage _
(lstAPI.hwnd, LB_SETHORIZONTALEXTENT, lngExtent, 0&)
```

Step 11

Save and run the application. Pressing the button now sends a message to the list box telling the box to set a virtual width three times larger than the actual physical width. When the virtual width is increased, the list box automatically creates a horizontal scroll bar.

Exercise 8-2: Changing Window Shapes

Window handles allow manipulation of a window in many ways. In this exercise, we will examine how to change the shape of a window. Even though most windows encounter are rectangular, the Windows operating system allows a window to take on any shape. We will demonstrate this capability by creating an oval `CommandButton`.

API CALLS

Step 1

Create a new directory in the File Explorer called **VB BOOTCAMP\EXERCISE8-2**. Start a new Visual Basic Standard EXE project. Add a Standard Module to the project by selecting **PROJECT/ADD MODULE** from the menu. The Standard Module is used to keep the declaration statements for API calls.

Step 2

In the Add-in manager, load the API Text Viewer, which can subsequently be accessed by selecting **ADD-INS/API VIEWER**. When the API Text Viewer is visible, load the declarations by selecting **FILE/LOAD TEXT FILE...** and selecting **WIN32API.TXT** as the file to load. When the file is loaded, all the API declarations are available. In the API Text Viewer, locate the following API calls:

```
CreateEllipticRgn
SetWindowRgn
```

Step 3

Return to Visual Basic and paste the declarations in the [General][Declarations] section of the Standard Module. The following code is pasted in:

```
Declare Function CreateEllipticRgn Lib "gdi32" _
   (ByVal X1 As Long, ByVal Y1 As Long, _
   ByVal X2 As Long, ByVal Y2 As Long) As Long
```

```
Declare Function SetWindowRgn Lib "user32" _
  (ByVal hWnd As Long, ByVal hRgn As Long, _
  ByVal bRedraw As Boolean) As Long
```

CHANGING THE WINDOW SHAPE

Step 4

The intent of this exercise is to create an oval button. In creating this button, we will use bitmaps to give the button the appearance of a border. The bitmaps are located on the CD-ROM, but need to be added to a resource file for use with the button. To create the resource file, load the VB6 Resource Editor from the Add-in manager by selecting **ADD-INS/ADD-IN MANAGER** from the menu.

Step 5

Start the Resource Editor by selecting **TOOLS/RESOURCE EDITOR...** from the menu. In the Resource Editor, add the bitmap files **UP.BMP** and **DOWN.BMP**. These bitmaps should have identifiers of 101 and 102 respectively. Once the bitmaps are loaded, save the resource file so it becomes part of the project.

Step 6

Drop a single button onto Form1. Set the properties for this single button as shown in the list below. Note that the size of the button is critical since the bitmaps we will use are sized for this button.

Name	cmdRegion
Caption	Clip Me!
Left	2205
Top	1665
Height	1005
Width	1995
Style	1-Graphical.

Step 7

Changing the shape of a window consists of defining a new shape and then applying it to the window. The function CreateEllipticRgn creates an oval that defines the new shape. The function SetWindowRgn is used to apply a defined shape to a window. CreateEllipticRgn returns a handle to the defined shape while SetWindowRgn takes the shape handle and a window handle to set the new shape. The code to accomplish this is integrated under the click event of cmdRegion. Add the following code to cmdRegion_Click to change the shape:

```
Static blnClipped As Boolean
Dim lngRegion As Long
Dim lngResult As Long
Dim lngX As Long, lngY As Long
```

```
If blnClipped Then
  'Restore Window to Normal
  lngResult = SetWindowRgn(cmdRegion.hWnd, 0&, True)


  'Change Button Caption
  cmdRegion.Caption = "Clip Me!"
  Set cmdRegion.Picture = LoadPicture("")

Else
  'Define the Region to Clip
  lngX = Int((cmdRegion.Width) / Screen.TwipsPerPixelX) - 4
  lngY = Int((cmdRegion.Height) / Screen.TwipsPerPixelY) - 3

  'Create the Region
  lngRegion = CreateEllipticRgn(4, 4, lngX, lngY)

  'Clip it!
  lngResult = SetWindowRgn(cmdRegion.hWnd, lngRegion, True)

  'Change Button Caption
  cmdRegion.Caption = ""
  Set cmdRegion.Picture = LoadResPicture(101, vbResBitmap)

End If


'Toggle the state
blnClipped = Not blnClipped
```

Step 8

After the button changes shape, we use the two bitmaps to show button-down and button-up states. Therefore, we need to swap the images under the MouseDown and MouseUp events. Add code to these two events so that the final code is as follows:

```
Private Sub cmdRegion_MouseDown(Button As Integer, Shift As Integer, _
  X As Single, Y As Single)
    If cmdRegion.Caption = "" Then
      Set cmdRegion.Picture = LoadResPicture(102, vbResBitmap)
    End If
End Sub


Private Sub cmdRegion_MouseUp(Button As Integer, Shift As Integer, _
```

```
   X As Single, Y As Single)
     If cmdRegion.Caption = "" Then
       Set cmdRegion.Picture = LoadResPicture(101, vbResBitmap)
     End If
 End Sub
```

Step 9

Save and run the project. Try clicking on the button.

Exercise 8-3: Subclassing Windows

Subclassing windows makes it possible to replace the default Window Function with a custom one. This permits examination of the messages entering a window and action when one is of interest. This exercise uses subclassing to create a status bar that shows a menu definition when the mouse passes over a menu selection.

ADDING THE API CALLS

Step 1

Create a subdirectory called **VB BOOTCAMP\EXERCISE8-3** using the File Explorer and then start a new Standard EXE project in Visual Basic 6.0. Add a Standard Module to the project.

Step 2

Minimize Visual Basic and start the API Text Viewer. In the API Text Viewer, locate, select, and copy the following functions and constants:

```
SetWindowLong
CallWindowProc
Const GWL_WNDPROC
Const WM_MENUSELECT
```

Step 3

Return to Visual Basic and paste the function and constant declarations into the Standard Module. Add the comments and variables shown to produce the following code:

```
Option Explicit
'This API function is used to change the structure
'of a window. To subclass, we must change the
'address of the "windows function" for the window
'we want to subclass.
Public Declare Function SetWindowLong Lib "user32" Alias _
"SetWindowLongA" (ByVal hwnd As Long, _
ByVal nIndex As Long, ByVal dwNewLong As Long) As Long
```

```
'This API function allows us to pass along the
'intercepted messages to the default "windows
'function" after we are through with them.
Public Declare Function CallWindowProc Lib "user32" Alias _
"CallWindowProcA" (ByVal lpPrevWndFunc As Long, ByVal hwnd As Long,_
    ByVal Msg As Long, ByVal wParam As Long, ByVal lParam As Long) _
    As Long

'API Constant used for nIndex argument of SetWindowLong.
'This tells SetWindowLong that we are changing the information
'regarding the address of the "windows function".
Public Const GWL_WNDPROC = -4

'This Message is used to detect a menu selection
Public Const WM_MENUSELECT = &H11F

'A variable to store the address of the default
'windows function we are subclassing
Public lpPrevWndProc As Long
```

BUILDING THE INTERFACE

Step 4

Select Form1 to begin building the user interface. Add a menu to the form by selecting **TOOLS/MENU EDITOR...** from the menu. Add the following menu structure to Form1:

Menu Name	Menu Caption
mnuMenus	Menu
mnuOne	One
mnuTwo	Two
mnuThree	Three

Step 5

Add a label control called lblStatus to Form1. Position the label so that it occupies the bottom of the form as a status bar. Add two command buttons to Form1. Name them cmdHook and cmdUnhook. Give them captions Hook and Unhook respectively.

HOOKING AND PROCESSING MESSAGES

Step 6

Open the Standard Module and define a new function called WindowProc. Add arguments to the function such that the final definition appears in the module as follows:

```
Public Function WindowProc(ByVal hw As Long, ByVal uMsg As Long, _
ByVal wParam As Long, ByVal lParam As Long) As Long
End Function
```

Step 7

The new function will be used as the Window Function to subclass Form1. When Form1 is hooked, all messages will be sent to this function. In this function, we want to detect a message that indicates the mouse is over a menu item in the Form1 menu. This message is WM_MENUSELECT. When we detect this message, a description of the menu item is written to the status bar of Form1. Add the following code inside WindowProc to detect the message and print the status description:

```
'This is the function that will intercept
'all of the messages from the subclassed
'window.
'We look for the WM_MENUSELECT message which
'fires when the user puts the mouse over the menu
If uMsg = WM_MENUSELECT Then
  Select Case Right$(Hex$(wParam), 1)
  Case 0
  Form1.lblStatus.Caption = ""
  Case 2
  Form1.lblStatus.Caption = "Menu One"
  Case 3
  Form1.lblStatus.Caption = "Menu Two"
  Case 4
  Form1.lblStatus.Caption = "Menu Three"
  End Select
End If
'After the messages are intercepted, we pass them
'along to the original default function so that it can
'actually handle them.
WindowProc = CallWindowProc _
(lpPrevWndProc, hw, uMsg, wParam, _
lParam)
```

Step 8

Hooking the window is done under the Click event of cmdHook. Add the following code to the click event:

```
lpPrevWndProc = SetWindowLong(Form1.hWnd, GWL_WNDPROC, _
AddressOf WindowProc)
```

Unhooking is done under the Click event of cmdUnhook using the following code:

```
Dim lngTemp As Long
lngTemp = SetWindowLong(Form1.hWnd, GWL_WNDPROC, _
lpPrevWndProc)
```

Step 9

Save and run the project. Try passing the mouse over the menus. Now click the **Hook** button and pass the mouse over the menus again.

FOR THE CERTIFIED PRO

Pro 8-1: GetTickCount

1. The `GetTickCount` API Call needs no arguments and it returns the number of milliseconds since Windows started. Use this to time the difference between an explicit property assignment and one that uses the default property.
2. Test the following lines of code in a loop to measure the difference is performance over several calls.

```
Label1.Caption=Text1.Text
Label1=Text1
```

Pro 8-2: SetCursorPos

1. The `SetCursorPos` API call positions the mousepointer by x, y coordinates measured in pixels.
2. Use this call to set the mouse to the upper left corner of a form when the form is clicked.
3. Then position the mouse to the upper left corner of a CommandButton when the button is pushed.

Pro 8-3: GetUserName

1. Use the `GetUserName` API call to populate a log in form with the user's name.
2. Base the log-in form on the `frmLogin` template in VB.

PREPARING FOR CERTIFICATION

Topics for further reading
    AddressOf
    API Functions
    Accessing DLLs and the Windows API

CERTIFICATION QUIZ

1. Messages are processed in a window by the:
   a.   Window Procedure
   b.   Window Function
   c.   Window Handle
   d.   Window Caption

2. Windows messages are:
   a.   long integers
   b.   function pointers
   c.   window handles
   d.   Window Functions

3. What API function places a message in the message queue?
   a.   EnumChildWindows
   b.   Send Message
   c.   PostMessage
   d.   WM_MENUSELECT

4. Subclassing refers to:
   a.   sending messages to a window
   b.   firing VB events
   c.   replacing the default Window Function
   d.   AddressOf

5. Callbacks are used by windows to:
   a.   periodically call a function
   b.   call a function after an event
   c.   call a function when data is available
   d.   call a function based on time

ANSWERS TO QUESTIONS

   1.   b
   2.   a
   3.   c
   4.   c
   5.   a

UNDERSTANDING CLASSES AND INSTANCES

Familiarity with the fundamentals of forms and standard modules including loading and unloading forms is required.

SKILLS COVERED

- Cert (3): Use multiple form instances to build applications
- Cert (3.a): Create new instances of a Visual Basic form
- Cert (3.b): Destroy instances of a Visual Basic form

Visual Basic has been around since 1991 and in that time has gained wide popularity as a Windows development platform. In the early days, VB could be used to create applications through forms and functions. That is still true today. VB has continued to grow in power by adding new features, most of which have been directed toward improving VB's object orientation. In spite of the improvements, many developers are mystified by object concepts—particularly classes and instances. In this chapter, we will introduce the concepts of classes and instances using familiar VB components such as forms. The amount of power available from a simple VB form may be a surprise.

Consider the simple act of loading a Visual Basic form. This can be accomplished using the `Load` command. If we want the form both to load and be displayed, we might use the `Show` command. Examine the following code carefully.

```
Form1.Show
```

This simple code contains a great deal of complexity and power. When most VB developers look at the code and try to imagine what must be happening inside VB, they think about it in more or less the following manner:

`Form1.Show` causes VB to go to the hard drive, find the form named Form1, load it into memory, and display it.

This is not at all what happens. But this is what VB allows users to think has happened. When VB was first created, its purpose was to make Windows programming more accessible to developers, since 1991 Windows development was difficult. To write a Windows application required the C language and the Windows SDK. When the small x in the upper right corner of a VB form is clicked, a form is summarily dismissed without regard for state. In 1991, that function had to be coded. It felt like months just to create a "Hello, World!" program in Windows.

Visual Basic made life a lot easier. It takes care of items like the ControlBox for us. This is good, but in creating VB, the people at Microsoft made strategic decisions about VB's functionality. They decided to hide many of the more gruesome details of Windows programming from the VB developer. This made life easier but less powerful. Now, as VB gains more and more object-oriented features, understanding some of the hidden programming behavior becomes critical.

When the code `Form1.Show` is executed, Visual Basic does not load and display Form1, but rather uses Form1 like a blueprint to create a new form. VB uses the Form1 created at design time as a template to produce an exact duplicate of the form in memory. Then, just to hide all this, VB promptly names the form it built in RAM with the same name as the template built at design time—Form1.

All the issues surrounding VB form creation address a very important topic in VB—classes and instances. The classic metaphor for classes and instances is that of a cookie cutter and cookies. If there is cookie dough spread out on the counter, a favorite cookie cutter can be used to make as many cookies as required. Each cookie looks exactly the same and has the characteristics of the cutter being used. Change the cookie cutter and the look of the cookie changes, but all the new cookies look alike and are based on the new cutter. Because we are developers and have to have our own lingo, we call the cookie cutter a *class* and the cookie an *instance*.

This metaphor applies exactly to how VB creates a new form when the code `Form1.Show` is executed. Visual Basic uses the Form1 created at design time like a cookie cutter or class. This class is taken to the dough, the memory, and a new cookie is made, the form instance. The beauty of this process is that once we understand it, we can make as many cookies as we want.

THE LIFE CYCLE OF A FORM

When a form is used, it goes through definite steps. Normally, we are not bothered by details, but we can actually take manual control over the life of a form if we want to. This allows a great flexibility in both design and function. As an example, we will examine the life of a form step by step through custom code.

DECLARING OBJECT VARIABLES

Before we can manually create a form, we must have a variable declared that can represent the form in our code. This is called an object variable. The purpose of the object variable is to act as a surrogate for the form instance we will create. Object variables have the scoping rules of any variable in VB. We can declare them as Public, Private, or Dim. The following code declares a variable capable of representing an instance of Form1:

```
Public MyForm As Form1
```

This code, may seem strange at first. The last time we checked, VB did not have an intrinsic data type known as Form1. But here we are declaring a variable As Form1. The reason this is legal is because Form1 is in the same project as my code. We can use any object we want in this way, causing a variable to represent all kinds of things in VB. Here are other legal object variables. Study each carefully.

```
Public MyForm As Form
Public MyTextBox As TextBox
Public MyControl As Control
Public MyScreen As Screen
Public MyFont As StdFont
Public MyPicture As StdPicture
```

Object variables can be declared As Form, which allows the variable to represent any form in the application. Variables can also be declared against specific types of controls like As TextBox or As ListBox. These declarations can then be used to pass controls to custom functions and subroutines. Variables can also be declared as any system object, such as Screen, Printer, the standard font object, and the standard printer object. Object variables are useful ways to code. For example, the following code accepts any ListBox control as an argument and searches it for a given text entry from a TextBox.

```
Public Function SearchList(MyList As ListBox, _
    MyText As TextBox) As Boolean
  SearchList = False
Dim I As Integer
  For I = 0 To MyList.ListCount-1
  If MyList.List(I) = MyText.Text Then SearchList = True
Next
End Sub
```

CREATING INSTANCES

Once an object variable is declared (e.g. as Form1), we can use it to represent an existing object as in the preceding example or we can create a new object from the class. Creating a new object from a class is called *instancing* and is accomplished through the use of the keyword New. The New keyword is perhaps the most important keyword in VB. It clearly shows the relationship between classes and instances. The following code is used to create a new instance from an existing class called Form1.

```
Public MyForm As Form1
Set MyForm = New Form1
```

Notice the use of the Set keyword with the New keyword. Set is always required when setting the value of an object variable. This line of code sets the object variable MyForm equal to a new instance of class Form1. Form1 is the cookie cutter and MyForm is the cookie. The important thing here is to use this line of code to create as many instances of a form as required—just declare a variable for each instance and there can be multiple copies of Form1.

Whenever a form is instanced using the New keyword, the form receives the Initialize event. This is used to notify a class that a new instance has been created. In this way the class can take any steps necessary to prepare the new instance for use. After the event, choose to load and show the form with this code:

```
Load MyForm
MyForm.Show
```

DESTROYING INSTANCES

When a form is finished being used, one might think of unloading it. Unloading a form is not enough to recover the memory used by the instance. VB provides a special keyword for destroying instances called Nothing. When an instance is set to Nothing, all the memory used by the instance is returned to the heap. VB also fires the Terminate event to notify the class that the instance memory is being reclaimed.

```
Unload MyForm
Set MyForm = Nothing
```

Whenever multiple instances of a class are created, it makes sense to have a way to manage the instances. Visual Basic provides such a mechanism, known as a *collection*. Collections are similar to arrays except that they hold objects and provide methods and properties that manipulate all the objects at once.

Visual Basic supports two built-in collections—Forms and Controls. The Forms collection is the collection of all forms currently loaded in the project. Nothing special needs to be done to get a form into the Forms collection. Visual Basic puts a form in the collection as soon as it is loaded. Once it is loaded, the Forms collection can be used to loop through every form in the project. The following code adds the name of every form in the project to a ListBox called List1.

```
Dim MyForm As Form
For Each MyForm In Forms
  List1.AddItem MyForm.Name
Next
```

This same technique applies to controls. For any given form selected, VB supports a Controls collection that has references to every control on the form. Just as all the forms in a project are visible in forms collection, Controls can be used to see all the controls on a form. VB also supports building custom collections with the Collection Object. We will discuss this in Chapter 14.

UNDERSTANDING OBJECT MODELS

Once the fundamentals of creating instances from classes become clear, that knowledge can be used for the rapid creation of powerful applications that take advantage of dozens of preexisting classes in other applications. Most familiar applications are already built on the concept of objects. This includes the entire office suite and most third-party products. When an application is constructed of objects, those objects are often made available through a mechanism known as an *object model*.

Object models are hierarchical representations of the classes that make up an application. These models show not only the names of the classes, but also the relationship the classes have to each other. Figure 9-1 shows a piece of the object model associated with Microsoft Excel. In this figure, the classes are presented in a vertical hierarchical fashion. Each box in the model represents a class and its position in the model shows its dependency on other classes.

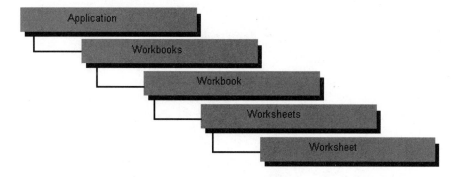

Figure 9-1 A partial Excel object model.

Examine the Excel product and notice that it is built on the concept of workbooks and worksheets. These are readily visible in the user interface (Figure 9-2) where groups of spreadsheets are organized into workbooks through the use of tabs. This organization is correctly reflected in the Excel object model. Note that it does not make sense in this scheme to have a worksheet unless a workbook has been defined to hold the sheet. This reality is also reflected in the object model, where the Worksheet class below the Workbook class is in the vertical model.

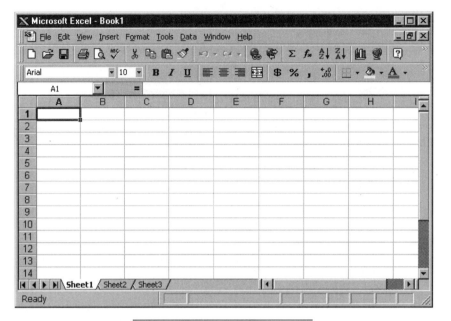

Figure 9-2 The Excel user interface.

The lifecycle of instances created from an object model like Excel is similar to the life of forms created using the New keyword. In order to use the model, a variable must be declared, and an instance created before calling the appropriate properties and methods. To that extent the object model is the same. Before using an object model from Visual Basic, tell the VB environment about the model. Visual Basic can find out about object models when a *reference* to the model is set. References allow Visual Basic to examine the system registry for information about the objects to be used. Setting a reference is accomplished by selecting **PROJECT/REFERENCES...** from the menu to reveal the References dialog (Figure 9-3).

The References dialog lists all the applications on a machine that are created from objects which can be accessed from Visual Basic. Open this dialog and notice that there are dozens of entries representing many applications, entries not only for products like Excel, but also for Word, PowerPoint, and other members of the Office suite. There are even entries for many third-party products as well as specialized entries representing components designed to perform data access. In fact, there are even some entries already selected which represent the language engine of Visual Basic itself.

Once a reference to any of these items is set, Visual Basic is given complete knowledge of the objects as well as their properties, events, and methods. For the items selected, VB also provides a tool to examine the object models, the Object Browser (Figure 9-4). The Object Browser shows the object model. Access the Browser by selecting **VIEW/OBJECT BROWSER...** from the menu. In the Object Browser, select the model to examine and the class to use. The Browser responds by listing all the properties, events, and methods for that class.

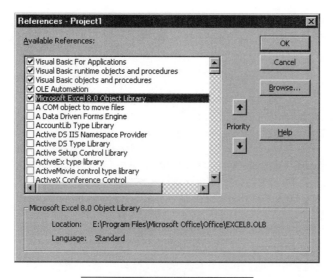

Figure 9-3 The References dialog.

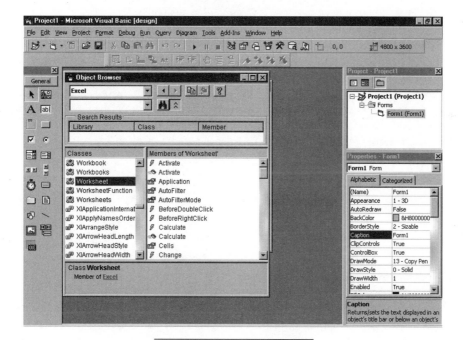

Figure 9-4 The Object Browser.

To begin using an object model, start by creating an instance of the first object in the model, often referred to as the *top-level* object. This object represents the entry point into the model.

Once this is created help create instances of other objects. A top-level object can be created much as an instance of a form is created. The following code declares a variable and creates an instance of the top-level object in Excel, called the *Application* object.

```
Dim objExcel As Excel.Application
Set objExcel = CreateObject("Excel.Application")
```

In the first line of code, we declare a variable as the type of object we want to create. In creating a form, declare a variable as Form1 or Form2, but when an external set of objects is used, the class name must be qualified with the name of the application that contains the classes. In this case we qualify the Application class using the word `Excel`. This syntax is similar to that in all object models. In the second line of code, we create an instance of the Application object. Here we use the `CreateObject` function which performs much the same service as the New keyword. After the instance is created, we can use all the properties, events, and methods of the object in our Visual Basic application.

Check It Out 9-1: Using Excel Objects

1. Create a new directory in the File Explorer called **VB BOOTCAMP\CHECK IT OUT 9-1**. Start a new Standard EXE project in Visual Basic.
2. Before using the Excel object model, set a reference to it so that Visual Basic can find the objects. From the Visual Basic menu, select **PROJECT/REFERENCES**. In the References dialog, place a check mark next to Microsoft Excel Object Library and close the dialog.
3. Before we create the objects, we must define variables for the objects. The objects are generally defined in the form `Server.Class`, however, the Object or Variant data type can also be usesd to hold instances. Add the following code to the [General][Declarations] section of Form1 to declare the variables:

```
'Declare variables
Private objExcel As Object
Private objBooks As Object
Private objBook As Object
Private objSheets As Object
Private objSheet As Object
```

4. In order to use the spreadsheet object, use the objects in the object model to create the sheet. The top-level object in the Excel object model is the Application object. We can instantiate the Application by using the `CreateObject` function in Visual Basic. After this object is created, it is a matter of calling properties and methods to create the rest of the objects. Add the following code to the `Form_Initialize` event of Form1 to create the objects:

```
Set objExcel = CreateObject("Excel.Application")
Set objBooks = objExcel.Workbooks
```

```
Set objBook = objBooks.Add
Set objSheets = objBook.Worksheets
Set objSheet = objSheets.Add
```

5. When the objects are no longer needed, thay should be destroyed. We will do this in the Terminate event of Form1 in case the application terminates prematurely. Add the following code to the Terminate event. Note that if the application is ended by selecting **RUN/END** from the menu, this code will not run.

```
Set objSheet = Nothing
Set objSheets = Nothing

objBook.Close SaveChanges:=False
Set objBook = Nothing
Set objBooks = Nothing

objExcel.Quit
Set objExcel = Nothing
```

6. Once the objects are created, it is a simple matter to call methods to borrow the functionality contained inside the objects. Build a GUI for the application with the following controls and set the properties as shown in Figure 9-5. Use the item list to set properties for the controls at design time.

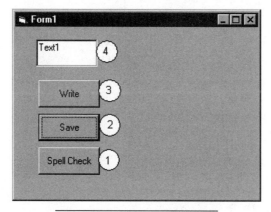

Figure 9-5 Form1 and Controls.

Item 1—CommandButton

Name	cmdSpellCheck
Caption	Spell Check

Item 2—CommandButton

Name	cmdSave
Caption	Save

Item 3—CommandButton

Name	cmdWrite
Caption	Write

Item 4 —TextBox

Name	txtData

7. The Write button is designed to make it possible to write data to cell A1 of the spread sheet. In the click event of cmdWrite, add the following code:

```
'Setting the value of a cell
objSheet.Cells(1, "A").Value = txtData.Text
MsgBox "Data Saved to Sheet"
```

8. The Save button will save the spreadsheet as a file named **data.xls**. Add the following code to the click event of cmdSave:

```
'Save the sheet
objSheet.SaveAs (App.Path & "\data.xls")
MsgBox "Sheet Saved"
```

9. The Spell Check button uses the Excel spell checker to check your stored word. Add the following code to the click event of cmdSpellCheck:

```
'Spell checking
objSheet.CheckSpelling
```

10. Save and run the application. It is a good idea to minimize the VB environment before running the spell check. This makes it easier to access the Spell Check dialog.

Exercise 9-1: Instancing Forms

Forms in Visual Basic are just like all other VB objects, they are actually templates or classes that can be instantiated at run time. This means that a form created at design time can be used at run time to stamp out copies of the form. In this exercise, we will use form instancing to create a simple Visual Basic Word processor.

MULTIPLE DOCUMENT INTERFACE

Step 1

Create a new directory using the File Explorer called **VB BOOTCAMP\EXERCISE9-1**. Start a new Standard EXE project in Visual Basic.

The Word Processor we will construct will be modeled after Microsoft Word, a Multiple Document Interface (MDI) application. MDI applications are those that have one large parent window containing several smaller child windows. Visual Basic makes it quite easy to create MDI applications. To place a parent window in the application, select **PROJECT/ADD MDI FORM** from the menu. Only one MDI Form is allowed per application. After placing the MDI Form in the application, look at the Project menu and notice the menu selection is now gray.

With most MDI applications, the parent window covers the entire screen. This can be made to happen by changing the `WindowState` property of the MDI Form to 2-Maximized. Change the WindowState property now.

Step 2

Making a regular form part of the MDI application is as simple as setting one property. Select **Form1** and press **F4** for the properties. Change the MDIChild property to True, which makes the form a child of the MDI Form. Now save and run the application to see the fundamental MDI behavior.

SUB MAIN

Step 3

In this application, we want to control when a child form is displayed. We will do this by starting our application from `Sub Main`. From the menu select **PROJECT/ADD MODULE** to add a standard module. With the code window visible, select **TOOLS/ADD PROCEDURE** and add a `Public Sub` named `Main`. This is the routine we will use to start the application. To start from `Sub Main`, select **Project-Properties** from the menu. In the General tab, set the startup object as `Sub Main` and close the Options dialog.

Step 4

When the application loads, all we want to do is display the large parent window. To accomplish this, add the following code to the `Sub Main` routine:

```
MDIForm1.Show
```

Save and run the application. The parent window should be covering the entire screen.

INSTANCING THE FORM

Step 5

In order to create a word processor, we will have to make a File menu and attach it to the parent window so that it can be used with any active document. Select the MDI Form in the design environment and open the Menu Editor by selecting **Tools/Menu Editor** from the menu. In the Menu Editor, build a file menu according to the following data:

Menu Name	Menu Caption
mnuFile	&File
mnuFileNew	&New

mnuFileOpen	&Open...
mnuFileSaveAs	Save &As
mnuFileBar	—
mnuFileExit	E&xit

Step 6

The Exit menu choice will destroy all open instances of forms and end the application. Add the following code to the Click event of the Exit menu to end the application:

```
Dim f As Form

'Unload all the forms except the MDI Form
For Each f In Forms
  If TypeOf f Is Form1 Then
  Unload f
  Set f = Nothing
End If
Next

'Unload MDI Form
Unload Me
End
```

Step 7

To simulate a blank document for our word processor, we will use a textbox to cover the entire front of Form1. The user can type into the textbox, which will automatically wrap the text. Add a textbox to Form1. In the Resize event of Form1, add the following code to resize the text box when the form is resized:

```
'Resize the Text Box
With Text1
  .Height = Me.ScaleHeight
  .Width = Me.ScaleWidth
  .Left = 0
  .Top = 0
End With
```

Step 8

In order to make the text wrap, change the following properties of Text1:

```
MultiLine     True
ScrollBars    2-Vertical
```

Step 9

Every time the user selects the New menu item, we will create an instance of Form1 as the new document. Add the following code to the Click event of `mnuFileNew` to generate the new blank document:

```
Dim f As Form1
Static n As Integer

'Create a new instance
Set f = New Form1
f.Text1.Text = ""
n = n + 1
f.Caption = "Document " & Format$(n)
f.Show
```

Save and run the project. Test the instancing of forms using the menu.

FILE OPERATIONS

Step 10

The menu supports saving and opening files in the word processor. In order to access the file system, we will use the Common Dialog control. Check the toolbox by using the tool tips to determine if the Common Dialog control is loaded. If not, place the Common Dialog control in the project by selecting **Project-Components** from the menu and checking the Microsoft Common Dialog Control entry.

When the Common Dialog Control is in the toolbox, add it to the MDIForm. Select the control and press **F4** to reveal the properties. The `Filter` property is used to filter out all files that do not match the selected filter. In the case of our word processor, we filter out all files that do not have a `.TXT` extension. Set the properties as follows:

```
FileName        *.txt
Filter  VB Word Processor(*.txt)|*.txt
```

Step 11

When the SaveAs menu is selected, we want to let the user save the document. We will use the Common Dialog Control to save the file. This Control is used to present built-in Windows dialogs to the user. The Common Dialog Control can show dialogs that allow file saving and opening. Add the following code under the Click event of the `mnuFileSaveAs` menu:

```
Dim strFile As String

'Open common dialog
CommonDialog1.ShowSave
strFile = CommonDialog1.FileName
```

```
'Save the File as text
Open strFile For Output As #1
 Print #1, MDIForm1.ActiveForm.Text1.Text
Close #1
```

Step 12

When the Open menu is selected, we want to allow the user to open the text file. Add the following code to the `mnuFileOpen` Click event to open the file.

```
Dim strFile As String
Dim strText As String

'Open common dialog
CommonDialog1.ShowOpen
strFile = CommonDialog1.FileName
If UCase$(Right$(strFile,3))<>"TXT" Then Exit Sub
'Create a New Instance for the Document
'This line of code makes a call to the
'same code that is used when you select
'new from the menu. It's perfectly legal
'to call an event-handling subroutine
'directly from code this way!
Call mnuFileNew_Click

'Open the File as text
Open strFile For Input As #1
 Do Until EOF(1)
  Line Input #1, strText
  Me.ActiveForm.Text1.Text = _
   Me.ActiveForm.Text1.Text & strText & vbCrLf
 Loop
Close #1
```

Step 13

Save and run the project. Create, save, and open several documents.

Exercise 9-2: Using the Word Object Model

Visual Basic permits creation and use of many different kinds of objects. In this exercise, we will create objects found in the Microsoft Word object model.

REFERENCING THE OBJECT MODEL

Step 1

Create a new directory using the File Explorer called **VB BOOTCAMP\EXERCISE9-2**. Start a new Standard EXE project in Visual Basic.

Step 2

Before the Word object model can be used, the application must be installed on the machine and a reference set in Visual basic. Open the References dialog by selecting **PROJECT/REFERENCES...** from the menu. In the References dialog, set a reference to **Microsoft Word 8.0 Object Library** and **Microsoft Office 8.0 Object Library**. Close the References dialog.

Step 3

Open the Object Browser by selecting **VIEW/OBJECT BROWSER...** from the menu. In the Object Browser, choose to examine the Word library. Notice all of the different objects available through this model. Close the Object Browser.

BUILDING THE APPLICATION

Step 4

Select Form1 from the Project window. Build the interface shown in Figure 9-6 on Form1. Use the item list below to set properties for the controls at design time.

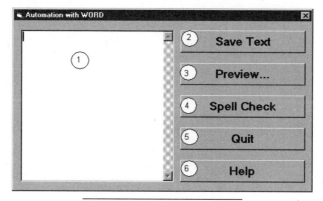

Figure 9-6 Form1 and controls.

Item 1— TextBox

Name	txtWord
Multiline	True
Scrollbars	2-Vertical

Item 2—CommandButton

Name	cmdSave

Caption	Save Text

Item 3—CommandButton

Name	cmdPreview
Caption	Preview...

Item 4—CommandButton

Name	cmdSpell
Caption	Spell Check

Item 5—CommandButton

Name	cmdQuit
Caption	Quit

Item 6—CommandButton

Name	cmdHelp
Caption	Help

Step 5

In order to use the model, it will be necessary to declare some variables as objects found in Word. In the [General][Declarations] section, declare the following variables:

```
Public objApplication As Word.Application
Public objDocument As Word.Document
Public objAssistant As Office.Assistant
```

Step 6

When the application starts, we want to create a new document in Word so that it can be edited from Visual Basic. Creating the new document is matter of creating an instance of the Document object. Add the following code to the Form_Load event to create a new document from Visual Basic:

```
'Create the New Document
Set objApplication = CreateObject("Word.Application")
Set objDocument = objApplication.Documents.Add
Set objAssistant = objApplication.Assistant
```

Step 7

The Save Text button writes whatever is typed into the TextBox into the new document object. Add the following code to the click event of cmdSave to save the text.

```
'Write to the new doc
objDocument.Content.Text = txtWord.Text
MsgBox "Text Saved to Document!", vbOKOnly, "Word"
```

Step 8

The Preview button is designed to permit viewing the actual Word document as it will appear when printed. Add the following code to the Click event of `cmdPreview` to set up the print preview.

```
'Show Document
objDocument.PrintPreview
objApplication.Visible = True
objApplication.Activate
```

Step 9

The Spell Check button performs spell checking on the Word document. Add the following code to `cmdSpell_Click` to implement spell checking.

```
'Check Spelling
objDocument.CheckSpelling
txtWord.Text = objDocument.Content.Text
```

Step 10

The Quit button causes the Word application to quit so we can shut down our VB application. Add the following code to the Click event of `cmdQuit` to shut down Word. ***DO NOT*** end the application by selecting **RUN/END** from the VB menu; if you select that, the code will not run

```
'Quit
objApplication.Quit SaveChages:=False
```

Step 11

A click on the Help button brings up the Office Assistant. Add the following code to the Click event of `cmdHelp` to show the Office Assistant:

```
'Show the Assistant
objApplication.Visible = True
objApplication.Activate
objAssistant.Help
```

Step 12

Save the work and run the project. Type text into the TextBox and press the **Save Text** button. Once text is saved, try previewing the document. With the document visible, press the **Spell Check** button. Finally, bring up Office Assistant for help. Then quit Word.

FOR THE CERTIFIED PRO

Pro 9-1: This lab will build a spreadsheet application similar to Microsoft Excel. Create this application to meet the following specifications:

1. The application will be a Multiple Document Interface project.

2. The application will present multiple spreadsheets created by using a Microsoft FlexGrid control maximized to cover a Visual Basic form.
   a. The spreadsheet grid should have 11 rows and 11 columns
   b. The first row should be a fixed row that labels the columns of the grid as **A** through **J**
   c. The first column should be a fixed column that labels the rows as **1** through **10**
   d. The grid should completely cover its form even when the form is resized.
   e. A user must be able to create as many spreadsheets as they want.
   f. Users must be able to use a menu to create new sheets, save sheets, and open saved sheets.
   g. All file operations must be completely protected from common run-time errors.
   h. Users will edit any cell in the sheet by double-clicking the cell and entering data through a custom input box created as a Visual Basic form and shown modally.
   i. The grid should initially be filled with all zeroes.
   j. The grid should not accept any input except numbers.
3. The main parent window must contain all menu choices. These menu choices should include New, Open, Save, and Exit. The Exit function should check for any unsaved files and prompt users to save them. On the menu, include a Window List of open documents.

PREPARING FOR CERTIFICATION

Topics for Further Reading
    Creating a Reference to an Object
    Navigating Object Models

CERTIFICATION QUIZ

1. What code creates a new instance of Form1 into the variable `MyForm`?
   a. `Set Form1 = New MyForm`
   b. `Set MyForm = New Form1`
   c. `Set New MyForm = Form1`
   d. `Set New Form1 = MyForm`

2. What code destroys the object `MyForm`?
   a. `Unload MyForm`
   b. `Set MyForm = New Form1`
   c. `Set MyForm = Nothing`
   d. `Destroy MyForm`

3. What variable declaration can represent any form?
   a. `Public MyForm As Form`
   b. `Private MyForm As Form`
   c. `Public MyForm As Forms`
   d. `Private MyForm As Forms`

4. Given the code `Form1.Show`, what is the firing order of events?
   a. Load, Initialize, Paint, Resize
   b. Load, Initialize, Resize, Paint
   c. Initialize, Load, Paint, Resize
   d. Initialize, Load, Resize, Paint

5. Given the following code, what is the firing order of events?

   ```
   Unload Form1
   Set Form1 = Nothing
   ```

   a. Unload then Terminate
   b. Terminate then Unload
   c. Terminate only
   d. Unload only

6. Which data types can hold a reference to an Excel spreadsheet?
   a. Enumeration
   b. Variant
   c. Object
   d. Control

7. What is the name of the first object in a model?
   a. top-app
   b. top-gun
   c. top-most
   d. top-level

8. What information is given by an object model?
   a. Properties
   b. Methods
   c. Class names
   d. Class relationships

9. What are the arguments for the CreateObject function?
   a. Registry Location
   b. Class ID
   c. Class Name
   d. Server Location

10. Which lines create an instance of a Word Application?
    a. `Set objApplication = New Word.Application`
    b. `Set objApplication = CreateObject_`
        `("Word.Application")`
    c. `Set objApplication = CreateObject Word.Application`
    d. `Set objApplication = New "Word.Application"`

ANSWERS TO CERTIFICATION QUIZ

1. b
2. c
3. a, b
4. d
5. a.
6. b, c
7. d
8. a, b, c, d
9. c, d
10. a, b

THE DATA ENVIRONMENT

Those who begin this chapter, should be familiar with fundamental data access concepts. If ODBC and OLEDB are not familiar, return to the introduction to data access in Chapter 5.

SKILLS COVERED

- 70-176 (2): Design Visual Basic components to access data from a database
- 70-176(11): Use data binding to display and manipulate data from a data source
- 70-175(15): Use data binding to display and manipulate data from a data source

The Data Environment designer is a new feature of Visual Basic 6.0 that permits ADO connections and queries at design time in a graphical interface. The Data Environment is more flexible than the ADO Data Control and affords the ability to define multiple connections to data sources within a single environment. It can also be used as a data source for bound controls or to create data reports.

To begin to use the Data Environment, make it available in Visual Basic IDE. Enable the Data Environment from the Components dialog (Figure 10-1) which is opened by selecting **PRO-JECT/COMPONENTS...** from the menu. All the designers that ship with Visual Basic are located on the Designers tab of the components dialog. Select the **Data Environment** and press **OK**. The Data Environment then appears under the PROJECT menu in the VBIDE. Note that the first four designers added to VB appear directly under the PROJECT menu, though, additional ones are placed under the PROJECT/MORE ACTIVEX DESIGNERS... menu.

Figure 10-1 The Components dialog.

After the Data Environment is available, add it to the project. When the Data Environment is added, a hierarchical layout with a root labeled **DataEnvironment1** and a new connection in the environment labeled **Connection1** will be visible. The connection as created contains no meaningful information. To set up the connection, right-click on it and select **PROPERTIES** from the popup menu. This presents a tabbed dialog which makes it possible to establish a data link and is exactly the same as the one used in the File Explorer to create Data Link files.

Once the properties for the connection are filled out (Figure 10-2), a data link has been established within the Data Environment. The Data Environment permits adding as many Data Links as desired by right-clicking the environment and selecting **ADD CONNECTION** from the pop-up menu. Once the connection is added, create a query associated with the connection by adding a new Command object to the environment. Right-click the connection on which the query is to run and choose **ADD COMMAND** from the popup menu. Once the command is added, access the properties of the command by right-clicking. A choice to view the command properties, will reveal a tabbed dialog that permits creation of a command against the associated connection.

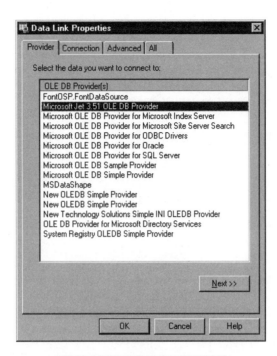

Figure 10-2 Data Link Properties.

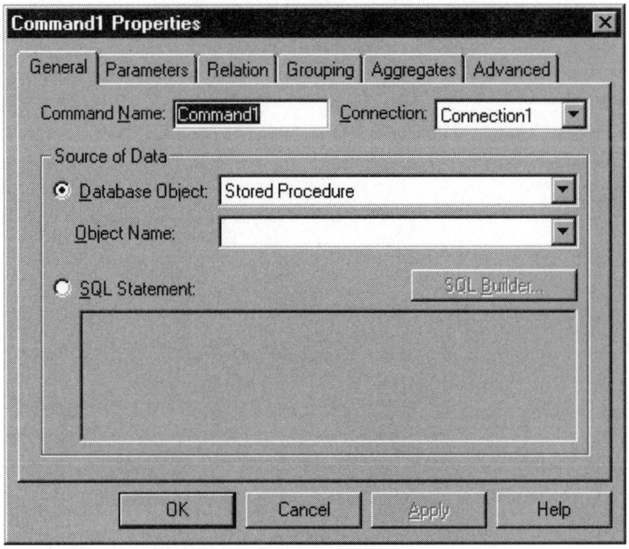

Figure 10-3 Command object properties.

The command properties (Figure 10-3) permits creation of queries that use SQL statement, stored procedures, or proprietary query languages for nonrelational data stores. Essentially, the full power of ADO is available in these dialogs. The beauty of the Data Environment is that establishing connections and running queries requires very little code. Most of the parameters are simply set in the tabbed dialogs of the Data Environment. If fact, the Data Environment supports drag-and-drop data binding with forms in an application.

The Data Environment allows dragging any command or field onto a form. When this happens, Visual Basic responds by placing a new visual element on the form. The type of visual element placed is set by Visual Basic based on the data type represented by a field. The control associated with a field can be changed by right-clicking the field in the Data Environment and selecting **PROPERTIES**. In the properties, it is possible to pick from a list of possible controls that can bind to the data type represented by the field.

Check It Out 10-1: Data Environment Basics

1. Start a new Visual Basic Standard EXE project.
2. If the Data Environment is not already available under the PROJECT menu, open the components dialog and select **Data Environment** from the Designers tab.
3. Add a Data Environment object to the project by selecting **PROJECT/DATA ENVIRONMENT** from the menu. (Note that the Data Environment may be under PROJECT/MORE ACTIVEX DESIGNERS… if several designers have already been added to Visual Basic.)
4. Right-click on **Connection1** and select **PROPERTIES** from the popup menu. This will open the Data Links properties dialog. In the Provider tab, choose **Microsoft JET 3.51 OLE DB Provider**. This will facilitate connection to a Microsoft Access database.
5. In the Connection tab, use the ellipsis in the Select or Enter a Database Name box to locate the file BIBLIO.MDB. Press the **Test Connection** button to verify that the data link is correctly established.
6. Press the **OK** button to save the data link.
7. Right-click on **Connection1** and select **ADD COMMAND** from the popup menu. This will place a new command object under the connection.
8. Right-click on the **Command1** object and select **PROPERTIES** from the popup menu. This will open the tabbed dialog for the command properties.
9. In the General tab, select to base the command on an SQL statement. In the SQL box type the following statement:

```
SELECT * FROM Publishers
```

10. Press the **OK** button to save the Command definition.
11. From the Project window select Form1 and make it visible. Now carefully select the **Restore** button from the VBIDE so that both the Data Environment and the Form are visible. Figure 10-4 shows the setup to achieve.

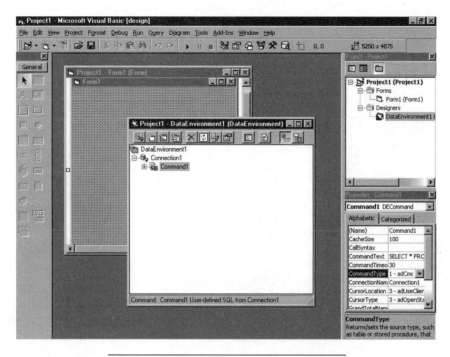

Figure 10-4 The Data Environment and Form1.

12. With the Form and the Data Environment visible, drag the **Command1** object from the Data Environment onto the surface of Form1. Visual Basic responds by immediately building an interface that shows the data defined by Command1.

13. With the interface built, all that remains is to create the code to navigate the recordset. Add two CommandButtons to Form1 for navigation. The complete interface is shown in Figure 10-5. Use the Item list below to set the Name and Caption of each button.

Item 1—CommandButton

Name   cmdPrev

Caption   Previous

Item 2—CommandButton

Name   cmdNext

Caption   Next

14. The navigation of the recordset is accomplished by adding code under each button. Add code under the buttons so that the final code appears as follows:

```
Private Sub cmdNext_Click()
  With DataEnvironment1.Recordsets(1)
    .MoveNext
```

```
      If .EOF Then .MoveLast
   End With
End Sub

Private Sub cmdPrev_Click()
   With DataEnvironment1.Recordsets(1)
      .MovePrevious
      If .BOF Then .MoveFirst
   End With
End Sub
```

15. Run the project and navigate the recordset using the buttons.

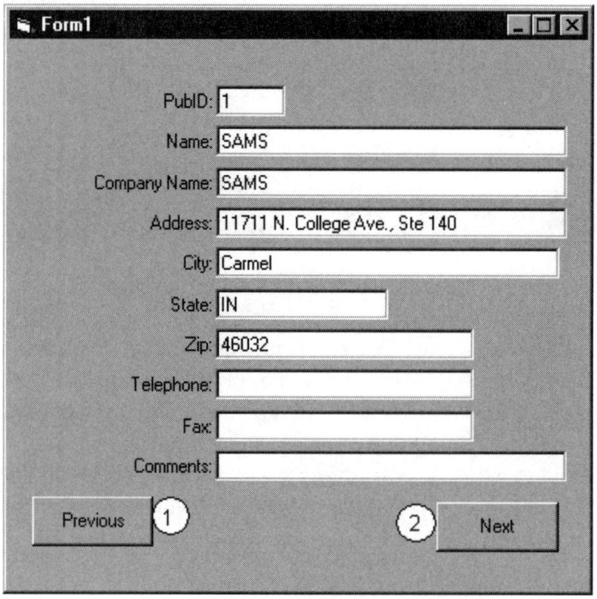

Figure 10-5 The complete Form1.

The Data Environment works as well with stored procedures in SQL Server as it does with simple SQL statements in Microsoft Access. Using a stored procedure is a matter of selecting the stored procedure in the Command properties. Connection objects can connect to SQL Server by using the appropriate provider. It will be necessary to enter additional information such as the machine where SQL Server is located and a UserID, but the Data Link dialog prompts for all necessary information. When it is completed, a new command object can be added to access the SQL Server connection.

When stored procedures are used, it will often be necessary to pass input parameters to make the query run. Input parameters are handled under the Parameters tab of the Command properties. In this tab specify key information about the parameter direction and data type. When the query is run, it will appear as a method of the Data Environment and the parameter will be an argument.

As an example of using stored procedures with the Data Environment (Figure 10-6), consider calling a stored procedure named `sp_GetTitlesByCompany`. This procedure is designed to return book titles from the SQL Server PUBS database given a company name. We can easily establish a connection to SQL Server using a Data Link and then insert a command for the stored procedure. Under the new command we select to base the command on a stored procedure and select the name of the procedure from the list.

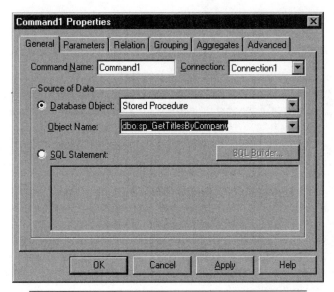

Figure 10-6 A Stored Procedure as a Command object.

Once the stored procedure command is created, it can be run from code and the results retrieved. All Connection and Command objects defined in the Data Environment are available as collections of the Data Environment. This means properties like UserID and password can easily be set from code. Also, all command objects run as methods of the Data Environment. For our stored procedure command, we need to pass a UserID and password as a first order of business. This can be done by referencing the collection of connections in the Data Environment as follows:

```
DataEnvironment1.Connection1.ConnectionString = "UID=sa;PWD=;"
```

To execute the stored procedure, address the command object as a method and pass the expected argument in the same line. The following line of code passes the argument along with wildcard characters to locate any publisher in the database containing the key word:

```
DataEnvironment1.Command1 "%Moon%"
```

After we execute the command, we expect to receive results. The DataEnvironment automatically creates the recordset as a new object. In the Data Environment, access the associated results by prefixing the command name with the letters *rs*. Therefore, the default name Command1 creates a recordset named rsCommand1. Once the records are available, loop through them as with any set of records. In the following code, we simply put the titles returned in the recordset into a list.

```
Do While Not DataEnvironment1.rsCommand1.EOF
   lstTitles.AddItem DataEnvironment1.rsCommand1!Title
   DataEnvironment1.rsCommand1.MoveNext
Loop
```

HIERARCHICAL CURSORS

One of the powerful new features of ADO is the ability to create data hierarchies, which make it easy to create master/detail views where one recordset contains details for a parent recordset. In this scenario, the Data Environment permits creation of a new child query as a field of an existing query. The resulting hierarchical recordset can then be bound to a grid for display.

Check It Out 10-2: Command Hierarchies

1. Start a new Visual Basic Standard EXE project.
2. If the Data Environment is not already available under the PROJECT menu, open the Components dialog and select the **Data Environment** from the Designers tab.
3. Add a Data Environment object to the project by selecting **PROJECT/DATA ENVIRONMENT** from the menu. (Note that the Data Environment may be under PROJECT/MORE ACTIVEX DESIGNERS… if several designers have already been added to Visual Basic.)
4. Right-click on the **Connection1** object to open the Data Link properties. In the Provider tab, choose **Microsoft JET 3.51 OLE DB Provider**. This will make it possible to connect to a Microsoft Access database.
5. In the Connection tab, use the ellipsis in the Select or Enter a Database Name box to locate the file BIBLIO.MDB. Press the **Test Connection** button to verify that the Data Link is correctly established.
6. Press the **OK** button to save the Data Link.
7. Right-click on **Connection1** and select **ADD COMMAND** from the popup menu. This will place a new command object under the connection.
8. Right-click on the **Command1** object and select **PROPERTIES** from the popup menu. This will open the tabbed dialog for the command properties.
9. In the General tab, rename the Command object Publishers. Select to base the command on an SQL statement. In the SQL box type the following statement:

```
SELECT PubId, Name FROM Publishers
```

10. Press the **OK** button to save the command definition.
11. Now we will add a child command to the Publishers command. Right-click on the **Publishers** command and select **ADD CHILD COMMAND** from the popup menu. A new Command object will be added as a field of the Publishers command.
12. Right-click on the new child command object and select **PROPERTIES** from the popup menu. In the General tab, change the Command name to `Titles`. Select to base the query on an SQL Statement and type the following statement into the SQL box:

```
SELECT * FROM Titles
```

13. Notice that the query used has no relationship information showing that titles are related to publishers. To establish this link, we use the Relation tab. Open this tab and check the **Relate to Parent Command** box. In the relation definition, choose to relate the PubId fields and press the **Add** button. Select **OK** to close the dialog.
14. Now that the hierarchy is defined, use the Data Environment as a source to bind to a display grid. Visual Basic 6.0 provides a special grid designed just to display these hierarchical structures and this control is available through the Components dialog as the Microsoft Hierarchical FlexGrid Control 6.0 (OLEDB). Add this control to the toolbox and place it on Form1.
15. In the properties of the FlexGrid, set the DataSource property to **DataEnvironment1** and the DataMember property to **Publishers**.
16. Run the project. The hierarchical data should be visible in the grid. Use the + and – signs in the grid to expand and collapse the hierarchy.

In addition to creating hierarchies, it is also possible to specify groupings and aggregate functions for the hierarchy. This facilitates grouping the display of titles by subject, for example. The aggregate functions then make it possible to show information such as the count of all books in a subject or the average price of a book in a given subject category.

THE MICROSOFT DATA TOOLS

Creating SQL statements can be tedious at best. Fortunately for VB programmers, we have tools to help. Visual Basic 6.0 ships with a graphical database interface known as the Microsoft Data Tools. These tools are specifically designed to help create SQL statements for use in applications. They can also be used in combination with the Data Environment to create command objects.

Begin using the data tools by opening the Data View window (Figure 10-7), which can be accessed by selecting **VIEW/DATA VIEW WINDOW** from the menu. The data view shows data links that result from data links files or from Data Environment objects. These data links make it easy to view the structure of any database.

Once a data link is visible in the data view, it is possible to view any part of the database structure. For example, examine table data by expanding the tables folder and double clicking an item. Or examine and edit stored procedures within Visual Basic. All the table data and stored procedure definitions are fully editable from within Visual Basic.

Figure 10-7 The Data View window.

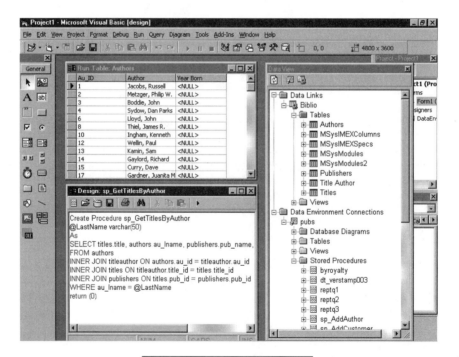

Figure 10-8 Microsoft Data Tools.

In addition to viewing and editing data, the data tools (Figure 10-8) also facilitate creation of queries as SQL statements. In order to create an SQL statement, start with one table open in the data tools. Next, make the SQL building panes visible by selecting **VIEW/SHOW PANES** from the menu. The data tools have design panes (Figure 10-9) for the raw SQL statement, table relationships, and a grid tool for building SQL. It is generally helpful to have all of these panes open when building queries.

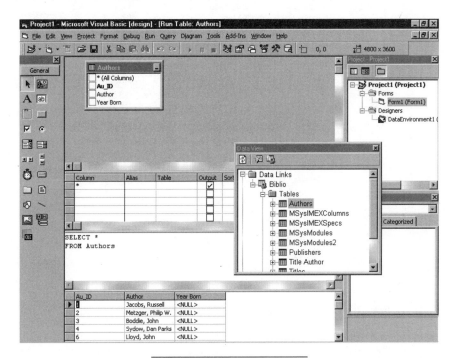

Figure 10-9 The design panes.

Once the design panes are visible, drag the tables to be queried from the Data View window to the diagram pane. A list of all fields in the table and relationships to other tables will be visible. To build a SELECT query, just check the boxes next to the fields to be included in the query. The data tools automatically construct an SQL statement (Figure 10-10) in the SQL pane.

Run any statement by selecting **QUERY/RUN** and view the results in the results pane. The data tools support the creation of SELECT, INSERT, UPDATE, and DELETE statements. Set the type of query to be created by selecting **QUERY/CHANGE TYPE** from the menu.

Check It Out 10-3: Building Queries

1. Start a new Standard EXE project in Visual Basic.
2. Open the Data View window by selecting **VIEW/DATA VIEW WINDOW** from the menu.
3. In the data view, right click the **Data Links** folder and select **ADD DATA LINK...** from the popup menu.

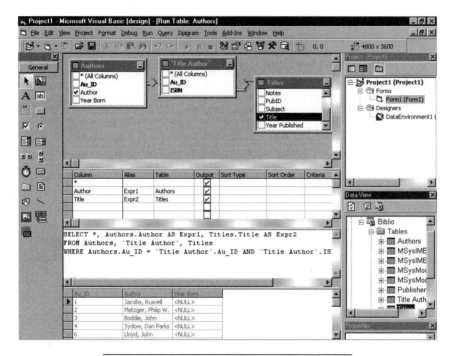

Figure 10-10 Creating an SQL SELECT statement.

4. Using the data links property sheet, establish a new data link to the BIBLIO database. On the Provider tab choose the **Microsoft Jet 3.51 OLE DB Provider**. On the Connection tab, use the ellipsis to select the **BIBLIO.MDB** file. Close the dialog.

5. The Biblio database should now be visible in the data view window as `DataLink1`. Open the tables folder for the data link and double click on the Authors table.

6. Open the design panes by selecting **VIEW/SHOW PANES** for the DIAGRAM, SQL, GRID, and RESULTS panes. With all the panes visible, the following SQL statement should appear in the SQL pane:

```
SELECT * FROM Authors
```

7. Drag the `TitleAuthor` and `Titles` tables from the Data View window to the diagram pane. See the tables and their relationships to other tables should be visible.

8. Use the checkboxes in the table and select **Author** from Authors and **Title** from Titles. No other fields should be selected. The following SQL statement should be visible:

```
SELECT Authors.Author AS Expr1, Titles.Title
FROM Authors, 'Title Author', Titles
WHERE Authors.Au_ID = 'Title Author'.Au_ID AND 'Title
    Author'.ISBN = Titles.ISBN
```

9. Run the query by selecting **QUERY/RUN** from the menu. Observe the results of the query in the results pane.

The data tools can also be used to create diagrams of SQL Server and Oracle databases. For these, there will be a folder labeled Database Diagrams in the Data View window. View any diagram in the folder or create a new one. New database diagrams are created by right-clicking the folder and selecting **NEW DIAGRAM** in the popup menu. To build the diagram, simply drag and drop tables from the Data View window into the blank diagram pane in Visual Basic. The table relationships are shown for each table dropped. Once the diagram is created, it can be printed.

The diagram view can also be used to examine and change structural information about the database. For example, add or delete columns from a table, or remove the table entirely from the database. For even more design power, right-click on any table in the data view and select **DESIGN**. The design view affords the complete ability to alter a table in any way. Add or delete columns or change data types. All of this is done through mouse clicks alone.

Finally, the data view can be used to create commands inside a Data Environment object. If there is a Data Environment in the project, drag tables, views, or stored procedures to the Data Environment window. For each object dropped, a new command is created in the Data Environment. These commands can then be bound to elements on a form as we described above.

Check It Out 10-4: The Data Tools and Data Environment

1. Start a new Standard EXE project in Visual Basic.

2. Open the Data View window by selecting **VIEW/DATA VIEW WINDOW** from the menu.

3. In the data view, right-click the Data Links folder and select **ADD DATA LINK...** from the popup menu.

4. Using the Data Links property sheet, establish a new data link to the BIBLIO database. On the Provider tab choose the **Microsoft Jet 3.51 OLE DB Provider**. On the Connection tab, use the ellipsis to select the **BIBLIO.MDB** file. Close the dialog.

5. The Biblio database should now be visible in the Data View window as `DataLink1`.

6. In the data view, push the toolbar to Add a Data Environment to the Current Project. A new Data Environment designer should appear in the Project Explorer.

7. From the data view, open the **Views** folder. Drag the **All Titles** view from the data view to the Data Environment. A new connection and command should appear.

8. Now show Form1. Make Form1 and the Data Environment visible together by selecting **WINDOW/TILE HORIZONTALLY** from the menu. With the windows next to each other, drag the **AllTitles** command onto Form1. A new interface will be built on the form.

9. Run the application. To complete the application, add navigation controls to the form.

THE DATA REPORT DESIGNER

Historically, Visual Basic has had weak reporting capabilities. This weakness was generally overcome by third-party reporting products like Crystal Reports. In version 6.0 of Visual Basic a built-in reporting engine known as the Data Report Designer has been introduced (Figure 10-11).

The simplest way to use the Data Report Designer is to think of it as a bound object. As with a grid control, a Data Environment object can be bound to the Data Report Designer to create a report on a recordset.

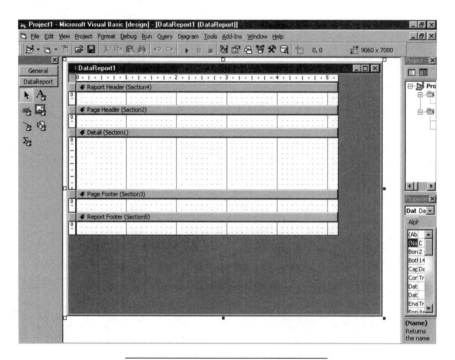

Figure 10-11 The Data Report Designer.

Check It Out 10-5: Creating a Report

1. Start a new Visual Basic Standard EXE project.
2. If the Data Environment or Data Report are not already available under the PROJECT menu, open the **Components** dialog and select the objects from the Designers tab.
3. Add a Data Environment object to the project by selecting **PROJECT/DATA ENVIRONMENT** from the menu. (Note that the Data Environment may be under PROJECT/MORE ACTIVEX DESIGNERS… if there are already several designers added to Visual Basic.)

4. Right-click on the **Connection1** object to open the Data Link properties. In the Provider tab, choose **Microsoft JET 3.51 OLE DB Provider**. This will make it possible to connect to a Microsoft Access database.

5. In the Connection tab, use the ellipsis in the Select or Enter a Database Name box to locate the file `BIBLIO.MDB`. Press the **Test Connection** button to verify that the Data Link is correctly established.

6. Press the **OK** button to save the Data Link.

7. Right-click on **Connection1** and select **ADD COMMAND** from the popup menu. This will place a new command object under the connection.

8. Right-click on the **Command1** object and select **PROPERTIES** from the popup menu. This will open the tabbed dialog for the command properties.

9. In the General tab, select to base the command on an SQL statement. In the SQL box type the following statement:

```
SELECT * FROM Publishers
```

10. Press the **OK** button to save the command definition.

11. Add a Data Report object to the project by selecting **PROJECT/DATA REPORT** from the menu. (Note that the Data Report may be under PROJECT/MORE ACTIVEX DESIGNERS… if several designers have already been added to Visual Basic.)

12. Connect the Data Environment to the Data report by setting the DataSource property of the Data Report to `DataEnvironment1`. Designate the query to show in the report by setting the Data Member property to `Command1`.

13. Right-click on the Report Designer and choose **RETRIEVE STRUCTURE** from the popup menu. This will cause the Report Designer to reflect the hierarchy in the Data Environment. For this simple query, we have not built a hierarchical structure, but if we had relationships between command objects, the Report Designer would create sections to reflect the relationships.

14. Select the **Detail** section of the Report Designer. From the toolbox, add a Report TextBox control by double-clicking the control. Add a Report Label control as well. Set the design-time properties of these two controls as shown in the item list below:

Item 1—Report Label

Name	lblName
Caption	Name

Item 2—Report TextBox

Name	txtName
DataMember	Command1
DataField	Company Name

15. The report is run by calling the `Show` method of the Report Designer. For this example, we will run the report in the Load event of Form1. Add the following code to the `Form_Load` event to run the report:

```
DataReport1.Show
```

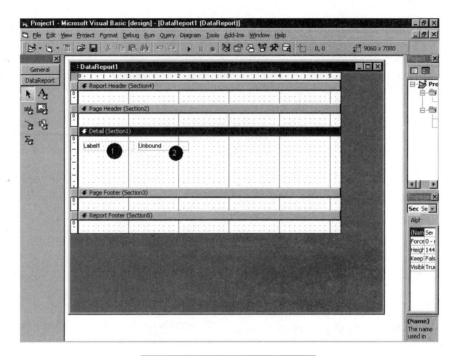

Figure 10-12 The report interface.

THE USERCONNECTION OBJECT

Along with the Data Environment, Visual Basic also provides a `UserConnection` object designer for use with the Remote Data Objects and ODBC. This object is the predecessor to the Data Environment and is considerably more limited in scope. Each designer attempts to provide the full power of a data access technology while limiting the requirement to write code.

In order to make the `UserConnection` object available, select it in the **Components** dialog. Once it is inserted, the `UserConnection` can be used to establish a connection to a DSN and to set up query objects. Accessing the objects is accomplished through Property sheets (Figure 10-13) where it is possible to specify the DSN and cursor driver as well as SQL statements and stored procedures.

When a `UserConnection` object is added to a project, it represents a single connection to an ODBC data source. Multiple connections cannot be represented in the same designer. To specify the connection, right-click the **UserConnection** and select **PROPERTIES** from the popup menu. A tabbed dialog will appear where information about the connection can be set.

Once the connection is defined, add to the designer queries in the form of SQL statements or stored procedures. This is done by pushing the **Insert Multiple Queries** button which appears on the top of the designer. The insert queries move generates the Query dialog, to be used to select stored procedures or build SQL statements.

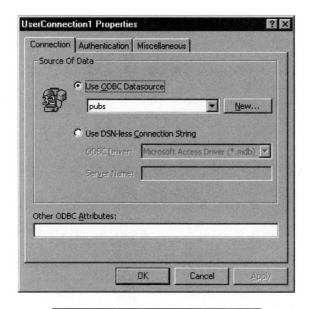

Figure 10-13 The Connection properties.

The `UserConnection` cannot be used as a source for data binding. This means specific code must be written using the properties and methods of the `UserConnection`. As with the `DataEnvironment`, however, queries defined in the designer can be called as methods and parameters can be passesd as arguments of those methods. For organizations still using ODBC, the designer offers advantages, though, it is much weaker than its ADO counterpart.

Exercise 10-1: The Data Environment

The Data Environment provides a quick and easy way to create data applications with OLEDB technology. In this exercise, we will investigate the Data Environment and the Report Designer.

THE DATA ENVIRONMENT

Step 1

Create a new directory in the File Explorer called **VB BOOTCAMP\EXERCISE10-1**. Start a new Visual Basic Standard EXE project.

Step 2

If the Data Environment is not already available under the PROJECT menu, open the **Components** dialog and select the **Data Environment** from the **Designers** tab. Add a Data Environment object to the project by selecting **PROJECT/DATA ENVIRONMENT** from the menu. (Note that the Data Environment may be under **PROJECT/MORE ACTIVEX DESIGNERS...** if several designers have already been added to Visual Basic.)

Step 3

In the Data Environment, right-click on the **Connection1** object. When the Data Link properties appear, select **Microsoft Jet 3.51 OLE DB Provider**.

Step 4

On the Connection tab, locate the Select or Enter a Database Name box. Press the **ellipsis** and locate BIBLIO.MDB. Test the connection with the **Test Connection** button. When the Data Link is correctly established, press **OK** to close the tabbed dialog.

Step 5

In the Data Environment, right-click on the **Connection1** object and select **RENAME** from the popup menu. Rename the connection **Biblio**.

Step 6

Right-click on the **Biblio** connection and choose **ADD COMMAND** from the menu. This will place a new command object called Command1 in the Data Environment. Right-click the **Command** object and select **RENAME** from the popup menu. Rename the Command object to Publishers.

Step 7

Right click the **Publishers** command and select **PROPERTIES** from the popup menu. This will bring up the tabbed dialog for the Command properties. In the General tab, select to base the query on an SQL statement. In the Data Environment, the question mark can be used in an SQL statement to indicate that a parameter should be passed to the statement. Each question mark is filled by arguments passed in the order they appear in the SQL statement. In the SQL box, type the following query:

```
SELECT PubID, Name FROM Publishers WHERE Name LIKE ?
```

Step 8

In order to define the parameter to be passed, use the Parameters tab, where there will be a parameter defined as Param1. This parameter is originally defined as a numeric value. Change the data type to String. Set the following values in the Parameter tab:

Data Type	adVarChar
Host Data Type	String
Size	255

Step 9

Create a child recordset for the Publishers command by right-clicking on the command and selecting **ADD CHILD COMMAND** from the popup menu. This child command will be used to display books associated with a selected publisher. When the child command is added, it will be named Command1.

Step 10

Before defining the new child command, create an SQL statement to use with the command. This SQL statement is going to join title and author information for the selected publisher.

Step 11

Open the Data View window by selecting **VIEW/DATA VIEW WINDOW** from the menu. In the data view, locate the Data Environment Connections folder. In this folder, the connection named `Biblio` should be visible. Open this connection and locate the Tables folder. In the folder, locate the Titles table. Double-click the **Titles** table to display it in the Microsoft Data Tools.

Step 12

With the Titles table visible, open the Data Tools panes by selecting **VIEW/SHOW PANES** from the menu. Open each of the four panes under this menu item. It may be necessary to click on the Titles table data to activate the SHOW PANES menu items.

Step 13

Once all the Data Tool panes are visible, drag the Title Author and Authors tables into the diagram pane of the Data Tools. When the tables are in the diagram panes, check carefully to verify that the Titles table is related to the Title Author table by the ISBN field and the Title Author table is related to the Authors table by the Au_ID field. If either of these relationships is missing, drag from the appropriate field into the Title Author table to recreate the relationship.

Step 14

To build the appropriate query, check the **PubID** and **Title** fields in the Titles table and the Author field in the Authors table. Next, examine the grid pane. The Data Tools automatically add an entry with an asterisk which forces a return of all fields in the query. We do not want to return all the fields so highlight the row containing the asterisk and press the **Delete** key. The Data Tools create the following query:

```
SELECT Titles.PubID AS Expr1, Titles.Titles As Expr2, Authors.Author
    AS Expr3
FROM Titles, 'Title Author', Authors
WHERE Titles.ISBN = 'Title Author'.ISBN AND 'Title Author'.Au_ID =
    Authors.Au_ID
```

Step 15

Copy the query created by the Data Tools onto the clipboard by highlighting the entire statement and selecting **EDIT/COPY** from the menu.

Step 16

Double click the Data Environment in the Project Explorer. Right-click the child command and select **PROPERTIES** from the popup menu. Immediately change the name of the command in the General tab to Titles. Select to base this query on an SQL Statement and paste the query from the data tools into the SQL box by selecting **EDIT/PASTE** from the menu.

Step 17

Click on the **Relation** tab where the PubID field from both the Publishers and Titles commands will be visible. Press the **Add** button to accept the suggested relation between the parent and child command. Press **OK** to preserve the work.

Step 18

Close all the open windows and save the project.

BUILDING THE USER INTERFACE

Step 19

Use the Components dialog to make the Hierarchical FlexGrid control available in the toolbox. Select **PROJECT/COMPONENTS** from the menu and locate the Microsoft Hierarchical FlexGrid Control 6.0 (OLEDB). Check this control and press the **OK** button.

Step 20

Open Form1. Create a GUI using a Label, a TextBox, a CommandButton, and a FlexGrid control. Figure 10-14 shows the final form. Use the Item list below to set design-time properties for the controls in the Properties window.

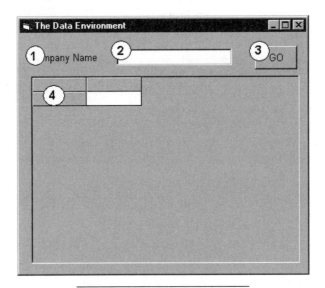

Figure 10-14 Form1 and controls.

Item 1—Label

Name	lblCompany
Caption	Company Name

Item2— TextBox

Name	`txtCompany`
Text	`micro`

Item3—CommandButton

Name	`cmdGO`
Caption	GO
Default	True

Item 4—Hierarchical FlexGrid

Name	`grdTitles`
AllowUserResizing	`1-flexResizeColumns`
DataSource	`DataEnvironment1`
DataMember	`Publishers`
FixedCols	0

Step 21

Click on the **Hierarchical FlexGrid** control on Form1. In the Properties window, locate the Custom property. Press the **ellipsis** that appears to reveal the tabbed Custom Property dialog. Locate the Bands tab in the Custom Property dialog. Select **Band0 (Publishers)** and then uncheck the **PubID** field (which is `Expr1`) so it will not be displayed. Also uncheck the **PubID** field for `Band1`.

Step 22

Change the column names in Band1 from `Expr2` and `Expr3` to `Title` and `Author` respectively. This can be done by selecting under the **Column Caption** heading for Band1. As with changing a file name in the File Explorer, gently click twice to enter **Edit** mode. When done, press the **OK** button. The grid should now show columns for Publisher, Title, and Author.

Step 23

When the application first starts, the TextBox contains the text `micro`, a suggested string for a search. When the button is pressed, whatever text is in the TextBox is used to run the Publishers command. Any company that has this text in its name will be returned and shown in the grid. Add the following code to the `cmdGO_Click` event to run the search and show the results.

```
MousePointer = vbHourglass
With DataEnvironment1

  'Close the current recordset
  .rsPublishers.Close

    'Run the new recordset
  .Publishers "%" & txtCompany.Text & "%"
```

```
End With

'Show new set in grid
Set grdTitles.DataSource = DataEnvironment1
grdTitles.CollapseAll

MousePointer = vbDefault
```

Step 24

Save the work and run the project. Use `micro` as a search string or try others such as `hill` or `mill`.

GENERATING A REPORT

Step 25

If the Data Report Designer is not already available under the PROJECT menu, open the components dialog and select the **Data Report Designer** from the Designers tab. Add Data Report Designer object to the project by selecting **PROJECT/DATA REPORT** from the menu. (Note that the Data Report Designer may be under PROJECT/MORE ACTIVEX DESIGNERS... if several designers have already been added to Visual Basic.)

Step 26

Connect the Data Report Designer to the Data Environment object by setting the `Data-Source` property of the Data Report to **DataEnvironment1** and the `DataMember` property to **Publishers**.

Step 27

This report will represent hierarchical data, so we have to reflect that structure in the report. Get the structure by right-clicking on the **Data Report Designer** and selecting **RETRIEVE STRUCTURE** from the popup menu. There will be a confirmation dialog to which the response should be **Yes**.

Step 28

Now examine the Report Designer. Notice that Visual Basic has created a hierarchical structure on the page that represents the structure in the data hierarchy. These sections make it possible to dictate the display of the report header, page header, publisher information, title information, page footer, and report footer.

Step 29

Select the **Report Header** section. Into this section drop a Report Label from the Data Report section of your toolbox. Change the `Caption` to read **Book Report**. The Font style and may be changed as required.

Step 30

Select the **Group** header. Into this section drop a Report TextBox from the toolbox. Set the `DataMember` property to **Publishers** and the `DataField` property to **Name**.

Step 31

Select the **Detail** section of the report. Into this section drop two Report TextBoxes. Place the controls side by side in the Detail section. Select the first TextBox and set its `DataMember` property to **Titles** and its `DataField` property to **Expr2**. Select the second TextBox and set its `DataMember` property to **Titles** and its `DataField` property to **Expr3**.

Step 32

Save the work.

Step 33

Open Form1. With Form1 visible, create a menu for Form1 by selecting **TOOLS/MENU EDITOR** from the menu. In the Menu Editor, build a Report menu with items Preview and Print. Use the Item list below to set the properties in the Menu Editor.

    Item 1—Menu
Name	`mnuReport`
Caption	Report

    Item 2—Menu
Name	`mnuPreview`
Caption	Preview

    Item 3—Menu
Name	`mnuPrint`
Caption	Print

Step 34

Previewing the report is done with the `Show` method. Under the click event of `mnuPreview`, add the following code:

```
DataReport1.Show
```

Step 35

Printing the report is done with the `PrintReport` method. Under the click event of `mnuPrint`, add the following code:

```
DataReport1.PrintReport
```

Step 36

Save and run the application. Try showing the report.

Exercise 10-2: The User Connection Designer

Visual Basic offers many different data access techniques. In this exercise, we will investigate RDO features through the `UserConnection` object.

SETTING UP THE ODBC DATA SOURCE

Step 1

Before using the ODBC API, set up an ODBC data source. In this exercise, we will be interacting with the Microsoft Access database BIBLIO.MDB that ships with Visual Basic.

Establishing the data source is not a Visual Basic, but rather a Windows Operating System function. Setup is done using the ODBC Administrator utility found in Windows. Locate the ODBC Administrator in the Control Panel, where there will be an icon labeled ODBC. Double click on this icon to start the ODBC Administrator.

Step 2

Starting the ODBC Administrator will generate the Data Sources dialog box, which lists all the ODBC data sources currently available on the machine. In order to create a new data source, select the **System DSN** tab. Push the **Add** button. The Create New Data Source dialog now visible lists all the ODBC drivers available on the machine. For this exercise, select the **Microsoft Access ODBC driver** from the list and press **Finish**.

Step 3

The ODBC Setup dialog will appear. In this dialog, define the new data source. First provide a name for the data source. This can be any name, but for this exercise, name the data source `BIBLIO`.

Next, select the **BIBLIO.MDB** database by pushing the **Select** button and navigating the file system to find the BIBLIO.MDB file. Select this file. Then push the **OK** button and back out of the ODBC Administrator. The data source has now been defined.

CREATING THE GUI

Step 4

Create a new subdirectory called **VB BOOTCAMP \EXERCISE10-2** for this Visual Basic project using the File Explorer. Start a new Visual Basic Standard EXE project. Construct a graphic user interface on Form1 as shown. Use the Item list to set design time properties for the controls. See Figure 10-15.

> **Item 1—Form**
>
> BorderStyle   3 'Fixed Dialog
>
> Caption   User Connection Object with Microsoft Access
>
> **Item 2— CommandButton**
>
> Caption   First
>
> Name   cmdMoveFirst

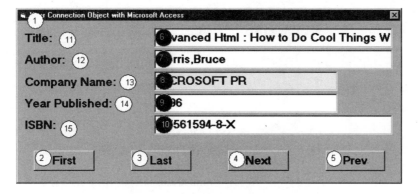

Figure 10-15 Form and Controls.

Item 3—CommandButton

Caption	Last
Name	cmdMoveLast

Item 4—CommandButton

Caption	Next
Name	cmdMoveNext

Item 5—CommandButton

Caption	Prev
Name	cmdMovePrevious

Item 6—TextBox

Name	txtFields
Index	0

Item 7—TextBox

Name	txtFields
Index	1

Item 8—TextBox

Name	txtFields
Index	2

Item 9—TextBox

Name	txtFields
Index	3

Item 10—TextBox

Name	txtFields
Index	4

Item11—Label

Name	lblFields
Caption	Title
Index	0

Item12—Label

Name	lblFields
Caption	Author
Index	1

Item13—Label

Name	lblFields
Caption	Company Name
Index	2

Item14—Label

Name	lblFields
Caption	Year Published
Index	3

Item15—Label

Name	lblFields
Caption	ISBN
Index	4

THE USER CONNECTION OBJECT

Step 5

In this section, use the UserConnection object to access the functionality of RDO. Select **Project/Components...** from the menu to display the Component dialog. In the Component dialog, select the **Designers** tab. In the Designers tab, ensure the **Microsoft UserConnection** object is selected. Add a new UserConnection to the project by selecting **Project/More ActiveX Designers/Microsoft UserConnection** from the menu. A new UserConnection object should appear.

Step 6

The UserConnection object gives graphical access to an RDO connection and makes it possible to define the ODBC connection and queries/stored procedures without writing extra code. Microsoft estimates that the UserConnection can reduce code by up to a factor of 10 for data connections with RDO.

Step 7

In the Properties of the UserConnection, connect to the **BIBLIO ODBC** data source by selecting it under the Use ODBC Datasource option. When the connection is defined, close the Properties dialog for the UserConnection. Name the new UserConnection object **conData**.

Step 8

Right-click on the UserConnection icon in the workspace area to reveal a popup menu. Select **Insert Query** from this menu to add a new query to the UserConnection. The new query dialog will appear and permit definition of the query. Name the new query **AllTitles**.

Select the option **Based on User-Defined SQL** and add the following SQL statement to the query designer (to construct the query using the data tools, it will be necessary to create a data link to use them.):

```
SELECT Titles.Title, Titles.ISBN, Authors.Author, Titles.[Year
Published], Publishers.[Company Name] FROM Publishers, Titles,
Authors, [title author] WHERE((((Authors.Au_ID = [title
author].Au_ID) AND ([title author].ISBN = Titles.ISBN)) AND
(Titles.PubID = Publishers.PubID))) ORDER BY Titles.Title
```

Step 9

Close the Query designer to save the new query definition in the UserConnection. Saving the SQL this way obviates having to create it in several lines of code. It is stored with the UserConnection object.

CODING THE APPLICATION

Step 10

Open the Code window for frmUserConnection. In the [General][Declarations] section, define the following variables for the RDO Connection and Resultset objects:

```
'This variable is for the User Connection
Private m_Connection As conData
'This variable is for the Resultset
Private m_Resultset As RDO.rdoResultset
```

Step 11

The database connection is made in the Form_Load event. After the connection is made, we run the predefined SQL query contained in the UserConnection. Add the following code to the Form_Load event to access the data source:

```
'Establish the Connection
Set m_Connection = New conData
m_Connection.EstablishConnection
'Get Results
Set m_Resultset = m_Connection.rdoQueries("AllTitles"). _
```

```
OpenResultset(rdOpenDynamic)
'Fill Form
ShowData
```

The ShowData routine is used to populate the textboxes with data. Create a new procedure as follows to show the data:

```
Public Sub ShowData()
'This routine shows data in the Text Boxes
txtFields(0).Text = m_Resultset!Title
txtFields(1).Text = m_Resultset!Author
txtFields(2).Text = m_Resultset![Company Name]
txtFields(3).Text = m_Resultset![Year Published]
txtFields(4).Text = m_Resultset!ISBN

End Sub
```

Step 12

The remainder of the code provides the functionality for the buttons. Add the following code to activate the buttons:

```
Private Sub cmdMoveFirst_Click()
 m_Resultset.MoveFirst
 ShowData
End Sub
Private Sub cmdMoveLast_Click()
 m_Resultset.MoveLast
 ShowData
End Sub
Private Sub cmdMoveNext_Click()
 m_Resultset.MoveNext
 If m_Resultset.EOF Then
 Beep
 m_Resultset.MoveLast
 Else
 ShowData
 End If
End Sub

Private Sub cmdMovePrevious_Click()
 m_Resultset.MovePrevious
 If m_Resultset.BOF Then
 Beep
 m_Resultset.MoveFirst
```

```
      Else
      ShowData
      End If
End Sub
```

Step 13
Save the project and run it.

FOR THE CERTIFIED PRO

Pro 10-1: Data Hierarchies

1. Create a hierarchical view in a Data Environment for the SQL Server pubs data-base that relates authors to book titles.
2. Show the relationship in a hierarchical flexgrid control.

Pro 10-2: Data-Reports

1. Create a Data Report for the above exercise.

PREPARING FOR CERTIFICATION

Topics for Further Reading
    About the Data Environment Designer
    The Data View Window and Visual Database Tools
    Hierarchical Cursors and Data Shaping
    Writing Reports with the Microsoft Data Report Designer

CERTIFICATION QUIZ

1. A Data Link is represented in the Data Environment by which object?
   a. Data Environment
   b. Connection
   c. Command
   d. UserConnection

2. Which data sources can be used as Data Links?
   a. ODBC database
   b. SQL Server
   c. Microsoft Access
   d. Microsoft Index Server

3. How can a parameter be specified to pass for a Command object?
   a. Include a * in the SQL statement
   b. Include a % in the SQL statement
   c. Include a ? in the SQL statement
   d. Include a / in the SQL statement

4. When defining a parameter for a command, which of the following should be set?
   a. Data Type
   b. Source Data Type
   c. Host Data Type
   d. Size

5. Which lines of code will execute a command named `MyQuery` in a Data Environment named `DataEnvironment1`?
   a. `DataEnvironment1("MyQuery")`
   b. `DataEnvironment1.MyQuery`
   c. `DataEnvironment1.Execute`
   d. `DataEnvironment1.Commands("MyQuery").Execute`

6. Given a command named `MyQuery`, what is the name of the recordset produced when the query runs?
   a. `MyRecordset`
   b. `RMyQuery`
   c. `Recordset`
   d. `rsMyQuery`

7. Which objects have the ability to display a hierarchical cursor?
   a. TextBox
   b. Hierarchical FlexGrid Control
   c. DataReport
   d. DataGrid

8. How can a new Data Link be bought into the Data View Window?
   a. Right-click the Data View window
   b. Add a new DataEnvironment to the project
   c. Add a new UserControl to the project
   d. Add a Report Designer to the project

9. For which databases does VB support diagram creation?
   a. Microsoft Access
   b. Microsoft FoxPro
   c. SQL Server
   d. Oracle

10. Which query types are supported by the Microsoft Data Tools?
    a. SELECT
    b. INSERT
    c. UPDATE
    d. DELETE

11. Which properties must be set in the Data Report Designer to report from a Data Environment?
    a. DataField
    b. DataMember
    c. DataSource
    d. DataBindings

12. How is the hierarchy of the Data Environment reflectd in a Data Report designer?
    a. Drag the Data Environment to the Report designer
    b. Use the RETRIEVE STRUCTURE menu item
    c. Set the Structure property to the Data Environment object
    d. Drag Command objects to the Report designer

13. Which data sources can be used with the UserConnection object?
    a. Data Links
    b. Text Files
    c. ODBC sources
    d. Excel files

14. How many connections can exist in one `UserConnection` object?
    a. 1
    b. 5
    c. 10
    d. Unlimited

15. Which objects can bind to the `UserConnection` object?
    a. DataEnvironment
    b. Data Report
    c. Grid Control
    d. None

ANSWERS TO CERTIFICATION QUIZ

1. b
2. a, b, c, d
3. c
4. a, c, d
5. b, d
6. d
7. b, c

8. a, b
9. c, d
10. a, b, c, d
11. b, c
12. b
13. c
14. a
15. d

REMOTE DATA OBJECTS

Those who begin this chapter, should be familiar with the concepts of ODBC and know how to create a DSN in the ODBC Administrator and use objects from an object model.

SKILLS COVERED

- 70-175 (34): Access and manipulate data using the Execute Direct model
- 70-175 (35): Access and manipulate data using the Prepare/Execute model
- 70-175 (36): Access and manipulate data by using the Stored Procedures model
- 70-175 (36.a): Use a stored procedure to execute a statement on a database
- 70-175 (36.b): Use a stored procedure to return records to a Visual Basic application
- 70-175 (37): Retrieve and manipulate data by using different cursor locations
- 70-175 (38): Retrieve and manipulate data by using different cursor types
- 70-175 (40): Manage database transactions to ensure data consistency and recoverability

■   70-175 (43): Use appropriate locking strategies to ensure data integrity

Understanding data access principles is probably the single most important skill a Visual Basic developer can possess. The bulk of all programs written today concern data access in one form or another. This statement is particularly true for a business application running on an enterprise network. Databases are the backbone of business applications, and success as a VB programmer depends on this knowledge. Although VB 6.0 ships with advanced data tools that implement the OLEDB technology, ODBC technology is still widely used and represents an important domain of knowledge. In this chapter, we will examine the high-performance object model for accessing ODBC data sources.

THE REMOTE DATA OBJECTS MODEL

Visual Basic 6.0 provides a fast and powerful mechanism for accessing ODBC data sources through code known as the Remote Data Objects (RDO), an ActiveX Component that consists of several classes supporting all the features of ODBC. It is easy to use this component to query and update ODBC sources with the speed and control required for enterprise applications.

Understanding RDO comes from understanding the objects contained within it. These objects together form the RDO Object Model (Figure 11-1), which is used graphically to represent the features of RDO, much as object models as Excel or even Visual Basic itself. The objects contained in RDO are specialized for data access using ODBC.

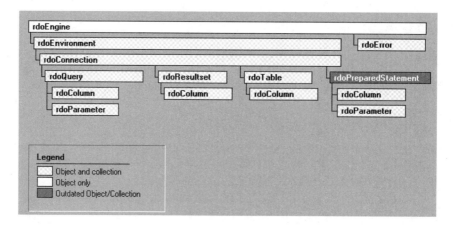

Figure 11-1 The RDO Object Model.

THE RDOENGINE OBJECT

The top-level object in the RDO model is the `rdoEngine` object, represents the entire RDO component. It contains information such as the version of RDO. It is not necessary explicitly to create an `rdoEngine` object, since RDO provides the first one automatically.

The `rdoEngine` object gives access to the rest of the objects in the model. In addition, it can be used to create new DSN entries on the fly through the `rdoRegisterDataSource` method. This method takes all the information necessary to create a new DSN. The following code creates a DSN for use against the Pubs database. Note that this code assumes SQL Server is running on the same machine as the code.

```
Dim strTemp As String
strTemp = "Description=Test DSN" & Chr$(13) & "SERVER=(local)" & _
    Chr$(13) & "Database=pubs"
rdoEngine.rdoRegisterDataSource "MyTestPubs", "SQL Server", True, _
    strTemp
```

THE RDOERROR OBJECT

The `rdoError` object is used to determine whether an operation on a data source has resulted in an error. The errors trapped by the `rdoError` object are not Visual Basic errors, but rather those that occur at the database server. There may not be a trappable runtime error for these errors. Instead, the `rdoErrors` collection can be examined after an operation to determine success or failure. The following code shows how:

```
Dim objError As RDO.rdoError
Dim strError As String
'Simple Error Handling
'Collect Errors
   For Each objError In rdoEngine.rdoErrors
      strError = strError & vbCrLf & objError.Description
   Next
'Display Errors
MsgBox "The following errors occurred: " _
   & vbCrLf & strError, vbOKOnly, "User Connection Object"
```

Whenever an error is generated by the database engine, the `rdoEngine` object fires an `InfoMessage` event, which indicates the need to examine the `rdoErrors` collection for messages. Generally, database engine messages are informational and thus safe to ignore, but always examine the collection just the same.

THE RDOENVIRONMENT OBJECT

The `rdoEnvironment` object represents a security context inside which a database can be accessed. Use this to specify User IDs and passwords or perform database transactions. An `rdoEnvironment` is not generally created directly, since the first one appears automatically. It is possible to create additional environments that are automatically managed through a collection.

THE RDOCONNECTION OBJECT

Most of the real functionality of RDO begins with the `rdoConnection` object, which is used to establish a connection with an ODBC data source. Once the data source is defined, the properties and methods of the `rdoConnection` can be used to communicate with the database server. The simplest access requires only that the object be instantiated, the name of the data source be set as it appears in the ODBC Administrator, and the connection be established:

```
Set m_Connection = New RDO.rdoConnection
m_Connection.Connect = "DSN=Biblio;"
m_Connection.EstablishConnection
```

THE RDOQUERY OBJECT

The `rdoQuery` object can be used to execute SQL queries on an open ODBC data source. Executing queries can be done with simple SQL statements in code or from precompiled stored procedures supported by a database like SQL Server. Parameters for stored procedures are managed using the `rdoParameter` object. At its most fundamental, the `rdoQuery` object needs only to know what connection to query and the SQL statement to use in the query:

```
'Create SQL Statement
Dim strSQL As String
strSQL = "SELECT * FROM Publishers"
'Create Query
Dim m_Query As RDO.rdoQuery
Set m_Query = New RDO.rdoQuery
Set m_Query.ActiveConnection = m_Connection
m_Query.SQL = strSQL
'Run Query
m_Query.Execute
```

THE RDORESULTSET OBJECT

The `rdoResultset` object is used to manage records returned from an open ODBC connection. Resultsets can be returned from an `rdoQuery` object or the `OpenResultset` method of an `rdoConnection` object. In any case, the most recently created record set can be accessed through the `LastQueryResults` property of the `rdoConnection` object:

```
Set m_Resultset = m_Connection.LastQueryResults
```

Once the `rdoResultset` is obtained, navigate the records using the `MoveFirst`, `MoveLast`, `MoveNext`, and `MovePrevious` methods, which permit scrolling through the records for display and update purposes. Once the record pointer is moved to the correct position, read the data from the record and show it in a Visual Basic form using the `rdoColumn` object.

THE RDOTABLE OBJECT

The `rdoTable` object represents a table in an ODBC data source. Its use is quite limited. This object is not particularly useful for normal database applications, but can be helpful in determinimg the structure of a data source. Generally, we work with `rdoResultset` objects to retrieve data from the data source. Visual Basic specifically discourages use of the `rdoTable` object as it is intended to support backward compatibility and future support is not guaranteed.

THE RDOCOLUMN OBJECT

The `rdoColumn` object represents a field in a returned recordset. Use this object to access the value for a particular field in a particular record. This object also returns information such as the data type or size of a field.

THE RDOPARAMETER OBJECT

The `rdoParameter` object represents a parameter passed into or received from a stored procedure. Although RDO offers many shorthand calls to stored procedures that do not require a parameter object, this object is useful when it is necessary to specify more detail for an argument or when receiving an output parameter from a stored procedure.

RDO EVENTS

Along with the properties and methods of RDO, the object model also supports several useful events which notify when an asynchronous activity completes or permits customizing the application behavior during database operations. Accessing any of the supported events is accomplished by declaring variables against the model using the `WithEvents` keyword. When declared this way, supported RDO events automatically appear in the code window.

```
Private WithEvents m_Connection As RDO.rdoConnection
```

CONNECTING TO DATA SOURCES

Using RDO from Visual Basic begins by properly referencing the RDO object model and connecting to a data source. Referencing the RDO object model is accomplished using the References dialog (Figure 11-2) just as it is for any COM object. The reference for RDO is listed as Microsoft Remote Data Object 2.0.

Once a reference is established, connect to a data source using the `rdoConnection` object. The process of using this object is the same as that for using any COM object. First declare a variable as an `rdoConnection`. Next, instantiate the object, and finally, call the properties and methods to accomplish the connection. When making the DSN connection, it is necessary to manage several key aspects, including the `Connect` string and the cursor driver.

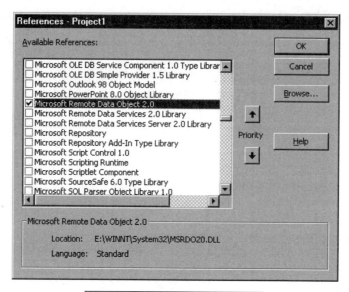

Figure 11-2 The References dialog.

ODBC CONNECT STRINGS

ODBC Connect strings are used during the connection process to pass key information to the ODBC driver for accessing the data source. This information can contain the DSN name, User ID, and Password as well as other key information. Table 11-1 shows all the possible arguments for a Connect string.

Connect string arguments are optional and ODBC can even automatically request missing parameters required for a connection. Typically, the ODBC Connect string is passsed through the Connect property of the `rdoConnection` object. The following code shows a sample string for an SQL Server data source called Publications:

```
Set m_Connection = New RDO.rdoConnection
m_Connection.Connect = "DSN=Publications;UID=sa;PWD=;"
```

In addition to the standard DSN connection using the ODBC Administrator, RDO also supports DSN-less connections, which are made without defining the DSN in the ODBC Administrator. Instead, all the data necessary to connect to the database are provided as part of the Connect string. The following code connects to a SQL Server database named *pubs* without using a DSN:

```
Set m_Connection = New RDO.rdoConnection
m_Connection.Connect = _
"DRIVER={SQL Server};SERVER=(local);DATABASE=pubs;UID=sa;PWD=;DSN=;"
```

Note that the Connect string provides additional information such as the ODBC driver to use and the server where the database can be found. Normally, this information is entered into the

ODBC Administrator, but when provided as part of the Connect string, it removes the requirement for a DSN.

Table 11-1 ODBC Connect String Arguments

Argument	Description
DSN	The ODBC data source name
UID	The database User ID
PWD	The database password
DRIVER	The ODBC driver
DATABASE	The name of the database to connect with
SERVER	The machine name of the database server
WSID	The machine name of the database client
APP	The name of the EXE File

CURSOR DRIVERS

Once the DSN is identified, the cursor driver to use with the connection should be specified. It determines where and how records returned from a database query are maintained. In general, the records may be maintained on either the client or the server. It is also possible to retrieve the actual record information or simply a set of record identifiers, known as keys, that map to the results of a query. The cursor driver is selected by setting the `CursorDriver` property of the `rdoConnection` object to one of the following constants: `rdUseIfNeeded`, `rdUseODBC`, `rdUseServer`, `rdUseClientBatch`, or `rdUseNone`. The following code shows a typical example of establishing the cursor driver:

```
Set m_Connection = New RDO.rdoConnection
m_Connection.Connect = "DSN=Publications;UID=sa;PWD=;"
m_Connection.CursorDriver=rdUseClientBatch
```

The `CursorDriver` property affects all the queries run on a connection and can only be set before the connection is actually made. After the connection is made, the property is read-only. To change the cursor driver, open a new connection to the database. The following sections describe the cursor driver options in detail.

rdUseIfNeeded

This option allows the ODBC driver to select the cursor to use. The driver may select client-side or server-side cursors. If it is available, RDO will select a server-side cursor. Server-side cursors store records returned from queries on the server where the database is located. The records are placed in temporary storage and returned to the client in groups as needed.

rdUseODBC

This option uses the standard ODBC cursor driver that places all retrieved records on the client machine. If the results are too large to fit in RAM, they are placed on the disk until all records are retrieved. Because all records are returned directly to the client, scrolling the records can be faster if the records all exist in memory. However, if large result sets are returned to the client, resources may quickly be exhausted and there may be delays while records are written and read from disk.

rdUseServer

This option forces the use of server-side cursors for all result sets. These cursors are excellent for use with larger result sets that may exhaust client resources if returned through a client-side cursor. However, make sure that the machine running the database has the capability to handle large data sets from multiple users. This can be an issue if hundreds of users are accessing the same database and they are all returning thousands of records.

rdUseClientBatch

This cursor driver causes records to be returned to the client just as with the `rdUseODBC` option, but has more capabilities than that option. It is designed to support such features as multitable updates and is really an upgrade to the `rdUseODBC` option. Employ this option as a preference when using client-side cursors.

rdUseNone

This option prevents the use of cursors and simply returns the records to the client one at a time when requested. It is the lightest and fastest of all cursors and should be used whenever possible. In order to maintain speed, however, this cursor driver only allows records to be navigated in one direction—forward. This cursor driver is ideal for populating list boxes from lookup lists.

ESTABLISHING THE CONNECTION

Once the Connect string and cursor driver are set, it is time to make the connection to the data source, through the `EstablishConnection` method of the `rdoConnection` object. The `EstablishConnection` method has the arguments prompt, read-only, and options.

The prompt argument determines whether or not ODBC should prompt users for arguments not provided in the Connect string. The prompting consists of dialog boxes that users may fill out to specify missing arguments from the Connect string. Table 11-2 shows a complete list of the prompting arguments.

The read-only argument is a simple Boolean value that indicates whether the connection is opened for read-only access. If it is opened as read-only, no updates are permitted. This argument is optional and the default is False.

The options argument permits specifying whether the connection should be opened asynchronously. If the connection should be opened asynchronously so that programmatic control returns to the application immediately, specify the constant `rdAsyncEnable`, RDO will start opening the connection and notify when the connection is complete through its event-handling structure, described later.

Establishing a complete connection requires setting the Connect string and cursor driver before calling the `EstablishConnection` method. The following code shows a typical connection example that incorporates all of the features discussed:

```
Set m_Connection = New RDO.rdoConnection
m_Connection.Connect = _
"DRIVER={SQL Server};SERVER=(local);DATABASE=pubs;UID=sa;PWD=;DSN=;"
m_Connection.CursorDriver = rdUseClientBatch
m_Connection.EstablishConnection rdAsyncEnable
```

Table 11-2 ODBC Prompt Options

Constant	Description
rdDriverPrompt	Always shows the Prompt dialog using the arguments of the Connect string and the dialog
rdDriverNoPrompt	Never shows the Prompt dialog. Incomplete connect information raises an error
rdDriverComplete	Raises the ODBC dialog if the Connect string does not contain sufficient information
rdDriverCompleteRequired	Raises the ODBC dialog if the Connect string does not contain sufficient information; also disables controls in the dialog where information entry is not required

RDOCONNECTION EVENTS

RDO supports a number of events related to the `rdoConnection` object. These provide the application with notification (e.g., when the application connects or disconnects from a data source). They can be particularly useful when the application engages in asynchronous connection. Under asynchronous connections, programmatic control returns immediately to the application, even before the actual connection is made. This feature allows the application to continue processing, but no queries can be run until the connection is complete. The `Connect` event provides notification that the connection has been established so that queries may be run. Table 11-3 shows a complete list of events supported by the connection object.

In order to use the event model of RDO, declare the `rdoConnection` variable `With-Events`. This keyword was covered in detail earlier in the book in creating custom events for Class Modules. When used with RDO, it enables all of the events for RDO in the VB code window.

Table 11-3 rdoConnection Object Events

Event	Description
BeforeConnect	Fires just before connecting to a DSN
Connect	Fires after connecting to a DSN
Disconnect	Fires after disconnecting from a DSN
QueryComplete	Fires immediately after a query completes
QueryTimeout	Fires when elapsed time exceeds the value set in the QueryTimeout property
WillExecute	Fires just before a query executes

Check It Out 11-1: Using RDO Events

1. Start a new Standard EXE project in Visual Basic.
2. Set a reference to RDO by selecting **Project/References...** from the menu.
3. In the References dialog, select **Microsoft Remote Data Object 2.0**.
4. Close the dialog.
5. Open the Code window for Form1. In the [General][Declarations] section, declare a variable as an rdoConnection object using the following code:

```
Private WithEvents m_Connection As RDO.rdoConnection
```

6. Examine the Object box in the code window. The object m_Connection should be listed in the dropdown combo. Select this object.
7. Examine the Procedure box. All the events associated with the rdoConnection should be visible. Select any of these events and write code in them.

UNDERSTANDING CURSORS

Once the SQL statement or stored procedure to execute is created, use the rdoQuery object to run the statement against an ODBC data source. To use an rdoQuery object, instantiate it and set the SQL property to the statement to be run. The Execute method then runs the statement against the DSN specified by the ActiveConnection property.

```
Set m_Query = New RDO.rdoQuery
Set m_Query.ActiveConnection = m_Connection
m_Query.SQL = "SELECT * FROM Customers"
m_Query.CursorTye = rdOpenStatic
m_Query.Execute
```

When a query is run and records are returned, the limitations of the cursor driver selected when the connection was made bind the transaction. Within these limitations, `rdoQuery` objects can then specify the type of cursor to employ. A cursor is different from a cursor driver. The driver sets boundaries inside which the `rdoQuery` object must operate, but the `CursorType` property refines the features of the resulting `rdoResultset` object. These features include scrolling and update capabilities. The `CursorType` is defined by the constants `rdOpenForwardOnly`, `rdOpenStatic`, `rdOpenKeyset`, and `rdOpenDynamic`.

RDOPENFORWARDONLY

The `rdOpenForwardOnly` option produces a set of records that can only be scrolled in the forward direction using the `MoveNext` method of the `rdoResultset` object. This cursor is the lightest and fastest of all those available, but is also the most limiting. It is always generated in conjunction with the `rdUseNone` cursor driver. This cursor is ideal for populating lookup lists or read-only data.

RDOPENSTATIC

The `rdOpenStatic` option produces a set of records that is fully scrollable, but has a static membership. This option generates a snapshot of the data at a moment in time. As updates are made to the database, they are not reflected in the recordset. The returned records may exist on the client or the server depending on the cursor driver selected.

RDOPENKEYSET

The `rdOpenKeyset` option produces not records, but rather a set of keys that reference records. The membership of the keyset is fixed, but the set is fully scrollable. The keyset will accept updates to the records it references through methods of the `rdoResultset` object such as Edit and Delete. These cursors may be built on either the client or the server depending on the cursor driver selected.

RDOPENDYNAMIC

The `rdOpenDynamic` option produces a keyset just like the rdOpenKeyset, but this option produces a result that dynamically reflects all changes made to the records either through methods of the `rdoResultset` or through direct changes via SQL UPDATE statements. This is the heaviest and slowest of all the cursors and is generally not used in an enterprise application.

MANAGING RESULTSETS

When a query is executed, it will be necessary to access the resulting records. RDO provides an object that permits access to the results of the last query. This result set is referenced through the `LastQueryResults` property of the `rdoConnection` object.

```
Dim m_Connection As RDO.rdoConection
Dim m_Query As RDO.rdoQuery
Dim m_Resultset As RDO.rdoResultset
Set m_Connection = New RDO.rdoConnection
m_Connection.Connect = "DSN=BIBLIO"
m_Connection.CursorDriver = rdUseClientBatch
m_Connection.EstablishConnection
Set m_Query = New RDO.rdoQuery
Set m_Query.ActiveConnection = m_Connection
m_Query.SQL = "SELECT * FROM Publishers"
m_Query.CursorTye = rdOpenStatic
m_Query.Execute
Set m_Resultset = m_Query.OpenResultset
```

Once the rdoResultset is captured, the records can be directly manipulated through methods of the rdoResultset object. Depending on the cursor type created, use the Move-First, MoveLast, MoveNext, and MovePrevious methods to scroll through the records. Once the desired record is selected, the data can be read out and placed in ActiveX controls for display.

To populate a GUI with the results of a query, choose to display all of the results at once, as in a grid, or to display the results one at a time in a detail view. In either case, there are accepted routines that can be used to produce the desired output. If, for example, there is a set of records that represent customer data, displaying all at once is done by looping through the rdoResultset object and populating the grid. The following code shows how to add customer data to a grid from a resultset named m_Resultset:

```
Do Until m_Resultset.EOF
  Grid1.AddItem m_Resultset.rdoColumns.Item ("Company Name").Value
  M_Resultset.MoveNext
Loop
```

Displaying records one at a time requires the combination of Move methods and a common routine used for display. This routine populates an individual control based on the current record pointer. Whenever data are read from the database, be careful of NULL values, which can cause run-time errors if an attempt is made to assign them to a TextBox. Instead, concatenate an empty string on the end of every field read to prevent NULL values. The following code shows a routine that populates a series of TextBoxes in a control array from a resultset called m_Resultset. The bang operator (!) is used to specify the name of the database field to place in the TextBox.

```
txtFields(0).Text = m_Resultset!Title & vbNullString
txtFields(1).Text = m_Resultset!Au_lname & vbNullString
txtFields(2).Text = m_Resultset!Pub_Name & vbNullString
txtFields(3).Text = m_Resultset!PubDate & vbNullString
txtFields(4).Text = m_Resultset!Title_ID & vbNullString
```

Some applications may require image data to be stored in the database. When image data are stored, they are broken down into constituent bytes. This type of data is referred to as a binary large object (BLOB). BLOB data requires some work to access from Visual Basic since the image control is not capable of directly receiving a stream of bytes. Instead, read the data from the database and write out a file. The file can then be loaded into an image control using the `LoadPicture` function.

Bytes can be manipulated using the `GetChunk` and `AppendChunk` methods which make it possible to read and write, will be respectively retrieved, using binary fields in the database. Generally, chunk data will be retrieved a little at a time to perform operations. However, all the data may be retrieved at once as in the case of displaying an image.

OPTIMISTIC BATCH OPERATIONS

Up to this point, we have discussed fairly typical types of RDO operations. If we were to survey the Visual Basic applications in use today, we would find that most applications open a connection at the beginning of the session and maintain it open until the user exits the application. In between, the program typically reads and writes using cursor operations as explained earlier in this chapter. This type of architecture works well for applications with just one user, though there will be significant difficulty in attempting to move cursor-based applications into the multi-user realm.

Adding users to an application is referred to as *scaling* an application. Scalability firmly depends upon the correct management of system resources. Today, the single biggest mistake made by VB programmers building multi-user applications is that they still rely upon cursor-based solutions, which do not scale well because they do not manage resources well. Consider the typical strategy of opening a connection to the database at the beginning of an application. If a connection is opened for every user that starts a multi-user application, there will be a large number of connections to maintain on the database. Although we can debate the exact number of connections possible, the mere act of giving each user a connection limits scalability to the total number of connections allowed by the server.

The solution to scaling a database application is not to use cursors at all. This statement is still stunning to many VB programmers who cannot understand how to perform data access without a cursor. The answer is simple. Instead of opening a connection for the entire session, open a connection only when one is needed to read or write to the database. This process makes it possible to use a small number of connections and thus increases the total number of possible users into the application.

When developers hear that they should open and close connections to the database, they rightfully respond that such operations are expensive and can cause the system to run slowly. This is true and therefore we will want to develop strategies that minimize the expense of sharing connections among many users. Anyone serious about this type of development should be sure to read Chapter 21 on the Microsoft Transaction Server which offers even more strategies for scaling.

For now, we will focus attention on a simple methodology for scaling known as *optimistic batch updating*. Optimistic batch updating refers to a cursorless data access strategy that allows clients to receive batches of database records, scroll them, modify them, and return them to the database for updating without keeping a connection constantly open. This is accomplished by *disconnecting* a set of records from the associated database. The steps to accomplish optimistic batch processing are:

1. Connect to a database.
2. Run a query on the database that returns records. These records are returned directly into the client's memory.
3. Disconnect the client from the database. The records returned from the original query remain in the client's memory, but are no longer associated with any particular database. We say they are *disconnected*.
4. The client browses the records and modifies them—unaware that the associated database connection no longer exists.
5. When the client is done with the data, they are returned to the database by establishing a new connection and sending the data back as a batch.
6. When the batch data arrives on the server, the changes are committed to the database as a batch and the connection is once again broken.

Those who have never before used optimistic batches, probably have some concerns at this point. First, there is the concern that while batch operations are in process, the underlying data might be changed by another user. This results in a *collision* when the batch update occurs. Second is the concern about *data aging*, the fact that since a batch is disconnected, it does not reflect any changes made to the data since it was retrieved. These concerns are legitimate and represent scenarios in which batch updating does not work well.

Before choosing to use batch updating, determine whether the application is suited for this approach. First determine whether the probability of collision is high. Suppose, for example, that the application is designed to fulfill orders from a warehouse. The warehouse has purchasing agents responsible for fulfilling orders in certain categories like household goods or industrial products. If the purchasing agent for household goods does not fulfill orders for industrial products, what is the likelihood of a collision? Clearly it is low. What if, on the other hand, this is an insurance application for a hospital. In this case, billing for recent patients in the hospital is being provided. The likelihood that several different departments at the hospital need to access the same recent patient record is probably high. In the first case, optimistic batch updating should work well. In the second example, there may be too many collisions to make it feasible. Data aging issues can also affect the programmer. For example, it would not be advisable to use batch updating to make an application to buy and sell stocks. Clearly, real-time data is critical in such a program.

Implementing optimistic batch updating requires setting the cursor driver to `rdUseClientBatch`. This cursor driver does not really result in a cursor at all since it facilitates batch processing. Also set the lock type to `rdConcurBatch`. This makes it possible to lock records when the batch is processed. Disconnecting the recordset is done by setting the `ActiveConnection` property of the `rdoResultset` to `Nothing`. After this is done, close the database connection if desired. The following code shows the basic steps to retrieve data.

```
'Establish the Connection
```

```
Set m_Connection = New RDO.rdoConnection
m_Connection.Connect = "UID=sa;PWD=;DSN=pubs;"
m_Connection.CursorDriver = rdUseClientBatch
m_Connection.EstablishConnection

'Create Query
Set m_Query = New RDO.rdoQuery
Set m_Query.ActiveConnection = m_Connection
m_Query.SQL = "SELECT * FROM Titles'"
m_Query.CursorType = rdOpenDynamic
m_Query.LockType = rdConcurBatch

'Run Query
Set m_Resultset = m_Query.OpenResultset

'Disconnect Resultset
Set m_Resultset.ActiveConnection = Nothing
```

Once the disconnected recordset is created, the client may freely navigate the data and edit the records. Editing these records changes only the data in the client's memory. It has no effect on the database itself. Making changes to the database requires a reconnection of the recordset and a batch update. The following code shows the essential steps.

```
'Establish the Connection
Set m_Connection = New RDO.rdoConnection
m_Connection.Connect = "UID=sa;PWD=;DSN=pubs;"
m_Connection.CursorDriver = rdUseClientBatch
m_Connection.EstablishConnection

'Update Resultset
Set m_Resultset.ActiveConnection = m_Connection
m_Resultset.UpdateBatch
```

Once the batch update operation is performed, examine the `BatchCollisionCount` property to determine how many of the rows sent back did not get updated. Once it is known that collisions occurred, resolve the collisions by using the `BatchCollisionRows` property, which provides an array of bookmarks to the collisions so they can be resolved.

Exercise 11-1: RDO Basics

RDO offers a flexible and powerful model for accessing ODBC data sources. In this exercise, we will investigate the fundamentals of RDO and create a cursor-based application that connects to the BIBLIO database.

SETTING UP THE ODBC DATA SOURCE

Step 1

Before using the ODBC API, set up an ODBC data source for use. In this exercise, we will be interacting with the Microsoft Access database `BIBLIO.MDB` that ships with Visual Basic.

Establishing the data source is not a Visual Basic, but rather a Windows OS function. Setup is done using the ODBC Administrator utility found in Windows. In the Control Panel, there will be an icon labeled ODBC. Double click on this icon to start the ODBC Administrator.

Step 2

When the ODBC Administrator is started, the ODBC Data Source Administrator dialog box will be visible. This dialog box lists all of the ODBC data sources currently available on the machine. In order to create a new data source, click the **System DSN** tab and push the **Add** button. This will reveal the Create New Data Source dialog, which lists all the ODBC drivers available on the machine. For this exercise, select the **Microsoft Access ODBC drivers** and press **Finish**.

Step 3

When **Finish** is pressesd, the ODBC Setup dialog will be visible. Here the new data source can be defined. First, provide a name for the data source. This can be any name, but for this exercise, name the data source `BIBLIO`.

Next, select the **BIBLIO.MDB** database by pushing the **Select** button and navigating the file system to find the BIBLIO.MDB file. Select this file and then push the **OK** button and back out of the ODBC Administrator. The data source has now been defined.

CREATING THE GUI

Step 4

Using the Windows File Explorer, create a new directory **VB BOOTCAMP\EXERCISE11-1**. Start a new Standard EXE project in Visual Basic.

Step 5

The interface for this application consists of Labels, TextBoxes, and CommandButtons. The Labels and TextBoxes are all part of control arrays. Create the interface as shown in Figure 11-3. Use the Item list below to set the design time properties for each object.

>
> **Item 1—Label**
>
> | | |
> |---|---|
> | Name | lblLabels |
> | Index | 0 |
> | Caption | Title |
>
> **Item 2—Label**
>
> | | |
> |---|---|
> | Name | lblLabels |
> | Index | 1 |

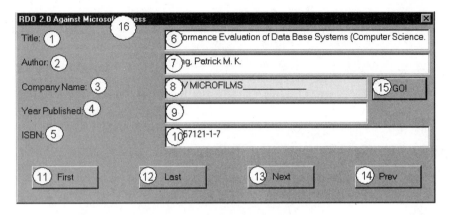

Figure 11-3 The Form interface.

Caption	Author

Item 3—Label

Name	lblLabels
Index	2
Caption	Company Name

Item 4—Label

Name	lblLabels
Index	3
Caption	Year Published

Item 5—Label

Name	lblLabels
Index	4
Caption	ISBN

Item 6—TextBox

Name	txtFields
Index	0
Text	<empty>

Item 7—TextBox

Name	txtFields
Index	1
Text	<empty>

Item 8—TextBox

Name	txtFields

Index	2
Text	\<empty\>
BackColor	Yellow

Item 9—TextBox

Name	txtFields
Index	3
Text	\<empty\>

Item 10—TextBox

Name	txtFields
Index	4
Text	\<empty\>

Item 11—CommandButton

Name	cmdMoveFirst
Caption	First

Item 12—CommandButton

Name	cmdMoveLast
Caption	Last

Item 13—CommandButton

Name	cmdMoveNext
Caption	Next

Item 14—CommandButton

Name	cmdMovePrevious
Caption	Previous

Item 15—CommandButton

Name	cmdGo
Caption	GO!
Default	True

Item 16—Form

Name	frmRDO2
Caption	RDO 2.0 Against Microsoft Access
BorderStyle	3-Fixed Dialog

CODING THE APPLICATION

Step 6

Before writing code using RDO, set a reference to the object model. Open the References dialog by selecting **PROJECT/REFERENCES…** from the menu. In the dialog, set a reference to **Microsoft Remote Data Objects 2.0**. Press the **OK** button.

Step 7

Just as with any object model, it will be necessary to declare variables to hold the objects to be created. This exercise also shows how to perform an asynchronous query with RDO. This means that a query will be run and then an event will be received when the query completes. Asynchronous queries allow users to continue working even while a query runs. In the [General][Declarations] section of frmRDO2, add the following code to declare variables for rdoConnection, rdoQuery, and rdoResultset objects.

```
'This variable is for the Connection
Private WithEvents m_Connection As RDO.rdoConnection

'These variables are for the query and resultset
Private m_Query As RDO.rdoQuery
Private m_Resultset As RDO.rdoResultset
```

Step 8

This exercise uses control arrays. Instead of addressing these arrays using integer index numbers, create an enumerated type to represent the index numbers. Add the following code to the [General][Declarations] section to declare the enumeration for use with the control arrays.

```
'Enumeration for Fields
Private Enum enmFields
  ntsTitle
  ntsAuthor
  ntsCompanyName
  ntsYearPublished
  ntsISBN
End Enum
```

Step 9

This example is intended to demonstrate a classic two-tier approach using cursors. Therefore, we will open a connection when the form is loaded and hold the connection throughout the session. Add the following code to the Form_Load event to open the database connection.

```
'Establish the Connection
Set m_Connection = New RDO.rdoConnection
m_Connection.Connect = "DSN=Biblio;"      'DSN Name
m_Connection.CursorDriver = rdUseServer    'Server-Side Cursor
m_Connection.EstablishConnection
```

Step 10

When the form is unloaded, we use the Terminate event to close the connection to the database. Add the following code to the Form_Terminate event to close the database connection:

```
'Close Connection
On Error Resume Next
```

```
m_Resultset.Close
Set m_Resultset = Nothing
m_Connection.Close
Set m_Connection = Nothing
```

Step 11

Most of the work in this exercise is done under the click event of the cmdGO button. The idea is to enter the partial name of a publisher into the Company Name field—which appears with a yellow background on the form—and the application will search the database for publishers containing the partial string. The form then returns a resultset with all the matching entries in the database. The most complicated part of this code is creating the SQL statement correctly. Carefully add the following code to the cmdGO_Click event to run the query based on a value typed into the Company Name field.

```
'Create SQL Statement
Dim strSQL As String

strSQL = ""
strSQL = strSQL & "SELECT Titles.Title, Titles.ISBN, _
          Authors.Author, "
strSQL = strSQL & "Titles.[Year Published], _
          Publishers.[Company Name] "
strSQL = strSQL & "FROM Publishers, Titles, Authors, _
          [title author] "
strSQL = strSQL & "WHERE Authors.Au_ID = [title author].Au_ID "
strSQL = strSQL & "AND [title author].ISBN = Titles.ISBN "
strSQL = strSQL & "AND Titles.PubID = Publishers.PubID "
strSQL = strSQL & "AND Publishers.[Company Name] "
strSQL = strSQL & "LIKE " & Chr$(39) & "%"
strSQL = strSQL & txtFields(ntsCompanyName) & "%" & Chr$(39)

'Create Query
Set m_Query = New RDO.rdoQuery
m_Query.SQL = strSQL                    'SQL Statement
m_Query.CursorType = rdOpenStatic       'Static Cursor
m_Query.Prepared = True                 'Create Prepared Statement
m_Query.KeysetSize = 20                 'Return 20 Rows at a time
m_Query.MaxRows = 100                   'Max Rows for Query
Set m_Query.ActiveConnection = m_Connection

'Run Query Asynchronously
Set m_Resultset = m_Query.OpenResultset(Options:=rdAsyncEnable)
```

Step 12

When the results of the query are returned, we will display them in the array of TextBox controls with a custom subroutine called `ShowData`. Add this sub by selecting **TOOLS/ADD PROCEDURE...** from the menu. In the Add Procedure dialog, create a new Private Sub named **ShowData**. Press **OK**. After the procedure is created, add code to display the resultset so that the final procedure looks like the following code:

```
Private Sub ShowData()

   'This routine shows data in the Text Boxes
   txtFields(ntsTitle).Text = m_Resultset!Title
   txtFields(ntsAuthor).Text = m_Resultset!Author
   txtFields(ntsCompanyName).Text = m_Resultset![Company Name]
   txtFields(ntsYearPublished).Text = m_Resultset![Year Published]
   txtFields(ntsISBN).Text = m_Resultset!ISBN

End Sub
```

Step 13

The query is run asynchronously by virtue of the `rdAsyncEnable` option set in the `OpenResultset` method. We will find out that the query has completed when an event fires. Access the `QueryComplete` event by selecting `m_Connection` from the Object box in the Code window and `QueryComplete` from the Procedure box. The `QueryComplete` event fires for every asynchronous query when it finishes running. As an argument, the event passes in the `rdoQuery` object that just finished running. Using this event, add the following code to handle the resultset when the query finishes running:

```
'This fires when the async query is completed
If m_Resultset.BOF And m_Resultset.EOF Then
   MsgBox "No Results!", vbOKOnly, "RDO 2.0"
Else
   ShowData
End If
```

Step 14

Once the results are received, navigate them using the buttons on the bottom of the form by using the `MoveFirst`, `MoveLast`, `MoveNext`, and `MovePrevious` methods of the `rdoResultset`. This code is similar for each of the buttons. The following code shows the four events and their associated code:

```
Private Sub cmdMoveFirst_Click()
   'Change Active Record
   m_Resultset.MoveFirst
   ShowData
```

```
End Sub

Private Sub cmdMoveLast_Click()
   'Change Active Record
   m_Resultset.MoveLast
   ShowData
End Sub

Private Sub cmdMoveNext_Click()

   'Change Active Record
   m_Resultset.MoveNext

     If m_Resultset.EOF Then
     Beep
     m_Resultset.MoveLast
   Else
     ShowData
   End If

End Sub

Private Sub cmdMovePrevious_Click()

   'Change Active Record
   m_Resultset.MovePrevious

   If m_Resultset.BOF Then
     Beep
     m_Resultset.MoveFirst
   Else
     ShowData
   End If

End Sub
```

Step 15

Save and run the application. Try entering partial search strings in the Company Name field and pressing the **GO** button. Try the strings `micro` and `hill` for results. Navigate the results using the buttons.

Exercise 11-2: Binary Large Objects

Applications often need to store image data. BLOBs are used to store images in a database. This exercise uses the pubs database in SQL Server to display company logos stored in the database. Note that access to a SQL Server database will be required for this exercise.

SETTING UP THE ODBC DATA SOURCE

Step 1

This exercise uses SQL Server's test database named *pubs*. Locate the ODBC Administrator under the Control Panel icon. In the Control Panel will be an icon labeled ODBC. Double click on this icon to start the ODBC Administrator.

Step 2

Starting the ODBC Administrator will reveal the ODBC Data Source Administrator dialog box, which lists all the ODBC data sources currently available on the machine. In order to create a new data source, select the **System DSN** tab, and push the **Add** button. This action will reveal the Create New Data Source dialog, which lists all the ODBC drivers available on the machine. For this exercise, select the SQL Server ODBC drivers from the list and press **Finish**.

Step 3

This will reveal the ODBC Setup dialog, where the new data source can be defined. First, provide a name for the data source. This can be any name, but for this exercise, name the data source **PUBS**. Continue to follow the dialog as it prompts for information for the DSN. The exact settings will differ depending upon the installation. Many of the settings will not affect this exercise, but be sure to name the DSN and provide the name of the machine where the SQL Server installation resides.

CREATING THE GUI

Step 4

Using the Windows File Explorer, create a new directory called **VB BOOTCAMP\ EXERCISE11-2**. Then start a new Standard EXE project in Visual Basic.

Step 5

Create a user interface with two CommandButtons and one Image control as shown in Figure 11-4. Use the Item list below to set design time properties for the objects.

Figure 11-4 The Form interface.

Item 1—Form

Name	`frmBlob`
Caption	BLOB Data in SQL Server

Item 2—Image

Name	`imgLogo`

Item 3—CommandButton

Name	`cmdPrev`
Caption	Previous

Item 4—CommandButton

Name	`cmdNext`
Caption	Next

CODING THE APPLICATION

Step 6

This application is a simple read-only application that uses RDO objects for data access. We create `rdoConnection`, `rdoQuery`, and `rdoResultset` objects. Add the following code to the [General][Declarations] section of Form1 to declare the appropriate variables.

```
'This variable is for the Connection
Private m_Connection As RDO.rdoConnection


'This variable is for the Recordset
Private m_Query As RDO.rdoQuery
Private m_Resultset As RDO.rdoResultset
```

Step 7

The PUBS database has a table named `pub_info` which contains a field named logo that has image data. The data represents bitmap images of company logos. Add the following code to the `Form_Load` event to retrieve the image data in an `rdoResultset` object. Note the code has a call to a function named `ShowLogo` which is not defined until the next step.

```
'Show Form
Show
DoEvents
Screen.MousePointer = vbHourglass

'Establish the Connection
Set m_Connection = New RDO.rdoConnection
m_Connection.Connect = "DSN = Pubs; UID = SA; PWD ="
m_Connection.CursorDriver = rdUseServer
m_Connection.EstablishConnection
```

```
'Create Query
Set m_Query = New RDO.rdoQuery
Set m_Query.ActiveConnection = m_Connection
m_Query.SQL = "SELECT pub_id,logo FROM pub_info"
m_Query.CursorType = rdOpenStatic

'Run Query
Set m_Resultset = m_Query.OpenResultset
m_Resultset.MoveFirst
ShowLogo

Screen.MousePointer = vbDefault
```

Step 8

Because an image control cannot directly receive a byte stream from the database, we will read the image and create a file. The GetChunk method reads the data and the LoadPicture function loads the image control. Create a procedure to perform this task by selecting **TOOLS/ADD PROCEDURE...** from the menu. In the Procedure dialog, create a Sub named ShowLogo. Press the **OK** button and add code to create the routine shown below:

```
Private Sub ShowLogo()

  Dim byteBlob() As Byte
  Dim lngSize As Long

  'Get size of BLOB
  lngSize = m_Resultset!Logo.ColumnSize
  If lngSize = 0 Then
    imgLogo.Picture = LoadPicture("")
    Exit Sub
  End If

  'Get BLOB
  byteBlob() = m_Resultset!Logo.GetChunk(lngSize)

  'Kill the exisitng file
  On Error Resume Next
  Kill App.Path & "\blob.dat"
  On Error GoTo 0

  'Write out the new file
  Open App.Path & "\blob.dat" For Binary As #1
    Put #1, , byteBlob()
  Close #1
```

```
'Load Picture
imgLogo.Picture = LoadPicture(App.Path & "\blob.dat")

End Sub
```

Step 9

Navigating the recordset is done with the two CommandButtons which use the `MoveNext` and `MovePrevious` methods. The following code shows the click events for each button:

```
Private Sub cmdNext_Click()
  m_Resultset.MoveNext
  If m_Resultset.EOF Then m_Resultset.MoveLast
  ShowLogo
End Sub

Private Sub cmdPrev_Click()
  m_Resultset.MovePrevious
  If m_Resultset.BOF Then m_Resultset.MoveFirst
  ShowLogo
End Sub
```

Step 10

Save and run the application. Use the CommandButtons to navigate the recordset.

Exercise 11-3: Batch Updating with RDO

Batch updating permits creation of a scalable two-tier application using RDO. This application demonstrates this technology against the SQL Server database pubs. Note that a SQL Server must be available to work this exercise.

Step 1

This exercise uses SQL Server's test database named *pubs*. Locate the ODBC Administrator under the Control Panel icon. In the Control Panel, find an icon labeled **ODBC**. Double click on this icon to start the ODBC Administrator.

Step 2

Starting the ODBC Administrator will reveal the ODBC Data Source Administrator dialog box, which lists all the ODBC data sources currently available on the machine. In order to create a new data source, push the **Add** button. This action will reveal the Add Data Source dialog, listing all the ODBC drivers available on the machine. For this exercise, select the **SQL Server ODBC drivers** from the list and press **Finish**.

Step 3

Pressing **Finish** will reveal the ODBC Setup dialog, where the new data source can be defined. First, provide a name for the data source. This can be any name, but for this exercise, name the data source **PUBS**. Continue to follow the dialog as it prompts for information for the DSN.

Exact settings will differ depending upon the installation. Many of the settings will not affect this exercise, but to name the DSN and provide the name of the machine where the SQL Server installation resides.

CREATING THE GUI

Step 4

Using the Windows File Explorer, create a new directory **VB BOOTCAMP\EXERCISE11-3**. Start a new Standard EXE project in Visual Basic.

Step 5

The interface for this application consists of Labels, TextBoxes, and CommandButtons. The Labels and TextBoxes are all part of control arrays. Create the interface as shown in Figure 11-5. Use the Item list below to set the design time properties for each object.

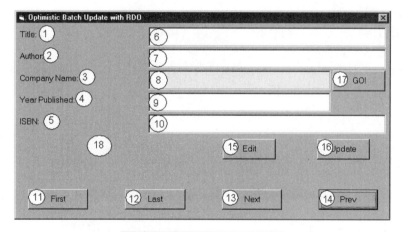

Figure 11-5 The Form interface.

Item 1—Label

Name	lblLabels
Index	0
Caption	Title

Item 2—Label

Name	lblLabels
Index	1
Caption	Author

Item 3—Label

Name	lblLabels

Index	2
Caption	Company Name

Item 4—Label

Name	lblLabels
Index	3
Caption	Year Published

Item 5—Label

Name	lblLabels
Index	4
Caption	ISBN

Item 6—TextBox

Name	txtFields
Index	0
Text	<empty>

Item 7—TextBox

Name	txtFields
Index	1
Text	<empty>

Item 8—TextBox

Name	txtFields
Index	2
Text	<empty>
BackColor	Yellow

Item 9—TextBox

Name	txtFields
Index	3
Text	<empty>

Item 10—TextBox

Name	txtFields
Index	4
Text	<empty>

Item 11—CommandButton

Name	cmdMoveFirst
Caption	First

Item 12—CommandButton

Name	cmdMoveLast
Caption	Last

Item 13—CommandButton

Name	cmdMoveNext
Caption	Next

Item 14—CommandButton

Name	cmdMovePrevious
Caption	Previous

Item 15—CommandButton

Name	cmdEdit
Caption	Edit

Item 16—CommandButton

Name	cmdUpdate
Caption	Update

Item 17—CommandButton

Name	cmdGo
Caption	GO!
Default	True

Item 18—Form

Name	frmBatch
Caption	Optimistic Batch Updating
BorderStyle	3-Fixed Dialog

CODING THE APPLICATION

Step 6

Before writing code using RDO, set a reference to the object model. Open the references dialog by selecting **PROJECT/REFERENCES...** from the menu. In the dialog, set a reference to **Microsoft Remote Data Objects 2.0**. Press the **OK** button.

Step 7

Just as with any object model, it will be necessary to declare variables to hold the objects to be created. In the [General][Declarations] section of frmBatch, add the following code to declare variables for rdoConnection, rdoQuery, and rdoResultset objects:

```
'Variables
Private m_Connection As RDO.rdoConnection
```

```
Private m_Query As RDO.rdoQuery
Private m_Resultset As RDO.rdoResultset
```

Step 8

This exercise uses control arrays. Instead of addressing these arrays using integer index numbers, create an enumerated type to represent the index numbers. Add the following code to the [General][Declarations] section to declare the enumeration for use with the control arrays:

```
'Enumeration for Fields
Private Enum enmFields
  ntsTitle
  ntsAuthor
  ntsCompanyName
  ntsYearPublished
  ntsISBN
End Enum
```

Step 9

Most of the work in this exercise is done under the Click event of the cmdGO button. The idea is to enter the partial name of a publisher into the Company Name field—which appears with a yellow background on the form; the application will search the database for publishers containing the partial string. The form then returns a resultset with all the matching entries in the database. The database connection is both made and broken in this single event.

```
Dim strSQL As String

'Establish the Connection
Set m_Connection = New RDO.rdoConnection
m_Connection.Connect = "DSN = Pubs; UID = SA; PWD ="
m_Connection.CursorDriver = rdUseClientBatch
m_Connection.EstablishConnection

'Create Query
Set m_Query = New RDO.rdoQuery
Set m_Query.ActiveConnection = m_Connection

strSQL = ""
strSQL = strSQL & "SELECT authors.au_id, authors.au_lname,"
strSQL = strSQL & "publishers.pub_id, publishers.pub_name,"
strSQL = strSQL & "titles.title_id , titles.Title, titles.pubdate "
strSQL = strSQL & "From authors "
strSQL = strSQL & "INNER JOIN titleauthor ON authors.au_id =
          titleauthor.au_id "
strSQL = strSQL & "INNER JOIN titles ON titleauthor.title_id =
```

```
            titles.title_id "
strSQL = strSQL & "INNER JOIN publishers ON titles.pub_id =
            publishers.pub_id "
strSQL = strSQL & "WHERE pub_name LIKE "
strSQL = strSQL & Chr$(39) & "%" & txtFields(ntsCompanyName).Text
            & "%" & Chr$(39)

m_Query.SQL = strSQL
m_Query.CursorType = rdOpenDynamic
m_Query.LockType = rdConcurBatch

'Run Query
Set m_Resultset = m_Query.OpenResultset
ShowData

'Disconnect Resultset
Set m_Resultset.ActiveConnection = Nothing
m_Connection.Close
Set m_Connection = Nothing
```

Step 10

When the results of the query are returned, we will display them in the array of TextBox controls, with a custom subroutine called ShowData. Add this sub by selecting **TOOLS/ADD PROCEDURE...** from the menu. In the Add Procedure dialog, create a new Private Sub named **ShowData**. Press **OK**. After the procedure is created, add code to display the resultset so that the final procedure looks like the following code:

```
Private Sub ShowData()

   'This routine shows data in the Text Boxes
   txtFields(ntsTitle).Text = m_Resultset!Title
   txtFields(ntsAuthor).Text = m_Resultset!au_lname
   txtFields(ntsCompanyName).Text = m_Resultset!pub_name
   txtFields(ntsYearPublished).Text = m_Resultset!pubdate
   txtFields(ntsISBN).Text = m_Resultset!Title_id

End Sub
```

Step 11

Once the results are received, navigate them using the buttons on the bottom of the form. This is done by using the MoveFirst, MoveLast, MoveNext, and MovePrevious methods of the rdoResultset. This code is similar for each of the buttons. The following code shows the four events and their associated code:

```
Private Sub cmdMoveFirst_Click()
```

```
    'Change Active Record
    m_Resultset.MoveFirst
    ShowData
End Sub

Private Sub cmdMoveLast_Click()
    'Change Active Record
    m_Resultset.MoveLast
    ShowData
End Sub

Private Sub cmdMoveNext_Click()

    'Change Active Record
    m_Resultset.MoveNext

    If m_Resultset.EOF Then
        Beep
        m_Resultset.MoveLast
    Else
        ShowData
    End If

End Sub

Private Sub cmdMovePrevious_Click()

    'Change Active Record
    m_Resultset.MovePrevious

    If m_Resultset.BOF Then
        Beep
        m_Resultset.MoveFirst
    Else
        ShowData
    End If

End Sub
```

Step 12

Once the records are on the client, they can be edited in memory. When they have been edited, the changes do not persist in the database. This is done through an explicit update. Add the following code to the `cmdEdit_Click` event to edit the records locally:

```
    'Edit the record locally
```

```
m_Resultset.Edit

  m_Resultset!Title = txtFields(ntsTitle).Text
  m_Resultset!Au_lname = txtFields(ntsAuthor).Text
  m_Resultset!pub_name = txtFields(ntsCompanyName).Text
  m_Resultset!pubdate = txtFields(ntsYearPublished).Text
  m_Resultset!title_id = txtFields(ntsISBN).Text

m_Resultset.Update
```

Step 13

Once the records are edited, they can be returned as a batch to the server for updating under the click event of the `cmdUpdate` button. Add the following code to reconnect the recordset to the database and submit the changes:

```
'Reconnect the resultset
Set m_Connection = New RDO.rdoConnection
m_Connection.Connect = "DSN = Pubs; UIS = SA; PWD ="
m_Connection.CursorDriver = rdUseClientBatch
m_Connection.EstablishConnection
Set m_Resultset.ActiveConnection = m_Connection

'Update Results
m_Resultset.BatchUpdate

'Look for collisions
MsgBox "Update complete." _
  & vbCrLf & m_Resultset.BatchCollisionCount _
  & " collisions detected.", vbOKOnly + vbInformation, "Batch
    Updates"

'Disconnect the Resultset
Set m_Resultset.ActiveConnection = Nothing
```

Step 14

Save and run the application. Try entering partial search strings in the Company Name field and pressing the **GO** button. Try the strings `micro` and `hill` for results. Navigate the results using the buttons.

Try making a change to the records by typing into the text fields and pressing **Edit**. Now end the application. Run the application again and see if the changes persisted. Now make an edit and update the database. Check the changes to see if they persisted.

FOR THE CERTIFIED PRO

Pro 11-1: RDO Objects and Collections

1. Use the RDO Objects and Collections to look at the database structure for any access database.
2. From a menu on a Form, allow a user to select an access database and view all of the tables in a Listbox.
3. When a table is selected from the list, populate a second ListBox with the column names from the table.
4. Use a TextBox to allow users to run SQL queries on the databsse and view the results in a grid.

PREPARING FOR CERTIFICATION

Topics for Further Reading
    Remote Data Objects and Collections
    Data Access Using Remote Data Objects

CERTIFICATION QUIZ

1. Name all the different kinds of ODBC data sources.
   a. User DSN
   b. Folder DSN
   c. File DSN
   d. System DSN

2. Which type of data source is available to all users of a single machine?
   a. User DSN
   b. Folder DSN
   c. File DSN
   d. System DSN

3. What methods can create an `rdoResultset`?
   a. `rdoConnection.OpenResultset`
   b. `rdoConnection.LastQueryResults`
   c. `rdoQuery.OpenResultset`
   d. `rdoQuery.LastQueryResults`

4. What keyword is used to include RDO events in your code?
   a. `HaveEvents`
   b. `RaiseEvents`
   c. `WithEvents`
   d. `Event`

5. What arguments are valid parts of an ODBC Connect string?
   a. TIME
   b. PWD
   c. DSN
   d. UID

6. Which constants are valid cursor drivers in RDO?
   a. rdDoNotUse
   b. rdUseIfNeeded
   c. rdUseClientBatch
   d. rdUseOnly

7. Which is a valid DSN-less Connect string?
   a. "DRIVER={SQL Server}; DSN=;SERVER=(local);
      DATABASE=pubs;UID=sa;PWD=;"
   b. "DRIVER={SQL Server};SERVER=(local);
      DSN=;DATABASE=pubs;UID=sa;PWD=;"
   c. "DRIVER={SQL Server};SERVER=(local);DATABASE=pubs;
      DSN=;UID=sa;PWD=;"
   d. "DRIVER={SQL Server};SERVER=(local);
      DATABASE=pubs;UID=sa;PWD=;DSN=;"

8. What constants represent valid cursors in RDO?
   a. rdOpenForwardOnly
   b. rdOpenStatic
   c. rdOpenKeyset
   d. rdOpenDynamic

9. Which cursors are available for use if the cursor driver is selected as rdUseNone?
   a. rdOpenForwardOnly
   b. rdOpenStatic
   c. rdOpenKeyset
   d. rdOpenDynamic

10. Which of the following methods are available to a cursor designated as
    rdOpenForwardOnly?
    a. MoveFirst
    b. MoveLast
    c. MoveNext
    d. MovePrevious

11. If the cursor driver is set to rdUseIfNeeded, which type of cursor is preferred?
    a. Server
    b. ClientBatch
    c. ODBC
    d. ForwardOnly

12. Which cursor type is fully updatable and has dynamic membership?
- a. `rdOpenForwardOnly`
- b. `rdOpenStatic`
- c. `rdOpenKeyset`
- d. `rdOpenDynamic`

13. What types of queries can be used with the `UserConnection` object?
- a. SQL queries
- b. Stored procedures
- c. SQL parameter queries
- d. SQL UPDATE queries

ANSWERS TO CERTIFICATION QUIZ

1. a, c, d
2. d
3. a, b, c
4. c
5. b, c, d
6. b, c
7. a, b, c, d
8. a, b, c, d
9. a
10. c
11. a
12. d
13. a, b, c, d

ACTIVE DATA OBJECTS

Those who begin this chapter, should be familiar with OLEDB technology including Data Links and should also be well versed in the principles of object models including instantiation and object variables. Data Links, OLEDB fundamentals, and object models were covered in previous chapters.

SKILLS COVERED

- 70-175 (34): Access and manipulate data using the Execute Direct model
- 70-175 (35): Access and manipulate data using the Prepare/Execute model
- 70-175 (36): Access and manipulate data by using the Stored Procedures model
- 70-175 (36.a): Use a stored procedure to execute a statement on a database
- 70-175 (36.b): Use a stored procedure to return records to a Visual Basic application
- 70-175 (37): Retrieve and manipulate data by using different cursor locations
- 70-175 (38): Retrieve and manipulate data by using different cursor types

- 70-175 (39): Use the ADO Errors collection to handle database errors
- 70-175 (40): Manage database transactions to ensure data consistency and recoverability
- 70-175 (43): Use appropriate locking strategies to ensure data integrity

Active Data Objects (ADO) is a set of objects contained in a dynamic link library which implement the OLEDB specification. This is the same technology used by the ADO data control and the Data Environment. ADO, however, is not abstracted through a visual tool. Instead, objects must be instantiated and managed manually. This will lead to much greater control over data access, all the operations will have to be coded. In the end, the rewards in flexibility and performance will be well worth the added effort.

ACTIVE DATA OBJECTS MODEL

Understanding ADO begins by examining the object model that implements it (Figure 12-1). Those accustomed to other models will find ADO much simpler and streamlined. Unlike RDO, ADO does not have an engine or environment object. Instead the primary focus is on individual connections, queries, and results.

Because ADO is an implementation of the OLEDB specification, the objects in ADO are used to access both relational and non-relational data stores in what is referred to as Universal Data Access (UDA). This means that the model itself must be extremely flexible since it is intended to be used by any data source. Regardless of the data source accessed, ADO always follows a connection, query, recordset perspective. However, no one can predict all the features an object model like ADO should have, since it is supposed to be capable of accessing anything. Therefore, ADO contains not only fixed objects, but also dynamic collections of Property objects whose membership changes depending upon what data source accessed.

THE CONNECTION OBJECT

The first object in the ADO model is the `Connection` object, which is capable of making a connection to any data source for which an OLEDB provider is registered on the system. OLEDB providers are similar to ODBC drivers in that they enable the communication between ADO and the selected data source. Without the appropriate provider, ADO cannot be used.

Visual Basic ships with a number of OLEDB providers which register on the system when VB is installed. These providers are really COM objects that implement the OLEDB specification. Providers are entered in the System Registry so they can be located when called for by an associated Data Link file. Data Link files designate the appropriate provider through a string name used to identify the provider. This string name is a unique name that can be referenced either by a Data Link file or directly in the VB code to access a data store. The following code shows the text of a typical Data Link file created to connect to the SQL Server pubs database.

```
[oledb]
; Everything after this line is an OLE DB initstring
Provider=SQLOLEDB.1;Persist Security Info=False;User ID=sa;Initial
Catalog=pubs;Data Source=(local)
```

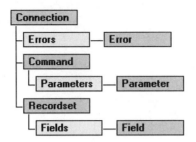

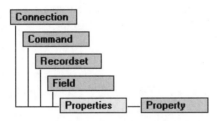

Figure 12-1 The ADO model.

In the Data Link file there is a single text string containing multiple field/value pairs which contain all the information necessary to connect to a UDA source. For example, the Provider=SQLOLEDB.1 portion designates that the Data Link uses the OLEDB provider for SQL Server. This cryptic string SQLOLEDB.1 is the programmatic identifier for the COM object which acts as the OLEDB provider. In general, all OLEDB providers use such strings to identify themselves. These strings are not easy to find, therefore, the simplest way to use them is to create a Data Link file from the File Explorer where the process is done using a wizard-like interface. However, programmers will occasionally want more control over connection strings, so knowing the exact syntax for a provider is important. Table 12-1 shows the strings for several common providers.

Table 12-1 OLEDB Provider Strings

Data Source	Provider Name
Microsoft Generic ODBC Driver	MSDASQL
Microsoft SQL Server	SQLOLEDB
Microsoft Oracle Provider	MSDAORA
Microsoft Access	Microsoft.Jet.OLEDB.3.51

continued on next page

Data Source	Provider Name
Microsoft Directory Services	AdsDSObject
Microsoft Index Server	MSIDXS
Microsoft Site Server	MSSEARCHSQL

In addition to the provider name, a properly formed Data Link can contain many other pieces of information. This information may be generic to many providers, such as the user name and password, or more specific information is required by the provider. All this implies that a good reference is required for any provider to be used. Fortunately, the MSDN documentation that ships with Visual Studio '98 contains help on each of the most common drivers.

Check It Out 12-1: Creating a Data Link File

1. Data Link Files are created in the File Explorer. Start the File Explorer and locate the directory **/PROGRAM FILES/COMMON FILES/SYSTEM/OLE DB/DATA LINKS**. This is where the Data Link files are normally created.
2. Select this new directory and choose **NEW/MICROSOFT DATA LINK** from the File Explorer menu.
3. Rename the file **BIBLIO.UDL** and press **Enter**.
4. Right-click the new file and select **PROPERTIES...** from the popup menu.
5. Click on the **Provider** tab and choose **Microsoft JET 3.51 OLEDB Provider**.
6. Click on the **Connection** tab. Use the **ellipsis** under Select or Enter Database Name to locate the BIBLIO.MDB database.
7. Press the **Test Connection** button to test the new Data Link.
8. Press **OK** to save the Data Link for use with the rest of this chapter.

Once a Data Link is established or the parameters required to access the provider directly from code are understood, you can use the `Connection` object to establish a connection to the selected data store. Establishing a connection requires creating an instance of the `Connection` object and setting the properties required to access the provider. The following code shows how a connection to the Biblio database might be established using ADO.

```
Dim m_Connection As ADODB.Connection
Set m_Connection = New ADODB.Connection
m_Connection.Provider = "Microsoft.Jet.OLEDB.3.51"
m_Connection.ConnectionString = _
   "Data Source=E:\Program Files\DevStudio\VB\Biblio.mdb"
m_Connection.Open
```

In the example, we declare a variable as a `Connection` object and create an instance using the `New` keyword. Once the instance is created, we set the `Provider` property to the name of the OLEDB provider to be used. The `ConnectionString` property then uses the Data Source key to point to the location of the database. Finally, the `Open` method uses the information to establish a connection to the designated data source with the designated provider. In this way, we specify all the information necessary to connect to the database directly in our code. However, we could also use a Data Link file to establish the connection. Because a Data Link contains all of the necessary information already, all we have to do is tell the `Connection` object which Data Link file to use. Specifying a Data Link file is done by using the `File Name` key to point to the UDL file where the Data Link is defined

```
Dim m_Connection As ADODB.Connection
Set m_Connection = New ADODB.Connection
m_Connection.ConnectionString = _
    "File Name=E:\Program Files\Common Files\System\OLE DB\Data
Links\Pubs.udl"
```

THE COMMAND OBJECT

The `Command` object used to run queries on an open connection. It is intended to be a very flexible object that can run commands against many different data sources. For this reason, use of the command object differs slightly from use of other query objects such as the `rdoQuery` object. However, it is still possible to use the SQL query language if using the `Command` object against relational data sources, is required.

The simplest, way to use a `Command` object is by setting three properties: `Active-Connection`, `CommandType` and `CommandText`. The `ActiveConnection` property is set to point to a previously-created `Connection` object. `CommandType` is the property that sets what kind of command will be executed. This might be an SQL statement or a stored procedure as well as some sort of proprietary command recognized by only one specific OLEDB provider. The following code shows how to run a simple SQL query against a relational database.

```
Set m_Command = New ADODB.Command
m_Command.CommandType = adCmdText
m_Command.CommandText = strSQL
m_Command.ActiveConnection = m_Connection
m_Command.Execute
```

The above example assumes a previously-created `Connection` named `m_Connection` and an SQL statement defined using the variable `strSQL`. The `CommandType` is set to the intrinsic constant `adCmdText` which means that we will be providing the command as a text string directly from our code. To use a stored procedure, set the property to `adCmdStoredProc`. The `CommandText` property is then set to the SQL statement to be run and the command is performed using the `Execute` method.

Commands work on non-relational OLEDB providers as well. It is not possible to use the SQL query language to run a query on a non-relational provider. SQL only works on realtional databases that support the SQL standard. SQL is simply not flexible enough to be used on a non-relational data store like the Microsoft Active Directory Service or Microsoft Index Server. When using ADO against these types of sources, it will be necessary to use a proprietary query language invented by the creator of the provider. This once again means that a good reference is vital to successfully interacting with OLEDB providers. As an example of how non-relational providers implement query languages, consider the following query which instructs the Microsoft Index Server to search the entire contents of the C drive for files containing the keyword BOOTCAMP.

```
SELECT Filename FROM SCOPE( 'DEEP TRAVERSAL OF " _
   & Chr(34) & "C:" & Chr(34) & _
   " ') WHERE CONTAINS(Contents,'"BOOTCAMP"') >0
```

THE RECORDSET OBJECT

The Recordset object represents records returned from the execution of a Command. ADO creates recordsets with return data for both relational and non-relational data stores. This is a significant advantage since data can be manipulated with identical methods, regardless of the source.

Recordset objects can be created in ADO in several different ways. The simplest way to get records is to run a single query using the Open method of the Recordset object. This method does not require a Connection or Command object to run. ADO simply creates a temporary connection and executes the command.

Check It Out 12-2: Returning Recordsets

1. Before continuing, make sure the Data Link file from Check It Out 12-1 has been created.
2. Start a new Standard EXE project in Visual Basic.
3. Set a reference to the ADO model by selecting **PROJECT/REFERENCES...** from the menu. In the References dialog, check the reference for **Microsoft ActiveX Data Objects 2.0 Library**. Push the **OK** button.
4. Drop a ListBox onto Form1.
5. In the Form_Load event run a query using just a Recordset object by adding the following code.

```
Dim m_Recordset As ADODB.Recordset
Set m_Recordset = New ADODB.Recordset
m_Recordset.Open "SELECT Name FROM Publishers", _
"File Name=<Your Data Link Path>\Biblio.udl"

Do While Not m_Recordset.EOF
  List1.AddItem m_Recordset!Name
  m_Recordset.MoveNext
Loop
```

6. Run the code and the list will fill with the names of all the Publishers. This code demonstrates how to return records with just the Open method.

Often, when returning data, it will be useful to have explicit access to the data connection for a given recordset. To preserve the connection, simply create a Connection object directly and then run the query. If the query is simple, it can still be executed without a Command object. Once the Connection object has been created, it can present an argument to the Open method or the ActiveConnection property of the Recordset object can be explicitly set. In general, ADO makes it possible to set properties and then call a method with no arguments, or to omit setting properties and call methods with an argument list. In the following code, we return the names of all publishers by setting properties and calling methods with no arguments.

```
Dim m_Connection As ADODB.Connection
Dim m_Recordset As ADODB.Recordset

Set m_Connection = New ADODB.Connection
m_Connection.ConnectionString = "File Name = Biblio.udl"
m_Connection.Open

Set m_Recordset = New ADODB.Recordset
Set m_Recordset.ActiveConnection = m_Connection
m_Recordset.Source = "SELECT Name FROM Publishers"
m_Recordset.Open
```

Setting properties before calling methods results in more lines of code since each property is set individually. However, the resulting code can be more readable than sending all properties as arguments. Notice also that the relationship between the Connection and the Recordset is established through the ActiveConnection property. With this property, it is possible to reuse the Recordset object against another connection later. To pass all parameters as arguments in the method, the following code, which is equivalent to the previous example, could be used:

```
Dim m_Connection As ADODB.Connection
Dim m_Recordset As ADODB.Recordset

Set m_Connection = New ADODB.Connection
m_Connection.Open "File Biblio.udl"

Set m_Recordset = New ADODB.Recordset
m_Recordset.Open "SELECT Name FROM Publishers", m_Connection
```

Although ADO offers two techniques for setting arguments, never use them together. The results may be unpredictable if, for example, the SQL statement for a Recordset is set in the Source property and then a different string is passed to the Open method. Choose a style and stick with it.

Once records are returned from a source, navigate them with standard methods. These methods should be familiar to those who have used any of the data access models before. Moving the cursor is done with the `MoveFirst`, `MoveLast`, `MoveNext`, and `MovePrevious` methods. Check to see if this is the beginning or end of the current set by using the `BOF` and `EOF` properties. Changes to the recordset are accomplished using the `AddNew`, `Update`, and `Delete` methods.

In addition to accessing data from `Connection` objects, ADO affords the ability to save recordsets to disk and access them later. This means that a `Recordset` object can be turned into a binary file and the data retrieved later using the `Open` method. This feature makes it possible to persist a recordset between sessions so the data are remembered even after the machine is turned off.

Check It Out 12-3: Persisting Recordsets

1. Before continuing, make sure the Data Link file from Check It Out 12-1 has been created.
2. Start a new Standard EXE project in Visual Basic.
3. Set a reference to the ADO model by selecting **PROJECT/REFERENCES...** from the menu. In the References dialog, check the reference for **Microsoft ActiveX Data Objects 2.0 Library**. Push the **OK** button.
4. Add controls to the toolbox by selecting **PROJECT/COMPONENTS...** from the menu. In the Components dialog, select the **Microsoft Common Dialog Control 6.0** and the **Microsoft Data Grid Control 6.0**. Press the **OK** button.
5. Create a user interface as shown in Figure 12-2. Use the Item list to set properties at design time.

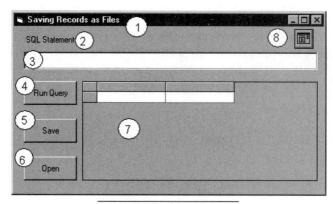

Figure 12-2 Form Interface.

Item 1—Form

Name	`frmFile`
Caption	Saving Records as Files

Item 2—Label

Name   lblQuery

Caption   SQL Statement

Item 3—TextBox

Name   txtQuery

Text   SELECT * FROM Publishers

Item 4—CommandButton

Name   cmdRun

Caption   Run Query

Item 5—CommandButton

Name   cmdSave

Caption   Save

Item 6—CommandButton

Name   cmdOpen

Caption   Open

Item 7—DataGrid

Name   grdResults

Item 8—CommonDialog

Name   dlgData

6. Run any query on the data source by typing the query into the TextBox and pushing the **Run Query** button. When the query is run, the results will be displayed in the grid. Add the following code to the cmdRun_Click event to run the query and display the results.

```
Dim m_Recordset As ADODB.Recordset
Set m_Recordset = New ADODB.Recordset
m_Recordset.CursorLocation = adUseClient
m_Recordset.CursorType = adOpenStatic
m_Recordset.Open txtQuery.Text, "File Name=<Your Data Link
    Path>\Biblio.udl"

Set grdResults.DataSource = m_Recordset
```

7. Saving the recordset to a file is done with the Save method. Use the Common Dialog control to select a location. Add the following code to the cmdSave_Click event to save the records to a file.

```
On Error GoTo SaveErr

  'Get Recordset
```

```
Dim m_Recordset As ADODB.Recordset
Set m_Recordset = grdResults.DataSource
Set grdResults.DataSource = Nothing

'Get FileName
Dim strFilename As String

dlgData.Filter = "Recordset Files(*.dat)|*.dat||"
dlgData.FileName = "Records"
dlgData.ShowSave
strFilename = dlgData.FileName

'Save Records
m_Recordset.Save strFilename
Exit Sub

SaveErr:
    MsgBox Err.Description
    Exit Sub
```

8. Once the records are saved to the file, they are no longer dependent upon any connection to the data source. To open the saved data, use the `Open` method with the filename as the argument. Add the following code to the `cmdOpen_Click` event to open the saved file and display the records.

```
On Error GoTo OpenErr

    'Get FileName
Dim strFilename As String

dlgData.Filter = "Recordset Files(*.dat)|*.dat||"
dlgData.FileName = "Records"
dlgData.ShowOpen
strFilename = dlgData.FileName

'Open Records
Dim m_Recordset As ADODB.Recordset
Set m_Recordset = New ADODB.Recordset
m_Recordset.Open strFilename

'Set Recordset
Set grdResults.DataSource = m_Recordset

Exit Sub
```

```
OpenErr:
  MsgBox Err.Description
  Exit Sub
```

9. Run the application. Execute the default query and save the data as a file. Once the data is saved, end the application. Then restart the application and open the saved file.

THE FIELD OBJECT

The Field object represents a column contained in a returned set of records. It gives access to the data returned in a set of records as well as structural information like the data type and size of the field. As with objects in other models, the Field object can be accessed through its associated collection or directly by name. The following code shows how to read a field named LastName from a recordset. All the following lines are equivalent.

```
MsgBox m_Recordset.Fields.Item("LastName").Value
MsgBox m_Recordset.Fields.Item("LastName")
MsgBox m_Recordset.Fields("LastName")
MsgBox m_Recordset!LastName
```

THE PARAMETER OBJECT

The Parameter object represents a parameter passed to a stored procedure by ADO. Use this object to call stored procedures and utilize both input and output parameters. Calling stored procedures is slightly different than using a straight SQL statement even without parameter objects. Once the connection is established, set the CommandType property of the Command object to adCmdStoredProc and the CommandText property to the name of the procedure to be run. The following code shows a simple call to the system stored procedure sp_who which returns information about current users of SQL Server:

```
'Variables
Dim m_Connection As ADODB.Connection
Dim m_Command As ADODB.Command
Dim m_Recordset As ADODB.Recordset

'Open Connection
Set m_Connection = New ADODB.Connection
m_Connection.Provider = "SQLOLEDB"
m_Connection.ConnectionString = "Data Source=(local);Database=master;UID=sa;PWD=;"
m_Connection.Open

'Create Command
Set m_Command = New ADODB.Command
```

```
m_Command.CommandType = adCmdStoredProc
m_Command.CommandText = "sp_Who"
Set m_Command.ActiveConnection = m_Connection

'Create Recordset
Set m_Recordset = New ADODB.Recordset
Set m_Recordset = m_Command.Execute
```

If the stored procedure requires the use of parameter objects, either create them directly or pass them as arguments to the Execute method of the Command object. The following code shows the Execute method for running the sp_who procedure against just the system administrator log in.

```
Set m_Recordset = m_Command.Execute(Parameters:= "sa")
```

When parameters are passed in line with the Execute method, they can only be used as input parameters. Using output parameters requires the explicit construction of a Parameter object. Parameters are built by creating an instance of the Parameter object and adding it to the Parameters collection for the associated Command object.

As an example, assume we have created a stored procedure. This stored procedure is added to the pubs database in SQL server and returns the average price of all the books in the Titles table. The price is returned as an output parameter from the stored procedure. The stored procedure is declared in SQL Server as follows:

```
CREATE PROCEDURE sp_AveragePrice
@Value smallmoney OUTPUT
AS
SELECT @VALUE = AVG(Price) FROM Titles
```

In order to run the procedure, we connect to the pubs database as usual and create a Command object. Once the Command is created, we use the Parameter object to build the output parameter. The following code shows how the output parameter is created to call the stored procedure:

```
Set m_Parameter = New ADODB.Parameter
m_Parameter.Direction = adParamOutput
m_Parameter.Type = adCurrency
```

The Direction property of the Parameter object is used to specify input or output. The type is used to define the data type expected by the stored procedure. ADO provides intrinsic constants for all the various SQL Server data types that might need to be declared. Once the parameter is created, add it to the Parameters collection for the Command object. This is accomplished by the following code:

```
objCommand.Parameters.Append m_Parameter
```

Once the collection of parameters is complete, the `Execute` method of the `Command` is called. When the procedure is executed, the output parameter value is changed by the stored procedure. When the procedure returns, use the value of the `Parameter`. The following code shows the average price in a message box:

```
MsgBox "The average price is: " & Format$(m_Command.Parameters(0),
        "Currency")
```

ADO EVENTS

ADO provides a significant event model to use to receive information about the state of the application. It is divided into events associated with the `Connection` and events associated with the `Recordset`. Although the `Connection` and `Recordset` support many different events for operations as varied as transactions and asynchronous queries, in connection to a database and running a query, the following events will be received:

Connection_WillConnect

This event fires before ADO connects to the specified data source. It passes in the information that will be used to establish the connection. This information may be modified before the connection is established.

Connection_ConnectComplete

This event fires after ADO has successfully connected to the data source. It can also be used to receive notification when an asynchronous connection is established. Asynchronous connections are enabled by using the `adAsyncConnect` option.

Recordset_WillMove

This event fires when the query causes the cursor to move to the first record. When this event fires, the move is just about to take place.

RecordsetMoveComplete

This event fires when ADO has finished moving the cursor in the new recordset.

Connection_ExecuteComplete

This event fires when the query being run is completed and the records are returned. It is a particularly useful event since it may be used to receive notification when an asynchronous query has completed asynchronous queries; it can be executed in ADO by using the `adAsyncExecute` parameter in the `Execute` method.

Check It Out 12-4: Asynchronous Operations

1. Before continuing, make sure the Data Link file from Check It Out 12-1 has been created.
2. Start a new Standard EXE project in Visual Basic.

3. Set a reference to the ADO model by selecting **PROJECT/REFERENCES...** from the menu. In the references dialog, check the reference for **Microsoft ActiveX Data Objects 2.0 Library**. Push the **OK** button.

4. Add a control to the toolbox by selecting **PROJECT/COMPONENTS...** from the menu. In the components dialog, select the **Microsoft Data Grid Control 6.0**. Press the **OK** button.

5. Add a data grid control to Form1.

6. In order to use the event model of ADO, declare variables `WithEvents`. Add the following code to the [General][Declarations] section of Form1 to use the event model:

```
Private WithEvents m_Connection As ADODB.Connection
Private WithEvents m_Recordset As ADODB.Recordset
```

7. We connect asynchronously to the data source when the form loads. Because it is an asynchronous connection, we will make the form appear immediately and then wait for the data. Add the following code to the `Form_Load` event to establish the connection.

```
'Show Form
Show
Refresh

'Connect Asynchronously
Set m_Connection = New ADODB.Connection
m_Connection.ConnectionString = "File Name=<Your Data Link
            Path>\Biblio.udl"
m_Connection.Open Options:=adAsyncConnect
```

8. When the connection is made, the `ConnectComplete` event will fire. When this happens, we will run the query asynchronously and wait for the results. Add the following code to the `m_Connection_ConnectComplete` event to run the query.

```
'Query Asynchronously
If pConnection Is m_Connection Then
   Set m_Recordset = New ADODB.Recordset
   m_Recordset.CursorLocation = adUseClient
   m_Recordset.CursorType = adOpenStatic
   m_Recordset.Source = "SELECT * FROM Publishers"
   Set m_Recordset.ActiveConnection = pConnection
   m_Recordset.Open Options:=adAsyncExecute
End If
```

9. When the query is finished, ADO fires the `ExecuteComplete` event. When this event fires, we can populate the grid with the returned data. Add the following code to the `m_Connection_ExecuteComplete` event to show the results.

```
'Display Data
If pRecordset Is m_Recordset Then
  Set DataGrid1.DataSource = pRecordset
End If
```

10. Run the application. Note how the form appears and then the grid is filled.

ADO CURSOR FEATURES

When the ADO model is used, specify the location and type of cursor for use with recordsets. ADO makes it possible to specify location through the `CursorLocation` property available through the `Connection` or `Recordset` object. This property accepts one of two values: `adUseClient` and `adUseServer`. Server-side are the default in ADO and are good for applications where maximum flexibility is required, including the need to see changes to the database reflected in recordsets. Client cursors are the best choice for scalability, they use fewer shared resources and support optimistic batch updating through disconnected recordsets.

Once the location is set, specify the particular features of the cursor through the `CursorType` property, which is set through the `Recordset` object and affects only recordsets opened after the property is set. The `CursorType` property supports the following values:

```
adOpenForwardOnly
```

The forward only cursor setting creates a recordset that can be traversed only once in the forward direction. This is the default `CursorType` setting and is not truly a cursor at all. This type of cursor is referred to as a *fire hose* cursor because it sends all records to the application all at once in a stream. This type is excellent for scalable applications where the data are traversed one time and a structure such as a lookup list is filled. This cursor type is only available with server cursor locations.

adOpenStatic

The static cursor provides a snapshot of the data which can be scrolled in the forward and backward directions. This type does not make visible any underlying data changes made by other users. This type is useful for scalable applications where data must be brought to the client and scrolled through. This cursor is the only setting available with both server and client locations. In a client cursor, this is the only setting supported; however, setting the type to any other value will not cause an error. The cursor type simply changes after the connection to `adOpenStatic`.

adOpenKeyset

The keyset cursor adds additional features. With a keyset type, data changes made by other users to the underlying recordset will be visible. Records added by other users are not made visible to this cursor, but deleted records deleted by other users become unavailable to this cursor. This cursor type is useful for cursor-based applications and is only available to server cursor locations.

adOpenDynamic

This cursor has the most features of any cursor type. The dynamic cursor causes all additions, deletions, and changes by other users to be reflected in the recordset. This is also the most expensive of all the cursors, requiring significantly more resources to maintain it. This cursor type is only available from server cursor locations.

Although the cursor type affects the features available to any cursor, not all OLEDB providers may support all possible features of a cursor. ADO therefore provides a mechanism for testing a `Recordset` object to determine what specific features are supported by the underlying cursor. The `Supports` method of the `Recordset` object is used to return Boolean values that indicate support for certain features. For example, to find out if the underlying recordset supports adding new records use the following code where `blnResults` is a Boolean and `objRecordset` is a `Recordset` object:

```
blnResults = objRecordset.Supports(adAddNew)
```

When calling the `Supports` method, combine options by adding them together and passing the total as an argument. In this case, the method returns True if all of the specified features are supported. Table 12-2 list all the possible arguments for the `Supports` method.

Table 12-2 Cursor Option Constants

Constant	Description
adAddNew	Supports the AddNew method
adApproxPosition	Supports the AbsolutePosition and AbsolutePage properties
adBookmark	Supports the Bookmark property
adDelete	Supports the Delete method
adHoldRecords	Get more records for the set without committing existing pending changes
adMovePrevious	Supports Move, MoverFirst, MovePrevious, and GetRows methods
adResync	Supports the Resync method
adUpdate	Supports the Update method
adUpdateBatch	Supports the UpdateBatch and CancelBatch methods

UNDERSTANDING DISCONNECTED RECORDSETS

Like RDO, ADO supports batch optimistic updating using disconnected recordsets. Those unfamiliar with the concepts of batch updating should refer to the discussion in Chapter 11. In this section, we focus on the features of ADO that support scalability and partitioning with the `Recordset` object. In general, a disconnected recordset is created by setting the `Active-Connection` property of the `Recordset` object to `Nothing`. Once the `Active-Connection` is set to `Nothing`, the `Recordset` object can be passed as a return value from a function and the `Recordset` can even be passed between applications operating on different machines.

Check It Out 12-5: Passing Recordsets

1. Before continuing, make sure the Data Link file from Check It Out 12-1 has been created.

2. Start a new ActiveX DLL project in Visual Basic. This type of project is covered in more detail later, but essentially allows another project to call functions that are defined here. We will also use a class module in this project to contain the functions. At this point, just recognize that this project allows sharing of the functions written.

3. Set a reference to the ADO model by selecting **PROJECT/REFERENCES...** from the menu. In the References dialog, check the reference for **Microsoft ActiveX Data Objects 2.0 Library**. Push the **OK** button.

4. Project1 uses the class module to run a query and create a `Recordset` object. With the class module selected, add a new procedure by selecting **TOOLS/ADD PROCEDURE** from the menu. Add a new Public Function named **Query**. When the function is added, specify that it should return a `Recordset` object. At the finish the function definition should appear in the class module as shown.

```
Public Function Query() As ADODB.Recordset

End Function
```

5. The `Query` function will run a query on the data source, and return a disconnected `Recordset`. Add the following code to the `Query` function to return the `Recordset` object to a calling client.

```
Dim objRecordset As ADODB.Recordset
Set objRecordset = New ADODB.Recordset
objRecordset.CursorLocation = adUseClient
objRecordset.CursorType = adOpenStatic
objRecordset.Open "SELECT * FROM Publishers", "File Name = <Your
    Data Link Path>\Biblio.udl"
Set Query = objRecordset
```

6. Add a new project to the application by selecting **FILE/ADD PROJECT** from the menu. In the Project dialog, select to **add a new Standard EXE project**. Be careful to add a project and not simply start a new project. Both Project1 and Project2 should be visible in the Project Explorer simultaneously.

7. Right-click **Project2** in the File Explorer. Select **SET AS START UP** from the menu. This will cause Project2 to be the first project to run.

8. Set a reference to the ADO model in Project2 by selecting **PROJECT/REFER-ENCES...** from the menu. In the References dialog, check the reference for **Microsoft ActiveX Data Objects 2.0 Library**. Push the **OK** button.

9. Add a control to the toolbox in Project2 by selecting **PROJECT/COMPO-NENTS...** from the menu. In the components dialog, select the **Microsoft Data Grid Control 6.0**. Press the **OK** button.

10. Add a new data grid to Form1 in Project2.

11. Project2 is going to call the `Query` function contained in Project1 and get the `Recordset` object as a return value. This `Recordset` will then be displayed in the grid. Add the following code to the `Form_Load` event of Form1 in Project2 to get the data:

```
Dim MyRecordset As ADODB.Recordset
Dim MyObject As Object

Set MyObject = CreateObject("Project1.Class1")
Set MyRecordset = MyObject.Query

Set DataGrid1.DataSource = MyRecordset
```

12. Run the application. The grid will fill with data showing how `Recordset` objects can be passed from one project to another.

Passing recordset objects is a good strategy for creating partitions. Partitioning an application refers to building separate tiers where data, business logic, and user interface are managed. These systems are typically called *n-tier* applications and represent the state-of-the-art in scalable, multi-user applications. In these applications, `Recordsets` can be passed from tier to tier where they may be edited or displayed. When the user is finished, the changes can be sent back to the database.

Changes to disconnected `Recordset` objects can be applied to the original database by reconnecting the `Recordset` and calling the `UpdateBatch` method. Reconnecting is done by creating a new `Connection` object and setting the `ActiveConnection` property of the `Recordset`. The following code shows how a disconnected `Recordset` might be reconnected to SQLServer and the changes applied:

```
'Reconnect the resultset
Set m_Connection = New ADODB.Connection
m_Connection.Provider = "MSDASQL"
m_Connection.ConnectionString = "Data Source=pubs;SERVER=(local);
    UID=sa;PWD=;"
m_Connection.CursorLocation = adUseClient
m_Connection.Open

'Update Results
```

```
m_Resultset.MarshalOptions = adMarshalModifiedOnly
Set m_Resultset.ActiveConnection = m_Connection
m_Resultset.UpdateBatch
```

In the above example, m_Connection is a Connection object and m_Recordset is a Recordset object. The Recordset object had previously been disconnected by setting its ActiveConnection property to Nothing. Once the connection is reestablished, the ActiveConnection property is set. The MarshalOptions property of the recordset specifies that only changed records should be sent to the database. Unchanged records are not sent, which cuts down on network traffic. Note that when the UpdateBatch method is to be used, the Recordset must have been opened using a client cursor location with a cursor type of adOpenStatic, and the LockType property must be set to adLockBatchOptimistic. The following code shows how this type of Recordset object might originally be created:

```
m_Resultset.CursorLocation = adUseClient
m_Resultset.CursorType = adOpenStatic
m_Resultset.LockType = adLockBatchOptimistic
```

Exercise 12-1: Active Data Objects (ADO)

ADO, the latest data access strategy from Microsoft, is unique because it has the ability to query both relational and non-relational data sources. In this exercise, we will use the optimistic batch update capabilities of ADO to create a simple, scalable, two-tier application.

SETTING UP THE DATA LINK

Step 1

Before using ADO, set up the Data Link file for use. In this exercise, we will be interacting with the SQL Server database "pubs." Establishing the data link is not a Visual Basic, but rather a Windows Operating System function. Set up is done using the File Explorer utility found in Windows. Start the File Explorer.

Step 2

Data Links can be defined anywhere on the computer, though they are commonly kept in the directory **\PROGRAM FILES\COMMON FILES\SYSTEM\OLE DB\DATA LINKS**. Locate this directory in the File Explorer. If the directory does not exist, you should create it.

Step 3

Select the **DATA LINKS** folder in the left-hand pane and choose **FILE/NEW/MICROSOFT DATA LINK FILE** from the menu. After selecting the menu, notice that a new Data Link file has been created. Edit the name of the file to **PUBS.UDL**.

Step 4

Right click **PUBS.UDL** and select **PROPERTIES...** from the popup menu. This dialog is where the information required by the OLEDB provider is specified. In the Provider tab choose **Microsoft OLE DB Provider for SQL Server**. Push the **Next** button.

Step 5

In the Connection tab, select the name of the server where the pubs database resides. Provide a user name and password to access the SQL Server. Finally, enter the name "pubs" as the database to use with this data link.

Step 6

Test the new connection by pressing the **Test Connection** button. When the connection tests satisfactorily, press the **OK** button.

CREATING THE GUI

Step 7

Using the Windows File Explorer, create a new directory **VB BOOTCAMP\EXERCISE12-1**. Start a new Standard EXE project in Visual Basic.

Step 8

The interface for this application consists of Labels, TextBoxes, and CommandButtons. The Labels and TextBoxes are all part of control arrays. Create the interface as shown in Figure 12-3. Use the Item list below to set the design time properties for each object.

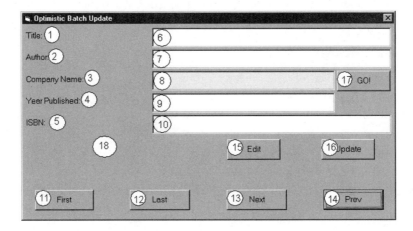

Figure 12-3 The Form interface.

Item 1—Label

Name	lblLabels
Index	0
Caption	Title

Item 2—Label

Name	lblLabels

Index	1
Caption	Author

Item 3—Label

Name	lblLabels
Index	2
Caption	Company Name

Item 4—Label

Name	lblLabels
Index	3
Caption	Year Published

Item 5—Label

Name	lblLabels
Index	4
Caption	ISBN

Item 6—TextBox

Name	txtFields
Index	0
Text	<empty>

Item 7—TextBox

Name	txtFields
Index	1
Text	<empty>

Item 8—TextBox

Name	txtFields
Index	2
Text	<empty>
BackColor	Yellow

Item 9—TextBox

Name	txtFields
Index	3
Text	<empty>

Item 10—TextBox

Name	txtFields
Index	4
Text	<empty>

Item 11—CommandButton

Name	`cmdMoveFirst`
Caption	First

Item 12—CommandButton

Name	`cmdMoveLast`
Caption	Last

Item 13—CommandButton

Name	`cmdMoveNext`
Caption	Next

Item 14—CommandButton

Name	`cmdMovePrevious`
Caption	Previous

Item 15—CommandButton

Name	`cmdEdit`
Caption	Edit

Item 16—CommandButton

Name	`cmdUpdate`
Caption	Update

Item 17—CommandButton

Name	`cmdGo`
Caption	GO!
Default	True

Item 18—Form

Name	`frmBatch`
Caption	Optimistic Batch Updating
BorderStyle	3-Fixed Dialog

CODING THE APPLICATION

Step 9

Now that the GUI is completed, we can populate it using ADO technology. Before using ADO, set a reference to it. Select **PROJECT/REFERENCES...** from the VB menu and locate the entry **Microsoft Active Data Objects 2.0**. Select the library and close the References dialog.

Step 10

ADO defines two key objects for accessing data: `Connection` and `Recordset`. We will use these objects by declaring variables of these types in the [General][Declarations] section of `frmBatch`. Add the following code to declare these variables:

```
'This variable is for the Connection
Private m_Connection As ADODB.Connection

'This variable is for the Recordset
Private m_Resultset As ADODB.Recordset

'Enumeration for Fields
Private Enum enmFields
  ntsTitle
  ntsAuthor
  ntsCompanyName
  ntsYearPublished
  ntsISBN
End Enum
```

Step 11

When the form loads, we establish a connection to the database using ADO. Add the following code to the `Form_Load` event to create a `Connection` object and connect to the Data Link file you built earlier. Note that the cursor location is set to `adUseClient` to facilitate batch processing.

```
'Show Form
Show
DoEvents

'Establish the Connection
Set m_Connection=New ADODB.Connection
m_Connection.ConnectionString="File Name=_
    <Your Data Link Path>/pubs.udl"
m_Connection.CursorLocation=adUseClient
m_Connection.Open
```

Step 12

After the connection is established, type a partial company name into the **Company Name** field and press the **GO** button. ADO will then query the data source for entries containing that string. Note how the database connection is disconnected after the query is run so that another user can have it. This technique is critical to scalability. Add the following code to the `cmdGO_Click` event to run the query:

```
'Create Query
Dim strSQL As String

strSQL = ""
```

```
strSQL = strSQL & "SELECT titles.title, authors.au_lname, "
strSQL = strSQL & "publishers.pub_name, titles.pubdate, "
strSQL = strSQL & "titles.title_id "
strSQL = strSQL & "FROM titles, authors, "
strSQL = strSQL & "publishers, titleauthor "
strSQL = strSQL & "WHERE authors.au_is = titleauthor.au_id "
strSQL = strSQL & "AND titleauthor.title_id = titles.title_id "
strSQL = strSQL & "AN titles.pub_id = publishers.pub_id "

'Run Query
'NOTE the propery settings required for a batch update!!!!
Set m_Resultset = New ADODB.Recordset
m_Resultset.ActiveConnection = m_Connection
m_Resultset.Source = strSQL
m_Resultset.CursorLocation = adUseClient
m_Resultset.CursorType = adOpenStatic
m_Resultset.LockType = adLockBatchOptimistic

m_Resultset.Open
ShowData

'Disconnect Resultset
Set m_Resultset.ActiveConnection = Nothing
m_Connection.Close
Set m_Connection = Nothing
```

Step 13

Displaying the current record is done by reading the field objects and putting them into the TextBoxes through a custom procedure called ShowData. Add this procedure by selecting **TOOLS/ADDPROCEDURE** from the menu. Create a Public Sub and add code so that the final results appear as follows:

```
Public Sub ShowData()

    'This routine shows data in the Text Boxes
    txtFields(ntsTitle).Text = m_Resultset!title & vbNullString
    txtFields(ntsAuthor).Text = m_Rsultset!au_lname & vbNullString
    txtFields(ntsCompanyName).Text = m_Resultset!pub_name _
        & vbNullString
    txtFields(ntsYearPublished).Text = m_Resultset!pubdate _
        & vbNullString
    txtFields(ntsISBN).Text = m_Resultset!title_id & vbNullString
```

```
End Sub
```

Step 14

Once the records have been returned, navigate through them using the buttons at the bottom of the form. This navigation is similar to that in any other data access object model like RDO or DAO. Add the following code to navigate the records:

```
'Navigation Code
Private Sub cmdMoveFirst_Click()
  m_Resultset.MoveFirst
  ShowData
End Sub

Private Sub cmdMoveLast_Click()
  m_Resultset.MoveLast
  ShowData
End Sub

Private Sub cmdMoveNext_Click()
  m_Resultset.MoveNext
  If m_Resultset.EOF Then
    Beep
    m_Resultset.MoveLast
  Else
    ShowData
  End If
End Sub

Private Sub cmdMovePrevious_Click()
  m_Resultset.MovePrevious
  If m_Resultset.BOF Then
    Beep
    m_Resultset.MoveFirst
  Else
    ShowData
  End If
End Sub
```

Step 15

Under batch updating, records can be edited at will, but the changes will only occur to the batch on the client machine. Since there is no longer a connection to the database, any changes made must ultimately be submitted to the server for reconnection with the data source. Add the following code to the `cmdEdit_Click` event to make local changes to records not yet committed to the database.

```
'Edit the record locally
m_Resultset!Title = txtFields(ntsTitle).Text
m_Resultset!au_lname = txtFields(ntsAuthor).Text
m_Resultset!pub_name = txtFields(ntsCompanyName).Text
m_Resultset!pubdate = txtFields(ntsYearPublished).Text
m_Resultset!title_id = txtFields(ntsISBN).Text

m_Resultset.Update
```

Step 16

After local changes are complete, submit the changes to the database. Submitted changes are synchronized with the database through the use of primary table keys. ADO identifies these keys through the `JOIN` clause of the associated SQL statement. Add the following code to the `cmdUpdate_Click` event to send changes back to the server.

```
'Reconnect the resultset
Set m_Connection=New ADODB.Connection
m_Connection.ConnectionString="File Name=_
    <Your Data Link Path>/pubs.udl"
m_Connection.CursorLocation=adUseClient
m_Connection.Open
Set m_Resultset.ActiveConnection=m_Connection

'Update Results
m_Resultset.MarshalOptions=adMarshalModifiedOnly
m_Resultset.UpdateBatch

'Disconnect the Resultset
Set m_Resultset.ActiveConnection=Nothing
```

Step 17

Save the project and run it. When testing the project, try making changes locally, but terminating the application before updating the server. What happens? The try a complete update to verify the application works.

Exercise 12-2: Non-relational Data Stores

This exercise demonstrates how to use ADO to query the Microsoft Index Server. Index Server must be installed and operational before this exercise begins. This normally entails installing the Internet Information Server and Index Server through the NT 4.0 Option Pack. While this book is not intended to teach these products, interested readers can gain valuable experience with ADO through this exercise.

SETTING UP THE DATA LINK

Step 1

Before accessing the Index Server, set up Data Link file for use. Establishing the data link is not a Visual Basic, but rather a Windows Operating System function. Set up is done using the File Explorer utility found in Windows. Start the File Explorer.

Step 2

Data Links can be defined anywhere on the computer, through they are commonly kept in the directory **\PROGRAM FILES\COMMON FILES\SYSTEM\OLE DB\DATA LINKS**. Locate this directory in the File Explorer.

Step 3

Select the **DATA LINKS** folder in the left-hand pane and choose **FILE/NEW/MICROSOFT DATA LINK FILE** from the menu. After the menu is selected, notice that a new Data Link file has been created. Edit the name of the file to **INDEX SERVER.UDL**.

Step 4

Right-click **INDEX SERVER.UDL** and select **PROPERTIES...** from the popup menu. This dialog is where the information required by the OLEDB provider is specified. In the Provider tab choose **Microsoft OLEDB Provider for Microsoft Index Server**. Push the **Next** button.

Step 5

In the Connection tab, set the Data Source to **WEB**. Test the new connection by pressing the **Test Connection** button. When the connection tests satisfactorily, press the **OK** button.

BUILDING THE INTERFACE

Step 6

Using the File Explorer, create a new directory **VB BOOTCAMP\EXERCISE 12-2**. Start a new Standard EXE project in Visual Basic.

Step 7

This application will be a search engine capable of searching a Web site using the Microsoft Index Server. In order for the project to work, it must be on the same machine as the Index Server. The interface for the search screen is shown in Figure 12-4. Create this interface using the Item list below to set design-time properties in the Properties window.

Item 1—Form

Name	frmIndex
Caption	Index Server
BorderStyle	3-Fixed Dialog

Item 2—ListBox

Name	lstPages

Item 3—TextBox

Name   `txtSearch`

Text   \<empty\>

Item 4—CommandButton

Name   `cmdSearch`

Caption   Search

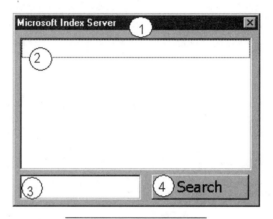

Figure 12-4 Form Interface.

CODING THE APPLICATION

Step 8

Set a reference to ADO before using it. Select **PROJECT/REFERENCES...** from the VB menu and locate the entry **Microsoft Active Data Objects 2.0**. Select the library and close the References dialog.

Step 9

All of the code in this exercise is placed under the `cdmSearch_Click` event. You will add this code one piece at a time, but each piece appears in order under the click event. Start with the code to connect to the Microsoft Index Server. This code is similar to connecting to any source and includes a reference to the Data Link file created earlier.

```
'Variables
Dim objConnection As ADODB.Connection
Dim objCommand As ADODB.Command
Dim objRecordset As ADODB.Recordset

'Open Connection
Set objConnection = New ADODB.Connection
objConnection.ConnectionString = _
```

```
    "File Name=<Your Data Link Path>\Index Server.udl;"
objConnection.Open
```

Step 10

This next part creates the actual query. Note that the query syntax is very different from standard SQL syntax even though it has a SELECT statement. This syntax is described in detail in the documentation for the Microsoft Index Server, however, some explanation is in order. Examine the code below and notice that the query statement asks to select the filenames from SCOPE ('DEEP TRAVERSAL OF, this statement means that the Index Server should search a given file path and every directory under it. If a SHALLOW TRAVERSAL OF is specified then it only searches the directory specified. In the code substitute the exact path on the drive to the area to be searched (e. g., C:\INETPUB\WWWROOT).

```
'Prepare Command
Set objCommand = New ADODB.Command
objCommand.CommandType = adCmdText
objCommand.Prepared = False

objCommand.CommandText = _
"SELECT Filename FROM SCOPE( 'DEEP TRAVERSAL OF " _
& Chr(34) & "<Your Path to the Web Site> & Chr(34) & _
" ') WHERE CONTAINS(Contents,'" _
& txtSearch.Text & "') >0"

Set objCommand.ActiveConnection = objConnection
```

Step 11

Now add the code that actually runs the query and returns results. The beauty of ADO is that even non-relational data is returned as a Recordset object. Add the following code to show the resulting files in the list:

```
'Execute Command
Set objRecordset = objCommand.Execute

'Build List
lstPages.Clear
Do While Not objRecordset.EOF
  lstPages.AddItem objRecordset("Filename")
  objRecordset.MoveNext
Loop
```

Step 12

Save and run the application. Type a search word into the TextBox and press the button. The files returned from the search will appear in the ListBox.

FOR THE CERTIFIED PRO

Pro 12-1: ADO Basics

1. Create an application that displays all of the Titles from the BIBLIO.MDB database in a grid.

Pro 12-2: Disconnected Recordsets

1. Create an application that runs a query to return the names of all Publishers in the BIBLIO.MDB database as a disconnected Recordset.
2. Save the Recordset as a file.

PREPARING FOR CERTIFICATION

Topics for Further Reading
  ADO Overview
  ADO Programming Model with Objects

CERTIFICATION QUIZ

1. Which of the following are legitimate OLEDB providers?
    a. MSDASQL
    b. SQLOLEDB
    c. MSDAORA
    d. MSIDXS

2. Which of the following is the default OLEDB provider for ADO?
    a. MSDASQL
    b. SQLOLEDB
    c. MSDAORA
    d. MSIDXS

3. What methods can create a Recordset?
    a. `Connection.Open`
    b. `Recordset.Open`
    c. `Command.Execute`
    d. `Query.Run`

4. What keyword is used to include ADO events in your code?
    a. `HaveEvents`
    b. `RaiseEvents`
    c. `WithEvents`
    d. `Event`

5. What arguments are valid parts of an OLEDB connect string?
   a. Data Source
   b. PWD
   c. DSN
   d. File Name

6. Which constants are valid cursor locations in ADO?
   a. `adDoNotUse`
   b. `adUseServer`
   c. `adUseClientBatch`
   d. `adUseClient`

7. Which is a valid ADO Connect string?
   a. `"File Source=Biblio.mdb;"`
   b. `"Data File=Biblio.udl"`
   c. `"File Name=Biblio.udl"`
   d. `"DRIVER={SQL Server};SERVER=(local);`
      `DATABASE=pubs;UID=sa;PWD=;DSN=;"`

8. What constants represent valid cursors in ADO?
   a. `adOpenForwardOnly`
   b. `adOpenStatic`
   c. `adOpenKeyset`
   d. `adOpenDynamic`

9. Which cursors are available for use if the cursor driver is selected as `adUseClient`?
   a. `adOpenForwardOnly`
   b. `adOpenStatic`
   c. `adOpenKeyset`
   d. `adOpenDynamic`

10. Which of the following methods are available to a cursor designated as `adOpenForwardOnly`?
    a. `MoveFirst`
    b. `MoveLast`
    c. `MoveNext`
    d. `MovePrevious`

11. What `LockType` is required for batch updates?
    a. `adLockReadOnly`
    b. `adLockPessimistic`
    c. `adLockOptimistic`
    d. `adLockBatchOptimistic`

12. Which cursor type is fully updatable and has dynamic membership?
   a. `adOpenForwardOnly`
   b. `adOpenStatic`
   c. `adOpenKeyset`
   d. `adOpenDynamic`

13. What types of queries can be used with the `Command` object?
   a. SQL queries
   b. Stored procedures
   c. SQL parameter queries
   d. SQL UPDATE queries

ANSWERS TO CERTIFICATION QUIZ

1. a, b, c, d
2. a
3. b, c
4. c
5. a, b, d
6. b, d
7. c, d
8. a, b ,c ,d
9. b
10. c
11. d
12. d
13. a, b, c, d

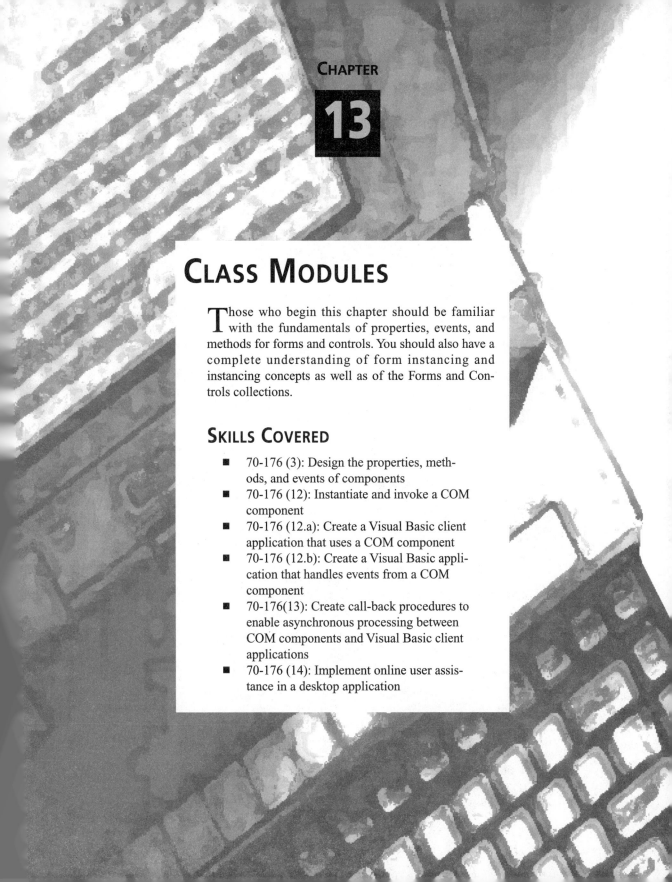

CLASS MODULES

Those who begin this chapter should be familiar with the fundamentals of properties, events, and methods for forms and controls. You should also have a complete understanding of form instancing and instancing concepts as well as of the Forms and Controls collections.

SKILLS COVERED

- 70-176 (3): Design the properties, methods, and events of components
- 70-176 (12): Instantiate and invoke a COM component
- 70-176 (12.a): Create a Visual Basic client application that uses a COM component
- 70-176 (12.b): Create a Visual Basic application that handles events from a COM component
- 70-176(13): Create call-back procedures to enable asynchronous processing between COM components and Visual Basic client applications
- 70-176 (14): Implement online user assistance in a desktop application

- 70-176 (14.c): Implement messages from a server component to a user interface
- 70-176 (16): Create a COM component that implements business rules or logic
- 70-176 (19): Debug a COM client written in Visual Basic
- 70-176 (28): Implement project groups to support the development and debugging process
- 70-176 (28.a): Debug DLLs in process
- 70-175 (4): Design the properties, methods, and events of components
- 70-175 (16): Instantiate and invoke a COM component
- 70-175 (16.a): Create a Visual Basic client application that uses a COM component
- 70-175 (16.b): Create a Visual Basic application that handles events from a COM component
- 70-175 (17): Create call-back procedures to enable asynchronous processing between COM components and Visual Basic client applications
- 70-175 (18): Implement online user assistance in a distributed application
- 70-175 (18.c): Implement messages from a server component to a user interface
- 70-175 (21): Create a COM component that implements business rules or logic
- 70-175 (25): Debug Visual Basic code that uses objects from a COM server
- 70-175 (48): Implement project groups to support the development and debugging process
- 70-175 (48.a): Debug DLLs in process

According to Microsoft, there are millions of Visual Basic programmers worldwide, and in many cases, these programmers each have several years of experience with the product. However, the majority of these same programmers have little or no experience with classes and object-oriented principles. The gap between VB programmers who use forms with functions and those who use classes with methods is startlingly wide. A Visual Basic programmer should understand that classes represent the gateway to every advanced feature in the product.

As with every technology a programmer tries to learn, the first roadblock to understanding classes is the terminology. In fact, the terminology associated with classes is particularly daunting. Words like *polymorphism* and *encapsulation* strike fear into the hearts of students, and instructors do not always have the patience to demystify the concepts. The result is that object-oriented (OO) principles are often guarded like a secret scroll of knowledge that can only be read by the worthy.

Object-oriented principles are not difficult. They are sensible implementations in software of attributes possessed by entities in the real world. That is what makes OO so powerful—the ability to model the real world.

Consider the state of programming without the benefit of OO. In Visual Basic, this limits users to Forms, Standard Modules, Functions, and Subroutines. In the real world, an application (e.g. a database application) consists of forms with textboxes as front ends mapped to fields in a database. The primary tools for building the application logic are the procedures—functions and subs. It is possible to identify something in the real world that is a function or subroutine? Maybe, but it is difficult to do. The best answer we have heard is a *play* in football. The play is reusable, and it is a procedure. It defines precisely how to process a sequence of events. But this is an extremely limited example that does not seem to generalize well to all kinds of business applications. Therefore, we conclude that reusable procedures do not model real-world problems well.

Now consider the same problem using software objects. It is possible to identify anything in the real world that is an object? Everything is an object: cups, pens, this book, computers, etc. Objects model the real world extremely well. They provide the kind of one-to-one mapping that permits identifying and manipulating the key entities of a business problem such as customers and invoices. Classes are also highly reusable entities that should ease development and maintenance of even complex systems.

With all of these advantages, why are many business programmers slow to adopt classes in their development efforts? Some developers have very strong negative reactions to the concept. We have seen COBOL programmers stand up in the middle of lecture and heatedly ask, "This is all wonderful, but can't I just do this with a function?" Our experience is that many developers have been using poor tools for so long, they are nearly incapable of recognizing the magnitude of OO as a tool. This chapter will help bridge the gap.

ENCAPSULATION

Many times when we teach programmers OO principles for the first time, they respond as if OO is a lightning bolt that radically changed software instantaneously. We prefer, however, to think of OO as a natural evolutionary step that grew logically from existing data structures. Imagine the dawn of programming (well, maybe not that far back) when data could only be managed through single variables. Somewhere along the lines, a programmer must have said "These variables are cool, but I'd really like to be able to manage lots of these variables together in a nice package." The response to this request was the variable array.

Variable arrays are great because they make it possible to take similar data and manage it in one place. If there is a series of customer names, it is possible to create an array called Names and index it: Names(1), Names(2), etc. This satisfied the ancient programmer for only a short period before he or she said, "Hey, these arrays are cool, but I have arrays that are related like Names() and Addresses() that I want to manage in a nice package." The response to this request was the user-defined type.

User-defined types are great because they help define several different types of data and keep them together. It is also possible to create an array of user-defined types to manage the many occurrences of data. Our customer array might look like this:

```
Type Customer
    Name As String
    Address As String
End Type


Public MyCustomers As Customer(10)
```

This satisfied the ancient programmer for only a short period before he or she said, "Hey, these user-defined types are cool, but I still have to pass them to the functions I want to call. I want to keep the data and the related functions together in one nice package." The response to this request was the class.

Classes are great for managing data and related functions because they are kept together in one package. This concept of bundling all the related functions and data is known as encapsulation and is a natural outgrowth of the desire to manage related items; it has its roots in the declaration of the very first variable. In Visual Basic, encapsulation appears through the implementation of properties, events, and methods. Each property, event, and method is directly associated with a class whether that class is a Form, an ActiveX Control, or a Class Module.

Check It Out 13-1: Classes Are Everywhere

1. Visual Basic supports classes in many ways—not just Class Modules. In fact, every Form and ActiveX Control is an instance of a class.
2. Start a new Standard EXE project in Visual Basic.
3. Place six TextBoxes on Form1.
4. Open the **Object** box in the Properties window and look at the entries for the six text boxes. Each entry has a name (e.g., Text1, Text2, etc.) and each entry shows the control class (i.e., TextBox). Every control used in VB is an instance of a class defined in the toolbox.

BUILDING A SIMPLE CLASS

When classes are used in Visual Basic, it is important to recognize the difference between two very different skills—object building and object using. Object building is the design and construction of classes; object using is simply exercising the functionality of a class. In this section, we will examine the fundamentals of class construction.

Classes are built around the Visual Basic Class Modules, which can be added to any project by selecting **PROJECT/ADD CLASS MODULE** from the menu. Initially, Class Modules appear remarkably similar to Standard Modules in that they are code windows with no GUI. The difference between Class Modules and Standard Modules lies in the fact that Class Modules can be instantiated at run time whereas Standard Modules cannot. In fact, the only way to use Class Modules is to instantiate them. They cannot be called directly like a function or variable in a Standard Module. Class Modules also do not support Form concepts like loading or unloading.

In Visual Basic the Form, Standard Module, and Class Module make up the three major components from which projects are built. Each one of these components has a special role to play in an application. Much about their respective roles is defined by two characteristics: instantiation and user interface. Forms obviously have a user interface. They can be instantiated at run time. Standard Modules, on the other hand, do not have a GUI nor can they be instantiated at run time. Finally Class Modules do not have a GUI, but they can be instantiated at run time. These fundamental differences allow each component to perform different tasks in a VB application.

CREATING PROPERTIES

In a Class Module, it is possible to create custom properties, which are data members of the class much like the declared members of a user-defined type. Consider the following user-defined type that represents a customer:

```
Type Customer
  FirstName As String
  LastName As String
  Address1 As String
  Address2 As String
  City As String
  State As String
  Zip As String
End Type
```

This user-defined type can easily be converted into a class by taking the definitions for all the variables in the type and placing them in the [General][Declarations] section of a Class Module named Customer. The only difference is that the variables must be scoped with the Public keyword. The result is the following code:

```
Public FirstName As String
Public LastName As String
Public Address1 As String
Public Address2 As String
Public City As String
Public State As String
Public Zip As String
```

Because the variables are declared with the Public keyword, they are available to the entire project. However, since classes must always be instanced before they can be used, the variables are always accessed through full qualification. This means that if an instance of the Customer class is named MyCustomer, we can access the variables using the following code:

```
MyCustomer.FirstName = "John"
MyCustomer.LastName = "Smith"
MyCustomer.Address1 = "432 Washington Ave"
MyCustomer.Address2 = "2nd Floor"
MyCustomer.City = "North Haven"
MyCustomer.State = "CT"
MyCustomer.Zip = "06473"
```

Just as for user-defined types, we can create an array of class instances to hold the many different customers we may need to access. The big difference here is that classes are typically managed in a collection rather than an array. These collections can function exactly like the Forms and Controls collections provided by VB.

CREATING METHODS

If Class Modules function similarly to user-defined types, why use them? Wouldn't it be simpler just to create user-defined types that do not require instancing? If we were just managing data, this argument might have some validity, but classes manage more than data, they also manage the procedures that work with the data. In Visual Basic, we know these functions as methods.

Methods are really just functions and subroutines defined inside a Class Module. The routines are defined using the `Public` keyword as we did for the variables we used to store data. Because of the Public declaration, they also have project scope and require full qualification when addressed. Thus a function called `SendInvoice` is called for an instance of the `Customer` class with the following code:

```
MyCustomer.SendInvoice
```

THE LIFE CYCLE OF A CLASS MODULE

Once created, a Class Module can be accessed by the project. Now is when we put on our "object-using" hat. This skill is fundamentally different from design because Class Modules are used in a manner similar to the way we use any object in Visual Basic. Therefore, more senior developers are typically object builders while junior personnel can be object users. This allows senior people to develop strong functional blocks that can be used by anyone on the team.

Using a class consists of three simple steps: declare a variable, instantiate the object, and call properties or methods. These steps are always the same regardless of how complicated the object designs become. Bear this in mind in learning to use classes—*object using never changes*. The only things to learn that are new pertain largely to object construction. This is another significant advantage because once people learn to use objects, they can use any object.

DECLARING OBJECT VARIABLES

The first step in using any class is to declare an object variable against the class to be used. Visual Basic provides many different ways to declare these variables, and each syntax has implications for the performance and behavior of the application. The simplest syntax is to declare the variable as the name of the class required. For a class named `Employee`, we might use the following code:

```
Public MyEmployee As Employee
```

Declaring a variable as the class to be used allows Visual Basic to examine code closely and verify that the properties and methods addressed in code are actually members of the class declared. Visual Basic can do this only when the variable is specifically declared as the class of interest. This is known as *early binding* and has a positive impact on not only code maintenance, but also performance. Early bound variables allow the Visual Basic compiler to implement optimizations for the particular class because VB knows at compile time what properties and methods are available.

Many times when we review code written by newcomers to OO principles, we find mistakes in variable declaration. For example, many developers declare object variables with the Object data type. So for a `Customer` class, we might find this code:

```
Public MyCustomer As Object
```

This is bad coding. When variables are declared As Object, they may represent any object—not just the intended class. Because VB does not know what object is wanted, it cannot implement any compile-time error checking for property and method calls or implement any optimizations. In fact, VB cannot check the property and method calls until run time when the object is actually instantiated. This is called *late binding*.

In addition to declaring variables As Object, VB also supports many other built-in object types that can be declared. Any variable may be declared as the class name of any control. So declarations As TextBox or As ListBox are perfectly legal. For more generic declarations, declare variables As Control or even As Form to represent any form or control in the project. Visual Basic also supports font and picture objects that can be declared As StdFont or As StdPicture. All these examples are early-bound declarations. Only As Object or As Variant declarations result in late binding.

INSTANTIATING THE OBJECT

The second step in the life of a class is instantiating the object. Instantiation is done in several different ways. Our recommendation is to instantiate all object variables using the New keyword on a separate line. This syntax uses the object variable and class name to create an instance. Thus, the Customer class might be instantiated as follows:

```
Public MyCustomer As Customer
Private Sub Form_Load()
    Set MyCustomer = New Customer
End Sub
```

This technique is known as *manual instantiation* because the object instance must be explicitly created on a separate line. The value of manual instantiation is that if any property or method of an object is called before it is properly instantiated, a trappable runtime error is received, specifically, Error 91, Object Variable or With Block Variable not Set.

Many VB developers do not use manual instantiation. Instead, we often see code in which the New keyword is used on the same line as the variable declaration. At first, this syntax seems compact and beneficial. After all, it saves a line of code required to instantiate the object. This syntax, however, has significant impact on the behavior of the application. When object variables are declared with the New keyword, they are instantiated as soon as any code in the application addresses a property or method of the object. This is known as *automatic instantiation*. Therefore, the following code is sufficient to declare and instantiate an object:

```
Public MyCustomer As New Customer
Private Sub Form_Load()
    MyCustomer.Name="John Smith"
End Sub
```

The problem with automatic instantiation is that it is easy to cause instances to be created when they are not desired. Remember, under manual instantiation, there is a trappable runtime error if there is an attempt to address an object not yet instantiated. Under automatic instantiation, there would be no error, instead, VB would create a new instance. This may not be desirable.

Finally, we also see the function `CreateObject()` used to make object instances. `CreateObject` is similar to the `New` keyword in that it returns a new object instance. The companion function `GetObject()` can be used to retrieve a reference to an object that has already been instantiated by another process.

Regardless of how an object is instantiated, Visual Basic notifies the class through the `Initialize` event. The `Initialize` event always fires when a class instance is created. In the `Initialize` event, it is possible to set the default values for properties of the class or perform other functions necessary to initialize the instance.

CALLING PROPERTIES OR METHODS

Once the object is instantiated, any of the available properties and methods may be called. When use of the object is finished, it should be set equal to `Nothing` to release the memory used by the object. The following code would destroy an instance of the `Customer` class:

```
Set MyCustomer = Nothing
```

When an instance is destroyed using the `Nothing` keyword, the class is notified through the `Terminate` event, which allows the class to clean up before it is destroyed. Use this event to destroy other objects and forms used by the class.

UNDERSTANDING OBJECT VARIABLE SCOPE

Object variables, like all variables declared, are affected by the scoping rules. Public object variables are available to an entire project and Private variables are reserved for the component in which they are defined. Understanding how scoping impacts the functionality of an application is critical to building robust classes.

As we discussed earlier, an object variable can be destroyed by setting it equal to the keyword `Nothing`. Not only can they be destroyed this way, but all declared object variables that have not yet been instantiated are also equal to nothing. Test for the existence of an object instance by using the `Is` operator. For example, the following code tests to see if an object variable has been instantiated:

```
If MyCustomer Is Nothing Then
  MsgBox "No Customer!"
End If
```

The `Is` operator is an extremely powerful feature that you will use often when programming objects. This operator can also be used in conjunction with other keywords that return information about the class of an object. Visual Basic supports two operators for determining an object's class: `TypeOf` and `TypeName`. `TypeOf` returns a Boolean based on a test class; `TypeName` returns a string.

```
If TypeOf MyCustomer Is Customer Then
  MsgBox TypeName(MyCustomer)
End If
```

The object operators are useful, but beg some questions regarding the exact nature of an object variable. Although we use variables such as `MyCustomer` here to reference an instance of the `Customer` class, the object variable itself does not contain the actual class information. Instead, it contains only a *reference* to the class—a long integer pointer to an address in memory.

Consider what happens when an instance of an object is created using the `New` keyword. When the line of code is executed, Visual Basic reads the class information from the Class Module constructed at design time and looks for a place in memory large enough to hold an instance. When it finds a suitable place in memory, an instance is created and the address of the instance is stored in the object variable. This reference then gives access to all the features of the class.

This is not, however, the end of the story. Whenever an instance is created from Visual Basic, the object itself keeps track of how many variables in the program are referencing the instance. This is known as *reference counting*. If we create an instance and then reference it twice, the reference count for the object would go up to two.

```
Public MyReference1 As Customer
Public MyReference2 As Customer

Private Sub Form_Load()
    'Instance Created and First Reference set
    Set MyReference1 = New Customer
    'Set a second reference
    Set MyReference2 = MyReference1
End Sub
```

Setting multiple references in a project is quite common as objects access one another, but the real impact of this code occurs when the objects are destroyed. The reason for concern is that the `Terminate` event of any Class Module only fires after all of the reference variables in code are set to `Nothing`. This means that setting one of the preceding references to `Nothing` is not enough to fire the `Terminate` event.

```
Private Sub Form_Unload()
    'The Terminate Event will not yet fire
    Set MyReference1 = Nothing
    'Now the Terminate Event will Fire!
    Set MyReference2 = Nothing
End Sub
```

The impact of reference counting is that the memory used by an object instance is not released until all the object variables are set to `Nothing`. Fortunately, Visual Basic helps out considerably in the management of instance memory through scoping rules. When an object variable loses scope, this has the same effect as setting the variable to `Nothing`. By definition, when a

Visual Basic application terminates, all variables lose scope. Therefore, exiting a VB application will always destroy all objects created by the application even if the instances were never set to Nothing. This feature, known as *garbage collection*, is one of the best features of Visual Basic and completely relieves the VB programmer from the burden of strict memory management.

Like so many features of Visual Basic, classes can be used at many different levels. In the previous chapter, we examined the fundamentals of classes, including properties and methods. Classes have many more features, however, that make them more robust and functional. In this chapter, we will cover the advanced features of classes and how to implement them.

USING PROPERTY PROCEDURES

We have already learned that classes are similar to user-defined types with the addition of functions known as methods. We also know that in the simplest construction of a class, Public variables can be used to represent properties of the class. Although Public variables can be used, they present some difficulties when constructing more complex classes.

PERFORMING DATA VALIDATION

Suppose you need to create an Employee class for tracking information about employees in a database. This class might have several properties such as Name, Age, Height, Weight, and Hair-Color. If you wanted, you could simply implement these in a Class Module as Public variables.

```
Public Name As String
Public Age As Integer
Public Height As Integer
Public Weight As Integer
Public HairColor As String
```

When using the object, all that is necessary is to declare a variable, instantiate the object, and set the properties. As long as things go right, there will be no problem. But suppose that a user of the application accidentally enters the data for the Name property into the field reserved for the HairColor property. The results can be problematic. In fact, the HairColor property is declared As String, so it can take any legal string value—not just valid colors for hair. The problem, then, with Public variables as properties is that we cannot adequately validate the entered data.

In order to properly validate property values, we need to introduce a new type of procedure known as a Property procedure. Property procedures are special procedures in Visual Basic designed to read and write property values to a class. Adding property procedures to a class is done from the TOOLS/ADD PROCEDURE dialog.

When Property procedures are added to a class, name the procedure with the name of the property to be created. When the Add Procedure dialog is closed, Visual Basic actually generates two different procedures. This procedure pair contains one procedure for reading the variable called Property Get and one procedure for writing the variable called Property Let. The following code shows the HairColor property declared with Property procedures:

```
Public Property Get HairColor() As Variant
End Property
Public Property Let HairColor(ByVal vNewValue As Variant)
End Property
```

Notice that Visual Basic declares both procedures as Public, which means they are accessible from outside the class. This is exactly the behavior we want, since the procedures will allow reading and writing to a class property. Since these procedures provide all the public access required, we can change the scope of the Public variable we declared earlier to Private. We might also want to give it an appropriate prefix to indicate that it is now a private variable. Private variables are often called *members* of a class, so we typically use an m_ prefix.

```
Private m_HairColor As String
```

The `Property Get` routine can be thought of as a function—it returns a value. In Visual Basic, the `Property Get` defaults to returning a type Variant, but we want to return the proper type for `HairColor`, which is `String`. Similarly, the `Property Let` behaves like a subroutine that takes an argument. Visual Basic also defaults the argument to Variant, but we will change that as well. The final code should appear as follows properly to declare the `HairColor` property with Property procedures:

```
Public Property Get HairColor() As String
End Property
Public Property Let HairColor(ByVal vNewValue As String)
End Property
```

When `Property Get` is called, we intend to return the property value. This is done by setting the function equal to the value of the `HairColor` variable in our code. In this way, `Property Get` returns a value just as a function does. When `Property Let` is called, we want to store the entered data in the Private data member. Thus, the final code for a basic property declaration would appear as follows:

```
Public Property Get HairColor() As String
    HairColor = m_HairColor
End Property
Public Property Let HairColor(ByVal vNewValue As String)
    m_HairColor=vNewValue
End Property
```

The interesting thing about Property procedures is that the calling client does not need to know that Property procedures have been used in the class. The client's calling syntax remains the same. Simply declare a variable, instantiate the object, and call the properties. The following code would create an object and set `HairColor` using the Property procedures.

```
Dim MyEmployee As Employee
Set MyEmployee = New Employee
```

```
MyEmployee.HairColor = "Brown"
```

Although we have made the class code more complex, we really have not changed the fundamental problem. Nothing in our efforts with Property procedures will prevent a wayward client from trying to send the Name data to the `HairColor` property. However, now we can place validation code in the `Property Let` procedure to deal with the problem.

```
Public Property Let HairColor(ByVal vNewValue As String)
    If vNewValue = "Black" Or vNewValue = "Brown" Then
    m_HairColor = vNewValue
    End If
End Property
```

This strategy allows us to perform validation on the submitted data and save it to the private data member only when it is valid. This technique is known as *data hiding*. Any feature of VB can be used to validate this data. It can be simple as shown here or more complex, such as reading a database table. The point is that there is all of the power and flexibility of VB to perform data validation.

INCORPORATING BUSINESS RULES

Data validation is not the only reason to use Property procedures. Property procedures also support the implementation of business rules. These rules can trigger actions based on the changes to properties. For example, suppose we had created an `Order` class for a computer repair shop to track work orders. This class might have a property called `Model` that tracks the type of computer we are repairing. In our business, if the model is an x386 or earlier, we charge a 15% premium for the work. Creating the property could be done with the following code.

```
Private Enum enmModel
    x286
    x386
    x486
    Pentium
End Enum
Private m_Model As enmModel
Public Property Get Model() As enmModel
    Model = m_Model
End Property
Public Property Let Model(ByVal NewModel As enmModel)
    m_Model = NewModel
    If m_Model < x486 Then Price = Price * 0.15
End Property
```

The business rule changes the `Price` property if `Model` is less than x486. This is typical of a business rule. All businesses have these rules, and they generally take the form of If...Then statements. These statements are easily created in a Property procedure.

CONTROLLING READING AND WRITING

Property procedures provide one last feature to classes—the ability to create read-only and write-only properties. By default, Visual Basic always creates Property procedures as Public. However, nothing stops us from changing the scope to Private for either `Property Let` or `Property Get`. Changing the scope of `Property Let` from Public to Private creates a read-only property. Changing `Property Get` creates a write-only property. In either case, if a client attempts to read or write data in an inappropriate manner, Visual Basic will raise a trappable runtime error in the client. This means the classes work exactly the same as other controls and classes in VB.

SETTING PROCEDURE ATTRIBUTES

Properties and methods of objects inside Visual Basic often have special behavior. Perhaps the best-known example of this is the Default property, a property of a class that receives an argument when no property is explicitly called. The Text property of a TextBox or the Caption property of a Label are common examples. These properties can be accessed without explicit code because they are designated as the default.

```
Text1 ="Hello"
Label1 = "World!"
```

Designating special behavior for properties and methods of classes is supported in Visual Basic through the Procedure Attributes dialog. The Procedure Attributes dialog provides a way to tag a procedure—either a property or a method—as the default member of a class. In the dialog, simply select the procedure to designate as the default. Click on the **Advanced** button for the selected procedure and set the ProcedureID dropdown to (default). Now access this member implicitly through code.

GENERATING EVENTS

So far, we have spent time discussing properties and methods, but very little has been said about creating custom events. Visual Basic supports a simple and powerful set of keywords for creating and using custom events in classes. These keywords make it possible to build events into classes and receive notification through event-handling subroutines in clients.

Custom events begin inside a Class Module. In the [General][Declarations] section of a Class Module, define events for the class to generate. Defining the classes is done with the `Event` keyword. To create an event inside the Employee class that fires whenever a property is set to an invalid value, use the following code:

```
Event PropertyError()
```

Once defined, this event can be fired inside any client using the Employee class. Firing the event is done with the `RaiseEvent` keyword, which is used in code wherever the event should fire. Imagine that we wanted to improve the data validation for the `HairColor` property to include raising an event when `HairColor` is incorrectly set. The following code uses the `RaiseEvent` keyword to notify clients when entered data is not valid:

```
Public Property Let HairColor(ByVal vNewValue As String)
    If vNewValue = "Black" Or vNewValue = "Brown" Then
        m_HairColor = vNewValue
    Else
        RaiseEvent PropertyError
    End If
End Property
```

On the client side, we would like to see an event-handling subroutine appear in the code window so that we can code action when the error occurs. Normally, we expect to see event procedures in the Procedure box associated with an object selected from the Object box. However, this does not happen automatically for classes. To get Class Module custom events to show in a client's code window, it is necessary to declare the object variable `WithEvents`. `WithEvents` is a special keyword that causes all of the events in a class to be made available to a client. The following code is sufficient to access all of the `Employee` class events.

```
Private WithEvents MyEmployee As Employee
```

Once declared `WithEvents`, the variable `MyEmployee` appears in the Object box of the code window. All the events associated with the object appear in the Procedure box. It is then possible to code these events just as for any other event handler.

COMPONENT OBJECT MODEL

During our discussion of Class Modules, we examined how to use classes inside projects. The classes we have constructed so far have been for the private use of a single project. This use of classes, however, is extremely limited and does not take advantage of all that classes have to offer. Not only can classes be used within an application, but also across applications.

Although the idea of creating software out of classes may be new to many VB programmers, it is certainly not new to software in general. Most modern software is constructed through classes. In fact, most of the familiar programs are based on classes, including not only Visual Basic itself, but also Word, Excel, PowerPoint, and Microsoft Access. All these programs—and most other Windows applications—are constructed through classes.

The reason that classes inside other applications are valuable is that VB actually has the ability to use the classes located in these other applications as if they were part of the Visual Basic language. A spell checker can be borrowed from Excel. The true power of classes comes from using them across applications.

The reason that we can use objects across applications is that all these objects support a common set of interfaces that allow them to communicate. Just like the interfaces created in VB, interfaces to other classes support polymorphism through standard interfaces that allow objects to communicate in Windows, called the Component Object Model (COM). Nearly all the classes in all the applications that run under Windows support COM. It allows the Visual Basic application to instantiate and call any class from any application.

In order to use classes from a COM-enabled application, Visual Basic must be told about the application and its classes. In the VB environment, any COM-enabled application may be used by setting a reference to the program. References are used to allow Visual Basic to examine all the classes, properties, events, and methods that a COM-enabled application has to offer. All the COM-enabled applications can be seen and references to them set using the References dialog, which is accessed by selecting **PROJECT/REFERENCES…** from the menu.

Once an application in the References dialog has been selected, all the objects contained inside the application are usable. Variables can be declared against the objects. The objects can be instantiated. Properties and methods can be called and events received. All the functionality of the object becomes available as if it were built into Visual Basic.

The problem, of course, is that the References dialog does not show the objects inside an application, it merely lists all the applications that are COM enabled. A developer learns about the objects that are actually inside the application by using another utility called the Object Browser, which shows all the classes, properties, events, and methods for any given COM-enabled application. Access the Object Browser by selecting **VIEW/OBJECT BROWSER** from the menu.

Check It Out 13-2: Using the Object Browser

1. Start a new Visual Basic Standard EXE project.
2. Open the References dialog by selecting **PROJECT/REFERENCES** from the menu.
3. In the References dialog, set a reference to the **Microsoft Visual Basic 6.0 Extensibility model** to be able to see many of the COM-enabled objects inside VB itself. Close the References dialog.
4. Open the Object Browser by selecting **VIEW/OBJECT BROWSER** from the menu.
5. At the top of the Object Browser, will be an entry marked <All Libraries>. Drop this box and select **VBIDE** to examine the objects inside VB.
6. In the Classes list, locate the class **VBE**. This class represents the entire Visual Basic product. Select this object and note the entries in the Members of VBE list. These members represent all properties, methods, and events in the VBE object.
7. Locate the Name property of VBE. Notice the small blue globe that appears next to the property. This globe indicates that the Name property is the default member for class VBE.

The Object Browser is a good utility for examining objects, but does not provide all the information necessary to understand the relationships between objects in an application. The objects in the browser are typically listed in alphabetical order, the least helpful presentation. Far better than an alphabetical representation is a hierarchical, graphical representation. This style of presentation is called the object model of an application.

This presentation style is much more meaningful to a developer who can easily see the logical relationship of classes. Notice that the Document class falls under the Application class in the model. This indicates that Application objects contain Document objects. This makes perfect sense since in Word, the application contains documents. Typically, this level of documentation is in the Help file for the target product.

Check It Out 13-3: Using the Word Object Model

Word 8.0 must be installed for this exercise.

1. Start a new Standard EXE project in Visual Basic.
2. Open the References dialog by selecting **PROJECT/REFERENCES** from the menu.
3. In the References dialog, set a reference to **Microsoft Word 8.0 Object Library**.
4. Declare variables for the Application and Document classes by placing the following code in the [General][Declarations] section of Form1:

```
Private objApplication As Word.Application
Private objDocument As Word.Document
```

5. Place a CommandButton and a TextBox on Form1. Use these controls to print the contents of the TextBox through Word when the CommandButton is pressed.
6. Create the new Word document by placing the following code in the Load event of Form1:

```
'Create the New Document
Set objApplication = New Word.Application
Set objDocument = objApplication.Documents.Add
```

7. Print the contents of the TextBox by placing the following code in the Click event of Command1

```
'Print the contents of the TextBox
objDocument.Content.Text = Text1.Text
objDocument.PrintOut
```

8. Run the project.

CREATING ACTIVEX COMPONENTS

We have seen that classes can be created as private entities inside an application. In Visual Basic, however, it is also possible to create classes that can be used by other applications. These projects allow construction of classes with their own object models; and these classes can be deployed to other developers.

In Visual Basic, classes that can be used by other applications are constructed using the ActiveX DLL or ActiveX EXE project type. The ActiveX DLL and ActiveX EXE types differ in performance and behavior. ActiveX DLLs are also called in-process servers because they run in the same memory space as the calling client. ActiveX EXEs are out-of-process servers and run in a separate memory space from the client. This is important, because running in the same memory space as a client is much more efficient. In fact, ActiveX DLLs can run over twenty times faster than ActiveX EXEs. The single biggest performance impact in Visual Basic development is the selection of ActiveX DLL versus ActiveX EXE.

With the tremendous advantages of ActiveX DLLs, why is an ActiveX EXE even an option? The answer is that only ActiveX EXEs can run on machines separate from the calling client. By definition an in-process server must be on the same machine as the client. These issues are discussed in detail in Chapter 16.

Creating and using ActiveX components is a matter of building classes into a separate project and setting a reference to the project inside a Standard EXE project. This works the same for ActiveX components as it does for any other COM-enabled application like Excel. To other developers, these objects work exactly the same way as any others.

Exercise 13-1: Class Module Fundamentals

The class module makes it possible to create custom objects in VB. These objects may then be reused in every project built. In this exercise, we will examine the fundamental concepts associated with object construction and usage.

BUILDING A CLASS

Step 1

Using the File Explorer, create a new directory **VB BOOTCAMP\EXERCISE13-1**. Start a new Visual Basic Standard EXE project. Insert a Class Module into the project by selecting **PROJECT/ADD CLASS MODULE** from the menu. Change the name of the class module from the default Class1 to **Employee**. Use this object to track employees in a mythical company.

Step 2

Every class that is created will have properties and methods. Properties describe the object being created; methods allow manipulation of the object. For the `Employee` class, we will define several properties to describe the employee. These properties can be added by creating Public variables in the [General][Declarations] section of the class module. Add the following code to the [General][Declarations] section to describe the employee:

```
Public Name As String
Public Salary As Currency
Public Title As String
```

Step 3

Once the properties are defined, we will need a way to interact with the employees created. Interacting is done through methods of the class. Methods are defined by creating Public subroutines or functions in the class. Add a new subroutine to the class by selecting **TOOLS/ADD PROCEDURE** from the menu. In the Insert Procedure dialog select the following options:

Name	Promote
Type	Sub
Scope	Public

Step 4

In the Promote subroutine, we will pass an argument that specifies the new position for the employee. At our mythical company, we use numeric codes to identify the position and salary of an employee. Therefore, we need to add an argument to the `Promote` method to indicate the new position for the employee. Add the argument to the routine so that the subroutine definition looks like this:

```
Public Sub Promote(intPosition As Integer)
End Sub
```

Step 5

Once the argument is defined, we have to take action to establish the new position for the employee. We will change the salary and title of the employee based on the new position code. Add the following code to the `Promote` method:

```
Select Case intPosition
  Case 1
    Title = "Programmer"
    Salary = 35000
  Case 2
    Title = "Team Leader"
    Salary = 40000
  Case 3
    Title = "Manager"
    Salary = 60000
  Case 4
    Title = "Department Head"
    Salary = 100000
  Case 5
    Title = "CIO"
    Salary = 300000
End Select
```

Step 6

Whenever an instance of a class is created in Visual Basic, the class receives the `Initialize` event, which makes it possible to initialize the values of any property in the class. In this way, default values can be established for the class. Simply set the variables in the Initialize event, which is found by selecting **Class** from the Object box and **Initialize** from the Procedure box. Add the following code to the `Initialize` event to set default values for the class:

```
Title = "Programmer"
Salary = 35000
```

USING THE CLASS MODULE IN A PROJECT

Step 7

Now that the class is built, we will create a GUI to utilize the class. The GUI will be built on Form1 and will consist of one list box, three labels, and two buttons. Figure 13-1 shows the completed form. Use the Item list below to set the design-time properties for the controls.

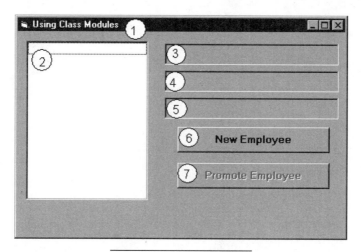

Figure 13-1 Form interface.

Item 1—Form

Caption   Classes

Item 2—ListBox

Name   lstEmployees

Item 3—Label

BorderStyle 1'Fixed Single

Name   lblName

Item 4—Label

BorderStyle 1'Fixed Single

Name   lblTitle

Item 5—Label

BorderStyle 1'Fixed Single

Name   lblSalary

Item 6—CommandButton

Caption	New Employee
Name	cmdNew

Item 7—CommandButton

Caption	Promote Employee
Name	cmdPromote

Step 8

When working with objects, we must keep track of many instances. Visual Basic provides a special built-in `Collection` object to use to store objects. Add the following code to the [General][Declarations] section of Form1 to define the collection and a variable to represent any single instance:

```
Private m_Employee As Employee
Private Employees As Collection
```

Step 9

When the application is first loaded, no employee objects are created. The application will start with a blank list. Add the following code to the `Form_Load` event of Form1:

```
'Clear the List box
lstEmployees.Clear

'Clear the Labels
lblName.Caption = ""
lblTitle.Caption = ""
lblSalary.Caption = ""

cmdPromote.Enabled = False
Set Employees = New Collection
```

Step 10

After initializing the controls, the user can create a new employee. Creating the employee will generate an instance of the `Employee` class, add the new employee to the collection, and place the employee in the list box. Add the following code to the Click event of `cmdNew` to generate a new employee:

```
Dim m_Employee As Employee
'Instantiate the Employee
Set m_Employee = New Employee

'Get a Name for the employee
m_Employee.Name = InputBox("Enter a Name")
```

```
'Place the Employee in the List
lstEmployees.AddItem m_Employee.Name

'Add Employee to the Collection
employees.Add m_Employee
```

Step 11

When an employee is selected from the List box, the information for that employee is displayed in the label controls. We also want to be able to promote the currently selected employee. Add the following code to the Click event of lstEmployees to display the employee information and enable the promote button:

```
'Display Info
lblName.Caption = Employees.Item(lstEmployees.ListIndex + 1).Name
lblTitle.Caption = Employees.Item(lstEmployees.ListIndex + 1).Title
lblSalary.Caption = Format$(Employees.Item(lstEmployees.ListIndex _
+ 1).Salary, "Currency")

'Enabled Promote Button
cmdPromote.Enabled = True
```

Step 12

Promoting an employee is a simple matter of calling the Promote method. In the Click event of cmdPromote, add the following code to call the Promote method:

```
Dim m_Employee As Employee
Dim intPosition As Integer
'Get new position code
intPosition = Val(InputBox("Enter New Position Code"))

'Promote employee
Set m_Employee = Employees.Item(lstEmployees.ListIndex + 1)
m_Employee.Promote intPosition

'Refresh Display
lblName.Caption = Employees.Item(lstEmployees.ListIndex + 1).Name
lblTitle.Caption = Employees.Item(lstEmployees.ListIndex + 1).Title
lblSalary.Caption = Format$(Employees.Item(lstEmployees.ListIndex _
    + 1).Salary, "Currency")
```

Step 13

Save and run the application.

Exercise 13-2: ActiveX Components

Class Modules are extremely powerful components in VB. They support reusable features like DLL and EXE creation. This exercise examines some of these advanced features.

BUILDING AN ACTIVEX DLL

Step 1

Using the File Explorer, create a new directory **VB BOOTCAMP\EXERCISE13-2**. Start a new Visual Basic ActiveX DLL project. Change the Name of the Class Module from the default Class1 to **Employee**. We will use this object to track employees in a mythical company.

Step 2

Every class created will have properties and methods. Properties describe the object being created; methods allow manipulation of the object. For the Employee class, we will define several properties to describe the employee. These properties are added by creating Property procedures in the class. Add the following code to the [General][Declarations] section to declare the Private data members that will be used by the Property procedures:

```
Private m_Name As String
Private m_Salary As Currency
Private m_Title As String
```

Step 3

Each of the Private variables has to be wrapped in a Public property procedure. Using the **TOOLS/ADD PROCEDURE** dialog, create the following code to access the Private data members. Be careful to note the type declarations of the procedures.

```
Public Property Get Name() As String
  Name = m_Name
End Property
Public Property Let Name(ByVal strName As String)
  m_Name = strName
End Property
Public Property Get Salary() As Currency
  Salary = m_Salary
End Property
Public Property Let Salary(ByVal curSalary As Currency)
  m_Salary = curSalary
End Property
Public Property Get Title() As String
  Title = m_Title
End Property
Public Property Let Title(ByVal strTitle As String)
  m_Title = strTitle
End Property
```

Step 4

Many objects have default members. For the `Employee` class, we will make the Name property the default through the Procedure Attributes dialog. From the menu select **TOOLS/PROCEDURE ATTRIBUTES**. In the dialog, select **Name** and push the **Advanced** button. In the ProcedureID box, select **(Default)**. Close the dialog by pushing **OK**.

Step 5

This class will have an event called `BadCode` that will notify calling clients when they enter a bad promotion code and is declared in the [General][Declarations] section of the `Employee` class. Add the following code to declare the event:

```
Event BadCode()
```

Step 6

Once the properties are defined, we will need a way to interact with the employees created. Interacting is done through methods of the class. Methods are defined by creating Public subroutines or functions in the class. Add a new subroutine to the class by selecting **TOOLS/ADD PROCEDURE** from the menu. In the Insert Procedure dialog select the following options:

Name	Promote
Type	Sub
Scope	Public

Step 7

In the `Promote` subroutine, we will pass an argument that specifies the new position for the employee. At our mythical company, we use numeric codes to identify the position and salary of an employee. Therefore, we need to add an argument to the `Promote` method to indicate the new position for the employee. Add the argument to the routine so that the subroutine definition looks like this:

```
Public Sub Promote(ByVal intPosition As Integer)
End Sub
```

Step 8

Once the argument is defined, we must take action to establish the new position for the employee. We will change the salary and title of the employee based on the new position code. If any promotion code is illegal, the `BadCode` event is fired. Add the following code to the `Promote` method:

```
Select Case intPosition
  Case 1
  Title = "Programmer"
  Salary = 35000
  Case 2
  Title = "Team Leader"
```

```
    Salary = 40000
    Case 3
    Title = "Manager"
    Salary = 60000
    Case 4
    Title = "Department Head"
    Salary = 100000
    Case 5
    Title = "CIO"
    Salary = 300000
    Case Else
    RaiseEvent BadCode
End Select
```

Step 9

Whenever an instance of a class is created in Visual Basic, the class receives the `Initialize` event, which makes it possible to initialize the values of any property in the class. In this way, we can establish default values for the class. Simply set the variables in the `Initialize` event, which is found by selecting **Class** from the Object box and Initialize from the Procedure box. Add the following code to the `Initialize` event to set default values for the class.

```
Title = "Programmer"
Salary = 35000
```

CALLING THE DLL FROM A CLIENT

Step 10

Now that the ActiveX DLL is built, we will create a GUI to utilize the class. The GUI will be built in a Standard EXE. Add a Standard EXE to the application by selecting **FILE/ADD PROJECT** from the menu.

We want the application to start from the `Load` event of Form1. Set the Standard EXE as the startup project. Right-click on **Project2** from the Project window and select **Set As Start-up** from the menu. Next, select **PROJECT/PROPERTIES** from the menu and set Startup Object to Form1.

We also need to reference the `Employee` class in Project1 from Project2. With Project2 active, set the reference by selecting **PROJECT/REFERENCES...** from the menu. In the References dialog, set a reference to Project1.

Step 11

The GUI for Form1 will consist of one list box, three labels, and two buttons. Place these controls on the form. Figure 13-2 shows the completed form. Use the Item list below to set the design-time properties for each control.

Item 1—Form

Caption   ActiveX Components

Item 2—ListBox

Name   lstEmployees

Item 3—Label

BorderStyle   1'Fixed Single

Name   lblName

Item 4—Label

BorderStyle   1'Fixed Single

Name   lblTitle

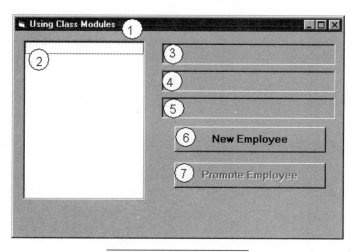

Figure 13-2 Form interface.

Item 5—Label

BorderStyle   1'Fixed Single

Name   lblSalary

Item 6—CommandButton

Caption   New Employee

Name   cmdNew

Item 7—CommandButton

Caption   Promote Employee

Name   cmdPromote

Step 12

The `Employee` class supports an event called `BadCode` that notifies calling clients when they have entered a bad promotion code. We want to receive this event, so we declare the `Employee` object `WithEvents`. Add the following code to the [General][Declarations] section of Form1:

```
Private WithEvents m_Employee As Employee
```

Step 13

When we work with objects, we must keep track of many instances. Visual Basic provides a special built-in `Collection` object to use to store objects. Add the following code to the [General][Declarations] section of Form1 to define the collection:

```
Private Employees As Collection
```

Step 14

When the application is first loaded, no `Employee` objects are created. The application will start with a blank list. Add the following code to the `Form_Load` event of Form1:

```
'Clear the List box
lstEmployees.Clear

'Clear the Labels
lblName.Caption = ""
lblTitle.Caption = ""
lblSalary.Caption = ""

'Disable the Promote button
cmdPromote.Enabled=False
'Create instance of the Collection
Set Employees = New Collection
```

Step 15

After initializing the controls, the user can create a new employee. Creating the employee will generate an instance of the `Employee` class, add the new employee to the collection, and place the employee in the list box. Add the following code to the Click event of `cmdNew` to generate a new employee:

```
'Instantiate the Employee
Set m_Employee = New Employee

'Get a Name for the employee
m_Employee.Name = InputBox("Enter a Name")

'Place the Employee in List
```

```
lstEmployees.AddItem m_Employee.Name

'Add Emkployee to Collection
Employees.Add m_Employee
```

Step 16

When an employee is selected from the list box, the information for that employee is displayed in the label controls. We also want to be able to promote the currently selected employee. Add the following code to the Click event of lstEmployees to display the employee information and enable the promote button:

```
'Display Info
lblName.Caption = Employees(lstEmployees.ListIndex + 1)
lblTitle.Caption = Employees(lstEmployees.ListIndex + 1).Title
lblSalary.Caption = Format$(Employees(lstEmployees.ListIndex _
    + 1).Salary, "Currency")

'Enabled Promote Button
cmdPromote.Enabled = True
```

Step 17

Promoting an employee is a simple matter of calling the Promote method. In the Click event of cmdPromote, add the following code to call the Promote method:

```
Dim intPosition As Integer

'Get new position code
intPosition = Val(InputBox("Enter New Position Code"))

'Promote employee
Set m_Employee = Employees(lstEmployees.ListIndex + 1)
m_Employee.Promote intPosition

'Refresh Display
lblName.Caption = Employees(lstEmployees.ListIndex + 1)
lblTitle.Caption = Employees(lstEmployees.ListIndex + 1).Title
lblSalary.Caption = Format$(Employees(lstEmployees.ListIndex _
    + 1).Salary, "Currency")
```

Step 18

If the entered promotion code is bad, we expect a call to BadCode. We will place a simple message box in this event to notify us of the problem. Add the following code under the m_Employee_BadCode event.

```
MsgBox "Bad Promotion Code entered!"
```

Step 19

Save and run the application.

FOR THE CERTIFIED PRO

This specification describes a database application against the Biblio database using ADO and Visual Basic class modules. Create this application to meet the following specifications:

1. Create an ActiveX DLL that contains classes named **Publisher** and **Title**. Each class should be created to represent the associated table contained in BIBLIO.MDB. Provide properties for each class that map to the fields in the table.

2. Create a third class in the ActiveX DLL named **Engine**. This class will be used to create and manage collections of Publishers and Titles.

   The Engine class should contain two private collection variables named Publishers and Titles.

   a. Create a method of the Engine class called `CreatePublishers` that when called fills the Publishers collection with all the Publisher entries from BIBLIO.MDB. This method creates an instance of the Publisher class for each row in the table and adds it to the collection.

   b. Create a method of the Engine class called `CreateTitles` that takes a `Long Integer` as an argument. The `Long Integer` argument will be a Publisher ID. This method will populate the Titles collection with all the Titles associated with the PublisherID.

   c. When either `CreatePublishers` or `CreateTitles` is called, use ActiveX Data Objects (ADO) to establish a connection to BIBLIO.MDB, read the appropriate data, and close the connection. Use a resulting `Recordset` to build the collections. These methods should return a collection object to the calling client.

3. Create a Front End to use the ActiveX DLL.

   a. The Front End should be a separate Standard EXE with a reference set to the above ActiveX DLL.

   b. The Front End should start up and present all the Publishers in a list. Fill this list by using the collection object returned from the `CreatePublishers` method.

   c. When the user selects a Publisher from the list, populate a Microsoft Flex Grid control with all of the associated Titles using the collection returned from the `CreateTitles` method.

4. When the application is complete, build and test setup disks.

PREPARING FOR CERTIFICATION

Topics for Further Reading
   Creating Your Own Classes
   Programming with Objects

CERTIFICATION QUIZ

1. Class Modules support which of the following events?
    a. Load
    b. Unload
    c. Initialize
    d. Terminate

2. Name the components that can be instantiated.
    a. Standard Module
    b. Class Module
    c. StdFont
    d. Form

3. Which of the following could be a method of a class?
    a. `Public Sub Walk()`
    b. `Private Sub Form_Load`
    c. `Private Sub Talk()`
    d. `Public Function Talk() As String`

4. Which Declarations are early bound?
    a. `Public MyObject As StdPicture`
    b. `Public MyObject As Control`
    c. `Public MyObject`
    d. `Private MyObject As New Customer`

5. In the following code, on what line does the Initialize event fire?
    a. `Public MyCustomer As New Customer`
    b. `Private Sub Form_Load()`
    c. `MyCustomer.Name = "John"`
    d. `End Sub`

6. In the following code, on what line does the Initialize event fire?
    a. `Public MyCustomer As Customer`
    b. `Private Sub Form_Load()`
    c. `Set MyCustomer = New Customer`
    d. `End Sub`

7. Given the following code, how many instances are created?
    ```
    Public MyForm1 As Form
    Public MyForm2 As Form
    Set MyForm1 = New Form1
    Set MyForm2 = New Form1
    ```
    a. 0
    b. 1
    c. 2
    d. 3

8. Given the following code, how many instances are created?

```
Public MyForm1 As Form
Public MyForm2 As Form
Set MyForm1 = New Form1
Set MyForm2 = MyForm1
```

a. 0
b. 1
c. 2
d. 3

9. Given the following code, how many instances are created?

```
Public MyForm1 As Class1
Public MyForm2 As Class1
Set MyForm1 = CreateObject("Project1.Class1")
Set MyForm2 = GetObject("Project1.Class1")
```

a. 0
b. 1
c. 2
d. 3

10. Given the following code, how many instances are created?

```
Public MyForm As Class1
Public MyCollection As New Collection
Set MyForm1 = New Class1
MyCollection.Add MyForm
```

a. 0
b. 1
c. 2
d. 3

11. Which of the following are advantages of Property procedures?
a. Allows data validation
b. Allows events to be raised
c. Allows business rule creation
d. Allows read-only property creation

12. Class events can be declared:
a. in a Procedure
b. at the project level
c. in [General][Declarations]
d. in the Object Browser

13. What keyword causes a custom class event to fire?
  a. `GenerateEvent`
  b. `RaiseEvent`
  c. `FireEvent`
  d. `LoadEvent`

ANSWERS TO CERTIFICATION QUIZ

1. a, c, d
2. c
3. b
4. d
5. c
6. a
7. a, b, c, d
8. a, b, c
9. a, b, c, d
10. d
11. c, d
12. b, c, d
13. a, d

ADVANCED COMPONENT DESIGN

Those who begin this chapter, must have a complete and thorough understanding of all class module principles previously presented. This is an advanced chapter that describes how to construct reusable ActiveX components and requires an understanding of OOP and COM.

SKILLS COVERED

- 70-176 (1): Assess the potential impact of the logical design on performance, maintainability, extensibility, and availability
- 70-176 (20): Compile a project with class modules into a COM component
- 70-176 (20.a): Implement an object model within a COM component
- 70-176 (20.b): Set properties to control the instancing of a class within a COM component

- 70-175 (1): Given a conceptual design, apply the principles of modular design to derive the components and services of the logical design
- 70-175 (19): Implement error handling for the user interface in distributed applications
- 70-175 (19.c): Determine how to send error information from a COM component to a client computer
- 70-175 (30): Compile a project with class modules into a COM component
- 70-175 (30.a): Implement an object model within a COM component
- 70-176 (30.b): Set properties to control the instancing of a class within a COM component

Visual Basic is a powerful professional programming tool masquerading in a drag-and-drop environment. Up to this point, we have examined many features of VB that can be used for rapid creation of applications. In this chapter, we take on the true professional features. This chapter is not for beginners or even most intermediate programmers, but for the advanced developer with significant experience.

POLYMORPHISM

Paramount in any discussion of classes is the concept of communication between the classes. Classes can often be thought of as *black boxes* of functionality. No one is quite sure what is inside, but we know how to make them work. This is exactly analogous to objects in the real world. Consider a television set. How many people are qualified to explain in detail how the internals of a television work? And yet, even though we do not know how they work, we can still use them. This is because we understand the controls that are on the front of the set. We understand the effect of adjusting the volume or changing the channels. In object-oriented terms we say that we understand the *interface* of the television.

Interfaces are a critical concept in dealing with software objects just as they are in dealing with television sets. If we understand the interface of an object, then we understand how to make it work even if we do not understand how it works. On televisions, functions are performed through knobs and switches. In software objects, functions are performed through properties and methods. If we had a software class called `Television`, it might have a method called `On`.

Interestingly, objects often have methods with the same names. This is not surprising and also reflects real-world objects. How many appliances are there with On/Off switches? And yet each switch does something different. Turn the television on and get a picture and sound. Turn a light on and get light. It is not necessary to learn a new skill to turn on an appliance. Even if an object that was never before seen were to appear; a power switch on the device would send a familiar message. Furthermore the label on the switch implies a guarantee to the user that the expected function is built into the object.

The concept of software objects that have the same methods but perform different functions is called *polymorphism*. This word is routinely misdefined but simply states that objects can have identical interfaces, but perform different functions. Why should a developer care? The primary reason is that polymorphic behavior allows one object to manipulate the interface of another without exactly knowing the nature of the function to perform. Just as we know how to operate switches on devices we have not seen before, polymorphism allows manipulation of software objects that have not been seen before.

Polymorphism is primarily implemented through inheritance in languages like Java and C++. Inheritance is the ability to define a new class based on an old class. This allows us to define an Employee class from a Human class. Unfortunately, Visual Basic does not support inheritance. Instead, VB implements polymorphism through interfaces. Interfaces are nothing more than the set of all properties and methods of a class. Using this definition, every class has at least one interface because every class has at least one set of properties and methods. In Visual Basic, the set of properties and methods defined in a class is called the default interface. While every class has at least one interface, VB now allows a class to have more than one using the keyword `Implements`.

The `Implements` keyword makes it possible to specify additional interfaces for the class to use. Predefined sets of properties and methods can be grabbed and immediately made a part of the class. These predefined interfaces come from other classes. Implements permits taking the default interface from any class and use it in another one. This is desirable to factor out common interface elements that define classes much as switches on appliances do.

Suppose we wanted to create software objects that represented a television and a light bulb. We already know each has a switch to turn it on, so it seems reasonable that each should have a method called `SwitchOn`. Without interfaces, we would have to provide a Public method to each class to implement the `SwitchOn` method. Furthermore, if we wanted to turn on one of the appliances, we would have to know specifically which one we wanted to turn on. The following code could be used to execute the `SwitchOn` method for both classes:

```
Public MyTelevision As Television
Public MyLightBulb As LightBulb
Set MyTelevision = New Television
Set MyLightBulb = New LightBulb
MyTelevision.SwitchOn
MyLightBulb.SwitchOn
```

We could simplify this code somewhat by placing all the appliances into a Collection object and using the For Each...Next loop to execute the On method for each class. But because each class is different, we are forced to declare a variable `As Object` so that it can represent any class. This means that our code will have a late-bound object variable that prevents the compiler from verifying our method call as well as implementing optimizations at compile time.

```
Dim MyAppliance As Object
For Each MyAppliance in MyCollection
    MyAppliance.SwitchOn
Next
```

What we really want is a way to factor out the common interface elements and use early binding when dealing with object variables. Interfaces provide that and more. Sticking with the same example, we will add a class to our project called the `IAppliance` class, which contains the definition of the common interface elements for all appliances. This will be our interface class, and by convention interfaces always begin with a capital *I*. In the class, we define the properties and methods for the interface, but we do not put any code in the routines.

```
Public Sub SwitchOn ()
End Sub
```

When defining an interface, we rarely put code in the property and method declarations. The interface serves only as the definition for which properties and methods are in the interface— not the functionality. To define functionality along with the interface, Visual Basic would have to support inheritance. This concept of properties and methods with no code may seem strange, but it is absolutely driven by the lack of inheritance. If VB had inheritance, we would be explaining polymorphism quite differently. An interface with no code is also called an *abstract class*.

Once the interface is defined as a separate class, we can use the collection of properties and methods in another class, with the `Implements` keyword. To use the interface, simply declare it in the [General][Declarations] section with the `Implements` keyword.

```
Implements IAppliance
```

Once we implement the `IAppliance` interface in the `Television` and `LightBulb` classes, a funny thing happens. The interface name appears in the Object box and all the properties and methods of the class appear in the Procedure box. In this way, we have a complete list of all the properties and methods available. The following code shows the declaration for the `SwitchOn` method as it might appear in the `Television` or `LightBulb` class:

```
Implements IAppliance
Private Sub IAppliance_SwitchOn()
End Sub
```

Notice that when we implement an interface, the properties and methods appear as Private in the implementing class. This is because the `IAppliance` class contains the Public elements for any class implementing `IAppliance`. If the properties and methods appeared as Public in the implementing class, then they could be called directly without the interface at all.

Implementing an interface represents a contract between the developer and the compiler. When an interface is implemented, we are promising the compiler that all the properties and methods in the interface will appear in the `Television` or `LightBulb` class. Remember that when we talked about the label next to the On/Off switch we said that represented a guarantee that the switch would perform the intended function. Interfaces are the same guarantee. We must place some code (at least a comment mark) in every property and method of the interface or it will not compile. Once implemented, however, interfaces greatly improve code performance. First of all, they make possible the use of early binding. Remember the example of using a collection to hold all appliances? With interfaces, the code that used late binding becomes early bound.

```
Dim MyAppliance As IAppliance
For Each MyAppliance in MyCollection
```

```
MyAppliance.SwitchOn
Next
```

Now the object variable is declared As IAppliance. This variable is capable of representing any object that implements IAppliance. Furthermore, the compiler recognizes the interface and makes the variable early bound. The compiler error checks method calls and improves speed—a big plus.

The code is also now able to deal with objects it has never seen before. If we build a Zorkometer class, we can be assured that the preceding collection code will work without recoding provided our new Zorkometer class implements IAppliance. Our code knows how to turn the Zorkometer on even though it has never seen it before.

CREATING OBJECT RELATIONSHIPS

One of the biggest advantages of using objects to construct applications is that objects more closely model the real world than do simple functions. A key feature of entities in the world is that they have relationships to one another. Relationships are obvious in every business problem and trying to model them is certainly not new. Anyone who has created even a simple database understands relationships.

Objects have two primary relationships which are common in applications: parent/child and one-to-many. The parent/child relationship defines a dependency between two objects. That is, one object should not exist unless another is created first. An example of this is the relationship between a student and a teacher. It makes no sense to have a student if there is no teacher. We say the student object is dependent upon the teacher object. One-to-many relationships are often associated with these dependencies. In our example, we know that a student is dependent upon a teacher, but that there are also many students for a single teacher. Thus we find that most business problems are defined by parent/child and one-to-many relationships.

Parent/child and one-to-many are certainly not the only relationships that objects can have. For example, we might want to model the fact that a student may take many different classes. From this perspective a single student can be associated with many teachers while a teacher is associated with many students. This relationship is a many-to-many relationship. This relationship is more difficult to model, and is generally created as a series of one-to-many relationships. The scope of the business problem is generally narrowed until a single one-to-many relationship is defined. In other words, part of the application may reflect one teacher with many students while another part may reflect one student with many teachers. This works because in the first case we are dealing with the classes an instructor will teach while the second scenario involves courses a student will take. It is unlikely that the application will want to deal with both scenarios simultaneously.

Modeling these relationships requires that we understand not only how the real entities are related in the business problem, but also the mechanics of how to code these relationships. As an example, let us create a simple object model that can be used to represent customers who purchase software products. Before we begin writing code, we model the relationships graphically. Figure 14-1 shows the object model.

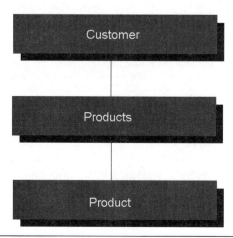

Figure 14-1 Customers and Products in an object model.

Object models are typically drawn in a vertical hierarchy which is intended to reflect the parent/child and one-to-many relationships in the model. Objects drawn lower in the model are dependent upon higher-level objects. Thus our model indicates that a Product object should not exist unless it is associated with a Customer object. The model also shows the one-to-many relationship between a Customer and a Product object. The object Products is a collection class designed to be a container for all the Product objects associated with a single Customer object. In this way, we can expand the model both horizontally and vertically until it adequately represents the business problem being solved.

In order to build a set of classes in Visual Basic that represents the model drawn, we understand the mechanics of creating the two key relationships. For simplicity, we will focus on the relationships separately. First, we will create a parent/child relationship between a single customer and a single product. Then we will create the collection class that will allow a customer to be associated with many products.

Our model is simple enough to start creating. We will begin at the top of the model and create a Customer class, a straightforward object with properties and methods that adequately define a Customer. This implementation can be as complex as desired, but for our example we will define a single property called Name, which would be created through the use of a Private data member and a set of Property procedures.

```
Private m_Name As String

Public Property Get Name() As String
   Name = m_Name
End Property

Public Property Let Name(ByVal strName As String)
   m_Name = strName
End Property
```

The dependent relationship is actually created when we define the `Product` class. Once the new class is added to the model, we can establish a dependency through the use of the Instancing property of the `Product` class. The Instancing property determines several different features affecting how an instance of the class is created. The following settings are available.

PRIVATE

When the Instancing property is set to Private, the associated class model is considered private to the application and cannot be seen by any other project. This means that even if the class is created in an ActiveX EXE or ActiveX DLL, no client will be able to create an instance of the class. This setting is used for classes in components intended as helper classes within the project.

PUBLICNOTCREATABLE

When the Instancing property is set to `PublicNot Creatable`, the associated class module can be seen by other applications, though those applications cannot create an instance of the class. This means that client applications can declare variables against this class and receive this class as a return value from a function. Clients cannot, however, use the `New` keyword or the `CreateObject` function to get an instance. This setting is the primary way to create the parent/child relationship. We will investigate this further.

SINGLEUSE

When the `Instancing` property is set to `SingleUse`, the associated class module can be seen and created by external clients, though each time a client creates an instance, a new copy of the entire component is created. This setting is for use with ActiveX EXE components only and affects the way in which these components scale. Scaling VB applications is covered later in Chapter 20.

GLOBALSINGLEUSE

When the Instancing property is set to `GlobalSingleUse`, the associated class module behaves just as it does when set to `SingleUse` with the exception that clients can call the component directly without creating an instance. Classes whose methods may be called without being instanced are referred to as *static* classes and behave more like function libraries and less like true classes.

MULTIUSE

When the Instancing property is set to `MultiUse`, the associated class module may be seen and created by an external client. Classes set to `MultiUse` service all client calls through a single copy of the ActiveX DLL or ActiveX EXE. This setting has an impact on the way in which the application scales for many users. Scaling is discussed in Chapter 20.

GLOBALMULTIUSE

When the Instancing property is set to `GlobalMultiUse`, the associated class module behaves just like `MultiUse` with the exception that the class is a static class. Therefore, the methods may be called without creating an instance of the class.

As we indicated, the `PublicNotCreatable` setting is used to establish parent/child relationships. Before we can establish the relationship, we should clearly understand what this setting accomplishes. We stated earlier that classes set to `PublicNotCreatable` can be seen but not created. From a practical standpoint, this means that the following operation is illegal in a client a class named `MyClass` where the `Instancing` property is set to `PublicNotCreatable`.

```
Set MyObject = CreateObject("Project1.MyClass")
Set MyObject = New MyClass
```

How can we get a reference to a child class if we cannot create an instance of it? Have the parent class return a reference from a method call. In this way, we must create the parent class first and then use the method of the parent to create the child. The following code shows the definition of a method in the `Customer` class that might create a dependent `Product` object:

```
Public Function CreateProduct() As Product
```

Check It Out 14-1: Parent/Child Relationships

1. Create a new ActiveX DLL project in Visual Basic. Multi-object components are most often created as ActiveX DLLs and ActiveX EXEs so they can be reused in different applications.
2. Change the name of Class1 to **Customer**.
3. Add a new class to the project by selecting **PROJECT/ADD CLASS MODULE** from the menu. Name this new class **Product**. Set the `Instancing` property of class Product to `PublicNotCreatable`.
4. In the code window for the Product class, add a property named Title as a Private data member wrapped in Property Procedures. The final code should appear as follows:

```
Private m_Title As String

Public Property Get Title() As String
  Title = m_Title
End Property

Public Property Let Title(ByVal strTitle As String)
   m_Title = strTitle
End Property
```

5. Open the code window for the `Customer` class. In this class, we will implement a function to create a dependent `Product` class. Add a Public function named

CreateProduct. This function should return a Product class. The following code shows the final function which creates a local instance of the Product class and returns it to the calling client:

```
Public Function CreateProduct_
    (strTitle As String) _
    As Project1.Product
    'Create a local instance
    Dim objProduct As Product
    Set objProduct = New Product

    'Set the property
    objProduct.Title = strTitle

    'Return the instance
    Set CreateProduct = objProduct
End Function
```

6. Add a new Standard EXE project to the application by selecting **FILE/ADD PROJECT** from the menu. This project will be a client for the object model.

7. Set a Reference to the ActiveX DLL project by selecting **PROJECT/REFER- ENCES** from the menu. In the References dialog, set a reference to **Project1** and push the **OK** button.

8. Right-click on **Project2** in the Project Explorer and select **SET AS START UP** from the popup menu. This will cause the client project to start first.

9. Open the code window for Form1 in Project2. The client will create an instance of the Customer and use it to get a Product instance. Add the following code to the Form_Load event to create the instances.

```
'Create a Customer
Dim objCustomer As Project1.Customer
Set objCustomer = New Project1.Customer

'Create a Product
Dim objProduct As Project1.Product
Set objProduct = objCustomer.CreateProduct("Visual Basic")

'Display Title
MsgBox "The Product Title is " & objProduct.Title
```

10. Run the application. There will be a message showing the title of the new product.

11. In order to prove that the Instancing property has truly created a dependency, try to modify the code to create a Product instance directly. This can be done by changing the line where the CreateProduct method is called as follows:

```
Set objProduct = New Project1.Product
```

12. Now run the code again. What happens?

Although the `Instancing` property makes it possible to implement a strict parent/child relationship, we may not always want to build dependencies rigidly. The latest trend in object model design is away from tightly-bound dependencies to a philosophy known as *standalone* objects. Standalone simply means that dependent objects can be created freely without having to create a parent object. However, the dependent object can be associated with a parent through a property.

Continuing with our example with teachers and students, sometimes in an application, we may want the ability to create a student without the requirement to create a teacher. This may occur, for example, when we need to deal with personal information about the student like address and phone number. Part of the application may be responsible for mailing a newsletter to all students. In this case, we just want student information—not teacher information. In a related scenario, we may want the ability to associate the student with a different teacher, as when the student changes classes. In these cases, tightly bound relationships may work against the developer.

Standalone objects are created by setting the `Instancing` property of all objects in the model to a value which allows creation such as `MultiUse`. If both the teacher and the student had Instancing properties set to `MultiUse`, we might be able to create them with the following code:

```
Dim MyTeacher As Teacher
Dim MyStudent As Student
Set MyTeacher = New Teacher
Set MyStudent = New Student
```

Once the objects are created, we may want to relate them and this would be done through a property of the `Teacher` class, normally named the same as the dependent object—in this case `Student`. Therefore all we have to do is set the `Student` property of the teacher.

```
Set MyTeacher.Student = MyStudent
```

Once set, the property forms the relationship between the objects. Now we can easily call properties and methods of the `Student` class using the `Teacher` class. We can also associate the student with a different teacher just by setting one property. We can even separate the student from all `Teacher` objects by setting the `Student` property of each `Teacher` object to `Nothing`. Standalone objects are considerably more flexible than traditional dependency models and are therefore preferred.

Once we have mastered the parent/child relationship we proceed to create one-to-many relationships. In our example, it is clear that we will want the ability to associate more than one student with a teacher. One-to-many relationships are built using collections. You are already familiar with several of the built-in collections found in Visual Basic, such as Forms and Controls. Additionally, you have worked with the `Collection` object to hold many instances. In this section, we teach you how to build a custom collection that is more powerful than any of the previous collections used.

Although past exercises in this book have used the built-in Collection object as a means to store multiple instances, this object has some limitations that advanced programmers will want to overcome. First and foremost, the VB Collection object is not a homogenous collection. It can hold objects of any type all together. We may be interested in keeping a collection of Student objects, though nothing really stops the programmer from putting anything into a collection. We can never guarantee that a Collection object just holds one type of class.

Second, Collection objects in VB do not permit adding custom properties and methods. We get the Add, Item, Remove, and Count members, but what if we want more? For example, suppose we wanted to create a Dismiss method which would dismiss all the students in the collection from the class. The VB Collection object gives us no way to create these custom methods. What we need is the ability to inherit all the features of the Collection object and then add or modify as we see fit. Unfortunately, as we know, Visual Basic does not support implementation inheritance. We cannot simply inherit from the Collection object to build our own collection.

In the absence of true implementation inheritance, Visual Basic programmers must use a workaround to simulate inheriting the features of the Collection object. This technique is known as *containment*, the process of creating a Private instance wrapped inside a VB class module. The class module is coded to reproduce every property and method of the contained class and delegates work to the contained class. Where appropriate, the class module can override the default functionality of the contained class.

Building a custom collection begins by defining a private Collection object in the [General][Declarations] section of a Class Module. Declaring a private object is similar to declaring any private variable. We already understand that Property procedures are Public accessor and mutator functions that work with a private member variable. The purpose of declaring a member variable as Private is to hide the data from clients so that they must use the Property procedures. Custom collection classes are built on the same principle. We will hide the Collection object functionality and force clients through our custom public interface. The following code declares a private collection for our class:

```
Private objCollection As New Collection
```

In the code above, we use automatic instantiation to create the private collection. This is permissible since we understand clearly the scope of our private collection. To be more formal and use manual instantiation, create and destroy the collection in the Initialize and Terminate events of the class In any case, once the private collection is defined, we must provide a public interface, which should reproduce all the properties and methods supported by the underlying collection with appropriate modifications to overcome the inherent weaknesses of the Collection object.

The public interface to any custom collection should consist of the methods Add, Item, and Remove and the Count property. These four members make up the minimum public interface for any collection created. When these members are implemented, they will delegate to the identical method found in the collection. Of the four standard collection methods, the most interesting is the Add method. Consider the Add method as it is found in the Collection object. This method has the following signature:

```
object.Add item,key,before,after
```

Notice that the original Add method allows users to pass in the item that they want added to the collection. This function signature means that the collection will accept any type of object the user wants to pass. We want to prevent this type of use and instead restrict the collection to one type of object. Recalling our use of students and teachers, we might want to make a collection that accepts only students. In order to create this type of collection, we will create a method Add for our collection, but it will have a different signature.

```
Public Function Add() As Student
```

Notice that the above signature does not accept any arguments. This is the simplest way to prevent unwanted objects from entering the collection. Then how is a student ever actually added to the collection? The collection creates the new student and returns it to the calling client through the return value of the Add method. The following code shows the complete Add method:

```
Public Function Add() As Student

   'Create Student
   Dim objStudent As Student
   Set objStudent = New Student

   'Add to private collection
   objCollection.Add objStudent

   'Return Student to client
   Set Add = objStudent

End Function
```

Examine the above code carefully. Since the method does not accept an object as argument, the method itself creates a new Student object. In our method, the new student would simply have all the default values set, but we could create the Add method with arguments for the properties of the newly-created object. The key, however, is only to create the object within the collection. Once created, the new object is added to the private collection for safekeeping. Finally, the object is returned to the client by the function. Once the client has the object, it can easily be modified, but the point is that this method can only produce Student objects. Therefore, the custom collection is guaranteed to be homogenous.

Once the Add method is created, building the other members is fairly straightforward. The Item, Remove, and Count members are implemented as simple delegations to the underlying private collection. The following code shows how to create a read-only Count property that delegates to the private collection.

```
Public Function Count() As Long
   Set Count = objCollection.Count
End Function
```

We want our collection to have the four required members and to behave exactly like the collections we have used before in Visual Basic. This means that we need to implement two important behaviors in our classes. The first is a default member. Collections always exhibit the Item method as the default member. Consider accessing the `Fields` collection in an ADO Recordset object. Because Item is the default member, the following two lines of code are equivalent:

```
MyRecordset.Fields.Item("Field1")
MyRecordset.Fields("Field1")
```

Another key feature of collections found in models like ADO is the ability to utilize the For Each...Next loop to iterate through all of the members of a collection. VB classes do not support this type of functionality natively. We need to be able to write code that allows us to look at each member of a custom collection. The following code might be executed to graduate each student from a teacher:

```
Dim objStudent As Student
For Each objStudent in objTeachers.Students
   objStudent.Graduate
Next
```

Designating the `Item` method as the default member of a custom collection is a matter of using the Procedure Attributes dialog. We have discussed in detail how to set default members. Setting the `Item` method as the default is a standard expected by developers.

Solving the second problem of support for the For Each...Next structure is a little more complicated. In fact, this is perhaps the most hare-brained operation in all Visual Basic because it involves the use of a magic number and delegating to an unfamiliar interface. Support for the For Each...Next syntax is provided by an enumerator object for every collection. Unfortunately, we cannot write a custom enumerator object in Visual Basic. Instead, we must delegate to the underlying private collection, by providing a method in our class called NewEnum. NewEnum is the standard name for the method that provides enumeration. Actually, the standard name for the enumerator method is _NewEnum. The underscore means that the method is hidden in the type library—we cannot see it using the object browser unless we specifically ask to view hidden members. We can view the hidden _NewEnum method by opening the Object Browser and finding the `Collection` object in the VBA library. After selecting the `Collection` object, right click in the object browser and select **VIEW HIDDEN MEMBERS** from the popup menu. Figure 14-2 shows the _NewEnum method.

In order to provide a method that can support enumeration, we must create a method named NewEnum, make it hidden, and give it a special magic number identifier in the Procedure Attributes dialog. We start with the method definition. For any collection that will support For Each...Next, simply add this code to the custom collection class.

```
Public Property Get NewEnum() As IUnknown
   Set NewEnum = MyCollection.[_NewEnum]
End Property
```

Next, we set the attributes for the method in the Procedure Attributes dialog. In this dialog, select the NewEnum method and push the **Advanced** button. The dialog opens to reveal advanced settings. Check the **Hide this Member** box and then type the magic number –4 into the Procedure ID box. Figure 14-3 shows the complete dialog.

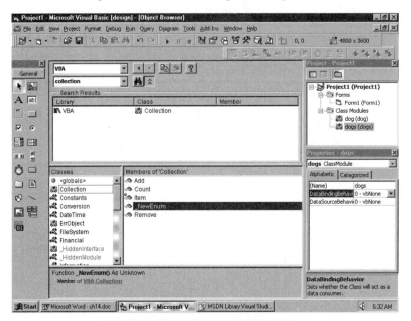

Figure 14-2 The _NewEnum method.

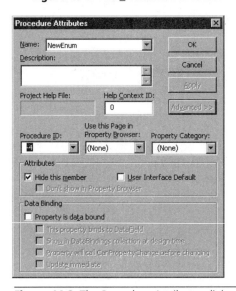

Figure 14-3 The Procedure Attributes dialog.

Creating a custom collection class is obviously an advanced skill complete with its own special requirements. The process of enabling the For Each...Next syntax is nothing short of ugly. Fortunately, we do have tools in Visual Basic that make building object models easier. The primary tool for object model construction is an add-in known as the Class Builder utility (Figure 14-4). Class Builder provides a graphical interface that builds objects and collections in a hierarchical model. To use the utility, simply activate it through the Add-In Manager. Once it is enabled, the Class Builder can be opened from the New Menu item under the Add-Ins menu. This menu opens a window where a new object model can be defined.

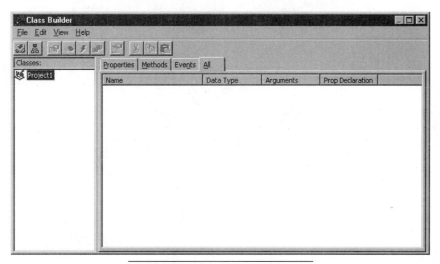

Figure 14-4 The Class Builder Utility.

The Class Builder shows a tree view on the left that represents the object model and an object view on the right showing properties and methods for objects. Creating a new model is a matter of adding objects and collections with custom properties and methods. When this is done, Class Builder will then build the code for the new objects.

Check It Out 14-2: Class Builder

1. Create a new ActiveX DLL project in Visual Basic.
2. If the Class Builder utility is not already loaded, open the Add-In Manager by selecting **ADD-INS/ADD-IN MANAGER** from the menu. In the Add-In Manager, activate the **Class Builder utility** and push **OK**.
3. Class Builder does not like to deal with class modules that already exist in a project. Therefore, right-click on the default **Class1** in the Project Explorer and select **REMOVE CLASS1** from the menu.
4. Now the ActiveX DLL should have no classes in it. Open the Class Builder utility to build a new object model by selecting **ADD-INS/CLASS BUILDER UTILITY...** from the menu.

5. We will build a simple model relating customers and products. Start by selecting **FILE/NEW/CLASS...** from the Class Builder menu. The Class Module Builder dialog (Figure 14-5) will appear.

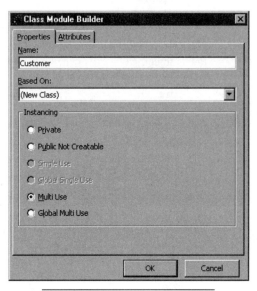

Figure 14-5 Class Module Builder.

6. In the Class Module Builder, name the new class **Customer** and push **OK**. The Customer class should appear in the tree view diagram.

7. With the Customer class active, select **FILE/NEW/COLLECTION...** from the menu. This will bring up the Collection Builder dialog. In this dialog, name the new collection **Products**. In the right side of the dialog, select to base the collection on a new class. Name the new class **Product**. Push the **OK** button.

8. Class Builder is now ready to build the object model. To generate the code, simply select **FILE/UPDATE PROJECT** from the menu. When Class Builder is through generating code, close the dialog and examine the code. Class Builder has stubbed out code for all the objects and collections along with complete support for the _NewEnum method.

OBJECT PERSISTENCE

We know from the earliest introduction to objects in Visual Basic that they are capable of managing application state through the use of properties. However, state management in VB objects is limited to the life of the object. When the object variable is set to Nothing, the data in the properties is destroyed. Object persistence is a feature of class modules that makes it possible to create objects that remember state beyond the life of the object itself.

Object persistence is enabled in VB through the use of the Persistable property of a class module. The normal setting is 0 – NotPersistable; setting this property to 1 – Persistable, adds three new events to a class module: `InitProperties`, `ReadProperties`, and `WriteProperties`. These events provide notification that tells the program when the first instance of an object is created as well as when the object should persist or depersist its state.

The `InitProperties` event fires for a persistent class the first time an instance of a particular class is created in the application. This event can be used to set the initial property values for the class. For a persistent object, the `InitProperties` event serves roughly the same purpose as the `Initialize` event for a non-persistent object. When a client sets the associated object variable to `Nothing`, the persistent class receives the `WriteProperties` event, which tells the instance that it is about to be destroyed and should therefore write its state to a persistent medium like the hard disk. When new instances of the class are subsequently created, they receive the `ReadProperties` event, which provides notification to the class that state information is available in a persistent format and it should be read. The following code shows the function signatures associated with the three new events..

```
Private Sub Class_InitProperties()
End Sub


Private Sub Class_ReadProperties(PropBag As PropertyBag)
End Sub


Private Sub Class_WriteProperties(PropBag As PropertyBag)
End Sub
```

Each persistent object has associated with it a special object used solely to manage persistent state. This object is known as a `PropertyBag`. The `PropertyBag` object is passed as an argument into the `ReadProperties` and `WriteProperties` events. Visual Basic programmers familiar with ActiveX controls projects know that the `PropertyBag` is used with controls to remember the values set into the control at design time. Similarly, programmers can use the `PropertyBag` for persistent classes to remember property values set at run time.

In an ActiveX control, the `PropertyBag` is used to maintain an in-RAM copy of the FRM file which represents any form. When a project is saved, the contents of the `Property-Bag` are stored in the FRM file. Persistent objects work slightly differently because in the latter case, we are trying to save properties set at run time—not design time. Therefore, we have to use a separate and distinct `PropertyBag` object to read and write run-time values to disk. This is indeed confusing, but each persistent object actually has two `PropertyBag` objects associated with it. One is used to manage state while the component is in memory, and the other is used to read and write to the hard drive.

We will start with the `PropertyBag` associated with the `ReadProperties` and `WriteProperties` events. When either of these events is called, the persistent object should read or write to the `PropertyBag` as appropriate. We will assume that an object named `Product` has a property called `Discount` which indicates the percentage discount received by customers who order 100 units or more of a product. This discount must be able to be changed, but it will not change often. Therefore, every time we create an instance of the Product class, we want to remember the latest discount in effect.

When we start the application for the first time and create an instance of the Product class, the InitProperties event will fire because no other instance has ever been created. In the InitProperties class, we set the value of the Discount property to some default. If the Product class has its Persistable property set to 1 – Persistable, then the following code sets the initial value of the property.

```
Private Sub Class_InitProperties()
   Discount = 10
End Sub
```

Now the user can change the value of the discount to reflect a new pricing policy set by the company. Let us say the discount is being raised to 15%. This would be accomplished through a Property Let procedure as follows.

```
Public Property Let Discount (dblDiscount As Double)
   m_Discount = dblDiscount
   PropertyChanged "Discount"
End Property
```

Examine the property procedure carefully. The above code assumes a Private data member named m_Discount for managing the property, but the more important line is the call to the Propertychanged method. The PropertyChanged method is called to indicate that a class has *dirty* properties. That is, the class needs to save its state. After PropertyChanged is called, any attempt to destroy the associated instance by setting the object variable to Nothing results in a call the WriteProperties so that the object can save its state to the PropertyBag. The following code shows how this might happen:

```
Private Sub Class_WriteProperties(PropBag As PropertyBag)
   PropBag.WriteProperty "Discount", Discount, 10
End Sub
```

The WriteProperty method of the PropertyBag is used to store the value of a property in the PropertyBag before it is lost. The WriteProperty method takes the name of the property as the first argument. The second argument is the value of the property and the final argument is the default value. This preserves the value of the property in the bag and if the component stays in memory, so will the PropertyBag. Therefore, subsequent instances of the Product class will not fire the InitProperties event when created, but will instead fire the ReadProperties event. The ReadProperties event retrieves the property values for the new instance from the PropertyBag. In this way, the new instance will use the latest value of the Discount property without requiring some sort of database or recoding effort to change the discount.

```
Private Sub Class_ReadProperties(PropBag As PropertyBag)
   Discount = PropBag.ReadProperty("Discount", 10)
End Sub
```

The only rub in this whole process is that the `PropertBag` used by the instance is only capable of remembering data in RAM. This works fine as long as the component remains in memory, however, what happens when the component unloads? We must create a separate instance of the `PropertyBag` and use it to write the data to the hard drive. This is done by writing the contents of the `PropertyBag` to a Binary file. The following code shows how an `Instance` of the Product class named MyProduct might be written to a Binary file.

```
Dim m_PropertyBag As PropertyBag
Set m_PropertyBag = New PropertyBag


m_PropertyBag.WriteProperty "Publisher", MyPublisher


'Write the Bag to a file
Dim vContents As Variant
vContents = m_PropertyBag.Contents


Open App.Path & "\Publisher.dat" For Binary As #1
   Put #1, , vContents
Close #1
```

Note how the above code saves the entire instance to the `PropertyBag`. The instance is then saved to disk using the `Contents` property of the `PropertyBag`. Once this is done, subsequent application sessions can read the contents from the hard drive by reversing the process.

```
Dim m_PropertyBag As PropertyBag
Dim MyProduct As Product
Dim vContents As Variant
Dim bytObject() As Byte

Set m_PropertyBag = New PropertyBag

Open App.Path & "\Login.dat" For Binary As #1
   Get #1, , vContents
Close #1


bytObject = vContents


m_PropertyBag.Contents = bytObject


Set MyProduct = m_PropertyBag.ReadProperty("Product")
```

Exercise 14-1: Polymorphism

As we have noted, polymorphism is the ability for an object variable to represent instances from many different classes. The `Form` keyword is a perfect example of an object variable that can represent many different instances. The `Form` variable has the ability to represent any VB form—Form1, Form2, Formx, MyForm, etc. Polymorphism provides a powerful mechanism for reusing objects in VB.

DEFINING INTERFACES

Step 1

Using the File Explorer, create a new directory in the File Explorer called **VB BOOTCAMP\EXERCISE14-1**. Start a new Standard EXE project in Visual Basic.

Step 2

Visual Basic creates polymorphic behavior in class modules through the use of *interfaces*, the collection of properties and methods that define a class. In early Visual Basic, classes could be defined, but no mechanism existed to standardize the interfaces of the classes created. Standardizing the interfaces in VB leads to easier reuse of the objects you create.

Step 3

In this exercise, we will create two classes: `Instructor` and `Student`. These classes will share some characteristics defined by an interface we will call `IHuman`. By implementing the `IHuman` interface in both classes, we will standardize their behavior and improve reuse. Insert a new Class Module into the project by selecting **PROJECT/ADD CLASS MODULE**. Name the new class `IHuman`.

Step 4

In this new class, we will define the common properties and methods for both Instructors and Students. This common set of properties and methods will be the Human Interface, which will support three common properties (`Name`, `Age`, and `Height`) as well as two common methods (`Talk` and `Walk`). The common properties are added to the interface using property procedures, and the methods are added with subroutines. Add the following code to the `IHuman` class to create the properties and methods interface:

```
'Common Properties
Public Property Get Name() As String
End Property


Public Property Let Name(ByVal strName As String)
End Property


Public Property Get Age() As Integer
End Property
```

```
Public Property Let Age(ByVal intAge As Integer)
End Property

Public Property Get Height() As Integer
End Property

Public Property Let Height(ByVal intHeight As Integer)
End Property

'Common Methods
Public Sub Talk()
End Sub

Public Sub Walk()
End Sub
```

Step 5

Note that in the above code, the procedures have no code in them. This is because the IHuman interface represents only a standard definition for an interface. Classes that define interfaces but do not have code are called *abstract classes*. All other classes that subsequently implement the IHuman interface must contain the properties and methods defined by the Abstract class with appropriate code.

THE INSTRUCTOR CLASS

Step 6

Add a new class module to the application and name it Instructor. The Instructor class will use all of the standard properties and methods defined by the Human interface. In order to invoke the interface, we use the VB keyword Implements. Add the following code to the [General][Declarations] section of the Instructor class:

```
Implements IHuman
```

Step 7

Now drop down the Object Box inside the Instructor class. There should be an entry for IHuman. Select the interface and look in the Procedure Box. See the properties and methods? Interfaces represent a *promise* on the part of the class to implement every property and method defined in the interface. Failure to do so will result in a compile error. Therefore, code must be added to each of the procedures in the Proc box. Using these procedures, add the following code to the Instructor class:

```
'Private Data Members
Private m_Name As String
```

```
Private m_Age As Integer
Private m_Height As Integer

Private Property Let IHuman_Age(ByVal RHS As Integer)
  m_Age = RHS
End Property

Private Property Get IHuman_Age() As Integer
  IHuman_Age = m_Age
End Property

Private Property Let IHuman_Height(ByVal RHS As Integer)
  m_Height = RHS
End Property

Private Property Get IHuman_Height() As Integer
  IHuman_Height = m_Height
End Property

Private Property Let IHuman_Name(ByVal RHS As String)
  m_Name = RHS
End Property

Private Property Get IHuman_Name() As String
  IHuman_Name = m_Name
End Property

Private Sub IHuman_Talk()
  MsgBox "Class Dismissed!"
End Sub

Private Sub IHuman_Walk()
  MsgBox "I'm Leaving!"
End Sub
```

Step 8

Add a new class to the project and name it Student. The Student will also implement the
IHuman interface. Add the following code to the [General][Declarations] section:

```
Implements IHuman
```

Step 9

Just like the Instructor class, the Student must also implement each part of the IHuman interface. Add the following code to implement the interface in the Student class:

```
'Private Data Members
Private m_Name As String
Private m_Age As Integer
Private m_Height As Integer


Private Property Let IHuman_Age(ByVal RHS As Integer)
  m_Age = RHS
End Property


Private Property Get IHuman_Age() As Integer
  IHuman_Age = m_Age
End Property


Private Property Let IHuman_Height(ByVal RHS As Integer)
  m_Height = RHS
End Property


Private Property Get IHuman_Height() As Integer
  IHuman_Height = m_Height
End Property


Private Property Let IHuman_Name(ByVal RHS As String)
  m_Name = RHS
End Property


Private Property Get IHuman_Name() As String
  IHuman_Name = m_Name
End Property


Private Sub IHuman_Talk()
  MsgBox "Snore..."
End Sub


Private Sub IHuman_Walk()
  MsgBox "I'm Outta Here!"
End Sub
```

USING POLYMORPHISM

Step 10

Now that the classes are defined, use them in a front end and implement polymorphic behavior. First build a front end to interact with the objects. Figure 14-6 shows the user interface. Using Form1, create the interface. Use the Item List below to set the design time properties for the controls.

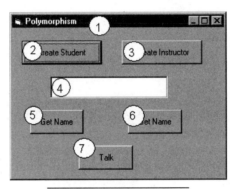

Figure 14-6 Form Interface.

Item 1—Form

Name	frmPoly
Caption	Polymorphism

Item 2—CommandButton

Name	cmdStudent
Caption	Create Student

Item 3—CommandButton

Name	cmdInstructor
Caption	Create Instructor

Item 4—TextBox

Name	txtName

Item 5—CommandButton

Name	cmdGetName
Caption	Get Name

Item 6—CommandButton

Name	cmdSetName
Caption	Set Name

Item 7—CommandButton

Name   cmdTalk
Caption   Talk

Step 11

Remember, polymorphism is the ability for one type of variable to represent several other object types. In our case the objects we want to represent are all based on the IHuman interface. Therefore, we must declare a variable of type IHuman. Add the following code to the [General][Declarations] section of the form to declare the variable:

```
'Polymorphic Variable
Private m_Person As IHuman
```

Step 12

When we create a Student or Instructor, we use the m_Person variable to activate the IHuman interface. Add the following code to the click event of cmdInstructor and cmdStudent as shown to instantiate the objects with the IHuman interface activated:

```
Private Sub cmdInstructor_Click()


    'Create Instructor
    Set m_Person = New Instructor
    MsgBox "Instructor Created!"


End Sub


Private Sub cmdStudent_Click()


    'Create Student
    Set m_Person = New Student
    MsgBox "Student Created!"


End Sub
```

Step 13

Once the IHuman interface is active, call any of the properties or methods of the interface without regard for whether the m_Person variable contains an Instructor or a Student. This is polymorphism! Add the folowing code to the form to call some of the properties and methods:

```
Private Sub cmdGetName_Click()
    txtName.Text = m_Person.Name
End Sub


Private Sub cmdSetName_Click()
```

```
    m_Person.Name = txtName.Text
End Sub

Private Sub cmdTalk_Click()
  m_Person.Talk
End Sub
```

Step 14

Run the project and create an `Instructor`, then a `Student`. Try calling some methods of the class. Now go back and examine the code until it is completely clear how it was created.

Exercise 14-2: Object Models

Building components with collections and objects is the objective of every VB programmer. Components form the backbone of RAD development. A well-designed component should be reusable over and over again. This exercise builds a complete object model with custom collections and objects that implement a code fragment repository.

CREATING THE OBJECT MODEL

Step 1

Using the File Explorer, create a new directory **VB BOOTCAMP\EXERCISE14-2**. Under this directory create two new directories named **\CLIENT** and **\SERVER**. Now start a new ActiveX DLL project in Visual Basic.

Step 2

If the Class Builder utility is not already loaded, open the Add-In Manager by selecting **ADD-INS/ADD-IN MANAGER** from the menu. In the Add-In Manager, activate the Class Builder utility and push **OK**.

Step 3

Class Builder does not like to deal with class modules that already exist in a project. Therefore, right-click on the default **Class1** in the Project Explorer and select **REMOVE CLASS1** from the menu. Now the ActiveX DLL should have no classes in it. Open the Class Builder utility to build a new object model by selecting **ADD-INS/CLASS BUILDER UTILITY...** from the menu.

Step 4

Our object model begins with a class named Library. The `Library` object represents an instance of the code fragment library. A single library can contain many fragments. Add the Library class by selecting **FILE/NEW/CLASS** from the Class Builder menu. In the Class Module Builder dialog, name the class **Library** and push the **OK** button.

Step 5

In the Class Builder, make sure the Library class is selected and click on the **Methods** tab. Add a new method to the Library class by selecting **FILE/NEW/METHOD** from the Class Builder menu. In the Method Builder dialog, name the new method **Connect**. Press the + button to add a new argument for the method. Name the argument **FileName** and change the data type to **String**. Press **OK** to add the argument and then **OK** again to add the new method.

Step 6

In the Class Builder, make sure the Library class is selected. Create a new collection under the Library class by selecting **FILE/NEW/COLLECTION** from the Class Builder menu. In the Collection Builder dialog, name the new collection **Fragments**. On the right side of the dialog, select the option to base the collection on a new class and name the new class Fragment. Press the **OK** button.

Step 7

Three objects should be visible in the Class Builder: Library, Fragments, and Fragment. Double-click on any item in the tree to expand or collapse the tree branch. Expand the tree until the Fragment class is visible.

Step 8

With the Fragment class selected, add a new property by selecting **FILE/NEW/PROPERTY** from the Class Builder menu. In the Property Builder dialog, name the new property **Value** and change the data type to **String**. Press the **OK** button.

Step 9

The fundamental object model for our code fragment repository is complete. Have the Class Builder generate the code for the new model by selecting **FILE/UPDATE PROJECT** from the menu. After the code is generated, save the work to the /SERVER directory created earlier.

CODING THE OBJECT MODEL

Step 10

Although the Class Builder gives us a great jump on the coding effort, we still have to write the code for much of the actual functionality of the repository. Our repository will be done in a simple text file which will keep a line for each fragment of code. We want the Library class to remember the file name associated with the repository. Add the following variable definition to the [General][Declarations]section of the Library class to hold the file name.

```
Private m_FileName As String
```

Step 11

After the Library object is instanced, the Connect method can be used to open a file for the repository. This method opens a file and loads all the code fragments into a collection. If the file name passed to the Connect method does not exist, then the method simply initializes the collection and saves the name of the file for writing later. Add the following code to the `Connect` method to access the file repository.

```
On Error GoTo ConnectErr

    'Variables
    Dim intFile As Integer
    Dim strCode As String

    m_FileName = FileName
    intFile = FreeFile

    'Open File
    Open FileName For Input As #intFile

      'Read in all code fragments
      Do While Not EOF(intFile)
        Line Input #intFile, strCode
        Fragments.Add _
          Left$(strCode, 9), _
          Right$(strCode, Len(strCode) - 9), _
          Left$(strCode, 9)
      Loop

    Close #intFile

  Exit Sub

ConnectErr:
    'We could get an error if the file does not exist
    If Fragments.Count > 0 Then
      MsgBox Err.Description
    End If
  Exit Sub
```

Step 12

When the `Library` object is terminated, we write all the code fragments back out to the file. We add this code to the `Terminate` event for the `Library` class. This event already has some code in it to destroy the associated `Fragments` collection, however, we will replace the existing code with the following code.

```
On Error GoTo TerminateErr
```

```
'Variables
Dim intFile As Integer
Dim strCode As String
Dim objFragment As Fragment

intFile = FreeFile

'Open File
Open m_FileName For Output As #intFile

  'Write out all code fragments
  For Each objFragment In Fragments
    'Get Code Fragment
    strCode = objFragment.Key & objFragment.Value

    'Write to file
    Print #intFile, strCode
  Next

Close #intFile

'Destroy the collection
Set mvarFragments = Nothing
Exit Sub


TerminateErr:
If Fragments.Count > 0 Then
    MsgBox Err.Description
  End If
  Exit Sub
```

CREATING THE CLIENT

Step 13

Now add a new Standard EXE project to the application by selecting **FILE/ADD PROJECT** from the menu. When the new project is added, right-click on it in the Project Explorer and pick **SET AS START UP** from the popup menu. Save the new project in the **\CLIENT** directory created earlier.

Step 14

In order to use the Library, set a reference in the client project. Select **PROJECT/REFERENCES** from the VB menu and set a reference to **Project1** from Project2.

Step 15

The user interface for the fragment repository consists of a TextBox, ListBox, and Command-Button. Figure 14-7 shows the complete interface. Use the Item list below to build set the design-time properties for the controls.

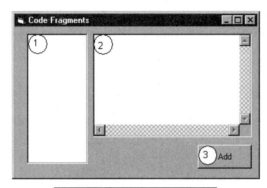

Figure 14-7 The Form Interface.

Item 1—ListBox

Name   lstFragments

Item 2—TextBox

Name   txtFragment

MultiLine   True

Scrollbars   3-Both

Text   <empty>

Item 3—CommandButton

Name   cmdAdd

Caption   Add

Step 16

Before we can use the objects in the model, we need to declare some variables. Add the following code to the [General][Declarations] section of Form1 to define the needed variables:

```
Private m_Library As Project1.Library
Private m_Fragment As Project1.Fragment
```

Step 17

When the form first loads, we create an instance of the Library class to open the repository file and initialize the objects model. Add the following code to the Form_Load event of Form1.

```
'Create a new library
Set m_Library = New Project1.Library
```

```
m_Library.Connect App.Path & "\fragments.txt"

'Fill List Box
For Each m_Fragment In m_Library.Fragments
  lstFragments.AddItem m_Fragment.Key
Next
```

Step 18

In order to add a code fragment to the model, the user types or pastes the code into the TextBox and presses the **Add** button. This creates a new `Fragment` object in the collection and saves the code. Add the following code to the Click event of `cmdAdd` to add a new fragment.

```
Dim strKey As String
strKey = "Item " & Format$(lstFragments.ListCount + 1, "0000")

'Add a new Fragment
Set m_Fragment = m_Library.Fragments.Add _
  (strKey, txtFragment.Text, strKey)

'Add to List
lstFragments.AddItem m_Fragment.Key
txtFragment.Text = ""
```

Step 19

Retrieving a code fragment is done by clicking on the `Fragment` key in the ListBox. The key is then used to access the associated `Fragment` object in the collection. Add the following code to the `lstFragments_Click` event to retrieve a code fragment.

```
'Show Code in TextBox
txtFragment.Text = _
m_Library.Fragments(lstFragments.List(lstFragments.ListIndex)).Value
```

Step 20

Save the project and run it. Try typing some code into the TextBox and pressing the **Add** button. Now try clicking on the `Fragment` key in the ListBox to retrieve the code fragment. Shut down the application by clicking on **ControlBox** and then restart to verify that the repository is working.

Exercise 14-3: Object Persistence

Object persistence allows us to create objects that remember their state even after the application is terminated. This exercise creates an ActiveX DLL that remembers the name of the last person to log into an application.

CREATING THE PERSISTENT OBJECT

Step 1

Using the File Explorer, create a new directory **VB BOOTCAMP\EXERCISE14-3**. Start a new ActiveX DLL project in Visual Basic.

Step 2

Select **Class1** from the Project Explorer and immediately change the class name to CLogin. In the Properties window, set the Persistable property to **1 – Persistable**. Changing the Persistable property will make the InitProperties, ReadProperties, and Write-Properties events available to this class.

Step 3

This class uses a simple property called UID to remember the user name of the last person to log in to the application. This name will then appear in the log in dialog when the application is next run. Create a UID property by selecting **TOOLS/ADD PROCEDURE** from the menu. Add a property procedure named UID.

Step 4

Add a Private data member to the [General][Declarations] section for the UID property and code the fundamental reading and writing functionality for the procedure. The following code shows the resulting code for implementing the property. Note that the Property Let procedure makes a call to the PropertyChanged method to notify the class that the property is dirty.

```
Private m_UID As String

Public Property Get UID() As String
   UID = m_UID
End Property

Public Property Let UID(ByVal strUID As String)
   m_UID = strUID

   'Calling This method will mark
   'the property as dirty
   PropertyChanged "UID"
End Property
```

Step 5

From the object box in the code window for CLogin, select **Class**. In the procedure box, add the events InitProperties, ReadProperties, and WriteProperties to the class definition.

Step 6

The `InitProperties` event will fire the first time the application is run and the `PropertyBag` is empty. In this event, we initialize the `UID` property to an empty string. Add the following code to the `InitProperties` event to initialize the property:

```
UID=""
```

Step 7

The `WriteProperties` event fires whenever the property is dirty and the instance is about to be destroyed. This event writes the value of the `UID` property to the `PropertyBag`. Add the following code to the `WriteProperties` event to save the `UID` property:

```
PropBag.WriteProperty "UID", UID, ""
```

Step 8

The `ReadProperties` event fires whenever a new instance of `CLogin` is created and the `ProprtyBag` has data in it. This will occur when the application is run each time after the first run. Add the following code to the `ReadProperties` event to read the contents of the `PropertyBag`:

```
UID = PropBag.ReadProperty("UID", "")
```

CREATING THE CLIENT

Step 9

Add a new Standard EXE project to the application by selecting **FILE/ADD PROJECT** from the menu. When the new project appears in the Project Explorer, right-click it and select **SET AS START UP** from the menu.

Step 10

Select **Project2** from the Project Explorer and open the references dialog by choosing **PROJECT/REFERENCES** from the menu. In the references dialog, set a reference to the ActiveX DLL in Project1.

Step 11

Figure 14-8 shows the log in screen for this exercise. Build this form using the Item list below to set design-time properties for the controls.

Item 1—Form

Name	frmLogIn
Caption	Log In
BorderStyle	3 - Fixed Dialog
ControlBox	False

Item 2—CommandButton

Name	cmdLogIn

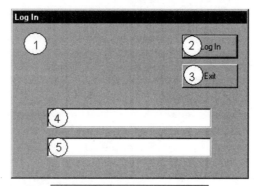

Figure 14-8 The Log In Screen.

Caption	Log In
Default	True

Item 3—CommandButton

Name	cmdExit
Caption	Exit
Cancel	True

Item 4—TextBox

Name	txtUID
Text	<empty>

Item 5—TextBox

Name	txtPassword
Text	<empty>
PasswordChar	*

Step 12

The front end needs to create both an instance of CLogin for the application and a PropertyBag object for reading and writing to disk. These instances are managed by private variables in the form. Add the following variables to the [General][Declarations] section of frmLogin.

```
Private m_Login As CLogin
Private m_PropertyBag As PropertyBag
```

Step 13

When the application starts, a new instance of CLogin is created. If a PropertyBag file exists, then the form reads it and sets properties for the object. If the PropertyBag does not exist, then a new instance of CLogin is created with default property settings. Add the following code to the Form_load event of frmLogIn to create a new instance of CLogin:

```
On Error GoTo LoadErr

   'Depersist Object
   Dim vContents As Variant
   Dim bytObject() As Byte

   ' Instantiate the PropertyBag
   Set m_PropertyBag = New PropertyBag

   'Read the file contents into a Variant.
   Open App.Path & "\Login.dat" For Binary As #1
     Get #1, , vContents
   Close #1

   'Assign the Variant to a Byte array.
   bytObject = vContents

   'Assign to the PropertyBag Contents property.
   m_PropertyBag.Contents = bytObject

   ' Instantiate the object from the PropertyBag
   Set m_Login = m_PropertyBag.ReadProperty("Login")

   'Put UID in TextBox
   txtUID.Text = m_Login.UID

   Exit Sub

LoadErr:
   'Any errors result in a new instance
   Set m_Login = New CLogin
   Exit Sub
```

Step 14

When the **Log In** button is pushed, this application sets the UID property of the CLogin instance. This will cause the instance to be marked as dirty so the ReadProperties and WriteProperties events will fire. Add the following code to the Click event of cmdLogIn to set the property:

```
m_Login.UID = txtUID.Text
MsgBox "Thanks for the log in!", vbOKOnly + vbInformation, "Log In"
```

Step 15

When the form exits, it destroys the instance of CLogin. In order to save the properties, they are written to a Binary file using the client's PropertyBag. Add the following code to the click event of the cmdExit button to write the instance to disk:

```
'Instance the Property Bag
Set m_PropertyBag = New PropertyBag

'Write the Class to the Bag
m_PropertyBag.WriteProperty "Login", m_Login

'Write the Bag to a file
Dim vContents As Variant
vContents = m_PropertyBag.Contents

Open App.Path & "\Login.dat" For Binary As #1
  Put #1, , vContents
Close #1

Set m_Login = Nothing
End
```

Step 16

Save the work and run the project. Enter your name in the **UID TextBox**. Type into the **Password** box and it will show asterisks, but it does not do anything in this exercise. Push the **Log In** button and then end the application by pushing the **Exit** button. Rerun the application and verify your name appears in the log in screen.

FOR THE CERTIFIED PRO

Pro 14-1: The following specification describes an object model to represent a group of students in a classroom.

1. Build an object model with Students as the top level object; it manages all of the Student instances. Student is a dependent object, and may not be instantiated directly by the object user. The goal is to get each Student instance to talk.

2. Create a Student class that has a Name property and a Talk method. The response of the Talk method on a Student named Gary should be My name is Gary. This object will be a dependent object, and should not be available to be instanced from the form with the New keyword. After a variable on the form has a reference to a Student instance, the code on the form must not be allowed to change the value of the Name property.

3. Create a `Students` collection class. This class should have the same property and methods of a VB Collection object. However, the `Add` method will need to accept an argument containing the student's name that is to be created.

4. Make a form with a CommandButton that can use the `Students` collection class to create a `Student` instance, based on a name typed into a TextBox. Use another CommandButton to invoke the `Talk` method on the `Student` instance for the Student whose name is in the TextBox, and present the message on the screen. Create the form in such a way as to allow for the creation of any number of students, and the `Talk` method is invoked only on the Student whose name is currently in the TextBox.

Preparing for Certification

Topics for Further Reading
  Organizing Objects: The Object Model
  Providing Polymorphism by Implementing Interfaces
  Persisting a Component's Data

Certification Quiz

1. Polymorphism in VB is best defined as:
   a. deriving one class from another through inheritance
   b. classes with similar properties but different types
   c. the default interface of a class
   d. classes with the same methods, but different functions

2. Abstract classes in VB:
   a. cannot be created
   b. have properties, but no methods
   c. have members, but no code
   d. have code, but no members

3. When a class implements an interface, it:
   a. must include every member of the interface
   b. can use all of the code in the interface parent
   c. becomes an abstract class
   d. no longer has a default interface

4. Interfaces have which of the following advantages?
   a. They allow early binding.
   b. They allow reuse.
   c. They support guaranteed callback methods.
   d. They help enforce standard coding practices.

5. An object model:
   a.   shows object names
   b.   shows object relationships
   c.   shows object members
   d.   shows object size

6. Dependent objects are created by setting the `Instancing` property to:
   a.   `Public, Not Creatable`
   b.   `Private`
   c.   `GlobalMultiUse`
   d.   `MultiUse`

7. Free-standing objects are created by setting the `Instancing` property to:
   a.   `Public, Not Creatable`
   b.   `Private`
   c.   `GlobalMultiUse`
   d.   `MultiUse`

8. In order to support the [_NewEnum] interface, a custom collection must:
   a.   set Instancing to Public, Not Creatable
   b.   set the ProcedureID to –4
   c.   create a custom NewEnum property
   d.   hide the NewEnum member

9. The `PropertyBag` can store what kind of data?
   a.   String
   b.   Object
   c.   Variant
   d.   Any data type

10. Which events are added when the `Persistable` property is set to 1 – Persistable?
   a.   `Initialize`
   b.   `InitProperties`
   c.   `ReadProperties`
   d.   `WriteProperties`

ANSWERS TO CERTIFICATION QUIZ

   1.   d
   2.   c
   3.   a
   4.   a, b, c, d
   5.   a, b
   6.   a
   7.   d
   8.   b, c, d
   9.   d
   10.   b, c, d

15

DATA BOUND AND REMOTE CLASSES

T hose who begin this chapter, should have a complete understanding of ActiveX components including ActiveX DLL and ActiveX EXE design and construction. This chapter describes how to use these components to create application partitions that permit creation of distributed applications with DCOM.

SKILLS COVERED

- 70-176 (22): Register and unregister a COM component
- 70-175 (2): Assess the potential impact of the logical design on performance, maintainability, extensibility, scalability, availability, and security
- 70-175 (3): Design Visual Basic components to access data from a database in a multi-tier application
- 70-175 (32): Register and unregister a COM component

- 70-175 (50): Use the Package and Deployment Wizard to create a setup program that installs a distributed application, registers COM components, and allows for uninstall
- 70-175 (51): Register a component that implements DCOM
- 70-175 (52): Configure DCOM on a client computer and on a server computer
- 70-175 (53): Plan and implement floppy disk-based deployment or compact disk deployment for a distributed application
- 70-175 (55): Plan and implement network-based deployment for a distributed application
- 70-175 (58): Deploy application updates for distributed applications

We have said from the very beginning of this book that Visual Basic is built from the ground up to create distributed applications. Put simply, a distributed application is one in which different components execute on different machines yet work in concert to create a complete application. Fundamental to the idea of distributing applications is the notion of *partitioning*. This refers to the design of distributed components that provides separation and reuse. In many ways partitioning can be thought of as encapsulation at the ActiveX EXE level. Instead of simply encapsulating the members of a class, we will encapsulate several classes in a component.

In the previous chapter we started the process of partitioning by creating custom object models. In a distributed application, these types of object models represent the fundamental unit of distribution. However, just creating and distributing object models is not enough to achieve a truly partitioned application design. Partitioning requires a mechanism for exchanging data between components that allows for easy substitution of components within the distributed application.

We can step back from the technology for a moment and discuss an imaginary business entity which performs medical laboratory analysis for several hospitals. Our imaginary business receives medical samples through the mail via overnight delivery, performs analysis on the samples, and returns results through the same overnight delivery service. In many ways, the relationship of the hospital to the laboratory mirrors the relationships of components in a distributed application.

We can think of both the hospital and the laboratory as ActiveX components running on different machines. This is a nice parallel because the hospital and the laboratory are physically separated from each other. The hospital and laboratory are also encapsulated entities: they each perform a specialized function somewhat independent of the other. The hospital specializes in patient care while the laboratory specializes in analysis. Therefore, the hospital looks like a black box to the laboratory and the lab looks like a black box to the hospital. The hospital simply sees the lab as a unit that receives work and outputs data. The laboratory sees the hospital as a client requesting services.

As far as the relationship between the two entities is concerned, we could easily model each one using the object model skills covered in previous chapters. However, that alone would not create a true application partition. The critical piece required for partitioning is actually provided by the package delivery service, which contains the information passed between the two entities. In one direction, the package contains a sample. In the other direction, it contains data. However, none of the people at the package delivery service actually care what is in the package. They deliver the package based on the address without regard for the nature of the data contained within. It is not until the package is opened by the recipient that the data actually become meaningful.

The key to creating any partitioned application is to create a standard *package* that carries data between the distributed components. Because this package is standardized, it is independent of the component receiving the data. So, for example, the hospital could easily choose to change the provider of laboratory services and still keep the same package delivery service. This eases the process of change resulting in simpler maintenance of the overall system.

Visual Basic provides a number of ways to create standardized packages that contain data. In the simplest form, a delimited string could be used to transfer data between components. In the most complex form, disconnected ADO Recordsets or even custom objects could be used to transfer data. The key is that the package must be standardized. This chapter presents a number of Visual Basic technologies that lend themselves to creating partitions. We will examine the technologies in detail and then later we will create truly distributed applications.

DATA BINDING BEHAVIOR

Data binding technology has come a long way since the first Data Control. In fact, binding has matured to the point where it can be considered for serious development. Chief among the improvements in data binding is the support for binding provided by class modules. Through the `DataBindingBehavior` property, classes have the ability to bind to data. A bound class can become an excellent mechanism for transferring data between application partitions.

Class modules support two different styles of data binding based on the `DataBinding-Behavior` property setting. Setting the property to `vbSimpleBound` allows a property from a class to bind directly to a field in a recordset. This means that as a recordset is navigated, the properties of the associated class change automatically without writing any code. Classes can also be bound to an entire recordset by setting the `DataBindingBehavior` property to `vbComplexBound`. Complex-bound classes directly access the recordset and completely encapsulate data access. Both simple and complex binding can enhance application partitioning and encapsulation.

To create a simple-bound class module, set the `DataBindingBehavior` property and construct the properties of the class to be bound. Building a bound class is almost the same as building a normal class module. The only difference is that the code to update the properties of the class need not be written since the data binding takes care of that.

Once the class is written, the underlying data source must be assocsiated with the properties of the class module. This association is done through the `BindingCollection` object. The `Binding` collection is the glue that connects a data source to a property. In order to associate a data field with a property there must be an instance of the data source, the class, and the Binding Collection. When the three instances have been created, the `Add` method of the `BindingCollection` is called to complete the association.

As an example, imagine an ADO `Recordset` object named `objRecordset` to be bound to a class named `MyClass`. Since this is simple binding, tell the `BindingCollection` object the name of the field in the recordset and the name of the property in the class to bind.

If the field name is `Book Title` and the class property is `Title`, then the following code will bind the data and the property:

```
Dim objBind As New MSBind.BindingCollection
Set objBind.DataSource = objRecordset

objBind.Add MyClass, "Title", "Book Title"
```

Once the data field and the class property are bound, the value of the class property changes automatically whenever the underlying data set is navigated. The navigation of the data can occur with standard methods such as `MoveFirst`, `MoveLast`, `MoveNext`, and `MovePrevious`. When these methods of the recordset are called, the property changes to follow suit. The recordset can also be updated when the client changes the property value of the class directly. This occurs by having the class call the `PropertyChanged` method from its `Property Let` procedure. Calling the `PropertyChanged` method of a bound class notifies the underlying data set that it should update to reflect the new value set into the class. The `PropertyChanged` method becomes a member of any class where the `DataBinding-Behavior` property is set to `vbSimpleBound`.

Simple binding is a good technique to use when the underlying class data is a fixed set of fields. However, if the class is capable of using more than one set of data, complex binding is more suitable. Complex binding allows a class to use any number of recordsets from a calling client. Complex-bound classes are created by setting the `DataBindingBehavior` to `vbComplexBound`. When the class is designated as complex bound, Visual Basic adds a `DataSource` and `DataMember` property to the class. These properties appear as property procedures in the [General] [Declarations] section of the class. In many ways, a complex bound class behaves like a grid control. The user simply specifies the `DataSource` and `DataMember` while the class manages all the data. The following code shows the procedures added to the class when it is designated as complex bound:

```
Public Property Get DataSource() As DataSource

End Property


Public Property Set DataSource(ByVal objDataSource As DataSource)

End Property


Public Property Get DataMember() As DataMember

End Property


Public Property Let DataMember(ByVal DataMember As DataMember)

End Property
```

The `DataSource` and `DataMember` properties will accept as arguments any object that implements the `DataSource` or `DataMember` interface as appropriate. The `DataSource` interface is supported by ADO `Connection` objects and custom data sources. The `DataMember` is typically a string that represents an SQL statement or possibly a custom query object for a custom source. Custom sources are covered in the next section, so for this discussion, we will limit the `DataSource` to an ADO `Connection` object and the `DataMember` to an SQL statement.

Once the property procedures are added to the class, set the values from an external client and use Private variables internally to manage them. The class then has an ADO `Connection` and an SQL statement so it can generate an ADO `Recordset` internally. This recordset can then be used for any purpose, but will usually be presented to external clients through a collection of properties. Since the class does not know at the outset what SQL statement will be sent to the `DataMember` property, hard-coded properties cannot be designed for the class, a pseudo collection can be created that reads from the fields of the resulting recordset. The following code shows how an ADO `Recordset` named `objRecordset` might be exposed by a complex bound class:

```
Public Function Properties (strPropertyName As String) As Variant
    Properties = objRecordset.Fields(strPropertyName).Value
End Function
```

The `Properties` collection ends up simply wrapping the `Fields` collection of the record-set. Why wrap the recordset in the class instead of simply dealing with the recordset directly? The primary reason is because a class module can implement custom interfaces needed by the application. This makes it possible to partition the application and use a custom class to transfer data between application partitions. For example, the organization may define an interface named `ICarryData`. Any class that implements `ICarryData` can be sent as an argument or return value from clients in the application. Since clients demand an object with this interface, you cannot simply send a client a recordset instead, a complex-bound class that wraps the recordset and provides the interface must be sent.

DATA SOURCE BEHAVIOR

Along with having the ability to behave as a data consumer, class modules can also function as custom data sources for providing access to any type of data—not simply a relational database. Creating a custom data source is done by setting the `DataSourceBehavior` property of a public class to `1-vbDataSource`. Setting this property adds the event `GetDataMember` to the class module and allows the class to be passed as an argument wherever a `DataSource` argument is required.

As an example of creating a custom data source, we will build a data source that can be used to find all the available printers on the network. The data source begins by creating a new ActiveX DLL project and setting the `DataSourceBehavior` property to `1-vbData-Source`. Although the class module provides the `DataSource` interface, it is still necessary to create a way to manage the data information within the class. This is typically accomplished through the use of a disconnected ADO `Recordset` object. In the `Initialize` event of the class module, we can create a standalone recordset and fill it with the data required. The following code shows how to create an ADO `Recordset` object and fill it with the names of the available printers:

```
'Create a new recordset
Set m_Recordset = New ADODB.Recordset
m_Recordset.Fields.Append "DeviceName", adBSTR, 255
m_Recordset.Open

'Populate the Recordset
Dim objPrinter As Printer

For Each objPrinter In Printers
  m_Recordset.AddNew
  m_Recordset!DeviceName = objPrinter.DeviceName
  m_Recordset.Update
Next


m_Recordset.MoveFirst
```

Note how the above code creates an ADO `Recordset` object out of thin air. It does not require a database connection, just an instance. Of course, when the recordset is created this way, it has no data in it. In fact, it has no structure either. The fields that will make up the recordset as well as populate it with data must be defined. The `Append` method of the `Fields` collection makes it possible to add new field definitions to the recordset and to make them one of many available data types. ADO supports intrinsic constants for all recognized data types. In our case, we simply used a string of 255 characters.

Once defined, data is added to the recordset in the usual way via the `AddNew` method. In our example, we simply loop through all of the available printers and populate the recordset. Once the data are contained within a private recordset, we are ready to expose it through the custom data source.

Exposing the data is the work of the `GetDataMember` event. This event is called whenever a client tries to bind to the custom data source using the `BindingCollection` object. Two arguments are passed into the event. The first is the `DataMember` argument, which is a string. This argument is the query the client wants to run. This might be an SQL statement or a definable custom query statement. The second argument is a `By Reference` argument called `Data`. In the `GetDataMember` event, the query is received via the `DataMember` argument and a reference returned to the underlying data source by setting the `Data` argument. For our simple example, we only recognize one query—`"SELECT * FROM Printers"`. The following code shows how to detect this query and return the recordset we built earlier:

```
Private Sub Class_GetDataMember_
        (DataMember As String, Data As Object)
```

```
If DataMember = "SELECT * FROM Printers" Then
  Set Data = m_Recordset
End If

End Sub
```

The logic in this event could be expanded to accept many different and more complex queries. Because the decision to return data is completely under your control. You could build your own query language that allows you to ask for printers available by domain or machine name for example. Remember that when building any query language that Visual Basic is case sensitive in text comparisions by default. Therefore, the Option Compare Text may be a desirable feature in the class module.

Since a recordset will likely contain more than one piece of data, navigation methods should be provided for the data source. These can be the classic MoveFirst, MoveNext, MoveLast, and MovePrevious methods. The following code shows the MoveNext method for our sample data source:

```
Public Sub MoveNext()
  m_Recordset.MoveNext
  If m_Recordset.EOF Then m_Recordset.MoveLast
End Sub
```

Once the data source is complete, clients may use it through the BindingCollection object, which takes the DataMember and DataSources as properties and then binds them to a client. The client may be a display device like a TextBox or another class module functioning as a bound client. In the case of an attempt to partition the application, the data source is normally contained within a class module as we have described. The following code shows how the data source might be bound to the "Name" property of a client class instance called MyPrinter.

```
m_BindCollection.DataMember = "SELECT * FROM Printers"
Set m_BindCollection.DataSource = m_DataSource
m_BindCollection.Add MyPrinter, "Name", "DeviceName"
```

CREATING DISTRIBUTED SETUPS

Creating distributed applications begins with a strong component-based design and the creation of object models. However, the key to communication between distributed components is the ability to create an instance of a remote object on a client machine. This process is commonly referred to as *remoting*. Visual Basic offers several mechanisms for creating remote instances within code, though all the mechanisms use the Distributed Component Object Model (DCOM).

DCOM is a technology that has received a lot of press and we work with many clients who are using it in one form or another to build distributed applications. However, many Visual

Basic programmers are still mystified by the technology so we will provide a brief explanation here along with the fundamentals necessary to create a remote instance using Visual Basic.

DCOM is a distributed version of COM technology. This book has spent considerable time examining the implementation of COM in the VB environment, and it is essentially the backbone of all our applications. The key to understanding COM and DCOM is to understand that these technologies rely completely on entries made within the operating system registry to locate and create instances of classes. Whether a local or a remote instance is required, there must be at least minimum entries present in the system registry.

The key entries for any object begin under the HKEY_CLASSES_ROOT key of the registry. Examine this key by running any of the several available registry editing tools on the system. The two common editors are REGEDIT and REGEDT32. Both these utilities make it possible to examine the entries in the system registry. Examine the HKEY_CLASSES_ROOT key to find an alphabetical listing of all of the COM objects registered for use on the system. These objects are listed using an English-name identifier called the *Programmatic Identifier* or ProgID. For Visual Basic projects, the ProgID is simply the name of the VB project followed by the name of the class module (e. g., Project1.Class1). Visual Basic uses ProgID names in code to create instances. This is the argument provided when an instance is created using the New keyword.

English names work well for humans, however, computers hate them. One reason is because they have no guarantee of uniqueness. Nothing prevents many programmers from all creating ActiveX DLLs with ProgIDs of Project1.Class1. To solve the problem of unique naming, each component in the registry is assigned a unique number known as a globally-unique identifier (GUID). This number is used by the COM subsystem to identify and create an instance of any particular class. The GUID associated with any ProgID if found directly beneath it in the registry. This GUID is commonly referred to as the class identifier or CLSID (Figure 15-1).

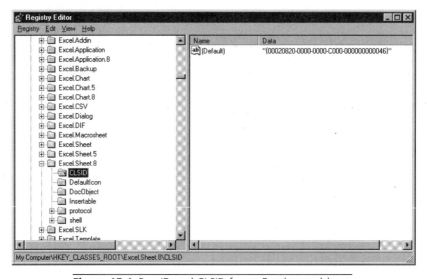

Figure 15-1 ProgID and CLSID for an Excel spreadsheet.

Many Visual Basic programmers are well aware of the use of ProgIDs and CLSIDs to create instances. They are less knowledgeable about how this system is used to create remote instances. Imagine an object used to programmatically create E-Mail. For this discussion, the ProgID of the object will be `VBMail.Connector`. This object does not reside locally on the machine, but is installed on a Windows/NT server machine on the network. This object would be useful in an application being created to send E-Mail whenever a fatal error occurs in the application. How can the application create an instance of the `VBMail.Connector` object and instruct it to send mail reporting a fatal error condition?

Perhaps the simplest way to create a remote instance is through the `CreateObject` function, which takes two arguments. The first is the ProgID of the object to be instantiated and the second is the name of the computer where the object is located. Thus, to create a remote instance of the `VBMail.Connector` object on a server called `Server1`, the following code would accomplish the task:

```
Dim MyObject As Object
Set MyObject = CreateObject("VBMail.Connector","Server1")
```

At first glance, it appears as though the above code will run from any client machine with network access to the machine `Server1`. However, DCOM always requires an entry of some sort on the client machine before a remote instance can be created. Therefore, the client machine must have at least an entry for the ProgID and CLSID before the above code will run. We discuss later how to create setups that ensure these registry entries are made, but for now simply recognize that the `CreateObject` function alone is not enough to create the remote instance.

In most cases, installing registry entries on the client machine to permit remote instances will result in more entries than simply the ProgID and CLSID. Although many other entries may be associated with a remote object, the most important of these is the `RemoteServerName` entry, which is placed in the registry by the client setup program. When this entry is present, the client machine can create a remote instance of the object without providing the machine name argument in `CreateObject`. Similarly, a client can also use the `New` keyword to create an instance. Thus the following lines of code will create a remote instance if the `VBMail.Connector` object has a registry entry for `RemoteServerName`:

```
Dim MyObject As VBMail.Connector
Set MyObject = New VBMail.Connector
```

The advantage of using the `New` keyword syntax above is that it is early bound. Because the client machine has the registry entries in place, Visual Basic can early bind to the component which is more efficient and less error prone. The drawback of the above code, however, is that the registry entries for the remote component are much more extensive as this is necessary to support the early binding. Again, the process of making these entries is handled during the setup which we cover next. The key is to understand that at a minimum the ProgID, CLSID, and `RemoteServerName` are required if the `CreateObject` method is not used with the machine name provided.

On the other hand, one of the advantages of the `CreateObject` syntax is lack of hardwiring to a particular machine. Imagine that many users are actively trying to create instances of the VBMail.Connector object. The total load on the Server1 machine could be eased by providing the exact same object on a machine name Server2. In this case, client software could search for the machine with the lowest traffic and create the remote instance there. Thus, the primary advantage of the CreateObject function is that it allows manual load balancing of the distributed application. When the RemoteServerName entry is used in the registry, only one machine can be used.

Once the components for the application are designed and the components to distribute are chosen, setup routines will have to be created that install the components on the desired machines. Generally, the Packaging and Distribution Wizard can easily create setups for the distributed components with no special effort by the programmer. The trick in setting up a distributed application is to build the client setup. It is, after all, the client software that must have the key registry settings before remote instances can be created.

The client setup begins when the distributed component is being created. It is the distributed component that has the detailed knowledge of the registry entries the client will require. The component can be made to provide these registry entries in what is known as a VBR file, which is essentially a macro capable of making client registry entries. To cause a component to generate a VBR file, open the project properties dialog and select the **Component** tab. On the tab, check the option **Remote Server Files**. If this option is checked, the component will build a VBR file when it is compiled.

Once the VBR file is made, create the client application and reference this file. In normal setups where an ActiveX component is installed, the Packaging and Distribution Wizard will attempt to distribute the actual ActiveX component. However, when a distributed setup is creatd, the VBR file acts as a surrogate for the component. Figure 15-2 shows the Included Files step in the Package and Deployment Wizard. In this step, the reference to the distributed ActiveX EXE is unchecked and the VBR file is added manually.

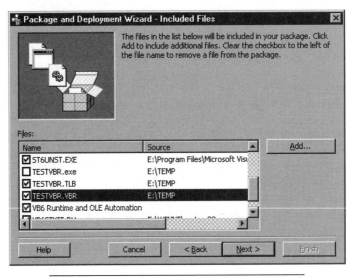

Figure 15-2 The Package and Deployment Wizard.

When a VBR file is added to the setup, the Wizard prompts to specify information about the remote component. Most of the information is provided from the VBR file, though it is usually necessary to specify the name of the machine where the component will reside (Figure 15-3). This ensures a `RemoteServerName` entry will be made on the client machine during installation.

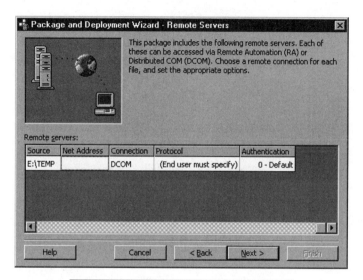

Figure 15-3 Remote Component Attributes.

After the setups are completed, the software for the client and distributed components can be installed as appropriate. There is one last concern even after the components are installed. Whenever a remote call is made to an object, the network security features of Windows/NT can prevent successful instancing unless the calling client has permission to call the remote object. Permissions for DCOM calls are managed through the DCOM configuration utility (Figure 15-4), which is run by typing **DCOMCNFG** at the command line. DCOMCNFG makes it possible to establish permissions on an object so it can be called remotely. In this utility, set the users and services that have permission to create and use the object.

Components can be installed using the Package and Deployment Wizard, though it will occasionally be useful to deploy components by hand. Deploying a component is a matter of copying the ActiveX DLL or ActiveX EXE to the target computer and registering the component directly from the command line in the operating system. To register an ActiveX EXE, run the component from the command line. Since the component is an EXE, it will start and run. Visual Basic ActiveX EXE components automatically make registry entries when run from the command line. Unregistering the component is accomplished by running the EXE from the command line with the /UNREGSERVER flag. For example, the following code unregisters an EXE named MYCOMPONENT.EXE:

```
MYCOMPONENT.EXE /UNREGSERVER
```

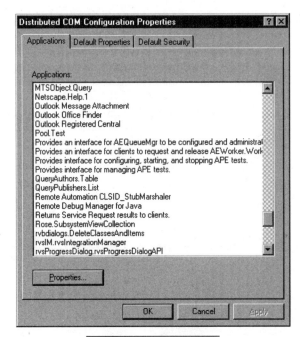

Figure 15-4 DCOMCNFG.

Because ActiveX DLL components cannot run on their own and instead require a host process, they cannot simply be registered by execution. Visual Basic provides a utility specifically to register and unregister ActiveX DLL components called REGSVR32.EXE. To register a component simply run the utility and provide the target DLL as an argument. To remove the component from the registry, run the REGSVR32 utility with the /u flag. The following code shows how to register and unregister a DLL named MYCOMPONENT.DLL.

```
REGSVR32.EXE MYCOMPONENT.DLL
REGSVR32.EXE /U MYCOMPONENT.DLL
```

Exercise 15-1: Simple Data Binding

Data Binding makes it possible to use class modules to wrap data access without writing the code to manipulate the properties. This exercise uses simple data binding to display data from the pubs database. It requires SQL Server to complete.

SETTING UP THE DATA LINK

Step 1

Before using data binding, set up a Data Link file for use. In this exercise, we will be interacting with the Microsoft SQL Server database "pubs." Establishing the data link is not a Visual Basic function, but rather a Windows Operating System function. If a Data Link file has been established for the pubs database, skip this section. Otherwise, start the Windows File Explorer.

Step 2

Data Links can be defined anywhere on the computer; they are commonly kept in the directory \PROGRAM FILES\COMMON FILES\SYSTEM\OLE DB\DATA LINKS. Locate this directory in the File Explorer.

Step 3

Select the **DATA LINKS** folder in the left-hand pane and choose **FILE/NEW/MICROSOFT DATA LINK FILE** from the menu. After the menu is selected, notice that a new Data Link file has been created. Edit the name of the file to `PUBS.UDL`.

Step 4

Right-click **PUBS.UDL** and select **PROPERTIES...** from the popup menu. This dialog is the information required by the OLEDB provider is specified. In the Provider tab choose **Microsoft OLEDB Provider for SQL Server**. Push the **Next** button.

Step 5

In the Connection tab, set the server name to the name of the machine with the SQL Server installation. If the installation is on the same machine as the project, simply enter **(local)** as the name. Set the user ID and password for access and set the database name as "pubs."

Step 6

Test the new connection by pressing the **Test Connection** button. When the connection tests satisfactorily, press the **OK** button.

CREATING THE BOUND CLASS

Step 7

Using the Windows File Explorer, create a new directory **VB BOOTCAMP\EXERCISE15-1**. Start a new Standard EXE project in Visual Basic.

Step 8

This example will bind a class to an ADO `Recordset` object. In order to accomplish the bind, set a reference to both ADO and the `BindingCollection` object. Set these references by selecting **PROJECT/REFERENCES** from the menu. In the references dialog, set a reference to **Microsoft ActiveX Data Objects 2.0 Library** and **Microsoft Data Binding Collection**. Press the **OK** button.

Step 9

Add a new class to the project by selecting **PROJECT/ADD CLASS MODULE** from the menu. In the Properties window for the new class, set the `DataBindingBehavior` property to **vbSimpleBound**. Also change the name of the class module to **Publishers**.

Step 10

To make a bound class, you must create instances of the data source, the class module, and the BindingCollection. While declaring variables, create one for the data-bound property Name. In the [General][Declarations] section of the class, declare variables for the data source and BindingCollection as follows:

```
'Data Binding/Source
Private m_Recordset As ADODB.Recordset
Private m_BindCollection As MSBind.BindingCollection


'Data members
Private m_Name As String
```

Step 11

Creating the properties for binding is done in the standard way through the use of property procedures. A property procedure is normally created for each property to be bound. In this example, create a Name property to bind to the recordset. Add this property as a property procedure as follows:

```
Public Property Get Name() As String
   Name = m_Name
End Property


Public Property Let Name(ByVal strName As String)
   m_Name = strName
End Property
```

Step 12

Although it is technically possible to use the BindingCollection from anywhere in the project, the best way to bind the class is to create the Recordset in the Initialize event of the class. In this way, the underlying data source can be hidden from the client. In this exercise, we enhance the binding by using a disconnected recordset. The recordset is created in the Initialize event and sent back to the database in the Terminate event. Add the following code to the Initialize event of the class:

```
'Create Disconnected Recordset
Set m_Recordset = New ADODB.Recordset
m_Recordset.CursorLocation = adUseClient
m_Recordset.CursorType = adOpenStatic
m_Recordset.LockType = adLockBatchOptimistic
m_Recordset.Source = "SELECT * FROM Publishers"
m_Recordset.Open _
       ActiveConnection:="File Name=<Your Data Link Path>\pubs.udl"
```

```
'Bind Properties to the Recordset
Set m_BindCollection = New MSBind.BindingCollection
Set m_BindCollection.DataSource = m_Recordset
m_BindCollection.Add Me, "Name", "Pub_Name"
```

Step 13

Updating the batch is done with a single method call in the `Terminate` event of the class. Add the following code to the `Terminate` event to call the `UpdateBatch` method:

```
m_Recordset.UpdateBatch
```

Step 14

Although we have used standard techniques for creating the disconnected recordset and performing a batch update, it is still not clear exactly how the data goes from the recordset to the property or how property changes made by a client are reflected in the underlying recordset. Reflecting the underlying recordset happens automatically and essentially requires no work; notifying the underlying recordset that an external client has changed the data requires action. The underlying recordset receives notification of external changes through the `Property-Changed` method, which should be called any time the external client changes the data. The simplest way to accomplish this is to place the method call in the `Property Let` procedure. Add the following code as the first line of the `Property Let Name` procedure:

```
PropertyChanged "Name"
```

Step 15

The only functionality left to code for the class module is the navigation control. Navigating the class is done through custom methods. These can be named anything, so we use the standard `MovePrevious` and `MoveNext` methods. Add the following code to the class module to manipulate the underlying recordset within the class:

```
Public Sub MoveNext()
  m_Recordset.MoveNext
  If m_Recordset.EOF Then m_Recordset.MoveLast
End Sub

Public Sub MovePrevious()
  m_Recordset.MovePrevious
  If m_Recordset.BOF Then m_Recordset.MoveFirst
End Sub
```

CREATING THE CLIENT

Step 16

Save the work and open Form1 to build the client. Figure15-5 shows the user interface for this exercise. Use the Item list below to set the properties for the controls at design time.

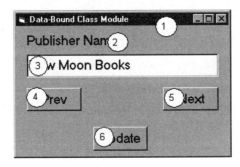

Figure 15-5 The Form Interface.

Item 1—Form

Name   frmPublisher

Caption   Data-Bound Class Module

Item 2—Label

Name   lblPublisher

Caption   Publisher Name

Item 3—TextBox

Name   txtPublisher

Item 4—CommandButton

Name   cmdPrev

Caption   Prev

Item 5—CommandButton

Name   cmdNext

Caption   Next

Item 6—CommandButton

Name   cmdUpdate

Caption   Update

Step 17

Since the class module encapsulates all data access, the client can simply create an instance of the Publishers class to access the data. This significantly simplifies the data management for the calling client. Add the following variable declaration to the [General][Declarations] section of Form1:

```
Private m_Publishers As Publishers
```

Step 18

The new instance is created when the form loads. Add the following code to the `Form_Load` event to create the instance and then reflect the `Name` property of the class in the TextBox:

```
'Create new instance
Set m_Publishers = New Publishers
txtPublisher.Text = m_Publishers.Name
```

Step 19

The Prev and Next buttons perform navigation by calling methods of the class. Add code to the click events of `cmdPrev` and `cmdNext` so that the final code appears as follows:

```
Private Sub cmdNext_Click()
  m_Publishers.MoveNext
  txtPublisher.Text = m_Publishers.Name
End Sub


Private Sub cmdPrev_Click()
  m_Publishers.MovePrevious
  txtPublisher.Text = m_Publishers.Name
End Sub
```

Step 20

The last thing the client must do is make changes to the data. All the client needs to do is change the value of the property. The data binding takes care of the rest. Add the following code to the click event of `cmdUpdate` to change a value:

```
m_Publishers.Name = txtPublisher.Text
```

Step 21

Save the work and run the project. Navigate the recordset. Then try making a change and ending the application by clicking the **ControlBox**.

Exercise 15-2: Creating a Custom Data Source

Visual Basic makes it possible to create data sources that expose almost any kind of data. Data sources created through class modules can be bound to clients with the `Binding-Collection` object. This exercise creates a simple data source to expose all of the available fonts.

CREATING THE DATA SOURCE

Step 1

Using the Windows File Explorer, create a new directory **VB BOOTCAMP\EXERCISE15-2** Start a new ActiveX DLL project in Visual Basic. Change the name of this project to

FontSource by selecting **PROJECT/PROPERTIES** from the menu. Type the new project name into the General tab and close the dialog.

Step 2

Change the name of the default Class1 to **Provider**. Set the DataSourceBehavior of the class to **1 – vbDataSource**. This will make the GetDataMember event available in procedure box of the Code window.

Step 3

This example uses a standalone ADO recordset to contain the source data; it will be necessary to set a reference to ADO. Set this reference by selecting **PROJECT/REFERENCES** from the menu. In the references dialog, set a reference to **Microsoft ActiveX Data Objects 2.0 Library**. Press the **OK** button.

Step 4

In order to create the ADO recordset and fill it with font information, we use a private variable. Add the following code to the [General][Declarations] section to declare the recordset variable:

```
Private m_Recordset As ADODB.Recordset
```

Step 5

The recordset is created and filled with data when the class is initialized. We can create the recordset by simply using the New keyword to generate an instance. After the instance is created, the Append method is used to add a new field to the Fields collection. Finally, the AddNew method is used to populate the recordset. Add the following code to the Initialize event of the class to create the recordset:

```
'In this event, the provider builds a
'data set by creating an ADODB recordset
'full of the appropriate data

'Create a new recordset
Set m_Recordset = New ADODB.Recordset
m_Recordset.Fields.Append "FontName", adBSTR, 255
m_Recordset.Open

'Populate the Recordset
Dim i As Integer

For i = 0 To Screen.FontCount - 1
  m_Recordset.AddNew
  m_Recordset!FontName = Screen.Fonts(i)
  m_Recordset.Update
Next
```

```
m_Recordset.MoveFirst
```

Step 6

External clients send queries to the data source and retrieve data via the `GetDataMember` event. This event is available in the procedure list for the Class object. Add this event to the Code window. In this event, we will be checking the `DataMember` argument to see what query was passed in. This data source only recognizes one query: `"SELECT * FROM FONTS"`. We could accept more complex queries and build a new recordset based on the query passed in. However, the job of this data source is relatively simple. Add the following code to the `Get-DataMember` event to receive the query and return data. Note that the query must be in all capital letters since we use the `UCase$` function. Add the Option Compare Text statement could be added to the [General][Declarations] section to force case-insensitive text coparisons.

```
If UCase$(DataMember) = "SELECT * FROM FONTS" Then
   Set Data = m_Recordset
End If
```

Step 7

The data source is navigated via two Public methods: `MovePrevious` and `MoveNext`. Add these methods as Public subroutines using the procedure dialog box by selecting **TOOLS/ADD PROCEDURE** from the menu. In these routines, add code to navigate the ADO recordset object. The final code for the methods appears as follows:

```
Public Sub MoveNext()
   m_Recordset.MoveNext
   If m_Recordset.EOF Then m_Recordset.MoveLast
End Sub


Public Sub MovePrevious()
   m_Recordset.MovePrevious
   If m_Recordset.BOF Then m_Recordset.MoveFirst
End Sub
```

CREATING THE DATA CLIENT

Step 8

Add a new Standard EXE project to the application by selecting **FILE/ADD PROJECT** from the menu. Immediately right-click on the new project in the Project Explorer and select **SET AS START UP** from the menu.

Step 9

Open the References dialog for Project2 by selecting **PROJECT/REFERENCES** from the menu. In the References dialog, set a reference to the data source in the `FontSource` project and set a reference to the Binding Collection object which appears as **Microsoft Data Binding Collection**. Press **OK** to close the dialog.

Step 10

Figure 15-6 shows the user interface of the client. Create this interface on the form in the Standard EXE project. Use the Item list below to set the design-time properties for the controls on the form.

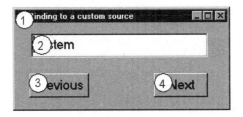

Figure 15-6 The Client Interface.

Item 1—Form

Name	`frmBind`
Caption	Binding to a custom source

Item 2—TextBox

Name	`txtFonts`
Text	<empty>

Item 3—CommandButton

Name	`cmdPrev`
Caption	Previous

Item 4—CommandButton

Name	`cmdNext`
Caption	Next

Step 11

In order to bind the TextBox to the data source, we need to create an instance of the `Provider` class and the `DataBinding` object. In the [General][Declarations] section of `frmBind`, add the following declarations:

```
Private m_BindCollection As MSBind.BindingCollection
Private m_DataSource As FontSource.Provider
```

Step 12

The data binding occurs immediately in the `Load` event of the form, which creates an instance of the data source and `DataBinding` object. The result is a call to the `GetDataMember`

method of the Provider class to retrieve the data in the recordset. Add the following code to the
`Form_Load` event of `frmBind` to complete the data binding:

```
'Create Objects
Set m_BindCollection = New MSBind.BindingCollection
Set m_DataSource = New FontSource.Provider

'Assign the provider to the binding collection
m_BindCollection.DataMember = "SELECT * FROM Fonts"
Set m_BindCollection.DataSource = m_DataSource

'Bind the text
m_BindCollection.Add txtFonts, "Text", "FontName"
```

Step 13

Navigating the data source is done under the Click event of each of the two buttons. This code
is a simple call to the appropriate method of the Provider class. In the click event of each button, add code so that the final result appears as follows:

```
Private Sub cmdNext_Click()
   m_DataSource.MoveNext
End Sub

Private Sub cmdPrev_Click()
   m_DataSource.MovePrevious
End Sub
```

Step 14

Save the work and run the project. It should be possible to use the buttons on the form to navigate the set of available system fonts.

Exercise 15-3: Distributed Applications

Visual Basic is an excellent tool for creating distributed applications. Using VB alone, create at
least an ActiveX EXE and a Standard EXE to investigate this technology. This exercise builds
an application that will make it possible to get system information from any computer on a network. Although this application can be built with just one machine, this exercise works best
with a network and permission to install components on it.

CREATING THE DISTRIBUTED COMPONENT

Step 1

Using the Windows File Explorer, create a new directory **VB BOOTCAMP\EXERCISE15-3**.
Under this directory, create a directory **\CLIENT** and a directory **\SERVER**. Under the

\CLIENT and \SERVER directories create directories called **\CODE** and **\SETUP**. Figure 15-7 shows the complete folder structure to build.

Figure 15-7 Exercise Folder structure.

Step 2

Start a new ActiveX EXE project in Visual Basic. Change the name of this project to **SystemInfo** by selecting **PROJECT/PROPERTIES** from the menu. Type the new project name into the General tab. Click on the component tab and check the **Remote Server Files** box to generate the VBR file when this component is compiled. Close the dialog.

Step 3

Change the name of the default class module in the project to **CData**. This class will be the public interface to a distributed component that reports system information for a machine. Save the project to the **\SERVER\CODE** directory created earlier.

Step 4

This component is going to return system information to the calling client. The system information will be retrieved using a simple API call—GlobalMemoryStatus. This API call uses a user-defined type to house information about the memory resources of a computer. Add the following code to the [General][Declarations] section of CData to make the API Call available:

```
'API Call
Private Declare Sub GlobalMemoryStatus Lib "kernel32" _
    (lpBuffer As MEMORYSTATUS)

'Structure for data
Private Type MEMORYSTATUS
    dwLength As Long
    dwMemoryLoad As Long
    dwTotalPhys As Long
    dwAvailPhys As Long
    dwTotalPageFile As Long
    dwAvailPageFile As Long
```

```
      dwTotalVirtual As Long
      dwAvailVirtual As Long
   End Type
```

Step 5

This class will provide a single method call to retrieve the data structure. This application is partitioned by using a standalone ADO Recordset object to transfer the data from the distributed component to the calling client. To create the recordset, set a reference to the ADO model. Open the References dialog by selecting **PROJECT/REFERENCES...** from the menu. Set a reference to **Microsoft ActiveX Data Objects 2.0 Library**. Push the **OK** button.

Step 6

The single method call to gather information is a function that returns the recordset object. Create this function by selecting **TOOLS/ADD PROCEDURE...** from the menu. In the procedure dialog, create a procedure named Retrieve and make it Public. Add the procedure to CData and then modify it to return an ADO Recordset object. The final function signature should appear as follows:

```
Public Function Retrieve() As ADODB.Recordset
End Function
```

Step 7

The Retrieve function creates a new recordset and fills it with data from the results of the GlobalMemoryStatus function. The results are returned to the client in the recordset. In this way, the client does not need intimate knowledge of how the data were gathered. Changes to the component will not affect the client as long as the client receives a recordset as the return value from the component. This fact could be guaranteed through the use of an interface to describe the contract between the partitions. In this case, add the following code to the retrieve method to get the data and send it to the client:

```
On Error GoTo RetrieveErr

   'Variables
   Dim objMemory As MEMORYSTATUS
   Dim objRecordset As ADODB.Recordset

   'Get System Data
   objMemory.dwLength = Len(objMemory)
   GlobalMemoryStatus objMemory

   'Build Recordset
   Set objRecordset = New ADODB.Recordset

   With objRecordset.Fields
```

```
      .Append "MemoryLoad", adBigInt
      .Append "TotalPhys", adBigInt
      .Append "AvailPhys", adBigInt
      .Append "TotalPageFile", adBigInt
      .Append "AvailPageFile", adBigInt
   End With

   'Fill Recordset with data
   objRecordset.Open
   objRecordset.AddNew
   objRecordset!MemoryLoad = objMemory.dwMemoryLoad
   objRecordset!TotalPhys = objMemory.dwTotalPhys
   objRecordset!AvailPhys = objMemory.dwAvailPhys
   objRecordset!TotalPageFile = objMemory.dwTotalPageFile
   objRecordset!AvailPageFile = objMemory.dwAvailPageFile
   objRecordset.MoveFirst

   'Return recordset
   Set Retrieve = objRecordset
   Exit Function

RetrieveErr:
   Set Retrieve = Nothing
```

Step 8

Save the project and make an EXE by selecting **FILE/MAKE SYSTEMINFO.EXE**.

CREATING THE CLIENT

Step 9

Start a new Standard EXE project in Visual Basic. Do not add this project to the ActiveX EXE project.

Step 10

Change the name of the form in the new project to **frmClient**. Open the project properties for the new project and name the project **InfoClient**. Save the project to the **\CLIENT\CODE** directory created earlier.

Step 11

Open the References dialog by selecting **PROJECT/REFERENCES** from the menu. In the references dialog, set a reference to the **Microsoft ActiveX Data Objects Library 2.0** and to **SystemInfo**.

Step 12

Create a user interface for the client software as shown in Figure 15-8. Use the Item list to set the design-time properties for the controls.

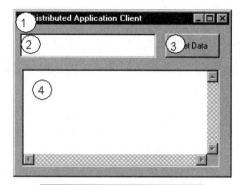

Figure 15-8 The client interface.

Item 1—Form

Name	frmClient
Caption	Distributed Application Client

Item 2—TextBox

Name	txtComputer
Text	<empty>

Item 3—CommandButton

Name	cmdData
Caption	Get Data

Item 4—TextBox

Name	txtData
Text	<empty>
MultiLine	True
Scrollbars	3-Both

Step 13

In the form, the user can type the name of any computer in the top TextBox and press the **Get Data** button. The code under the Click event of the button creates an instance of the object on the machine using the name entered in the TextBox and returns the ADO Recordset. The data are then displayed in the multi-line TextBox. Add the following code to the click event of cmdData to get the data:

```
'Variables
```

```
Dim m_Recordset As ADODB.Recordset
Dim m_Field As ADODB.Field
Dim m_SystemInfo As SystemInfo.CData

'Retrieve the Data
Set m_SystemInfo = _
    CreateObject("SystemInfo.CData", txtComputer.Text)
Set m_Recordset = m_SystemInfo.Retrieve

'Display the data
txtData.Text = txtComputer.Text & vbCrLf

For Each m_Field In m_Recordset.Fields
  txtData.Text = txtData.Text & m_Field.Name & ": " & _
      m_Field.Value & vbCrLf
Next
```

Step 14

Save the work and create an EXE by selecting **FILE/MAKE INFOCLIENT.EXE** from the menu.

CREATING THE SETUPS

Step 15

If it is not already available in the VB environment, go to the **Add-In Manager** and activate the Package and Deployment Wizard. When the Wizard is available, start it by selecting **ADD-INS/PACKAGE AND DEPLOYMENT WIZARD…** from the menu.

Step 16

When the wizard starts, choose to create a new package by pushing the **Package** button. Any miscellaneous messages from the Wizard as it starts are not critical.

Step 17

In the Package Type step choose to create a **Standard Setup Package**. Push **Next**.

Step 18

In the Package Folder step, choose to build the setup for the client in the **\CLIENT\SETUP** directory created earlier. Push **Next**. There may be a dialog about missing dependency information. This dialog is not critical and may be dismissed by pressing the **OK** button.

Step 19

In the Included Files step, locate the entry for **SYSTEMINFO.EXE**. This is going to be the distributed component and should not be installed on the client machine. Uncheck this item.

Now press the **Add** button and manually add the **SYSTEMINFO.VBR** file in place of the distributed component. Press **Next**.

Step 20

The Package and Deployment Wizard will present the Remote Servers step, where a table of information retrieved from the VBR file will be visible. The information should all be filled out with the exception of the Net Address column. A RemoteServerName entry for the distributed component in the client registry, could be entered here, but this application uses the CreateObject function to specify the server, so leave it blank. If this entry is left blank, there will be a prompt during the installation process for a machine name. If the setup is run later, be prepared to specify a machine, though the CreateObject function can override this entry. Press **Next**.

Step 21

In the Cab Options step, specify to build the setup as a single CAB file. Press **Next**.

Step 22

In the Installation Title step, change the installation title to **VB BOOTCAMP Distributed App**. Press **Next**.

Step 23

In the Start Menu Items step, accept the default settings by pressing **Next**.

Step 24

In the Install Locations step, accept the defaults by pressing **Next**.

Step 25

In the Shared Files step, accept the defaults by pressing **Next**.

Step 26

In the Finished! step, press **Finish** to build your setup.

Step 27

Open the SystemInfo project and run the Package and Deployment Wizard to create a setup for the distributed component. When the wizard starts, select to create a new package by pushing the **Package** button.

Step 28

In the Package Type step choose to create a **Standard Setup Package**. Push **Next**.

Step 29

In the Package Folder step, choose to build the setup for the client in the **\SERVER\SETUP** directory created earlier. Push **Next**. There will be a dialog asking about inclusion of special files for Remote Automation (RA) support. RA is the predecessor to DCOM. This component uses DCOM, not RA, so do not distribute these files.

Step 30

Accept the default settings for all of the additional steps in the Wizard by pushing the **Next** button. Push the **Finish** button to build the CAB file and set up for the distributed component.

FOR THE CERTIFIED PRO

Pro 15-1: Distributed Setups

1. Create the installations in Exercise 15-3.
2. Install these components on distributed machines on the network.
3. Verify that communication between client and the server is possible. This process may involve adjusting settings on the distributed component's server via DCOMC-NFG.

PREPARING FOR CERTIFICATION

Topics for Further Reading
   Creating Data Sources
   ActiveX Components Standards and Guidelines

CERTIFICATION QUIZ

1. Simple bound classes:
    a. Bind to an entire recordset
    b. Bind to an ActiveX control
    c. Bind to a ADO data control
    d. Bind a single property to a field

2. Complex bound classes:
    a. Bind to an entire recordset
    b. Bind to an ActiveX control
    c. Bind to an ADO data control
    d. Bind a single property to a field

3. The `BindingCollection` object:
    a. Binds a data source to a class
    b. Binds a data source to a form
    c. Binds a data field to a property
    d. Binds a data field to an ActiveX control

4. Complex bound classes support which properties:
   a. `DataField`
   b. `DataSource`
   c. `DataValue`
   d. `DataMember`

5. Setting the `DataSource` property of a class to `vbDataSource` adds what event to the class?
   a. `GetDataValue`
   b. `GetDataMember`
   c. `GetDataField`
   d. `GetDataSource`

6. What entries are required on a client machine to allow remote component creation?
   a. `ProgID`
   b. `CLSID`
   c. `CodeID`
   d. `RemoteServerName`

7. If a client has a `RemoteServerName` entry, specifying a machine name in the `CreateObject` function results in the remote object being created
   a. on the machine designated by `RemoteServerName`.
   b. on the machine designated by the `CreateObject` function.
   c. and failing with a Can't Create ActiveX Component Error.
   d. on the local machine.

8. When creating a distributed setup what file is used to add client registry entries?
   a. EXE file
   b. DLL file
   c. VBR file
   d. REG file

9. The DCOMCNFG Utility sets:
   a. Launch Permissions
   b. Access Permissions
   c. Edit Permissions
   d. Running Account

ANSWERS TO CERTIFICATION QUIZ

1. d
2. a, c
3. c, d
4. b, d
5. b
6. a, b, d

7. b
8. c
9. a, b, c, d

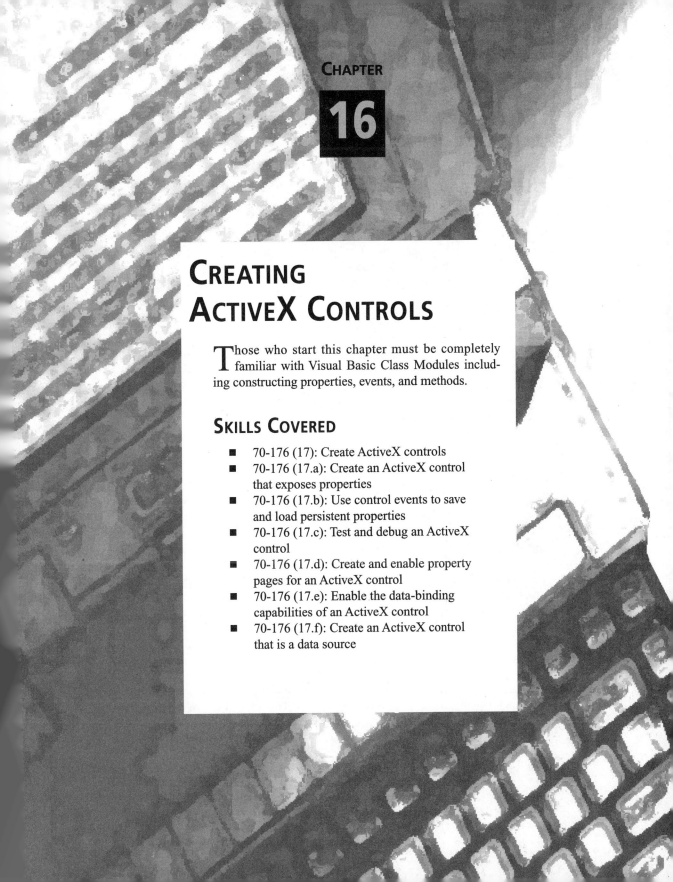

CREATING ACTIVEX CONTROLS

Those who start this chapter must be completely familiar with Visual Basic Class Modules including constructing properties, events, and methods.

SKILLS COVERED

- 70-176 (17): Create ActiveX controls
- 70-176 (17.a): Create an ActiveX control that exposes properties
- 70-176 (17.b): Use control events to save and load persistent properties
- 70-176 (17.c): Test and debug an ActiveX control
- 70-176 (17.d): Create and enable property pages for an ActiveX control
- 70-176 (17.e): Enable the data-binding capabilities of an ActiveX control
- 70-176 (17.f): Create an ActiveX control that is a data source

- 70-176 (28): Implement project groups to support the development and debugging process
- 70-176 (28.a): Debug DLLs in process
- 70-175 (22): Create ActiveX controls
- 70-175 (22.a): Create an ActiveX control that exposes properties
- 70-175 (22.b): Use control events to save and load persistent properties
- 70-175 (22.c): Test and debug an ActiveX control
- 70-175 (22.d): Create and enable property pages for an ActiveX control
- 70-175 (22.e): Enable the data-binding capabilities of an ActiveX control
- 70-175 (22.f): Create an ActiveX control that is a data source
- 70-175 (48): Implement project groups to support the development and debugging process
- 70-175 (48.b): Test and debug a control in process

Ever since Visual Basic was first released, it has contained reusable elements. These elements have undergone many changes over the years, but the philosophy of reuse has been a cornerstone of VB development from the beginning. Throughout this book, we have reused elements that exist inside VB's toolbox. Over time these elements have gone by many names, including such generic descriptions as *objects* or *controls*.

Stepping back a couple of versions, you may have been familair with the toolbox elements in Visual Basic 3.0 known as Visual Basic Extensions (VBXs). Under Visual Basic 3.0, VBXs were proprietary reusable components that could only be used in a VB application. When Microsoft developed Visual Basic 4.0, VBXs were changed radically. The value of reusable components in Windows had been proven by the VBX, and Microsoft wanted to extend the reuse to all of its visual development tools. Hence the VBX standard was scrapped in favor of an open standard known as OLE Custom Controls or OCXs. OCXs are unique because although VBXs can only be used in Visual Basic, OCXs can be used by all visual tools and any third-party tools that support the standard, such as Borland's Delphi. OCXs ushered in a new era of reuse in Windows development, but more changes were to follow.

Not long after Visual Basic 4.0 was introduced, the drumbeat of the Internet was starting to be heard at Microsoft. Microsoft considered their current suite of tools and tried to determine which ones could easily map to Internet development. One of the first candidates for conversion was the OCX. Microsoft reasoned that what the OCX did for cross-language development, it could now do for Internet development. The OCX standard was modified slightly to allow controls to be hosted by a Web browser, and the ActiveX control was born.

Visual Basic now has the ability to create these ActiveX controls,a significant advance for VB developers. When controls are created, not only can they be used in Visual Basic, FoxPro and C++, but they can also be used on the Internet. This section teaches the fundamentals of control development in VB.

Control Creation Fundamentals

Creating an ActiveX Control begins by selecting the ActiveX Control project template in Visual Basic. This template contains the structure required to create a control. When the project is first started, a single gray area appears. This area resembles a Visual Basic form, but has no border, no title bar, and no control buttons. In fact, this area is not a form at all, but rather one of the new family of visual elements called a Designer.

Designers are used in Visual Basic as visual elements that help programmers create objects. The ActiveX Control Designer (Figure 16-1) is embodied in a special object called the `UserControl` object which contains all the plumbing necessary to create a true ActiveX Control. In fact, if a control were compiled now, it would be a real ActiveX control that could be distributed—it would just be invisible and have no functionality.

When an ActiveX Control is created using VB, three different approaches are possible. The first is to draw a custom control. The `UserControl` object contains custom drawing methods that will facilitate creation of circles, lines, and points.

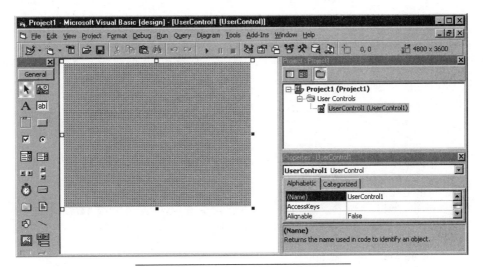

Figure 16-1 The ActiveX Control Designer.

Another choice is to use existing Visual Basic controls to create a new control. For example, a TextBox and a Vertical Slider can be used to create a spin button or a TextBox and ListBox can be used for a new ComboBox. Any existing control may be used as a component in a new control. Existing controls incorporated into new controls are called Constituent controls.

Constituent Control: any control placed on a UserControl object for the purpose of creating a new ActiveX Control in Visual Basic.

BACKGROUND

The third option is to extend the functionality of a single control. For example, take a TextBox, retain all its existing features, but add a new Mask property for restricting data input and create a Masked Edit control. Extending one control in an ActiveX Control project is called *subclassing a control*.

Subclassing: creating a new object that has all the original properties and methods of an existing object while adding some custom features.

BACKGROUND

Regardless of which method is chosen to create the new control, the process of coding the project remains largely unchanged. The only issue becomes properly redrawing a control when it is resized by the user. Resizing is a major issue in control design that should be tackled as a first order of business for any new control.

Whenever a user of the control resizes it, the `UserControl` object receives a `UserControl_Resize()` event. Constituent controls do not automatically resize when the `UserControl` object resizes. That functionality must be coded in the `Resize` event. A single control can be subclassed by forcing the value of the constituent control's `Height` and `Width` properties to match the new `Height` and `Width` of the `UserControl` object. However, if multiple constituent controls are in use, there must be careful planning of how to resize them for the correct effect.

Check It Out 16-1: Control Resizing

1. Start a new ActiveX Control project in Visual Basic 6.0.
2. Drop a TextBox on the `UserControl` object, and place it in the upper left corner.
3. Resize the `UserControl` object so that it is completely covered by the TextBox.
4. Close all open windows in the project.
5. Add a new project to the group by selecting **FILE/ADD PROJECT...** from the menu. In the New Project dialog, select to **add a new Standard EXE project**.
6. Look in the toolbox for the new project and identify the icon for the new control. Put the mouse over the control and the ToolTip should read UserControl1. This is the new control in action.
7. Add the control created to Form1 in the Standard EXE project by double clicking on the control in the toolbox.
8. Try resizing the control on Form1. Does the TextBox resize or just the UserControl designer?
9. Now add the following code to the `UserControl_Resize` event:

```
Text1.Height=UserControl.Height
Text1.Width=UserControl.Width
```

10. Close all the open windows and then reopen Form1. Now resize the control on Form1.

ADDING PROPERTIES

ActiveX Control properties are created in the project much as properties are created in VB Class Modules. To create new properties, use property procedures. These properties can then show up in the Properties window of the Visual Basic environment. Properties for controls come from several sources. Some are provided to a control by its container, others come from Constituent controls, and still others may be custom properties.

EXTENDER PROPERTIES

Not all properties of an ActiveX Control come from the control itself. Some are actually given to the control by the container that hosts it. This is true of the ActiveX Controls created in Visual Basic. Containers often provide properties that are meaningful to the container, but not necessarily to the control. Consider the `TabIndex` property, which specifies the order in the tab sequence for a control. The control itself is not particularly concerned with its tab order, but the hosting Form is definitely interested. The Form must respond to events related to the tab order, such as `GotFocus` and `LostFocus`. Therefore, the Form extends the `TabIndex` property to a control to track these events.

Visual Basic 6.0 affords access to all the properties extended to the ActiveX control through a special object called the `Extender` object which can be used in the Visual Basic ActiveX control project to affect any of the extended properties. In most cases, the `Extender` will never be addressed directly since the `Extender` properties are generally not a concern.

Check It Out 16-2: Extender Properties

1. Start a new ActiveX Control project in Visual Basic 6.0.
2. Drop a CommandButton on the `UserControl` object, and place it in the upper left corner.
3. Resize the `UserControl` object so that it is completely covered by the CommandButton.
4. In the `Resize` event of the `UserControl` object, add the following code:

```
Extender.Left=0
Extender.Top=0
Command1.Height=UserControl.ScaleHeight
Command1.Width=UserControl.Scale Width
```

5. Close all open windows in the project.
6. Add a new project to the group by selecting **FILE/ADD PROJECT...** from the menu. In the New Project dialog, select to **add a new Standard EXE project**.
7. Look in the toolbox for the new project and identify the icon for the new control. Put the mouse over the control and the ToolTip should read UserControl1.
8. Add the control created to Form1 in the Standard EXE project by double clicking on the control in the toolbox.
9. Try resizing the control on Form1. Does the control resize?

CONSTITUENT CONTROL PROPERTIES

When a control is first created with Visual Basic, it may seem likely to contain all the properties, events, and methods of the Constituent controls that are contained on the `UserControl` object. All controls used as part of the `UserControl` are considered private to the control project. Therefore, none of them appear as properties of the control unless you explicitly write code to expose them. This is done by wrapping the property of the Constituent Control in a Property Procedure. For example, to expose the Text property of a Constituent Control Text1, use the following code:

```
Public Property Get Text()As String
   Text=Text1.Text
End Property
Public Property Let Text(strText As String)
   Text1.Text=strText
End Property
```

The process of creating a set of Property Procedures for each Constituent Control property can be quite laborious. Fortunately, Visual Basic provides a Wizard to ease the work. It exists as an Add-In under the Add-In Manager dialog in Visual Basic and is called the ActiveX Control Interface Wizard (Figure 16-2).

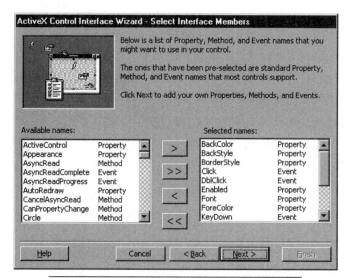

Figure 16-2 The ActiveX Control Interface Wizard.

CUSTOM PROPERTIES

Custom properties are as simple to create in the ActiveX control project as they are in any Visual Basic Class module. Custom properties are created by adding a pair of Property Procedures to the control and providing a Private variable to retain the property state. Every time a Property Procedure is added to the control project, Visual Basic automatically adds the property to the Properties window.

Check It Out 16-3: Adding Custom Properties

1. Start a new ActiveX Control project in Visual Basic 6.0.
2. Drop a TextBox on the `UserControl` object, and place it in the upper left corner.
3. Resize the `UserControl` object so that it is completely covered by the TextBox.
4. Add a Property Procedure called `MyProperty`. Create the Property Procedures with the following code:

```
Private m_MyProperty As String
Public Property Let MyProperty(strMyProperty As String)
    M_MyProperty = strMyProperty
End Property
Public Property Get MyProperty() As String
    MyProperty = m_MyProperty
End Property
```

5. Close all the project windows
6. Add a new project to the group by selecting **FILE/ADD PROJECT...** from the menu. In the New Project dialog, select to **add a new Standard EXE project**.
7. Look in the toolbox for the new project and identify the icon for the new control. Put the mouse over the control and the ToolTip should read UserControl1.
8. Add the control created to Form1 in the Standard EXE project by double clicking on the control in the toolbox.
9. Examine the Properties window for the new property. Try changing its value.

READ-ONLY AND WRITE-ONLY PROPERTIES

Often ActiveX controls support a number of special types of properties. For example, some properties are available only for reading or writing, but not both. These types of properties can be created in ActiveX controls as well. As is the case for many features in ActiveX controls, read-only or write-only properties are created exactly as Class modules are.

As an example, suppose we wanted to create a read-only property for a custom TextBox called `Length`. The `Length` property will return the length of the text in our control as a read-only property. Users of our control can call this property at run time, but they cannot write to it. Creating the property requires a pair of Property procedures, but to make the property read-only, we must alter the scoping qualifier of `Property Let` from Public to Private. The following code shows how to create the `Length` property:

```
Private Property Let Length(intLength As Integer)
End Property
Public Property Get Length() As Integer
End Property
```

Run time-Only and Design Time-Only Properties

Creating properties available only at design time or run time is accomplished through the use of a special object called the `Ambient` object which is responsible for providing information to the ActiveX control regarding the state of the form hosting the control. In the case of properties, the `UserMode` property of the `Ambient` object is used to determine if the control is being hosted at design time or run time. If the hosting application is in Visual Basic, then `Ambient.UserMode` is False. If the hosting application is currently executing, then `Ambient.UserMode` is True.

In order to enforce design time or run time behavior, check the value of `UserMode` and then either raise an error or execute the requested functionality. To create a design time-only property called `Style` that accepts an integer to change the look of the control would require two Property procedures, as we have discussed. However, creating Property procedure pairs will make the same property available at run time as well. Therefore, we must check `Ambient.UserMode` in `Property Let` as follows:

```
Private m_Style As Integer
Public Property Let Style (intStyle As Integer)
   If Ambient.UserMode = False Then
     m_Style = intStyle
   Else
     Err.Raise vbOjbectError, UserControl1, _
         "Not available at run-time"
   End If
End Property
```

Use the same strategy to create run time-only properties. If an error is raised at run time, then the control container is responsible for trapping and handling the error just like any VB control. If an error is raised at design time, use a message box as a display. No other special code is required.

Procedure Attributes

Along with property behaviors such as read only or write only, many properties also exhibit special characteristics beyond those already described. These special behaviors are not easily categorized and can exist at both design time and run time. As examples, consider `Default` property behavior and the `Caption` property behavior.

All VB programmers should be familiar with the behavior of `Default` properties, which receive values from code implicitly even when not called explicitly. The `Text` property of a TextBox is a good example. Access the `Text` property of any TextBox implicitly with the following code:

```
Text1 = "New Technology Solutions"
```

To implement this type of behavior in the controls, use Procedure Attributes, a catch-all dialog that makes it possible to designate certain properties in the control as having special behaviors

(Figure 16-3). To designate a property as the default for the control, select **TOOLS/PROCE-DURE ATTRIBUTES...** from the menu. In the Procedure Attributes dialog, select the property to make as the default and press the **Advanced** button. Under the advanced setting, locate the ProcedureID. Then select default as the ProcedureID.

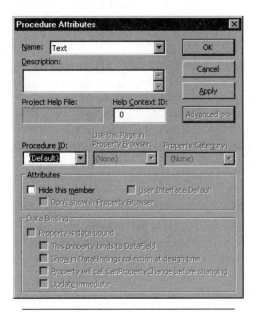

Figure 16-3   Procedure Attributes dialog.

The `Caption` property has special behavior that can also be implemented with the Procedure Attributes dialog. At design time it automatically sends characters one at a time to the target control. To check on this behavior, try dropping a Label control and changing the `Caption` property. Notice how each letter enters the Caption independently. The controls we make in Visual Basic do not have this behavior by default. To simulate the `Caption` property, set the appropriate procedure attribute to Caption in the Procedure Attributes dialog.

SAVING PROPERTY VALUES WITH THE PROPERTYBAG

As controls are used in the Visual Basic design environment, the values of their properties will be changed from the defaults specified. This is a natural part of the design process. Like other controls in Visual Basic, these changes will need to be saved as part of the project so that they can be remembered when the project is saved and later opened. Saving properties for controls is the function of a special object called the `PropertyBag`. Using the `PropertyBag` correctly depends on a complete understanding of the life cycle of a control.

When the control is used in the Visual Basic environment, it receives several events throughout its life. The most important of these are `InitProperties`, `WriteProperties`, and `ReadProperties`. These events are fired in the `UserControl` object, and they make it possible to set default property values, save properties, and retrieve properties respectfully.

INITPROPERTIES

When an ActiveX Control is first dropped on a VB form from the ToolBox, the control is notified through the `InitProperties` event of the `UserControl` object. This event permits setting the default property values for the control. Setting these values is a matter of coding them in the event:

```
Public Sub UserControl_InitProperties
   Border = 1
   Size = 2
End Sub
```

Any properties set in `InitProperties` reflect the defaults that will always be seen when the control is first dropped. Some properties, however, have special behavior when dropped on a form. Certain properties such as those associated with Fonts actually accept the values currently in use by the form. The properties are called Ambient properties.

Check It Out 16-4: Ambient Properties

1. Start a new Standard EXE project in Visual Basic.
2. Change the `Font` property of Form1 to **Times New Roman** size **16**.
3. Drop a Label Control on Form1.
4. What happened to the `Font` and `ForeColor` properties of Label1?
5. Change the `Font` of Form1 to **Arial 10**.
6. Change the `ForeColor` of Form1 to **Red**.
7. Drop another Label control on Form1.
8. What happened?

Ambient properties are controlled in the ActiveX Control project through the `Ambient` object. We used the `UserMode` property of the `Ambient` object earlier to help create run time only and design time-only properties. We can also use it to synchronize our controls with the hosting container. The `Ambient` object allows us to read the `Font`, `ForeColor`, `BackColor`, and `DisplayName` of the control on the container. To synchronize the control with the container, the following code could be used:

```
UserControl_InitProperties
   On Error Resume Next
   Set Font = Ambient.Font
   ForeColor = Ambient.ForeColor
   BackColor = Ambient.BackColor
   Text = Ambient.DisplayName
End Sub
```

In this code note the error handling. Always use error handling before addressing the `Ambient` object because the properties of the object may not be available for every container. For example, when using this code for a downloaded component in Internet Explorer, expect to receive run time errors. For the most part, we can discard any errors that occur here, so the code just resumes on the next line.

WRITE PROPERTIES

Whenever a user saves the current project, the control is notified through the `WriteProper-ties` event, which signals that it is time to save the properties of the control to persistent file storage. Visual Basic saves the properties of controls as plain ASCII text inside the FRM file that represents the hosting form. VB will also save properties to the FRM file, if it is instructed to save control properties when they are dirty and write to the correct code.

Telling Visual Basic that a control has dirty properties that need saving is done in the `Property Let` procedure for any property to be saved. Inside a `Property Let` for the control, tell Visual Basic that the property has been changed by calling the `Property-Changed` method of the `UserControl` and providing the name of the changing property. The following code notifies the Visual Basic design environment that the Text property of a custom control has changed:

```
Public Property Let Text(strText As String)
   Text1.Text = strText
   PropertyChanged "Text"
End Property
```

When `PropertyChanged` is called, Visual Basic will make sure that the user of the control is prompted to save any changes before they leave the current project. This generates the familiar Save Changes? dialog box. When the user saves changes, there is a call to `WriteProperties`, where the `PropertyBag` object is used to write to the FRM file of the hosting form. The `WriteProperty` method of the `PropertyBag` takes as arguments the name of the property to save, the value of the property, and the default value.

```
Private Sub UserControl_WriteProperties (PropBag As PropertyBag)
   PropBag.Write Property "MyProperty",MyProperty,"MyDefault"
End Sub
```

Visual Basic writes the property to the FRM file only if the current value is different from the default. In this way, VB can save file space by not writing properties that will already be set correctly next time in the `ReadProperties` event. When reading from the `PropBag`, always use error handling because FRM files are saved as ASCII text and can be edited, so that the integrity of the FRM file cannot be guaranteed when reading from it.

READPROPERTIES

The `ReadProperties` event is fired when the control is created because a project was opened in Visual Basic. In this case, the control is created in the opening of the project and the prompt is to read properties out of the `PropertyBag`. This is a simple matter of using the `ReadProperty` method of the `PropertyBag` and selecting the properties accordingly. The `ReadProperty` method takes as arguments the name of the property to read and its default value. Once again, use error handling when reading from the `PropertyBag`:

```
Private Sub UserControl_ReadProperties (PropBag As PropertyBag)
  MyProperty = PropBag.ReadProperty("MyProperty","MyDefault")
End Sub
```

ADDING EVENTS

Just as with other ActiveX controls used in Visual Basic, the controls created also support event generation. Once defined inside the control, the events become available to any hosting application and will even appear automatically in the Visual Basic code window at design time. Furthermore, event definition in ActiveX controls follows the same rules as event definition in any VB Class module.

Adding a new event definition is done in the [General][Declarations] section of the `User-Control` object with the `Event` keyword. Simply name the event and any required arguments using the following syntax:

```
Event EventName(Arg1, Arg2, Arg3,…)
```

Once the event is defined, fire it from the control using the `RaiseEvent` keyword. This command can be used from any sub or function and immediately causes the event handling routine in the hosting form to execute. The following syntax fires the event:

```
RaiseEvent EventName
```

Check It Out 16-5: Defining Events

1. Start a new ActiveX Control project in Visual Basic 6.0.
2. Drop a TextBox on the `UserControl` object, and place it in the upper left corner.
3. Resize the `UserControl` object so that it is completely covered by the TextBox.
4. Add an event declaration to the [General][Declarations] section of the `UserControl` object with the following code:

   ```
   Event TextChanged(strText As String)
   ```

5. In the Change event of Text1 raise the custom event with the following code:

   ```
   RaiseEvent TextChanged (Text1.Text)
   ```

6. Add a new project to the group by selecting **FILE/ADD PROJECT...** from the menu. In the New Project dialog, select to **add a new Standard EXE project**.
7. Look in the toolbox for the new project and identify the icon for the new control. Put the mouse over the control and the ToolTip should read UserControl1.
8. Add the control created to Form1 in the Standard EXE project by double clicking on the control in the toolbox.
9. Open the Code window for Form1 and select **UserControl11** from the Object box. Note that the events declaration for the custom event is visible in the Code window.

ADDING METHODS

Methods in ActiveX control projects are generated by defining Public Subs or Functions in the `UserControl` object. The Public routines may be subsequently called from any container hosting the control. This technique is exactly the same as defining methods for Class modules.

BUILDING SPECIAL FEATURE CONTROLS

In addition to the standard control creation features, Visual Basic supports the construction of special features into controls such as data binding or invisible controls. These features are generally created by changing properties of the `UserControl` object or by selecting appropriate procedure attributes. These special features represent additions to the control and do not affect the creation of properties, events, and methods as previously discussed.

DATA BOUND CONTROLS

Perhaps the most complex of the special features to add is data binding. Data bound controls have the ability to connect to a Visual Basic data control to receive database information. Controls can be created to add, edit, update, and delete from an associated database.

Creating a bound control begins just as creating any other control does. Keep in mind at the outset which properties will be data bound. Once the control is built, set data binding features in the Procedure Attributes dialog. Simply select the property to bind from the Name list in the dialog and check the **Property is Data Bound** option.

Underneath the data binding option is a series of three suboptions that further specify the behavior of the data-bound control. The first, titled "This Property Binds to DataField" is used to specify that this property should appear alone under the `DataField` property. The `DataField` property is generally used when a control has just a single bound property.

The second suboption is titled "Show in DataBindings Collection At Design Time" and determines whether the bound property appears in the Properties window under the `DataBindings` property. `DataBindings` normally contains a list of all bindable properties, if more than one exists.

The third suboption is titled "Property Will Call CanPropertyChange Before Changing" and specifies that the control will check with the container to see if the property can be changed. Bound properties may not be able to change if, for example, the database is opened for read-only access. Unfortunately, however, the current version of Visual Basic always returns True when this function is called, so it is of little use.

CONTAINER CONTROLS

Visual Basic also supports creating controls that act as containers for other controls. The Frame control in Visual Basic is an example of a container control. When a new control is placed in a container, it moves with the container and cannot be removed. Setting up the control as a container is a simple matter of setting the `ControlContainer` property of the `UserControl` object to True.

Once a control is designated as a container, it may be desirable to perform functions on the other controls that reside in the container. Any hosted control may be programmatically manipulated through the `ContainedControls` collection accessible through the `UserControl` object. For example, to set all the controls in the container to resize proportionally when the container resizes, the following code could be used:

```
Private m_HeightScale As Integer
Private m_WidthScale As Integer
Private Sub UserControl_Resize()

    Dim objControl As Control

    For Each objControl In UserControl.ContainedControls
  objControl.Left = Int(objControl.Left * (Width / m_WidthScale))
  objControl.Top = Int(objControl.Top * (Height / m_HeightScale))
  objControl.Width = Int(objControl.Width * (Width / m_WidthScale))
  objControl.Height = _
      Int(objControl.Height * (Height / m_HeightScale))
    Next
    'Save New Dimensions
    m_HeightScale = Height
    m_WidthScale = Width
End Sub
```

INVISIBLE CONTROLS

Visual Basic also makes it possible to build controls that are invisible at run time. An example is the Timer control, which is used to fire code at a given interval. In the case of the timer, no user interface is necessary, so the control can be invisible at run time but provide an interface at design time for setting properties. To make the control invisible at run time, set the `InvisibleAtRuntime` property of the `UserControl` object to True.

Although invisible controls can be created in Visual Basic 6.0, they probably should not be. The reason is that invisible controls are essentially ActiveX DLLs with more overhead. If the functionality of an ActiveX DLL is required, create one instead of an invisible control. The performance will be more satisfactory.

UTILIZING PROPERTY PAGES

Although the Properties window offers an excellent way to set most properties, it is not always flexible enough to meet the needs of all controls. In many cases, controls have a special property called `Custom` that allows access to a special interface for setting properties. This interface is called a Property Page or Property Sheet. This is a feature that we can add to our own controls.

Just like the ActiveX Control project itself, Property Pages are created through a special object. The `PropertyPage` object can be easily added to the ActiveX Control project by selecting **PROJECT/ADD PROPERTY PAGE...** from the menu. When a `PropertyPage` object is added, it appears as a blank gray designer area similar to the `UserControl` object.

Each `PropertyPage` object included in the ActiveX Control project represents one tab in a tabbed dialog. The collection of these tabs makes the Custom Property dialog. The job is to design the property pages so that common control features are grouped together. Typical tabs might include General, Fonts, and Colors.

SHOWING PROPERTIES ON THE PAGE

Property Pages have key events used to manage control settings. In Visual Basic, if a `PropertyPage` object is associated with an ActiveX Control, then a Custom property will appear in the VB Properties window. This `Custom` property has an ellipsis associated with it. When the button is pushed, the `PropertyPage` object is notified through the `SelectionChanged` event. In fact, the page receives this event any time the group of selected controls are changed.

When the `SelectionChanged` event fires, populate the page with the current values of the control properties. Accessing the group of controls is done with the `SelectedControls` collection. By convention the first selected control is used to populate the page. If, for example, Masked Edit controls were selected, the following code would populate an option button called `optMask` using the Mask Property:

```
Private Sub PropertyPage_SelectionChanged()
  optMask(SelectedControls(0).Mask) = True


End Sub
```

Notice that the page is populated using `SelectedControls(0)`. This is the typical technique and results in the expected control behavior in the Visual Basic design environment. When using the `SelectedControls` collection, always assume that it is populated solely with the class of controls handled by the page. Visual Basic will automatically disable Property Pages if controls of different classes are selected in the environment.

APPLYING PROPERTY CHANGES

When a `PropertyPage` object is open, users interact with the controls placed on it to set property values. When a property is changed, the code notifies the Visual Basic environment by calling the `Changed` method of the `PropertyPage` object. Calling this method causes the Apply button of the page to activate. Typically, the `Change` method would be called in the `Changed` or `Clicked` event of the GUI elements in the page.

Once the Apply button is active, users can click on the button to set all the new property values into the group of selected controls. When the Apply button is pushed, the page is notified through the `ApplyChanges` event of the `PropertyPage` object. In this event, apply all the changes to each control in the `SelectedControls` collection. For example, the following code applies the changes from a page with an option button called `optMask` to all `MaskEdit` controls in the `SelectedControls` collection:

```
Private Sub PropertyPage_ApplyChanges()
  Dim objControl As MaskEdit
  For Each objControl In SelectedControls
    'Mask Property
    If optMask(0).Value Then objControl.Mask = 0
    If optMask(1).Value Then objControl.Mask = 1
    If optMask(2).Value Then objControl.Mask = 2
  Next
End Sub
```

ATTACHING PAGES TO CONTROLS

Once the `PropertyPage` objects are constructed, they may be attached to the ActiveX Control. Attaching pages is done with the `PropertyPages` property of the `UserControl` object. This opens a dialog for attaching pages to the Custom property. Attaching any `PropertyPage` object is done by checking the associated checkbox.

Pages can also be attached to individual properties. This is typically done when a property is complicated enough to warrant its own interface. The Procedure Attributes dialog makes it possible to specify a page for any property created. Standard pages can also be specified for properties such as pictures, colors, or fonts. Visual Basic sets these automatically whenever a property is created with a return value of `StdFont`, `OLE_COLOR`, or `StdPicture`.

Exercise 16-1: A Complete ActiveX Control

This example builds a Picture Button control from two image controls. In this exercise, we will learn to manage the initializing, saving, and retrieving of properties for the ActiveX control. At the end, there will be a fully functional control.

CONTROL FUNDAMENTALS

Step 1

Create a new directory for this project called **\VB BOOTCAMP\EXERCISE 16-1**. Start Visual Basic 6.0 and begin a new ActiveX Control project. Name the new `UserControl` object **Pbutton** and place two image controls on the User Control object. Change the properties as follows:

Control	Name	Index
Image1	imgPButton	0
Image2	imgPButton	1

Step 2

Add a picture to each image control as shown next. These images should be available in the Visual Basic directories if the graphic files have been installed.

Control	Picture

```
imgPButton(0)   lightoff.ico
imgPButton(1)   lighton.ico
```

Step 3

Move the images to the upper left corner of the User Control and resize the User Control around the images. The image controls should be placed directly on top of each other. The images represent the two states of the Picture Button control.

Step 4

Set the properties for the images to establish the initial appearance of the button as follows:

Name	Visible	BorderStyle
imgPButton(0)	True	0-None
imgPButton(1)	False	1-Fixed Single

Step 5

Close all the open code windows and designers, and save the ActiveX Control project as **PBUTTON.VBP**.

Step 6

Add a new Standard EXE to Visual Basic using the **FILE/ADD PROJECT** menu. Right click the Project explorer on the Standard EXE project and select **Set as StartUp**. Save the Standard EXE project as **TEST.VBP** and the project group as **PBUTTON.VBG**.

Using the toolbox, place a new instance of the PButton Control on Form1 in the TEST.VBP project. The off light bulb image should be visible in the control. Now switch to the ActiveX Control project.

The button will not be sizable—it will always look like a toolbar button. In the Code window for the User Control, select the **Resize** event. Add the following code to the event to prevent the control from resizing:

```
Private Sub UserControl_Resize()
Height = imgPButton(1).Height
Width = imgPButton(1).Width
End Sub
```

CONTROL PROPERTIES

Step 7

For this control, we will create a `MousePointer` property and use this property to completely investigate the process of initializing, saving, and restoring property values in the design environment. Add the following code to expose the `MousePointer` property of the Pbutton Control:

```
Public Property Get MousePointer() As MousePointerConstants
   MousePointer = imgPButton(0).MousePointer
End Property
```

```
Public Property Let MousePointer_
        (ByVal intNewMouse As MousePointerConstants)
    imgPButton(0).MousePointer = intNewMouse
    imgPButton(1).MousePointer = intNewMouse
End Property
```

The Property Procedures permit reading and writing the property, but what determines the initial value of the property when the control is first placed on a form? Visual Basic provides several events that are important to the life cycle of a control. These events control the initialization, saving, and restoring of properties when projects are opened and closed inside Visual Basic. These are the key events:

- `UserControl_InitProperties()` called when a control is first dropped on a form.
- `UserControl_WriteProperties()` called when the user saves the VB project.
- `UserControl_ReadProperties()` called when an existing VB project is opened.

TIP

InitProperties, WriteProperties, and ReadProperties make it possible to control the initialization, saving, and restoring of properties to the ActiveX Control.

Step 8

When a user of your ActiveX Control first places an instance on a form in a new VB project, `UserControl_InitProperties()` is called. In this event, you can set the initial value for your property. Add the following code to `UserControl_InitProperties()` to set the initial value for the `MousePointer` property:

```
Private Sub UserControl_InitProperties()
    MousePointer = vbDefault
End Sub
```

Once the ActiveX Control is instantiated, Visual Basic must know if any of the control properties are changed. Calling the `PropertyChanged` method of the `UserControl` does this. The `PropertyChanged` method tells the VB environment that the form is dirty. This is vital because VB will not save the changed values of the control unless it is told to. To do this add the following line of code to the end of the `Property Let MousePointer` procedure:

```
PropertyChanged "MousePointer"
```

Step 9

Whenever a user saves changes to a project, Visual Basic must save any properties for the control. Control properties are saved as part of the FRM file that defines the form hosting the control. To save space in the FRM file, VB only saves properties for a control if the saved value is different from the default value. VB can be told to save properties by the `WriteProperties` event that fires whenever the user of the control saves changes to a project. In order to write the properties to the FRM file, use the `WriteProperty` method of the `PropBag` object. Add the following code to the `WriteProperties` event to save the `MousePointer` property:

```
Private Sub UserControl_WriteProperties(PropBag As PropertyBag)
    PropBag.WriteProperty "MousePointer", MousePointer, vbDefault
End Sub
```

The syntax for writing properties with the `PropBag` object is:

```
PropBag.WriteProperty name, value, default
```

Step 10

When a project that uses the control is opened for editing, the properties for the control must be read from the FRM file and set into the control. Visual Basic does this by using the `ReadProperties` event and the `PropBag` object. Add the following code to the `ReadProperties` event to restore the properties to the ActiveX control:

```
Private Sub UserControl_ReadProperties(PropBag As PropertyBag)
    MousePointer = PropBag.ReadProperty("MousePointer", vbDefault)
End Sub
```

The syntax for reading properties with the `PropBag` object is:

```
property=PropBag.ReadProperty name, default
```

CONTROL EVENTS

Step 11

For this control, we want to add a `Click` event that will fire when the button is pushed. We must also track the state of the button so that the image can be changed accordingly. Add the following code to the [General][Declarations] section to declare the `Click` event:

```
Event Click()
```

Fire the `Click` event and change the images by adding the following code to the Click event of `imgPButton`:

```
Private Sub imgPButton_Click(Index As Integer)
    'Swap images
    If Index = 0 Then
      imgPButton(0).Visible = False
      imgPButton(1).Visible = True
    Else
      imgPButton(0).Visible = True
```

```
        imgPButton(1).Visible = False
     End If
     RaiseEvent Click
  End Sub
```

Step 12

Save the project group. Run the project group and test the button. There should be a functioning two-state button.

THE TOOLBOX ICON

Step 13

Stop the project and switch to the ActiveX Control project. Add a toolbox icon by selecting the UserControl properties and setting the ToolBoxBitmap property to **PBUTTON.BMP**, which is found on the companion CD-ROM. Use any custom bitmap for the toolbox as long as it is 15 pixels wide and 16 pixels high.

THE ABOUT BOX

Step 14

Creating an About box for the control is a matter of creating a form for the box. Insert a new About dialog into the ActiveX Control project by selecting **PROJECT/ADD FORM** from the menu. When prompted, select to **add a new About dialog**.

To display the About box, add a custom method to the ActiveX Control project to display the form. Using the **TOOLS/ADD PROCEDURE** dialog, add a new Sub called **ShowAbout** and place code in it to create the following:

```
Public Sub ShowAbout()
   frmAbout.Show vbModal
End Sub
```

This procedure must be called by VB whenever a user selects the About property from the Properties window. This connection is made through the Procedure Attributes dialog. Select **TOOLS/PROCEDURE ATTRIBUTES** from the menu, and then select **ShowAbout** from the procedure list.

Click on the **Advanced** button and select **AboutBox** in the ProcedureID box. Check **Hide this Member** so that the subroutine cannot be called externally. This is important because the About box is not functionality we want called from VB code. Now close the dialog box.

Step 15

Save the project group and switch to TEST.VBP. Test the About box by clicking on the **About** property in the Properties window.

Exercise 16-2: Creating Property Pages

When an ActiveX Control is created, the user can be allowed to manipulate the control properties through a custom interface known as a Property Page. These pages are found on many commercially available controls under the Custom property. In this exercise, we will create a rotating Moon control with custom Property Pages.

CONTROL FUNDAMENTALS

Step 1

Create a new directory for this project called **\VB BOOTCAMP\EXERCISE 16-2**. Start Visual Basic 6.0 and begin a new ActiveX Control project. Name the new `UserControl` object **Moon**.

Step 2

Place eight image controls on the User Control object. Change the properties as follows:

Control	Name	Index
Image1	imgMoon	0
Image2	imgMoon	1
Image3	imgMoon	2
Image4	imgMoon	3
Image5	imgMoon	4
Image6	imgMoon	5
Image7	imgMoon	6
Image8	imgMoon	7

Step 3

Add a picture to each control using the eight moon icons that ship with Visual Basic or the moon icons for this exercise from the CD-ROM. Change the Visible property of each control to False.

Step 4

Place a Timer Control on the form and name it **tmrMoon**. Set the Interval property to **500**.

Step 5

Move the images to the upper left corner of the User Control and resize the User Control around the images. The image controls should be placed directly on top of each other with the Top and Left properties set to zero. We do not want the user to be able to resize this control, so add the following code to the `UserControl_Resize()` event to prevent resizing:

```
Private Sub UserControl_Resize()
    Height = imgMoon(0).Height
    Width = imgMoon(0).Width
End Sub
```

Step 6

When the control runs, we want it to cycle the moon images. Add the following code to the Timer event of `tmrMoon` to cycle the images:

```
Private Sub tmrMoon_Timer()
    Static intPhases As Integer
    imgMoon(intPhases).Visible = False
    intPhases = intPhases + 1
    If intPhases > 7 Then intPhases = 0
    imgMoon(intPhases).Visible = True
End Sub
```

Step 7

Save the project. Close the open windows. Add a Standard EXE to the project group by selecting **FILE/ADD PROJECT** from the menu. In the Standard EXE, place a moon control on Form1. Immediately, the moon should by cycling through its phases. Save the Standard EXE as **TEST.VBP** and the project group as **MOON.VBG** using the **FILE/SAVE PROJECT GROUP** menu.

CONTROL PROPERTIES

TIP

Throughout this section, the control behavior may be erratic until all the code is in the project. If necessary, try dropping new copies of the control into the test project whenever there is a significant change to the property code.

Step 8

In this exercise, we will implement several properties for the moon control. We will start by creating them normally, and then add the custom property pages. To control the moon, we will create Enabled, Speed, and Direction properties.

Switch to the ActiveX Control project. Create the `Enabled` property by using the **TOOLS/ADD PROCEDURE** dialog and add a Property procedure called **Enabled**. The `Enabled` property is a special property implemented by the `Extender` object; however, the Extender will not provide an `Enabled` property unless one is specifically created. Add the following code to create the `Enabled` property:

```
Public Property Get Enabled() As Boolean
   Enabled = UserControl.Enabled
End Property

Public Property Let Enabled(ByVal blnEnabled As Boolean)
   'Implement Enabled
   UserControl.Enabled = blnEnabled
```

```
    'Affect animation
    tmrMoon.Enabled = blnEnabled
    PropertyChanged "Enabled"
End Property
```

TIP

Although provided by the `Extender` object, the `Enabled` property is not implemented unless a property procedure by that name is created and the Enabled property of the `UserControl` object is set in code.

Step 9

In order to make the `Enabled` property work correctly, assign it to the Enabled ID using the **TOOLS/PROCEDURE ATTRIBUTES** dialog. In the dialog, select the procedure and push the **Advanced** button to locate the Procedure ID box. In the Procedure ID box, select **Enabled**. Save the project and try changing the `Enabled` property of the control in **TEST.VBP**.

Step 10

The `Speed` property determines the time interval for the animation sequence. This value is sent to the `Interval` property of the `Timer` control. Add a Property Procedure called **Speed** and the following code to create the property:

```
Public Property Get Speed() As Integer
    Speed = tmrMoon.Interval
End Property
Public Property Let Speed(ByVal intSpeed As Integer)
    If intSpeed < 0 Then intSpeed = 0
    tmrMoon.Interval = intSpeed
    PropertyChanged "Speed"
End Property
```

Save the project and switch to **TEST.VBP**. Change the `Speed` property and watch the results.

Step 11

The `Direction` property determines the rotation direction for the moon. This is an enumerated property with values `ClockWise` and `CounterClockWise`. To use the enumerated values, add the following code to the [General][Declarations] section of the `UserControl` object:

```
Public Enum enmDirection
    ClockWise
    CounterClockWise
End Enum


Private m_Direction As enmDirection
```

Create the `Direction` property with a Property Procedure and the following code:

```
Public Property Get Direction() As enmDirection
  Direction = m_Direction
End Property
Public Property Let Direction(ByVal enmNewDir As enmDirection)
  m_Direction = enmNewDir
  PropertyChanged "Direction"
End Property
```

To use the `Direction` property, change the code in the `Timer` event of `tmrMoon` so that it appears as follows:

```
Private Sub tmrMoon_Timer()
  Static intPhases As Integer
  imgMoon(intPhases).Visible = False
  If m_Direction = CounterClockWise Then
    intPhases = intPhases + 1
    If intPhases > 7 Then intPhases = 0
  Else
    intPhases = intPhases - 1
    If intPhases < 0 Then intPhases = 7
  End If
  imgMoon(intPhases).Visible = True
End Sub
```

Save the project and try out the new properties.

Step 12

In order properly to manage the properties across development sessions, code must be added to the `InitProperties`, `WriteProperties`, and `ReadProperties` events. The following code will allow the properties to be saved and restored:

```
Private Sub UserControl_InitProperties()
imgMoon(0).Visible = True
Enabled = True
Direction = ClockWise
Speed = 500
End Sub


Private Sub UserControl_ReadProperties(PropBag As PropertyBag)
Enabled = PropBag.ReadProperty("Enabled", True)
Direction = PropBag.ReadProperty("Direction", ClockWise)
Speed = PropBag.ReadProperty("Speed", 500)
End Sub
```

```
Private Sub UserControl_WriteProperties(PropBag As PropertyBag)
PropBag.WriteProperty "Enabled",Enabled, True
PropBag.WriteProperty "Direction", Direction, ClockWise
PropBag.WriteProperty "Speed", Speed, 500
End Sub
```

Save the project and switch to the **TEST.VBP** project. Delete the moon control on Form1 and drop a new one. Try changing the Enabled, Speed, and Direction properties.

ADDING PROPERTY PAGES

Step 13

Now that the Moon control behavior is well defined, we can create a custom Property Page for graphically controlling the property values at design time. Insert a Property Page into the ActiveX Control project by activating the project and selecting **PROJECT/ADD PROPERTY PAGE**. Be sure to add a new blank page and do not use any of the Property Page wizards.

Add the following controls to the property page:

1   Checkbox
2   Option Buttons
2   Labels
1   Horizontal Scroll Bar

Step 14

Change the Properties of the Controls as follows:

Property Page	
Caption	Moon
Name	ppgMoon
Height	3500
Width	4700
ScrollBar	
Name	scrSpeed
Height	285
Left	225
Max	1000
Top	2970
Value	500
Width	4245
OptionButton	
Caption	CounterClockWise

Height	330
Name	optDirection
Left	180
Index	1
Top	2070
Width	2265

OptionButton

Caption	Clockwise
Height	330
Name	optDirection
Left	180
Index	0
Top	1620
Width	2265

CheckBox

Caption	Enabled
Height	330
Left	180
Name	chkEnabled
Top	540
Width	2265

Label

Caption	Speed
Height	240
Left	225
Name	lblSpeed
Top	2655
Width	1905

Label

Caption	Direction
Height	285
Left	135
Name	lblDirection
Top	1215
Width	2310

Step 15

Save the Property Page as **MOON.PAG**.

Now that the Property Page interface is created, attach the page to the Moon control. In the ActiveX Control project, select the `UserControl` object and display its properties. Locate the property called Property Pages and open the Property Pages dialog.

In the dialog, place a check mark next to the `ppgMoon` Property Page. Save the project and examine the `Custom` property of the Moon control in TEST.VBP. When you press the **ellipsis**, the new Property Page should be visible, but not yet functional.

Step 16

Switch to the ActiveX Control project and open the Code window for the Property Page. When a user of the control selects a control, the Property Page must reflect the values of the selected control. In order to do this, the Property Page supports an event called `SelectionChanged`. When this event fires, the page must be updated to the new values. The following code reads the properties from the first control in the selection and populates the page:

```
Private Sub PropertyPage_SelectionChanged()
  'Enabled
  chkEnabled.Value = -1 * SelectedControls(0).Enabled

  'Direction
  If SelectedControls(0).Direction = ClockWise Then
    optDirection(0).Value = True
  Else
    optDirection(1).Value = True
  End If

  'Speed
  If SelectedControls(0).Speed > 1000 _
  Then SelectedControls(0).Speed = 1000
  scrSpeed.Value = SelectedControls(0).Speed
End Sub
```

Step 17

Visual Basic needs to know whenever a user changes the control properties by using the Property Page. Alert VB to changes by calling the `Change` method for the Property Page. This is analogous to calling the `PropertyChanged` method for a `UserControl` object. When the `Change` method is called, VB automatically enables an Apply button for the page. Add the following code to the Click event for the checkbox and option buttons and the `Change` event for the scroll bar:

```
PropertyPage.Changed = True
```

Step 18

Updating the properties is done whenever the user presses the **Apply** button or selects **OK**. Pressing these buttons fires the `ApplyChanges` event in the Property Page. In this event, we add code to update all the controls in the selection. Add the following code to the Property Page to update the selected controls:

```
Private Sub PropertyPage_ApplyChanges()
  Dim ctlMoon As UserControl
  For Each ctlMoon In SelectedControls
    'Enabled
    ctlMoon.Enabled = -1 * chkEnabled.Value
    'Direction
    If optDirection(0) Then
      ctlMoon.Direction = ClockWise
    Else
      ctlMoon.Direction = CounterClockWise
    End If
    'Speed
    ctlMoon.Speed = scrSpeed.Value
  Next
End Sub
```

Step 19

Save the project and try out the new Property Page.

FOR THE CERTIFIED PRO

Pro 16-1: Grid Control

1. Create a custom ActiveX Control that can show a grid of up to 100 rows and 100 columns.
2. Provide a "Rows" and "Cols" property to set the number of rows and columns to display.
3. Provide properties "Row" and "Col" to set an Active cell and a "Text" property to read or write data.

PREPARING FOR CERTIFICATION

Topics for Further Reading
    Creating ActiveX Controls
    Building ActiveX Controls
    Creating Property Pages for ActiveX Controls

CERTIFICATION QUIZ

1. Which object provides properties to ActiveX Controls hosted in a container?
   a. `UserMode` object
   b. `Extender` object
   c. `Ambient` object
   d. `PropertyPage` object

2. Name all the types of ActiveX Controls that can be created in Visual Basic.
   a. Owner drawn
   b. User created
   c. Single subclass
   d. Multiple constituent

3. When a constituent control is used in an ActiveX Control project, what mechanism is used to expose properties?
   a. Inheritance
   b. Polymorphism
   c. Encapsulation
   d. Containment

4. What type of procedure is used to create a control method?
   a. Subroutines
   b. Functions
   c. Property procedures
   d. Friendly procedures

5. What object allows a control to synchronize with its container?
   a. `Extender`
   b. `PropertyPage`
   c. `UserMode`
   d. `Ambient`

6. What property is used to determine whether an ActiveX control is in the design environment?
   a. `DesignMode`
   b. `RunMode`
   c. `UserMode`
   d. `OwnerMode`

7. Where is a control designated as data bound?
   a. The Procedure Attributes dialog
   b. The `UserControl` Property sheet
   c. The Project options
   d. The Project window

8. Where is a control designated as a container?
   a.   The Procedure Attributes dialog
   b.   The UserControl Property sheet
   c.   The Project options
   d.   The Project window

9. Where are new control events declared?
   a.   Project options dialog
   b.   In a Standard Module added to the control project
   c.   In the `RaiseEvent` routine of the `UserForm` object
   d.   In the [General][Declarations] section of the `UserControl` object

10. What event fires when a control is first placed on a form?
   a.   `ReadProperties`
   b.   `InitProperties`
   c.   `WriteProperties`
   d.   `SaveProperties`

11. What event fires when a project is saved?
   a.   `ReadProperties`
   b.   `InitProperties`
   c.   `WriteProperties`
   d.   `SaveProperties`

12. What event fires when a project is opened?
   a.   `ReadProperties`
   b.   `InitProperties`
   c.   `WriteProperties`
   d.   `SaveProperties`

13. What collection is used to set the properties for controls from a Property page?
   a.   `GroupedControls`
   b.   `ChosenControls`
   c.   `PickedControls`
   d.   `SelectedControls`

14. What event fires when the Apply button of a PropertyPage object is pressed?
   a.   `FixChanges`
   b.   `SetChanges`
   c.   `ApplyChanges`
   d.   `GetChanges`

15. What happens to a Property Page if controls from different classes are selected?
   a.   The page is disabled.
   b.   Only controls of the same class are used.
   c.   A trappable runtime error occurs.
   d.   Nothing

ANSWERS TO CERTIFICATION QUIZ

1. b
2. a, c, d
3. d
4. a, b
5. d
6. c
7. a
8. b
9. d
10. b
11. c
12. a
13. d
14. c
15. a

CREATING
ACTIVEX DOCUMENTS

Those who read this chapter need to be familiar with how to use the Internet Explorer. It is also helpful to have some understanding such of Internet systems as Internet Information Server.

SKILLS COVERED

- 70-176 (18): Create an active document
- 70-176 (18.a): Use code within an ActiveX document to interact with a container application
- 70-176 (18.b): Navigate to other ActiveX documents
- 70-176 (32): Plan and implement Web-based deployment for a desktop application
- 70-175 (20): Use an active document to present information within a web browser
- 70-175 (23): Create an active document
- 70-175 (23.a): Use code within an ActiveX document to interact with a container application

- 70-175 (23.b): Navigate to other ActiveX documents
- 70-175 (54): Plan and implement Web-based deployment for a distributed application.

An ActiveX Document, like just about every project type in Visual Basic, is a COM object. This project type, however, creates a special kind of COM object that can only be hosted in certain containers. The containers that host ActiveX Documents are known appropriately as ActiveX Document Container applications. Currently, only three applications have the ability to host ActiveX Documents. These are the Office Binder, a Visual Basic Tool Window, and the Internet Explorer version 3.0 and later. The Internet Explorer is the primary container for these applications and is the focus of this chapter.

ACTIVEX DOCUMENTS FUNDAMENTALS

In setting out to create an ActiveX Document project, notice the option to select or create either an ActiveX Document DLL or an ActiveX Document EXE. The difference between these two projects is the same as between an ActiveX DLL or ActiveX EXE project. The ActiveX Document DLL runs in the process space of the container while the ActiveX Document EXE runs in its own separate memory space. Just like regular ActiveX components, ActiveX Document DLLs can run significantly faster than their out-of-process counterparts.

When creation of an ActiveX Document has been selected, Visual Basic begins the project with another special designer object. The foundation for every ActiveX Document is the `UserDocument` object, which contains all the plumbing necessary for the project to be an ActiveX Document. All that is necessary is to focus on the functionality.

The `UserDocument` object is similar to a form in Visual Basic: build a GUI on it and write code behind the events. When this is done, run the Document, but it will not run stand-alone as a regular VB application will. Instead, Visual Basic creates a special Internet page that can show in Internet Explorer. This page is called a Visual Basic Document or VBD and this file is used by Internet Explorer to access the functionality of the project.

During the debugging process, Visual Basic creates a temporary VBD for use. However, this process is masked by the fact that the project appears to run directly from within Visual Basic. This is because Visual Basic creates the temporary VBD file and then opens Internet Explorer and displays the document. In this way, the debugging process is very similar to debugging any application in VB.

Check It Out 17-1: Creating a Simple ActiveX Document

1. Start a new ActiveX Document DLL project in Visual Basic.
2. On UserDocument1, place a command button and change the Caption to **Push Me!**.
3. In the Click event of the button, place a Message Box statement with the classic `"Hello, World!"` announcement.

```
Public Sub Command1_Click()
```

```
      MsgBox "Hello, World!"
  End Sub
```

4. Run the project: the Debugging tab of the project properties will prompt the selection **Start Component**.
5. Visual Basic runs and displays your application in the Internet Explorer.

DATA PERSISTENCE IN ACTIVEX DOCUMENTS

Developing an application for the Internet can be difficult regardless of the technology chosen to implement the solution because the function of the Internet is fundamentally different from that of an enterprise network. In particular, the relationship between client and server is handled differently.

Imagine utilizing any Web server from within a browser. Browser users type the Internet address or Uniform Resource Locator (URL), into the browser and a page appears. From the perspective of the server, each client request is a separate and distinct transaction, and the server maintains no history of the transactions. Each Web page requested is unrelated to any requested before. The server hands out Web pages to clients in response to their requests, but takes no responsibility for remembering the state of any transaction. This is the basic difficulty of Web design.

If an application is built for the Web, in any technology, users may come to the site to use this application, but how long will they stay? Suppose you have created an online catalog that allows a virtual shopping cart to be used. The user goes through the departments of the catalog, which are represented by different Web pages, and then finally expects to go to one last page to pay the bill. Imagine that the user has viewed three different catalog pages, but before checking out, gets bored and decides to go to the Microsoft site for a while. At this point, should the application remember any items that were selected before the user left the site? When users come back to the site, should their shopping lists still exist or do they have to start over? What if they are gone for 5 minutes, 5 hours, or 5 days? When is it proper to stop remembering the information for them?

The problem gets even worse. Imagine that someone is three pages through a ten-page application. On page three, they simply use the browser to set a bookmark. Now, they turn off their machine and go on vacation. One week later, they start up the browser and immediately use the bookmark to jump right into the middle of the application. Now what happens? The inherent statelessness of the Internet makes application design difficult.

Overcoming the limitations of the Internet is done by creating various means for causing data to persist in ActiveX Documents. The techniques used to remember state fall into two categories: managing state for an individual document and managing state for an entire set of documents. The techniques are not always pretty, but they are functional.

THE LIFE CYCLE OF AN ACTIVEX DOCUMENT

In order to understand how state is maintained for an individual document, we must understand the life cycle of a document. The life of a `UserDocument` is marked by several key events identical to the events received by an ActiveX Control created in Visual Basic. For those who have read the chapter on ActiveX Control creation, these events will be familiar.

THE INITPROPERTIES EVENT

The `InitProperties` event of the `UserDocument` object fires for the ActiveX Document the first time it is rendered in the browser. This property is used to initialize any data the document needs. For example, it might be desirable to clear the fields of a data input form or provide some default values for a list. The `InitProperties` event is similar to the `Form_Load` event for a regular VB form.

While the definition of `InitProperties` seems to make sense at first, it actually falls quite short. When, after all, is the "first time" a Web page is viewed. Is it the first time any user views it? The first time for each user? And what if a user returns to the document later? How much time must go by before `InitProperties` fires again? Once again, the questions surrounding the development process all concern the management of state.

The answer to this issue lies in understanding how the Internet Explorer manages Web pages. Internet Explorer actually remembers the last five Web pages it viewed in RAM. This RAM cache should not be confused with disk cache. The last five Web pages viewed by Internet Explorer are in memory. Therefore, the definition of the first time a Web page is viewed is any time it is not in RAM cache. `InitProperties` fires whenever the `UserDocument` is requested by the browser and the document is not currently in the RAM cache.

THE WRITEPROPERTIES EVENT

The `WriteProperties` event of the `UserDocument` object fires whenever someone leaves the document. This event is designed to let the document know to save data to persistent storage because the user is leaving. When data are saved to persistent storage from a `UserDocument` object, a special object in Visual Basic known as the `Property Bag` is used by both `UserDocuments` and `UserControls` to save data to persistent storage just before the instance is destroyed. Saving the data is done with the `WriteProperty` method of the `PropBag` object. The following code writes data called `MyData` to the `Property Bag`:

```
PropBag.WriteProperty "MyData","This is my data"
```

The `Property Bag` normally saves data to RAM until the user elects to save a document. To prompt the user to save a document, let the Internet Explorer know that the particular document is dirty. Notifying the container that the current ActiveX Document is dirty is accomplished through the `PropertyChanged` method of the `UserDocument` object. Using this method will force a dialog prompting the user to save the current document to the hard drive when the page is exited. The `PropertyChanged` method is generally used in any `Property Let` procedure.

THE READPROPERTIES EVENT

The `ReadProperties` event of the `UserDocument` object fires whenever the user returns to an ActiveX Document that was previously saved. This event provides notification to the document that it should read the `Property Bag` for data. Reading the `Property Bag` is accomplished through the `ReadProperty` method of the `PropBag` object. The following code reads data called `MyData` from `PropBag`:

```
MyVar = PropBag.ReadProperties("MyData")
```

UTILIZING ASYNCHRONOUS DOWNLOADING

Whenever content is created for the Internet, size is an important factor. Often, Internet sites are filled with large files that must be downloaded before the application can function. ActiveX Documents provide a mechanism for minimizing the impact of downloads known as asynchronous downloads, which provide the ability for the application to function while downloading files over the Internet.

Asynchronous downloads are fairly simple to initiate and manage. The key to success is knowing when a download can be initiated. In ActiveX Documents, asynchronous downloading is available after the ActiveX Document is fully sited in the Internet Explorer. When a document is fully sited, it is visible in the browser and its `Show` event fires. Therefore, asynchronous downloads are not available until the `Show` event fires.

Once the document is sited, an asynchronous download may be initiated through the `AsyncRead` method of the `UserDocument` object. This methods takes as arguments the URL of the file to download, a file type specifier, and an alias for the data being loaded. The alias is used later to identify when the download is complete. Because the download is asynchronous, the alias is used in conjunction with the `AsyncReadComplete` event to notify the document when the data download is finished. In the `AsyncReadComplete` event, the download may be identified by the alias and the data used wherever required.

DISTRIBUTING ACTIVEX DOCUMENTS

Perhaps one of the most compelling reasons to use ActiveX Documents is the ease with which they may be distributed to a client. ActiveX Documents, by definition, are distributed using the Internet to download the required components. The setup can be created easily using the Setup Wizard.

Once the ActiveX Documents are created and compiled, use the Internet Setup option of the Package and Deployment Wizard to create and distribute the setup. The Package and Deployment Wizard walks through the process with little fanfare. There are only a couple of areas where special attention is required. Specifically, the Package and Deployment Wizard uses a cabinet (extension .CAB) file as the container for all downloaded components, and requires information about the project design before it can build the CAB file correctly. The Package and Deployment Wizard Safety Settings are where key options must be specified.

In this dialog, the ActiveX Document may be marked as Safe for Initialization and Safe for Scripting. These two checkboxes are a verification on the part of the designer that the ActiveX Documents cannot be used to damage a client computer. This is not a certification that the software is free of viruses, but rather that the design of the software will not allow someone else to use it for nefarious purposes. For example, if an ActiveX Document performing file access is created, there is nothing inherently damaging about the component. However, someone else might use the file access capabilities to overwrite the AUTOEXEC.BAT, doing irreparable harm to the client. Therefore, checking the safety boxes requires a significant amount of thought on the part of the designer to ensure that the active content cannot be misused.

The second part of safety, verifying the software virus free, is done through a process known as Authenticode, an administrative process of verifying or *signing* active content to ensure it is safe to operate. Authenticode works on a dual-key encryption scheme in which Internet Explorer holds the public key and the software author holds the private key. When the active content is downloaded, the Internet Explorer can interrogate the component and determine if it is properly signed by the manufacturer. If it is, then the user sees the verification certificate. If not, the user is presented with a warning dialog cautioning that the active content is not known to be safe.

The tools required to sign active content are contained in the Internet Explorer Client SDK, or the InetSDK. The InetSDK is available as a free download from the Microsoft site at **www.microsoft.com/ie**. In order to sign the software a, developer needs to have not only the code signing tools, but also a private key to use with the tools. Digital certificate keys are not assigned by Microsoft, but by an independent company known as Verisign through its website at www.verisign.com.

Once the Setup Wizard has completed creating the Internet download, the resulting files can be examined. The output of the Wizard consists of three files: a CAB file, a VBD file, and an HTML file. The process of downloading the components requires that a user navigate to the HTML file created by the Setup Wizard. The HTML file references the CAB file, causing Internet Explorer to download all of the components designated by the CAB file. Once the supporting components are downloaded and installed, Internet Explorer is redirected to the VBD file to display the ActiveX Document.

Exercise 17-1: ActiveX Document Fundamentals

ActiveX Documents are special components that run inside ActiveX Document Containers. ActiveX Document Containers include the Internet Explorer, the Office Document Binder, and Visual Basic dockable windows. Although other containers can be used, ActiveX Documents are primarily used inside the Internet Explorer to create rich Visual Basic interfaces that can run on the Intranet.

GRAPHIC USER INTERFACE

Step 1

Create a new directory called **\VBBOOTCAMP\EXERCISE 17-1** using the File Explorer. Start a new ActiveX Document DLL project in Visual Basic. When the project starts, an ActiveX Document designer known as a UserDocument object will be visible. The User-Document object is like a Visual Basic form that can be hosted by the Internet Explorer.

ActiveX Documents can only be hosted by Internet Explorer 3.01 and higher. Make sure to have the correct version of IE running.

Step 2

On the UserDocument, place two image controls, a label control, and a timer control. Change the properties of the controls as follows:

UserDocument

BackColor	White
Name	Bfly
Height	3915
Width	6990

Label

BackStyle	Transparent
Name	lblBFly
Alignment	2-Centered
Caption	ActiveX Documents
Left	225
Top	180
Height	420
Width	6360
FontName	Arial
FontSize	14
FontBold	True

Image Controls

Name	imgBFly(0), imgBFly(1)
Visible	False
Left	0
Top	2745
Height	1155
Width	1155

Timer Control

Name	tmrBFly
Interval	250

Step 3

Set the Project Properties by selecting **PROJECT/PROJECT1 PROPERTIES....** Change the name of the project to **ActDoc**.

ASYNCHRONOUS DOWNLOADS

Step 4

ActiveX Documents used inside the Internet Explorer have the ability to asynchronously download content from a Web site. In this exercise, we will use the async download technique to place images in image controls. Asynchronous downloading is available after the ActiveX Document has initialized. Therefore, we will place the download code in the Show event of the UserDocument. The Show event fires after the document is visible in the browser. When Show fires, the ActiveX Document is sited and asynchronous downloading is available. Add the following code to the Show event of the UserDocument object to download the image files:

```
Dim strURL1 As String
Dim strURL2 As String


'Async data can be read from a file or URL
strURL1 = _
    "[Your Required Files Root Directory]\Required Files\BFly1.bmp"
strURL2 = _
    "[Your Required Files Root Directory]\Required Files\BFly2.bmp"


'The AsyncRead method starts the download
'NOTE: The Name you give the data in CASE SENSITIVE
UserDocument.AsyncRead strURL1, vbAsyncTypeFile, "BFly1"
UserDocument.AsyncRead strURL2, vbAsyncTypeFile, "BFly2"
```

Step 5

The AsyncReadComplete event of the UserDocument object fires when the file download is complete. In this event, we can read the file into the appropriate image control. Add the following code to the AsyncReadComplete event of the UserDocument object:

```
'Load the images
'Again, be careful to note the case sensitivity of the names!!
If AsyncProp.PropertyName = "BFly1" Then
  imgBFly(0).Picture = LoadPicture(AsyncProp.Value)
ElseIf AsyncProp.PropertyName = "BFly2" Then
  imgBFly(1).Picture = LoadPicture(AsyncProp.Value)
End If
```

CREATING THE ANIMATION

Step 6

The animation is controlled by the timer. The position of the images is tracked by two variables. Add the following variable definitions to the [General][Declarations] section to track the image position:

```
Private m_Top As Integer
Private m_Left As Integer
```

Step 7

Before the animation begins, the initial placement of the images is calculated. Add the following code to the `Initialize` event of the `UserDocument` to set the initial values:

```
'Set the initial values for Top and Left
m_Top = Height - imgBFly(0).Height
m_Left = 0
lblBFly.ZOrder
imgBFly(0).Visible = True
```

Step 8

When the timer fires, the images are alternated to generate the animation. Add the following code to the `Timer` event to create the animation:

```
'Calculate new positions
m_Top = m_Top - 100
m_Left = m_Left + 100

If m_Top < 0 Then
 m_Top = Height - imgBFly(0).Height
 m_Left = 0
End If
'Move images
imgBFly(0).Top = m_Top
imgBFly(0).Left = m_Left
imgBFly(1).Top = m_Top
imgBFly(1).Left = m_Left
'Animate the Butterfly
If imgBFly(0).Visible Then
  imgBFly(0).Visible = False
  imgBFly(1).Visible = True
Else
  imgBFly(0).Visible = True
  imgBFly(1).Visible = False
End If
```

VIEWING THE DOCUMENT

Step 9

Start the ActiveX Document by selecting **RUN/START** from the menu. Visual Basic then creates a special file that can be accessed by the Internet Explorer. This document has a .VBD extension and is created in the root directory of the Visual Basic installation. The Internet

Explorer will download the butterfly images asynchronously and start your animation. This technique is excellent for large files that take time to download across the Internet. Your users can start working in the Web page while data is downloading in the background.

PREPARING FOR CERTIFICATION

Topics for Further Reading
    Creating an ActiveX Document
    Building ActiveX Documents

CERTIFICATION QUIZ

1. What types of ActiveX Documents can you create?
    a.   ActiveX DLL
    b.   ActiveX EXE
    c.   ActiveX Document DLL
    d.   ActiveX Document EXE

2. What features are supported by an ActiveX Document DLL?
    a.   Modeless forms
    b.   Modal forms
    c.   Property bags
    d.   Asynchronous download

3. What features are supported by an ActiveX Document EXE?
    a.   Modeless forms
    b.   Modal forms
    c.   Property bags
    d.   Asynchronous download

4. How many documents are kept in memory by Internet Explorer?
    a.   10
    b.   15
    c.   7
    d.   5

5. What method is used to mark an ActiveX Document as dirty?
    a.   `DocumentChanged`
    b.   `BrowserChanged`
    c.   `PropertyChanged`
    d.   `ValueChanged`

6. What events fire when an ActiveX Document is first viewed?
   a. `ReadProperties`
   b. `WriteProperties`
   c. `Initialize`
   d. `InitProperties`

7. What events fire when an ActiveX Document is dismissed?
   a. `ReadProperties`
   b. `WriteProperties`
   c. `Initialize`
   d. `InitProperties`

8. What features tell Internet Explorer that an ActiveX Document cannot be used to harm a client?
   a. Safe for Scripting
   b. Safe for Startup
   c. Safe for Initialization
   d. Safe for Properties

9. What program is used to mark active components as virus free?
   a. Supercode
   b. Genuinecode
   c. Authenticode
   d. Vericode

10. Name all the files created by an Internet setup.
    a. HTML
    b. CAB
    c. DLL
    d. VBD

ANSWERS TO CERTIFICATION QUIZ

1. c, d
2. a, b, c, d
3. a, b, c, d
4. d
5. c
6. c, d
7. b
8. a, c
9. c
10. a, b, d

WEB CLASSES

This chapter introduces Web Classes as a means to creating Internet applications with Visual Basic. It does not attempt to explain all the surrounding Internet technology like Internet Information Server or Visual InterDev. Those who begin this chapter, should already be familiar with the basic aspects of the Internet including Web servers and browsers. Some knowledge of HTML is also helpful. Finally, it is extremely important to have access to a Web server locally. This Web server might be the personal Web server for Windows or Internet Information Server running on Windows/NT.

SKILLS COVERED

- 70-176 (32): Plan and implement Web-based deployment for a desktop application
- 70-175 (14): Create dynamic Web pages by using Active Server Pages (ASP)
- 70-175 (54): Plan and implement Web-based deployment for a distributed application.
- Cert (4): Use Web Classes to create IIS Applications

- Cert (4.a): Use the events of a Web Class to manage user requests
- Cert (4.b): Use Web Items to respond to user requests
- Cert (4.c): Use the IIS Application object model to control program flow
- Cert (4.d): Use Web Classes to manage state in an Internet application
- Cert (4.e): Use IIS applications to create browser-independent applications

Web Classes are the backbone of a particular type of Visual Basic project known as an IIS application. IIS stands for Internet Information Server—Microsoft's Web server—and as such the name is an attempt to identify the key feature of a Web Class application. Specifically, Web Class applications run on the server. Because Web Classes operate on the Web server—as opposed to being downloaded to the client—they are browser independent. That means they can run in Internet Explorer and Netscape Navigator. This is perhaps the biggest reason to recommend this type of Internet project since all the other Internet projects available in VB run solely inside the Internet Explorer. This chapter examines Web Class applications in detail to show how to create browser-independent Internet applications with Visual Basic.

WEB CLASS FUNDAMENTALS

IIS Applications are a combination of compiled Visual Basic code and HTML pages. Since the application is intended to be browser independent, the output to the browser must be pure HTML. Web Classes represent the compiled code portion of the IIS application. Their function is to receive requests from client browsers and process them. The results of the process may be a prewritten HTML page or dynamically generated HTML directly from the Web Class.

IIS Applications begin, as any other, by selection from the New Project dialog. When the new project is started, Visual Basic presents a default Web Class to work with. The Web Class is one of many designers included with Visual Basic (Figure 18-1). Double click on it in the Project Explorer and the designer opens to reveal the design-time interface.

Figure 18-1 The Web Class Designer.

The Web Class designer consists of three main parts: the root of the class, HTML Templates, and custom Web items. The root of the class receives user input and begins the processing of a request. The response to any request may be generated by the root of the Web Class, processed as an HTML Template, or dynamically created through a custom Web item.

Although the IIS application attempts to abstract Internet development to the point where a developer can be somewhat ignorant of Web technologies, the truth is that Web Classes are inextricably linked to Active Server Pages (ASP) technology. Although this book cannot possibly teach the exhaustive topic of ASP in one chapter, readers must understand some of what ASP accomplishes in order to see how Web Classes fit into an overall application design.

While the root of the Web Class acts as the starting point for code in an IIS project, it is not the first thing that happens when as IIS application is run on the Internet. As we will see later, when an IIS application is deployed to the Internet, the Package and Deployment Wizard generates a generic ASP page that is posted on the Internet site. This page is used to launch the IIS application. The ASP page is necessary because the final deployment of an IIS application is actually as an ActiveX DLL. Therefore, the application will require a host to launch and load the DLL before any processing can begin. The following listing shows a typical ASP page generated by the Package and Deployment Wizard:

```
<%
Response.Buffer=True
Response.Expires=0


If (VarType(Application("~WC~WebClassManager")) = 0) Then
Application.Lock
If (VarType(Application("~WC~WebClassManager")) = 0) Then
Set Application("~WC~WebClassManager") = _
Server.CreateObject("WebClassRuntime.WebClassManager")
End If
Application.UnLock
End If
Application("~WC~WebClassManager").ProcessNoStateWebClass _
    "HelloWebClass.hello", _
Server, _
Application, _
Session, _
Request, _
Response
%>
```

This ASP page accomplishes two important prerequisites before any of the IIS application code is executed. First of all, this page ensures that an instance of the Web Class Manager exists on the site. The Web Class Manager is an object used to handle multiple Web Classes that may be created and deployed to a site. The second thing this page does is to instruct the Web Class Manager to create an instance of the DLL that houses the IIS application. Therefore, whenever a client uses an IIS application, they actually call an ASP page similar to the one above (Figure 18-2). This page starts the Web Class Manager and instructs it to create an instance of the Web Class. At that point, the code will begin to execute.

Once the application receives a call, the Web Class follows a predictable life cycle similar to that of other objects in Visual Basic like the form. The first event a Web Class fires after the user makes a request from the ASP page is the Initialize event. This has the same significance as it does in a Class module. Initialize is notification that an instance of the Web Class has been created. The BeginRequest event is the next to fire. Remember that the purpose of a Web Class is primarily to process user requests. The `BeginRequest` event marks the beginning of the processing. Use this event to get or initialize data that may be needed to process the request. For example, an online catalog might read a database to access special pricing features currently in effect. The Start event fires after the `BeginRequest` event. This is the primary event used to process a request and can include an HTML response, processing code, or calling a Web item. When the processing is completed, the `EndRequest` event fires followed by the `Terminate` event when the instance is destroyed.

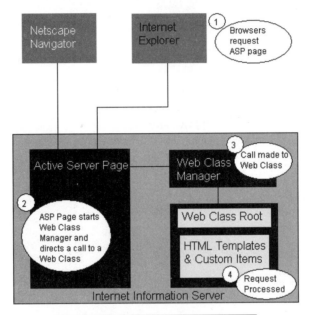

Figure 18-2 Typical IIS Application Flow.

Check It Out 18-1: Web Class Events

1. Start a new Web Class project in Visual Basic
2. Select the default Web Class in the Project Explorer and push the **View Code** button. In the Code window, notice that the Start event for the Web Class has already been coded.
3. Drop the object box in the code window and select the `WebClass` object. In the procedure box, add the `Initialize`, `BeginRequest`, `EndRequest`, and `Terminate` events to the Web Class.
4. In each of these events, write a `Debug.Print` statement to track the firing order of the events. For example, in the `Initialize` event write `Debug.Print Initialize`.
5. Run the application by selecting **RUN/START**.

6. When the application starts, there will be a prompt with the **Debugging** tab of the Project Properties dialog. Since this project is a DLL it cannot run on its own, but must be started by another application. Accept the default selecting **Start Component** to have VB start the DLL.

7. Visual Basic may ask permission to create a virtual directory for the application before it runs. A virtual directory allows the Web server to locate and start the project without deploying it to the Internet.

8. When the application starts, the Internet Explorer browser will open and reveal the Web page generated by the `Start` event of the Web Class. In the browser, note the Web address accessed; an ASP page has actually been accessed.

9. Now examine the Immediate Window in Visual Basic. The five events in the life of the Web Class should all have executed.

Visual Basic makes creating and debugging IIS applications easy because they can be run directly from within Visual Basic. VB makes this possible by creating virtual directories for Web projects. Virtual Directories appear in the directory structure of a Web site, but actually exist somewhere else on the hard drive. For example, saving a Web Class and then running it will cause VB to prompt to create a virtual directory where the project is saved. This effectively allows a browser to use the content in the directory. In our case, this is the Web Class. Look at a list of all virtual directories by accessing the Internet Service Manager for Internet Information Server. Figure 18-3 shows typical virtual directories on IIS.

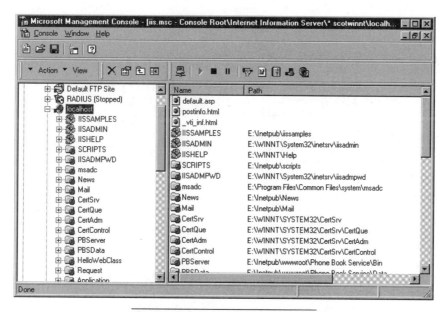

Figure 18-3 Virtual Directories in IIS.

RESPONDING THROUGH WEB ITEMS

Responding to a user request can be as simple as coding an HTML page in the `Start` event of the Web class. In fact, the `Start` event already has code in it when a new IIS application is created. This code uses the `Write` method of the `Response` object to generate an HTML output stream. The `Response` object is part of the IIS Application object model. Those who have developed in Active Server Pages before will also recognize the object as part of the ASP model. In fact, the `Response` object works in Visual Basic largely the same way it works in ASP. The `Write` method generates HTML output from a process.

```
With Response
.Write "<html>"
.Write "<body>"
.Write
    "<h1><font face=""Arial"">WebClass1's Starting Page</font></h1>"
.Write
    "<p>This response was created in the Start event of _
    WebClass1.</p>"
.Write "</body>"
.Write "</html>"
End With
```

The code above is the default code from the Start event of any new Web Class. This code also shows how cumbersome a Web Class can be to use. Because the `Write` method is used over and over to generate an HTML output, your code can become bloated soon after attaining even a moderate level of complexity. Add to that the fact that any changes to this code require a recompile of the application and we have the makings for a rocky maintenance road.

Fortunately, raw HTML is not the only option we have for responding to user requests. The preferred method of response is instead to use an HTML Template. An HTML Template is a prewritten HTML file into which programmatic replacements of key content can be made. In this way, it is not necessary to constantly code the mundane portions of a page like the `<TITLE></TITLE>` tag. In fact, the philosophy behind IIS applications is not to create the HTML Templates, but rather to use content provided by a web master. This does not prevent us from creating custom HTML Templates, but for a developer who is the content author as well as the programmer, Visual InterDev is a better solution than Web Classes.

Adding an HTML Template to a Web Class is done through the designer. In the designer, right-click the **HTML Template WebItems** folder and select **ADD HTML Template....** Use the file dialog to locate HTML pages required in the application. Once added, these templates can be used directly to respond to the user. Of course, when the Web Class starts, the HTML Template is never called directly, so it must be invoked from within the Web Class. This is accomplished by using the `NextItem` property. For a Web Class, simply delete the default code in the `Start` event and then substitute a call to the HTML Template. When a call is made to an HTML Template, the `Respond` event of the template object fires so a response can be formulated using the template. The simplest way to create a response from a template is to use the `WriteTemplate` method which creates an HTML output that exactly matches the template. This essentially returns the page to the user.

Check It Out 18-2: Using an HTML Template

1. Start a new IIS Application in Visual Basic. Save this project to a temporary directory before adding an HTML Template.
2. In the Designer view, right click on the **HTML Template WebItems** folder and add the HTML Template **FADETEXT.HTM** from the CD-ROM. Name the item **FadeText** in the designer. **FADETEXT.HTM** is a Web page built on Dynamic HTML technology and shows some simple interactive effects.
3. In WebClass1, delete all the code in the `Start` event and add the following code:

```
Set WebClass.NextItem = FadeText
```

4. Now select **FadeText** from the object box and Visual Basic will insert the `Respond` event. Generate a response from the template by placing the following code in the `Respond` event:

```
FadeText.WriteTemplate
```

5. Select **RUN/START** from the menu. Visual Basic will respond by presenting the **Debugging** tab of the properties dialog. Accept the default **Start Component** by pressing the **OK** button.
6. Visual Basic may also prompt with a dialog to create a virtual directory. Accept the default by pushing the **OK** button.
7. A Web page will open in the Internet Explorer showing the HTML Template. Try moving the mouse over the text in the page for a quick look at Dynamic HTML in action. This effect is not generated by code, but instead by the HTML page itself. Note that this page is not technically a browser-independent page since it uses HTML recognized only in Internet Explorer, but it is just an example.

When a template is used, it is rare simply to want to return the HTML as it appears in the template. Usually, some aspect of the template needs modification to customize the response. Customizing responses with HTML Templates is done through a special *replacement tag*, a symbol used in the HTML Template to designate where new content should be placed when generated by the Web Class. The form of the replacement tag is determined by the `TagPrefix` property of the HTML Template. Normally, the `TagPrefix` property is set to `WC@`, but this can be changed to any arbitrary symbol. Once it is set, use the prefix to create replacement tags, which take the form of the prefix plus a name. For example, the following shows a snippet of HTML code that designates an area to be replaced inside of a header tag:

```
<H2>The current time is <WC@Time> put current time
here</WC@Time></H2>
```

When the HTML Template is called through the `NextItem` property, the `Respond` event will fire. However, before the `Respond` event, the HTML Template will receive the `ProcessTag` event. The `ProcessTag` affords a chance to make programmatic substitutions for the tags in the template. The `ProcessTag` event passes in the name of the tag and the current contents of the tag. The following code shows how to replace the `<WC@Time>` tag with the current time.

```
Private Sub MyTemplate_ProcessTag _
    (ByVal TagName As String, TagContents As String, _
        SendTags As Boolean)
    If TagName = "WC@Time" Then
        TagContents = Now
    End If
End Sub
```

When the `TagContents` argument is sent to the `ProcessTag` event, it contains the value originally between the tags. Use this information to help make a replacement. For example, the data might contain the primary key of a database table. The key could be used to locate the data to put in the template. Once the value of the `TagContents` argument is set, those data are used to replace both the tags and the content in the template.

In more advanced applications, it might be desirable to replace the tag with some content as well as another replacement tag. This sets up a recursive replacement scheme where the template can be scanned for replacements over and over until no more replacement tags are found. In order to enable this type of recursive replacement, set the `ReScanReplacements` property to True. The following code could be used to replace the tag with the current time, and provide a mechanism for adding a greeting later:

```
Private Sub MyTemplate_ProcessTag _
    (ByVal TagName As String, TagContents As String, _
        SendTags As Boolean)
    If TagName = "WC@Time" Then
        TagContents = Now & _
            "<WC@greeting>Place Greeting Here</WC@greeting>"
    End If
End Sub
```

Recursive code can be very useful for inserting many elements such as when a grid needs to be filled with the results of a database query. In addition to inserting a new tag during recursive replacement, we can also reinsert the same tag. This is done by setting the `SendTags` argument to True. This might be desirable if the first replacement is used as a key for the second replacement. Replacing the tag with the current time plus the original tag itself is accomplished with the following code:

```
Private Sub MyTemplate_ProcessTag _
    (ByVal TagName As String, TagContents As String, _
        SendTags As Boolean)
    If TagName = "WC@Time" Then
        TagContents = Now
```

```
        End If
    SendTags=True
End Sub
```

Along with data, one of the key elements to replace are anchor tags, which allow navigation of an HTML page. Because IIS applications run locally when they are debugged and are later deployed to a Web server, hard-coded anchor tags will prevent the application from working correctly. Therefore, there should be a way dynamically to generate anchor tags for other Web items. This is done with the URLFor function, which returns the unifrom resource locator, URL (Web address) for a given Web item. Thus, if there is a replacement tag named WC@Location and it must contain the address of an HTML Template named MyTemplate, the following code could be used in the ProcessTag event.

```
Private Sub MyTemplate_ProcessTag _
    (ByVal TagName As String, TagContents As String, _
        SendTags As Boolean)
    If TagName = "WC@Location" Then
        TagContents = URLFor(MyTemplate)
    End If
End Sub
```

Check It Out 18-3: Processing Tags

1. Start a new IIS Application project in Visual Basic. Immediately save this project to a temporary directory.
2. This example fills an HTML table with the results of a query. Open the references dialog by selecting **PROJECT/REFERENCES** from the menu. Set a reference to **Microsoft ActiveX Data Objects 2.0 Library**. Close the dialog.
3. Open the Web Class designer. Right-click the **HTML Templates Web Items** folder and add the template file **PUBLISHERS.HTM** to the project from the CD-ROM. This template has a skeleton HTML table with replacement tags already inserted. Name the new template **Publishers**.
4. Open the Code window. In the Start event for WebClass1, remove the default code and insert a call to the **Publishers** template with the following code:

```
Set WebClass.NextItem = Publishers
```

5. This example uses the Biblio database to display information about publishers. Add the following code to the [General][Declarations] section to declare an ADO Recordset object:

```
Private m_Recordset As ADODB.Recordset
```

6. Database connections should be made in the BeginRequest event and then released in the EndEvent request. Add the following code to the BeginRequest event to retrieve the records:

```
Set m_Recordset = New ADODB.Recordset
m_Recordset.Open "SELECT * FROM Publishers", _
"Provider=Microsoft.Jet.OLEDB.3.51;Data Source = _
   <Path to biblio.mdb>\biblio.mdb"
```

7. In the EndRequest event, close the recordset using the following code.

```
m_Recordset.Close
Set m_Recordset = Nothing
```

8. In the Object box locate the Publishers object. This will cause Visual Basic to insert the Respond event. In the Respond event, generate the output with the following code:

```
Publishers.WriteTemplate
```

9. Now add the ProcessTag event for the Publishers template from the Procedure list. In this event, we will perform recursive tag replacement until the entire record-set has been placed in the page. Add the following code to the ProcessTag event to publish the data.

```
Publishers.ReScanReplacements = True

Select Case TagName
  Case "WC@Name"
    TagContents = m_Recordset!Name & ""
  Case "WC@Address"
    TagContents = m_Recordset!Address & ""
  Case "WC@City"
    TagContents = m_Recordset!City & ""
  Case "WC@State"
    TagContents = m_Recordset!State & ""
  Case "WC@Zip"
    TagContents = m_Recordset!Zip & ""
    m_Recordset.MoveNext
  Case "WC@Row"
    If m_Recordset.EOF Then
      TagContents = ""
    Else
      TagContents = TagContents & "<WC@Row>" & TagContents _
              & "</WC@Row>"
    End If
End Select
```

10. Select **RUN/START** from the menu. Visual Basic will respond by presenting the Debugging tab of the Properties dialog. Accept the default **Start Component** by pressing the **OK** button.

11. Visual Basic may also prompt with a dialog to create a virtual directory. Accept the default by pushing the OK button.

12. The open Internet Explorer will be visible with a table of publisher information.

Although replacing tags in an HTML Template provides significant flexibility, it is only one of the features required to create a complete application. Along with creating responses, Web Classes provide a powerful mechanism for controlling navigation. This mechanism is known as a Template Web Item event, which makes it possible to create an event when a user interacts with the server through HTML tags like anchors and forms. For example, there can be notification when a user submits a form to the application. An event can be directly attached to an entire HTML Template. This feature makes it possible to cause the Respond event of an HTML Template to be automatically triggered if the user makes a particular request.

Before template events can be usesd, the events to trap and how the Web Class should connect with them must be identified. Event candidates consist of any tag in the HTML Template that contains a reference to the server. This includes anchor tags, forms, and images. When an HTML Template contains such tags, the Web Class designer lists (Figure 18-4) the tags in the list view portion of the designer. This list view, can be used to connect a tag as an event in code or directly to another HTML Template.

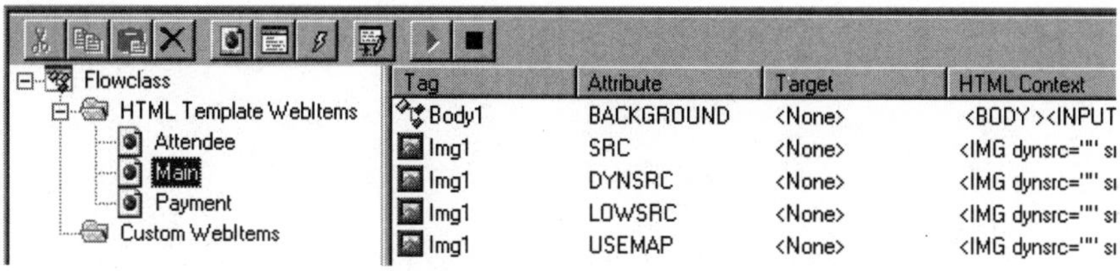

Figure 18-4 Event Candidates in the Web Class Designer.

Connecting an event is done by first selecting the HTML Template whose tags need to be seen. The event candidate tags are then listed in the designer, and it is possible to right-click on the tag to be connected. After the right-click, a popup menu permits selection to connect the tag to a custom event or another HTML Template. Custom events subsequently appear in the Code window, while connecting to another template causes the Respond event for the target template to fire when the user interacts with the selected tag.

Check It Out 18-4: Connecting Events

1. Start a new IIS Application project in Visual Basic. Immediately save this project to a temporary directory.

2. Open the Web Class designer. Right-click the **HTML Templates Web Items** folder and add the template file **EVENTS.HTM** to the project from the CD-ROM. Name the new template **Events**.

3. When you add the **EVENTS.HTM** file, Visual Basic will list the tags that are candidates for events. Locate the entry **Hyperlink1** in the list view. This entry corresponds to an anchor tag in the HTML Template. Right-click this entry and select **CONNECT TO CUSTOM EVENT**. A new event will appear in the tree view.

4. Open the Code window. In the `Start` event for WebClass1, remove the default code and insert a call to the Publishers template with the following code:

```
Set WebClass.NextItem = Events
```

5. Drop the Object box in the Code window and select the `Events` object. Visual Basic will open the `Respond` event. For this example, we simply want to send the template so the user can click the anchor tag. Add the following code to return the template to the browser:

```
Events.WriteTemplate
```

6. Now drop the Procedure box in the Code window and locate the entry for Hyperlink1. Select this entry and Visual Basic will write code for the custom event. Add the following code to the `Events_Hyperlink` event to generate a response to the user.

```
With Response
   .Write "<HTML>"
   .Write "<HEAD>"
   .Write "<TITLE>Event Response</TITLE>"
   .Write "</HEAD>"
   .Write "<BODY>"
   .Write "<H2>You clicked the anchor</H2>"
   .Write "</BODY>"
   .Write "</HTML>"
End With
```

7. Select **RUN/START** from the menu. Visual Basic will respond by presenting the Debugging tab of the Properties dialog. Accept the default **Start Component** by pressing the **OK** button.

8. Visual Basic may also prompt with a dialog to create a virtual directory. Accept the default by pushing the **OK** button.

9. The Internet Explorer will show the first page with the anchor. Click the **anchor**; this will run the code in the custom event to generate the return page.

Along with connecting events associated with tags in the HTML Template, Visual Basic permits creating custom events not directly part of any HTML Template. In this way an event can be created for anything desired. To create a custom event, right-click the **HTML Template** and select **ADD CUSTOM EVENT** from the menu. This will add a new event under the HTML Template and make it available in the Code window.

Once the new custom event is defined, specify how it is activated. This type of event can be associated with any tag that takes a Web address as an attribute. The address is placed into a Web page using the URLFor function. If there are an HTML Template named `MyTemplate` and a custom event named `MyEvent`, the following code shows how to create an anchor tag as a response using the URLFor function:

```
With Response
    .Write "<HTML>"
    .Write "<HEAD>"
    .Write "<TITLE>Custom Event</TITLE>"
    .Write "</HEAD>"
    .Write "<BODY>"
    .Write "<A HREF=" & URLFor(MyTemplate, "MyEvent") & _
        ">Click Here</A>"
    .Write "</BODY>"
    .Write "</HTML>"
End With
```

When constructing event initiators for a Web page with the URLFor function, it is possible to use the name of a predefined event as shown above or to create an event dynamically. Dynamically created events were not created at design time, but were passed to the Web page anyway, by using an event name in the URLFor function that is not associated with any particular Web item. Any event created in this way, will fire the UserEvent event for the associated Web item.

While HTML Templates are the workhorses of IIS applications, it is also possible to define custom Web items that are not separate files, but instead are part of the code in the application. A custom Web item differs from an HTML Template in that the entire response must be created in code. This entails an arduous process of writing HTML tags in code and using the Write method of the Response object to generate the output. The good thing about custom Web items is that they are very useful for generating reusable HTML. They can be used to generate standard head and foot sections for HTML pages with things like company information or standard copyright notices.

Check It Out 18-5: Custom Web Items

1. Start a new IIS Application project in Visual Basic. Immediately save this project to a temporary directory.

2. Open the Web Class designer. Right-click the **Custom Web Items** folder select **ADD CUSTOM WEB ITEM** from the menu. Change the name of the new item to Header. Add two more custom Web items and change their names to **WebBody** and **Footer**.

3. Open the Code window. In the Start event for WebClass1, remove the default code and insert a call to the Publishers template with the following code:

```
Set WebClass.NextItem = Header
```

4. Drop the Object box and select **Header** from the list. Visual Basic will insert the `Respond` event. Repeat this action to insert the `Respond` events for the WebBody and Footer items as well.

5. In the `Header_Respond` event, we create a standard header. After the header is generated, we redirect the next call to the WebBody item to construct the body of the page. Add the following code to the `Header_Respond` event to generate the header.

```
With Response
   .Write "<HTML>"
   .Write "<HEAD>"
   .Write "<TITLE>Standard Header</TITLE>"
   .Write "</HEAD>"
End With
Set WebClass.NextItem = WebBody
```

6. The WebBody item generates the body of the Web page and then redirects the processing to the Footer item to finish the page. Add the following code to `WebBody_Respond` to generate the body of the page:

```
With Response
   .Write "<BODY>"
   .Write "<H2>Body Text</H2>"
   .Write "</BODY>"
End With
Set WebClass.NextItem = Footer
```

7. The last routine to run is the `Respond` event of the Footer item. This code finishes the page. Add the following code to the `Footer_Respond` event:

```
Response.Write "</HTML>"
```

8. Run the application. A simple Web page will be generated. In the browser, select **VIEW/SOURCE** and examine the actual HTML generated by the WebClass. The cumulative effect of all three custom Web items will be visible.

IIS APPLICATION OBJECT MODEL

Along with Web Classes and Web Items, IIS applications provide an object model to access to manage common tasks associated with Internet applications. These objects come directly from ASP technology. For those who have worked with ASP before, the objects will be familiar. The IIS application object model is a flat model consisting of the six objects: Response, Application, Request, Session, Server, and BrowserType. Along with the fact that the model has no hierarchy, the object model also differs from a standard model in that instances of the objects do not need to be created. In many ways, the objects in the model behave like system objects.

That is, they are available to the application by name any time. Each of the objects has its own particular uses in an application and many different properties and methods. In this section we cover the objects and some of the most common uses for them.

RESPONSE OBJECT

We have already used the Response Object in this chapter. It is the principal object used to generate an HTML output from the application. The `Write` method of the Response Object is used to write HTML to the output stream. The application can continue to write to the output stream as long as the `NextItem` property of the Web Class is set. HTML is continually sent to the client until the execution of the Last Respond event in the application.

It is possible to affect how the HTML is sent to the client through the `Buffer` property of the `Response` object. Setting this property to True causes the application to buffer the entire HTML stream and then send it to the client all at once. This can speed overall processing; however, for applications that take a long time to generate the HTML, the user may be left with a blank screen for a noticeable amount of time. Balance the utility of this property against the processing time.

Besides generating output, the `Response` object can also be used to affect how the output is handled. For example, the `Expires` method of the `Response` object makes it possible to indicate when a page should be considered expired by a receiving browser. When a page is expired, it will no longer be used from the client-side cache, but will be reloaded from the server. It is possible to designate that a page generated never be cached by using the following code:

```
Response.Expires = 0
```

Expiring a page a soon as it is loaded by a client browser causes the browser always to return to the server for a new copy of the page each time it is requested. This behavior is actually critical to many business applications. Imagine the disaster for a stock quote application, if the browser keeps retrieving the last quote from cache instead of going back to the server for the latest quote.

APPLICATION AND SESSION OBJECT

The Application and Session objects are capable of remembering state information. We have not yet discussed the use of variables and state information in an IIS application, but it is a significant issue for any Internet application and is fundamentally different from managing state in a normal VB application.

In consideration of state management in any Internet application, it is important to realize that the Internet is essentially a stateless medium. At its heart, the Internet has no capability to remember variable information. Generally, a browser connects to a Web site, requests a page, receives the response, and terminates the connection. Each request by a browser is a stateless transaction with the Web server. Think of a Web page transaction as a file copy operation. The file is copied from server to client and the transaction ends. There is no record or memory that the transaction took place.

The problem gets even worse for state management on the Internet because the Internet has no clear definition of what constitutes an *application*. When an application starts in Windows, there is a clear beginning—double-click an icon on the desktop. There is also a clear ending—select **FILE/EXIT** from the menu. Nowhere on the Internet is there the metaphorical equivalent of the beginning and ending of an application. Each transaction is singular unto itself with no memory of other transactions. And yet, we do know that Web sites seem to remember information. We order books or personalize home pages and the Web site seems to remember the information. The secret here is that in most cases the Web sites are not remembering anything—the user is.

State management for Internet applications is largely handled through *cookies*, pieces of information written to the hard drive of the client computer. When a home page is personalized for a site visited, the site does not remember the personalization settings, the user does. The information is written as a cookie to the hard drive and retrieved by the site the next time the user returns. That is why most Internet applications require cookies to work. If cookies are disabled or the browser lives behind a firewall that prevents their use, many Web applications will not function correctly.

The purpose of the `Application` and `Session` objects is to abstract the management of cookies so that they appear to function like regular variables in the application. These objects are used to create programmatic variables, but they really generate cookies. The `Application` object creates a variable simultaneously available to all users of the application while the `Session` object creates variables reserved for a single user. Creating a variable with the `Application` or `Session` object is a simple matter of naming the variable and setting its value. The following lines of code show how to create an Application variable named `MyVar1` and a Session variable named `MyVar2`:

```
Application("MyVar1")=10
Session("MyVar2")="Test"
```

`Application` and `Session` variables are essentially variants. They can be used to represent any data type. They also do not need to be explicitly declared. The act of setting their value causes them to be defined. Note that each Application or Session variable is handled as a member of the object. It is always accessed through the `Application` or `Session` object and never directly by name.

Because the `Application` object is available to all the browsers using the IIS application, concurrency issues are a concern. To handle these issues, the `Application` object provides the `Lock` and `Unlock` methods. Before setting the value of an Application variable, lock the `Application` object. After the variable is set, the object can be unlocked so it may be accessed by another user.

APPLICATION VARIABLES

Application variables are good for use as *hit counters* for the application. Since each user of the application can access the variable, the following simple code can count the number of hits for the Web Class:

```
Private Sub WebClass_Start()

'Change Value
  Application.Lock
  Application("HitCount")=Application("HitCount")+1
  Application.UnLock

End Sub
```

The scope of an Application variable is the life of the application. This may seem obvious, but we just got through saying that an application cannot be easily defined on the Internet. In fact, applications are defined arbitrarily in the Microsoft world. The definition of an application is said to be a virtual directory and all the Web pages or IIS applications are contained within it. This means that an application is said to start the first time any user selects a Web page from within a virtual directory. So the first time the IIS application receives an Initialize event, that marks the start of the application. However, the IIS application is an ActiveX DLL and is unloaded from memory after each request. The application is said to end 20 minutes after the last user makes a request from the Web Class. Therefore, Application variables exist from the first request to the Web Class until 20 minutes after the last request.

Those familiar with ASP will understand the Application variable life completely, but for VB programmers who have not programmed the Internet before, this is a bizarre way to define variable life. Keep in mind that this definition is a necessity that comes out of the inherent statelessness of the Internet.

When variables are created and used, most of the time there is less interest in Application level variables and more interest in variables assigned to a particular user. The variables are created by the Session object. Because the ActiveX DLL is unloaded after each request, there must be a way to remember the state of the user between calls to the Web Class. This is done with the Session variable, which is available from the first call to the Web Class until that particular user stops making requests in excess of 20 minutes.

The alternative to using Application and Session variables is to set up the Web Class so that it is never unloaded from memory. Do this by setting the StateManagement property of the Web Class to wcRetainInstance. Then skip using Application and Session variables and instead simply use Regular VB variables declared in the [General][Declarations] section of the Web Class. While this may seem immediately more natural—BEWARE! This strategy is fraught with danger because only server-side resources are now being used instead of client-side cookes to remember state. Typically, the instance of the Web Class DLL lives for as long as the application lives. Once again this means 20 minutes after the last user makes a request of the Web Class. The Web Class can be manually unloaded by using the ReleaseInstance method. All things considered, our recommendation is to use the Application and Session objects.

REQUEST OBJECT

The Request object is the object used to gain access to data submitted by a user to the Web Class. Users submit data in Internet applications in one of two ways—through a form or though a hyperlink. Perhaps a user has been on the Internet and filled out a form to place an order. In this process, information is entered in TextBoxes and a button is pressed to Submit the form. Submitting a form sends the data from the form to the Web server for processing. The Request object makes it possible to access that data in the IIS application. Data can also be submitted to a server by clicking a hyperlink that contains data within it. This happens, for example, when selecting from a list of search results to see a Web page. The Request object also affords access to data submitted through a hyperlink.

A Web page creates a form for submission through the use of the <FORM> tag, which contains various input elements like text and options. When a form is filled out and submitted, a special attribute of the <FORM> tag called ACTION directs the submitted form to a particular Internet address. The application at this address must then be ready to handle the submitted data. In an IIS application, tag replacements are used to specify the address of the Web Item which is to handle the data. When the form is submitted, the submitted data can then be accessed using the Request object in the Respond event of the designated Web item.

Imagine an IIS application with an HTML Template named FORM.HTM. This HTML Template already has a form defined that was created by the web master. The ACTION attribute also has a replacement tag designated as WC@Action. The form can be sent to a user and Web Item can be named FormProcess to receive the data by using the following code:

```
If TagName="WC@Action" Then TagContents=URLFor("FormProcess")
```

The user can then fill out the form and submit it as normal. When this happens the Respond event of the Web Item FormProcess is fired. In this event the submitted data can be accessed using the Request object, which contains all the submitted data in a collection called Form. The members of the collection are accessed by the names given them in the form. For example, if a form contains a TextBox named txtName, the submitted data for this field can be accessed with the following code.

```
Request.Form("txtName")
```

Remember, the philosophy of the IIS Application is that the VB Programmer is given HTML Templates by the Web master. To this end, the programmer must work with the Web master to add, where necessary, replacement tags such as the ACTION attribute of the <FORM> tag. The Web master must also provide a list of the names used for elements in the form so that these can be incorporated in the code.

As we stated, forms are not the only mechanism for submitting data. HTML pages can be created to submit data to an application when a hyperlink is clicked. These data are referred to as "QueryStrings" and can be accessed using the Request object. The Request object supports these data through a separate collection. Once again, the field name of the data being submitted must be known, but once it is known, it is accessed through the QueryString collection. As an example, imagine that a search results page shows hyperlinks the user can click. When the hyperlink is clicked, it submits data called "PageName" that designates the page desired. Navigation to the page could be forced by using the Redirect method of the Response object and retrieving the name of the page from the QueryString as follows:

```
Response.Redirect Request.QueryString("PageName")
```

Finally, do not forget that events can always be associated with any form or anchor tag. When an event is associated, a custom event can be generated upon form submission and this can then be used to process the submitted data with the Request object. This technique eliminates the need for tag replacements in the ACTION attribute since the IIS application handles it.

Check It Out 18-6: The Request Object

1. Start a new IIS Application project in Visual Basic. Immediately save this project to a temporary directory.

2. Open the Web Class designer. Right click on the **HTML Template Web Items** folder and select **ADD HTML Template** from the pop-up menu. Add the HTML Template REQUEST.HTM from the CD-ROM. Name the template **RequestForm** in the designer.

3. Right-click the **RequestForm** template and choose **EDIT HTML Template**. Examine the template and locate the replacement tag WC@action. This is the tag that will hold the address for submitting the form contained in the template. Do not actually edit the template, but simply close it after examining the HTML.

4. Right-click on the **Custom Web Items** folder in the designer and select **ADD CUSTOM WEB ITEM** from the pop-up menu. This will add a new custom Web Item. Name the new item **Echo**. This will be the item used to process the form submitted from the HTML Template.

5. Open the Code window. In the Start event for WebClass1, remove the default code and insert a call to the Publishers template with the following code:

```
Set WebClass.NextItem = RequestForm
```

6. When the NextItem property is set, the ProcessTag event of the Request-Form item will fire. In this event, we want to replace the WC@action tag with the address of the custom item Echo. This will cause the form contents to be sent to the custom item. Add the following code to the RequestForm_ProcessTag event.

```
If TagName = "WC@action" Then TagContents = _
     "<form method=post action=" _
  & URLFor("Echo") & ">"
End If
```

7. After the ProcessTag event fires, the Respond event will fire for the RequestForm item. In this event, we simply want to send the template to the client. Add the following code to the RequestForm_Respond event to send the form to the browser:

```
RequestForm.WriteTemplate
```

8. When the form is filled out and submitted by the user, it is sent to the Echo item. This causes the Respond event to fire for this item. In this event, we simply

examine the contents of the submitted form and build a response page that echoes this information back to the client. Although we are performing a simple function here to illustrate form processing, nothing prevents performing more sophisticated processing such as accessing a database. Add the following code to the `Echo_Respond` event to generate the response page:

```
'Header
With Response
   .Write "<HTML>"
   .Write "<HEAD>"
   .Write "<TITLE>Echo A Request</TITLE>"
   .Write "</HEAD>"
   .Write "<BODY>"
   .Write "<CENTER>"
   .Write "<H1>Here is your information</H1>"
   .Write "<TABLE>"
End With


'Echo submitted form
Dim vItem As Variant
For Each vItem In Request.Form
  With Response
     .Write "<TR>"
     .Write "<TH>"
     .Write vItem
     .Write "</TH>"
     .Write "<TD>"
     .Write Request.Form(vItem)
     .Write "</TD>"
     .Write "</TR>"
  End With
Next


'Footer
With Response
   .Write "</TABLE>"
   .Write "</CENTER>"
   .Write "</BODY>"
   .Write "</HTML>"
End With
```

9. Save the work and run the application. There should be a form with several text fields. Fill out the form and submit it. A Response page should appear with the information.

SERVER OBJECT

The `Server` object can be used to create instances of ActiveX components for an application through the `CreateObject` method of the server. The `CreateObject` method takes as an argument the ProgID of the COM object to be created. It works essentially the same way as VB's own `CreateObject` function with one important difference. The `CreateObject` method of the Server allows IIS to detect the threading model of the components created and synchronize the threads during calls from clients. In IIS applications, always create instances of external COM objects using this method.

BROWSERTYPE OBJECT

The `BrowserType` object detects the browser that is making a request from the application. This is a critical operation for sites where it is desirable to customize responses based on the make and model of the requesting browser. The object is remarkably simple to use. For example, the following code returns a string with the make and model of the requesting browser:

```
Dim strBrowser
strBrowser = BrowserType.Browser & " " & BrowserType.Version
```

Once this information is available, the HTML response can be customized for the browser. Although this chapter does not attempt to discuss all the intricate aspects of Internet development, many of the Microsoft technologies are not supported by Netscape Navigator. So if the browser is Internet Explorer, version 4.0 for example, it might be desirable to use ActiveX controls or Microsoft Dynamic HTML as a response. Neither of these technologies is supported by Netscape. Table 18-1 gives a listing of the key properties supported by the `BrowserType` object.

Table 18-1 BrowserType Properties

Property Name	Description
Browser	Returns a string identifying the make of the browser
Version	Returns a string with the version number of the browser
Frames	Returns True if supported
Tables	Returns True if supported
Cookies	Returns True if supported
BackgroundSounds	Returns True if supported
VBScript	Returns True if supported
JavaScript	Returns True if supported
JavaApplets	Returns True if supported
ActiveXControls	Returns True if supported

Exercise 18-1: Web Classes

Web Classes are a server-side Internet solution capable of creating browser-independent solutions. In this project, we will create a mock bookstore that uses Web classes to publish the Biblio database and take orders for books. This exercise requires a Web server available locally to run the application.

Step 1

Using the File Explorer, create a new directory **VB BOOTCAMP/EXERCISE 18-1**.

Step 2

Start a new IIS application in Visual Basic. Open the project properties by selecting **PROJECT/PROJECT1 PROPERTIES** from the menu. In the Properties dialog, change the name of the application to **Bookstore**. Close the dialog. Save the project to the directory created.

Step 3

Open the Web Class designer. Right-click on the **HTML Template Web Items** folder and select **ADD HTML Template** from the pop-up menu. Locate the file **HOME.HTM** on the CD-ROM and add it to the project. Rename the item **Home** in the designer. This is the home page of the application. It is a form that permits searching for books in the Biblio database.

Step 4

Right-click on the **HTML Template Web Items** folder and select **ADD HTML Template** from the popup menu. Locate the file **BOOKS.HTM** on the CD-ROM and add it to the project. Rename the item **Books** in the designer. This is the template that will show the results of the search.

Step 5

Right-click on the **Custom Web Items** folder and select **ADD CUSTOM WEB ITEM** from the popup menu. Name the item **Details** in the designer. This is the item that will show the details of a selected book.

Step 6

Open the Code window for the Web Class and remove the default code found in the `Start` event. Now add the following code to cause the Home HTML Template to be processed:

```
Set WebClass.NextItem = Home
```

Step 7

The Home HTML Template contains a tag is used to replace the `ACTION` attribute of the form so that the submitted contents can be directed to a Web item. In the `Home_ProcessTag` event, add the following code to direct the submitted form data to the Books HTML Template:

```
If TagName = "WC@action" Then _
    TagContents = "<form method=post action=" _
  & URLFor("Books") & ">"
End If
```

Step 8

After the tags are replaced, the `Respond` event fires. In this event, we simply want to send the home page to the browser. Add the following code to the `Home_Respond` event to generate the HTML output:

```
Home.WriteTemplate
```

Step 9

Save the work and run the application. At this point, there should be the home page and a form making it possible to submit a query to find a book. After verifying the application works, stop the application and return to the design environment.

Step 10

After the search form is filled out and submitted, we want to access a the Biblio database to search for books. We will use ADO to perform the query operation. Open the References dialog by selecting **PROJECT/REFERENCES** from the menu. Set a reference to **Microsoft ActiveX Data Objects 2.0 Library**. Close the dialog.

Step 11

When the form is submitted, the Books HTML Template is invoked. In the `ProcessTag` event, we fill the page with the results of the query. This requires running the query and replacing tags in an HTML table to show the results. We also want to be able to allow a user to click on one of the books in the table and see a detail screen about the book. We will place a hyperlink in the table that creates a run-time event for each book in the list. Add the following code to the `Books_ProcessTag` event to run the query and build the results:

```
Static blnStatic As Boolean

'This is the query. We use a static variable to
'run this just the first time. This is necessary
'because this procedure uses recursive tag
'replacements to publish the search results
If Not blnStatic Then
  'Run Query
  Dim strSQL As String
  Static objRecordset As ADODB.Recordset

  'Build Query
  strSQL = "SELECT * FROM [All Titles] WHERE "
  strSQL = strSQL & "(Author LIKE '%" & _
          Request.Form("txtAuthor") & "%' AND "
  strSQL = strSQL & "Title LIKE '%" & _
          Request.Form("txtTitle") & "%' AND "
  strSQL = strSQL & "[Company Name] LIKE '%" & Request.Form _
```

```
                    ("txtPublisher") & "%' )"

      'Run Query
      Set objRecordset = New ADODB.Recordset
      objRecordset.CursorLocation = adUseClient
      objRecordset.CursorType = adOpenForwardOnly
      objRecordset.MaxRecords = 30
      objRecordset.Open strSQL, _
        "Provider=Microsoft.Jet.OLEDB.3.51;Data _
            Source=<Your Path>\
Biblio.mdb"
End If


'Generate Return Page
Books.ReScanReplacements = True
blnStatic = True

'Build a table of data
Select Case TagName
  Case "WC@ISBN"
    TagContents = "<A HREF=" & Chr$(34) & _
      URLFor(Details, (objRecordset!ISBN)) & Chr$(34) & _
      ">" & objRecordset!ISBN & "</A>"
  Case "WC@Title"
    TagContents = objRecordset!Title & ""
  Case "WC@Author"
    TagContents = objRecordset!Author & ""
  Case "WC@Publisher"
    TagContents = objRecordset![Company Name] & ""
    objRecordset.MoveNext
  Case "WC@Row"
    If objRecordset.EOF Then
      TagContents = ""
    Else
      TagContents = TagContents & "<WC@Row>" & TagContents _
          & "</WC@Row>"
    End If
End Select
```

Step 12

Once the table is generated, we want to send the page back to the browser. Add the following code to the Books_Respond event to send generate the output:

```
Books.WriteTemplate
```

Step 13

Save the results and run the application. Try typing **MICRO** into the publisher field and running a search. A table of books should be returned. Once the application is working, end and return to design mode.

Step 14

Now that a table of book results is generated, we expect the user to click on one of the books to see more details. Because the hyperlinks we generated contained dynamic events, we will receive notification through the UserEvent event of the Details item. In this event, we can run a query to get the book details. Add the following code to the Details_UserEvent event to run the query and generate the details page:

```
'Run Query
Dim strSQL As String
Static objRecordset As ADODB.Recordset

'Build Query
strSQL = "SELECT * FROM Titles WHERE ISBN = " & _
        Chr$(34) & EventName & Chr$(34)

'Run Query
Set objRecordset = New ADODB.Recordset
objRecordset.CursorLocation = adUseClient
objRecordset.CursorType = adOpenForwardOnly
objRecordset.Open strSQL, _
   "Provider=Microsoft.Jet.OLEDB.3.51;Data _
       Source=<Your Path>\Biblio.mdb"

'Generate HTML
With Response
   .Write "<HTML>"
   .Write "<HEAD>"
   .Write "<TITLE>Details</TITLE>"
   .Write "</HEAD>"
   .Write "<BODY>"
   .Write "<H2>Here are the details for your book</H2>"
   .Write "<P>" & objRecordset!Title & "</P>"
   .Write "<P>" & objRecordset!Description & "</P>"
   .Write "</BODY>"
   .Write "</HTML>"
End With
```

Step 15

Save and run the project. Try searching for books and then clicking on the results to see the book details.

FOR THE CERTIFIED PRO

Pro 18-1: Web Classes

1. Create an IIS application that allows users to register for a technical seminar. The application should have a home page that lists the available seminars and offers a from to register.
2. When the form is submitted, record the registration as a line in a text file.
3. Provide an administrator's page that presents an attendance sheet for any given seminar.

PREPARING FOR CERTIFICATION

Topics for Further Reading
    Developing IIS Applications
    Web Class Events
    The Object Model for IIS Applications

CERTIFICATION QUIZ

1. Web Classes are compiled as
    a.   ActiveX EXEs
    b.   Active X DLLs
    c.   Standard EXEs
    d.   HTML

2. Web Classes are loaded
    a.   directly into the browser
    b.   directly into a Web page
    c.   by the Web Class Manager
    d.   by an Active Server Page

3. The Web Class Manager is loaded
    a.   directly into the browser
    b.   directly into a Web page
    c.   by the Web Class Manager
    d.   by an Active Server Page

4. The correct order of events for a Web Class is
   a. Initialize, Start, BeginRequest, EndRequest, Terminate
   b. Terminate, Start, Initialize, BeginRequest, EndRequest
   c. Initialize, BeginRequest, Start, EndRequest, Terminate
   d. Initialize, Start, BeginRequest, Terminate, EndRequest

5. A virtual directory
   a. appears on a Web site, but is actually somewhere on the hard drive.
   b. is only created when an IIS application is debugged.
   c. appears on the network, but is actually on the Web site.
   d. is the place to store temporary files.

6. HTML Templates are
   a. compiled components called by an IIS application.
   b. created dynamically by Web Classes.
   c. downloaded by Web Classes for use in the project.
   d. any Web page.

7. Replacement tags are identified by
   a. the prefix "WC".
   b. the tag <REPLACE>.
   c. being bolded in the Web page according to the `Bold` property.
   d. a tag prefixed according to the `TagPrefix` property.

8. Web Classes have events that are
   a. an intrinsic part of the Web Class.
   b. created as custom events.
   c. received from user interaction with a Web page.
   d. created dynamically at run time.

9. Session Variables have a life of
   a. 5 minutes after the last request.
   b. 10 minutes after the last request.
   c. 15 minutes after the last request.
   d. 20 minutes after the last request.

10. What property of the `BrowserType` indicates the make of a browser
   a. Window
   b. Browser
   c. Document
   d. Version

ANSWERS TO CERTIFICATION QUIZ

1. b
2. c
3. d
4. c
5. a
6. d
7. d
8. a, b, c, d
9. d
10. b

DHTML APPLICATIONS

Those who begin this chapter should have a firm understanding of Internet concepts, including a general knowledge of servers and browsers. Although not absolutely necessary, an understanding of HTML is helpful. For those who have built DHTML applications in another tool, like Visual InterDev, this chapter will be much easier to understand.

SKILLS COVERED

- 70-176 (32): Plan and implement Web-based deployment for a desktop application
- 70-175 (54): Plan and implement Web-based deployment for a distributed application
- Cert (5): Use DHTML Applications to create intranet applications
- Cert (5.a): Use the DHTML designer to create Web front ends
- Cert (5.b): Use HTML pages in a DHTML application
- Cert (5.c): Navigate between pages in a DHTML application

■ Cert (5.d): Manage state in a DHTML application with cookies

DHTML applications are Visual Basic projects based upon Microsoft's Dynamic HTML client-side technology that allows Web pages to take on a heightened level of interactivity and functionality. Before proceeding, we should point out that DHTML applications only run in Internet Explorer (IE) 4.0 or later. These projects cannot be run in the Netscape Navigator. In many ways, the DHTML application is similar to the ActiveX Document project. Both are client-side technologies. Both require Internet Explorer. Both are encapsulated in ActiveX DLLs that must be downloaded from the server before they will run. DHTML applications, however, represent a new alternative to form-based user interfaces that has considerable support from Microsoft and is likely to become more important in future versions of Visual Basic.

DHTML FUNDAMENTALS

Like many of the Internet projects in Visual Basic, DHTML applications do not represent a new technology, but rather a new way of creating Web content. Programmers who use tools like Visual InterDev have been creating Dynamic HTML Web pages since the release of IE 4.0. The purpose of the DHTML application is to give the Visual Basic developer the ability to create Dynamic HTML Web pages without having to master the details of Web development. DHTML applications also represent an alternative to forms. Even if creating content for the Internet is not a goal, knowledge of DHTML is still necessary. Because the browser has been integrated into the operating system, DHTML can now be used as a standard interface to a Windows application. Some have gone so far as to say that the VB forms package is on its last leg.

When a DHTML application starts, Visual Basic provides a project that contains a standard module and a DHTML designer. The DHTML designer (Figure 19-1) is used to build the user interface while the standard module provides prebuilt functions for managing application state. We will discuss state management later in the chapter after we focus on the use of the DHTML designer. Figure 19-1 shows the designer in Visual Basic.

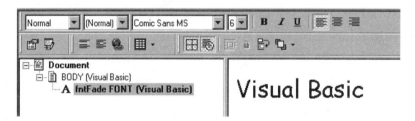

Figure 19-1 The DHTML Designer.

The DHTML designer consists of a two-pane editor which has an HTML outline view on the left and a WYSIWYG page layout on the right. This editor is used to create the user interface for a new DHTML Web page. Each DHTML designer corresponds to a single Web page. Add as many designers to the project as desired. Content for these designers can be saved in one of two ways. The Web pages can be saved as part of the final ActiveX DLL or as external HTML files. Pages can be saved externally, or pages that were generated in an external tool like Visual InterDev can be used. Specify how to save the pages using the editor's property sheet (Figure 19-2), which is available by pushing the leftmost button on the Editor toolbar.

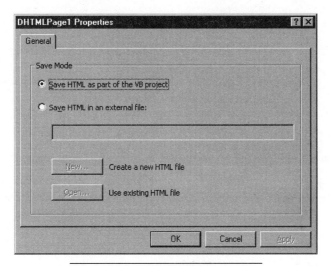

Figure 19-2 DHTML Editor properties.

When the designer is open, you'll notice that the toolbox activates a special tab labeled HTML. When you look at the items in the toolbox, you will see buttons, text fields, options, and other assorted fundamental input devices. At first, these items may seem to be a set of ActiveX controls. They are actually HTML tags masquerading as controls. Using one of the controls from the toolbox begins to build a Web page in the designer. So while dropping a button onto the designer is similar to placing ActiveX controls on a form, this is really just building a Web page.

Once a control is placed on the page, it appears in the WYSIWYG editor and under the HTML outline. Grab the control and rearrange it on the page just as you would with a form. It is even possible to double click the control to access a code window with events. However, the events supported by DHTML applications are slightly different from the ones in a Standard EXE with forms. Dropping an HTML button on the designer and double clicking it will reveal the `OnClick` event in the Code window. Why not just call this Click? The answer is that DHTML applications conform to the Internet standards for event naming. In Web pages, all the events begin with the word "On".

Things get even stranger with properties. For Visual Basic programmers, the property that designates the text on the face of the button is `Caption`. In DHTML applications the property is `Value`. In fact the `Value` property is a common one also used to designate the text in an HTML TextBox.

Check It Out 19-1: DHTML Fundamentals

1. Start a new DHTML project in Visual Basic. Immediately open the designer named DHTMLPage1.
2. From the toolbox, drop an HTML button on the designer, by double clicking the control in the toolbox.
3. The designer allows in-place editing of the button's caption. Try typing the new caption **Push Me!** directly into the button.
4. The button also appears with a hashed border, which can be used to move or resize the button. Try manipulating the button within the designer.
5. Double-click the button to enter the Code window. This should reveal the `OnClick` event. In this event, add the following simple code:

```
MsgBox "Hey, you clicked me!"
```

6. HTML controls not only have different names for events, they also have different events altogether. Drop the procedure box in the Code window to examine the various events supported by the HTML button. From the list, select the `OnMouseOver` and `OnMouseOut` events and add them to the Code window.
7. The `OnMouseOver` fires whenever the mouse passes into the boundary of the button. When this happens, we can affect the look and feel of the button. Changing the contents of a page is done through the DHTML object model. We will discuss this object model in detail later, but for now, add the following code to change the button when the mouse passes over it:

```
Button1.Style.Color = "Red"
```

8. When the mouse leaves the button, the `OnMouseOut` event fires. Add the following code to the `OnMouseOut` event to change the button back to its original color:

```
Button1.Style.Color = "Black"
```

9. Run the application. There will be a prompt with the Debugging tab of the Project properties. Accept the default start option by pushing the **OK** button. The Internet Explorer will start. Try passing the mouse over the button. Now push the button to test its functionality.

To build a Dynamic HTML application, it will undoubtedly be desirable to use more than one DHTML designer. Since each designer corresponds to a separate web page in the application, knowing how to navigate between the pages as well as to pass information will be necessary. These concepts are typically foreign to Visual Basic programmers who navigate between forms using the simple Show method and are used to an application's retaining state until it terminates.

As we pointed out in the chapter on Web Classes, Internet applications are essentially stateless and cannot remember information. Each transaction in the application is serving a Web page to the browser. The server is incapable of remembering any variable information. This is true in DHTML applications just as it is for Web Classes. Each designer in the application is a separate

Web page and cannot share state with other designers directly. It is not possible to declare a Public variable in a designer and access it from another designer. In fact, each page should be treated as a separate entity that can manage its own internal state as long as it is displayed in the browser. When the browser navigates away from the page, any stored information is lost.

Because the data in a designer cannot be shared with other designers directly, we need an indirect mechanism for sharing state. In DHTML applications, this state is shared exactly as it is with any Web page—through cookies. Cookies are state values written to the hard drive of the client's computer. In the case of a DHTML application, one designer leaves a cookie—or piece of data—and another designer can read it when it loads into the browser. The code for managing cookies is actually written when a new DHTML application starts and can be found in the standard module included with the project. This standard module, also contains two functions—GetProperty and PutProperty. The functions signatures for these routines are shown below:

```
Public Sub PutProperty _
(objDocument As HTMLDocument, _
strName As String, _
vntValue As Variant, _
Optional Expires As Date)
Public Function GetProperty _
(objDocument As HTMLDocument, _
strName As String) As Variant
```

While setting and retrieving cookies requires a simple call to the above functions, the arguments deserve a closer look. The first argument of each function is listed as type HTMLDocument. This argument refers to the document which is setting or getting the cookie value. In the next section, we will discuss the DHTML object model in detail, though understanding cookies requires understanding the two most important objects in a DHTML application—BaseWindow and Document. Together, these objects make it possible to reference the current browser and Web page which are required to use cookies.

BaseWindow is an object that refers to the browser itself. Think of BaseWindow as the frame inside which a Web page is displayed. The Document object is a reference to the actual web page. The current page can always be addressed with the following code:

```
BaseWindow.Document
```

This code is used as the first argument in both the GetProperty and PutProperty functions. The actual designer is never addressed in code. In fact, the designer cannot be addressed by name—that nets an error. Always refer to the currently active designer through the Document object. As we learn more about the DHTML object model, we will discover that BaseWindow and Document are the critical objects for manipulating Web pages in a browser.

Once there is a reference to the active document, use the arguments in the PutProperty function to save a field/value pair and give it an expiration date. When cookies are saved, they are managed in a special file by the browser, which keeps track of the expiration dates and automatically removes old cookies. While an expiration date is optional, it is a good idea to set one in order to prevent building up unwanted data and wasting hard-drive space.

Once a cookie is set, the application will typically move to another page to continue processing. An example of this type of workflow is the virtual shopping cart. In this scenario, imagine visiting an online site that sells catalog items. In this application, every page might represent a department such as Men's, Women's, Sporting Goods, or Housewares. Shop at each department to fill the shopping cart with goods. The items in the cart are remembered as cookies on the client machine. When shopping is finished, move to investigate the page where all the items are read out and tallied for sale.

Navigating between pages in a DHTML application requires the use of the `BaseWindow` object, which supports the `Navigate` method, used to move the browser to a new Web page. The `Navigate` method takes a single argument, which is the Uniform Resource Locator (URL) of the page to go to. This can be a complete web address or a relative address which navigates in relation to the current location. Thus the following are all valid statements:

```
BaseWindow.Navigate "http://www.vb-bootcamp.com"
BaseWindow.Navigate "default.asp"
BaseWindow.Navigate "../home.htm"
```

DHTML designers can also be the target of the `Navigate` method. When the DHTML application runs it creates Web pages for each of the designers in the project. The name of the Web page is created as a combination of the project name and the designer name followed by an HTML extension. Thus, for a project named DHTMLProject and a designer named Page1, the following code would navigate to the page:

```
BaseWindow.Navigate "DHTMLProject_Page1.html"
```

It is also possible to use the HTML Hyperlink, which can be found in the toolbox and represents an anchor tag in a Web page. Simply drop the control on the designer and assign it an address. When a user clicks the link at run time, this causes immediate navigation to the target page.

Check It Out 19-2: Navigation and State

1. Start a new DHTML application in Visual Basic.
2. Open the **DHTMLPage1** designer. Figure 19-3 shows the interface for the Web page. Build this interface in the designer and use the Item list to set the design-time properties.

   Item 1—HTML TextBox

ID	`txtName`
Value	empty

   Item 2—HTML Button

ID	`btnNext`
Value	Next

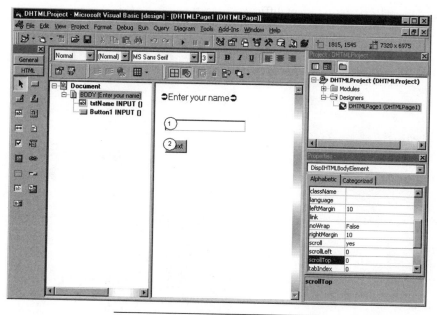

Figure 19-3 The DHTMLPage1 Interface.

3. Add a second designer to the application by selecting **PROJECT/ADD DHTML PAGE** from the menu. When the page is added, there will be a query whether to save the page within the project or as an external file. Choose to save the page within the project and press the **OK** button.

4. Figure 19-4 shows the interface for the second Web page. Build this interface in the designer and use the Item list to set the design-time properties.

Item 1—HTML TextBox

ID   `txtEMail`

Value   empty

Item 2—HTML Button

ID   `btnNext`

Value   Next

5. Add a third designer to the application by selecting **PROJECT/ADD DHTML PAGE** from the menu. When the page is added, there will be a query about saving the page within the project or as an external file. Choose to save the page within the project and press the **OK** button.

6. Figure 19-5 shows the interface for the third Web page. Build this interface in the designer and use the Item list to set the design-time properties.

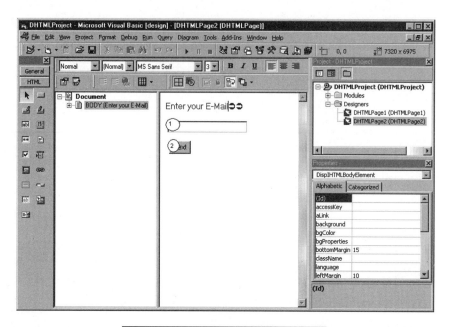

Figure 19-4 The DHTMLPage2 Interface.

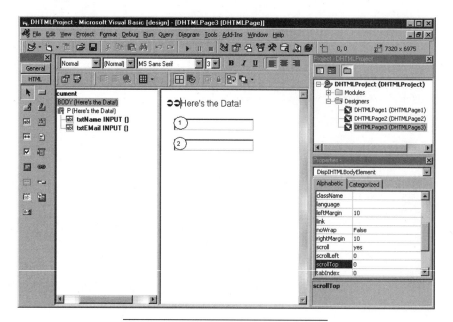

Figure 19-5 The DHTMLPage3 Interface.

Item 1—HTML TextBox

ID   txtName

Value   empty

Item 2—HTML TextBox

ID   txtEMail

Value   empty

7. Open the Code window for **DHTMLPage1**. In this page, write the data entered into the TextBox to a cookie and navigate to the second page. In the object box, locate the `btnNext` object. Selecting this object will add the `OnClick` event. Add the following code to the btnNext_OnClick event.

```
'Write the cookie
PutProperty BaseWindow.Document, "Name", txtName.Value,
         DateAdd("d", 1, Now)


'Navigate
BaseWindow.navigate "DHTMLProject_DHTMLPage2.html"
```

8. Open the Code window for **DHTMLPage2**. In this page, write the data entered into the TextBox to a cookie and navigate to the third page. Add the following code to the `btnNext_OnClick` event:

```
'Write the cookie
PutProperty BaseWindow.Document, "EMail", txtEMail.Value,
         DateAdd("d", 1, Now)


'Navigate
BaseWindow.navigate "DHTMLProject_DHTMLPage3.html"
```

9. Open the Code window for **DHTMLPage3**. In this page read the cookies left by the other two pages. When a page first loads, the `OnLoad` event of the `BaseWindow` fires. This event is similar to the `Form_Load` event for a form. Add the following code to the `BaseWindow_Onload` event to read and display the cookies:

```
txtName.Value = GetProperty(BaseWindow.Document, "Name")
txtEMail.Value = GetProperty(BaseWindow.Document, "EMail")
```

10. Run the application. There will be a prompt with the Debugging tab. Select the default start options by pressing the **OK** button. The first page in the application will start. In this page type your name and press the **Next** button.

11. The application navigates to the second page. In this page, enter the **E-Mail** address and press the **Next** button. The third page should appear and display the data entered in the first two pages.

THE DHTML OBJECT MODEL

Like most applications today, the Internet Explorer is constructed of software objects, and these objects are accessible through code. We call this collection of objects the DHTML object model and it is the key to moving beyond the basics with DHTML. Figure 19-6 shows the DHTML object model.

Figure 19-6 The DHTML Object Model.

The BaseWindow object is the cornerstone of the object model. We have already seen how this object allows us to navigate between pages in an application, but, it has many more uses. The BaseWindow represents any frame that contains a Web page. This includes the main window of the browser or any windows in a frame set. The BaseWindow object has properties and methods that permit manipulation of all the open windows in the browser as well as performing many utility functions such as setting up timers.

We will start our investigation of the BaseWindow object by examining its role in a frame set. Frame sets are familiar to most browser users as multiple Web pages shown in the browser.

This type of display often has a banner window, a navigational toolbar window, and a main window. Figure 19-7 shows a typical frame set.

Figure 19-7 A Frame Set.

The frame set shown actually contains four different windows. The main window of the browser contains the definition of the frame set while the three windows each contain visual information. While we cannot directly create a frame set definition in a DHTML application, we can use an existing Web page to define the frame set and then use DHTML designers to provide the visual content for the set. Frame sets are defined in HTML using the <FRAMESET> and <FRAME> tags, which define the size, numbers, and content of the frames. The following code shows the frame set definition that created Figure 19-7:

```
<HTML>
<HEAD>
<META NAME="GENERATOR" Content="Microsoft Visual Studio 6.0">
<TITLE></TITLE>

</HEAD>
<FRAMESET COLS="27%,73%">
 <FRAME SRC="toolbar.htm" NAME="TOOLBAR" SCROLLING="Yes"
        FRAMEBORDER="0">
 <FRAMESET ROWS="25%,75%">
  <FRAME SRC="banner.htm" NAME="BANNER" SCROLLING="No"
         FRAMEBORDER="0">
```

```
<FRAME SRC="home.htm" NAME="HOME" SCROLLING="Yes" FRAMEBORDER="0">
</FRAMESET>
</FRAMESET>
</HTML>
```

The <FRAMESET> tag defines the size and number of frames. The above page shows that one <FRAMESET> tag divides the page into columns at 27% and 73%. A second <FRAMESET> tag divides the second column into rows at 25% and 75%. The <FRAME> tags define the content for each page. This can be the name of an existing Web page or the generated name a designer will have at run time. The most important part of the definition, however, is the name. Each window in the frame set is given a name when it is created. Use these names, to programmatically manipulate any of the windows within the frame set.

Check It Out 19-3: Navigating Frame Sets

---

1. Start a new DHTML Project in Visual Basic.
2. Add three new DHTML designers to the application by selecting **PROJECT/ADD DHTML PAGE** from the menu. When the pages are added, there will be a query about saving the page within the project or as an external file. Choose to save the page within the project and press the **OK** button.
3. There should now be four DHTML designers in the project. Add a fifth designer to the application by selecting **PROJECT/ADD DHTML PAGE** from the menu. When the page is added, there will be a query about saving the page within the project or as an external file. Choose **Save as External File** and then press the **Open** button to locate an existing file. Locate and add the file **FRAMESET.HTM** from the CD-ROM. This page defined a frame set for this exercise.
4. Open the designer for **DHTMLPage1**. Figure 19-8 shows the user interface for this designer. This will be the navigational toolbar. Create this interface and use the Item list for setting design-time properties.

   Item 1—HTML Button

Name	btnPage1
Value	Page 1

   Item 2—HTML Button

Name	btnPage2
Value	Page 2

   Item 3—HTML Button

Name	btnPage3
Value	Page 3

5. Open the Code window for **DHTMLPage1**. In the Code window, write code to manipulate the frame set. The name of the main frame in the set is **Home**. This

window is accessible through the Frames collection of the `BaseWindow` object. Add the following code to the page to manipulate the frame set:

```
Private Function btnPage1_onclick() As Boolean
   BaseWindow.Parent.frames("Home").navigate "DHTMLProject_
             DHTMLPage2.html"
End Function


Private Function btnPage2_onclick() As Boolean
   BaseWindow.Parent.frames("Home").navigate "DHTMLProject_
             DHTMLPage3.html"
End Function


Private Function btnPage3_onclick() As Boolean
   BaseWindow.Parent.frames("Home").navigate "DHTMLProject_
             DHTMLPage4.html"
End Function
```

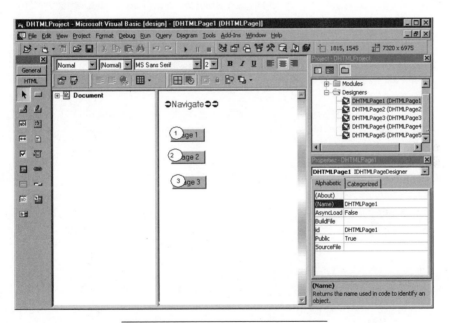

Figure 19-8 The DHTMLPage1 Interface.

6. Open each of the remaining designers and add text or graphics to identify them uniquely. The exact content is not critical. Just place text Page 1, Page 2, or Page 3 on the designer.

7. Save the work and run the application. When the application is run, the Debugging tab of the Project Properties dialog will appear. Select to start the application with **DHTMLPage5** which is the frame set definition. Press **OK**.

8. Try using the buttons on the page to navigate the pages.

Underneath the `BaseWindow` object is the `Document` object, which represents an HTML page being displayed inside a window. Each DHTML designer in the project eventually becomes a `Document` when it is displayed. As we have pointed out, the designer is converted to an HTML page when displayed in the browser, and it is at this point that the `Document` object becomes meaningful. In standard HTML applications, all code is written directly into the HTML page—there is no separate designer. However, since Visual Basic provides the designer as a precursor to the `Document` object, we are concerned not only with the `Document` object but also with the life cycle of the designer itself.

The designer supports four events familiar to Visual Basic programmers: `Initialize`, `Load`, `Unload`, and `Terminate`. The `Initialize` event fires when the ActiveX DLL that contains the designer is created. The final distribution of a DHTML application is always an ActiveX DLL. Typically this DLL may be created and destroyed many times in an application. When the `Initialize` event fires, it is not certain that all other objects on the page are available, so do not attempt to use object references from this event.

After the `Initialize` event, the designer fires the `Load` event. The `Load` event fires after the first element in the designer becomes visible. Once again, it is not certain that all the elements on the page are available in this event. Instead of using the `Load` event of the designer, use the `OnLoad` event of the `BaseWindow` to start any animations or interactions with elements on the page.

The `Unload` event fires when a user is leaving this designer for another page. In the `Unload` event, we can still reference all the objects on a page, so clean up should occur here if necessary. The `BaseWindow` object also supports an `OnUnload` event typically used for clean up in standard HTML pages. This event can be used by the application as well.

Finally, the `Terminate` event fires for the designer when the object is being destroyed, typically because the ActiveX DLL is unloading. This event is similar to the `Terminate` event in any class module. None of the objects on the Web page is available during this event, so do not depend upon it to manage data entered into the page.

Because the designer object is actually contained within the `Document` object at run time, it is not considered a proper member of the DHTML object model. Beneath the `Document` object, however, is access to all of the elements on the page. This entails user elements like text and buttons as well as formatting tags for fonts and tables. All these elements give wide control over the appearance and behavior of the Web pages. But it is possible to derive maximum benefit from DHTML, fundamental differences in event handling must be understood.

Events in DHTML have many radical differences from their Visual Basic counterparts. First and foremost, we have already seen that the names of events in DHTML routinely begin with the `On` keyword. Examples of this include `OnClick` and `OnLoad`. DHTML also has events that are not found at all in Visual Basic. For example, all elements in the designer support `OnMouseOver` and `OnMouseOut` events. These events fire when the mouse moves into or out of the graphical area of the element.

Another significant difference between Visual Basic and DHTML events is that DHTML events do not have arguments, while Visual Basic events regularly pass in arguments such as *x* and *y* coordinates for a mouse or ASCII code for a key press. DHTML arguments are read from a special object known as the Event object. When an event fires, key information may be read as a property of the Event object. The following code shows how to access the ASCII code for a keyboard interaction using the OnKeyPress event:

```
Private Sub Text1_onkeypress()
   MsgBox BaseWindow.Event.KeyCode
End Sub
```

DHTML's lack of arguments in event signatures is accompanied by support for a mechanism unseen in Visual Basic known as Event Bubbling. Event Bubbling allows events fired within an element to trigger related events in objects higher in the object model. For example, pushing an HTML button causes an OnClick event for the button, but will also fire an OnClick event for the Document which contains the button. The advantage of Event Bubbling is that it is possible to handle events for similar controls in one location rather than coding all the events separately. Suppose you want to change the color on any button in the page to red whenever the mouse passes over it. In Visual Basic, you would normally have to write the code for each button—or at best write a common function called by each button. In DHTML, all the buttons can be trapped at the Document level using the Document_OnMouseOver event.

To trap the events for many elements within the Document, there must be a way to identify the specific element that caused the event to fire. This is done through the SrcElement property of the event object. The SrcElement object, procures a reference to the exact item in the page that is causing an event to fire. The following code shows how you might trap all events at the Document level and change the color of the firing element:

```
Private Sub Document_onmouseover()
   With BaseWindow.event.srcElement.Style.Color = "red"
End Sub
```

In the above code, the SrcElement property returns a reference to the element that originally fired the bubbling event. The Style property allows access to the visual properties of the element. We will cover styles later, but for now the color is changed to red for any element the mouse passes over. Of course we may not want to change the color for every element the mouse passes over. We may just want to change it for buttons, or maybe for hyperlinks. The class of the firing element can be read through the TagName property. To change the color to red only for Input tags in the page, you write the following code:

```
Private Sub Document_onmouseover()

   With BaseWindow.event.srcElement
     If .tagName = "INPUT" Then
       .Style.Color = "red"
     End If
```

```
    End With

  End Sub
```

Elements are typically filtered by `TagName` and the visual behavior is changed based on the type of element. Sometimes it will be desirable to suppress the bubbling of events for a particular element. There might be one special button on the page that should not turn red when the mouse passes over. Bubbling can be suppressed for any event by using the `CancelBubble` property. Event bubbling makes it possible to handle the majority of behavioral events at the `Document` level while dealing with the exceptions at a lower level. The following code shows how the `OnMouseOver` bubble can be canceled for a button named `MyButton`:

```
Private Sub MyButton_onmouseover()
  BaseWindow.event.cancelBubble = True
End Sub
```

Check It Out 19-4: Event Bubbling

1. Start a new DHTML application in Visual Basic.
2. Open the designer for **DHTMLPage1**.
3. Figure 19-9 shows the designer with three hyperlinks in it. Place the three hyperlinks in the page. We will use event bubbling to change the color of these hyperlinks at the Document level.

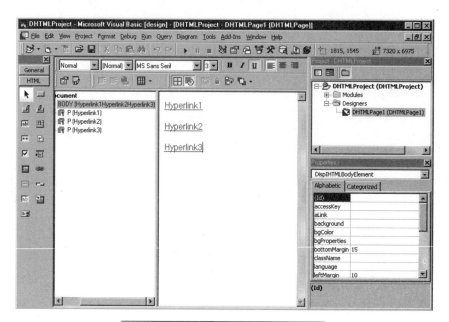

Figure 19-9 The DHTMLPage1 Interface.

4. Since all the hyperlinks will have the same behavior, we need not code them separately. Instead we will use the `Document` object to handle all the tags. Add the following code to handle the `OnMouseOver` and `OnMouseOut` events for the document:

```
Private Sub Document_onmouseover()

   With BaseWindow.event.srcElement
     If .tagName = "A" Then
       .Style.Color = "red"
     End If
   End With


End Sub


Private Sub Document_onmouseout()

   With BaseWindow.event.srcElement
     If .tagName = "A" Then
       .Style.Color = "blue"
     End If
   End With


End Sub
```

5. Run the application. Try moving the mouse over the hyperlinks and watch the behavior.

In the previous examples, we accessed the visual features of HTML elements through the `Style` property. Each element in the designer has a `Style` property which contains information about the appearance and position of the element. We can programmatically access the `Style` property for an element and then use sub properties to change characteristics of the element. The `Style` property allows access to features such as font, color, and size as well as left, top, height, and width.

Dynamic HTML is a broad topic that encompasses much more than Visual Basic. Many developers have used DHTML in Web pages and through tools like Visual InterDev before it was available in DHTML applications. Those who are serious about developing these applications from scratch will want to reference the Internet Explorer Software Development Kit (Inet SDK) and investigate the use of Visual InterDev. DHTML applications like IIS applications are primarily for developers creating simple applications or receiving Web pages from a Web master to be used as a starting point.

Exercise 19-1: DHTML Applications

This exercise uses a DHTML application to create a HelpDesk application. Use application to submit help requests and track their progress. This application uses a Microsoft Access database named **DHTMLHelpDesk.mdb** found on the CD-ROM.

Step 1

Using the File Explorer, create a new directory named **VB BOOTCAMP/EXERCISE19-1**. Copy the file **DHTMLHELPDESK.MDB** from the CD-ROM into the new directory.

Step 2

Within the same directory, create a Data Link file for the new database by selecting **FILE/NEW/MICROSOFT DATA LINK** from the menu in the File Explorer. This will create a new Data Link file. Rename the file **HELPDESK.UDL**.

Step 3

Right click the **HELPDESK.UDL** file and select **PROPERTIES** from the pop-up menu. This will open the Data Link properties dialog. In the Provider tab, select **Microsoft Jet 3.51 OLE DB Provider** and press the **Next** button.

Step 4

In the Connection tab, press the **ellipsis** next to the TextBox labeled **Select** or **Enter Database Name**. Use the file dialog to locate the database and select it. Push the **Test Connection** button. When the connection is set up, Press the **OK** button to close the dialog.

Step 5

Start a new DHTML application in Visual Basic.

Step 6

This project performs data access using the ActiveX Data Objects. Since this is a Help Desk application, we are assuming it is being used on an intranet. Since it is on an intranet, we can gain access to Data Link files and utilize standard ADO data access techniques. If we were creating this application for use on the Internet, it would be impossible to establish a data link across the Internet to files within the security boundary of a domain. For this reason, DHTML applications make excellent intranet systems.

In order to use ADO, we have to set a reference to the object model. Open the References dialog by selecting **PROJECT/REFERENCES** from the menu. In the References dialog, set a reference to **Microsoft ActiveX Data Objects 2.0 Library**. Close the dialog by pressing the **OK** button.

Step 7

Open the project properties dialog by selecting **PROJECT/DHTMLPROJECT PROPERTIES...** from the menu. In the Properties dialog, change the name of the project to **DHTMLHelpDesk**. Close the dialog by pressing the **OK** button.

Step 8

Open the designer for **DHTMLPage1**. In the Properties window, change both the Name and ID for the designer to **Request**. This is the page that will take Help Desk requests.

Step 9

Save the project into the directory created earlier.

Step 10

Figure 19-10 shows the complete interface for the Request designer. Begin building this page by typing the words **Enter your Request** at the top of the page.

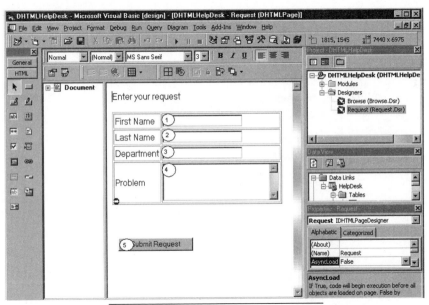

Figure 19-10 The complete Request page.

Step 11

On a new line in the designer, a table can be added to build the request form. Insert the table by selecting **INSERT TABLE** underneath the Table Operations button on the toolbar. Locate the button and use the down arrow to drop the appropriate menu. When the menu item is selected a two-by-two table will appear in the page.

Step 12

Locate the `<TABLE>` tag in the treeview of the designer. It may be necessary to expand the tree to find the table. Right click on the `<TABLE>` entry in the tree and select **PROPER-TIES...** from the menu. This will open the Table Properties dialog. In table properties, change the border size to 2. Close the dialog by pushing the **OK** button.

Step 13

Now move to the design view and very carefully click in one of the cells in the table. Be careful just to click inside the cell and not accidentally to select the entire table. Right-click the cell and select **INSERT ROW** from the menu. Add rows until the table has two columns and four rows.

Step 14

In the second column of the table, add HTML TextBoxes to the first four cells. In the last cell of the second column, add a `TextArea` control to create a memo field. In the first column of the table, label the input boxes with text by referring to Figure 19-10. Use the Item list below to set the properties for each item.

Item 1—HTML TextBox

ID	`txtFirstName`
Name	`txtFirstName`
Value	\<empty\>

Item 2—HTML TextBox

ID	`txtLastName`
Name	`txtLastName`
Value	\<empty\>

Item 3—HTML TextBox

ID	`txtDepartment`
Name	`txtDepartment`
Value	\<empty\>

Item 4—HTML TextArea

ID	`txtProblem`
Name	`txtProblem`
Value	\<empty\>

Step 15

Add an HTML Button to the designer. Position it as shown in Figure 19-10. Change the text on the button to read **Submit Request**. Using the properties page, change the ID of the button to **btnSubmit**.

Step 16

Double click on the **btnSubmit** button to open the code window. The event `btnSubmit_OnClick` should be visible in the code window. In this event, we will write code to submit the request using a simple INERT SQL statement. Add the following code to the `btnSubmit_OnClick` event to submit the request:

```
'Build SQL Statement
Dim strSQL As String
```

```
strSQL = "INSERT INTO Requests
(RequestDate,FirstName,LastName,Department,Problem,Status) "
strSQL = strSQL & "VALUES("
strSQL = strSQL & Chr$(34) & Now & Chr$(34) & ","
strSQL = strSQL & Chr$(34) & txtFirstName.Value & Chr$(34) & ","
strSQL = strSQL & Chr$(34) & txtLastName.Value & Chr$(34) & ","
strSQL = strSQL & Chr$(34) & txtDepartment.Value & Chr$(34) & ","
strSQL = strSQL & Chr$(34) & txtProblem.Value & Chr$(34) & ","
strSQL = strSQL & Chr$(34) & "Initiated" & Chr$(34) & ")"


'Open Connection
Dim objConnection As ADODB.Connection
Set objConnection = New ADODB.Connection


'Run SQL
objConnection.Open "File Name=<Your Path>\HelpDesk.udl"
objConnection.Execute strSQL
objConnection.Close


MsgBox "Thanks for submitting your request", vbOKOnly + _
       vbInformation, "Help Desk"
```

Step 17

Before running the application, open the database using the data tools in order to view the data as they are entered. Open the Data View window by selecting **VIEW/DATA VIEW WINDOW**. In the Data View window, right-click on the **Data Links** folder and select **ADD A DATA LINK**. This will bring up the Data Link properties. Add a data link to the DHTML-HelpDesk.MDB file. When it is added, it should be possible to examine the Requests table in the database.

Step 18

Save and run the application. When presented with the debugging tab, select the default options by pressing the **OK** button. When the application starts, try adding a new request to the database.

Step 19

After the request is added, end the application and open the Requests table in the Data View. Verify that the request was added to the database.

Step 20

Now we will create a page for viewing and tracking requests. Add a new designer to the application by selecting **PROJECT/ADD DHTML PAGE**. When prompted, select to save the page as part of the application. Press the **OK** button.

Step 21

This page uses optimistic batch updating to retrieve, browse and edit requests. Change the Name and ID of this page to **BROWSE**.

Step 22

Figure 19-11 shows the final page for editing and reviewing help requests. Start this page by typing **Request Maintenance Page** at the top of the page.

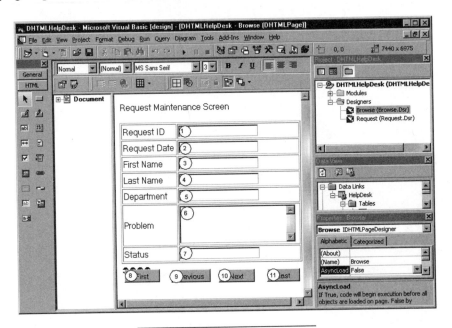

Figure 19-11 The Browse Designer.

Step 23

On a new line in the designer, we will add a table to build the maintenace form. Insert the table by selecting **INSERT TABLE** underneath the **Table Operations** button on the toolbar. Locate the button and use the down arrow to drop the appropriate menu. When the menu item is selected a two-by-two table will appear in the page.

Step 24

Now move to the design view and very carefully click in one of the cells in the table. Be careful just to click inside the cell and not accidentally to select the entire table. Right-click the cell and select **INSERT ROW** from the menu. Add rows until the table has two columns and seven rows.

Step 25

In the second column of the table, add HTML TextBoxes to the first five cells and the last cell. In the sixth cell of the second column, add a TextArea control to view the memo field. In the

first column of the table, label the input boxes with text by referring to Figure 19-11. Use the
Item list below to set the properties for each item.

Item 1—HTML TextBox

ID	`txtRequestID`
Name	`txtRequestID`
Value	\<empty\>

Item 2—HTML TextBox

ID	`txtRequestDate`
Name	`txtRequestDate`
Value	\<empty\>

Item 3—HTML TextBox

ID	`txtFirstName`
Name	`txtFirstName`
Value	\<empty\>

Item 4—HTML TextBox

ID	`txtLastName`
Name	`txtLastName`
Value	\<empty\>

Item 5—HTML TextBox

ID	`txtDepartment`
Name	`txtDepartment`
Value	\<empty\>

Item 6—HTML TextArea

ID	`txtProblem`
Name	`txtProblem`
Value	\<empty\>

Item 7—HTML TextBox

ID	`txtStatus`
Name	`txtStatus`
Value	\<empty\>

Step 26

Add six HTML buttons to the page to allow navigation of the recordset. These buttons should
be aligned as shown in Figure 19-11. Use the Item list below to set their ID and Value properties at design time.

Item 8—HTML Button

ID	btnMoveFirst
Name	btnMoveFirst
Value	First

Item 9—HTML Button

ID	btnMovePrev
Name	btnMovePrev
Value	Previous

Item 10—HTML Button

ID	btnMoveNext
Name	btnMoveNext
Value	Next

Item 11—HTML Button

ID	btnMoveLast
Name	btnMoveLast
Value	Last

Step 27

Open the Code window for the designer. In this application, we will declare private variables for the data access. Add the following code to the [General][Declarations] section to be used for data access:

```
Private m_Connection As ADODB.Connection
Private m_Recordset As ADODB.Recordset
```

Step 28

In the OnLoad event of the BaseWindow object, we will access the database and return all of the entries as a batch. We will then disconnect from the database and use the recordset for browsing and editing. Add the following code to the BaseWindow_OnLoad event to retrieve the data:

```
'Establish the Connection
Set m_Connection = New ADODB.Connection
m_Connection.ConnectionString = _
  "File Name=<Your Path>\HelpDesk.udl"
m_Connection.CursorLocation = adUseClient
m_Connection.Open

Set m_Recordset = New ADODB.Recordset
m_Recordset.ActiveConnection = m_Connection
m_Recordset.Source = "SELECT * FROM Requests"
```

```
m_Recordset.CursorLocation = adUseClient
m_Recordset.CursorType = adOpenDynamic
m_Recordset.LockType = adLockBatchOptimistic


m_Recordset.Open
ShowData


'Disconnect Resultset
Set m_Recordset.ActiveConnection = Nothing
m_Connection.Close
Set m_Connection = Nothing
```

Step 29

The data are displayed using a custom routine. Add this procedure by selecting **TOOLS/ADD PROCEDURE** from the menu. In the Add Procedure dialog, add a new Private Sub named **ShowData**. Add code to this procedure so that the final result appears as follows:

```
Private Sub ShowData()
   txtRequestID.Value = m_Recordset!RequestID & ""
   txtRequestDate.Value = m_Recordset!RequestDate & ""
   txtFirstName.Value = m_Recordset!FirstName & ""
   txtLastName.Value = m_Recordset!LastName & ""
   txtDepartment.Value = m_Recordset!Department & ""
   txtProblem.Value = m_Recordset!Problem & ""
   txtStatus.Value = m_Recordset!Status & ""
End Sub
```

Step 30

The buttons at the bottom of the page are used to navigate the records. This is simple navigational code using ADO methods. Write the following procedures to navigate the recordset:

```
Private Function btnMoveFirst_onclick() As Boolean
   m_Recordset.MoveFirst
   ShowData
End Function


Private Function btnMoveLast_OnClick() As Boolean
   m_Recordset.MoveLast
   ShowData
End Function


Private Function btnMoveNext_OnClick() As Boolean
   m_ Recordset.MoveNext
```

```
       If m_ Recordset.EOF Then
          Beep
          m_ Recordset.MoveLast
       Else
          ShowData
       End If
    End Function


       Private Function btnMovePrevious_OnClick() As Boolean
          m_ Recordset.MovePrevious
          If m_ Recordset.BOF Then
             Beep
             m_ Recordset.MoveFirst
          Else
             ShowData
          End If
       End Function
```

Step 31

Open the Project Properties dialog by selecting **PROJECT/DHTMLHELPDESK PROPER-TIES** from the menu. Select the **Debugging** tab and switch the Start Component from Request to Browse. Press **OK**.

Step 32

Run the application. The browse page should appear and the navigation buttons should be functional.

FOR THE CERTIFIED PRO

Pro 19-1:

1. After finishing exercise 19-1, add buttons to the Browse page for Editing the records and performing a batch update.

PREPARING FOR CERTIFICATION

Topics for Further Reading
    DHTML Application Development Process
    The Internet Explorer SDK available at **www.microsoft.com/ie**
    Inside Dynamic HTML by Scott Isaacs, Microsoft Press

CERTIFICATION QUIZ

1. DHTML applications run in which browsers?
   a. Internet Explorer 3.0
   b. Internet Explorer 4.0
   c. Netscape Navigator 3.0
   d. Netscape Navigator 4.0

2. DHTML applications run
   a. on the server.
   b. on the client.
   c. on both client and server.
   d. on neither client nor server.

3. DHTML designers
   a. represent many pages.
   b. are run in an ActiveX DLL.
   c. represent one Web page.
   d. can be stored in a toolbox.

4. DHTML application documents can be stored
   a. in the application.
   b. in a separate document.
   c. in both a separate document and in the application.
   d. in neither a separate document nor the application.

5. Which are valid events for an HTML button?
   a. `OnMouseOver`
   b. `OnMouseOut`
   c. `OnClick`
   d. `OnBlur`

6. Data in a DHTML application can be stored
   a. in designer-level variables.
   b. in cookies.
   c. in module-level variables.
   d. passed between designers.

7. If a browser shows three frames in a set, how many window objects are available?
   a. 1
   b. 2
   c. 3
   d. 4

8. Which are valid statements?

   a.   `BaseWindow.Navigate "http://www.microsoft.com"`

   b.   `BaseWindow.Navigate DHTMLPage1`

   c.   `BaseWindow.Navigate "DHTMLProject_DHTMLPage1.html"`

   d.   `BaseWindow.Navigate ../default.asp"`

9. What code returns a reference to the element causing an event?

   a.   `BaseWindow.Event.SourceElement`

   b.   `BaseWindow.Event.Element`

   c.   `BaseWindow.Event.SrcElement`

   d.   `BaseWindow.Event.Source`

10. What code suppresses event bubbling?

   a.   `BaseWindow.Event.Cancel = True`

   b.   `BaseWindow.Event.CancelBubble`

   c.   `BaseWindow.Event.CancelBubble = False`

   d.   `BaseWindow.Event.CancelBubble = True`

ANSWERS TO CERTIFICATION QUIZ

1. b
2. b
3. b, c
4. a, b
5. a, b, c, d
6. a, b, c
7. d
8. a, b, d
9. c
10. d

SCALING VISUAL BASIC APPLICATIONS

Those who begin this chapter, should have complete knowledge of OLEDB and Active Data Objects. They should also be able to build and use ActiveX DLL projects. Microsoft Transaction Server will be required to complete the Check It Out exercises and the final chapter exercise.

SKILLS COVERED

- 70-175 (7): Configure a server computer to run Microsoft Transaction Server (MTS)
- 70-175 (7.a): Install MTS
- 70-175 (7.b): Set up security on a system package
- 70-175 (8): Configure a client computer to use an MTS component
- 70-175 (8.a): Create packages that install or update MTS components on a client computer
- 70-175 (24): Design and create components that will be used with MTS

- 70-175 (26): Choose the appropriate threading model for a COM component
- 70-175 (27): Create a package by using the MTS Explorer
- 70-175 (27.a): Use the Package and deployment Wizard to create a package
- 70-175 (27.b): Import existing packages
- 70-175 (27.c): Assign Names to packages
- 70-175 (27.d): Assign security to packages
- 70-175 (28): Add components to an MTS package
- 70-175 (28.a): Set transactional properties of components
- 70-175 (28.b): Set security properties of components
- 70-175 (29): Use role-based security to limit use of an MTS package to specific users
- 70-175 (29.a): Create roles
- 70-175 (29.b): Assign roles to components or component interfaces
- 70-175 (29.c) Add users to roles
- 70-175 (56) Implement load balancing

Application partitioning and distributed components have been a focus of many parts of this book. Now we will examine a specific kind of partitioned application known as a three-tier application. In three-tier architecture, thin clients are created that access business objects distributed throughout the enterprise. These objects in turn access the data sources used in the application. The entire design is aimed at providing thin clients and robust, scalable applications. Figure 20-1 shows the fundamental architecture of a typical three-tier application.

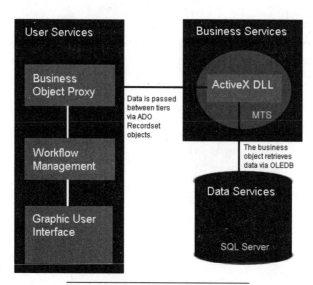

Figure 20-1 Three-Tier Architecture.

In a full-blown three-tier application, separate partitions are defined for Data Services, Business Services, and User Services. Data Services consist of the database and any stored procedures or triggers defined within. The Business Services typically consist of Visual Basic components that read and write to the database. Partitioning is achieved through OLE DB technology and the use of Active Data Objects. This means that you could change the business compnent without affecting the database or change the database and still use the same business object. User Services provides the interface to the user as well as workflow management. Data are typically passed from Business Services to User Services by using disconnected ADO Recordset objects. These recordsets are created by the Business layer and passed to User Services by using disconnected ADO Recordset objects. The key relationship between User Services and Business Services is that User Services never directly execute an SQL statement on the database. Instead, User Services call methods of the objects in Business Services which return a recordset. This provides partitioning between the User Services and Business Services.

Data are further abstracted through a workflow object which may convert a recordset into a collection so that it can be dealt with in an object-oriented fashion. User Services never bind directly to a recordset because that builds dependencies between layers and works against proper partitioning. We will see much more of partitioning and tiers as we work our way through the various scalability features of Visual Basic.

Visual Basic provides several features that allow business objects (typically ActiveX EXE projects) to scale. Many of these features are somewhat limited, but, depending on the number of users, VB may handle the projected load easily. However, as user load increases from one to hundreds or even thousands, system resources such as threads, database connections, and object instances play a major role in the overall performance of you enterprise.

SINGLE-USER APPLICATIONS

Single-user applications are the simplest to build in Visual Basic, and obviously have no scaling issues to worry about. In this type of application, developers might open a connection to a data source through ADO and leave the connection open throughout the session. Because the application has only one user, there need be no concern with monopolizing resources like data connections.

Similarly, threading is not an issue. Visual Basic differs from other languages in that, programmers cannot start a new thread within the application. Other languages (e.g., Visual C++) support multithreading, which allows an application to execute multiple lines of code nearly simultaneously. Multithreading means an application can perform more than one function at a time—as when printing while saving to a file. In Visual Basic, multiple functions are queued and executed in the order requested. This is not a problem for one user, but it can be for many users.

Memory usage is hardly a concern either. With only a single user, no one is competing for resources, so the application can be much less concerned with releasing objects not currently in use. Most of the business objects should be created as ActiveX DLLs to enhance speed, and they will run directly on the client. Perhaps the only real memory issue to be faced is returning a record set from the database that is larger than the available memory, so that disk caching results.

All in all, single-user applications are simple, and most Visual Basic programming reflects this style. Many VB developers simply do not understand scaling issues and continue to develop large applications as if they were being used by just a few people. Scaling requires breaking old habits.

MULTI-USER APPLICATIONS

Those who leave the world of single-user applications, must immediately concern themselves with conserving system resources. The business objects must be removed from the client and moved to the network. This means it is no longer possible to use ActiveX DLLs because they cannot be remotely accessed. Instead, ActiveX EXEs are used and calls to them are made through the Distributed Component Object Model (DCOM). At this point, several key features of ActiveX EXEs come into play.

Class Modules in ActiveX EXEs have a special property known as the Instancing property that helps business objects scale. This property has several settings we examined earlier in the book, but here we are concerned with two: Multi-Use and Single-Use. These settings determine how an ActiveX EXE behaves when its services are requested by many users at the same time.

MULTI-USE ACTIVEX EXE

Setting the Instancing property to Multi-Use causes the ActiveX EXE to produce a new instance of the requested class module each time a new client calls. All the created instances run together inside the same memory space occupied by the ActiveX EXE. This model is best described as *one server—many instances*.

The problem with a Multi-Use ActiveX EXE goes back to the single-threaded nature of Visual Basic. In the single-threaded business object, all the instances share the same memory space. Therefore, they cannot execute simultaneously on the one thread. This means that although each client has its own instance of the business object, VB cannot service more than one client at a time.

Imagine that the business object is responsible for querying a database and performing a multitable join. Suppose further that the operation takes six seconds to complete. Since the object cannot multithread, it must make each client wait in the queue while requests are processed in turn. The tenth person in the queue would wait 60 seconds for service. In fact, that person may never get service, since remote requests typically time out in 10 seconds based on the default value of the OLEServerBusyTimeout property of the App object.

Of course Visual Basic can alleviate some of the issues surrounding threads by selecting to support multithreading for a business object. However, multithreading is not a solution that allows an application to scale endlessly. Thread management can actually be quite expensive, as we will see.

SINGLE-USE ACTIVEX EXE

One solution to the problem of single-threaded business objects is to set the Instancing property to Single-Use. Unlike Multi-Use objects, Single-Use objects do not create multiple instances in the same memory space. Single-Use components create a whole new instance of the ActiveX EXE-one for each client that calls. When it is not possible to multithread, multi-tasking is required. This leads to a situation in which no client has to wait for service because a new instance of the ActiveX EXE is always created for each individual user.

The issue with Single-Use components, of course, is resource depletion. Each client is going to start a new copy of the component, which may rapidly consume system resources on the target machine. This is the same old story—performance versus resources.

APARTMENT THREADING

Another solution to the scaling problem lies in declaring the ActiveX to support multithreading through the apartment threading model. Supporting multithreading is done in the Properties dialog for the project. Select **Apartment Threading** in the Threading Model options and declare whether to provide a thread for each client or to utilize a thread pool.

Selecting apartment threading is not a panacea. The choice has significant consequences and design issues. Many people unfamiliar with multithreaded applications believe that multi-threaded applications always run faster and better than single-threaded applications. This is not necessarily true. Multithreaded applications must share the microprocessor resources, and the constant swapping can actually lead to poorer performance for an individual process while providing improved performance on the aggregate.

Threading works best when the number of active threads roughly matches the number of processors in the machine. If there is a single processor, this means there can be no more than one active thread at a time. Any more will actually lead to performance degradation.

Performance is also greatly affected by the threading options selected (Figure 20-2). Selecting **Thread per Object** causes the component to spawn a new thread for each client that calls. This can engender problems quickly as dozens of threads are created on a machine with just a single processor. It is better is to select **Thread Pool**, where threads can be limited to just a few and they will be reused when they are inactive. Thread pooling is one of the cornerstones of scalability.

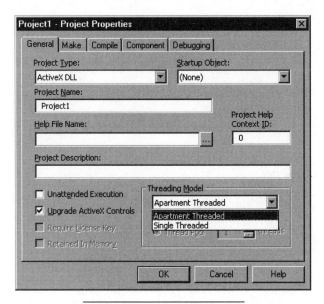

Figure 20-2 Threading Options.

THE MICROSOFT TRANSACTION SERVER

While the options built into Visual Basic provide some scaling features, they are generally not powerful enough to scale into large-enterprise applications. When applications are used by dozens of people, there must be concern with more than just the options that can be set in VB, specifically, with pooling three major resources: threads, object instances, and ODBC connections.

Providing control over the major resources is the job of the Microsoft Transaction Server (MTS). This provides all the resource and component management capabilities the application needs while requiring very few changes in the VB code. Best of all, there need be no concern with issues like Multi-Use versus Single-Use. Just create VB business objects and let MTS manage the details.

MTS does not even utilize ActiveX EXEs, but uses ActiveX DLLS instead. The reason for the change is that once an ActiveX DLL is placed under MTS control, MTS takes care of the surrogate out-of-process component. Microsoft Transaction Server provides all the DCOM capabilities that allow clients to call an object while managing resources that promote scalability and fault tolerance.

Installing the Microsoft Transaction Server is a fairly straightforward process. MTS ships as part of the Windows/NT 4.0 Option Pack. A standard installation is a matter of running the Option Pack installation on an existing Windows/NT 4.0 server. MTS also supports a Windows '98 version, though this version does not support the same level of security as the full-blown version does. MTS is also tightly integrated with the Internet Information Server (IIS). Install IIS version 4.0 and MTS is installed automatically.

Once MTS is installed, administrative can be accessed. The primary interface to MTS is the Transaction Server Explorer (Figure 20-3), which provides a way to add, remove, and manage components under the control of MTS. The MTS Explorer is built on the same GUI metaphor as the Windows File Explorer.

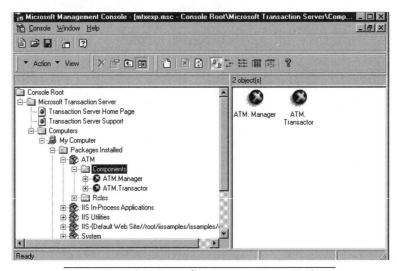

Figure 20-3 The Microsoft Transaction Server Explorer.

In the MTS Explorer, components on any machine in the enterprise can be viewed. The components are organized into a logical hierarchy that consists of machines, packages, and components. Components placed under MTS control reside inside a package, an administrative grouping of components that allows them to exist in the same security context. Inside a package, are installed one or more components, which can be nothing more than Visual Basic class modules compiled into an ActiveX DLL.

The process of placing an object under MTS control is relatively simple. First construct an ActiveX DLL project in Visual Basic. At the simplest level, the DLL created need not have any special features associated with it. Just create the DLL and provide at least one Public method in the Class Module. As a simple example, we compiled an ActiveX DLL to test MTS. This DLL called MyObject has one Class Module called Test. This class has one method called CallMe. The following is the complete code for MyObject.Test:

```
Public Function CallMe() As String
  CallMe = "I received your call!"
End Function
```

Once it is compiled into a DLL, it is placed under MTS control. In the MTS Explorer, we define a new package by clicking the Packages folder and selecting **FILE/NEW...** from the menu. In the Package Wizard (Figure 20-4) we can define a new package for the ActiveX DLL. Then MTS prompts for a name and creates the new package.

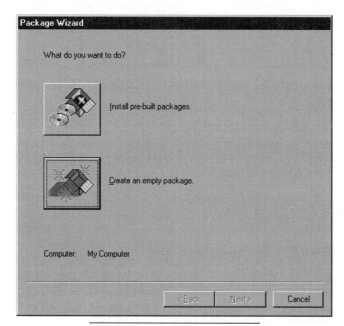

Figure 20-4 The Package Wizard.

Once the package is created, we can easily install the component by clicking on the new package to open it. Inside the package, we must click on the **Components** folder and select **FILE/NEW...** from the menu. In the Component Wizard (Figure 20-5), we then select to install our new component by picking it from a list of all registered components on the machine.

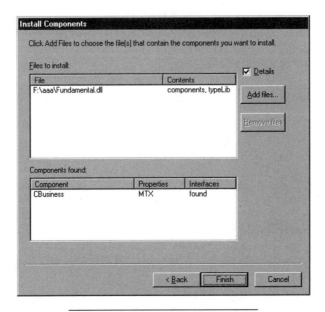

Figure 20-5 The Component Wizard.

At this point, the component is installed under MTS control. Now whenever the component is called by a VB application, MTS will intercept the request and process it using objects created from the MyObject ActiveX DLL. Now the object is available to all applications on the enterprise that support DCOM, and after the object is placed in MTS, the benefits of automatic thread pooling ensue.

Check It Out 20-1: MTS Fundamentals

1. Using the File Explorer, create a new directory called **VB BOOTCAMP\CHECK IT OUT20-1**. In Visual Basic, start a new ActiveX DLL project.
2. Open the Project Properties dialog by selecting **PROJECT/PROJECT1 PROPERTIES** from the menu. Change the name of the ActiveX DLL to **Fundamental**. While the dialog is open, verify that the Threading Model option is set to **Apartment Threaded**. Press the **OK** button to close the dialog.
3. In the Project Explorer, select **Class1**. Change the name of Class1 to **CBusiness**.
4. Add a method to the CBusiness object by selecting **TOOLS/ADD PROCEDURE** from the menu. In the Add Procedure dialog, create a Public Function named

Process. In this function add simple code to return a message to the calling client. The complete method code is shown below:

```
Public Function Process() As String
  Process = "MTS Fundamentals at work."
End Function
```

5. Compile the ActiveX DLL by selecting **MAKE/FUNDAMENTAL.DLL** from the menu.

6. Open the **Microsoft Transaction Server Explorer**. In the Explorer, locate a machine on which there is permission to create packages. Expand the view until the **Packages Installed** folder is visible under the appropriate computer icon. Right-click the folder and select **NEW/PACKAGE** from the menu. This will start the Package Wizard.

7. In the Package Wizard, select to **Create an Empty Package**. Press the **Next** button.

8. The Package Wizard will now prompt for a name. Type the name **My First Package**. Press the **Next** button.

9. The Package Wizard now prompts for information about the identity of the package. Run the package under a selected identity or use the identity of the calling client by selecting **Interactive User**. Press **Finish** to install the new package.

10. A new package appears in the tree view for the MTS Explorer. Expand the new package and locate the **Components** folder. Right-click this folder and select **NEW/COMPONENT** from the popup menu. This will start the Component Wizard.

11. In the Component Wizard, select **Install New Component**. This will bring up the screen shown in Figure 20-5. In this screen, select **Add Files** and use the File dialog to locate the file **FUNDAMENTAL.DLL** created earlier. When this file is selected, the Component Wizard shows the classes available within the DLL. Press **Finish** to add the component. Fundamental. CBusiness should now be visible as a member of the package.

12. Now start a new Standard EXE project in Visual Basic. Do not add this project to the ActiveX DLL, but rather start a completely new project.

13. This project will use the component created earlier. Set a reference to this component by selecting **PROJECT/REFERENCES** from the menu. In the References dialog, set a reference to **Fundamental**. Press **OK** to close the dialog.

14. Add a command button to the existing Form1. Double click the button to open the `Command1_Click` event in the code window. Under this event, add the following code to make a call to the MTS component:

```
Dim objBusiness As New Fundamental.CBusiness
MsgBox objBusiness.Process
```

15. Run the project by selecting **RUN/START**. When the project starts, click the button; there will be a delay as MTS starts up and loads the package. This is typical for the first call to an MTS component. Click the button a second or third time and

see MTS respond instantly. This fundamental processing is not difficult and immediately provides superior thread pooling features that help the application scale.

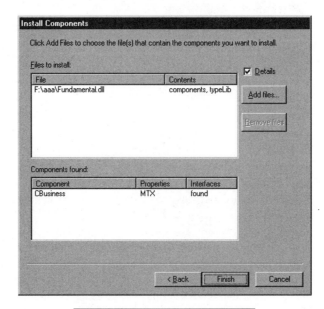

Figure 20-5 Selecting Components.

DATABASE CONNECTION POOLING

Database connection pooling is a requirement for scaling applications. In most Visual Basic
applications, developers do not concern themselves with database connection pooling. Frontend components routinely open connections at the beginning of a session and leave them open
until the application is terminated. Under MTS, database connections are not opened by the
front end or Web page, but rather by the business object itself. Therefore, the ActiveX DLLs
we create in Visual Basic must open a connection, read or write to the data source, and then
close the connection. The clients never access the database directly.

If the client never has direct access to a record set, then how can the data be retrieved?
Clients calling MTS objects rely on the objects to return data from a data source in a predictable format, which may be as simple as a delimited string or as complex as a collection of
objects. In any case, the business object is responsible for selecting records from the database,
packaging them and returning them to the client.

As a simple example, consider a business object that reads entries from a data source and
returns them as a delimited string. The client will then parse the returned string and place the
entries in a list box. This is a typical technique for creating lookup lists. This object is an
ActiveX DLL with one method. The business object uses the ActiveX Data Objects (ADO) to
access a data link created from the database. The component opens a connection to the data
source and reads out all required data. The data are added to a string delimited by pipe charac-

ters (|). In order to allow MTS to pool the database connection, the object opens a connection at the beginning of the function and simply allows the variable to lose scope at the end of the function.

```
'Open Connection
Dim objConnection As ADODB.Connection
Dim objResultset As ADODB.Recordset

Set objConnection = New ADODB.Connection
objConnection.ConnectionString = "File Name=C:\biblio.udl"
objConnection.Open

'Run Query
Set objResultset = New ADODB.Recordset
Set objResultset.ActiveConnection = objConnection
objResultset.Source = "SELECT Name FROM Publishers ORDER BY Name"
objResultset.CursorLocation = adUseClient
objResultset.CursorType = adOpenForwardOnly
objResultset.Open

'Create Return String
Dim strTemp As String
strTemp = ""

Do While Not objResultset.EOF
  strTemp = strTemp & objResultset!Name & "|"
  objResultset.MoveNext
Loop
```

The string is returned to a client through a call to the business object. The data are then parsed and added as entries to a list box. Other applications, such as Internet Web pages, may use the same object to fill a lookup list as well. The following code shows how the data are parsed back out of the returned string:

```
'Variables
Dim objQuery As MyObject.MyData

'Create the business object
Set objQuery = New MyObject.MyData

'Run the Query
Dim strReturn As String
strReturn = objQuery.GetDelimData
```

```
'Fill the ListBox
Dim intStart As Integer
Dim intCurrent As Integer
intStart = 1
intCurrent = 1

'Parse the returned string
Do While intCurrent < Len(strReturn)
 intCurrent = InStr(intStart, strReturn, "|")
 If intCurrent = 0 Then Exit Do
 List1.AddItem Mid$(strReturn, intStart, intCurrent - intStart)
 intStart = intCurrent + 1
Loop
```

As your application gets more complicated, it will be desirable to return more than just a simple list from a lookup table, you will want to return complete sets of records. In this case, we will use a disconnected ADO `Recordset` object to retrieve records and return them to the client. This follows the same general technique as producing a delimited string, but instead a disconnected recordset is passed. These recordsets are easily passed as return values from functions in the business object. The key to using them successfully is to disconnect the recordset before it is returned to the calling client.

```
Public Function GetData() As ADODB.Recordset
```

In the client, the recordset is used to populate a collection which in turn can fill a GUI element like a grid. In this way a complete set of data can be returned without having direct access to a database connection in the Web page. The page can also write data back by calling methods that perform SQL UPDATE functions inside Visual Basic business objects. Thus add, edit, and delete functionality can be provided through objects under MTS. These objects are subsequently available to all applications on the enterprise without rewriting.

OBJECT INSTANCE MANAGEMENT

The final concern when scaling applications is object instance management. Object management features in MTS allow for the creation and destruction of objects using the minimum amount of resources. Since resources are shared, the system is much more efficient. MTS provides for object instance management, but there must be changes to the business object in order to take full advantage of MTS.

Whenever a business object is created under MTS, a special object is also created to monitor the process. This is called an `ObjectContext`. It is responsible for observing the resource usage of a business object and notifying MTS when the object can be destroyed. Normally, objects are destroyed only after the client releases any reference being held in a variable.

However, if we change our code slightly, we can notify MTS directly that our object is ready to return to the pool and make its resources available to other users. Creating and destroying objects so that they exist for the absolute minimum amount of time is called Just-In-Time (JIT) activation and As-Soon-As-Possible (ASAP) deactivation. JIT/ASAP management is the most efficient way to use system resources.

Enabling JIT/ASAP pooling requires that the business object communicate directly with the `ObjectContext` assigned by MTS. This is done by using a special function called `GetObjectContext`, which is a member of the Transaction Server API. To access these functions, set a reference to MTS in the References dialog of Visual Basic. This reference is listed as Microsoft Transaction Server Type Library. Once the reference is set, use the **GetObjectContext** function to retrieve a reference to the **ObjectContext**. This function is a part of the MTS library.

```
Dim objContext As MTxAS.ObjectContext
Set objContext = GetObjectContext()
```

When the business object has a reference to the **ObjectContext**, it can easily tell MTS to recycle the object by calling the `SetComplete` method. This method causes MTS to place the business object back in the pool for reuse. When objects are reused this way, MTS can use just a few objects to service many clients simultaneously. Of course, recycling objects means that any data retained in the object are lost. Therefore, do not create business objects that cause data to persist. Instead save any required data in the client.

Check It Out 20-2: Returning Records

1. In the File Explorer, create a new directory called **VB BOOTCAMP/CHECK IT OUT20-2**.
2. Start a new ActiveX DLL project in Visual Basic.
3. Open the project properties by selecting **PROJECT/PROJECT1 PROPERTIES** from the menu. In the Properties dialog, change the name of the project to **MTS-Data**. Also be sure that the threading model is set to **Apartment Threaded**. Press **OK** to close the dialog.
4. In order to return recordsets, set a reference to the ADO library and the MTS library. Open the References dialog by selecting **PROJECT/REFERENCES** from the menu. In the References dialog, set a reference to **Microsoft ActiveX Data Objects 2.0 Library** and **Microsoft Transaction Server Type Library**. Press **OK** to close the dialog.
5. In the Project Explorer, select **Class1**. Change the name of Class1 to **Publishers**. We will use this class to return information about publishers from the Biblio database.
6. In a partitioned application, the client must not make direct SQL calls to the database. Instead, we will create a method that the business object will run. Add a method to the Publishers class by opening the Code window and selecting **TOOLS/ADD PROCEDURE** from the menu. In the Add Procedure dialog, select to add a **Public Function**

Named Query. Add this function by pressing the **OK** button and then modify it to return a recordset. The complete function signature is shown below:

```
Public Function Query() As ADODB.Recordset

End Function
```

7. Because MTS components use resources only when necessary, each method call must establish a connection to the database and then read data. Database connection pooling takes care of ensuring the connection is created efficiently. Add the following code to the `Query` method to read data from the database and return the records through a disconnected recordset:

```
On Error GoTo QueryErr

    'Declare Variables
    Dim objConnection As ADODB.Connection
    Dim objRecordset As ADODB.Recordset
    Dim objContext As MTxAS.ObjectContext

    'Get Object Context
    Set objContext = GetObjectContext

    'Connect to database
    Set objConnection = New ADODB.Connection
    objConnection.Provider = "Microsoft.Jet.OLEDB.3.51"
    objConnection.ConnectionString = _
        "Data Source=<Your Path>\Biblio.mdb"
    objConnection.CursorLocation = adUseClient
    objConnection.Open

    'Create Recordset
    Set objRecordset = New ADODB.Recordset
    objRecordset.Source = "SELECT * FROM Publishers"
    objRecordset.CursorType = adOpenStatic
    objRecordset.LockType = adLockBatchOptimistic
    Set objRecordset.ActiveConnection = objConnection
    objRecordset.Open

    Set objRecordset.ActiveConnection = Nothing

    'Return Records
    Set Query = objRecordset

    'Tell MTS we were successful
    objContext.SetComplete
```

```
    Exit Function

QueryErr:
    'Tell MTS we failed!
    objContext.SetAbort
    Set Query = Nothing

    'Write error to log
    App.StartLogging App.Path & "\mts.log", 2
    App.LogEvent Err.Description
```

8. Compile the ActiveX DLL by selecting **MAKE/MTSDATA.DLL** from the menu.
9. Open the **Microsoft Transaction Server Explorer**. In the Explorer, locate a machine on which there is permission to create packages. Expand the view until the **Packages Installed** folder is visible under the appropriate computer icon. Right-click the folder and select **NEW/PACKAGE** from the menu. This will start the Package Wizard.
10. In the Package Wizard, select **Create an Empty Package**. Push the **Next** button.
11. The Package Wizard will now prompt for a name. Type the name **Publisher Data**. Press the **Next** button.
12. The Package Wizard now prompts for information about the identity of the package. Run the package under a selected identity or use the identity of the calling client. Use the identity of the calling client by selecting **Interactive User**. Press **Finish** to install the new package.
13. A new package appears in the tree view for the MTS Explorer. Expand the new package and locate the **Components** folder. Right-click this folder and select **NEW/COMPONENT** from the popup menu. This will start the Component Wizard.
14. In the Component Wizard, select **Install New Component**. In this screen, select **Add Files** and use the file dialog to locate the file **MTSDATA.DLL** created earlier. When this file is selected, the Component Wizard shows the classes available within the DLL. Press **Finish** to add the component. `MTSData.Publishers` should be visible as a member of the package.
15. Now start a new Standard EXE project in Visual Basic.
16. This project will use the component created earlier. Set a reference to this component by selecting **PROJECT/REFERENCES** from the menu. In the references dialog, set a reference to **MTSData**. Since a recordset is returned from the function call, also set a reference to **Microsoft ActiveX Data Objects 2.0 Library**. Press **OK** to close the dialog.
17. Normal partitioning would require that the recordset be used to fill a custom collection of Publisher objects; however, for simplicity and to allow focus on the business object creation, display this recordset directly in a grid. Select **PROJECT/COMPONENTS** from the menu and locate the **Microsoft DataGrid Control (OLEDB) 6.0**. Check this control and add it to the toolbox by pressing the **OK** button.

18. Add a DataGrid control to Form1. Then doubleclick the form to open the `Form_Load` event. Add the following code to call the business object and display the results:

```
Dim objBusiness As MTSData.Publishers
Set objBusiness = New MTSData.Publishers

Set DataGrid1.DataSource = objBusiness.Query
```

19. Save and run the project. The grid should be visible filled with data.

ADDITIONAL MTS FEATURES

This chapter is intended as an overview of MTS technology, with emphasis on skills required to pass the certification exam. In this section, we touch on additional features of MTS that are important to a total solution. In particular, we will discuss security and transaction processing.

One of the best features of MTS is the fact that it abstracts the Windows/NT security system and makes it simple to build secure applications. Secure applications are those that make it possible to restrict the creation and use of objects in the business layer. Under each package created in MTS, will be a folder labeled Roles (Figure 20-6). The Roles folder is used to create definitions of user permissions for objects. Inside this folder, any number of roles can be created with names that are arbitrarily defined.

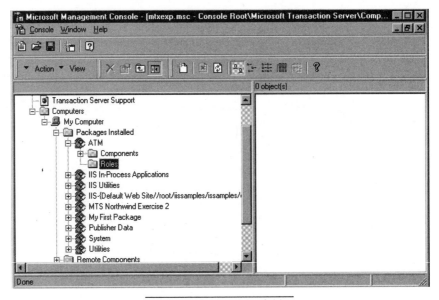

Figure 20-6 The Roles folder.

Roles are defined by right-clicking on the folder and selecting **NEW/ROLE** from the popup menu. A new role is essentially meaningless until a user is added to it. Users are added from the Window/NT list of users for a domain and are placed under the Roles folder in a folder marked Users (Figure 20-7). The Users folder associates Windows/NT user IDs with the role names defined for a package.

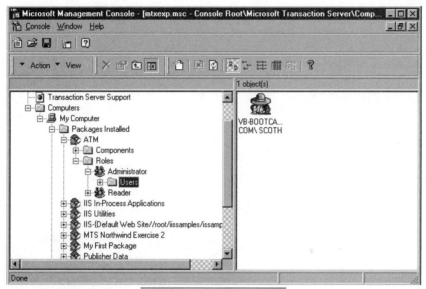

Figure 20-7 Users and Roles.

Once Windows/NT users are associated with a role, assign them permission to access an object by adding the role name to the Role Membership folder (Figure 20-8) under the component of interest. Assigning a role to the Role Membership folder of a component gives all Windows/NT users attached to the role permission to create and access instances of the component. Those who are not members of the allowed roles will receive a Visual Basic run-time error when creation of or access to an instance of the component is attempted.

Once the roles, user, and memberships are established, there is one last item to take care of. For any given package, security is normally not turned on. For roles to work, the properties dialog for a package must be entered and secuirty activated. This is done by right-clicking the package and selecting **PROPERTIES**. In the Properties dialog, select the **Security** tab. On the Security tab, check the box **Enable Authorization Checking**. (See Figure 20-9.)

Another important feature of MTS is the ability to automatically initiate and process transactions. This is done by setting the properties for a component on the Transaction tab of the properties dialog. Components in MTS support four options for transactions: Requires New Transaction, Requires Transaction, Supports Transactions, and Does Not Support Transactions. These attributes determine whether a component joins an existing transaction or starts a new one.

Requires New Transaction will cause a new transactional context to be created each time the component is called. A Transaction allows a component to join a transaction in process or start a new one if one has not been created. Supports Transactions allows a component to join an existing transaction or operate alone—outside a transaction. Does Not Support Transactions means the component will always operate alone.

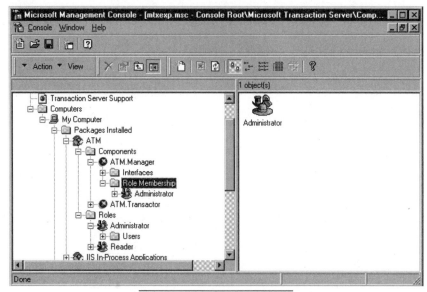

Figure 20-8 Role Membership.

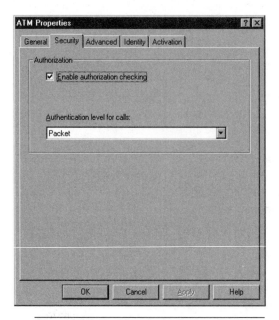

Figure 20-9 Enabling Authorization Checking.

While these properties can be set inside the MTS Explorer, Visual Basic offers them as properties of the class module. In the Properties window for any class, the property `MTSTransactionMode` will be visible. If this property is set in Visual Basic, then MTS will automatically set the property when the component is added to MTS. If the component is not added to MTS, this property has no meaning.

Exercise 20-1: Using Microsoft Transaction Server

Microsoft Transaction Server (MTS) is a product designed to manage all the overhead associated with scalable business applications. Use MTS immediately to gain the benefits of resource pooling and transaction processing. This exercise will show how to use MTS to build fault-tolerant, scalable applications.

SETTING UP THE DATA LINK

Step 1

Before using ADO, set up a Data Link file for use. In this exercise, we will be interacting with the Microsoft Access database **NWIND.MDB** that ships with Visual Basic. This database contains suppliers and products for a mythical company. Establishing the data link is not a Visual Basic function, but rather a Windows Operating System function. Setup is done using the File Explorer utility found in Windows. Start the File Explorer.

Step 2

Data Links can be defined anywhere on the computer, though they are commonly kept in the directory **\PROGRAM FILES\COMMON FILES\SYSTEM\OLE DB\DATA LINKS**. Locate this directory in the File Explorer. If the Data Links directory does not exist, create it.

Step 3

Select the **DATA LINKS** folder in the left-hand pane and choose **FILE/NEW/MICROSOFT DATA LINK** from the menu. After selecting the menu, notice that a new Data Link file has been created. Edit the name of the file to **NORTHWIND.UDL**.

Step 4

Right click **NORTHWIND.UDL** and select **PROPERTIES...** from the popup menu. This dialog is where to specify the information required by the OLEDB provider. In the Provider tab choose **Microsoft Jet 3.51 OLEDB Provider**. Press the **Next** button.

Step 5

In the Connection tab, locate the **NWIND.MDB** database file under **Select or Enter Database Name**. NWIND.MDB will be in the root of the Visual Basic installation.

Step 6

Test the new connection by pressing the **Test Connection** button. When the connection tests satisfactorily, press the **OK** button.

CREATING THE BUSINESS OBJECTS

Step 7

Using the File Explorer, create a new directory called **VB BOOTCAMP\EXERCISE20-1**. Beneath this new directory, create two new folders: one called **\CLIENT** and one called **\SERVER**.

Step 8

Start a new Visual Basic ActiveX DLL project. Select **Project/References...** from the menu and set a reference to the **Microsoft ActiveX Data Objects 2.0 Library** and **Microsoft Transaction Server Type Library**. Close the dialog by pressing the **OK** button.

Step 9

Change the properties of **Project1** by selecting **Project/Project1 Properties...** from the menu. In the Project Properties dialog, change the name of the project to **MTSObject** and change the description to **MTS Training Exercise Objects**. Ensure that the threading model is set to **Apartment Threaded**. Close the dialog by pressing the **OK** button.

Step 10

Change the name of the Class1 component to **Query**. This class will initiate a new transaction for each call that it receives. Set the `MTSTransactionMode` property to **4–RequiresNewTransaction**. Save the project in the **\SERVER** directory.

Step 11

Create a new method in the Query class by selecting **TOOLS/ADD PROCEDURE...** from the menu. In the Add Procedure dialog, set the following attributes:

> Name: `GetCategories`
> Type: Function:
> Scope: Public

Step 12

After inserting the new function, modify the function to return an ADO `Recordset` data type. The complete function should now look like this:

```
Public Function GetCategories() As ADODB.Recordset
End Sub
```

Step 13

The `GetCategories` method is used to return a recordset with the available categories in the NorthWind database. These categories will be used to populate a lookup table in the final application. Add the following code to the `GetCategories` method to generate the lookup list:

```
On Error GoTo GetCategoriesErr

    'Declare Variables
```

```vb
    Dim objConnection As ADODB.Connection
    Dim objRecordset As ADODB.Recordset
    Dim objContext As MTxAS.ObjectContext

    'Get Object Context
    Set objContext = GetObjectContext

    'Connect to database
    Set objConnection = New ADODB.Connection
    objConnection.ConnectionString = _
        "File Name=<Your Path>\northwind.udl"
    objConnection.CursorLocation = adUseClient
    objConnection.Open

    'Create Recordset
    Set objRecordset = New ADODB.Recordset
    objRecordset.Source = _
        "SELECT CategoryID ,CategoryName FROM Categories"
    objRecordset.CursorType = adOpenStatic
    objRecordset.LockType = adLockBatchOptimistic
    Set objRecordset.ActiveConnection = objConnection
    objRecordset.Open

    Set objRecordset.ActiveConnection = Nothing

    'Return Records
    Set GetCategories = objRecordset

    'Tell MTS we were successful
    objContext.SetComplete
    Exit Function

GetCategoriesErr:
    'Tell MTS we failed!
    objContext.SetAbort
    Set GetCategories = Nothing

    'Write error to log
    App.StartLogging App.Path & "\mts.log", vbLogToFile
    App.LogEvent Err.Description
```

Step 14

After all the category names are returned to the front end, the user will select a category and want to see the associated products from the data source for that category. This is accomplished with a method called `GetProducts`, which will return all the products in an ADO `Record-set` to the client. The client can then use the array to fill a grid. Add the `GetProduct` method by selecting **TOOLS/ADD PROCEDURE...** from the menu. In the Add Procedure dialog, set the following attributes:

> Name: `GetProducts`
>
> Type: Function
>
> Scope: Public

Change the `GetProducts` function to accept one argument and return a disconnected recordset with the data. The resulting function should look like this:

```
Public Function GetProducts(lngCategoryID As Long) _

    As ADODB.Recordset
End Function
```

Step 15

GetProducts uses the category ID to search for products and fill an ADO Recordset with results. It also uses JIT Activation to ensure that instances of the Query class are recycled as soon as possible. Add the following code to the `GetProducts` function to return a recordset of products to the client:

```
On Error GoTo GetProductsErr

    'Declare Variables
    Dim objConnection As ADODB.Connection
    Dim objRecordset As ADODB.Recordset
    Dim objContext As MTxAS.ObjectContext

    'Get Object Context
    Set objContext = GetObjectContext

    'Connect to database
    Set objConnection = New ADODB.Connection
    objConnection.ConnectionString = _
        "File Name=<Your Path>\northwind.udl"
    objConnection.CursorLocation = adUseClient
    objConnection.Open

    'Create Recordset
    Set objRecordset = New ADODB.Recordset
```

```
  objRecordset.Source = _
    "SELECT * FROM Products WHERE CategoryID=" & lngCategoryID
  objRecordset.CursorType = adOpenStatic
  objRecordset.LockType = adLockBatchOptimistic
  Set objRecordset.ActiveConnection = objConnection
  objRecordset.Open

  Set objRecordset.ActiveConnection = Nothing

  'Return Records
  Set GetProducts = objRecordset

  'Tell MTS we were successful
  objContext.SetComplete
  Exit Function

GetProductsErr:
  'Tell MTS we failed!
  objContext.SetAbort
  Set GetProducts = Nothing

  'Write error to log
  App.StartLogging App.Path & "\mts.log", vbLogToFile
  App.LogEvent Err.Description
```

PLACING THE BUSINESS OBJECT UNDER MTS CONTROL

Step 16

Now that the business object is complete, compile it by selecting **FILE/MAKE MTSOB-JECT.DLL** from the menu. When the DLL is created, save the work and exit Visual Basic.

Step 17

From the Start menu, start the Microsoft Transaction Server Explorer. In the MTS Explorer, select **My Computer** and **Packages Installed**. Add a new package to MTS by selecting **ACTION/NEW** from the menu. In the Package Wizard, select to install a new empty package. Press **Next**. Name the new package **MTS NorthWind Exercise**. Press **Next**. Set the package identity to **Interactive User**. Press **Finish**.

Step 18

Double click on the new package installed to reveal the **Components** folder. Now double click on the **Components** folder itself. Select **ACTION/NEW** from the menu to add a new component to the package. In the Component Wizard, select to import components already registered.

Locate the component `MTSObject.Query` and select it. Press **Finish**. The component is now registered and under control of the Microsoft Transaction Server.

CREATING THE FRONT END

Step 19

Start Visual Basic and select to create a new Standard EXE project. This project will be the front end to the business objects. Select **PROJECT1/PROPERTIES...** from the menu and change the project name to **FrontEnd**.

Step 20

Select **PROJECT REFERENCES...** from the menu and set a reference to the business object just created called **MTS Training Exercise Objects**. Also set a reference to ADO through the Microsoft ActiveX Data Objects 2.0 Library. Save the project in the **\CLIENT** directory.

Step 20

Whenever variables are used in the front end to refer to business objects, they should be declared at a high level of scope. The client can then seemingly hold a reference to the business object while the `SetComplete` method releases resources. Add the following variables to the [General][Declarations] section to manage the business object and recordset:

```
Private objRecordset As ADODB.Recordset
Private objBusiness As MTSObject.Query
```

Step 21

Add a list box to Form1 in the new project. Name the list box **lstCategories**. This list box will be used to show a list of all of the product categories. Filling the list is done by calling to the business object and retrieving the category names. When the recordset is received, fill the list. Add the following code to the `Form_Load` event to fill the list:

```
Set objBusiness = New MTSObject.Query
Set objRecordset = objBusiness.GetCategories

Do While Not objRecordset.EOF
  lstCategories.AddItem objRecordset!CategoryName & ""
  lstCategories.ItemData(lstCategories.NewIndex) = _
      objRecordset!CategoryID
  objRecordset.MoveNext
Loop
```

Step 22

Save the project and run it. Verify that the list box fills with product categories. Stop the project and return to design mode.

Step 23

Add a grid control to the project by selecting **PROJECT/COMPONENTS...** from the menu. In the Components dialog, select the **Microsoft DataGrid (OLEDB) 6.0** control. Press **OK** to add it to the toolbox. Place a grid control on the form and name it **grdProducts**. This grid will be used to see all the products in a given category. The grid will fill when a user clicks on a category. Add the following code to the Click event of lstCategories to finish the project:

```
Set objRecordset = objBusiness.GetProducts _
    (lstCategories.ItemData(lstCategories.ListIndex))
Set grdProducts.DataSource = objRecordset
```

Step 24

Save the project and run it. Try clicking on a product category in the list box.

FOR THE CERTIFIED PRO

Pro 20-1: Workflow Objects

After completing the exercise 20-1, provide further partitioning by creating a collection class for Products. Use the recordset returned from the business object to fill the collection. Then show the collection in the front end form.

INCREASING YOUR KNOWLEDGE

Topics for Further Reading

The Microsoft Transaction Server is covered in additional detail under the Books On-Line that ship with the product itself.

CERTIFICATION QUIZ

1. Which are valid settings for the Instancing Property?
   a. Multi-Use
   b. Many-Use
   c. Single-Use
   d. Mono-Use

2. What are valid selections for threading model in an ActiveX EXE?
   a. Threads per client
   b. Threads per object
   c. Thread pool
   d. Multi-thread

3. What threading model is supported by unattended execution?
   a. Free threaded
   b. Trailer threaded
   c. Home threaded
   d. Apartment threaded

4. What resources are pooled by the Microsoft Transaction Server (MTS)?
   a. Disk space
   b. Object instances
   c. ODBC connections
   d. Threads

5. What kind of components are used in MTS?
   a. ActiveX Document DLL
   b. ActiveX Document EXE
   c. ActiveX DLL
   d. ActiveX EXE

6. How is ODBC Connection pooling implemented in MTS?
   a. by using the function PoolConnection
   b. by managing connections in the business layer
   c. by managing connections in the client services layer
   d. by preventing data access with stored procedures

7. What method of the rdoResultset object puts records into an array?
   a. `GetRecords`
   b. `GetResults`
   c. `GetColumns`
   d. `GetRows`

8. What function is used to get a reference to the `ObjectContext`?
   a. `GetRef`
   b. `GetRows`
   c. `GetObjectContext`
   d. `GetContext`

9. What methods are used to tell MTS that an object can be pooled?
   a. `SetAbort`
   b. `SetComplete`
   c. `SetDone`
   d. `SetFinish`

10. What file is used to aid in remote client installs?
   a. VBR file
   b. VBD file
   c. MSC file
   d. MMM file

ANSWERS TO CERTIFICATION QUIZ

1. a, c
2. b, c
3. b, d
4. c, d
5. c
6. b
7. d
8. c
9. a, b
10. a

CREATING VISUAL BASIC ADD-INS

Those who begin this chapter, should have a thorough understanding of object models and ActiveX components.

SKILLS COVERED

- 70-176 (21): Use the Visual Component Manager to manage components
- 70-175 (31): Use the Visual Component Manager to manage components

Visual Basic Add-Ins are ActiveX components that can be used to extend the functionality of the Visual Basic Integrated Debugging Environment (VBIDE). Add-ins are built to add features that Visual Basic does not implement or to provide tools that are specific to a particular business. They are an excellent way to enhance productivity.

Visual Basic ships with several add-ins created by Microsoft. There is a complete list of these in the contents of the Add-In Manager, which is used to activate selected add-ins for use inside Visual Basic. Access the Add-In Manager by selecting **ADD-INS/ADD-IN MANAGER...** from the menu.

THE VISUAL BASIC OBJECT MODEL

Creating add-ins for Visual Basic requires an intimate knowledge of the VBIDE object model. The object model is a graphical representation of the objects contained inside VB. These objects make it simpler to communicate with and manipulate the components of a Visual Basic project. These objects can be used to add menu items to the VBIDE, change properties of forms and modules in a project, detect when projects are changed, and perform a host of other useful functions.

The VBIDE object model begins with the top-level object, VBE, that represents the current Visual Basic environment. This is a reference to the running instance of VB itself. This object is the gateway to all the other aspects of VBIDE. All the add-ins will begin by establishing a reference to this object.

After a reference to the VBE object is established, access one of several collections that represent projects and components inside VB. VBProjects is a collection of all the currently open projects inside VB. Because VB can open more than one project at a time, the collection can be used programmatically to examine and manipulate components inside any open project.

CodePanes is a collection of all of the currently visible code windows. Each time a new code window is open, VB adds it to the CodePanes collection. This collection makes it possible to access code in any open project and create tools that generate code. The CodePane itself is considered the window that contains the code module. In the VB object model, individual lines of code are accessed by using the CodeModule property of any selected CodePane object.

The set of all open windows including dockable windows is represented by the Windows collection, which affords programmatic access to a Window object for the purpose of managing display and real estate. You can easily pen and close windows from the add-in using this collection.

One of the key features of an add-in is the ability to place menu items and toolbars in the VBIDE. Establishing new menus and tools is done using CommandBar objects. CommandBar objects are are generic selection objects that can represent either buttons on a toolbar or menu items. In fact, CommandBar objects facilitate creation of all kinds of menu controls. Use CommandBar objects to place a ListBox control directly inside a menu or toolbar, for example. There is no limit to simple text and buttons. VB manages the set of all menu and toolbar controls through the CommandBars collection.

Once new menu items or tools are established, it will be important to know when a user selects the control. Detecting events inside VB is the function of the Events collection, which provides a number of interesting and useful events for the add-in. Visual Basic supports menu item and toolbar events through the CommandBarEvents object. Detect File events such as File Save actions through the FileControlEvents object. When users change the references in the References dialog, detect the action through the ReferenceEvents object. Detecting modified controls and components is accomplished through VBControlsEvents, SelectedVBControlsEvents, VBComponentsEvents, and VBProjectsEvents objects.

It is also necessary to understand the `Office` object model, which provides all the features the VB add-in will use to create toolbars and menus. These items are actually part of a shared library used not only by Visual Basic, but also by each member of the Office family. Look closely at various Office products, and notice that these applications have the same types of menu items and tools as VB supports. Office products, for example, can support lists and combo boxes just as VB does. This is because the menus are driven from the same common library.

Accessing these two critical object models from the VB add-in requires setting a reference to them in the References dialog. The VBIDE object model can be found in the References dialog listed as Microsoft Visual Basic 6.0 Extensibility. The `Office` model is listed as Microsoft Office 8.0 Object Library. To begin creating any add-in, start with an ActiveX DLL project and set a reference to these two libraries.

Once the references for these models are set, spend time examining them in the Object Browser, an excellent way to gain knowledge about the objects, properties, events, and methods of the two models. The VB extensibility library is listed as VBIDE in the Object Browser, whereas the Office 8.0 library is simply listed as Office. The Object Browser will be a frequent point of reference for those developing add-ins.

CONNECTING AN ADD-IN TO VB

Add-ins are made available to Visual Basic when they are listed in a special file used by the Add-In Manager. This file is called VBADDIN.INI and lists all the add-ins available to VB. It is the basis for the list generated when the Add-In Manager is selected from Visual Basic. Before the add-in can appear in the list, it must make an appropriate entry in this file.

VBADDIN.INI is an initialization file that contains only one section, dedicated to maintaining the list of available add-ins. Examine this file by opening it in Notepad. The file typically resides in the \WINDOWS directory on a system. It contains an entry for an add-in based on the ProgID of the primary connection class in the add-in. The value of each entry is either 1 for True or 0 for False and specifies whether the add-in should be immediately loaded when VB starts. Those not loaded immediately may be loaded at any time by using the Add-In Manager. Any add-ins left running when VB shuts down are automatically restarted when VB is run the next time. The following code shows a typical VBADDIN.INI file:

```
[Add-Ins32]
RealEstateAgent.Connect=1
AddProc.Connect=1
AttilaPro.Connector=0
WebDock.Connect=0
RVBAddInMenus.Connector=0
RVBAddIn.Connector=0
MTxAddIn2.RegRefresh=1
Dashboard.Connect=0
UnitMan.Connect=1
VBSDIAddIn.Connect=0
```

```
DataToolsAddIn.Connect=0
AppWizard.Wizard=0
WizMan.Connect=0
ClassBuilder.Wizard=0
AddInToolbar.Connect=0
ControlWiz.Wizard=0
DataFormWizard.Wizard=0
ActiveXDocumentWizard.Wizard=0
PropertyPageWizard.Wizard=0
APIDeclarationLoader.Connect=0
ResEdit.Connect=1
```

Normally, an entry for the add-in should be made during the installation process. An entry must also be made at design time so the add-in can be tested. The entry could be made by hand, but a simple way is to provide a helper function used only during debugging. This helper function is created in a standard module and can be called anything, but we use `AddToINI`. This function makes an API call to add the necessary entry for an add-in to the VBADDINI.INI. The following code shows a typical routine for a project titled `MyAddIn`:

```
Declare Function WritePrivateProfileString& _
Lib "kernel32" Alias "WritePrivateProfileStringA" _
(ByVal AppName$, ByVal KeyName$, _
ByVal keydefault$, ByVal FileName$)
Sub AddToINI()
  'Call this to update the INI in VBIDE
  Dim ErrCode As Long
  ErrCode = WritePrivateProfileString _
  ("Add-Ins32", "MyAddIn.Connect", "1", _
  "vbaddin.ini")
  Debug.Print "Added to VB INI file!"
End Sub
```

Once the routine is added to the project, execute it in Break mode to make the appropriate entry. Do this by starting the add-in and then immediately entering Break mode. In the Immediate window, type `AddToINI` and the routine responds with Added to VB INI file! Once this is finished, continue running the add-in for testing.

When an add-in is connecting to the VBIDE, VB expects to find a certain set of methods available in a class module that it can call to provide information. Therefore, the next step in connecting is to create a class with the desired methods. Although either an ActiveX EXE or ActiveX DLL project can be created as an add-in, ActiveX DLLs are much faster and are therefore the preferred method. When an ActiveX DLL is created, VB provides the project with a default class named Class1. Typically, we change the name of this class to Connect or Connector and use it as the primary class to receive input from the VBIDE. Note that the name of this class is arbitrary, but it must be properly reflected in the `AddToINI` routine or the add-in will not be properly registered with the VBADDIN.INI file.

Once the class module is named, provide a set of four guaranteed methods that VB can call when the add-in connects. From our previous work, we know how to guarantee that a class implements certain methods, through interfaces. In fact, the VBIDE object model provides an interface the class must implement to be an add-in, called `IDTExtensibility`. Therefore, every add-in must have a class that contains the following code in the [General][Declarations] section:

```
Implements IDTExtensibility
```

When the class implements this interface, four methods must be provided for the class: `OnConnection`, `OnDisconnection`, `OnStartupComplete`, and `OnAddinsUpdate`. `OnConnection` is called by the `VBIDE` when the add-in is first connected to VB. `OnDisconnection` is called when the add-in is disconnected. Both these methods may be called if VB starts up or shuts down, or when the add-in is manipulated in the Add-In Manager. The `OnStartupComplete` method is called when the complete startup of the `VBIDE` is finished. `OnAddinsUpdate` is called when changes to the VBADDINI.INI file are saved. These methods represent the starting point for much of what the add-in does.

MENUS AND TOOLBARS

When the add-in is connecting to the `VBIDE`, it will probably be desirable to add menu items and tools to the environment. The menu items and tools are typically removed again when the add-in disconnects. These items can be added and removed in the `OnConnection` and `OnDisconnection` methods respectively. Creating these items is done using the `Office` object model.

All the menu items and toolbars to interact with in VB are members of the `CommandBars` collection. This collection has members that give access to nearly everything that can be selected from in VB. The main toolbars are accessed by the names Standard, Edit, Debug, and Form Editor. The Main menu is accessed by the name Menu Bar. Through these, it is easy to add new items, delete items, and replace items.

Before placing items, declare a variable to represent the new item in the [General][Declarations] section of the primary `Connect` class. Typically objects are declared as `CommandBarControl` objects, but there are also special controls such as `CommandBarButton` and `CommandBarComboBox` objects. When these special objects are declared additional properties, events, and methods become available for the object. For example, declaring an object as `CommandBarComboBox` makes it possible to use the `AddItem` method to place items in a list on a toolbar. After the new items are declared, add them to the toolbar or menu of choice. The following code shows how to add a new button to the Standard toolbar in Visual Basic:

```
'Declare Toolbar Buttons and Menus
Public objCommandBar As Office.CommandBarControl
```

```
Private Sub IDTExtensibility_OnConnection _
(ByVal VBInst As Object, _
ByVal ConnectMode As VBIDE.vbext_ConnectMode, _
ByVal AddInInst As VBIDE.AddIn, Custom() As Variant)

  'Save instance of VB
  Set objVBE = VBInst

  'Create CommandBar
  Set objCommandBar = objVBE.CommandBars("Standard").Controls.Add _
  (msoControlButton, , , , True)
End Sub
```

Once the new control is attached to a menu or toolbar, to receive events from the control in the add-in declare a Handler object. Handlers are members of the VBIDE object model and are of type CommandBarEvents. The following code declares a Handler object for a new item:

```
Private WithEvents objMenuHandler As VBIDE.CommandBarEvents
```

Notice that the object is declared WithEvents. Creating the object this way enables the class module to receive events from the new control. All that is necessary is to connect the Handler object to the menu item of choice. The following code shows how to add a new menu item to the View menu in VB and trap when the item is clicked:

```
'Menu Item and Handler Objects
Public WithEvents objMenuHandler As VBIDE.CommandBarEvents
Public objMenu As Office.CommandBarControl

Private Sub IDTExtensibility_OnConnection(ByVal VBInst As Object, _
ByVal ConnectMode As VBIDE.vbext_ConnectMode, _
   ByVal AddInInst As VBIDE.AddIn, Custom() As Variant)
 'Save the vb instance
 Set m_VBIDE = VBInst
 'Build Menus
 Set objMenu = m_VBIDE.CommandBars("Menu Bar"). _
      Controls("View").CommandBar.Controls.Add(1, , , 1, True)
 objMenu.Caption = "&My Item"
 Set objMenuHandler = m_VBIDE.Events.CommandBarEvents(objMenu)
End Sub
```

With the Handler object in place, all that is necessary is to write the appropriate code in the Click event generated for the Handler object. This event is in the code module because the Handler object was declared WithEvents. After receiving the click, use the rest of the VB object model to manipulate the current project.

MANIPULATING PROJECT COMPONENTS

Menu items are not the only way to receive events in the add-in. Visual Basic 6.0 supports a wide range of events generated in response to user actions. These events can be very useful in creating tools that effectively manage the VB environment. When add-ins are created, it is often useful to know when a user is manipulating the current project. In particular, changes to the elements of a project may be of interest. Visual Basic makes it possible to discover, for example, when a user adds a new project, component, or control to the environment or to detect when one of these elements is removed or selected.

To set up the add-in to detect project events, declare an appropriate event-handling object using the `WithEvents` keyword. Declare objects that handle project, component, and control events based on the design of the add-in. The following lines of code declare events for all the supported project events:

```
Private WithEvents m_ProjectHandler As VBIDE.VBProjectsEvents
Private WithEvents m_ComponentHandler As VBIDE.VBComponentsEvents
Private WithEvents m_ControlsHandler As VBIDE.VBControlsEvents
Private WithEvents m_SelectedHandler As VBIDE.SelectedVBControlsEvents
```

Once the event handler is declared, connect it to the appropriate project in the VBIDE. Connecting the event handlers always begins by connecting the `VBProjectsEvents` object first. Connect an event handler to the current project using the following code:

```
Set m_ProjectHandler = VBE.Events.VBProjectsEvents
```

This line of code is typically included in the `OnConnection` method of the `IDTExtensibility` interface. When this event handler is connected, the add-in can receive four project events: `ItemAdded`, `ItemRemoved`, `ItemRenamed`, and `ItemActivated`. Use these events to take action in the add-in, but also use them to connect the event handler for the project components. For example, when the add-in receives the `ItemAdded` event, we know that a new project was added. Therefore, we must connect the component handler. The following code shows how this is done:

```
Private Sub m_ProjectHandler_ItemAdded _
(ByVal VBProject As VBIDE.VBProject)
  Set m_ComponentHandler = m_VBE.Events.VBComponentsEvents(VBProject)
End Sub
```

When the component events handler is connected, the add-in can receive six events related to forms and modules: `ItemAdded`, `ItemActivated`, `ItemReloaded`, `ItemRemoved`, `ItemRenamed`, and `ItemSelected`. These events can be used to take action when a user manipulates a form or module in the project. Also connect the controls events handler. When a new component is added, the `ItemAdded` event appears just for a new project. Then connect controls events through the following code:

```
Set ControlsHandler = _
```

```
objVBE.Events.VBControlsEvents _
(m_VBE.ActiveVBProject, m_VBComponent.Designer)
Set SelectedHandler = _
objVBE.Events.SelectedVBControlsEvents _
(m_VBE.ActiveVBProject, m_VBComponent.Designer)
```

Once the setup to receive events about the projects, components, and controls is accomplished, the add-in can easily manipulate these same components. Suppose, for example, creating an add-in that did nothing except change the BackColor of forms from the default color to white. Every time a user places a new form in the project, the add-in will automatically change the color. This can easily be done by detecting the `ItemAdded` event of the `Component Handler` object. Then, in the event, manipulate the currently selected component as follows:

```
Private Sub objCompHandler_ItemActivated_
    (ByVal VBComponent As VBIDE.VBComponent)
 If TypeOf VBComponent Is vbext_ct_VBForm Then
 VBComponent.Properties("BackColor").Value = &HFFFFFF
 End If
End Sub
```

It is also possible to modify the project code. The Visual Basic add-in model allows access to the Code windows of any component through the `CodePanes` and `VBComponents` collections. To access these collections, address the `CodeModule` property of any `CodePane` or `VBComponent`. As an example, the following code can be used to get a reference to the `CodeModule` object of the currently selected form or module:

```
Set objModule = m_VBE.ActiveCodePane.CodeModule
```

Once there is a reference to the `CodeModule`, VB provides a number of properties and methods that make it possible to generate code. The `AddFromFile` and `AddFromString` methods allow adding code to a module from either a saved file or a string variable. Delete code from a module using the `DeleteLines` method. Code replacement is accomplished by using the `ReplaceLine` method. VB also provides properties and methods to search a code module, count the lines in various sections, and manipulate the variable and procedure declarations. In general, a wide variety of coding tasks can be accomplished using the add-in architecture.

DISTRIBUTING THE ADD-IN

Distributing a Visual Basic Add-In is generally as easy as distributing any in-process ActiveX DLL project. Simply use the Setup Wizard that ships with Visual Basic to generate the distribution disks. The only rub in the entire procedure is that an add-in must have an entry in the VBADDIN.INI file before it can be seen inside the VB environment.

To make an entry in VBADDIN.INI, customize the setup created by the Setup Wizard, which actually uses a Visual Basic project to perform the installation. This project already exists in the VB installation. The project is SETUP1.VBP. Open this file directly in VB to modify the Setup Wizard.

The SETUP1.VBP project is specifically designed to be easily modified. Although the project has many pieces, everything that needs to be changed is kept in the Form_Load event of the form called frmSetup1. In this section, code can be added to make the appropriate entry in VBADDIN.INI. Typically, we place the code right after the label marked ExitSetup. The code looks the same as the code for registering the add-in during debugging:

```
ExitSetup:
'**********
'Custom Code for Add-In installation
'**********
Dim ErrCode As Long
ErrCode = WritePrivateProfileString _
("Add-Ins32", "MyAddIn.Connect", "1", _
"vbaddin.ini")
```

Once the new code is added, save the project and recompile it. After recompiling, run the Setup Wizard and distribute the add-in as an ActiveX DLL project. Because the Setup Wizard uses the compiled version of SETUP1.VBP, changes will become part of the installation. When the user sets up the add-in, the appropriate entries will be made to VBADDIN.INI. The only thing to remember is to comment out these lines of code before using the Setup Wizard to distribute any other application.

EXISTING ADD-INS

Although it is easy to create add-ins with Visual Basic, many useful add-ins already ship with the product. In many cases, these add-ins help solve design problems or simplify repetitive coding. In this section, we review the add-ins that ship with Visual Basic.

ACTIVEX CONTROL INTERFACE WIZARD

The ActiveX Control Interface Wizard (Figure 21-1) is an add-in designed to generate the laborious code required to subclass an ActiveX control. In the control creation portion of this book, we examined the required steps for subclassing and extending existing ActiveX controls. Because Visual Basic does not support inheritance, each property, event, and method of a subclassed control must be re-created by hand. This code is difficult to write accurately, which is why the add-in should be used automatically to generate the code.

ACTIVEX DOCUMENT MIGRATION WIZARD

The ActiveX Document Migration Wizard (Figure 21-1) is an add-in designed to create an ActiveX Document from an existing Visual Basic form. This is a helpful utility, but be aware that this tool actually changes the existing project. Therefore, be sure to back up any project before using this add-in.

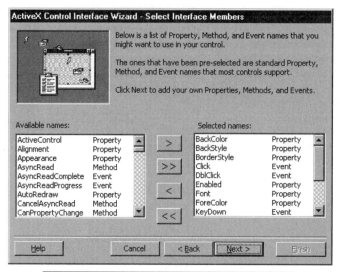

Figure 21-1 The ActiveX Control Interface Wizard.

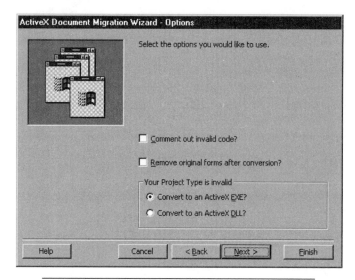

Figure 21-2 The ActiveX Document Migration Wizard.

API Viewer

The API Viewer (Figure 21-3) add-in is a utility for retrieving template function call definitions for the Windows API. Using this tool, search for, copy, and paste into code Declare Function statements, constants, and structures.

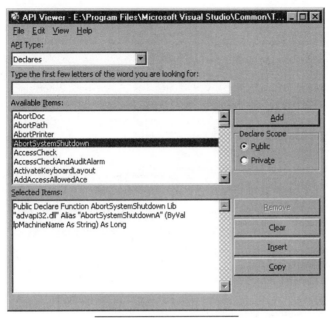

Figure 21-3 The API Viewer.

APPLICATION WIZARD

The Application Wizard (Figure 21-4) is an add-in that generates a framework for an MDI, SDI, or Explorer application. Using this add-in, it is easy to create the essentials of any application style including fundamental interfaces.

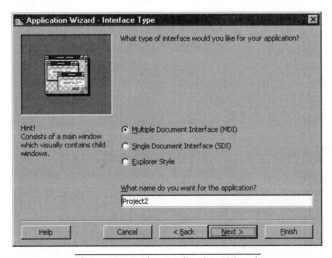

Figure 21-4 The Application Wizard.

CLASS BUILDER UTILITY

The Class Builder Utility (Figure 21-5) is perhaps one of the most useful add-ins that ships with Visual Basic. It makes it possible to design a complete object hierarchy of collections and objects. Design the hierarchy using visual elements in a tree structure. For each element, specify properties and methods. The utility also supports collections. When the hierarchy is defined, generate all the class modules and code necessary to implement the structure. The Class Builder even takes care of setting key procedure attributes for default members as well as implementing the For Each... syntax for collections.

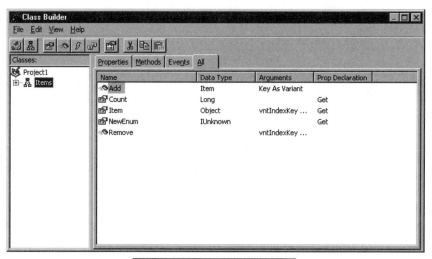

Figure 21-5 Class Builder Utility.

DATA FORM WIZARD

The Data Form Wizard (Figure 21-6) builds a data input form from a database definition. This tool makes it easy to construct data input forms. The forms, however, are relatively plain and consist of textboxes as the input mechanism. The add-in is a good starting point, but probably not useful in a wide range of applications.

DATA OBJECT WIZARD

The Data Object Wizard (Figure 21-7) is an add-in that creates classes with controls bound to them. This utility shows off some of the enhanced data binding features of Visual Basic. Use it to bind a workflow class to a data display in a partitioned application.

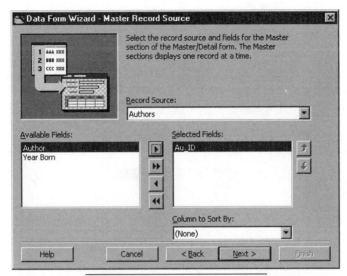

Figure 21-6 The Data Form Wizard.

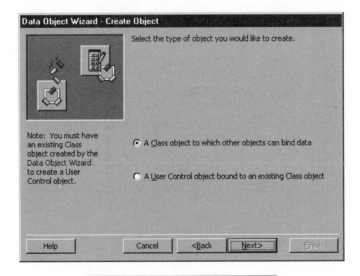

Figure 21-7 The Data Object Wizard.

PROPERTY PAGE WIZARD

The Property Page Wizard (Figure 21-8) helps construct Property Pages for ActiveX Control projects. These pages can then be attached to any property of the control and allow a graphical way to set design time properties. Property Pages are discussed in more detail in the ActiveX Control section of this book.

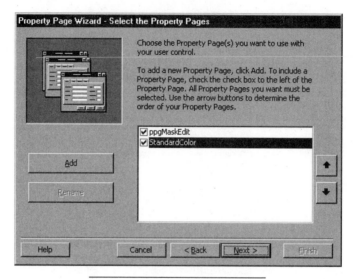

Figure 21-8 Property Page Wizard.

RESOURCE EDITOR

The Resource Editor (Figure 21-9) allows use of Windows Resources in applications. The resources include string tables, icons, and cursors. This add-in creates a resource file with an RES extension. The resource file is compiled as a part of the final project and may be read by the project at run-time. Resource files are covered in detail earlier in this book.

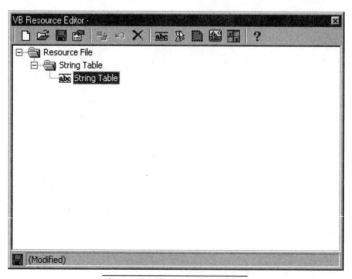

Figure 21-9 Resource Editor.

SQL DEBUGGING

The SQL debugging add-in (Figure 21-10) permits creating and debugging SQL stored procedures from within Visual Basic. Use it in conjunction with the Microsoft Data Tools, and gain a powerful set of tools for manipulating database elements. As with the Microsoft Data Tools, the best way to use the debugger is in conjunction with the Data Environment object. This makes it possible to move between the project, debugging, and the data tools easily.

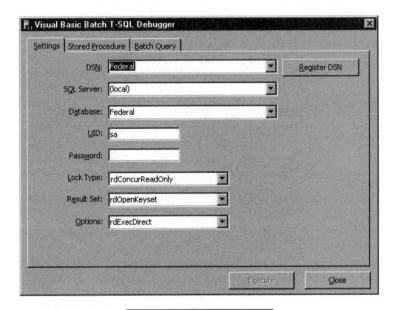

Figure 21-10 SQL Debugger.

VISUAL COMPONENT MANAGER

The Visual Component Manager (VCM) (Figure 21-11) included with every product in the Visual Studio suite is a repository for components, documentation, and models. Once a component is stored in the VCM, it may be shared with other developers and used in other tools. Components may be stored and sorted by type and key words. Developers may then search the VCM to locate reusable components needed an application.

Exercise 21-1: The VB Real Estate Agent

This exercise creates a useful add-in in Visual Basic 6.0 that manages the set of open windows. Use of Visual Basic throughout this book has helped us realize that managing screen real estate can be time-consuming. One key reason that VB has a cluttered environment is because it has no *full-screen* feature to clear away all the open windows. This add-in creates a full-screen feature and adds it to the VB menu.

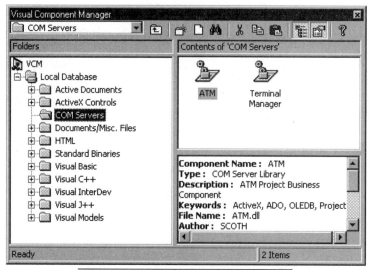

Figure 21-11 Visual Component Manager.

Add-ins are an advanced topic in Visual Basic. Those who begin this exercise, should be well-versed in topics such as interfaces and classes. All this knowledge is necessary to successful creation of an add-in. This particular exercise also makes use of several API calls to read and write to an initialization (INI) file.

Interfacing to the VBIDE

Step 1

Using the File Explorer, create a directory called **VB BOOTCAMP\EXERCISE21-1** for the project. Start a new ActiveX DLL project in Visual Basic. All add-ins are ActiveX components and essentially operate exactly as any component ever created.

Step 2

To communicate with the Visual Basic Integrated Debugging Environment (VBIDE), a reference must be set to the object library that defines the available VBIDE objects. Set the reference by choosing **PROJECT/REFERENCES...** from the menu. The References dialog should appear. In the References dialog, select **Microsoft Visual Basic 6.0 Extensibility**. This is the library for the VBIDE.

In addition to the VBIDE reference, we also need to set a special reference to help us manage menu items and toolbars. Menus and tools are managed from a central component for all Microsoft Office and VB menus. This library is the Microsoft Office 8.0 Object Library. Set a reference to this item as well.

Close the References dialog and open the Object Browser by selecting **VIEW/OBJECT BROWSER...** from the menu. With the Object Browser visible, select **VBIDE** from the library list to view the set of all objects in the VBIDE model. Scroll to the bottom of the object list and select the object **Windows**. This is the collection of VB's windows. We will use this collection to manage the available screen real estate. At the end, close the Object Browser.

Step 3

Select **Class1** from the Project Window and view its properties in the Properties window. Change the name of Class1 to **Connect**. This is the class we will use to communicate with the VBIDE.

To communicate with VB, we must implement a special interface that allows the VBIDE to contact our add-in when it is loaded by the user. The name of this interface is IDTExtensibility. To implement this interface, add the following code to the [General][Declarations] section of the Connect class:

```
'The Add-In Interface
Implements IDTExtensibility
```

Once this interface is implemented, select it from the Object box in the code window. This interface enforces four methods: OnConnection, OnDisconnection, OnStartup- Complete, and OnAddinsUpdate. Because this interface is implemented in our Con- nect class, we must have code for each of the four methods or the compile will fail. This add- in only uses two of the four methods, however, so we will simply place a comment in the unused methods. To add the unused methods, place the following code in the Connect class:

```
Private Sub IDTExtensibility_OnStartupComplete(Custom() As Variant)
  'Required
End Sub
Private Sub IDTExtensibility_OnAddInsUpdate(Custom() As Variant)
  'Required
End Sub
```

Connecting to the VBIDE

Step 4

The first thing any add-in must do is connect to the VBIDE. Connecting to the VBIDE allows our add-in to receive events from the environment, such as a user adding a new component or saving a project. Connecting is done with the OnConnection method. VB calls this method when the add-in is first loaded.

The primary purpose of the OnConnection method for this add-in is to set up the menu structure inside the VBIDE. Using objects found inside the VBIDE, we can easily add menu items to and delete menu items from the VB menu structure. For our add-in, we want to add a menu item to the View menu that a user can select to maximize the available work area. We also want to add a menu item to the Add-Ins menu that can be used to set some options for the add-in.

Before we can create the menus, we must declare object variables to manage them. Menus require two different objects to do their work: the Menu object and the Menu Handler object. The Menu object represents the actual menu; the Menu Handler object is used to trap when the user selects the menu. Declare these variables in the [General][Declarations] section of the Connect class as follows:

```
'Menus
Public WithEvents objMenuHandler As VBIDE.CommandBarEvents
Public objMenu As Office.CommandBarControl
Public WithEvents objFormMenuHandler As VBIDE.CommandBarEvents
Public objFormMenu As Office.CommandBarControl
```

Step 5

When the OnConnection method is called, we are passed an object reference to the running instance of Visual Basic. To preserve this reference, we store it in a Private variable. Declare that variable in the [General][Declarations] section of the Connect class as follows:

```
'Variables
Private m_VBIDE As VBIDE.VBE
```

Step 6

Now that the variables are all declared, we can connect to the VBIDE and create our menus. In the OnConnection method, we create the menus and attach the handlers. Add the following code to the OnConnection method to initialize the add-in:

```
'Save the vb instance
Set m_VBIDE = VBInst


'Build Menus
Set objMenu = m_VBIDE.CommandBars("Menu Bar"). _
Controls("View").CommandBar.Controls.Add(1, , , 1, True)
objMenu.Caption = "&Max Work Area"
Set objMenuHandler = m_VBIDE.Events.CommandBarEvents(objMenu)
Set objFormMenu = m_VBIDE.CommandBars("Menu Bar"). _
Controls("Add-Ins").CommandBar.Controls.Add(1, , , 3, True)
objFormMenu.Caption = "VB Real &Estate Agent..."
Set objFormMenuHandler = _
    m_VBIDE.Events.CommandBarEvents(objFormMenu)
```

Step 7

The IDTExtensibility interface also provides the OnDisconnection method, which is called when our add-in is unloaded. In this method, we must restore the menu structure and undo the changes we made in the OnConnection method. Add the following code to the OnDisconnection method to reset the VBIDE:

```
'Remove Menu Items
 objMenu.Delete
 objFormMenu.Delete
```

SPECIFYING OPTIONS

Step 8

When the add-in is in use, we want to allow users to select options that will specify which windows to close when the work area is maximized and which windows to open when the work area is restored. In this way, users can select, for example, to leave the toolbox visible while the screen is maximized working on a form.

All the options are selected as checkboxes in a special options form. When the add-in is unloaded, these options are written via API calls to an INI file. The INI file is subsequently read at startup to preserve the user's options. In this step, we will create the options form. The form consists of two frames with nine checkboxes in each frame. Add a new form to the project by selecting **PROJECT/ADD FORM...** from the menu. Name the new form **frmOptions**.

As far as the add-in is concerned, only the names of the checkboxes and form are important. Each of the checkboxes is a member of a two-element control array. Index zero is the checkbox associated with the Close frame, and Index one is associated with the Open frame. Construct the form in any way as long as the following controls are available:

```
fraOptions(0)
fraOptions(1)
chkImmediate(0)
chkImmediate(1)
chkLocals(0)
chkLocals(1)
chkWatch(0)
chkWatch(1)
chkProject(0)
chkProject(1)
chkProperties(0)
chkProperties(1)
chkBrowser(0)
chkBrowser(1)
chkLayout(0)
chkLayout(1)
chkToolbox(0)
chkToolbox(1)
chkColor(0)
chkColor(1)
cmdCancel
cmdOK
```

Step 9

The options are managed by reading from and writing to an INI file. This file is accessed through API calls defined inside a standard module. Add a new module to the project by selecting **PROJECT/ADD MODULE** from the menu. Name the new module **basRealEstate**.

Open the module. In this module define the routines necessary to read from and write to the INI file. Reading from and writing to the file are done with two API calls: `Write-PrivateProfileString` and `GetPrivateProfileString`. Obtain the function declarations for these calls by using the API text viewer that ships with Visual Basic. When the function declarations are identified, paste them into the [General][Declarations] section of the module as follows:

```
Declare Function WritePrivateProfileString& _
Lib "kernel32" Alias "WritePrivateProfileStringA" _
(ByVal AppName$, ByVal KeyName$, _
ByVal keydefault$, ByVal FileName$)
Declare Function GetPrivateProfileString Lib "kernel32" _
Alias "GetPrivateProfileStringA" _
    (ByVal lpApplicationName As String, _
ByVal lpKeyName As Any, ByVal lpDefault As String, _
ByVal lpReturnedString As String, ByVal nSize As Long, _
ByVal lpFileName As String) As Long
```

Step 10

The module contains two functions used to obtain information from the INI file called `CloseWindow` and `OpenWindow`. These two functions are used to determine if a particular window should be opened or closed on a maximize or restore operation. They take as an argument the type of window to get information about and return a Boolean value indicating whether the window should open or close. Add these two functions to the module using the following code:

```
Public Function CloseWindow(intType As Integer) As Boolean
  Dim strReturn As String * 255
  Dim lngErr As Long
  Dim strWindow As String
  CloseWindow = False
  strReturn = String$(255, Chr$(0))
  'Get Window Type
  Select Case intType
  Case vbext_wt_Watch
  strWindow = "Watch"
  Case vbext_wt_ToolWindow
  strWindow = "Toolbox"
  Case vbext_wt_PropertyWindow
```

```
    strWindow = "Property"
Case vbext_wt_ProjectWindow
    strWindow = "Project"
Case vbext_wt_Locals
    strWindow = "Locals"
Case vbext_wt_Immediate
    strWindow = "Immediate"
Case vbext_wt_ColorPalette
    strWindow = "Color"
Case vbext_wt_Browser
    strWindow = "Browser"
Case vbext_wt_Preview
    strWindow = "Layout"
End Select
'Read Flag
lngErr = GetPrivateProfileString(strWindow, "MaxClose", _
"NotFound", strReturn, Len(strReturn) + 1, _
   App.Path & "\RealEstate.ini")
'Return Value
If UCase$(Left$(strReturn, InStr(strReturn, _
   Chr$(0)) - 1)) = "-1" Then
CloseWindow = True
End If
End Function
Public Function OpenWindow(intType As Integer) As Boolean
 Dim strReturn As String * 255
 Dim lngErr As Long
 Dim strWindow As String
 OpenWindow = False
 strReturn = String$(255, Chr$(0))
 Get Window Type
 Select Case intType
 Case vbext_wt_Watch
 strWindow = "Watch"
 Case vbext_wt_ToolWindow
 strWindow = "Toolbox"
 Case vbext_wt_PropertyWindow
 strWindow = "Property"
 Case vbext_wt_ProjectWindow
 strWindow = "Project"
 Case vbext_wt_Locals
```

```
    strWindow = "Locals"
    Case vbext_wt_Immediate
    strWindow = "Immediate"
    Case vbext_wt_ColorPalette
    strWindow = "Color"
    Case vbext_wt_Browser
    strWindow = "Browser"
    Case vbext_wt_Preview
    strWindow = "Layout"
    End Select
    'Read Flag
    lngErr = GetPrivateProfileString(strWindow, "RestoreOpen", _
    "NotFound", strReturn, Len(strReturn) + 1, App.Path & _
        "\RealEstate.ini")
    'Return Value
    If UCase$(Left$(strReturn, InStr(strReturn, _
        Chr$(0)) - 1)) = "-1" Then
    OpenWindow = True
    End If
    End Function
```

Step 11

Although not related to managing options, the module also contains an important routine that
helps us test the add-in at design time. This routine is called AddToINI and is used to register
our add-in with the Visual Basic Add-In Manager. The Add-In Manager is responsible for displaying a list of all available add-ins. To be shown on the list, our add-in must make an entry in
a special file called **VBADDIN.INI**. Add the following code to the module to make this entry:

```
    Sub AddToINI()
    'Call this to update the INI in VBIDE
    Dim ErrCode As Long
    ErrCode = WritePrivateProfileString _
    ("Add-Ins32", "RealEstateAgent.Connect", "1", _
    "vbaddin.ini")
    Debug.Print "Added to VB INI file!"
    End Sub
```

Step 12

Close the module and save the work. Now open the Code window for the options form. In this
form, write routines used to display the current options in the checkbox groups. The data are
saved in the INI file for each window and specify its state when a maximize or restore operation is performed. Listing 16-3 shows a typical INI file for this add-in.

```
    [Immediate]
```

```
MaxClose=-1
RestoreOpen=0
[Locals]
MaxClose=-1
RestoreOpen=0
[Watch]
MaxClose=-1
RestoreOpen=0
[Project]
MaxClose=-1
RestoreOpen=-1
[Property]
MaxClose=-1
RestoreOpen=-1
[Browser]
MaxClose=-1
RestoreOpen=0
[Toolbox]
MaxClose=-1
RestoreOpen=-1
[Color]
MaxClose=-1
RestoreOpen=0
[Layout]
MaxClose=-1
RestoreOpen=0
```

Step 13

Before we can code the routines to update the options form, we must add constants to the form. These constants are simply used to track the mode for which we are saving options. Add the following constants to the [General][Declarations] section of frmOptions:

```
Private Const ntsMaxClose% = 0
Private Const ntsRestoreOpen% = 1
```

Step 14

Options are read from the INI file when the options form is first loaded. The options are read for each of the windows by making the appropriate API call. Read these options by adding the following code to the Form_Load event of frmOptions:

```
'Immediate
chkImmediate(ntsMaxClose).Value = _
CloseWindow(vbext_wt_Immediate) * -1
```

```
chkImmediate(ntsRestoreOpen).Value = _
OpenWindow(vbext_wt_Immediate) * -1
'Locals
chkLocals(ntsMaxClose).Value = _
CloseWindow(vbext_wt_Locals) * -1
chkLocals(ntsRestoreOpen).Value = _
OpenWindow(vbext_wt_Locals) * -1
'Watch
chkWatch(ntsMaxClose).Value = _
CloseWindow(vbext_wt_Watch) * -1
chkWatch(ntsRestoreOpen).Value = _
OpenWindow(vbext_wt_Watch) * -1
'Project
chkProject(ntsMaxClose).Value = _
CloseWindow(vbext_wt_ProjectWindow) * -1
chkProject(ntsRestoreOpen).Value = _
OpenWindow(vbext_wt_ProjectWindow) * -1
'Property
chkProperties(ntsMaxClose).Value = _
CloseWindow(vbext_wt_PropertyWindow) * -1
chkProperties(ntsRestoreOpen).Value = _
OpenWindow(vbext_wt_PropertyWindow) * -1
'Browser
chkBrowser(ntsMaxClose).Value = _
CloseWindow(vbext_wt_Browser) * -1
chkBrowser(ntsRestoreOpen).Value = _
OpenWindow(vbext_wt_Browser) * -1
'Layout
chkLayout(ntsMaxClose).Value = _
CloseWindow(vbext_wt_Preview) * -1
chkLayout(ntsRestoreOpen).Value = _
OpenWindow(vbext_wt_Preview) * -1
'Toolbox
chkToolbox(ntsMaxClose).Value = _
CloseWindow(vbext_wt_ToolWindow) * -1
chkToolbox(ntsRestoreOpen).Value = _
OpenWindow(vbext_wt_ToolWindow) * -1
'Color
chkColor(ntsMaxClose).Value = _
CloseWindow(vbext_wt_ColorPalette) * -1
```

```
chkColor(ntsRestoreOpen).Value = _
OpenWindow(vbext_wt_ColorPalette) * -1
```

Step 15

Options are written to the INI file when the user presses the **OK** button. If the user presses the **Cancel** button, options are not written. Add the following code to the `Click` event of the Cancel button to bypass the INI file:

```
Unload Me
```

Writing the options requires calling the API function and is essentially the reverse of the read operation. Add the following code to the `Click` event of the OK button to write the options:

```
Dim lngErr As Long
'Immediate
lngErr = WritePrivateProfileString _
("Immediate", "MaxClose", _
CStr(chkImmediate(ntsMaxClose).Value * -1), _
App.Path & "\RealEstate.ini")
lngErr = WritePrivateProfileString _
("Immediate", "RestoreOpen", _
CStr(chkImmediate(ntsRestoreOpen).Value * -1), _
App.Path & "\RealEstate.ini")
'Locals
lngErr = WritePrivateProfileString _
("Locals", "MaxClose", _
CStr(chkLocals(ntsMaxClose).Value * -1), _
App.Path & "\RealEstate.ini")
lngErr = WritePrivateProfileString _
("Locals", "RestoreOpen", _
CStr(chkLocals(ntsRestoreOpen).Value * -1), _
App.Path & "\RealEstate.ini")
'Watch
lngErr = WritePrivateProfileString _
("Watch", "MaxClose", _
CStr(chkWatch(ntsMaxClose).Value * -1), _
App.Path & "\RealEstate.ini")
lngErr = WritePrivateProfileString _
("Watch", "RestoreOpen", _
CStr(chkWatch(ntsRestoreOpen).Value * -1), _
App.Path & "\RealEstate.ini")
'Project
lngErr = WritePrivateProfileString _
```

```vb
("Project", "MaxClose", _
CStr(chkProject(ntsMaxClose).Value * -1), _
App.Path & "\RealEstate.ini")
lngErr = WritePrivateProfileString _
("Project", "RestoreOpen", _
CStr(chkProject(ntsRestoreOpen).Value * -1), _
App.Path & "\RealEstate.ini")
'Property
lngErr = WritePrivateProfileString _
("Property", "MaxClose", _
CStr(chkProperties(ntsMaxClose).Value * -1), _
App.Path & "\RealEstate.ini")
lngErr = WritePrivateProfileString _
("Property", "RestoreOpen", _
CStr(chkProperties(ntsRestoreOpen).Value * -1), _
App.Path & "\RealEstate.ini")
'Browser
lngErr = WritePrivateProfileString _
("Browser", "MaxClose", _
CStr(chkBrowser(ntsMaxClose).Value * -1), _
App.Path & "\RealEstate.ini")
lngErr = WritePrivateProfileString _
("Browser", "RestoreOpen", _
CStr(chkBrowser(ntsRestoreOpen).Value * -1), _
App.Path & "\RealEstate.ini")
'Layout
lngErr = WritePrivateProfileString _
("Layout", "MaxClose", _
CStr(chkLayout(ntsMaxClose).Value * -1), _
App.Path & "\RealEstate.ini")
lngErr = WritePrivateProfileString _
("Layout", "RestoreOpen", _
CStr(chkLayout(ntsRestoreOpen).Value * -1), _
App.Path & "\RealEstate.ini")
'Toolbox
lngErr = WritePrivateProfileString _
("Toolbox", "MaxClose", _
CStr(chkToolbox(ntsMaxClose).Value * -1), _
App.Path & "\RealEstate.ini")
lngErr = WritePrivateProfileString _
("Toolbox", "RestoreOpen", _
```

```
CStr(chkToolbox(ntsRestoreOpen).Value * -1), _
App.Path & "\RealEstate.ini")
'Color
lngErr = WritePrivateProfileString _
("Color", "MaxClose", _
CStr(chkColor(ntsMaxClose).Value * -1), _
App.Path & "\RealEstate.ini")
lngErr = WritePrivateProfileString _
("Color", "RestoreOpen", _
CStr(chkColor(ntsRestoreOpen).Value * -1), _
App.Path & "\RealEstate.ini")
Unload Me
```

HANDLING THE MENU EVENTS

Step 16

The only part of our add-in left to construct is the menu handling routines. These all fire in response to user interaction with the Visual Basic menu structure. In particular, we want to receive notification when the menu items we added to VB are clicked. The add-in tracks the currently active options in memory through several variables we must add before writing our menu routines. Add these variables to the [General][Declarations] section of the Connect class:

```
Private m_Immediate As Boolean
Private m_Locals As Boolean
Private m_Watch As Boolean
Private m_Project As Boolean
Private m_Properties As Boolean
Private m_Object As Boolean
Private m_Layout As Boolean
Private m_Toolbox As Boolean
Private m_Color As Boolean
```

Step 17

To open or close the windows, the user interacts with our menu item under the View menu. This item is tracked by the objMenuhandler object. Select the objMenuHandler object from the Object box in the Code window of class Connect. The Click event should be visible for this object. This is the event that will fire when the user selects the menu item. Add the following code to objMenuHandler_Click to open or close the designated windows:

```
'Open or Close Windows
  Dim objWindow As VBIDE.Window
  For Each objWindow In m_VBIDE.Windows
```

```
If objMenu.Caption = "&Max Work Area" Then
   If CloseWindow(objWindow.Type) Then
   objWindow.Close
End If
Else
   If OpenWindow(objWindow.Type) Then
   objWindow.Visible = True
End If
End If
Next
'Change Menu Item
If objMenu.Caption = "&Max Work Area" Then
   objMenu.Caption = "&Restore Work Area"
   Else
   objMenu.Caption = "&Max Work Area"
End If
```

Step 18

To change the selected options, the user interacts with our menu item under the Add-Ins menu. This menu item is tracked by the `objFormMenuHandler` object, which also has a `Click` event. Add the following code to this event to show the Options dialog:

```
frmOptions.Show
```

TESTING THE ADD-IN

Step 19

Make sure all the work is saved. While still inside the VB design environment, select **RUN/START** from the menu. The add-in will start, but nothing will happen. Enter **Break** mode by selecting **RUN/BREAK**. Now register the add-in by typing directly into the immediate debug window:

This calls the routine created earlier and writes to the VBADDIN.INI file. Now continue running the add-in by selecting **RUN/CONTINUE**. Minimize this copy of VB 5 and start another copy from the system Start menu. When the second copy starts, the add-in will automatically be loaded for use. It may be necessary to debug any mistakes made in creating the code.

Once a successful connection is made, use the View menu to try and maximize the work area. Also try the Options window under the Add-Ins menu.

PREPARING FOR CERTIFICATION

Topics for Further Reading

"Extending the Visual Basic Environment with Add-Ins"

CERTIFICATION QUIZ

1. Which are methods of the IDTExtensibility interface?
 a. `OnConnection`
 b. `OnStartupComplete`
 c. `OnDisconnection`
 d. `OnAddInsUpdate`

2. Which object represents the current instance of Visual Basic?
 a. VBIDE
 b. VBE
 c. VB
 d. VBD

3. What object allows VBIDE events to be trapped?
 a. ActiveEvents
 b. Events
 c. VBEvents
 d. VBEEvents

4. What ActiveX component contains toolbar and menu objects?
 a. VBIDE
 b. ADODB
 c. ODBC
 d. Office

5. What file contains the information for all registered add-ins?
 a. VBADDIN.INI
 b. ADDIN.INI
 c. ADD.INI
 d. VBADD.INI

6. What object allows access to the code in a project?
 a. `CodeWindow`
 b. `CodePanes`
 c. `CodeModules`
 d. `CodeModule`

7. What VB projects can perform as add-ins?
 a. ActiveX Documents
 b. ActiveX EXE
 c. ActiveX DLL
 d. ActiveX Control

8. What code can be used to access the main VB toolbar?
   a. `CommandBars("Main")`
   b. `ComandBars("Standard Menu")`
   c. `CommandBars("Main")`
   d. `CommandBars("Standard")`

9. Which object is used to generate project-level events?
   a. `VBEvents`
   b. `ProjectEvents`
   c. `VBProjectsEvents`
   d. `VBProjectEvents`

10. Which project must be modified when creating an add-in setup?
    a. SETUP132.VBP
    b. SETUP.VBP
    c. SETUP1.VBP
    d. SETUP32.VBP

ANSWERS TO CERTIFICATION QUIZ

1. a, b, c, d
2. b
3. c
4. d
5. a
6. d
7. a, b, c
8. d
9. c
10. b

EXAM MATRIX

TEST OVERVIEW

Visual Basic developers must now pass two exams specifically targeted at VB development before they can receive the Microsoft Certified Solution Developer certification. The VB exams fall into two categories: Desktop applications and distributed applications. The exam titles are 70-016: Designing and Implementing Desktop Applications and 70-175: Designing and Implementing Distributed Applications. In addition to the two Visual Basic exams, developers must pass the Solution Architecture exam and one elective. The complete requirements for certification can be found at **www.microsoft.com/mcp**.

70-176: DESIGNING AND IMPLEMENTING DESKTOP APPLICATIONS

Exam 70-176 is designed to assess your skills at developing desktop applications. The following matrix shows the skills being tested by this exam. These objectives appear at the beginning of appropriate chapters where they are covered. This matrix can also be used to identify your weak areas and where the material is covered in the book.

Skill	Description	Chapter
70-176 (1)	Assess the potential impact of the logical design on performance, maintainability, extensibility, and availability.	14
70-176 (2)	Design Visual Basic components to access data from a database.	10
70-176 (3)	Design the properties, methods, and events of components.	13
70-176 (4)	Establish the environment for source-code version control.	1
70-176 (5)	Install and configure Visual Basic for developing desktop applications.	1
70-176 (6)	Implement navigational design.	1,3,7
70-176 (6.a)	Dynamically modify the appearance of a menu.	3
70-176 (6.b)	Add a pop-up menu to an application.	3
70-176 (6.c)	Create an application that adds and deletes menus at run time.	7
70-176 (6.d)	Add controls to forms.	1
70-176 (6.e)	Set properties for command buttons, text boxes, and labels.	1
70-176 (6.f)	Assign code to a control to respond to an event.	1
70-176 (7)	Create data input forms and dialog boxes.	2,7
70-176 (7.a)	Display and manipulate data by using custom controls.	2
70-176 (7.b)	Create an application that adds and deletes controls at run time.	7
70-176 (7.c)	Use the Controls collection to manipulate controls at run time.	2
70-176 (7.d)	Use the Forms collection to manipulate forms at run time.	2
70-176 (8)	Write code that validates user input.	7
70-176 (8.a)	Create an application that verifies data entered by a user at the field level and the form level.	7
70-176 (8.b)	Create an application that enables or disables controls based on input in fields.	7
70-176 (9)	Write code that processes data entered on a form.	2
70-176 (9.a)	Given a scenario, add code to the appropriate form event. Events include Initialize, Terminate, Load, Unload, QueryUnload, Activate, and Deactivate.	2
70-176 (10)	Add an ActiveX control to the toolbox.	1

Skill	Description	Chapter
70-176 (11)	Use data binding to display and manipulate data from a data source.	5,10
70-176 (12)	Instantiate and invoke a COM component.	13
70-176 (12.a)	Create a Visual Basic client application that uses a COM component.	13
70-176 (12.b)	Create a Visual Basic application that handles events from a COM component.	13
70-176 (13)	Create call-back procedures to enable asynchronous processing between COM components and Visual Basic client applications.	13
70-176 (14)	Implement online user assistance in a desktop application.	7,13
70-176 (14.a)	Set appropriate properties to enable user assistance. Help contents include HelpFile, HelpContextID, and WhatsThisHelp.	7
70-176 (14.b)	Create HTML Help for an application.	7
70-176 (14.c)	Implement messages from a server component to a user interface.	13
70-176 (15)	Implement error handling for the user interface in desktop applications.	6
70-176 (15.a)	Identify and trap run-time errors.	6
70-176 (15.b)	Handle inline errors.	6
70-176 (16)	Create a COM component that implements business rules or logic. Components include DLLs, ActiveX controls, and active documents.	13
70-176 (17)	Create ActiveX controls.	16
70-176 (17.a)	Create an ActiveX control that exposes properties.	16
70-176 (17.b)	Use control events to save and load persistent properties.	16
70-176 (17.c)	Test and debug an ActiveX control.	16
70-176 (17.d)	Create and enable property pages for an ActiveX control.	16
70-176 (17.e)	Enable the data-binding capabilities of an ActiveX control.	16
70-176 (17.f)	Create an ActiveX control that is a data source.	16
70-176 (18)	Create an active document.	17
70-176 (18.a)	Use code within an active document to interact with a container application.	17
70-176 (18.b)	Navigate to other active documents.	17
70-176 (19)	Debug a COM client written in Visual Basic.	13

Skill	Description	Chapter
70-176 (20)	Compile a project with class modules into a COM component.	14
70-176 (20.a)	Implement an object model within a COM component.	14
70-176 (20.b)	Set properties to control the instancing of a class within a COM component.	14
70-176 (21)	Use Visual Component Manager to manage components.	21
70-176 (22)	Register and unregister a COM component.	15
70-176 (23)	Access and manipulate a data source by using ADO and the ADO Data control.	5
70-176 (24)	Given a scenario, select the appropriate compiler options.	1
70-176 (25)	Control an application by using conditional compilation.	1
70-176 (26)	Set watch expressions during program execution.	6
70-176 (27)	Monitor the values of expressions and variables by using the Debug window.	6
70-176 (27.a)	Use the Immediate window to check or change values.	6
70-176 (27.b)	Use the Locals window to check or change values.	6
70-176 (28)	Implement project groups to support the development and debugging process.	13
70-176 (28.a)	Debug DLLs in process.	13
70-176 (28.b)	Test and debug a control in process.	16
70-176 (29)	Given a scenario, define the scope of a watch variable.	6
70-176 (30)	Use the Package and Deployment Wizard to create a setup program that installs a desktop application, registers the COM components, and allows for uninstall.	7
70-176 (31)	Plan and implement floppy disk-based deployment or compact disc-based deployment for a desktop application.	7
70-176 (32)	Plan and implement Web-based deployment for a desktop application.	17,18,19
70-176 (33)	Plan and implement network-based deployment for a desktop application.	7
70-176 (34)	Fix errors, and take measures to prevent future errors.	6
70-176 (35)	Deploy application updates for desktop applications.	7

70-175: DESIGNING AND IMPLEMENTING DISTRIBUTED APPLICATIONS

Exam 70-175 is designed to asses your skills at developing distributed applications. These include both client/server and intranet applications. The following matrix shows the skills being tested by this exam. These objectives appear at the beginning of appropriate chapters where they are covered. This matrix can also be used to identify your weak areas and where the material is covered in the book.

Skill	Description	Chapter
70-175(1)	Given a conceptual design, apply the principles of modular design to derive the components and services of the logical design.	14
70-175(2)	Assess the potential impact of the logical design on performance, maintainability, extensibility, scalability, availability, and security.	15
70-175(3)	Design Visual Basic components to access data from a database in a multi-tier application.	15
70-175(4)	Design the properties, methods, and events of components.	13
70-175(5)	Establish the environment for source-code version control.	1
70-175(6)	Install and configure Visual Basic for developing distributed applications.	1
70-175(7)	Configure a server computer to run Microsoft Transaction Server (MTS).	20
70-175(7.a)	Install MTS.	20
70-175(7.b)	Set up security on a system package.	20
70-175(8)	Configure a client computer to use an MTS component.	20
70-175(8.a)	Create packages that install or update MTS components on a client computer.	20
70-175(9)	Implement navigational design.	1,3,7
70-175(9.a)	Dynamically modify the appearance of a menu.	3
70-175(9.b)	Add a pop-up menu to an application.	3
70-175(9.c)	Create an application that adds and deletes menus at run time.	7
70-175(9.d)	Add controls to forms.	1
70-175(9.e)	Set properties for command buttons, text boxes, and labels.	1
70-175(9.f)	Assign code to a control to respond to an event.	1
70-175(10)	Create data input forms and dialog boxes.	2,7

Skill	Description	Chapter
70-175(10.a)	Display and manipulate data by using custom controls.	2
70-175(10.b)	Create an application that adds and deletes controls at run time.	7
70-175(10.c)	Use the Controls collection to manipulate controls at run time.	2
70-175(10.d)	Use the Forms collection to manipulate forms at run time.	2
70-175(11)	Write code that validates user input.	7
70-175(11.a)	Create an application that verifies data entered by a user at the field level and the form level.	7
70-175(11.b)	Create an application that enables or disables controls based on input in fields.	7
70-175(12)	Write code that processes data entered on a form.	2
70-175(12.a)	Given a scenario, add code to the appropriate form event. Events include Initialize, Terminate, Load, Unload, QueryUnload, Activate, and Deactivate.	2
70-175(13)	Add an ActiveX control to the toolbox.	1
70-175(14)	Create dynamic Web pages by using Active Server Pages (ASP).	18
70-175(15)	Use data binding to display and manipulate data from a data source.	5,10
70-175(16)	Instantiate and invoke a COM component.	13
70-175(16.a)	Create a Visual Basic client application that uses a COM component.	13
70-175(16.b)	Create a Visual Basic application that handles events from a COM component.	13
70-175(17)	Create call-back procedures to enable asynchronous processing between COM components and Visual Basic client applications.	13
70-175(18)	Implement online user assistance in a distributed application.	7,13
70-175(18.a)	Set appropriate properties to enable user assistance. Help contents include HelpFile, HelpContextID, and WhatsThisHelp.	7
70-175(18.b)	Create HTML Help for an application.	7
70-175(18.c)	Implement messages from a server component to a user interface.	13
70-175(19)	Implement error handling for the user interface in distributed applications.	6
70-175(19.a)	Identify and trap run-time errors.	6

Skill	Description	Chapter
70-175(19.b)	Handle inline errors.	6
70-175(19.c)	Determine how to send error information from a COM component to a client computer.	6,14
70-175(20)	Use an active document to present information within a Web browser.	17
70-175(21)	Create a COM component that implements business rules or logic. Components include DLLs, ActiveX controls, and active documents.	13
70-175(22)	Create ActiveX controls.	16
70-175(22.a)	Create an ActiveX control that exposes properties.	16
70-175(22.b)	Use control events to save and load persistent properties.	16
70-175(22.c)	Test and debug an ActiveX control.	16
70-175(22.d)	Create and enable property pages for an ActiveX control.	16
70-175(22.e)	Enable the data-binding capabilities of an ActiveX control.	16
70-175(22.f)	Create an ActiveX control that is a data source.	16
70-175(23)	Create an active document.	17
70-175(23.a)	Use code within an active document to interact with a container application.	17
70-175(23.b)	Navigate to other active documents.	17
70-175(24)	Design and create components that will be used with MTS.	20
70-175(25)	Debug Visual Basic code that uses objects from a COM server.	13
70-175(26)	Choose the appropriate threading model for a COM component.	20
70-175(27)	Create a package by using the MTS Explorer.	20
70-175(27.a)	Use the Package and Deployment Wizard to create a package.	20
70-175(27.b)	Import existing packages.	20
70-175(27.c)	Assign names to packages.	20
70-175(27.d)	Assign security to packages.	20
70-175(28)	Add components to an MTS package.	20
70-175(28.a)	Set transactional properties of components.	20
70-175(28.b)	Set security properties of components.	20

Skill	Description	Chapter
70-175(29)	Use role-based security to limit use of an MTS package to specific users.	20
70-175(29.a)	Create roles.	20
70-175(29.b)	Assign roles to components or component interfaces.	20
70-175(29.c)	Add users to roles.	20
70-175(30)	Compile a project with class modules into a COM component.	14
70-175(30.a)	Implement an object model within a COM component.	14
70-175(30.b)	Set properties to control the instancing of a class within a COM component.	14
70-175(31)	Use Visual Component Manager to manage components.	21
70-175(32)	Register and unregister a COM component.	15
70-175(33)	Access and manipulate a data source by using ADO and the ADO Data control.	5
70-175(34)	Access and manipulate data by using the Execute Direct model.	11,12
70-175(35)	Access and manipulate data by using the Prepare/Execute model.	11,12
70-175(36)	Access and manipulate data by using the Stored Procedures model.	11,12
70-175(36.a)	Use a stored procedure to execute a statement on a database.	11,12
70-175(36.b)	Use a stored procedure to return records to a Visual Basic application.	11,12
70-175(37)	Retrieve and manipulate data by using different cursor locations. Cursor locations include client-side and server-side.	11,12
70-175(38)	Retrieve and manipulate data by using different cursor types. Cursor types include forward-only, static, dynamic, and keyset.	11,12
70-175(39)	Use the ADO Errors collection to handle database errors.	12
70-175(40)	Manage database transactions to ensure data consistency and recoverability.	11,12
70-175(41)	Write SQL statements that retrieve and modify data.	5
70-175(42)	Write SQL statements that use joins to combine data from multiple tables.	5
70-175(43)	Use appropriate locking strategies to ensure data integrity. Locking strategies include Read-Only, Pessimistic, Optimistic, and Batch Optimistic.	11,12

Skill	Description	Chapter
70-175(44)	Given a scenario, select the appropriate compiler options.	1
70-175(45)	Control an application by using conditional compilation.	1
70-175(46)	Set watch expressions during program execution.	6
70-175(47)	Monitor the values of expressions and variables by using the Debug window.	6
70-175(47.a)	Use the Immediate window to check or change values.	6
70-175(47.b)	Use the Locals window to check or change values.	6
70-175(48)	Implement project groups to support the development and debugging process.	13,16
70-175(48.a)	Debug DLLs in process.	13
70-175(48.b)	Test and debug a control in process.	16
70-175(49)	Given a scenario, define the scope of a watch variable.	6
70-175(50)	Use the Package and Deployment Wizard to create a setup program that installs a distributed application, registers the COM components, and allows for uninstall.	15
70-175(51)	Register a component that implements DCOM.	15
70-175(52)	Configure DCOM on a client computer and on a server computer.	15
70-175(53)	Plan and implement floppy disk-based deployment or compact disc-based deployment for a distributed application.	15
70-175(54)	Plan and implement Web-based deployment for a distributed application.	17,18,19
70-175(55)	Plan and implement network-based deployment for a distributed application.	15
70-175(56)	Implement load balancing.	20
70-175(57)	Fix errors, and take measures to prevent future errors.	6
70-175(58)	Deploy application updates for distributed applications.	15

PROFESSIONAL SKILLS

The following matrix shows additional skills covered in this book that are not specifically list-ed on the exam matrix. These skills are included in the book because they represent foundation knowledge or advanced knowledge that is required to create professional Visual Basic applications. As of this writing, the Visual Basic 6.0 exams are in beta, so there is a good chance that many of these skills may ultimately appear on the final certification exam. All of these items are covered completely in the book.

Skill	Description	Chapter
Cert (1)	Write code using the Visual Basic Language	4
Cert (1.a)	Use code structures to control program flow	4
Cert (1.b)	Use built-in functions to manipulate programmatic data	4
Cert (1.c)	Create custom functions to process data	4
Cert (1.d)	Use variables of differing data types to store and manipulate values	4
Cert (1.e)	Use constants to simplify code maintenance	4
Cert (2)	Use the Windows API to overcome limitations of Visual Basic	8
Cert (2.a)	Send messages to windows to affect their behavior	8
Cert (2.b)	Use the Windows API to return system and user information	8
Cert (2.c)	Subclass a Visual Basic form using the AddressOf keyword	8
Cert (3)	Use multiple form instances to build applications	9
Cert (3.a)	Create new instances of a Visual Basic form	9
Cert (3.b)	Destroy instances of a Visual Basic form	9
Cert (4)	Use Web Classes to create IIS Applications	18
Cert (4.a)	Use the events of a Web Class to manage user requests	18
Cert (4.b)	Use Web Items to respond to user requests	18
Cert (4.c)	Use the IIS Application object model to control program flow	18
Cert (4.d)	Use Web Classes to manage state in an Internet application	18
Cert (4.e)	Use IIS applications to create browser-independent applications	18
Cert (5)	Use DHTML Applications to create intranet applications	19
Cert (5.a)	Use the DHTML designer to create web front ends	19
Cert (5.b)	Use HTML pages in a DHTML application	19
Cert (5.c)	Navigate between pages in a DHTML application	19
Cert (5.d)	Manage state in a DHTML application with cookies	19

INDEX

SOFTWARE AND INFORMATION LICENSE

The software and information on this diskette (collectively referred to as the "Product") are the property of The McGraw-Hill Companies, Inc. ("McGraw-Hill") and are protected by both United States copyright law and international copyright treaty provision. You must treat this Product just like a book, except that you may copy it into a computer to be used and you may make archival copies of the Products for the sole purpose of backing up our software and protecting your investment from loss.

By saying "just like a book," McGraw-Hill means, for example, that the Product may be used by any number of people and may be freely moved from one computer location to another, so long as there is no possibility of the Product (or any part of the Product) being used at one location or on one computer while it is being used at another. Just as a book cannot be read by two different people in two different places at the same time, neither can the Product be used by two different people in two different places at the same time (unless, of course, McGraw-Hill's rights are being violated).

McGraw-Hill reserves the right to alter or modify the contents of the Product at any time.

This agreement is effective until terminated. The Agreement will terminate automatically without notice if you fail to comply with any provisions of this Agreement. In the event of termination by reason of your breach, you will destroy or erase all copies of the Product installed on any computer system or made for backup purposes and shall expunge the Product from your data storage facilities.

LIMITED WARRANTY

McGraw-Hill warrants the physical diskette(s) enclosed herein to be free of defects in materials and workmanship for a period of sixty days from the purchase date. If McGraw-Hill receives written notification within the warranty period of defects in material or workmanship, and such notification is determined by McGraw-Hill to be correct, McGraw-Hill will replace the defective diskette(s). Send request to:

Customer Service
McGraw-Hill
Gahanna Industrial Park
860 Taylor Station Road
Blacklick, OH 43004-9615

The entire and exclusive liability and remedy for breach of this Limited Warranty shall be limited to replacement of defective diskette(s) and shall not include or extend to any claim for or right to cover any other damages, including but not limited to, loss of profit, data, or use of the software, or special, incidental, or consequential damages or other similar claims, even if McGraw-Hill has been specifically advised as to the possibility of such damages. In no event will McGraw-Hill's liability for any damages to you or any other person ever exceed the lower of suggested list price or actual price paid for the license to use the Product, regardless of any form of the claim.

THE McGRAW-HILL COMPANIES, INC. SPECIFICALLY DISCLAIMS ALL OTHER WARRANTIES, EXPRESS OR IMPLIED, INCLUDING BUT NOT LIMITED TO, ANY IMPLIED WARRANT OF MER-CHANTABILITY OR FITNESS FOR A PARTICULAR PURPOSE. Specifically, McGraw-Hill makes no representation or warranty that the Product is fit for any particular purpose and any implied warranty of merchantability is limited to the sixty day duration of the Limited Warranty covering the physical diskette(s) only (and not the software or information) and is otherwise expressly and specifically disclaimed.

This Limited Warranty gives you specific legal rights, you may have others which may vary from state to state. Some states do not allow the exclusion of incidental or consequential damages, or the limitation on how long an implied warranty lasts, so some of the above may not apply to you.

This Agreement constitutes the entire agreement between the parties relating to use of the Product. The terms of any purchase order shall have no effect on the terms of this Agreement. Failure of McGraw-Hill to insist at any time on strict compliance with this Agreement shall not constitute a waiver of any rights under this Agreement. This Agreement shall be construed and governed in accordance with the laws of New York. If any provision of this Agreement is held to be contrary to law, that provision will be enforced to the maximum extent permissible and the remaining provisions will remain in force and effect.